Character Sketches

Fiction, and the Drama

Vol. 3

A Revised American Edition of the Reader's Handbook

Ebenezer Cobham Brewer,

(Editor: Marion Harland)

Alpha Editions

This edition published in 2024

ISBN : 9789366380384

Design and Setting By
Alpha Editions
www.alphaedis.com
Email - info@alphaedis.com

As per information held with us this book is in Public Domain.
This book is a reproduction of an important historical work. Alpha Editions uses the best technology to reproduce historical work in the same manner it was first published to preserve its original nature. Any marks or number seen are left intentionally to preserve its true form.

Contents

VOLUME III. ....- 1 -
CHARACTER SKETCHES OF ROMANCE, FICTION,
AND THE DRAMA. ....- 3 -

# VOLUME III.

CHARACTER SKETCHES OF ROMANCE, FICTION, AND THE DRAMA.

ARK TAPLEY, a serving companion of Martin Chuzzlewit, who goes out with him to Eden, in North America. Mark Tapley thinks there is no credit in being jolly in easy circumstances; but when in Eden he found every discomfort, lost all his money, was swindled by every one, and was almost killed by fevers, then indeed he felt it would be a real credit "to be jolly under the circumstances."—C. Dickens, *Martin Chuzzlewit* (1843).

Markham, a gentleman in the train of the earl of Sussex.—Sir W. Scott, *Kenilworth* (time, Elizabeth).

Markham (*Mrs.*), pseudonym of Mrs. Elizabeth Perrose (born Elizabeth Cartwright), authoress of *History of England*, etc.

Markleham (*Mrs.*), the mother of Annie. Devoted to pleasure, she always maintained that she indulged in it for "Annie's sake." Mrs. Markleham is generally referred to as "the old soldier."—C. Dickens, *David Copperfield* (1849).

Marksman, one of Fortunio's seven attendants. He saw so clearly and to such a distance, that he generally bandaged his eyes in order to temper the great keenness of his sight.—Comtesse D'Aunoy, *Fairy Tales* ("Fortunio," 1682).

Marlborough (*The duke of*), John Churchill. He was called by Marshal Turenne *Le Bel Anglais* (1650-1722).

Marlow (*Sir Charles*), the kind-hearted old friend of Squire Hardcastle.

Young Marlow, son of Sir Charles. "Among women of reputation and virtue he is the modestest man alive; but his acquaintances give him a very different character among women of another stamp" (act i. 1). Having mistaken Hardcastle's house for an inn, and Miss Hardcastle for the barmaid, he is quite at his ease, and makes love freely. When fairly caught, he discovers that the supposed "inn" is a private house, and the supposed barmaid is the squire's daughter; but the ice of his shyness being broken, he has no longer any difficulty in loving according to his station.—Goldsmith, *She Stoops to Conquer* (1773).

When Goldsmith was between 16 and 17 he set out for Edgworthstown, and finding night coming on, asked a man which was the "best house" in the town—meaning the best inn. The man pointed to the house of Sir Ralph Fetherstone (or *Mr. Fetherstone*), and Oliver, entering the parlor, found the master of the mansion sitting at a good fire. Oliver told him he desired to pass the night there, and ordered him to bring in supper. "Sir Ralph" knowing his customer, humored the joke, which Oliver did not discover till next day, when he called for his bill. (We are told in *Notes and Queries* that Ralph Fetherstone was only *Mr.*, but his grandson was *Sir Thomas*).

Marmaduke Wharne. Eccentric old Englishman long resident in America. Benevolent and beneficent, but gruff in manner and speech.—A. D. T. Whitney, *Leslie Goldthwaite's Summer* (1866).

Marmaduke (*Sir*). A man who has lost all earth can give—wealth, love, fame and friends, but thus comforts himself:

"I account it worth
All pangs of fair hopes crossed,—
All loves and honors lost,—
To gain the heavens, at cost
Of losing earth."
Theodore Tilton, *Sir Marmaduke's Musings* (1867).

Marmion. Lord Marmion was betrothed to Constance de Beverley, but he jilted her for Lady Clare, an heiress, who was in love with Ralph de Wilton. The Lady Clare rejected Lord Marmion's suit, and took refuge from him in the convent of St. Hilda, in Whitby. Constance took the veil in the convent of St. Cuthbert, in Holy Isle, but after a time left the convent clandestinely, was captured, taken back, and buried alive in the walls of a deep cell. In the mean time, Lord Marmion, being sent by Henry VIII. on an embassy to James IV. of Scotland, stopped at the hall of Sir Hugh de Heron, who sent a palmer as his guide. On his return, Lord Marmion commanded the abbess of St. Hilda to release the Lady Clare, and place her under the charge of her kinsman, Fitzclare of Tantallon Hall. Here she met the palmer, who was Ralph de Wilton, and as Lord Marmion was slain in the battle of Flodden Field, she was free to marry the man she loved.—Sir W. Scott, *Marmion* (1808).

Marmion (*Lord*), a descendant of Robert de Marmion, who obtained from William the Conqueror, the manor of Scrivelby, in Lincolnshire. This Robert de Marmion was the first royal champion of England, and the office remained in the family till the reign of Edward I., when in default of male issue it passed to John Dymoke, son-in-law of Philip Marmion, in whose family it remains still.

Marnally (*Bernard*). Good-looking Irish tutor at "Happy-go-Lucky," a country house. He is accused of murdering the infant children of a young widow with whom he is in love, but is acquitted and goes back to Ireland. Some years later, he revisits America, meets his old love and marries her.— Miriam Coles Harris, *Happy-go-Lucky* (1881).

Marner (*Silas*). Miser and misogynist in humble life, who finds a baby-girl in his cottage one night, and in bringing her up, learns to have patience with life and charity with his kind.—George Eliot, *Silas Marner.*

Ma′ro, Virgil, whose full name was Publius Virgilius Maro (B.C. 70-19).

Oh, were it mine with the sacred Maro's art
To wake to sympathy the feeling heart,
Like him the smooth and mournful verse to dress
In all the pomp of exquisite distress ...
Then might I ...
Falconer, *The Shipwreck*, iii. 5 (1756).

Mar′onites (3 *syl.*), a religious semi-Catholic sect of Syria, constantly at war with their near neighbors, the Druses, a semi-Mohammedan sect. Both are now tributaries of the sultan, but enjoy their own laws. The Maronites number about 400,000, and the Druses about half that number. The Maronites owe their name to J. Maron, their founder; the Druses to Durzi, who led them out of Egypt into Syria. The patriarch of the Maronites resides at Kanobin; the hakem of the Druses at Deir-el-kamar. The Maronites, or "Catholics of Lebanon," differ from the Roman Catholics in several points, and have a pope or patriarch of their own. In 1860 the Druses made on them a horrible onslaught, which called forth the intervention of Europe.

Marotte (2 *syl.*), a footman of Gorgibus; a plain bourgeois, who hates affectation. When the fine ladies of the house try to convert him into a fashionable flunky, and teach him a little grandiloquence, he bluntly tells them he does not understand Latin.

Marotte. Voilà un laquais qui demande si vous êtes au logis, et dit que son maître, vous venir voir.

Madelon. Apprenez, sotte, à vous énoncer moins vulgaiment. Dites: Voilà un nécessaire que demande si vous êtes en commodité d'etre visibles.

Marotte. Je n'entends point le Latin.—Molière, *Les Précieuses Ridicules*, vii. (1659).

Marphi′sa, sister of Roge′ro, and a female knight of amazing prowess. She was brought up by a magician, but being stolen at the age of seven, was sold to the king of Persia. When she was 18, her royal master assailed her honor; but she slew him, and usurped the crown. Marphisa went to Gaul to join the army of Agramant, but subsequently entered the camp of Charlemagne, and was baptized.—Ariosto, *Orlando Furioso* (1516).

Marphu′rius, a doctor of the Pyrrhonian school. Sganarelle consults him about his marriage; but the philosopher replies, "Perhaps; it is possible; it may be so; everything is doubtful;" till at last Sganarelle beats him, and

Marphurius says he shall bring an action against him for battery. "Perhaps," replies Sganarelle; "it is possible; it may be so," etc., using the very words of the philosopher (sc. ix.).—Molière, *Le Mariage Forcé* (1664).

Marplot, "the busy body." A blundering, good-natured, meddlesome young man, very inquisitive, too officious by half, and always bungling whatever he interferes in. Marplot is introduced by Mrs. Centlivre in two comedies, *The Busy Body* and *Marplot in Lisbon*.

That unlucky dog Marplot ... is ever doing mischief, and yet (to give him his due) he never designs it. This is some blundering adventure, wherein he thought to show his friendship, as he calls it.—Mrs. Centlivre, *The Busy Body*, iii. 5 (1709).

⁎ This was Henry Woodward's great part (1717-1777). His unappeasable curiosity, his slow comprehension, his annihilation under the sense of his dilemmas, were so diverting, that even Garrick confessed him the decided "Marplot" of the stage.—Boaden, *Life of Siddons*.

N. B.—William Cavendish, duke of Newcastle, brought out a free tranlation of Molière's *L'Etourdi*, which he entitled *Marplot*.

Marquis de Basqueville, being one night at the opera, was told by a messenger that his mansion was on fire. "Eh bien," he said to the messenger, "adressez-vous à Mme. la marquise qui est en face dans cette loge; car c'est affaire de ménage."—Chapus, *Dieppe et ses Environs* (1853).

Marrall (*Jack*), a mean-spirited, revengeful time-server. He is the clerk and tool of Sir Giles Overreach. When Marrall thinks Wellborn penniless, he treats him like a dog; but as soon as he fancies he is about to marry the wealthy dowager, Lady Allworth, he is most servile, and offers to lend him money. Marrall now plays the traitor to his master, Sir Giles, and reveals to Wellborn the scurvy tricks by which he has been cheated of his estates. When, however, he asks Wellborn to take him into his service, Wellborn replies, "He who is false to one master will betray another;" and will have nothing to say to him.—Massinger, *A New Way to Pay Old Debts* (1628).

Married Men of Genius. The number of men of genius unhappy in their wives is very large. The following are notorious examples:—Socratês and Xantippê; Saadi, the Persian poet; Dantê and Gemma Donati; Milton, with Mary Powell; Marlborough and Sarah Jennings; Gustavus Adolphus and his flighty queen; Byron and Miss Milbanke; Dickens and Miss Hogarth; etc. Every reader will be able to add to the list.

Mars, divine Fortitude personified. Bacchus is the tutelary demon of the Mahommedans, and Mars the guardian potentate of the Christians.—Camoens, *The Lusiad* (1569).

That Young Mars of Men, Edward the Black prince, who with 8,000 men defeated, at Poitiers, the French king, John, whose army amounted to 60,000—some say even more (A. D. 1356).

The Mars of Men, Henry Plantagenet, earl of Derby, third son of Henry, earl of Lancaster, and near kinsman of Edward III. (See DERBY.)

Marse' Chan. Brave Virginian soldier whose lady-love enacts "My Lady Disdain" until news is brought her that he has fallen in battle. Then she grieves for him as a widow for her husband, and when she dies, she is buried by him.—Thomas Nelson Page, *In Ole Virginia* (1887).

Mars of Portugal (*The*), Alfonso de Albuquerque, viceroy of India (1452-1515).

Mars Wounded. A very remarkable parallel to the encounter of Diŏmed and Mars in the *Iliad*, v., occurs in Ossian. Homer says that Diomed hurled his spear against Mars, which, piercing the belt, wounded the war-god in the bowels; "Loud bellowed Mars, nine thousand men, ten thousand, scarce so loud, joining fierce battle." Then Mars ascending, wrapped in clouds, was borne upwards to Olympus.

Ossian, in *Carrick-Thura*, says that Loda, the god of his foes, came like a "blast from the mountain. He came in his terror and shook his dusky spear. His eyes were flames, and his voice like distant thunder. 'Son of night,' said Fingal, 'retire. Do I fear thy gloomy form, spirit of dismal Loda? Weak is thy shield of cloud, feeble thy meteor sword.'" Then cleft he the gloomy shadow with his sword. It fell like a column of smoke. It shrieked. Then rolling itself up, the wounded spirit rose on the wind, and the island shook to its foundation."

Marseilles' Good Bishop, Henri François Xavier de Belsunce (1671-1775). Immortalized by his philanthropic diligence in the plague at Marseilles (1720-1722).

Charles Borromēo, archbishop of Milan a century previously (1576), was equally diligent and self-sacrificing in the plague of Milan (1538-1584).

Sir John Lawrence, lord mayor of London during the great plague, supported 40,000 dismissed servants, and deserves immortal honor.

Darwin refers to Belsunce and Lawrence in his *Loves of the Plants*, ii. 433.

Marshal Forwards, Blücher; so called for his dash in battle, and the rapidity of his movements, in the campaign of 1813 (1742-1819).

Marsi, a part of the Sabellian race, noted for Magic, and said to have been descended from Circê.

Marsis vi quadam genitali datum, ut serpentium virulentorum domitores sint, et incantationibus herbarumque succis faciant medelarum mira.—*Gellius*, xvi. 11.

Marsig´lio, a Saracen king, who plotted the attack upon Roland, "under the tree on which Judas hanged himself." With a force of 600,000 men, divided into three companies, Marsiglio attacked the paladin in Roncesvallês and overthrew him; but Charlemagne, coming up, routed the Saracen, and hanged him on the very tree under which he planned the attack.—Turpin, *Chronicle* (1122).

Marsilia, "who bears up great Cynthia's train," is the marchioness of Northampton, to whom Spenser dedicated his *Daphnaida*. This lady was Helena, daughter of Wolfgangus Swavenburgh, a Swede.

No less praiseworthy is Marsilia,
Best known by bearing up great Cynthia's train.
She is the pattern of true womanhead....
Worthy next after Cynthia [*queen Elizabeth*] to tread,
As she is next her in nobility.
Spenser, *Colin Clout's Come Home Again* (1595).

Mar´syas, the Phrygian flute-player. He challenged Apollo to a contest of skill, but being beaten by the god, was flayed alive for his presumption.

Mar´tafax and Ler´mites (3 *syl.*), two famous rats brought up before the White Cat for treason, but acquitted.—Comtesse D'Aunoy, *Fairy Tales* ("The White Cat," 1682).

Marta´no, a great coward, who stole the armor of Gryphon, and presented himself in it before King Norandi´no. Having received the honors due to the owner, Martano quitted Damascus with Origilla; but Aquilant unmasked the villain, and he was hanged (bks. viii., ix.).—Ariosto, *Orlando Furioso* (1516).

Marteau des Heretiques, Pierre d'Ailly; also called *L'Aigle de la France* (1350-1420).

Martel (*Charles*), Charles, natural son of Pépin d'Héristal.

M. Collin de Plancy says that this "palace mayor" of France was not called "Martel" because he *martelé* ("hammered") the Saracens under Abd-el-Rahman in 732, but because his patron saint was *Martellus* (or *St. Martin*).—*Bibliothèque des Légendes*.

Thomas Delf, in his translation of Chevreuil's *Principles of Harmony, etc., of Colors* (1847), signs himself "Charles Martel."

Martext (*Sir Oliver*), a vicar in Shakespeare's comedy of *As You Like It* (1600).

Martha:

"Yea, Lord! Yet man must earn
And woman bake the bread;
And some must watch and wake
Early for other's sake
Who pray instead."
Julia C. R. Dorr, *Afternoon Songs* (1885).

Martha, sister to "The Scornful Lady" (no name given).—Beaumont and Fletcher, *The Scornful Lady* (1616).

Martha, the servant-girl at Shaw's Castle.—Sir W. Scott, *St. Ronan's Well* (time, George III.).

Martha, the old housekeeper at Osbaldistone Hall.—Sir W. Scott, *Rob Roy* (time, George I.).

Martha, daughter of Ralph and Louise de Lascours, and sister of Diana de Lascours. When the crew of the *Urania* rebelled, Martha, with Ralph de Lascours (the captain), Louise de Lascours, and Barabas, were put adrift in a boat, and cast on an iceberg in "the Frozen Sea." The iceberg broke, Ralph and Louise were drowned, Barabas was picked up by a vessel, and Martha fell into the hands of an Indian tribe, who gave her the name of Orgari´ta ("withered corn"). She married Carlos, but as he married under a false name, the marriage was illegal, and when Carlos was given up to the hands of justice, Orgarita was placed under the charge of her grandmother, Mde. de Théringe, and [probably] espoused Horace de Brienne.—E. Stirling, *The Orphan of the Frozen Sea* (1856).

Martha, a friend of Margaret. She makes love to Mephistophelês, with great worldly shrewdness.—Goethe, *Faust* (1798).

Martha, alias ULRICA, mother of Bertha, who is betrothed to Hereward and marries him.—Sir W. Scott, *Count Robert of Paris* (time, Rufus).

Martha (The Abbess), abbess of Elcho Nunnery. She is a kinswoman of the Glover family.—Sir W. Scott, *Fair Maid of Perth* (time, Henry IV.).

Martha (Dame), housekeeper to major Bridgenorth.—Sir W. Scott, *Peveril of the Peak* (time, Charles II.).

Martha Hilton, serving-maid in the household of the widowed Governor Wentworth, until, on his sixtieth birthday, he surprised the guests assembled to do him honor by wedding her in their sight.—Henry Wadsworth Longfellow, *Lady Wentworth*.

Marthé, a young orphan, in love with Frédéric Auvray, a young artist who loves her in return, but leaves her, goes to Rome, and falls in love with another lady, Elena, sister of the Duke Strozzi. Marthé leaves the Swiss pastor, who is her guardian, and travels in midwinter to Rome, dressed as a boy, and under the name of Piccolino. She tells her tale to Elena, who abandons the fickle, false one, and Frédéric forbids the Swiss wanderer ever again to approach him. Marthé, in despair, throws herself into the Tiber, but is rescued. Frédéric repents, is reconciled, and marries the forlorn maiden.—Mons. Guiraud, *Piccolino* (an opera, 1875).

Marthon, an old cook at Arnheim Castle.—Sir W. Scott, *Anne of Geierstein* (time, Edward IV.).

Marthon, alias RIZPAH, a Bohemian woman, attendant on the Countess Hameline of Croye.—Sir W. Scott, *Quentin Durward* (time, Edward IV.).

Martian Laws (not *Mercian* as Wharton gives it in his *Law Dictionary*) are the laws collected by Martia, the wife of Guithelin, great grand-son of Mulmutius, who established in Britain the "Mulmutian Laws" (*q.v.*). Alfred translated both these codes into Saxon-English, and called the Martian code *Pa Marchitle Lage*. These laws have no connection with the kingdom of Mercia.—Geoffrey, *British History*, iii. 13 (1142).

Guynteline, ... whose queen, ... to show her upright mind,
To wise Mulmutius' laws her Martian first did frame.
Drayton, *Polyolbion*, viii. (1612).

Martigny (*Marie le comptesse de*), wife of the earl of Etherington.—Sir W. Scott, *St. Ronan's Well* (time, George III.).

Martin, in Swift's *Tale of the Tub*, is Martin Luther; "John" is Calvin; and "Peter" the pope of Rome (1704).

In Dryden's *Hind and Panther*, "Martin" means the Lutheran party (1687).

Martin, the old verdurer near Sir Henry Lee's lodge.—Sir W. Scott, *Woodstock* (time, Commonwealth).

Martin, the old shepherd in the service of the lady of Avenel.—Sir W. Scott, *The Monastery* (time, Elizabeth).

Martin, the ape in the beast-epic of *Reynard the Fox* (1498).

Martin (Dame), partner of Darsie Latimer at the fishers' dance.—Sir W. Scott, *Redgauntlet* (time, George III.).

Martin (Sarah), the prison reformer of Great Yarmouth. This young woman, though but a poor dressmaker, conceived a device for the reformation of prisoners in her native town, and continued for twenty-four years her earnest and useful labor of love, acting as schoolmistress, chaplain and industrial superintendent. In 1835, Captain Williams, inspector of prisons, brought her plans before the Government, under the conviction that the nation at large might be benefitted by their practical good sense (1791-1843).

Martin Weldeck, the miner. His story is read by Lovel to a picnic party at St. Ruth's ruins.—Sir W. Scott, *The Antiquary* (time, George III.).

Martine (3 *syl.*), wife of Sganarelle. She has a furious quarrel with her husband, who beats her, and she screams. M. Robert, a neighbor, interferes, says to Sganarelle, "Quelle infamie! Peste soit le coquin, de battre ainsi sa femme." The woman snubs him for his impertinence, and says, "Je veux qu'il me battre, moi;" and Sganarelle beats him soundly for meddling with what does not concern him.—Molière, *Le Médecin Malgré Lui* (1666).

Martival (*Stephen de*), a steward of the field at the tournament.—Sir W. Scott, *Ivanhoe* (time, Richard I.).

Martivalle (*Martius Galeotti*), astrologer to Louis XI. of France.—Sir W. Scott, *Quentin Durward* (time, Edward IV.).

Martyr King (*The*), Henry VI., buried at Windsor beside Edward IV.

Here o'er the Martyr King [*Henry VI.*] the marble weeps.
And fast beside him once-feared Edward [*IV.*] sleeps;
The grave unites where e'en the grave finds rest,
And mingled lie the oppressor and th'opprest.
Pope.

Martyr King (*The*), Charles I. of England (1600, 1625-1649).

Louis XVI. of France is also called Louis "the Martyr" (1754, 1774-1793).

Martyrs to Science.

Claude Louis, Count Berthollet, who tested on himself the effects of carbonic acid on the human frame, and died under the experiment (1748-1822).

Giordano Bruno, who was burnt alive for maintaining that matter is the mother of all things (1550-1600).

Galileo, who was imprisoned twice by the Inquisition for maintaining that the earth moved round the sun, and not the sun round the earth (1564-1642).

And scores of others.

Marvellous Boy (*The*), Thomas Chatterton (1752-1770).

I thought of Chatterton, the marvellous boy,
The sleepless soul that perished in his pride.
Wordsworth.

Marwood (*Alice*), daughter of an old woman who called herself Mrs. Brown. When a mere girl she was concerned in a burglary and was transported. Carker, manager in the firm of Dombey and Son, seduced her, and both she and her mother determined on revenge. Alice bore a striking resemblance to Edith (Mr. Dombey's second wife), and in fact they were cousins, for Mrs. Brown was "wife" of the brother-in-law of the Hon. Mrs. Skewton (Edith's mother).—C. Dickens, *Dombey and Son* (1846).

Marwood (Mistress), jilted by Fainall, and soured against the whole male sex. She says, "I have done hating those vipers—men, and am now come to despise them;" but she thinks of marrying to keep her husband "on the rack of fear and jealousy."—W. Congreve, *The Way of the World* (1700).

Mary, the pretty housemaid of the worshipful, the mayor of Ipswich (*Nupkins*). When Arabella Allen marries Mr. Winkle, Mary enters her service; but eventually marries Sam Weller, and lives at Dulwich, as Mr. Pickwick's housekeeper.—C. Dickens, *The Pickwick Papers* (1836).

Mary, niece of Valentine, and his sister Alice. In love with Mons. Thomas.—Beaumont and Fletcher, *Mons. Thomas* (1619).

Mary. The queen's Marys, four young ladies of quality, of the same age as Mary, afterwards "queen of Scots." They embarked with her in 1548, on board the French galleys, and were destined to be her playmates in childhood, and her companions when she grew up. Their names were Mary Beaton (or *Bethune*), Mary Livingston (or *Leuison*), Mary Fleming (or *Flemyng*), and Mary Seaton (*Seton* or *Seyton*).

*** Mary Carmichael has no place in authentic history, although an old ballad says:

Yestrien the queen had four Marys;
This night she'll hae but three:
There was Mary Beaton, and Mary Seaton,
And Mary Carmichael, and me.

*** One of Whyte Melville's novels is called *The Queen's Marys*.

Mary Anne, a slang name for the guillotine; also called *L'abbaye de monte-à-regret* ("the mountain of mournful ascent"). (See MARIANNE.)

Mary Anne, a generic name for a secret republican society in France. See MARIANNE.)—B. Disraeli, *Lothair*.

Mary Anne was the red-name for the republic years ago, and there always was a sort of myth that these secret societies had been founded by a woman.

The Mary-Anne associations, which are essentially republic, are scattered about all the provinces of France.—*Lothair*.

Mary Graham, an orphan adopted by old Martin Chuzzlewit. She eventually married Martin Chuzzlewit, the grandson, and hero of the tale.

Mary Scudder. Blue-eyed daughter of a "capable" New England housewife. From childhood she has loved her cousin. Her mother objects on the ground that James is "unregenerate," and brings Mary to accept Dr. Hopkins, her pastor. The doctor, upon discovering the truth, resigns his betrothed to the younger lover.—Harriet Beecher Stowe, *The Minister's Wooing* (1862).

Mary Stuart, an historical tragedy by J. Haynes (1840). The subject is the death of David Rizzio.

*** Schiller has taken Mary Stuart for the subject of a tragedy. P. Lebrun turned the German drama into a French play. Sir W. Scott, in *The Abbot*, has taken for his subject the flight of Mary to England.

Mary Tudor. Victor Hugo has a tragedy so called (1833), and Tennyson, in 1878, issued a play entitled *Queen Mary*, an epitome of the reign of the Tudor Mary.

Mary and Byron. The "Mary" of Lord Byron was Miss Chaworth. Both were under the guardianship of Mr. White. Miss Chaworth married John Musters, and Lord Byron married Miss Milbanke; both equally unfortunate. Lord Byron, in *The Dream*, refers to his love-affair with Mary Chaworth.

Mary in Heaven (*To*) and *Highland Mary*, lyrics addressed by Robert Burns to Mary Campbell, between whom and the poet there existed a strong attachment previous to the latter's departure from Ayrshire to Nithsdale. *Mary Morison*, a youthful effusion, was written to the object of a prior passion. The lines in the latter

Those smiles and glances let me see,
That make the miser's treasure poor,

resembles those in *Highland Mary*—

Still o'er those scenes my mem'ry wakes,
And fondly broods with miser care.

Mary of Mode´na, the second wife of James II. of England, and mother of "The Pretender."

Mamma was to assume the character and stately way of the royal "Mary of Modena."—Percy Fitzgerald, *The Parvenu Family*, iii. 239.

Mary Queen of Scots was confined first at Carlisle; she was removed in 1568 to Bolton; in 1569 she was confined at Tutbury, Wingfield, Tutbury, Ashby-de-la-Zouche, and Coventry; in 1570 she was removed to Tutbury, Chatsworth, and Sheffield; in 1577 to Chatsworth; in 1578 to Sheffield; in 1584 to Wingfield; in 1585 to Tutbury, Chartley, Tixhall, and Chartley; in 1586 (September 25) to Fotheringay.

⁎ She is introduced by Sir W. Scott, in his novel entitled *The Abbot*.

Schiller has taken Mary Stuart for the subject of his best tragedy, and P. Lebrun brought out in France a French version thereof (1729-1807).

Mary queen of Scots. The most elegant and poetical compliment ever paid to woman was paid to Mary queen of Scots, by Shakespeare, in *Midsummer Night's Dream*. Remember, the *mermaid* is "Queen Mary;" the *dolphin* means the "dauphin of France," whom Mary married; the *rude sea* means the "Scotch rebels;" and the *stars that shot from their spheres* means "the princes who sprang from their allegiance to Queen Elizabeth."

Thou remember'st
Since once I sat upon a promontory,
And heard a *mermaid*, on a *dolphin's* back,
Uttering such dulcet and harmonious breath,
That the *rude sea* grew civil at her song;
And certain *stars shot madly from their spheres*,
To hear the sea-maid's music.
Act ii. sc. 1 (1592).

These "stars" were the earl of Northumberland, the earl of Westmoreland, and the duke of Norfolk.

Mary, the Maid of the Inn, the delight and sunshine of the parish, about to be married to Richard, an idle, worthless fellow. One autumn night, two guests were drinking at the inn, and one remarked he should not much like to go to the abbey on such a night. "I'll wager that Mary will go," said the other, and the bet was accepted. Mary went, and, hearing footsteps, stepped into a place of concealment, when presently passed her two young men carrying a young woman they had just murdered. The hat of one blew off, and fell at Mary's feet. She picked it up, and flew to the inn, told her story, and then, producing the hat, found it was Richard's. Her senses gave way, and she became a confirmed maniac for life.—R. Southey, *Mary, the Maid of the Inn* (from Dr. Plot's *History of Staffordshire*, 1686).

Mary Pyncheon. (See PYNCHEON.)

Mary Woodcock. (See WOODCOCK.)

Mar´zavan, foster-brother of the Princess Badou´ra.—*Arabian Nights* ("Camaralzaman and Badoura").

Masaniello, a corruption of [Tom]maso Aniello, a Neapolitan fisherman, who headed an insurrection in 1647 against the duke of Arcos; and he resolved to kill the duke's son for having seduced Fenella, his sister, who was deaf and dumb. The insurrection succeeded, and Masaniello was elected by his rabble "chief magistrate of Portici;" but he became intoxicated with his greatness, so the mob shot him, and flung his dead body into a ditch. Next day, however, it was taken out and interred with much ceremony and pomp. When Fenella heard of her brother's death, she threw herself into the crater of Vesuvius.

※ Auber has an opera on the subject (1831), the libretto by Scribe. Caraffa had chosen the same subject for an opera previously.

Mascarille (3 *syl.*), the valet of La Grange. In order to reform two silly, romantic girls, La Grange and Du Croisy introduce to them their valets, as the "marquis of Mascarille" and the "viscount of Jodelet." The girls are taken with their "aristocratic visitors;" but when the game has gone far enough, the masters enter and unmask the trick. By this means the girls are taught a most useful lesson, and are saved from any serious ill consequences.—Molière, *Les Précieuses Ridicules* (1659).

※ Molière had already introduced the same name in two other of his comedies, *L'Etourdi* (1653) and *Le Dépit Amoureux* (1654).

Masetto, a rustic engaged to Zerlīna; but Don Giovanni intervenes before the wedding, and deludes the foolish girl into believing that he means to make her a great lady and his wife.—Mozart, *Don Giovanni* (libretto by L. da Ponte, 1787).

Mask´well, the "double dealer." He pretends to love Lady Touchwood, but it is only to make her a tool for breaking the attachment between Mellefont (2 *syl.*) and Cynthia. Maskwell pretends friendship for Mellefont merely to throw dust in his eyes respecting his designs to carry off Cynthia, to whom Mellefont is betrothed. Cunning and hypocrisy are Maskwell's substitutes for wisdom and honesty.—W. Congreve, *The Double Dealer* (1700).

Massasowat. The account given by Edward Winslow of the illness of Massasowat—the friendly Indian chief whose alliance with the pilgrim father ceased only with his life—is a curious contribution to colonial literature. The remedies and diet used by Winslow are so extraordinary as to give unintentional point to his remark—"We, with admiration, blessed GOD for giving his blessing to such rare and ignorant means."—Edward Winslow, *Good News from New England* (1624).

Mason (*William*). The medallion to this poet in Westminster Abbey was by Bacon.

Mason (*Lady*). She forges a will purporting to be by her husband, securing his estate to herself and her son. Nobody suspects the fraud for years. When inquiry arises, Lady Mason is engaged to a gallant old baronet who will not credit her guilt until, conscience-smitten, she throws herself at his feet and acknowledges all.

Lucius Mason. The priggish, good-looking youth for whom Lady Mason risks so much. When he learns the truth he is stern in his judgment of the unhappy woman.—Anthony Trollope, *Orley Farm.*

Master (*The*). Goethe is called *Der Meister* (1749-1832).

I beseech you, Mr. Tickler, not to be so sarcastic on "The Master."—*Noctes Ambrosiana.*

Master (The Old). Mythical personage, whose breakfast-table monologues are among the most charming that enliven the pages of Oliver Wendell Holmes's *Poet at the Breakfast Table.* "I think he suspects himself of a three-story intellect, and I don't feel sure that he isn't right."

Master Adam, Adam Billaut, the French poet (1602-1662).

Master Humphrey, the narrator of the story called "The Old Curiosity Shop."—C. Dickens, *Master Humphrey's Clock* (1840).

Master Leonard, grand-master of the nocturnal orgies of the demons. He presided at these meetings in the form of a three-horned goat with a black human face.—*Middle Age Demonology.*

Master, like Man (*Like*).

Such mistress, such Nan;
Such master, such man.
Tusser, xxxviii. 22.

Again:

Such master, such man; and such mistress, such maid;
Such husband and huswife; such houses arraid.
T. Tusser, *Five Hundred Points of Good Husbandry*, xxxix. 22 (1557).

Master Matthew, a town gull.—Ben Jonson, *Every Man in His Humor* (1598).

Master Stephen, a country gull of melancholy humor. (See MASTER MATTHEW).—Ben Jonson, *Every Man in His Humor* (1598).

Master of Sentences, Pierre Lombard, author of a book called *Sentences* (1100-1164).

Masters (*Doctor*), physician to Queen Elizabeth.—Sir W. Scott, *Kenilworth* (time, Elizabeth).

Masters (The Four): (1) Michael O'Clerighe (*or* Clery), who died 1643; (2) Cucoirighe O'Clerighe; (3) Maurice Conry; (4) Fearfeafa Conry; authors of *Annals of Donegal*.

Mat Mizen, mate of H.M. ship *Tiger*. The type of a daring, reckless, daredevil English sailor. His adventures with Harry Clifton, in Delhi, form the main incidents of Barrymore's melodrama, *El Hyder, Chief of the Ghaut Mountains*.

Mat-o'-the Mint, a highwayman in Captain Macheath's gang. Peachum says, "He is a promising, sturdy fellow, and diligent in his way. Somewhat too bold and hasty; one that may raise good contributions on the public if he does not cut himself short by murder."—Gay, *The Beggar's Opera*, i. (1727).

Matabrune (3 *syl.*), wife of King Pierron of the Strong Island, and mother of Prince Oriant, one of the ancestors of Godfrey of Bouillon.—*Mediæval Romance of Chivalry*.

Mathematical Calculators.

George Parkes Bidder, president of the Institution of Civil Engineers (1800-).

Jedediah Buxton, of Elmeton, in Derbyshire. He would tell how many letters were in any one of his father's sermons, after hearing it from the pulpit. He went to hear Garrick, in *Richard III.*, and told how many words each actor uttered (1705-1775).

Zerah Colburn, of Vermont, U. S., came to London in 1812, when he was eight years old. The duke of Gloucester set him to multiply five figures by three, and he gave the answer instantly. He would extract the cube root of nine figures in a few seconds (1804-).

Vito Mangiamele, son of a Sicilian shepherd. In 1839 MM. Arago, Lacroix, Libri, and Sturm examined the boy, then 11 years old, and in half a minute he told them the cube root of seven figures, and in three seconds of nine figures (1818-).

Alfragan, the Arabian astronomer (died 820).

Mathilde (2 *syl.*), heroine of a tale so called by Sophie Ristaud, Dame Cottin (1773-1807).

Mathilde (3 *syl.*), sister of Gessler, the tyrannical governor of Switzerland, in love with Arnoldo, a Swiss, who saved her life when it was imperilled by an avalanche. After the death of Gessler she married the bold Swiss.—Rossini, *Guglielmo Tell* (an opera, 1829).

Mathis, a German miller, greatly in debt. One Christmas Eve a Polish Jew came to his house in a sledge, and, after rest and refreshment, started for Nantzig, "four leagues off." Mathis followed him, killed him with an axe, and burnt the body in a lime-kiln. He then paid his debts, greatly prospered, and became a highly respected burgomaster. On the wedding night of his only child, Annette, he died of apoplexy, of which he had previous warning by the constant sound of sledge-bells in his ears. In his dream he supposed himself put into a mesmeric sleep in open court, when he confessed everything, and was executed.—J. R. Ware, *The Polish Jew*.

⁎ This is the character which first introduced H. Irving to public notice.

Math′isen, one of the three anabaptists who induced John of Leyden to join their rebellion; but no sooner was John proclaimed "the prophet-king" than the three rebels betrayed him to the emperor. When the villains entered the banquet-hall to arrest their dupe, they all perished in the flames of the burning palace.—Meyerbeer, *Le Prophète* (an opera, 1849).

Matilda, wife of the earl of Leicester, in the "first American tragedy regularly produced" in the United States.

She plans to poison her lord, a plot discovered and thwarted by him. In shame and remorse she stabs herself to the heart, praying Leicester to "pity her youthful paramour."—William Dunlap, *Leicester, A Tragedy* (1794).

Matilda, sister of Rollo and Otto, dukes of Normandy, and daughter of Sophia.—Beaumont and Fletcher, *The Bloody Brother* (1639).

Matilda, daughter of Lord Robert Fitzwalter.

⁎ Michael Drayton has a poem of some 650 lines, so called.

Matilda, daughter of Rokeby, and niece of Mortham. Matilda was beloved by Wilfred, son of Oswald; but she herself loved Redmond, her father's page, who turned out to be Mortham's son.—Sir W. Scott, *Rokeby* (1812).

Matsys (*Quintin*), a blacksmith of Antwerp. He fell in love with Liza, the daughter of Johann Mandyn, the artist. The father declared that none but an artist should have her to wife; so Matsys relinquished his trade, and devoted himself to painting. After a while, he went into the studio of Mandyn to see his picture of the fallen angel; and on the outstretched leg of one of the figures painted a bee. This was so life-like, that when the old man returned, he proceeded to frighten it off with his handkerchief. When he discovered the deception, and found out it was done by Matsys, he was so delighted that he at once gave Liza to him for wife.

Matthew Merrygreek, the servant of Ralph Roister Doister. He is a flesh-and-blood representative of "vice" in the old morality-plays.—Nicholas Udall, *Ralph Roister Doister* (the first English comedy, 1634).

Matthias de Monçada, a merchant. He is the father of Mrs. Witherington, wife of General Witherington.—Sir W. Scott, *The Surgeon's Daughter* (time, George II.).

Matthias de Silva (*Don*), a Spanish beau. This exquisite one day received a challenge for defamation, soon after he had retired to bed, and said to his valet, "I would not get up before noon to make one in the best party of pleasure that was ever projected. Judge, then, if I shall rise at six o'clock in the morning to get my throat cut."—Lesage, *Gil Blas*, iii. 8 (1715).

(This reply was borrowed from the romance of Espinel, entitled *Vida del Escudero Marços de Obregon*, 1618).

Mattie, maid servant of Bailie Nicol Jarvie, and afterwards his wife.—Sir W. Scott, *Rob Roy* (time, George I.).

Maud Muller, pretty, shy haymaker, of whom the judge, passing by, craves a cup of water. He falls in love with the rustic maiden, but dare not wed her. She, too, recollects him with tenderness, dreaming vainly of what might have been her different lot.

"Of all sad words of tongue or pen,
The saddest are these, 'It might have been.'"
J. G. Whittier, *Maud Muller*.

Bret Harte has written a clever parody upon Maud Muller,—"*Mrs. Judge Jenkins*."

"There are no sadder words of tongue or pen,
Than 'It is, but *it hadn't orter been!*'"

Maude, (1 *syl.*), wife of Peter Pratefast, "who loved cleanliness."

She kepe her dishes from all foulenes;
And when she lacked clowtes withouten fayle,
She wyped her dishes with her dogges tayll.
Stephen Hawes, *The Pastyme of Pleasure*, xxix. (1515).

Maugis, the Nestor of French romance. He was one of Charlemagne's paladins, a magician and champion.

⁎ In Italian romance he is called "Malagigi" (*q.v.*).

Maugis d'Aygremont, son of Duke Bevis d'Aygremont, stolen in infancy by a female slave. As the slave rested under a white-thorn, a lion and a leopard devoured her, and then killed each other in disputing over the infant. Oriande la fèe, attracted to the spot by the crying of the child, exclaimed, "by the powers above, the child is *mal gist* ('badly nursed')!" and ever after it was called Mal-gist or Mau-gis'. When grown to manhood, he obtained the enchanted horse Bayard, and took from Anthenor (the Saracen) the the sword Flamberge. Subsequently he gave both to his cousin Renaud (*Renaldo*). Romance of *Maugis d'Aygremont et de Vivian son Frère*.

*** In the Italian romance, Maugis is called "Malagigi," Bevis is "Buovo," Bayard is "Bayardo," Flamberge is "Fusberta," and Renaud is "Renaldo."

Maugrabin (*Zamet*), a Bohemian, hung near Plessis lés Tours.

Hayraddin Maugrabin, the "Zingaro," brother of Zamet Maugrabin. He assumes the disguise of Rouge Sanglier, and pretends to be a herald from Liège [*Le.aje*].—Sir W. Scott, *Quentin Durward* (time, Edward IV.).

Mau´graby, son of Hal-il-Maugrăby and his wife Yandar. Hal-il-Maugraby founded Dom-Daniel "under the roots of the ocean" near the coast of Tunis, and his son completed it. He and his son were the greatest magicians that ever lived. Maugraby was killed by Prince Habed-il-Rouman, son of the caliph of Syria, and with his death Dom-Daniel ceased to exist.—*Continuation of Arabian Nights* ("History of Maugraby").

Did they not say to us every day that if we were naughty the Maugraby would take us?—*Continuation of Arabian Nights*, iv. 74.

Maugys, a giant who kept the bridge leading to a castle in which a lady was besieged. Sir Lybius, one of the knights of the Round Table, did battle with him, slew him, and liberated the lady.—*Libeaux* (a romance).

Maul, a giant who used to spoil young pilgrims with sophistry. He attacked Mr. Greatheart with a club; but Greatheart pierced him under the fifth rib, and then cut off his head.—Bunyan, *Pilgrim's Progress*, ii. (1684).

Maul of Monks, Thomas Cromwell, visitor-general of English monasteries, which he summarily suppressed (1490-1540).

Maulstatute (*Master*), a magistrate.—Sir W. Scott, *Peveril of the Peak* (time, Charles II.).

Maun´drel, a wearisome gossip, a chattering woman.

Maundrels, vagaries, especially those of a person in delirium, or the disjointed gabble of a sleeper.

*** The word is said to be a corruption of Mandeville (*Sir John*), who published a book of travels, full of idle tales and maundering gossip.

Mauprat (*Adrien de*), colonel and chevalier in the king's army; "the wildest gallant and bravest knight of France." He married Julie; but the king accused him of treason for so doing, and sent him to the Bastille. Being released by the Cardinal Richelieu, he was forgiven, and made happy with the blessing of the king.—Lord Lytton, *Richelieu* (1839).

Mauprat, the last of a fierce race of French robber nobles. His wild nature is subdued into real nobility by his love for his beautiful cousin.—George Sand, *Mauprat* (1836).

Maurice Beevor (*Sir*), a miser, and (failing the children of the countess) heir to the Arundel estates. The countess having two sons (Arthur and Percy), Sir Maurice hired assassins to murder them; but his plots were frustrated, and the miser went to his grave "a sordid, spat-upon, revengeless, worthless, and rascally poor cousin."—Lord Lytton, *The Sea-Captain* (1839).

Mause (*Old*), mother of Cuddie Headrigg, and a covenanter.—Sir W. Scott, *Old Mortality* (time, Charles II.).

Mauso′lus, king of Caria, to whom his wife Artĕmisia erected a sepulchre which was one of the "Seven Wonders of the World" (B.C. 353).

The chief mausoleums besides this are those of Augustus; Hadrian (now called the castle of St. Angelo) at Rome; Henri II., erected by Catherine de Medicis; St. Peter the martyr, in the church of St. Eustatius, by G. Balduccio; that to the memory of Louis XVI.; and the tomb of Napoleon in Les Invalides, Paris. The one erected by Queen Victoria to Prince Albert may also be mentioned.

Mauthe Dog, a black spectre spaniel that haunted the guard-room of Peeltown in the Isle of Man. One day a drunken trooper entered the guard-room while the dog was there, but lost his speech, and died within three days.—Sir W. Scott, *Lay of the Last Minstrel*, vi. 26 (1805).

Mauxalin′da, in love with Moore, of Moore Hall; but the valiant combatant of the dragon deserts her for Margery, daughter of Gubbins, of Roth'ram Green.—H. Carey, *Dragon of Wantley* (1696-1743).

Mavortian, a soldier or son of Mavors (*Mars*).

Hew dreadfull Mavortian the poor price of a dinner.—Richard Brome, *Plays* (1653).

Mawworm, a vulgar copy of Dr. Cantwell "the hypocrite." He is a most gross abuser of his mother tongue, but believes he has a call to preach. He tells old Lady Lambert that he has made several sermons already, but "always does 'em extrumpery" because he could not write. He finds his "religious vocation" more profitable than selling "grocery, tea, small beer, charcoal, butter, brickdust, and other spices," and so comes to the conclusion that it "is sinful to keep shop." He is a convert of Dr. Cantwell, and believes in him to the last.

Do despise me; I'm the prouder for it. I like to be despised.—I. Bickerstaff, *The Hypocrite*, ii. 1 (1768).

Max, a huntsman, and the best marksman in Germany. He was plighted to Agatha, who was to be his wife, if he won the prize in the annual match. Caspar induced Max to go to the wolf's glen at midnight and obtain seven charmed balls from Samiel, the Black Huntsman. On the day of contest, while Max was shooting, he killed Caspar, who was concealed in a tree, and the king in consequence abolished this annual *fête*.—Weber, *Der Freischütz* (an opera, 1822).

Maxime (2 *syl.*), an officer of the Prefect Almachius. He was ordered to put to death Valerian and Tibur´cê, because they refused to worship the image of Jupiter; but he took pity on them, took them to his house, became converted and was baptized. When Valerian and Tiburcê were afterwards martyred, Maxime said he saw angels come and carry them to heaven, whereupon Almachius caused him to be beaten with rods "til he his lif gan lete."—Chaucer, *Canterbury Tales* ("Second Nun's Tale," 1388).

⁎ This is based on the story of "Cecilia" in the *Legenda Aurea*; and both are imitations of the story of Paul and the jailer of Philippi (*Acts* xvi. 19-34).

Maximil´ian (son of Frederick III.), the hero of the *Teuerdank*, the *Orlando Furioso* of the Germans, by Melchior Pfinzing.

.... [*here*] in old heroic days
Sat the poet Melchoir, singing Kaiser Maximilian's praise.
Longfellow, *Nuremberg*.

Maximin, a Roman tyrant.—Dryden, *Tyrannic Love*, or *the Royal Martyr*.

Maximus, (called by Geoffrey, "Maximian"), a Roman senator, who in 381, was invited to become king of Britain. He conquered Armorica (*Bretagne*), and "published a decree for the assembling together there of 100,000 of the common people of Britain, to colonize the land, and 30,000 soldiers to defend the colony." Hence Armorica was called, "The other Britain" or "Little Britain."—Geoffrey, *British History*, v. 14 (1142).

Got Maximus at length the victory in Gaul,
... where after Gratian's fall.
Armorica to them the valiant victor gave....
Which colony ... is "Little Britain" called.
Drayton, *Polyolbion*, ix. (1612).

Maxwell, deputy chamberlain at Whitehall.—Sir W. Scott, *Fortunes of Nigel* (time, James I.).

Maxwell (*Mr. Pate*), laird of Summertrees, called "Pate in Peril;" one of the papist conspirators with Redgauntlet.—Sir W. Scott, *Redgauntlet* (time, George III.).

Maxwell (*The Right Hon. William*), Lord Evandale, an officer in the king's army.—Sir W. Scott, *Old Mortality* (time, Charles II.).

May, a girl who married January, a Lombard baron 60 years old. She loved Damyan, a young squire; and one day the baron caught Damyan and May fondling each other, but the young wife told her husband his eyes were so defective that they could not be trusted. The old man accepted the solution—for what is better than "a fruitful wife and a confiding spouse?"—Chaucer, *Canterbury Tales* ("The Merchant's Tale," 1388).

May unlucky for Brides. Mary, queen of Scotland, married Bothwell, the murderer of her husband, Lord Darnley, on May 12.

Mense malum Maio nubere vulgus ait.
Ovid, *Fasti*, v.

May-Day (*Evil*), May 1, 1517, when the London apprentices rose up against the foreign residents and did incalcuable mischief. This riot began May 1, and lasted till May 22.

May Queen (*The*), a poem in three parts by Tennyson (1842). Alice, a bright-eyed, merry child, was chosen May queen, and, being afraid she might oversleep herself, told her mother to be sure to call her early.

I sleep so sound all night, mother, that I shall never wake,
If you do not call me loud when the day begins to break;
But I must gather knots of flowers, and buds and garlands gay,
For I'm to be queen o' the May, mother, I'm to be queen o' the May.

The old year passed away, and the black-eyed rustic maiden was dying. She hoped to greet the new year before her eyes closed in death, and bade her mother once again to be sure to call her early; but it was not now because she slept so soundly. Alas! no.

Good night, sweet mother; call me before the day is born.
All night I lie awake, but I fall asleep at morn;
But I would see the sun rise upon the glad New Year,
So, if you're waking, call me, call me early, mother dear.

The day rose and passed away, but Alice lingered on till March. The snow-drops had gone before her, and the violets were in bloom. Robin had dearly loved the child, but the thoughtless village beauty, in her joyous girlhood, tossed her head at him, and never thought of love, but now, that she was going to the land of shadows, her dying words were:

And say to Robin a kind word, and tell him not to fret;
There's many worthier than I, would make him happy yet.
If I had lived—I cannot tell—I might have been his wife;
But all these things have ceased to be, with my desire of life.

Maye (*The*), that subtle and abstruse sense which the goddess Maya inspires. Plato, Epicharmos, and some other ancient philosophers refer it to the presence of divinity. "It is the divinity which stirs within us." In poetry it gives an inner sense to the outward word, and in common minds it degenerates into delusion or second sight. Maya is an Indian deity, and personates the "power of creation."

Hartmann possède la Mâye ... il laisse pénétrer dans ses écrits les sentiments, et les pensées dont son âme est remplie, et cherche sans cesse à resoudre les antithèses.—G. Weber, *Hist. de la Littérature Allemande.*

Mayeux, a stock name in France for a man deformed, vain, and licentious, but witty and brave. It occurs in a large number of French romances and caricatures.

Mayflower, a ship of 180 tons, which in December, 1620, started from Plymouth, and conveyed to Massachusetts 102 puritans, called the "Pilgrim Fathers," who named their settlement New Plymouth.

... the *Mayflower* sailed from the harbor [*Plymouth*],
Took the wind on her quarter, and stood for the open Atlantic,
Borne on the sand of the sea, and the swelling hearts of the pilgrims.
Longfellow, *Courtship of Miles Standish*, v. (1858).

Men of the Mayflower, the Pilgrim Fathers, who went out in the *Mayflower* to North America in 1620.

Mayflower (Phœbe), servant at Sir Henry Lee's lodge.—Sir W. Scott, *Woodstock* (time, commonwealth).

Maylie (*Mrs.*), the lady of the house attacked burglariously by Bill Sykes and others. Mrs. Maylie is mother of Harry Maylie, and aunt of Rose Fleming, who lives with her.

She was well advanced in years, but the high-backed oaken chair in which she sat was not more upright than she. Dressed with the utmost nicety and precision in a quaint mixture of bygone costume, with some slight concession to the prevailing taste, which rather served to point the old style pleasantly than to impair its effect, she sat in a stately manner, with her hands folded before her.

Harry Maylie, Mrs. Maylie's son. He marries his cousin, Rose Fleming.—C. Dickens, *Oliver Twist* (1837).

Mayor of Garratt (*The*). Garratt is between Wandsworth and Tooting. The first mayor of this village was elected towards the close of the eighteenth century, and the election came about thus: Garratt Common had often been encroached on, and in 1780 the inhabitants associated themselves together to defend their rights. The chairman was called *Mayor*, and as it happened to be the time of a general election, the society made it a law that a new "mayor" should be elected at every general election. The addresses of these mayors, written by Foote, Garrick, Wilks, and others, are satires and political squibs. The first mayor of Garratt was "Sir" John Harper, a retailer of brickdust; and the last was "Sir" Harry Dimsdale, a muffin-seller (1796). In Foote's farce so called, Jerry Sneak is chosen mayor, son-in-law of the landlord (1763).

Mayors (*Lord*) who have founded noble houses:

	Lord Mayor.
AVELAND (*Lord*), from Sir Gilbert Heathcote	1711
BACON (*Lord*), from Sir Thomas Cooke, draper	1557
BATH (*Marquis of*), from Sir Rowland Heyward, cloth-worker	1570
BRAYBROOKE (*Lord*), from Sir John Gresham, grocer	1547
BROOK (*Lord*), from Sir Samuel Dashwood, vintner	1702
BUCKINGHAM (*Duke of*), from Sir John Gresham, grocer	1547
COMPTON (*Lord*), from Sir Wolston Dixie, skinner	1585
CRANBOURNE (*Viscount*), from Sir Christopher Gascoigne	1753
DENBIGH (*Earl of*), from Sir Godfrey Fielding, mercer	1452
DONNE (*Viscount*), from Sir Gilbert Heathcote	1711
FITZWILLIAM (*Earl of*), from Sir Thomas Cooke, draper	1557
PALMERSTON (*Lord*), from Sir John Houblon, grocer	1695
SALISBURY (*Marquis of*), from Sir Thomas Cooke, draper	1557
WARWICK (*Earl of*), from Sir Samuel Dashwood, vintner	1702
WILTSHIRE (*Earl of*), from Sir Godfrey Boleine	1457

(queen Elizabeth was his granddaughter).

Maypole (*The*), the nickname given to Erangard Melousine de Schulemberg, duchess of Kendal, the mistress of George I., on account of her leanness and height (1719, died, 1743).

Mazarin of Letters (*The*), D'Alembert (1717-1783).

Mazarine (*A*), a common council-man of London; so called from the mazarine-blue silk gown worn by this civil functionary.

Mazeppa (*Jan*), a hetman of the Cossacks, born of a noble Polish family in Podolia. He was a page in the court of Jan Casimir, king of Poland, and while in this capacity intrigued with Theresia, the young wife of a Podolian count, who discovered the amour, and had the young page lashed to a wild horse, and turned adrift. The horse rushed in mad fury, and dropped down dead in the Ukraine, where Mazeppa was released by a Cossack, who nursed him carefully in his own hut. In time the young page became a prince of the Ukraine, but fought against Russia in the battle of Pultowa. Lord Byron (1819) makes Mazeppa tell his tale to Charles XII. after the battle (1640-1709).

"Muster Richardson" had a fine appreciation of genius, and left the original "Mazeppa" at Astley's a handsome legacy [1766-1836].—Mark Lemon.

M. B. Waistcoat, a clerical waistcoat. M. B. means "Mark [*of the*] Beast;" so called because, when these waistcoats were first worn by Protestant clergymen (about 1830), they were stigmatized as indicating a popish tendency.

He smiled at the folly which stigmatized an M. B. waistcoat—Mrs. Oliphant, *Phœbe, Jun.*, ii. 1.

McGrath (*Miss Jane*), "is a woman. Uv course doorin' the war she wuz loyal ez she understood loyalty. She believed in her State. She hed two brothers which went into the Confedrit servis, and she gave 'em both horses. But wood any sister let her brother go afoot?... Her case is one wich I shel push the hardest.... Ef Congress does not consider it favorably it will show that Congress hez no bowels."—D. R. Locke's, *The Struggles—Social, Financial and Political—of Petroleum*, V. Nasby.

Meadows (*Sir William*), a kind country gentleman, the friend of Jack Eustace, and father of young Meadows.

Young Meadows left his father's home because the old gentleman wanted him to marry Rosetta, whom he had never seen. He called himself Thomas, and entered the service of Justice Woodcock as gardener. Here he fell in love with the supposed chamber-maid, who proved to be Rosetta, and their marriage fulfilled the desire of all the parties interested.—I. Bickerstaff, *Love in a Village*.

Charles Dignum made his *début* at Drury Lane, in 1784, in the character of "Young Meadows." His voice was so clear and full-toned, and his manner of singing so judicious, that he was received with the warmest applause.— *Dictionary of Musicians.*

Meagles (*Mr.*), an eminently "practical man," who, being well off, travelled over the world for pleasure. His party consisted of himself, his daughter Pet, and his daughter's servant called Tatty-coram. A jolly man was Mr. Meagles; but clear-headed, shrewd, and persevering.

Mrs. Meagles, wife of the "practical man," and mother of Pet.—C. Dickens, *Little Dorrit* (1857).

Meal-Tub Plot, a fictitious conspiracy concocted by Dangerfield for the purpose of cutting off those who opposed the succession of James, duke of York, afterwards James II. The scheme was concealed in a meal-tub in the house of Mrs. Cellier (1685).

Measure for Measure. There was a law in Vienna that made it death for a man to live with a woman not his wife; but the law was so little enforced that the mothers of Vienna complained to the duke of its neglect. So the duke deputed Angelo to enforce it, and, assuming the dress of a friar, absented himself awhile, to watch the result. Scarcely was the duke gone, when Claudio was sentenced to death for violating the law. His sister Isabel went to intercede on his behalf, and Angelo told her he would spare her brother if she would give herself to him. Isabel told her brother he must prepare to die, as the conditions proposed by Angelo were out of the question. The duke, disguised as a friar, heard the whole story, and persuaded Isabel to "assent in words," but to send Mariana (the divorced wife of Angelo), to take her place. This was done; but Angelo sent the provost to behead Claudio, a crime which "the friar" contrived to avert. Next day, the duke returned to the city, and Isabel told her tale. The end was, the duke married Isabel, Angelo took back his wife, and Claudio married Juliet, whom he had seduced.—Shakespeare, *Measure for Measure* (1603).

⁎⁎* This story is from Whetstone's *Heptameron* (1578). A similar story is given also in Giraldi Cinthio's third decade of stories.

Medam´othi, the island at which the fleet of Pantag´ruel landed on the fourth day of their voyage. Here many choice curiosities were bought, such as "the picture of a man's voice," an "echo drawn to life," "Plato's ideas," some of "Epicurus's atoms," a sample of "Philome´la's needlework," and other objects of *vertu* to be obtained nowhere else.—Rabelais, *Pantagruel*, iv. 3 (1545).

⁎⁎* *Medamothi* is a compound Greek word, meaning "never in any place." So *Utopia* is a Greek compound, meaning "no place;" *Kennaquhair* is a Scotch

compound, meaning "I know not where;" and *Kennahtwhar* is Anglo-Saxon for the same. All these places are in 91° north lat. and 180° 1' west long., in the Niltālê Ocean.

Medea, a famous sorceress of Colchis who married Jason, the leader of the Argonauts, and aided him in getting possession of the golden fleece. After being married ten years, Jason repudiated her for Glaucê; and Medea, in revenge, sent the bride a poisoned robe, which killed both Glaucê and her father. Medea then tore to pieces her two sons, and fled to Athens in a chariot drawn by dragons.

The story has been dramatized in Greek by Eurĭpĭdês; in Latin by Senĕca and by Ovid; in French by Corneille (*Médée*, 1635), Longepierre (1695), and Legouvé (1849); in English by Glover (1761).

Mrs. Yates was a superb "Medea."—Thomas Campbell.

Mede′a and Absyr′tus. When Medea fled with Jason from Colchis (in Asia), she murdered her brother, Absyrtus, and, cutting the body into several pieces, strewed the fragments about, that the father might be delayed in picking them up, and thus be unable to overtake the fugitives.

Meet I an infant of the duke of York,
Into as many gobbets will I cut it
As wild Medea young Absyrtus did.
Shakespeare, 2 *Henry VI.* act v. sc. 2 (1591).

Mede′a's Kettle. Medea, the sorceress, cut to pieces an old ram, threw the parts into her caldron, and by her incantations changed the old ram into a young lamb. The daughters of Pelias thought they would have their father restored to youth, as Æson had been. So they killed him, and put the body in Medea's caldron; but Medea refused to utter the needful incantation, and so the old man was not restored to life.

Change the shape, and shake off age. Get thee Medea's kettle, and be boiled anew.—W. Congreve, *Love for Love*, iv. (1695).

Médecin Malgré Lui (*Le*) a comedy by Molière (1666). The "enforced doctor" is Sganarelle, a faggot-maker, who is called in by Géronte to cure his daughter of dumbness. Sganarelle soon perceives that the malady is assumed in order to prevent a hateful marriage, and introduces her lover as an apothecary. The dumb spirit is at once exorcised, and the lovers made happy with "pills matrimoniac."

In 1723 Fielding produced a farce called *The Mock Doctor*, which was based on this comedy. The doctor he calls "Gregory," and Géronte "Sir Jasper." Lucinde, the dumb girl, he calls "Charlotte," and Anglicizes her lover, Léandre, into "Leander."

Medham (*"the keen"*), one of Mahomet's swords.

Medicine (*The Father of*), Aretæos of Cappadocia (second and third centuries).

*** Also Hippoc´rates, of Cos (B.C. 460-357).

Medina, the Golden Mean personified, Step-sister of Elissa (*parsimony*) and Perissa (*extravagance*). The three sisters could never agree on any subject.—Spenser, *Faëry Queen*, ii. (1590).

Medley (*Matthew*), the factotum of Sir Walter Waring. He marries Dolly, daughter of Goodman Fairlop, the woodman.—Sir H. P. Dudley, *The Woodman* (1771).

Medo´ra, the beloved wife of Conrad, the corsair. When Conrad was taken captive by the Pacha Seyd, Medora sat day after day expecting his return, and feeling the heart-anguish of hope deferred. Still he returned not, and Medora died. In the mean time, Gulnare, the favorite concubine of Seyd, murdered the pacha, liberated Conrad, and sailed with him to the corsair's island home. When, however, Conrad found his wife dead, he quitted the island, and went no one knew whither. The sequel of the story forms the poem called *Lara*.—Byron, *The Corsair* (1814).

Medo´ro, a Moorish youth of extraordinary beauty, but of humble race; page to Agramante. Being wounded, Angelica dressed his wounds, fell in love with him, married him, and retired with him to Cathay, where, in right of his wife, he became a king. This was the cause of Orlando's madness.—Ariosto, *Orlando Furioso* (1516).

When Don Roldan [*Orlando*] discovered in a fountain proofs of Angelica's dishonorable conduct with Medoro, it distracted him to such a degree that he tore up huge trees by the roots, sullied the purest streams, destroyed flocks, slew shepherds, fired their huts, pulled houses to the ground, and committed a thousand other most furious exploits worthy of being reported in fame's register.—Cervantes, *Don Quixote*, I. iii. 11 (1605).

Medu´sa (*The soft*), Mary Stuart, queen of Scots (1545-1577).

Rise from thy bloody grave,
Thou soft Medusa of the "Fated Line,"
Whose evil beauty looked to death the brave!
Lord Lytton, *Ode*, i. (1839).

Meeta, the "maid of Mariendorpt," a true woman and a true heroine. She is the daughter of Mahldenau, minister of Mariendorpt, whom she loves almost to idolatry. Her betrothed is Major Rupert Roselheim. Hearing of her father's captivity at Prague, she goes thither on foot to crave his pardon.—S. Knowles, *The Maid of Mariendorpt* (1838).

Meg, a pretty, bright, dutiful girl, daughter of Toby Veck, and engaged to Richard, whom she marries on New Year's Day.—C. Dickens, *The Chimes* (1844).

Meg Dods, the old landlady at St. Ronan's Well.—Sir W. Scott, *St. Ronan's Well* (time, George III.).

Meg Merrilees, a half-crazy sibyl or gypsy woman.—Sir W. Scott, *Guy Mannering* (time, George II.).

Meg Murdochson, an old gypsy thief, mother of Madge Wildfire.—Sir W. Scott, *Heart of Midlothian* (time, George II.).

Megid´don, the tutelar angel of Simon the Canaanite. This Simon, "once a shepherd, was called by Jesus from the field, and feasted Him in his hut with a lamb."—Klopstock, *The Messiah*, iii. (1748).

Megingjard, the belt of Thor, whereby his strength was doubled.

Megissog´won (*"the great pearl feather"*), a magician, and the Manĭto of wealth. It was Megissogwon who sent the fiery fever on man, the white fog, and death. Hiawatha slew him, and taught man the science of medicine. This great Pearl-Feather slew the father of Niko´mis (the grandmother of Hiawatha). Hiawatha all day long fought with the magician without effect; at nightfall the woodpecker told him to strike at the tuft of hair on the magician's head, the only vulnerable place; accordingly, Hiawatha discharged his three remaining arrows at the hair tuft, and Megissogwon died.

"Honor be to Hiawatha!
He hath slain the great Pearl-Feather;
Slain the mightiest of magicians—
Him that sent the fiery fever, ...
Sent disease and death among us."
Longfellow, *Hiawatha*, ix. (1855).

Megnoun. (See MEJNOUN.)

Meg´ra, a lascivious lady in the drama called *Philaster*, or *Love Lies a-bleeding*, by Beaumont and Fletcher (1608).

Meiklehose (*Isaac*), one of the elders of Roseneath parish.—Sir W. Scott, *Heart of Midlothian* (time, George II.).

Meiklewham (*Mr. Saunders*), "the man of law," in the managing committee of the Spa hotel.—Sir W. Scott, *St. Ronan's Well* (time, George III.).

Meister (*Wilhelm*), the hero and title of a novel by Goethe. The object is to show that man, despite his errors and short-comings, is led by a guiding hand, and reaches some higher aim at last (1821).

Meistersingers, or minstrel tradesmen of Germany. An association of master tradesmen to revive the national minstrelsy, which had fallen into decay with the decline of the minnesingers, or love minstrels (1350-1523). Their subjects were chiefly moral or religious, and constructed according to rigid rules. The three chief were Hans Rosenblüt (armorial painter, born 1450), Hans Folz (surgeon, born 1479), and Hans Sachs (cobbler, 1494-1574). The next best were Heinrich von Mueglen, Konrad Harder, Master Altschwert, Master Barthel Regenbogen (the blacksmith), Muscablüt (the tailor), and Hans Blotz (the barber).

Mej´noun and Lei´lah (2 *syl.*), a Persian love tale, the Romeo and Juliet of Eastern romance. They are the most beautiful, chaste, and impassionate of lovers; the models of what lovers would be if human nature were perfect.

When he sang the loves of Megnôun and Leileh ... tears insensibly overflowed the cheeks of his auditors.—W. Beckford, *Vathek* (1786).

Mela Dryfoos. Loud young lady of the gilded period, "physically too amiable and too well corporeally ever to be quite cross," but selfish and coarse and reposing confidently upon the importance given her by her father's money.—W. D. Howells, *A Hazard of New Fortunes* (1889).

Melan´chates (4 *syl.*), the hound that killed Actæon, and was changed into a hart.

Melanchates, that hound
That plucked Actæon to the grounde,
Gaue him his mortal wound, ...
Was chaungéd to a harte.
J. Skelton, *Philip Sparow* (time, Henry VIII).

Melantius, a rough, honest soldier, who believes every one is true till convicted of crime, and then is he a relentless punisher. Melantius and Diph´ilus are brothers of Evadnê.—Beaumont and Fletcher, *The Maid's Tragedy* (1610).

⁎ The master scene between Antony and Ventidius in Dryden's *All for Love* is copied from *The Maid's Tragedy*. "Ventidius" is in the place of Melantius.

Melchior, one of the three kings of Cologne. He was the "Wise Man of the East" who offered to the infant Jesus *gold*, the emblem of royalty. The other two were Gaspar and Balthazar. Melchior means "king of light."

Melchior, a monk attending the black priest of St. Paul's.—Sir W. Scott, *Anne of Geierstein* (time, Edward IV.).

Melchior (i.e. Melchior Pfinzing), a German poet who wrote the *Teuerdank*, an epic poem which has the kaiser Maximilian (son of Frederick III.) for its hero. This poem was the *Orlando Furioso* of the Germans.

Sat the poet Melchior, singing kaiser Maximilian's praise.
Longfellow, *Nuremberg*.

Melea´ger, son of Althæa, who was doomed to live while a certain log remained unconsumed. Althæa kept the log for several years, but being one day angry with her son, she cast it on the fire, where it was consumed. Her son died at the same moment.—Ovid, *Metam.*, viii. 4.

Sir John Davies uses this to illustrate the immortality of the soul. He says that the life of the soul does not depend on the body as Meleager's life depended on the fatal brand.

Again, if by the body's prop she stand—
If on the body's life her life depend,
As Meleager's on the fatal brand;
The body's good she only would intend.
Reason, iii. (1622).

Melesig´enes (5 *syl.*). Homer is so called from the river Melês (2 *syl.*), in Asia Minor, on the banks of which some say he was born.

... various measured verse,
Æolian charms and Dorian lyric odes,
And his who gave them breath, but higher sung,
Blind Melesigēnês, thence Homer called,
Whose poem Phœbus challenged for his own.
Milton, *Paradise Regained* (1671).

Melema *(Tito)*. Beautiful accomplished Greek adventurer who marries and is unfaithful to Romola. He dies by the hand of an old man who had been the benefactor of his infancy and youth, and whom he had basely deserted and ignored.—George Eliot, *Romola*.

Me´li *(Giovanni)*, a Sicilian, born at Palermo; immortalized by his eclogues and idylls. Meli is called "The Sicilian Theocritus" (1740-1815).

Much it pleased him to peruse
The songs of the Sicilian Muse—
Bucolic songs by Meli sung.
Longfellow, *The Wayside Inn* (prelude, 1863).

Meliadus, father of Sir Tristan; prince of Lyonnesse, and one of the heroes of Arthurian romance.—*Tristan de Leonois* (1489).

*** Tristan, in the *History of Prince Arthur*, compiled by Sir T. Malory (1470), is called "Tristram;" but the old minnesingers of Germany (twelfth century) called the name "Tristan."

Mel´ibe (3 *syl.*), a rich young man married to Prudens. One day, when Melibê was in the fields, some enemies broke into his house, beat his wife, and wounded his daughter Sophie in her feet, hands, ears, nose and mouth. Melibê was furious and vowed vengeance, but Prudens persuaded him "to forgive his enemies, and to do good to those who despitefully used him." So he called together his enemies, and forgave them, to the end that "God of His endeles mercie wole at the tyme of oure deyinge forgive us oure giltes that we have trespased to Him in this wreeched world."—Chaucer, *Canterbury Tales* (1388).

*** This prose tale is a liberal translation of a French story.—See *MS. Reg.*, xix. 7; and *MS. Reg.*, xix. 11, British Museum.

Melibee, a shepherd, and the reputed father of Pastorella. Pastorella married Sir Calidore.—Spenser, *Faëry Queen*, vi. 9 (1596).

"Melibee" is Sir Francis Walsingham. In the *Ruins of Time*, Spenser calls him "Melibœ." Sir Philip Sidney (the "Sir Calidore" of the *Faëry Queen*) married his daughter Frances. Sir Francis Walsingham died in 1590, so poor that he did not leave enough to defray his funeral expenses.

Melibœus, one of the shepherds in *Eclogue* i. of Virgil.

Spenser, in the *Ruins of Time* (1591), calls Sir Francis Walsingham "the good Melibœ;" and in the last book of the *Faëry Queen* he calls him "Melibee."

Melin´da, cousin of Sylvia. She loves Worthy, whom she pretends to dislike, and coquets with him for twelve months. Having driven her modest lover to the verge of distraction, she relents, and consents to marry him.—G. Farquhar, *The Recruiting Officer* (1705).

Mel´ior, a lovely fairy, who carried off, in her magic bark, Parthen´opex, of Blois, to her secret island.—*Parthenopex de Blois* (a French romance, twelfth century).

Melisen´dra (*The princess*), natural daughter of Marsilio, and the "supposed daughter of Charlemagne." She eloped with Don Gayferos. The king, Marsilio, sent his troops in pursuit of the fugitive. Having made Melisendra his wife, Don Gayferos delivered her up captive to the Moors at Saragossa. This was the story of the puppet-show of Master Peter, exhibited to Don

Quixote and his squire at "the inn beyond the hermitage."—Cervantes, *Don Quixote*, II. ii. 7 (1615).

Melissa, a prophetess who lived in Merlin's cave. Bradamant gave her the enchanted ring to take to Roge´ro; so, under the form of Atlantês, she went to Alcīna's isle, delivered Rogēro, and disenchanted all the captives in the island.

In bk. xix. Melissa, under the form of Rodŏmont, persuaded Agramant to break the league which was to settle the contest by single combat, and a general battle ensued.—Ariosto, *Orlando Furioso* (1516).

⁎ This incident of bk. xix. is similar to that in Homer's *Iliad*, iii. iv., where Paris and Menelāos agree to settle the contest by single combat; but Minerva persuades Pandăros to break the truce, and a general battle ensues.

Me´lita (now *Malta*). The point to which the vessel that carried St. Paul was driven was the "Porto de San Paolo," and according to tradition, the cathedral of Citta Vecchia stands on the site of the house of Publius, the Roman governor. St. Paul's grotto, a cave in the vicinity, is so named in honor of this great apostle.

Meli´tus, a gentleman of Cyprus, in the drama called *The Laws of Candy*, by Beaumont and Fletcher (1647).

Melizyus, king of Thessaly, in the golden era of Saturn. He was the first to tame horses for the use of man.

Melizyus (King) held his court in the Tower of Chivalry, and there knighted Graunde Amoure, after giving him the following advice:

And first *Good Hope* his legge harneyes should be;
His habergion, of *Perfect Ryhteousnes*,
Gird first with the girdle of *Chastitie*;
His rich placarde should be good busines,
Brodred with *Alms* ...
The helmet *Mekenes*, and the shelde *Good Fayeth*,
His swerde *God's Word*, as St. Paule sayeth.
Stephen Hawes, *The Passe-tyme of Pleasure*, xxviii. (1515).

Mell (*Mr.*), the poor, down-trodden second master at Salem House, the school of Mr. Creakles. Mr. Mell played the flute. His mother lived in an almshouse, and Steerforth used to taunt Mell with this "degradation," and indeed caused him to be discharged. Mell emigrated to Australia, and succeeded well in the new country.—C. Dickens, *David Copperfield* (1849).

Melle´font (2 *syl.*), in love with Cynthia, daughter of Sir Paul Pliant. His aunt, Lady Touchwood, had a criminal fondness for him, and, because he repelled her advances, she vowed his ruin. After passing several hair-breadth escapes from the "double dealing" of his aunt and his "friend," Maskwell, he succeeded in winning and marrying the lady of his attachment.—W. Congreve, *The Double Dealer* (1700).

Mellifluous Doctor (*The*), St. Bernard, whose writings were called "a river of paradise" (1091-1153).

Melnotte (*Claude*), a gardener's son, in love with Pauline, "the Beauty of Lyons," but treated by her with contempt. Beauseant and Glavis, two other rejected suitors, conspired with him to humble the proud fair one. To this end, Claude assumed to be the prince of Como, and Pauline married him, but was indignant when she discovered how she had been duped. Claude left her to join the French army, and, under the name of Morier, rose in two years and a half to the rank of colonel. He then returned to Lyons, and found his father-in-law on the eve of bankruptcy, and Pauline about to be sold to Beauseant to pay the creditors. Claude paid the money required, and claimed Pauline as his loving and truthful wife.—Lord L. B. Lytton, *Lady of Lyons* (1838).

Melo (*Juan de*), born at Castile in the fifteenth century. A dispute having arisen at Esaló'na upon the question whether Achillês or Hector were the braver warrior, the Marquis de Ville'na called out, "Let us see if the advocates of Achillês can fight as well as prate." At the word, there appeared in the assembly a gigantic fire-breathing monster, which repeated the same challenge. Every one shrank back except Juan de Melo, who drew his sword and placed himself before King Juan II. to protect him, "tide life, tide death." The king appointed him alcaydê of Alcala la Real, in Graná'da, for his loyalty.—*Chronica de Don Alvaro de Luna*.

Melrose (*Violet*), an heiress, who marries Charles Middlewick. This was against the consent of his father, because Violet had the bad taste to snub the retired tradesman, and considered vulgarity as the "unpardonable sin."

Mary Melrose, Violet's cousin, but without a penny. She marries Talbot Champneys; but his father, Sir Geoffrey, wanted him to marry Violet, the heiress.—H. J. Byron, *Our Boys* (a comedy, 1875).

Melusi'na, the most famous of the *fées* of France. Having enclosed her father in a mountain for offending her mother, she was condemned to become a serpent every Saturday. When she married the count of Lusignan, she made her husband vow never to visit her on that day, but the jealousy of the count made him break his vow. Melusina was, in consequence, obliged to leave her mortal husband, and roam about the world as a ghost till the day of doom. Some say the count immured her in the dungeon wall of his castle.—*Jean d'Arras* (fourteenth century).

*** The cry of despair given by the *fée* when she discovered the indiscreet visit of her husband, is the origin of the phrase, *Un cri de Mélusine* ("A shriek of despair").

Melvil (*Sir John*), a young baronet, engaged to be married to Miss Sterling, the elder daughter of a City merchant, who promises to settle on her £800,000. A little before the marriage, Sir John finds that he has no regard for Miss Sterling, but a great love for her younger sister, Fanny, to whom he makes a proposal of marriage. His proposal is rejected; and it is soon brought to light that Miss Fanny had been clandestinely married to Lovewell for four months.—Colman and Garrick, *The Clandestine Marriage* (1766).

Melville (*Major*), a magistrate at Cairnvreckan village.—Sir W. Scott, *Waverley* (time, George II.).

Melville (*Sir Robert*), one of the embassy from the privy council to Mary queen of Scots.—Sir W. Scott, *The Abbot* (time, Elizabeth).

Melville, the father of Constantia.—C. Macklin, *The Man of the World* (1764).

Melville (*Julia*), a truly noble girl, in love with Faulkland, who is always jealous of her without a shadow of cause. She receives his innuendos without resentment, and treats him with sincerity and forbearance (see act i. 2).—Sheridan, *The Rivals* (1775).

Melyhalt (*The Lady*), a powerful subject of King Arthur, whose domains Sir Galiot invaded; notwithstanding which the lady chose Sir Galiot as her fancy knight and chevalier.

Memnon, king of the Ethiopians. He went to the assistance of his uncle, Priam, and was slain by Achillês. His mother, Eos, inconsolable at his death, weeps for him every morning, and her tears constitute what we call dew.

Memnon, the black statue of King Amen′ophis III., at Thebes, in Egypt, which, being struck with the rays of the morning sun, gives out musical sounds. Kircher says these sounds are due to a sort of clavecin or Æolian harp enclosed in the statue, the cords of which are acted upon by the warmth of the sun. Cambyses, resolved to learn the secret, cleft the statue from head to waist; but it continued to utter its morning melody notwithstanding.

Memnon, "the mad lover," general of As′torax, king of Paphos.—Beaumont and Fletcher, *The Mad Lover* (1617).

Memnon, the title of a novel by Voltaire, the object of which is to show the folly of aspiring to too much wisdom.

Memnon's Sister. He′mera, mentioned by Dictys Cretensis.

Black, but such as in esteem
Prince Memnon's sister might beseem.
Milton, *Il Penseroso* (1638).

Memorable (*The Ever-*), John Hales, of Eton (1584-1656).

Memory. The persons most noted for their memory are:

Magliabecchi, of Florence, called "The Universal Index and Living Cyclopædia" (1633-1714).

P. J. Beronicius, the Greek and Latin improvisator, who knew by heart Horace, Virgil, Cicero, Juvenal, both the Plinys, Homer, and Aristophănês. He died at Middleburgh, in 1676.

Andrew Fuller, after hearing 500 lines twice, could repeat them without a mistake. He could also repeat verbatim a sermon or speech; could tell either backwards or forwards every shop sign from the Temple to the extreme end of Cheapside, and the articles displayed in each of the shops.

"Memory" Woodfall could carry in his head a debate, and repeat it a fortnight afterwards.

"Memory" Thompson could repeat the names, trades, and particulars of every shop from Ludgate Hill to Piccadilly.

William Ratcliff, the husband of the novelist, could repeat a debate the next morning.

Memory (The Bard of), Samuel Rogers, author of the *Pleasures of Memory* (1762-1855).

Men of Prester John's Country. Prester John, in his letter to Manuel Comnēnus, says his land is the home of men with horns; of one-eyed men (the eye being in some cases before the head, and in some cases behind it); of giants, forty ells in height (*i.e.* 120 feet); of the phœnix, etc.; and of ghouls who feed on premature children. He gives the names of fifteen different tributary states, amongst which are those of Gog and Magog (now shut in behind lofty mountains); but at the end of the world these fifteen states will overrun the whole earth.

Menalcas, any shepherd or rustic. The name occurs in the *Idylls* of Theoc´ritos, the *Eclogues* of Virgil, and the *Shepheardes Calendar* of Spenser.

Men´cia of Mosquera (*Donna*) married Don Alvaro de Mello. A few days after the marriage, Alvaro happened to quarrel with Don An´drea de Baesa and kill him. He was obliged to flee from Spain, leaving his bride behind, and his property was confiscated. For seven years she received no intelligence of his whereabouts (for he was a slave most of the time), but when seven years had elapsed the report of his death in Fez reached her. The young widow now married the marquis of Guardia, who lived in a grand castle near Burgos, but walking in the grounds one morning she was struck with the earnestness with which one of the under-gardeners looked at her. This man proved to be her first husband, Don Alvaro, with whom she now fled from the castle; but on the road a gang of robbers fell upon them. Alvaro was killed, and the lady taken to the robbers' cave, where Gil Blas saw her and heard her sad tale. The lady was soon released, and sent to the castle of the marquis of Guardia. She found the marquis dying from grief, and indeed he died the day following, and Mencia retired to a convent.—Lesage, *Gil Blas*, i. 11-14 (1715).

Mendo´za, a Jew prize-fighter, who held the belt at the close of the last century, and in 1791 opened the Lyceum in the Strand, to teach "the noble art of self-defence."

I would have dealt the fellow that abused you such a recompense in the fifth button, that my friend Mendoza could not have placed it better.—R. Cumberland, *Shiva, the Jew*, iv. 2 (1776).

There is a print often seen in old picture shops, of Humphreys and Mendoza sparring, and a queer angular exhibition it is. What that is to the modern art of boxing, Quick's style of acting was to Dowton's.—*Records of a Stage Veteran*.

Mendoza (Isaac), a rich Jew, who thinks himself monstrously wise, but is duped by every one. (See under ISAAC.)—Sheridan, *The Duenna* (1775).

Menech´mians, persons exactly like each other, as the brothers Dromio. So called from the Mencœchmi of Plautus.

Menec´rates (4 *syl.*), a physician of Syracuse, of unbounded vanity and arrogance. He assumed to himself the title of Jupiter, and in a letter to Philip, king of Macedon, began thus: "Menecratês Jupiter to King Philip, greeting." Being asked by Philip to a banquet, the physician was served only with frankincense, like the gods; but Menecratês was greatly offended, and hurried home.

Mengs (*John*), the surly innkeeper at Kirchhoff village.—Sir W. Scott, *Anne of Geierstein* (time, Edward IV.).

Menippee (*Satyre*), a famous political satire, written during the time of what is called in French History the Holy League, the objects of which were to exterminate the Huguenots, to confine the king (Henri III.) in a monastery, and to crown the duc de Guise. The satire is partly in verse, and partly in prose, and its object is to expose the perfidious intentions of Philip of Spain and the culpable ambition of the Guises.

It is divided into two parts, the first of which is entitled *Catholicon d'Espagne*, by Pierre Leroy (1593), exposing those who had been corrupted by the gold of Spain; the second part is entitled *Abrégé des Etats de la Ligue*, by Gillot, Pithou, Rapin and Passerat, published 1594.

*** Menippus was a cynic philosopher and poet of Gadara, in Phœnicia, who wrote twelve books of satires in prose and verse.

Varro wrote in Latin a work called *The Satires of Menippus* (*Satyræ Menippeæ*).

Mennibojou, a North American Indian deity.

Mentz (*Baron von*), a Heidelberg bully, whose humiliation at the hands of the fellow-student he has insulted is the theme of an exciting chapter in Theodore S. Fay's novel, *Norman Leslie* (1835).

Menteith (*the earl of*), a kinsman of the earl of Montrose.—Sir W. Scott, *Legend of Montrose* (time, Charles I.).

Mentor, a wise and faithful adviser or guide. So called from Mentor, a friend of Ulyssês, whose form Minerva assumed when she accompanied Telemachus in his search for his father.—Fénelon, *Télémaque* (1700).

Mephistoph´eles (5 *syl.*), the sneering, jeering, leering attendant demon of Faust in Goethe's drama of *Faust*, and Gounod's opera of the same name. Marlowe calls the name "Mephostophilis" in his drama entitled *Dr. Faustus*. Shakespeare, in his *Merry Wives of Windsor* writes the name "Mephostophilus;" and in the opera he is called "Mefistofele" (5 *syl.*). In the old demonology, Mephistophelês was one of the seven chief devils, and second of the fallen archangels.

Mephostophilis, the attendant demon of Faustus, in Marlowe's tragedy of *Dr. Faustus* (1589).

There is an awful melancholy about Marlowe's "Mephostophilis," perhaps more expressive than the malignant mirth of that fiend in the renowned work of Goethe.—Hallam.

Mephostophilus, the spirit or familiar of Sir John Faustus or [Dr.] John Faust (Shakespeare, *Merry Wives of Windsor*, 1596). Subsequently it became a term of reproach, about equal to "imp of the devil."

Mercedes, Spanish woman, who, to disarm suspicion, drinks the wine poisoned for the French soldiery who have invaded the town. She is forced to let her baby drink it, also, and gives no sign of perturbation until the invaders, twenty in number, have partaken of the wine, and the baby grows livid and expires before their eyes.—Thomas Bailey Aldrich, *Mercedes* (drama, 1883).

Mercer (*Major*), at the presidency of Madras.—Sir W. Scott, *The Surgeon's Daughter* (time, George II.).

Merchant of Venice (*The*), Antonio, who borrowed 3000 ducats for three months of Shylock, a Jew. The money was borrowed to lend to a friend named Bassanio, and the Jew, "in merry sport," instead of interest, agreed to lend the money on these conditions: If Antonio paid it within three months, he should pay only the principal; if he did not pay it back within that time, the merchant should forfeit a pound of his own flesh, from any part of his body the Jew might choose to cut it off. As Antonio's ships were delayed by contrary winds, he could not pay the money, and the Jew demanded the forfeiture. On the trial which ensued, Portia, in the dress of a law doctor, conducted the case, and, when the Jew was going to take the forfeiture, stopped him by saying that the bond stated "a pound of flesh," and that, therefore, he was to shed no drop of blood, and he must cut neither more nor less than an exact pound, on forfeit of his life. As these conditions were practically impossible, the Jew was nonsuited and fined for seeking the life of a citizen.—Shakespeare, *Merchant of Venice* (1598).

The story is in the *Gesta Romanorum*, the tale of the bond being ch. xlviii., and that of the caskets ch. xcix.; but Shakespeare took his plot from a Florentine novelette called *Il Pecorone*, written in the fourteenth century, but not published till the sixteenth.

There is a ballad on the subject, the date of which has not been determined. The bargain runs thus:

"No penny for the loan of it,
For one year shall you pay—
You may do me a good turn
Before my dying day;
But we will have a merry jest,
For to be talkêd long;
You shall make me a bond," quoth he,
"That shall be large or strong."

Merchant's Tale (*The*), in Chaucer, is substantially the same as the first Latin metrical tale of Adolphus, and is not unlike a Latin prose tale given in the appendix of T. Wright's edition of Æsop's fables. The tale is this:

A girl named May married January, an old Lombard baron, 60 years of age, but entertained the love of Damyan, a young squire. She was detected in familiar intercourse with Damyan, but persuaded her husband that his eyes had deceived him, and he believed her.—Chaucer, *Canterbury Tales* (1388).

Mercian Laws. (See MARTIAN.)

Mercilla, a "maiden queen of great power and majesty, famous through all the world, and honored far and nigh." Her kingdom was disturbed by a soldan, her powerful neighbor, stirred up by his wife Adicĭa. The "maiden queen" is Elizabeth; the "soldan," Philip of Spain, and "Adicia" is injustice, presumption, or the bigotry of popery.—Spenser, *Faëry Queen*, v. (1596).

Mercu´tio, kinsman of Prince Escalus, and Romeo's friend. An airy, sprightly, elegant young nobleman, so full of wit and fancy that Dryden says Shakespeare was obliged to kill him in the third act, lest the poet himself should have been killed by Mercutio.—Shakespeare, *Romeo and Juliet* (1598).

Mercutio of Actors (*The*), William Lewis (1748-1811).

Mercy, a young pilgrim, who accompanied Christiana in her walk to Zion. When Mercy got to the Wicket Gate, she swooned from fear of being refused admittance. Mr. Brisk proposed to her, but being told that she was poor, left her, and she was afterwards married to Matthew, the eldest son of Christian.—Bunyan, *Pilgrim's Progress*, ii. (1684).

Merdle (*Mr.*), banker, a skit on the directors of the Royal British bank, and on Mr. Hudson, "the railway king." Mr. Merdle, of Harley Street, was called the "Master Mind of the Age." He became insolvent, and committed suicide. Mr. Merdle was a heavily made man, with an obtuse head, and coarse, mean, common features. His chief butler said of him, "Mr. Merdle never was a gentleman, and no ungentlemanly act on Mr. Merdle's part would surprise me." The great banker was "the greatest forger and greatest thief that ever cheated the gallows."

Lord Decimus [*Barnacle*] began waving Mr. Merdle about ... as Gigantic Enterprise. The wealth of England, Credit, Capital, Prosperity, and all manner of blessings.—Bk. ii. 24.

Mrs. Merdle, wife of the bank swindler. After the death of her husband, society decreed that Mrs. Merdle should still be admitted among the sacred few; so Mrs. Merdle was still received and patted on the back by the upper ten.—C. Dickens, *Little Dorrit* (1857).

Meredith (*Mr.*), one of the conspirators with Redgauntlet.—Sir W. Scott, *Redgauntlet* (time, George III.).

Meredith (*Mr. Michael*), "the man of mirth," in the managing committee of the Spa hotel.—Sir. W. Scott, *St. Ronan's Well*. (time, George III.).

Meredith (*Sir*), a Welsh knight.—Sir W. Scott, *Castle Dangerous* (time, Henry I.).

Meredith (*Owen*), pseudonym of the Hon. Edward Robert Bulwer Lytton (Lord Lytton), author of *The Wanderer* (1859), etc. This son of Lord Bulwer Lytton, poet and novelist, succeeded to the peerage in 1873.

Me′rida (*Marchioness*), betrothed to Count Valantia.—Mrs. Inchbald, *Child of Nature*.

Meridarpax, the pride of mice.

Now nobly towering o'er the rest, appears
A gallant prince that far transcends his years;
Pride of his sire, and glory of his house,
And more a Mars in combat than a mouse;
His action bold, robust his ample frame,
And Meridarpax his resounding name.
Parnell, *The Battle of the Frogs and Mice*, iii. (about 1712).

Merid′ies or "Noonday Sun," one of the four brothers who kept the passages of Castle Perilous. So Tennyson has named him; but in the *History of Prince Arthur*, he is called "Sir Permōnês, the Red Knight."—Tennyson, *Idylls* ("Gareth and Lynette"); Sir T. Malory, *History of Prince Arthur*, i. 129 (1470).

Merion (*James*), New York lawyer, who plays the lover to three women, honestly believing himself enamoured of each.—Ellen Olney Kirke, *A Daughter of Eve* (1889).

Merle (*Madame*), a plausible woman with an ambition to be thought the incarnation of propriety, who carries with her the knowledge that she is the mistress of a man who has a wife, and that Madame Merle's illegitimate daughter is brought up by the step-mother, who knows nothing of the shameful story.—Henry James, *The Portrait of a Lady* (1881).

Merlin (*Ambrose*), prince of enchanters. His mother was Matilda, a nun, who was seduced by a "guileful sprite," or incubus, "half angel and half man, dwelling in mid-air betwixt the earth and moon." Some say his mother was the daughter of Pubidius, lord of Math-traval, in Wales; and others make her a princess, daughter of Demetius, king of Demet′ia. Blaise baptized the infant, and thus rescued it from the powers of darkness.

Merlin died spell-bound, but the author and manner of his death are given differently by different authorities. Thus, in the *History of Prince Arthur* (Sir T. Malory, 1470), we are told that the enchantress Nimue or Ninive inveigled the old man, and "covered him with a stone under a rock." In the *Morte d'Arthur* it is said "he sleeps and sighs in an old tree, spell-bound by Vivien." Tennyson, in his *Idylls* ("Vivien"), says that Vivien induced Merlin to take shelter from a storm in a hollow oak tree, and left him spell-bound. Others say he was spell-bound in a hawthorn bush, but this is evidently a blunder. (See MERLIN THE WILD.)

⁂ Merlin made "the fountain of love," mentioned by Bojardo in *Orlando Innamorato*, l. 3.

Ariosto, in *Orlando Furioso*, says he made "one of the four fountains" (ch. xxvi).

He also made the Round Table at Carduel for 150 knights, which came into the possession of King Arthur on his marriage with Queen Guinever; and brought from Ireland the stones of Stonehenge on Salisbury Plain.

Allusion is made to him in the *Faëry Queen*; in Ellis's *Specimens of Early English Metrical Romances*; in Drayton's *Polyolbion*; in *Kenilworth*, by Sir W. Scott, etc. T. Heywood has attempted to show the fulfilment of Merlin's prophecies.

Of Merlin and his skill what region doth not hear?...
Who of a British nymph was gotten, whilst she played
With a seducing sprite ...
But all Demetia thro' there was not found her peer.
Drayton, *Polyolbion*, v. (1612).

Merlin (The English), W. Lilly, the astrologer, who assumed the *nom de plume* of "Mer′linus Anglĭcus" (1602-1681).

Merlin the Wild, a native of Caledonia, who lived in the sixteenth century, about a century after the great Ambrose Merlin, the sorcerer. Fordun, in his *Scotichronicon*, gives particulars about him. It was predicted that he would die by earth, wood, and water, which prediction was fulfilled thus: A mob of rustics hounded him, and he jumped from a rock into the Tweed, and was impaled on a stake fixed in the river bed. His grave is still shown beneath an aged hawthorn bush at Drummelzier, a village on the Tweed.

Merlin's Cave, in Dynevor, near Carmarthen, noted for its ghastly noises of rattling iron chains, brazen caldrons, groans, strokes of hammers, and ringing of anvils. The cause is this: Merlin set his spirits to fabricate a brazen wall to encompass the city of Carmarthen, and as he had to call on the Lady of the Lake, bade them not to slacken their labor till he returned; but he never did return, for Vivien by craft got him under the enchanted stone, and kept him there. Tennyson says he was spell-bound by Vivien in a hollow oak tree, but the *History of Prince Arthur* (Sir T. Malory) gives the other version.—Spenser, *Faëry Queen*, iii. 3 (1590).

Merop's Son, a nobody, a *terræ filius*, who thinks himself somebody. Thus Phaëton (Merop's son), forgetting that his mother was an earthborn woman, thought he could drive the horses of the sun, but not being able to guide them, nearly set the earth on fire. Many presume like him, and think themselves capable or worthy of great things, forgetting all the while that they are only "Merop's son."

Why, Phaëton (for thou art Merop's son),
Wilt thou aspire to guide the heavenly car,
And with thy daring folly burn the world?
Shakespeare, *Two Gentlemen of Verona*, act iii. sc. 1 (1594).

Merrilees (*Meg*), a half-crazy woman, part sibyl and part gypsy. She is the ruler and terror of the gypsy race. Meg Merrilees was the nurse of Harry Bertram.—Sir W. Scott, *Gay Mannering* (time, George II.).

In the dramatized version of Scott's novel, Miss Cushman [1845-9] made "Meg Merrilees" her own. She showed therein indisputably the attributes of genius. Such was her power over the intention and feeling of the part, that the mere words were quite a secondary matter. It was the figure, the gait, the look, the gesture, the tone, by which she put beauty and passion into language the most indifferent.—Henry Morley.

Merry Andrew, Andrew Borde, physician to Henry VIII. (1500-1549).

⁎ Prior has a poem on *Merry Andrew*.

Merry Monarch (*The*), Charles II., of England (1630, 1660-1685).

Merry Mount. Name of the home of a certain Englishman, called in the chronicle "the pestilent Morton," who set up a May-pole in colonial Massachusetts.

"That worthy gentleman, Mr. John Endicott, ... visiting those parts, caused that May-pole to be cut down, and rebuked them for their profaneness ... so they now (or others) changed the name of their place, 'Merry Mount,' again, and called it 'Mount Dagon.'"—William Bradford, *History of the Plymouth Plantation* (1630-50).

Mer´rylegs, a highly trained, performing dog, belonging to Signor Jupe, clown in Sleary's circus. This dog leaves the circus when his master disappears, but several years afterwards finds its way back and dies.—C. Dickens, *Hard Times* (1854).

Merthyr Tydvil, a corruption of *Martyr St. Tidfil*, a Welsh princess who suffered martyrdom.

Merton (*Tommy*), one of the chief characters in *Sanford and Merton*, a tale for boys, by Thomas Day (1783-9).

Merton (*Tristram*). Thomas Babington Macaulay (Lord Macaulay), so signs the ballads and sketches which he inserted in *Knight's Quarterly Magazine*.

Mertoun (*Basil*), *alias* VAUGHAN, formerly a pirate.

Mordaunt Mertoun, son of Basil Mertoun. He marries Brenda Troil.—Sir W. Scott, *The Pirate* (time, William III.).

Merveilleuse [*Mair.vay. 'uze*], the sword of Doolin of Mayence. It was so sharp that, if placed edge downwards on a block of wood, it would cut through it of itself.

Mervett (*Gustavus de*), in *Charles XII.*, an historical drama by J. R. Planché (1826).

Mervyn (*Mr. Arthur*), guardian of Julia Mannering.—Sir W. Scott, *Guy Mannering* (time, George II.).

Messali´na, wife of the Emperor Claudius of Rome. Her name is a by-word for incontinency (A.D. *-48).

Messalina (The Modern), Catherine II. of Russia (1729-1796).

Messalina of Germany, Barbary of Cilley, second wife of Kaiser Sigismund of Germany (fifteenth century).

Messala. Haughty young Roman who feigns friendship for Ben-Hur, and betrays his confidence. In after years the scheme of revenge nursed by the ruined youth is fulfilled in the famous chariot-race.—Lew Wallace, *Ben Hur, A Tale of the Christ* (1880).

Messiah (*The*), an epic poem in fifteen books, by F. G. Klopstock. The first three were published in 1748, and the last in 1773. The subject is the last days of Jesus, His crucifixion and resurrection. Bk. i. Jesus ascends the Mount of Olives, to spend the night in prayer. Bk. ii. John the Beloved, failing to exorcise a demoniac, Jesus goes to his assistance; and Satan, rebuked, returns to hell, where he tells the fallen angels his version of the birth and ministry of Christ, whose death he resolves on. Bk. iii. Messiah sleeps for the last time on the Mount of Olives; the tutelar angels of the twelve apostles, and a description of the apostles are given. Satan gives Judas a dream, and then enters the heart of Caiaphas. Bk. iv. The council in the palace of Caiaphas decree that Jesus must die; Jesus sends Peter and John to prepare the Passover, and eats His Last Supper with His apostles. Bk. v. The three hours of agony in the garden. Bk. vi. Jesus, bound, is taken before Annas, and then before Caiaphas. Peter denies his Master. Bk. vii. Christ is brought before Pilate; Judas hangs himself; Pilate sends Jesus to Herod, but Herod sends Him again to Pilate, who delivers Him to the Jews. Bk. viii. Christ nailed to the cross. Bk. ix. Christ on the cross. Bk. x. The Death of Christ. Bk. xi. The vail of the Temple rent, and the resurrection of many from their graves. Bk. xii. The burial of the body, and death of Mary, the sister of Lazarus. Bk. xiii. The resurrection and suicide of Philo. Bk. xiv. Jesus shows Himself to His disciples. Bk. xv. Many of those who had risen from their graves show themselves to others. Conclusion.

Messiah, an oratorio by Handel (1749). The liberetto was by Charles Jennens, nicknamed "Soliman the Magnificent."

Metanoi´a, Repentance personified, by William Browne, in *Britannia's Pastorals*, v. (Greek, *mĕtanoia*, "repentance".)

Faire Metanoia is attending
To croune thee with those joys that know no ending.
Pastorals, v. 1 (1613).

Metasta´sio. The real name of this Italian poet was Trapassi (*death*). He was brought up by Gravina, who Grecized the name (1698-1782).

⁎ So "Melancthon" is the Greek form of *Schwarzerdê* ("black earth"); "Œcolampadius" is the Greek form of the German name *Hausschein*; "Desiderius Erasmus" is *Gheraerd Gheraerd* (the first "Gheraerd" is Latinized into *Desiderius*, and the latter is Grecized into *Erasmus*).

Meth´os, drunkenness personified. He is twin-brother of Gluttony, their mother being Caro (*fleshly lust*). In the battle of Mansoul, Methos is slain by Agnei´a (*wifely chastity*) spouse of Eucra´tês (*temperance*), and sister of Parthen´ia (*maiden chastity*). (Greek, *methê* or *methŭs* is "drunkenness.")—Phineas Fletcher, *The Purple Island*, vii., xi. (1633).

Met´ophis, the corrupt chief minister of Sesostris.

Il avait l'ame aussi corrumpue et aussi artificieuse que Sesostris était sincère et généreux.—Fénelon, *Télémaque* (1700).

Mexit´li, chief god and idol of the Az´tecas. He leaped full-grown into life, and with a spear slew those who mocked his mother, Coatlan´tona (4 *syl.*).

Already at [*his mother's breast*] the blow was aimed,
When forth Mexitli leapt, and in his hand
The angry spear.
Southey, *Madoc*, ii. 21 (1805).

⁎ Of course, it will be remembered that Minerva, like Mexitli, was born full-grown and fully armed.

Mezen´tius, king of the Tyrrhenians, who put criminals to death by tying them face to face with dead bodies.—Virgil, *Æneid*, viii. 485.

Mezzora´mia, an earthly paradise in Africa, accessible by only one road. Gaudentio di Lucca discovered the road, and lived at Mezzoramia for twenty-five years.—Simon Berington, *Gaudentio di Lucca*.

M. F. H., Master [*of the*] Fox-hounds.

Micaw′ber (*Mr. Wilkins*), a most unpractical, half-clever man, a great speechifier, letter writer, projector of bubble schemes, and, though confident of success, never succeeding. Having failed in everything in the old country, he migrated to Australia, and became a magistrate at Middlebay.—C. Dickens, *David Copperfield* (1849).

⁎ This truly amiable, erratic genius is a portrait of Dickens's own father, "David Copperfield" being Dickens, and "Mrs. Nickleby" (one can hardly believe it) is said to be Dickens's mother.

Mi′chael (2 *syl.*), the special protector and guardian of the Jews. This archangel is messenger of peace and plenty.—Sale's *Korân*, ii. notes.

⁎ That Michael was really the protector and guardian angel of the Jews we know from *Dan.* x. 13, 21; xii. 1.

Milton makes Michael the leader of the heavenly host in the war in heaven. The word means "God's power." Gabriel was next in command to the archangel Michael.

Go, Michael, of celestial armies prince
Paradise Lost, vi. 44 (1665).

⁎ Longfellow, in his *Golden Legend*, says that Michael is the presiding spirit of the planet Mercury, and brings to man the gift of prudence ("The Miracle-Play," iii., 1851).

Michael, the "trencher favorite" of Arden of Feversham, in love with Maria, sister of Mosby. A weak man, who both loves and honors Arden, but is inveigled by Mosby to admit ruffians into Arden's house to murder him.—Geo. Lillo, *Arden of Feversham* (1592).

Michael, God of Wind (*St.*). At the promontory of Malea is a chapel built to St. Michael, and the sailors say when the wind blows from that quarter it is occasioned by the violent motion of St. Michael's wings. Whenever they sail by that promontory, they pray St. Michael to keep his wings still.

St. Michael's Chair. It is said that any woman who has sat on Michael's chair (on St. Michael's Mount, in Cornwall), will rule her husband ever after.

Michael Angelo of Battle-Scenes (*The*), Michael Angelo Cerquozzi, of Rome (1600-1660).

Michael Angelo of France (*The*), Jean Cousin (1500-1590).

Michael Angelo des Kermesses, Peter van Laar, called *Le Bamboche*, born at Laaren (1613-1673).

Or *Michel-Ange des Bamboches*.

Michael Angelo of Music (*The*), Johann Christoph von Glück (1714-1787).

Michael Angelo of Sculptors (*The*), Pierre Puget (1623-1694).

Réné Michael Slodtz is also called the same (1705-1764).

Michael Angelo Titmarsh, one of the pseudonyms under which Thackeray contributed to *Frazer's Magazine* (1811-1863).

Michael Armstrong, "the factory boy." The hero and title of a novel by Mrs. Trollope (1839). The object of this novel is to expose what the authoress considered to be the evils of the factory system.

Michael Perez, the copper captain. (See PEREZ.)

Michael, the Stammerer, born at Armorium, in Phrygia, mounted the throne as emperor of Greece in A.D. 820. He used all his efforts to introduce the Jewish Sabbath and sacrifice.

I think I have proved ...
The error of all those doctrines so vicious ...
That are making such terrible work in the Churches
By Michael the Stammerer.
Longfellow, *The Golden Legend* (1851).

Michal, in the satire of *Absalom and Achitophel*, by Dryden and Tate, is meant for Catharine, the wife of Charles II.—Pt. ii. (1682).

Michelot, an unprincipled, cowardly, greedy man, who tries to discover the secret of "the gold-mine." Being procurator of the president of Lyons, his office was "to capture and arrest" those charged with civil or criminal offences.—E. Stirling, *The Gold-Mine, or Miller of Grenoble* (1854).

Micomico′na, the pretended queen of Micomicon. Don Quixote's adventure to Micomiconnia came to nothing, for he was taken home in a cage, almost as soon as he was told of the wonderful enchantments.—Cervantes, *Don Quixote*, I. iv. 2 (1605.)

Mi′das (*Justice*), appointed to adjudge a musical contest between Pol and Pan. He decides in favor of Pan, whereupon Pol throws off his disguise, appears as the god Apollo, and, being indignant at the decision, gives Midas "the ears of an ass."—Kane O'Hara, *Midas* (1764).

Edward Shuter (1728-1776) was pronounced by Garrick "the greatest comic actor;" and C. Dibdin says: "Nothing on earth could have been superior to his 'Midas.'"

Midas's Ears. The servant who used to cut the king's hair, discovering the deformity, was afraid to whisper the secret to any one, but, being unable to contain himself, he dug a hole in the earth, and, putting his mouth into it, cried out, "King Midas has ass's ears!" He then filled up the hole and felt relieved.

Tennyson makes the barber a woman:

No livelier than the dame
That whispered "Asses' ears" among the sedge.
Tennyson, *The Princess.*

Middleburgh (*Mr. James*), an Edinburgh magistrate.—Sir W. Scott, *Heart of Midlothian* (time, George II.).

Middlemas (*Mr. Matthew*), a name assumed by General Witherington.

Mrs. Middlemas, wife of the general (born Zelia de Monçada).

Richard Middlemas, alias *Richard Tresham,* a foundling, apprenticed to Dr Gray. He discovers that he is the son of General Witherington, and goes to India, where he assumes the character of Sadoc, a black slave in the service of Mde. Montreville. He delivers Menie Gray by treachery to Tippoo Saib, and Hyder Ali gives him up to be crushed to death by an elephant.—Sir W. Scott, *The Surgeon's Daughter* (time, George II.).

Middlewick (*Mr. Perkyn*), a retired butterman, the neighbor of Sir Geoffrey Champneys, and the father of Charles. The butterman is innately vulgar, drops his *h's* and inserts them out of place, makes the greatest geographical and historical blunders, has a tyrannical temper, but a tender heart. He turns his son adrift for marrying Violet Melrose, an heiress, who snubbed the plebeian father. When reduced to great distress, the old butterman goes to his son's squalid lodgings and relents. So all ends happily.

Charles Middlewick, son of the retired butterman, well educated, and a gentleman. His father wanted him to marry Mary Melrose, a girl without a penny, but he preferred Violet, an heiress.—H. J. Byron, *Our Boys* (1875).

Midge, the miller's son, one of the companions of Robin Hood. (See MUCH.)

Midge (*The*), a well-born but friendless waif, thrown at the age of thirteen upon the charity of Dr. Peters, an eccentric bachelor. She cares for his house and for him in quaint, womanly fashion, very bewitching, until she is grown. The suit of another and a younger man, makes the doctor know, to his cost, how well he loves her. He holds his peace, and marries Midge to her lover.

"Then he went into the big pantry. In the corner on the shelf, still lay the crock in which the Midge had hidden her head, heavy with childish grief, years before. The old stool stood before it. He sat down on it and rested his hot forehead on the cool rim of the jar.

"And that's the end of the story."—H. C. Bunner, *The Midge* (1886).

Midian Mara, the Celtic mermaid.

Midlo'thian (*The Heart of*), a tale of the Porteous riot, in which the incidents of Effie and Jeanie Deans are of absorbing interest. Effie was seduced by Geordie Robertson (*alias* George Staunton), while in the service of Mrs. Saddletree. She murdered her infant, and was condemned to death; but her half-sister, Jeanie, went to London, pleaded her cause before the queen, and obtained her pardon. Jeanie, on her return to Scotland, married Reuben Butler; and Geordie Robertson (then Sir George Staunton) married Effie. Sir George being shot by a gypsy boy, Effie (*i.e.* Lady Staunton), retired to a convent on the Continent.—Sir W. Scott, *Heart of Midlothian* (time, George II.).

Midshipman Easy. (See EASY.)

Midsummer Night's Dream. Shakespeare says there was a law in Athens, that if a daughter refused to marry the husband selected for her by her father, she might be put to death. Egēus (3 *syl.*), an Athenian, promised to give his daughter, Hermia, in marriage to Demētrius; but, as the lady loved Lysander, she refused to marry the man selected by her father, and fled from Athens with her lover. Demetrius went in pursuit of her, followed by Helĕna, who doted on him. All four came to a forest, and fell asleep. In their dreams a vision of fairies passed before them, and on awaking, Demetrius resolved to forego Hermia, who disliked him, and to take to wife Helena, who sincerely loved him. When Egeus was informed thereof, he readily agreed to give his daughter to Lysander, and the force of the law was not called into action (1592).

*** Several of the incidents of this comedy are borrowed from the *Diana* of Montemayor, a Spaniard (sixteenth century).

Midwinter (*Ozias*), the *alias* of another Allan Armadale. His father has murdered the father of the real Allan, and the son of the homicide resolves to keep his own identity a secret, while trying to atone to Allan for the wrong done him. He loves and marries the perfidious governess of Allan's betrothed.—Wilkie Collins, *Armadale*.

Miggs (*Miss*), the handmaiden and "comforter" of Mrs. Varden. A tall, gaunt young woman, addicted to pattens; slender and shrewish, of a sharp and acid visage. She held the male sex in utter contempt, but had a secret exception in favor of Sim Tappertit, who irreverently called her "scraggy." Miss Miggs always sided with madam against master, and made out that she was a suffering martyr, and he an inhuman Nero. She called ma'am "mim;" said her sister lived at "twenty-sivin;" Simon she called "Simmun." She said Mrs. Varden was "the mildest, amiablest, forgivingest-sperited, longest-sufferingest female in existence." Baffled in all her matrimonial hopes, she was at last appointed female turnkey to a county Bridewell, which office she held for thirty years, when she died.

Miss Miggs, baffled in all her schemes ... and cast upon a thankless, undeserving world, turned very sharp and sour ... but the justices of the peace for Middlesex ... selected her from 124 competitors to the office of turnkey for a county Bridewell, which she held till her decease, more than thirty years afterwards, remaining single all that time.—C. Dickens, *Barnaby Rudge* (1841).

Mign´on, a beautiful, dwarfish, fairy-like Italian girl, in love with Wilhelm, her protector. She glides before us in the mazy dance, or whirls her tambourine like an Ariel. Full of fervor, full of love, full of rapture, she is overwhelmed with the torrent of despair at finding her love is not returned, becomes insane, and dies.—Goethe, *Wilhelm Meister's Apprenticeship* (1794-6).

Sir W. Scott drew his "Fenella," in *Peveril of the Peak*, from this character; and Victor Hugo has reproduced her in his *Notre Dame*, under the name of "Esmeralda."

Mignonette:

"A pitcher of mignonette
In a tenement's highest casement
Queer sort of flower-pot—yet
That pitcher of mignonette
Is a garden in heaven set
To the little sick child in the basement,
The pitcher of mignonette.
In the tenement's highest casement."
Henry Cuyler Bunner, *Airs from Arcady and Elsewhere* (1884).

Migonnet, a fairy king, who wished to marry the princess brought up by Violenta, the fairy mother.

Of all dwarfs he was the smallest. His feet were like an eagle's, and close to the knees, for legs he had none. His royal robes were not above half a yard long, and trailed one-third part upon the ground. His head was as big as a peck, and his nose long enough for twelve birds to perch on. His beard was bushy enough for a canary's nest, and his ears reached a foot above his head.—Comtesse D'Aulnoy, *Fairy Tales* ("The White Cat," 1682).

Mikado (*of Japan*), the hero of Gilbert and Sullivan's opera "The Mikado." The plot turns upon the complications brought about the Mikado's severe laws against flirting:

"So he decreed in words succint,
That all who flirted, leered or winked,
Unless connubially linked,
Should forthwith be beheaded."

Mi′lan (*The duke of*), an Italian prince, an ally of the Lancastrians.—Sir W. Scott, *Anne of Geierstein* (time, Edward IV.).

Milan Decree, a decree of Napoleon Bonaparte, dated Milan, December 27, 1807, declaring "the whole British empire to be in a state of blockade, and prohibiting all countries from trading with Great Britain, or using any article made therein."

₊ As Britain was the best customer of the very nations forbidden to deal with her, this very absurd decree was a two-edged sword, cutting both ways.

Mildred, the bride, "fresh and fair as May," whom Philip, the pastor, installs as *Mistress of the Manse*, in Josiah Gilbert Holland's poem of that name (1874).

Mildmay (*Frank*), hero of sea-story bearing his name.—Frederick Marryatt.

Mile′sian Fables (*Milesiæ Fabulæ*), very wanton and ludicrous tales. Sir Edward Bulwer Lytton (Lord Lytton) published six of the *Lost Tales of Milētus* in rhymeless verse. He pretends he borrowed them from the scattered remnants preserved by Apollodo′rus and Conon, contained in the pages of Pausa′nias and Athenæus, or dispersed throughout the Scholiasts. The Milesian tales were, for the most part, in prose; but Ovid tells us that Aristi′dês rendered some of them into verse, and Sisenna into Latin.

Junxit Aristides Milesia carmina secum
Pulsus Aristides nec tamen urba sua est.

The original tales by Antonius Diog′enês are described by Photius. It appears that they were great favorites with the luxurious Sybarites. A compilation was made by Aristīdês, by whom (according to Ovid) some were versified also. The Latin translation by Sisenna was made about the time of the civil wars of Ma′rius and Sylla. Parthen′ius Nice′nus, who taught Virgil Greek, borrowed thirty-six of the tales, which he dedicated to Cornelius Gallus, and entitled *Erôtikôn Pathêmatôn* ("love stories").

Milesia Crimina, amatory offences. Venus was worshipped at Milētus, and hence the loose amatory tales of Antonius Diogenês were entitled *Milesiæ Fabulæ*.

Mile′sians, the "ancient" Irish. The legend is that Ireland was once peopled by the Fir-bolg or Belgæ from Britain, who were subdued by Milesians from Asia Minor, called the Gaels of Ireland.

Miles (*Throckmorton*), harum-scarum, brave, indiscreet, over-generous hero of Constance Cary Harrison's story, *Flower de Hundred* (1890).

Milford (*Colonel*), a friend of Sir Geoffrey Peveril.—Sir W. Scott, *Peveril of the Peak* (time, Charles II.).

Milford (*Jack*), a natural son of Widow Warren's late husband. He was the crony of Harry Dornton, with whom he ran "the road to ruin." Jack had a fortune left him, but he soon scattered it by his extravagant living, and was imprisoned for debt. Harry then promised to marry Widow Warren if she would advance him £6,000 to pay off his friend's debts with. When Harry's father heard of this bargain, he was so moved that he advanced the money himself; and Harry, being set free from his bargain, married the widow's daughter instead of the widow. Thus all were rescued from "the road to ruin."—Holcroft, *The Road to Ruin* (1792).

Milinowski, a portly, imposing American widow, who, after twenty years spent under the marital rule of a Prussian army officer, "takes kindly to the prose of life." She is the exemplary and not unkindly chaperone of *Miss Caroline Lester*, heroine of Charlotte Dunning's book *Upon a Cast* (1885).

Milk-Pail (*The*), which was to gain a fortune, (See PERRETTE.)

Millamant, the *prétendue* of Edward Mirabell. She is a most brilliant girl, who says she "loves to give pain, because cruelty is a proof of power; and when one parts with one's cruelty, one parts with one's power." Millamant is far gone in poetry, and her heart is not in her own keeping. Sir Wilful Witwould makes love to her, but she detests "the superannuated lubber."—W. Congreve, *The Way of the World* (1700).

Miller (*James*), the "tiger" of the Hon. Mr. Flammer. James was brought up in the stable, educated on the turf and *pavé*, polished and completed in the fives-court. He was engaged to Mary Chintz, the maid of Miss Bloomfield.—C. Selby, *The Unfinished Gentleman*.

Miller, (*Joe*), James Ballantyne, author of *Old Joe Miller, by the Editor of New J. M.*, three vols. (1801).

*** Mottley compiled a jest-book in the reign of James II., entitled *Joe Miller's Jests*. The phrase, "That's a Joe Miller," means "that's a jest from Mottley's book."

Miller (*Maximilian Christopher*), the Saxon giant; height eight feet. His hand measured a foot; his second finger was nine inches long; his head unusually large. He wore a rich Hungarian jacket and a huge plumed cap. This giant was exhibited in London in the year 1733. He died aged 60; was born at Leipsic (1674-1734).

Miller (*Draxy*), bonny daughter of a thriftless, honest man, whose energy in the effort to recover some hundreds of acres of woodland deeded to her in jest, and supposed to be unprofitable, leads to comfort for her father, and a happy marriage for herself.—*Saxe Holm Stories* (1886).

Miller of Mansfield (*The*), John Cockle, a miller and keeper of Sherwood Forest. Hearing the report of a gun, John Cockle went into the forest at night to find poachers, and came upon the king (Henry VIII.), who had been hunting, and had got separated from his courtiers. The miller collared him; but, being told he was a wayfarer, who had lost himself in the forest, he took him home with him for the night. Next day, the courtiers were brought to the same house, having been seized as poachers by the under-keepers. It was then discovered that the miller's guest was the king, who knighted the miller, and settled on him 1000 marks a year.—R. Dodsley, *The King and the Miller of Mansfield* (1737).

Miller of Trompington (*The*), Simon Simkin, an arrant thief. Two scholars undertook to see that a sack of corn was ground for "Solar Hill College," without being tampered with; so one stood at the hopper, and the other at the trough below. In the mean time, Simon Simkin let loose the scholars' horse; and while they went to catch it, he purloined half a bushel of the flour, which was made into cakes, and substituted meal in its stead. But the young men had their revenge; they not only made off with the flour, meal, and cakes without payment, but left the miller well trounced also.—Chaucer, *Canterbury Tales* ("The Reeve's Tale," 1388).

A trick something like that played off on the Miller of Trompington.—*Review of Kirkton*, xix. 253.

Miller on the Dee. "There was a Jolly Miller once lived on the River Dee," is a song by Isaac Bickerstaff, introduced in *Love in a Village*, i. 1 (1763).

Mills (*Miss*), the bosom friend of Dora. Supposed to have been blighted in early life in some love affair, and hence she looks on the happiness of others with a calm, supercilious benignity, and talks of herself as being "in the desert of Sahara."—C. Dickens, *David Copperfield* (1849).

Millwood (*Sarah*), the courtezan who enticed George Barnwell to rob his master and murder his uncle. Sarah Millwood spent all the money that George Barnwell obtained by these crimes, then turned him out of doors, and informed against him. Both were hanged.—George Lillo, *George Barnwell* (1732).

Milly, the wife of William Swidger. She is the good angel of the tale.—C. Dickens, *The Haunted Man* (1848).

Milo, an athlete of Croto´na, noted for his amazing strength. He could carry on his shoulders a four-year-old heifer. When old, Milo attempted to tear in twain an oak tree, but the parts, closing on his hands, held him fast, till he was devoured by wolves.

Milo (The English), Thomas Topham, of London (1710-1752).

Milton, introduced by Sir Walter Scott in *Woodstock* (time, Commonwealth).

Milton of Germany, Frederick Gottlieb Klopstock, author of *The Messiah*, an epic poem (1724-1803).

A very German Milton indeed.
Coleridge.

Milton's Monument, in Westminster Abbey, was by Rysbrack.

Milvey (*The Rev. Frank*), a "young man expensively educated and wretchedly paid, with quite a young wife and half a dozen young children. He was under the necessity of teaching ... to eke out his scanty means, yet was generally expected to have more time to spare than the idlest person in the parish, and more money than the richest."

Mrs. Milvey (Margaretta), a pretty, bright little woman, emphatic and impulsive, but "something worn by anxiety. She had repressed many pretty tastes and bright fancies, and substituted instead schools, soup, flannel, coals, and all the week-day cares and Sunday coughs of a large population, young and old."—C. Dickens, *Our Mutual Friend* (1864).

Minagro´bis, admiral of the cats in the great sea-fight of the cats and rats. Minagrobis won the victory by devouring the admiral of the rats, who had made three voyages round the world in very excellent ships, in which he was neither one of the officers nor one of the crew, but a kind of interloper.—Comtesse D'Aulnoy, *Fairy Tales* ("The White Cat," 1682).

Min´cing, lady's-maid to Millamant. She says *mem* for ma'am, *fit* for fought, *la'ship* for ladyship, etc.—W. Congreve, *The Way of the World* (1700).

Minikin (*Lord*), married to a cousin of Sir John Trotley, but, according to *bon ton*, he flirts with Miss Tittup; and Miss Tittup, who is engaged to Colonel Tivy, flirts with a married man.

Lady Minikin, wife of Lord Minikin. According to *bon ton*, she hates her husband, and flirts with Colonel Tivy; and Colonel Tivy, who is engaged to Miss Tittup, flirts with a married woman. It is *bon ton* to do so.—Garrick, *Bon Ton* (1760).

Minjekah´wun, Hiawatha's mittens, made of deer-skin. When Hiawatha had his mittens on, he could smite the hardest rocks asunder.

He [*Hiawatha*] had mittens, Minjekahwun,
Magic mittens made of deer-skin;
When upon his hands he wore them,
He could smite the rocks asunder.
Longfellow, *Hiawatha*, iv. (1855).

Minna and Brenda, two beautiful girls, the daughters of Magnus Troil, the old udaller of Zetland. Minna was stately in form, with dark eyes and raven locks; credulous and vain, but not giddy; enthusiastic, talented and warm-hearted. She loved Captain Clement Cleveland; but Cleveland was killed in an encounter on the Spanish main. Brenda had golden hair, a bloom on her cheeks, a fairy form, and a serene, cheerful disposition. She was less the heroine than her sister, but more the loving and confiding woman. She married Mordaunt Mertoun (ch. iii).—Sir W. Scott, *The Pirate* (time, William III.).

Minna von Barnhelm. A wealthy girl who is engaged to Major von Tellheim, a Prussian soldier. He loses his fortune, is wounded and suspected of dishonor, and from regard for Minna strives to break the engagement. Everything is righted, and they marry.—G. E. Lessing.

Minneha´ha ("*the laughing water*"), daughter of the arrow-maker of Daco´tah, and wife of Hiawatha. She was called Minnehaha from the waterfall of that name between St. Anthony and Fort Snelling.

From the waterfall, he named her
Minnehaha, Laughing Water.
Longfellow, *Hiawatha*, iv. (1855).

Minnesingers, the Troubadours of Germany during the Hohenstaufen period (1138-1294), minstrels who composed and sung short lyrical poems—usually in praise of women or in celebration of the beauties of nature—called *Minne*, or love songs. The names of nearly three hundred of these poets have come down to us, including all classes of society, the most famous being Dietmar von Aist, Ulrich von Lichenstein, Heinrich von Frauenlob, and above all Walther von der Vogelweid (1168-1230). Wolfram von Eschenbach, Gottfried von Strasburg, and Hartmann von der Aue are also classed among the Minnesingers, but their principal fame was won in the field of metrical romance.

⁎ The story runs that Vogelweid bequeathed his worldly all to a Wurtzburg monastery upon condition that they should feed the doves at noon every day upon his grave. The multiplying birds aroused the avaricious alarm of the abbot, who forbade the daily distribution.

"Time has long effaced the inscriptions
On the cloister's funeral stones,
And tradition only tells us
Where repose the poet's bones.
But around the vast cathedral
By sweet echoes mutiplied
Still the birds repeat the legend
And the name of Vogelweid."
H. W. Longfellow, *Walter von der Vogelweid* 186-.

Mino´na, "the soft blushing daughter of Torman," a Gaelic bard in the *Songs of Selma*, one of the most famous portions of Macpherson's *Ossian*.

Minor (*The*), a comedy by Samuel Foote (1760). Sir George Wealthy, "the minor," was the son of Sir William Wealthy, a retired merchant. He was educated at a public school, sent to college, and finished his training in Paris. His father, hearing of his extravagant habits, pretended to be dead, and, assuming the guise of a German baron, employed several persons to dodge the lad, some to be winners in his gambling, some to lend money, some to cater to other follies, till he was apparently on the brink of ruin. His uncle, Mr. Richard Wealthy, a City merchant, wanted his daughter, Lucy, to marry a wealthy trader, and as she refused to do so, he turned her out of doors. This young lady was brought to Sir George as a *fille de joie*, but she touched his heart by her manifest innocence, and he not only relieved her present necessities, but removed her to an asylum where her "innocent beauty would be guarded from temptation, and her deluded innocence would be rescued from infamy." The whole scheme now burst as a bubble. Sir George's father, proud of his son, told him he was his father, and that his losses were only fictitious; and the uncle, melted into a better mood, gave his daughter to his nephew, and blessed the boy for rescuing his discarded child.

Minotti, governor of Corinth, then under the power of the doge. In 1715 the city was stormed by the Turks; and during the siege one of the magazines in the Turkish camp blew up, killing 600 men. Byron says it was Minotti himself who fired the train, and that he perished in the explosion.—Byron, *Siege of Corinth* (1816).

Minstrel (*The*), an unfinished poem, in Spenserian metre, by James Beattie. Its design was to trace the progress of a poetic genius, born in a rude age, from the first dawn of fancy to the fullness of poetic rapture. The first canto is descriptive of Edwin, the minstrel; canto ii. is dull philosophy, and there, happily, the poem ends. It is a pity it did not end with the first canto (1773-4).

And yet poor Edwin was no vulgar boy,
Deep thought oft seemed to fix his infant eye.

Dainties he heeded not, nor gaude, nor toy,
Save one short pipe of rudest minstrelsy;
Silent when sad, affectionate, tho' shy;
And now his look was most demurely sad;
And now he laughed aloud, though none knew why.
The neighbors stared and sighed, yet blessed the lad;
Some deemed him wondrous wise, and some believed him mad.
Canto i. 16.

Minstrel (Lay of the Last). Ladye Margaret, "the flower of Teviot," was the daughter of Lord Walter Scott, of Branksome Hall. She loved Baron Henry, of Cranstown; but between the two families a deadly feud existed. One day the elfin page of Lord Cranstown inveigled the heir of Branksome Hall (then a lad) into the woods, where he fell into the hands of the English, who marched with 3000 men to Branksome Hall; but, being told that Douglas was coming to the rescue with 10,000 men, the two armies agreed to settle by single combat whether the lad should be given up to the mother or be made King Edward's page. The two champions were Sir Richard Musgrave (*English*) and Sir William Deloraine (*Scotch*). The Scotch champion slew Sir Richard, and the boy was delivered to his mother. It now turned out that Sir William Deloraine was Lord Cranstown, who claimed and received the hand of Ladye Margaret as his reward.—Sir W. Scott (1805).

Minstrel of the Border, Sir W. Scott; also called "The Border Minstrel" (1771-1832).

My steps the Border Minstrel led.
Wordsworth, *Yarrow Revisited.*

Great Minstrel of the Border.
Wordsworth.

Minstrel of the English Stage (*The Last*), James Shirley, last of the Shakespeare school (1594-1666).

⁎ Then followed the licentious French school, headed by John Dryden.

Minstrels (*Royal Domestic*).

Of William I., Berdie, called *Regis Jocula'tor.*

Of Henry I., Galfrid and Royer, or Raher.

Of Richard I., Blondel.

Mint Julep, a Virginian beverage, celebrated in song by Charles Fenno Hoffman (185-). A favorite variety of this drink is compounded of brandy, water, sugar, mint-leaves and pounded ice, and is called a "hail-storm."

"The draught was delicious, and loud the acclaim,
'Though something seemed wanting for all to bewail;
But JULEPS the drink of immortals became
When Jove himself added a handful of hail."
Charles Fenno Hoffman, *Poems* (1846).

Mintz, *alias* Araminta Sophronia—the best cook and housemaid in town—rules the Stackpole family with a rod of red-hot steel until the son of the house defies her by marrying the head scholar in the Boston Cooking School.—Augusta Larned, *Village Photographs* (1887).

Miol´ner (3 *syl.*), Thor's hammer.

This is my hammer, Miölner the mighty;
Giants and sorcerers cannot withstand it.
Sæmund Sigfusson, *Edda* (1130).

Miquelets (*Les*), soldiers of the Pyrenees, sent to co-operate with the dragoons of the *Grand Monarque* against the Camisards of the Cevennes.

Mir´abel, the "wild goose," a travelled Monsieur, who loves women in a loose way, but abhors matrimony, and especially dislikes Oria´na; but Oriana "chases" the "wild goose" with her woman's wiles, and catches him.—Beaumont and Fletcher, *The Wild-goose Chase* (1652).

Mirabel (*Old*). He adores his son, and wishes him to marry Oria´na. As the young man shilly-shallies, the father enters into several schemes to entrap him into a declaration of love; but all his schemes are abortive.

Young Mirabel, the son, called "the inconstant." A handsome, dashing young rake, who loves Oriana, but does not wish to marry. Whenever Oriana seems lost to him the ardor of his love revives; but immediately his path is made plain, he holds off. However, he ultimately marries her.—G. Farquhar, *The Inconstant* (1702).

Mirabell (*Edward*), in love with Millamant. He liked her, "with all her faults; nay, liked her for her faults, ... which were so natural that (in his opinion) they became her."—W. Congreve, *The Way of the World* (1700).

Not all that Drury Lane affords
Can paint the rakish "Charles" so well,
Or give such life to "Mirabell"
[*As Montague Talbot*, 1778-1831].
Crofton Croker.

Mirabella, "a maiden fair, clad in mourning weeds, upon a mangy jade unmeetly set, with a lewd fool called Disdain" (canto 6). Timias and Serena, after quitting the hermit's cell, meet her. Though so sorely clad and mounted, the maiden was "a lady of great dignity and honor, but scornful and proud." Many a wretch did languish for her through a long life. Being summoned to Cupid's judgment hall, the sentence passed on her was that she should "ride on a mangy jade, accompanied by a fool, till she had saved as many lovers as she had slain" (canto 7). Mirabella was also doomed to carry a leaky bottle, which she was to fill with tears, and a torn wallet, which she was to fill with repentance: but her tears and her repentance dropped out as fast as they were put in, and were trampled under foot by Scorn (canto 8).—Spenser, *Faëry Queen*, vi. 6-8 (1596).

⁎ "Mirabella" is supposed to be meant for Rosalind, who jilted Spenser, and who is called by the poet "a widow's daughter of the glen, and poor."

Mir´amont, brother of Justice Brisac, and uncle of the two brothers, Charles (the scholar) and Eustace (the courtier). Miramont is an ignorant, testy old man, but a great admirer of learning and scholars.—Beaumont and Fletcher, *The Elder Brother* (1637).

Miran´da, daughter of Prospero, the exiled duke of Milan, and niece of Antonio, the usurping duke. She is brought up on a desert island, with Ariel, the fairy spirit, and Cal´iban, the monster, as her only companions. Ferdinand, son of the king of Naples, being shipwrecked on the island, falls in love with her, and marries her.—Shakespeare, *The Tempest* (1609).

Identifying herself with the simple yet noble-minded Miranda in the isle of wonder and enchantment.—Sir W. Scott.

Miranda, an heiress, the ward of Sir Francis Gripe. As she must obtain his consent to her marriage before she could obtain possession of her fortune, she pretended to love him, although he was 64 years old; and the old fool believed it. When, therefore, Miranda asked his consent to marry, he readily gave it, thinking himself to be the man of her choice; but the sly little hussy laughed at her old guardian, and plighted her troth to Sir George Airy, a man of 24.—Mrs. Centlivre, *The Busy Body* (1709).

Mir´ja, one of the six Wise Men of the East, led by the guiding star to Jesus. Mirja had five sons, who followed his holy life.—Klopstock, *The Messiah*, v. (1771).

Mirror (*Alasnam's*), a mirror which showed Alasnam if "a beautiful girl was also chaste and virtuous." The mirror was called "the touchstone of virtue."—*Arabian Nights* ("Prince Zeyn Alasnam").

Mirror (Cambuscan's), a mirror sent to Cambuscan´, king of Tartary, by the king of Araby and Ind. It showed those who consulted it if any adversity were about to befall them; if any one they loved were friend or foe.—Chaucer, *Canterbury Tales* ("The Squire's Tale," unfinished.)

"Or call up him who left half-told,
The story of Cambuscan bold.
*　　*　　*　　*　　*
That owned the virtuous ring and glass."
Milton, *Il Penseroso*.

Mirror (Kelly's), Dr. Dee's speculum. Kelly was the doctor's speculator or seer. The speculum resembled a "piece of polished cannel coal."

Kelly did all his feats upon
The devil's looking-glass, a stone.
S. Butler, *Hudibras* (1663-78).

Mirror (Lao's), a looking-glass which reflected the mind as well as the outward form.—Goldsmith, *Citizen of the World*, xlv. (1759).

Mirror (Merlin's Magic) or Venus's looking-glass, fabricated in South Wales, in the days of King Ryence. It would show to those that looked therein anything which pertained to them, anything that a friend or foe was doing. It was round like a sphere, and was given by Merlin to King Ryence.

That never foe his kingdom might invade
But he it knew at home before he heard
Tidings thereof.

Britomart, who was King Ryence's daughter and heiress, saw in the mirror her future husband and also his name, which was Sir Artegal.—Spenser, *Faëry Queen*, iii. 2 (1590).

Mirror (Prester John's), a mirror which possessed similar virtues to that made by Merlin. Prester John could see therein whatever was taking place in any part of his dominions.

*** Dr. Dee's speculum was also spherical, and possessed a similar reputed virtue.

Mirror (Reynard's Wonderful). This mirror existed only in the brain of Master Fox. He told the queen lion that whoever looked therein could see what was being done a mile off. The wood of the frame was part of the same block out of which Crampart's magic horse was made.—*Reynard the Fox*, xii. (1498).

Mirror (Venus's), generally called "Venus's looking-glass," the same as [Merlin's magic mirror](#) (*q.v.*).

Mirror (Vulcan's). Vulcan made a mirror which showed those who looked into it the past, present, and future. Sir John Davies says that Cupid handed this mirror to Antin´ous, when he was in the court of Ulysses, and Antinous gave it to Penel´opê, who beheld therein the court of Queen Elizabeth and all its grandeur.

Vulcan, the king of fire, that mirror wrought ...
As there did represent in lively show
Our glorious English court's divine image
As it should be in this our golden age.
Sir John Davies, *Orchestra* (1615).

Mirror of King Ryence, a mirror made by Merlin. It showed those who looked into it whatever they wished to see.—Spenser, *Faëry Queen*, iii. (1590).

Mirror of Knighthood, a romance of chivalry. It was one of the books in Don Quixote's library, and the curé said to the barber:

"In this same *Mirror of Knighthood* we meet with Rinaldo de Montalban and his companions, with the twelve peers of France, and Turpin, the historian. These gentlemen we will condemn only to perpetual exile, as they contain something of the famous Bojardo's invention, whence the Christian poet Ariosto borrowed the groundwork of his ingenious compositions; to whom I should pay little regard if he had not written in his own language [*Italian*]."—Cervantes, *Don Quixote*, I. i. 6 (1605).

Mirror of all Martial Men, Thomas, earl of Salisbury (died 1428).

Mirrour for Magistraytes, begun by Thomas Sackville, and intended to be a poetical biography of remarkable Englishmen. Sackville wrote the "Induction," and furnished one of the sketches, that of Henry Stafford, duke of Buckingham (the tool of Richard III.). Baldwynne, Ferrers, Churchyard, Phair, etc., added others. Subsequently, John Higgins, Richard Nichols, Thomas Blenerhasset, etc., supplied additional characters; but Sackville alone stands out pre-eminent in merit. In the "Induction," Sackville tells us he was conducted by Sorrowe into the infernal regions. At the porch sat Remorse and Dread, and within the porch were Revenge, Miserie, Care, and Slepe. Passing on, he beheld Old Age, Maladie, Famine, and Warre. Sorrowe then took him to Achĕron, and ordered Charon to ferry them across. They passed the three-headed Cerbĕrus and came to Pluto, where the poet saw several ghosts, the last of all being the duke of Buckingham, whose "*complaynt*" finishes the part written by Thomas Sackville (1557). (See BUCKINGHAM.)

⁎ Henry Stafford, duke of Buckingham, must not be mistaken for George Villiers, duke of Buckingham 150 years later.

Mirza (*The Vision of*). Mirza, being at Grand Cairo on the fifth day of the moon, which he always kept holy, ascended a high hill, and, falling into a trance, beheld a vision of human life. First he saw a prodigious tide of water rolling through a valley with a thick mist at each end—this was the river of time. Over the river was a bridge of a thousand arches, but only three score and ten were unbroken. By these, men were crossing, the arches representing the number of years the traveller lived before he tumbled into the river.

Lastly, he saw the happy valley, but when he asked to see the secrets hidden under the dark clouds on the other side, the vision was ended, and he only beheld the valley of Bagdad, with its oxen, sheep, and camels grazing on its sides.—Addison, *Vision of Mirza* (*Spectator*, 159).

Misbegot (*Malcolm*), natural son of Sybil Knockwinnock, and an ancestor of Sir Arthur Wardour.—Sir W. Scott, *The Antiquary* (time, George III.).

Miser (*The*), a comedy by H. Fielding, a *réchauffé* of Molière's comedy *L'Avare*. Lovegold is "Harpagon," Frederick is "Cléante," Mariana is "Mariane," and Ramilie is "La Fléche." Lovegold, a man of 60, and his son Frederick, both wish to marry Mariana, and, in order to divert the old miser from his foolish passion, Mariana pretends to be most extravagant. She orders a necklace and ear-rings of the value of £3000, a petticoat and gown from a fabric which is £12 a yard, and besets the house with duns. Lovegold gives £2000 to break off the bargain, and Frederick becomes the bridegroom of Mariana.

Misers.—See *Dictionary of Phrase and Fable*.

Misere′re (*The*), sung on Good Fridays in Catholic churches, is the composition of Gregorio Allegri, who died in 1640.

Mishe-Mok′wa, the great bear slain by Mudjekeewis.—Longfellow, *Hiawatha*, ii. (1855).

Mishe-Nah′ma, the great sturgeon, "king of fishes," subdued by Hiawatha. With this labor, the "great teacher" taught the Indians how to make oil for winter. When Hiawatha threw his line for the sturgeon, that king of fishes first persuaded a pike to swallow the bait and try to break the line, but Hiawatha threw it back into the water. Next, a sun-fish was persuaded to try the bait, with the same result. Then the sturgeon, in anger, swallowed Hiawatha and canoe also; but Hiawatha smote the heart of the sturgeon with his fist, and the king of fishes swam to the shore and died. Then the sea-gulls opened a rift in the dead body, out of which Hiawatha made his escape.

"I have slain the Mishê-Nahma,
Slain the king of fishes" said he.
Longfellow, *Hiawatha*, vii. (1855).

Misnar, sultan of India, transformed by Ulin into a toad. "He was disenchanted by the dervise Shemshel′nar, the most "pious worshipper of Alla amongst all the sons of Asia." By prudence and piety, Misnar and his vizier, Horam, destroyed all the enchanters who filled India with rebellion, and, having secured peace, married Hem′junah, daughter of Zebenezer, sultan of Cassimir, to whom he had been betrothed when he was known only as the prince of Georgia.—James Ridley, *Tales of the Genii*, vi., vii. (1751).

Misog'onus, by Thomas Rychardes, the third English comedy (1560). It is written in rhyming quatrains, and not in couplets like *Ralph Roister Doister* and *Gammer Gurton's Needle*.

Miss in Her Teens, a farce by David Garrick (1753). Miss Biddy Bellair is in love with Captain Loveit, who is known to her only by the name of Rhodophil; but she coquets with Captain Flash and Mr. Fribble, while her aunt wants her to marry an elderly man by the name of Stephen Loveit, whom she detests. When the Captain returns from the wars, she sets Captain Flash and Mr. Fribble together by the ears; and while they stand fronting each other, but afraid to fight, Captain Loveit enters, recognizes Flash as a deserter, takes away his sword, and dismisses Fribble as beneath contempt.

Mississippi Bubble, the "South Sea scheme" of France, projected by John Law, a Scotchman. So called because the projector was to have the exclusive trade of Louisiana, on the banks of the Mississippi, on condition of his taking on himself the National Debt (incorporated 1717, failed 1720).

The debt was 208 millions sterling. Law made himself sole creditor of this debt, and was allowed to issue ten times the amount in paper money, and to open "the Royal Bank of France," empowered to issue this paper currency. So long as a 20-franc note was worth 20 francs, the scheme was a prodigious success, but immediately the paper money was at a discount, a run on the bank set in, and the whole scheme burst.

Miss Ludington. A beautiful girl changed by illness into "a sad and faded woman." She had a portrait painted from an ivory miniature of herself, taken before the change, and conceives the idea that *what she was once* must still exist somewhere. The phantasy is played upon by impostors, who undertake to materialize the fancied creature and introduce her as the soul-sister of the credulous spinster. The instrument of the audacious fraud becomes conscience stricken and reveals it.—Edward Bellamy, *Miss Ludington's Sister* (1884).

Mistletoe Bough (*The*). The song so called is by Thomas Haynes Bayley, who died 1839. The tale is this: Lord Lovel married a young lady, a baron's daughter, and on the wedding night the bride proposed that the guest should play "hide-and-seek." The bride hid in an old oak chest, and the lid, falling down, shut her in, for it went with a spring-lock. Lord Lovel sought her that night and sought next day, and so on for a week, but nowhere could he find her. Some years later, the old chest was sold, and, on being opened, was found to contain the skeleton of the bride.

Rogers, in his *Italy*, gives the same story, and calls the lady "Ginevra" of Modĕna.

Collet, in his *Relics of Literature*, has a similar story.

Another is inserted in the *Causes Célèbres*.

Marwell Old Hall (near Winchester), once the residence of the Seymours, and afterwards of the Dacre family, has a similar tradition attached to it, and "the very chest is said to be now the property of the Rev. J. Haygarth, rector of Upham."

Bramshall, Hampshire, has a similar tale and chest.

The great house at Malsanger, near Basingstoke, also in Hampshire, has a similar tradition connected with it.

Mi′ta, sister of Aude. She married Sir Miton de Rennes, and became the mother of Mitaine. (See next art.)—*Croquemitaine*, xv.

Mitaine, daughter of Mita and Miton, and godchild of Charlemagne. She went in search of Fear Fortress, and found that it existed only in the imagination, for as she boldly advanced towards it, the castle gradually faded into thin air. Charlemagne made Mitaine, for this achievement, Roland's squire, and she fell with him in the memorable attack at Roncesvallês. (See previous art.)—*Croquemitaine*, iii.

Mite (*Sir Matthew*), a returned East Indian merchant, dissolute, dogmatical, ashamed of his former acquaintances, hating the aristocracy, yet longing to be acknowledged by them. He squanders his wealth on toadies, dresses his livery servants most gorgeously, and gives his chairmen the most costly exotics to wear in their coats. Sir Matthew is forever astonishing weak minds with his talk about rupees, lacs, jaghires, and so on.—S. Foote, *The Nabob*.

Mithra or **Mithras**, a supreme divinity of the ancient Persians, confounded by the Greeks and Romans with the *sun*. He is the personification of Ormuzd, representing fecundity and perpetual renovation. Mithra is represented as a young man with a Phrygian cap, a tunic, a mantle on his left shoulder, and plunging a sword into the neck of a bull. Scaliger says the word means "greatest" or "supreme." Mithra is the middle of the triplasian deity: the Mediator, Eternal Intellect, and Architect of the world.

Her towers, where Mithra once had burned,
To Moslem shrines—oh shame!—were turned;
Where slaves, converted by the sword,
Their mean apostate worship poured,
And cursed the faith their sires adored.
Moore, *Lalla Rookh* ("The Fire-Worshippers," 1817).

Mithridate (3 *syl.*), a medicinal confection, invented by Damoc′ratês, physician to Mithrida′tês, king of Pontus, and supposed to be an antidote to all poisons and contagion. It contained seventy-two ingredients. Any panacea is called a "mithridate."

Their kinsman garlic bring, the poor man's mithridate.
Drayton, *Polyolbion*, xx. (1622).

Mithridate (3 *syl.*), a tragedy by Racine, (1673). "Monime" (2 *syl.*), in this drama, was one of Mdlle. Rachel's great characters.

Mithrida′tes (4 *syl.*), surnamed "the Great." Being conquered by the Romans, he tried to poison himself, but poison had no effect on him, and he was slain by a Gaul. Mithridatês was active, intrepid, indefatigable, and fruitful in resources; but he had to oppose such generals as Sulla, Lucullus, and Pompey. His ferocity was unbounded, his perfidy was even grand.

*** Racine has written a French tragedy on the subject, called *Mithridate* (1673); and N. Lee brought out his *Mithridatês* in English about the same time.

Mixit (*Dr.*), the apothecary at the Black Bear inn at Darlington.—Sir W. Scott, *Rob Roy* (time, George I.).

M'liss, brave, arch, and loving girl of the Wild West; the heroine of one of Bret Harte's most popular sketches.

M. M. Sketch (*An*), a memorandum sketch.

Mne′me (2 *syl.*), a well-spring of Bœo′tia, which quickens the memory. The other well-spring in the same vicinity, called *Lê′thê*, has the opposite effect, causing blank forgetfulness.—Pliny.

Dantê calls this river Eu′noê. It had the power of calling to the memory all the good acts done, all the graces bestowed, all the mercies received, but no evil.—Dantê, *Purgatory*, xxxiii. (1308).

Mo′ath, a well-to-do Bedouin, father of Onei′za (3 *syl.*), the beloved of Thalaba. Oneiza, having married Thalaba, died on the bridal night, and Moath arrived just in time to witness the mad grief of his son-in-law.—Southey, *Thalaba, the Destroyer*, ii., viii. (1798).

Mocca′sins, an Indian buskin.

He laced his moccasins [*sic*] in act to go.

Campbell, *Gertrude of Wyoming*, i. 24 (1809).

Mochingo, an ignorant servant of the Princess Ero′ta.—Beaumont and Fletcher, *The Laws of Candy* (1647).

Mock Doctor (*The*), a farce by H. Fielding (1733), epitomized from *Le Médecin Malgré Lui*, of Molière (1666). Sir Jasper wants to make his daughter marry a Mr. Dapper; but she is in love with Leander and pretends to be dumb. Sir Jasper hears of a dumb doctor, and sends his two flunkies to fetch him. They ask one Dorcas to direct them to him, and she points them to her husband, Gregory, a faggot-maker; but tells them he is very eccentric, and must be well beaten, or he will deny being a physician. The faggot-maker is accordingly beaten into compliance, and taken to the patient. He soon learns the facts of the case, and employs Leander as apothecary. Leander makes the lady speak, and completes his cure with "pills matrimoniac." Sir Jasper takes the joke in good part, and becomes reconciled to the alliance.

Mocking-Bird. "During the space of a minute, I have heard it imitate the woodlark, chaffinch, blackbird, thrush, and sparrow.... Their few natural notes resemble those of the nightingale, but their song is of greater compass and more varied."—Ashe, *Travels in America*, ii. 73.

Moclas, a famous Arabian robber, whose name is synonymous with "thief." (See ALMANZOR, the caliph.)

Mode (*Sir William*), in Mrs. Centlivre's drama, *The Beaux' Duel* (1703).

Mode´love (*Sir Philip*), one of the four guardians of Anne Lovely, the heiress. Sir Philip is an "old beau, that has May in his fancy and dress, but December in his face and his heels. He admires all new fashions ... loves operas, balls, and masquerades" (act i. 1). Colonel Freeman personates a French fop, and obtains his consent to marry his ward, the heiress.—Mrs. Centlivre, *A Bold Stroke for a Wife* (1717).

Modely, a man of the world, gay, fashionable, and a libertine. He had scores of "lovers," but never loved till he saw the little rustic lass named Aura Freehold, a farmer's daughter, to whom he proposed matrimony.—John Philip Kemble, *The Farm-house*.

Modish (*Lady Betty*), really in love with Lord Morelove, but treats him with assumed scorn or indifference, because her pride prefers "power to ease." Hence she coquets with Lord Foppington (a married man), to mortify Morelove and arouse his jealousy. By the advice of Sir Charles Easy, Lord Morelove pays her out in her own coin, by flirting with Lady Graveairs, and assuming an air of indifference. Ultimately, Lady Betty is reduced to common sense, and gives her heart and hand to Lord Morelove.—Colley Cibber, *The Careless Husband* (1704).

Modo, the fiend that urges to murder, and one of the five that possessed "poor Tom."—Shakespeare, *King Lear*, act iv. sc. 1 (1605).

Modred, son of Lot, king of Norway, and Anne, own sister of King Arthur (pt. viii. 21; ix. 9). He is always called "the traitor." While King Arthur was absent, warring with the Romans, Modred was left regent, but usurped the crown, and married his aunt, the queen (pt. x. 13). When Arthur heard thereof, he returned, and attacked the usurper, who fled to Winchester (pt. xi. 1). The king followed him, and Modred drew up his army at Cambula, in

Cornwall, where another battle was fought. In this engagement Modred was slain, and Arthur also received his death-wound (pt. xi. 2). The queen, called Guanhuma´ra (but better known as Guen´evere), retired to a convent in the City of Legions, and entered the order of Julius the Martyr (pt. xi. 1).—Geoffrey, *British History* (1142).

✶ This is so very different from the accounts given in Arthurian romance of Mordred, that it is better to give the two names as if they were different individuals.

Modred (Sir), nephew of King Arthur. He hated Sir Lancelot, and sowed discord among the knights of the Round Table. Tennyson says that Modred "tampered with the lords of the White Horse," the brood that Hengist left. Geoffrey of Monmouth says, he made a league with Cheldric, the Saxon leader in Germany, and promised to give him all that part of England which lies between the Humber and Scotland, together with all that Hengist and Horsa held in Kent, if he would aid him against King Arthur. Accordingly, Cheldric came over with 800 ships, filled "with pagan soldiers" (*British History*, xi. 1).

When the king was in Brittany, whither he had gone to chastise Sir Lancelot for adultery with the queen, he left Sir Modred regent, and Sir Modred raised a revolt. The king returned, drew up his army against the traitor, and in this "great battle of the West" Modred was slain and Arthur received his death-wound.—Tennyson, *Idylls of the King* ("Guinevere," 1858).

✶ This version is in accordance neither with Geoffrey of Monmouth (see previous art.), nor with Arthurian romance (see MORDRED), and is, therefore, given separately.

Modu, the prince of all devils that take possession of a human being.

Mado was the chief devil that had possession of Sarah Williams; but ... Richard Mainy was molested by a still more considerable fiend called *Modu*, ... the prince of all other devils.—Harsnett; *Declaration of Popish Impostures*, 268.

Modus, cousin of Helen; a "musty library, who loved Greek and Latin;" but cousin Helen loved the bookworm, and taught him how to love far better than Ovid could with his *Art of Love*. Having so good a teacher, Modus became an apt scholar, and eloped with Cousin Helen.—S. Knowles, *The Hunchback* (1831).

Mœ´chus, adultery personified; one of four sons of Caro (*fleshly lust*). His brothers were Pornei´us (*fornication*), Acath´arus and Asel´gês (*lasciviousness*). In the battle of Mansoul, Mœchus is slain by Agnei´a (*wifely chastity*), the spouse of Encra´tês (*temperance*) and sister of Parthen´ia (*maidenly chastity*).

(Greek, *moichos* "an adulterer.")—Phineas Fletcher, *The Purple Island*, xi. (1633).

Mœli′ades (4 *syl.*). Under this name William Drummond signalized Henry, prince of Wales, eldest son of James I., in the monody entitled *Tears on the Death of Mœliadës*. The word is an anagram of *Milês a Deo*. The prince, in his masquerades and martial sports, used to call himself "Mœliadês of the Isles."

Mœliadês, bright day-star of the West.
W. Drummond, *Tears on the Death of Mœliades* (1612).

The burden of the monody is:

Mœliadês sweet courtly nymphs deplore,
From Thulê to Hydaspês' pearly shore.

Moffat (*Mabel*), domestic of Edward Redgauntlet.—Sir W. Scott, *Redgauntlet* (time, George III.).

Mogg Megone. Indian sachem who, at the behest of a white girl, kills her betrayer, and brings his scalp to her. In the storm of anguished remorse awakened by the sight of the bloody trophy, the woman murders Megone in his sleep, and is henceforth banned by the church, driven by conscience, a miserable wanderer upon the earth.—John Greenleaf Whittier, *Mogg Megone*.

Moha′di (*Mahommed*), the twelfth imaum, whom the Orientals believe is not dead, but is destined to return and combat Antichrist before the consummation of all things.

*** Prince Arthur, Merlin, Charlemagne, Barbarossa, Dom Sebastian, Charles V., Elijah Mansur, Desmond of Kilmallock, etc., are traditionally not dead, but only sleeping till the fullness of time, when each will awake and effect most wondrous restorations.

Mohair (*The Men of*), the citizens of France.

The men of mohair, as the citizens were called.—*Asylum Christi*, viii.

Moha′reb, one of the evil spirits of Dom-Daniel, a cave "under the roots of the ocean." It was given out that these spirits would be extirpated by one of the family of Hodei′rah (3 *syl.*), so they leagued against the whole race. First, Okba was sent against the obnoxious race, and succeeeded in killing eight of them, Thalaba alone having escaped alive. Next, Abaldar was sent against Thalaba, but was killed by a simoom. Then Loba′ba was sent to cut him off, but perished in a whirlwind. Lastly, Mohareb undertook to destroy him. He assumed the guise of a warrior, and succeeded in alluring the youth to the very "mouth of hell;" but Thalaba, being alive to the deceit, flung Mohareb into the abyss.—Southey, *Thalaba, the Destroyer*, v. (1797).

Mohicans (*Last of the*), Uncas, the Indian chief, son of Chingachook, and called "Deerfoot."—J. F. Cooper, *The Last of the Mohicans* (a novel, 1826).

The word ought to be pronounced *Mo.hek´.kanz*, but is usually called *Mo.hĕ.kanz*.

Mohocks, a class of ruffians who at one time infested the streets of London. So called from the Indian Mohocks. At the Restoration, the street bullies were called Muns and Tityre Tus; they were next called Hectors and Scourers; later still, Nickers and Hawcabites; and lastly, Mohocks.

Now is the time that rakes their revels keep,
Kindlers of riot, enemies of sleep;
His scattered pence the flying Nicker flings,
And with the copper shower the casement rings;
Who has not heard the Scowerer's midnight fame?
Who has not trembled at the Mohock's name?
Gay, *Trivia*, iii. 321, etc. (1712).

Mohun (*Lord*), the person who joined Captain Hill in a dastardly attack on the actor, Mountford, on his way to Mrs. Bracegirdle's house, in Howard Street. Captain Hill was jealous of Mountford, and induced Lord Mohun to join him in this "valiant exploit." Mountford died next day, Captain Hill fled from the country, and Mohun was tried but acquitted.

The general features of this cowardly attack are very like that of the Count Koningsmark on Thomas Thynne of Lingleate Hill. Count Koningsmark was in love with Elizabeth Percy (widow of the earl of Ogle), who was contracted to Mr. Thynne; but before the wedding day arrived, the count, with some hired ruffians, assassinated his rival in his carriage as it was passing down Pall Mall.

*** Elizabeth Percy, within three months of the murder, married the duke of Somerset.

Moidart (*John of*), captain of the clan Ronald, and a chief in the army of Montrose.—Sir W. Scott, *Legend of Montrose*, (time, Charles I.).

Moi´na (2 *syl.*), daughter of Reutha´mir, the principal man of Balclu´tha, a town on the Clyde, belonging to the Britons. Moina married Clessammor (the maternal uncle of Fingal), and died in childbirth of her son Carthon, during the absence of her husband.—Ossian, *Carthon*.

Mokanna, the name given to Hakem ben Haschem, from a silver gauze veil worn by him "to dim the lustre of his face," or rather to hide its extreme ugliness. The history of this impostor is given by D'Herbelot, *Bibliothèque Orientale* (1697).

⁎⁎⁎ Mokanna forms the first story of *Lalla Rookh* ("The Veiled Prophet of Khorassan"), by Thomas Moore (1817).

Mokattam (*Mount*), near Cairo (Egypt), noted for the massacre of the Caliph Hakem B'amr-ellah, who was given out to be incarnate deity, and the last prophet who communicated between God and man (eleventh century). Here, also; fell in the same massacre his chief prophet, and many of his followers. In consequence of this persecution, Durzi, one of the "prophet's" chief apostles, led the survivors into Syria, where they settled between the Libanus and Anti-Libanus, and took the name of Durzis, corrupted into Druses.

As the khalif vanished erst,
In what seemed death to uninstructed eyes,
On red Mokattam's verge.
Robert Browning, *The Return of the Druses*, i.

Molay (*Jacques*), grand-master of the Knights Templar, as he was led to the stake, summoned the pope (Clement V.), within forty days, and the king (Philippe IV.), within forty weeks, to appear before the throne of God to answer for his death. They both died within the stated periods. (See SUMMONS TO DEATH.)

Molière (*The Italian*), Charlo Goldoni (1707-1793).

Molière (*The Spanish*), Leandro Fernandez Moratin (1760-1828).

Moll Cutpurse, Mary Frith, who once attacked General Fairfax on Hounslow Heath.

Moll Flanders, a woman of great beauty, born in the Old Bailey. She was twelve years a courtezan, five years a wife, twelve years a thief, eight years a convict in Virginia; but ultimately grew rich, and died a penitent in the reign of Charles II.

⁎⁎⁎ Daniel Defoe wrote her life and adventures, which he called *The Fortunes of Moll Flanders* (1722).

Molly, Jaggers's housekeeper. A mysterious, scared-looking woman, with a deep scar across one of her wrists. Her antecedents were full of mystery, and Pip suspected her of being Estella's mother.—C. Dickens, *Great Expectations* (1860).

Molly Maggs, a pert young housemaid, in love with Robin. She hates Polyglot, the tutor of "Master Charles," but is very fond of Charles. Molly tries to get "the tuterer Polypot" into a scrape, but finds, to her consternation, that Master Charles is in reality the party to be blamed.—J. Poole, *The Scapegoat*.

Molly Maguires, stout, active young men, dressed up in women's clothes, with faces blackened, or otherwise disguised. This secret society was organized in 1843, to terrify the officials employed by Irish landlords to distrain for rent, either by grippers, (*bumbailiffs*), process-servers, keepers, or drivers (*persons who impound cattle till the rent is paid.*—W. S. Trench, *Realities of Irish Life*, 82.

Molly Mog, an innkeeper's daughter at Oakingham, Berks. Molly Mog was the toast of all the gay sparks in the former half of the eighteenth century; but died a spinster at the age of 67 (1699-1766).

⁎ Gay has a ballad on this *Fair Maid of the Inn*. Mr. Standen, of Arborfield, the "enamoured swain," died in 1730. Molly's sister was quite as beautiful as "the fair maid" herself. A portrait of Gay still hangs in Oakingham Inn.

Molly Wilder, New England girl, who shelters and cares for a young French nobleman wrecked on the Cape Cod coast. A love affair and a clandestine marriage follow. The marriage is acknowledged when peace is established between the French and English.—Jane G. Austin, *A Nameless Nobleman* (1881).

Molmu′tius. (See MULMUTIUS.)

Moloch (*ch* = *k*), the third in rank of the Satanic hierarchy, Satan being first, and Beëlzebub second. The word means "king." The rabbins say the idol was of brass, with the head of a calf. Moloch was the god of the Am′monites (3 *syl.*), and was worshipped in Rabba, their chief city.

First Moloch, horrid king, besmeared with blood
Of human sacrifice, and parents' tears,
Though, for the noise of drums and timbrels loud,
Their children's cries unheard, that passed thro' fire
To his grim idol. Him the Ammonite
Worshipped in Rabba.
Milton, *Paradise Lost*, i. 392, etc. (1665).

Mo′ly (Greek, *môlu*), mentioned in Homer's *Odyssey*. An herb with a black root and white blossom, given by Hermês to Ulysses, to counteract the spells of Circê, (See HÆMONY.)

... that Mō′ly
That Hermês once to wise Ulysses gave.
Milton, *Comus* (1634).

The root was black,
Milk-white the blossom; Môly is its name

In heaven.
Homer, *Odyssey*, x. (Cowper's trans.).

Momus's Lattice. Momus, son of Nox, blamed Vulcan, because, in making the human form, he had not placed a window in the breast for the discerning of secret thoughts.

Were Momus' lattice in our breasts,
My soul might brook to open it more widely
Than theirs [i. e. *the nobles*].
Byron, *Werner*, iii., 1 (1822).

Mon or **Mona**, Anglesia, the residence of the Druids. Suetonius Paulīnus, who had the command of Britain in the reign of Nero (from A.D. 59 to 62), attacked Mona, because it gave succor to the rebellious. The frantic inhabitants ran about with fire-brands, their long hair streaming to the wind, and the Druids invoked vengeance on the Roman army.—See Drayton, *Polyolbion*, viii. (1612).

Mon´aco (*The king of*), noted because whatever he did was never right in the opinion of his people, especially in that of Rabagas, the demagogue: If he went out, he was "given to pleasure;" if he stayed at home, he was "given to idleness;" if he declared war, he was "wasteful of the public money;" if he did not, he was "pusillanimous;" if he ate, he was "self-indulgent;" if he abstained, he was "priest-ridden."—M. Sardou, *Rabagas* (1872).

Monaco. Proud as a Monegasque. A French phrase. The tradition is that Charles Quint ennobled every one of the inhabitants of Monaco.

Monaldini (*Signor*), rich, *bourgeois* citizen of Rome, who purchases, fits up and lets to desirable tenants an old palace.—Mary Agnes Tincker, *Signor Monaldini's Niece* (1879).

Monarch of Mont Blanc, Albert Smith; so-called, because for many years he amused a large London audience, night after night, by relating "his ascent of Mont Blanc" (1816-1860).

Monarque (*Le Grand*), Louis XIV., of France (1638, 1643-1715).

Monastery (*The*), a novel by Sir W. Scott (1820). *The Abbot* appeared the same year. These two stories are tame and very defective in plot; but the character of Mary queen of Scots, in *The Abbot*, is a correct and beautiful historical portrait. The portrait of Queen Elizabeth is in *Kenilworth*.

Monçada (*Matthias de*), a merchant, stern and relentless. He arrests his daughter the day after her confinement of a natural son.

Zilia de Monçada, daughter of Matthias, and wife of General Witherington.—Sir W. Scott, *The Surgeon's Daughter*, (time, George II.).

Monda´min, maize or Indian corn (*mon-da-min*, "the Spirit's grain").

Sing the mysteries of mondamin,
Sing the blessing of the corn-fields.
Longfellow, *Hiawatha*, xiii. (1855).

Mone´ses (3 *syl.*), a Greek prince, betrothed to Arpasia, whom for the nonce he called his sister. Both were taken captive by Baj´azet. Bajazet fell in love with Arpasia, and gave Monēsês a command in his army. When Tamerlane overthrew Bajazet, Monēsês explained to the Tartar king how it was that he was found in arms against him, and said his best wish was to serve Tamerlane. Bajazet now hated the Greek, and, as Arpasia proved obdurate, thought to frighten her into compliance by having Monēsês bow-strung in her presence; but the sight was so terrible that it killed her.—N. Rowe, *Tamerlane* (1702).

Money, a drama by Lord E. L. B. Lytton (1840). Alfred Evelyn, a poor scholar, was secretary and factotum of Sir John Vesey, but received no wages. He loved Clara Douglas, a poor dependent of Lady Franklin; proposed to her, but was not accepted, "because both were too poor to keep house." A large fortune being left to the poor scholar, he proposed to Georgina, the daughter of Sir John Vesey; but Georgina loved Sir Frederick Blount, and married him. Evelyn, who loved Clara, pretended to have lost his fortune, and, being satisfied that she really loved him, proposed a second time, and was accepted.

Moneytrap, husband of Araminta, but with a *tendresse* for Clarissa, the wife of his friend Gripe.—Sir John Vanbrugh, *The Confederacy* (1695).

Monflathers (*Miss*), mistress of a boarding and day establishment, to whom Mrs. Jarley sent little Nell, to ask her to patronize the wax-work collection. Miss Monflathers received the child with frigid virtue, and said to her, "Don't you think you must be very wicked to be a wax-work child? Don't you know it is very naughty to be a wax child when you might have the proud consciousness of assisting, to the extent of your infant powers, the noble manufacturers of your country?" One of the teachers here chimed in with "How doth the little—;" but Miss Monflathers remarked, with an indignant frown, that "the little busy bee" applied only to genteel children, and the "works of labor and of skill" to painting and embroidery, not to vulgar children and wax-work shows."—Charles Dickens, *The Old Curiosity Shop*, xxxi. (1840).

Monford, the lover of Charlotte Whimsey. He plans various devices to hoodwink her old father, in order to elope with the daughter.—James Cobb, *The First Floor* (1756-1818).

Monime (2 *syl.*), in Racine's tragedy of *Mithridate*. This was one of Mdlle. Rachel's great characters, first preformed by her in 1838.

Monim′ia, "the orphan," sister of Chamont, and ward of Lord Acasto. Monimia was in love with Acasto's son, Castalio, and privately married him. Polydore (the brother of Castalio) also loved her, but his love was dishonorable love. By treachery, Polydore obtained admission to Monimia's chamber, and passed the bridal night with her, Monimia supposing him to be her husband; but when the next day she discovered the deceit, she poisoned herself; and Polydore, being apprised that Monimia was his brother's wife, provoked a quarrel with him, ran on his brother's sword, and died.—Otway, *The Orphan* (1680).

More tears have been shed for the sorrows of "Belvidēra" and "Monimia," than for those of "Juliet" and "Desdemona."—Sir W. Scott, *The Drama*.

Monimia, in Smollett's novel of *Count Fathom* (1754).

Moniplies (*Richie*), the honest, self-willed Scotch servant of Lord Nigel Olifaunt, of Glenverloch.—Sir W. Scott, *Fortunes of Nigel* (time, James I.).

Monk (*General*), introduced by Sir Walter Scott in *Woodstock* (time, Commonwealth.

Monk (*The Bird Singing to a*). The monk is Felix, who listened to a bird for a hundred years, and thought the time only an hour.—Longfellow, *The Golden Legend*, ii. (1851).

Monk (*The*), a novel, by Sir Matthew G. Lewis (1794).

Monk Lewis. Matthew Gregory Lewis; so called from his novel (1773-1818).

Monk of Bury, John Lydgate, poet, who wrote the *Siege of Troy*, the *Story of Thebes*, and the *Fall of Princes* (1375-1460).

Nothynge I am experte in poetry,
As the monke of Bury, floure of eloquence.
Stephen Hawes, *The Passe-Tyme of Plesure* (1515).

Monk of Westminister, Richard, of Cirencester, the chronicler (fourteenth century).

This chronicle, *On the Ancient State of Britain*, was first brought to light in 1747, by Dr. Charles Julius Bertram, professor of English at Copenhagen; but the original being no better known than that of Thomas Rowley's poems, published by Chatterton, grave suspicions exist that Dr. Bertram was himself the author of the chronicles.

Monks (*The Father of*), Ethelwold, of Winchester (*-984).

Monks, alias Edward Leeford, a violent man, subject to fits. Edward Leeford, though half-brother to Oliver Twist, was in collusion with Bill Sykes, to ruin him. Failing in this, he retired to America, and died in jail.—C. Dickens, *Oliver Twist* (1837).

Monkbarns (*Laird of*), Mr Jonathan Oldbuck, the antiquary.—Sir W. Scott, *The Antiquary* (time, George III.).

Mon´ker and Nakir [*Na.keer*], the two examiners of the dead, who put questions to departed spirits respecting their belief in God and Mahomet, and award their state in after-life according to their answers.—*Al Korân*.

"Do you not see those spectres that are stirring the burning coals? Are they Monker and Nakir come to throw us into them?"—W. Beckford, *Vathek* (1786).

Monmouth, the surname of Henry V. of England, who was born in that town (1388, 1413-1422).

*** Mon-mouth is the *mouth of the Monnow*.

Monmouth (*The duke of*), commander-in-chief of the royal army.—Sir W. Scott, *Old Mortality* (time, Charles II.).

*** The duke of Monmouth was nicknamed "The Little Duke," because he was diminutive in size. Having no name of his own, he took that of his wife, "Scott," countess of Buccleuch. Pepys says: "It is reported that the king will be tempted to set the crown on the Little Duke" (*Diary*, seventeenth century).

Mon´ema, wife of Quia´ra, the only persons of the whole of the Guārani race who escaped the small-pox plague which ravaged that part of Paraguay. They left the fatal spot, and settled in the Modai woods. Here they had one son, Yerūti, and one daughter, Mooma, but Quiāra was killed by a jagŭar before the latter was born. Monĕma left the Mondai woods, and went to live at St. Joăchin, in Paraguay, but soon died from the effects of a house and city life.—Southey, *A Tale of Paraguay* (1814).

Mononia, when nature embellished the tint
Of thy fields and thy mountains so fair,
Did she ever intend that a tyrant should print
The footstep of slavery there?
T. Moore, *Irish Melodies*, i. ("War Song," 1814).

Monsieur, Philippe, Duc d'Orléans, brother of Louis XIV. (1674-1723).

*** Other gentlemen were Mons. A or Mons. B, but the regent was Mons. without any adjunct.

Similarly, the daughter of the duc de Chartres (the regent's grandson) was Mademoiselle.

Monsieur le Coadjuteur, Paul de Gondi, afterwards Cardinal de Retz (1614-1679).

Monsieur le duc, Louis Henri de Bourbon, eldest son of the prince de Condé (1692-1740).

Monsieur Thomas, a drama by Beaumont and Fletcher (1619).

Monsieur Tonson, a farce by Moncrieff. Jack Ardourly fails in love with Adolphine de Courcy in the street, and gets Tom King to assist in ferreting her out. Tom King discovers that his sweeting lives in the house of a French refugee, a barber, named Mons. Morbleu; but not knowing the name of the young lady, he inquires for Mr. Thompson, hoping to pick up information. Mons. Morbleu says no Mons. Tonson lives in the house, but only Mde. Bellegarde and Mdlle. Adolphine de Courcy. The old Frenchman is driven almost crazy by different persons inquiring for Mons. Tonson; but ultimately Jack Ardourly marries Adolphine, whose mother is Mrs. Thompson after all.

Taylor wrote a drama of the same title in 1767.

Monster (*The*), Renwick Williams, a wretch who used to prowl about London by night, armed with a double-edged knife, with which he mutilated women. He was condemned July 8, 1790.

Mont Rognon (*Baron of*), a giant of enormous strength and insatiable appetite. He was bandy-legged, had an elastic stomach, and four rows of teeth. He was a paladin of Charlemagne, and one of the four sent in search of Croquemitaine and Fear Fortress.—*Croquemitaine*.

Mont St. Michel, in Normandy. Here nine druidesses used to sell arrows to sailors to charm away storms. The arrows had to be discharged by a young man 25 years of age.

The Laplanders drove a profitable trade by selling winds to sailors. Even so late as 1814, Bessie Millie, of Pomōna (Orkney Islands), helped to eke out a livelihood by selling winds for sixpence.

Eric, king of Sweden, could make the winds blow from any quarter he liked by a turn of his cap. Hence, he was nicknamed "Windy Cap."

Mont Trésor, in France; so called by Gontran "the Good," king of Burgundy (sixteenth century). One day, weary with the chase, Gontran laid himself down near a small river, and fell asleep. The squire who watched his master, saw a little animal come from the king's mouth, and walk to the stream, over which the squire laid his sword, and the animal running across, entered a hole in the mountain. When Gontran was told of this incident, he said he had dreamt that he crossed a bridge of steel, and, having entered a cave at the foot of a mountain, entered a palace of gold. Gontran employed men to undermine the hill, and found there vast treasures, which he employed in works of charity and religion. In order to commemorate this event he called the hill Mont Trésor.—Claud Paradin, *Symbola Heroica*.

⁎ This story has been ascribed to numerous persons.

Mon′tague (3 *syl.*), head of a noble house in Verona, at feudal enmity with the house of Capŭlet. Romeo belonged to the former, and Juliet to the latter house.

Lady Montague, wife of Lord Montague, and mother of Romeo.— Shakespeare, *Romeo and Juliet* (1598).

Montalban.

Don Kyrie Elyson de Montalban, a hero of romance, in the *History of Tirante the White*.

Thomas de Montalban, brother of Don Kyrie Elyson, in the same romance of chivalry.

Rinaldo de Montalban, a hero of romance, in the *Mirror of Knighthood*, from which work both Bojardo and Ariosto have largely borrowed.

Montalban, now called Montauban (a contraction of *Mons Alba′nus*), in France, in the department of Tarn-et-Garonne.

Jousted in Aspramont or Montalban.
Milton, *Paradise Lost*, i. 583 (1665).

Montalban (The Count), in love with Volantê (3 *syl.*), daughter of Balthazar. In order to sound her, the count disguised himself as a father confessor; but Volantê detected the trick instantly, and said to him, "Come, come, count, pull off your lion's hide, and confess yourself an ass." However, as Volantê really loved him, all came right at last.—J. Tobin, *The Honeymoon* (1804).

Montanto (*Signor*), a master of fence and a great braggart.—Ben Jonson, *Every Man in His Humour* (1598).

Montargis (*The Dog of*), named Dragon. It belonged to Captain Aubri de Montdidier, and is especially noted for his fight with the Chevalier Richard Macaire. The dog was called Montargis, because the encounter was depicted over the chimney of the great hall in the castle of Montargis. It was in the forest of Bondi, close by this castle, that Aubri was assassinated.

Monte Christo (*Count*), convict who escapes from prison, and finds immense treasure, with which he does incredible things.

Assuming the title of "count," he adds the name of the island on which his treasure is buried, and plays the grande seignior in society, punishing his former persecutors and false friends, and rewarding his old allies. Finally he is brought to confess that man cannot play providence, and to recall the words "Vengeance is mine!"—Alexander Dumas, *Count of Monte Christo*.

Montenay (*Sir Philip de*), an old English knight.—Sir W. Scott, *Castle Dangerous* (time, Henry I.).

Montesi´nos, a legendary hero, who received some affront at the French court, and retired to La Mancha, in Spain. Here he lived in a cavern, some sixty feet deep, called "The Cavern of Montesinos." Don Quixote descended part of the way down this cavern, and fell into a trance, in which he saw Montesinos himself, Durandartê and Belerma under the spell of Merlin, Dulcin´ea del Toboso enchanted into a country wench, and other visions, which he more than half believed to be realities.—Cervantes, *Don Quixote*, II. ii. 5, 6 (1615).

. This Durandartê was the cousin of Montesinos, and Belerma the lady he served for seven years. When he fell at Roncesvallês, he prayed his cousin to carry his heart to Belerma.

Montespan (*The marquis de*), a conceited court fop, silly and heartless. When Louis XIV. took Mde. de Montespan for his concubine, he banished the marquis, saying:

Your strange and countless follies—
The scenes you make—your loud domestic broils—
Bring scandal on our court. Decorum needs
Your banishment.... Go!
And for your separate household, which entails
A double cost, our treasure shall accord you
A hundred thousand crowns.
Act iv. 1.

The foolish old marquis says, in his self-conceit:

A hundred thousand crowns for being civil
To one another! Well now, that's a thing
That happens but to marquises. It shows
My value in the state. The king esteems
My comfort of such consequence to France,
He pays me down a hundred thousand crowns,
Rather than let my wife disturb my temper!
Act v. 2.

Madame de Montespan, wife of the marquis. She supplanted La Vallière in the base love of Louis XIV. La Vallière loved the *man*, Montespan the *king*. She had wit to warm but not to burn, energy which passed for feeling, a head to check her heart, and not too much principle for a French court. Mde. de Montespan was the *protégée* of the Duke de Lauzun, who used her as a stepping-stone to wealth; but when in favor, she kicked down the ladder by which she had climbed to power. However, Lauzun had his revenge; and when La Vallière took the veil, Mde. de Montespan was banished from the court.—Lord E. L. B. Lytton, *The Duchess de la Vallière* (1836).

Montfauçon (*The Lady Calista of*), attendant of Queen Berengaria.—Sir. W. Scott, *The Talisman* (time, Richard I.).

Mont-Fitchet (*Sir Conrade*), a preceptor of the Knights Templar.—Sir W. Scott, *Ivanhoe* (time, Richard I.).

Montfort (*De*), the hero and title of a tragedy, intended to depict the passion of hate, by Joanna Baillie (1798). The object of De Montfort's hatred is Rezenvelt, and his passion drives him on to murder.

*** De Montfort was probably the suggestive inspiration of Byron's *Manfred* (1817).

Montgomery (*Mr.*), Lord Godolphin, lord high treasurer of England in the reign of Queen Anne. The queen called herself "Mrs. Morley," and Sarah Jennings, duchess of Marlborough, was "Mrs. Freeman."

Monthermer (*Guy*), a nobleman, and the pursuivant of King Henry II.—Sir W. Scott, *The Betrothed* (time, Henry II.).

Montjoie, chief herald of France.—Sir W. Scott, *Quentin Durward* (time, Edward IV.).

Montorio, the hero of a novel, who persuaded his "brother's sons" to murder their father by working on their fears, and urging on them the doctrine of fatalism. When the deed was committed, Montorio discovered that the young murderers were not his nephews, but his own sons.—Rev. C. R. Maturin, *Fatal Revenge* (1807).

Montreal d'Albano, called "Fra Moriale," knight of St. John of Jerusalem, and captain of the Grand Company in the fourteenth century, when sentenced to death by Rienzi, summoned his judge to follow him within the month. Rienzi was killed by the fickle mob within the stated period. (See SUMMONS TO DEATH.)

Montreville (*Mde. Adela*), or the Begum Mootee Mahul, called "the queen of Sheba."—Sir W. Scott, *The Surgeon's Daughter* (time, George II.).

Montrose (*The duke of*), commander-in-chief of the king's army.—Sir W. Scott, *Rob Roy*, xxxii. (time, George I.).

Montrose (*The Marquis of*).—Sir W. Scott, *Woodstock* (time, Commonwealth).

Montrose (James Grahame, earl of), the king's lieutenant in Scotland. He appears first disguised as Anderson, servant of the earl of Menteith.—Sir W. Scott, *Legend of Montrose* (time, Charles I.).

Monuments *(The)*, Poor family in London.

Father, a convict who gets out of prison on a ticket-of-leave.

Mother, Hester, an honest washerwoman, afterwards in almshouse, and blind.

Claude, Bright young fellow, educated by Lady Mildred Eldredge.

Melenda, a work-girl, fierce and virtuous, starving, yet independent.

Joe, plumber and house-decorator, typical British workman.

Polly, adopted by Lady Mildred, called "Violet," and brought up with her own daughter.

Sam, a red-hot socialist, ready with impracticable plans of leagues and reformation.—Walter Besant, *Children of Gibeon* (1890).

Montserrat *(Conrade, marquis of)*, a crusader.—Sir W. Scott, *The Talisman* (time, Richard I.).

Moody *(John)*, the guardian of Peggy Thrift, an heiress, whom he brings up in the country, wholly without society. John Moody is morose, suspicious, and unsocial. When 50 years of age, and Peggy 19, he wants to marry her, but is out-witted by "the country girl," who prefers Belville, a young man of more suitable age.

Alithea Moody, sister of John. She jilts Sparkish, a conceited fop, and marries Harcourt.—*The Country Girl* (time, Garrick, altered from Wycherly).

Mooma, youngest sister of Yerūti. Their father and mother were the only persons of the whole Guarāni race who escaped a small-pox plague which ravished that part of Paraguay. They left the fatal spot and lived in the Mondai woods, where both their children were born. Before the birth of Mooma, her father was eaten by a jagŭar, and the three survivors lived in the woods alone. When grown to a youthful age, a Jesuit priest persuaded them to come and live at St. Joăchin (3 *syl.*); so they left the wild woods for a city life. Here the mother soon flagged and died. Mooma lost her spirits, was haunted with thick-coming fancies of good and bad angels, and died. Yerūti begged to be baptized, received the rite, cried, "Ye are come for me! I am ready;" and died also.—Southey, *A Tale of Paraguay* (1814).

Moon (Man in the), said to be Cain, with a bundle of thorns.

Now doth Cain with fork of thorns confine
On either hemisphere, touching the wave

Beneath the towers of Seville. Yesternight
The moon was round.
Dantê, *Hell*, xx. (1300).

Moon (Minions of the), thieves or highwaymen. (See MOON'S MEN.)

Moon and Mahomet. Mahomet made the moon perform seven circuits round Caaba or the holy shrine of Mecca, then enter the right sleeve of his mantle and go out at the left. At its exit, it split into two pieces, which reunited in the centre of the firmament. This miracle was performed for the conversion of Hahab, the Wise.

Moon-Calf, an inanimate, shapeless human mass, said by Pliny to be engendered of woman only.—*Nat. Hist.*, x. 64.

Moon's Men, thieves or highwaymen, who ply their vocation by night.

The fortune of us that are but moon's men doth ebb and flow like the sea.—Shakespeare, 1 *Henry IV*. act i. sc. 2 (1597).

Moonshine (*Saunders*), a smuggler.—Sir W. Scott, *Bride of Lammermoor* (time, William III.).

Moore (*Mr. John*), of the Pestle and Mortar, Abchurch Lane, immortalized by his "worm-powder," and called the "Worm Doctor."

Moors. The Moors of Aragon are called Tangarins; those of Granāda are Mudajares; and those of Fez are called Elches. They are the best soldiers of the Spanish dominions. In the Middle Ages, all Mohammedans were called *Moors*; and hence Camoens, in the *Lusiad*, viii., called the Indians so.

Mopes (*Mr.*), the hermit, who lived on Tom Tiddler's Ground. He was dirty, vain, and nasty, "like all hermits," but had landed property, and was said to be rich and learned. He dressed in a blanket and skewer, and, by steeping himself in soot and grease, soon acquired immense fame. Rumor said he murdered his beautiful young wife, and abandoned the world. Be this as it may, he certainly lived a nasty life. Mr. Traveller tried to bring him back into society, but a tinker said to him "Take my word for it, when iron is thoroughly rotten, you can never botch it, do what you may."—C. Dickens, *A Christmas Number* (1861).

Mopsus, a shepherd, who, with Menalcas, celebrates the funeral eulogy of Daphnis.—Virgil, *Eclogue*, v.

Mora, the betrothed of Oscar, who mysteriously disappears on his bridal eve, and is mourned for as dead. His younger brother, Allan, hoping to secure the lands and fortune of Mora, proposes marriage, and is accepted. At the wedding banquet, a stranger demands "a pledge to the lost Oscar," and all accept it except Allan, who is there and then denounced as the murderer of his brother. Oscar then vanishes, and Allan dies.—Byron, *Oscar of Alva*.

Moradbak, daughter of Fitead, a widower. Hudjadge, king of Persia, could not sleep, and commanded Fitead, his porter and jailer, under pain of death, to find some one to tell him tales. Fitead's daughter, who was only 11, undertook to amuse the king with tales, and was assisted in private by the sage Abou'melek. After a perfect success, Hudjadge married Moradbak, and at her recommendation, Aboumelek was appointed overseer of the whole empire.—Comte de Caylus, *Oriental Tales* (1743).

Morakan'abad, grand vizier of the Caliph Vathek.—Beckford, *Vathek* (1784).

Moral Philosophy (*The Father of*), Thomas Aquinas (1224-1274).

Moran, Son of Fithil, one of the scouts in the army of Swaran, king of Lochlin (*Denmark*).—Ossian, *Fingal*.

Moran's Collar, a collar for magistrates, which had the supernatural power of pressing the neck of the wearer if his judgments deviated from strict justice, and even of causing strangulation if he persevered in wrong doing. Moran, surnamed "the Just," was the wise counsellor of Feredach, an early king of Ireland.

Morat, in *Aurungzebe*, a drama by Dryden (1675).

Edward Kynaston [1619-1687] shone with uncommon lustre in "Morat" and "Muley Moloch." In both these parts he had a fierce, lion-like majesty in his port and utterance, that gave the spectators a kind of trembling admiration.—Colley Cibber.

Morbleu! This French oath is a corrupt contraction of Mau'graby; thus, *maugre bleu, mau'bleu*. Maugraby was the great Arabian enchanter, and the word means "barbarous," hence a barbarous man or barbarian. The oath is common in Provence, Languedoc, and Gascoigne. I have often heard it used by the medical students at Paris.

Probably it is a punning corruption of *Mort de Dieu*.

Mordaunt, the secretary, at Aix, of Queen Margaret, the widow of Henry VI. of England.—Sir W. Scott, *Anne of Geierstein* (time, Edward IV.).

Mor'decai (*Beau*), a rich Italian Jew, one of the suitors of Charlotte Goodchild, but, supposing the report to be true that she has lost her fortune, he calls off and retires.—C. Macklin, *Love à-la-Mode* (1759).

Mordecai. Earnest young Jew, supporting himself by repairing watches, jewelry, etc. He is devoted to his race, proud of his lineage, and versed in all pertaining to Hebrew history. He dies of consumption.—George Eliot, *Daniel Deronda*.

Mordent, father of Joanna, by a former wife. In order to marry Lady Anne, he deserts Joanna and leaves her to be brought up by strangers. Joanna is placed under Mrs. Enfield, a crimp, and Mordent consents to a proposal of Lennox to run off with her. Mordent is a spirit embittered with the world—a bad man, with a goading conscience. He sins and suffers the anguish of remorse; does wrong, and blames Providence because when he "sows the wind he reaps the whirlwind."

Lady Anne, the wife of Mordent, daughter of the earl of Oldcrest, sister of a viscount, niece of Lady Mary, and one of her uncles is a bishop. She is wholly neglected by her husband, but, like Griselda (*q.v.*), bears it without complaint.—Holcroft, *The Deserted Daughter* (1784, altered into *The Steward*).

Mordred (*Sir*), son of Margawse (sister of King Arthur), and Arthur, her brother, while she was the wife of Lot, king of Orkney (pt. i. 2, 35, 36). The sons of Lot himself and his wife were Gaw´ain, Agravain, Ga´heris, and Gareth, all knights of the Round Table. Out of hatred to Sir Launcelot, Mordred and Agravain accuse him to the king of too great familiarity with Queen Guenever, and induce the king to spend a day in hunting. During his absence, the queen sends for Sir Launcelot to her private chamber, and Mordred and Agravain, with twelve other knights, putting the worst construction on the interview, clamorously assail the chamber, and call on Sir Launcelot to come out. This he does, and kills Agravain with the twelve knights, but Mordred makes his escape and tells the king, who orders the queen to be burnt alive. She is brought to the stake, but is rescued by Sir Launcelot, who carries her off to Joyous Guard, near Carlisle, which the king besieges. While lying before the castle, King Arthur receives a bull from the pope, commanding him to take back his queen. This he does, but as he refuses to be reconciled to Sir Launcelot, the knight betakes himself to Benwick, in Brittany. The king lays siege to Benwick, and during his absence leaves Mordred regent. Mordred usurps the crown, and tries, but in vain, to induce the queen to marry him. When the king hears thereof, he raises the siege of Benwick, and returns to England. He defeats Mordred at Dover, and at Barondown, but at Salisbury (*Camlan*) Mordred is slain fighting with the king, and Arthur receives his death-wound. The queen then retires to a convent at Almesbury, is visited by Sir Launcelot, declines to marry him, and dies.—Sir T. Malory, *History of Prince Arthur* iii. 143-174 (1470).

*** The wife of Lot is called "Anne" by Geoffrey, of Monmouth (*British History*, viii. 20, 21); and "Bellicent" by Tennyson, in *Gareth and Lynette*.

This tale is so very different from those of Geoffrey of Monmouth, and Tennyson, that all three are given. (See MODRED.)

Mor´dure (2 *syl.*), son of the emperor of Germany. He was guilty of illicit love with the mother of Sir Bevis, of Southampton, who murdered her husband and then married Sir Mordure. Sir Bevis, when a mere lad, reproved his mother for the murder of his father, and she employed Saber to kill him; but the murder was not committed, and young Bevis was brought up as a shepherd. One day, entering the hall where Mordure sat with his bride, Bevis struck at him with his axe. Mordure slipped aside, and the chair was "split to shivers." Bevis was then sold to an Armenian, and was presented to the king, who knighted him and gave him his daughter Josian in marriage.—M. Drayton, *Polyolbion*, ii. (1612).

Mordure (2 *syl.*), Arthur's sword, made by Merlin. No enchantment had power over it, no stone or steel was proof against it, and it would neither break nor bend. (The word means "hard biter.")—Spenser, *Faëry Queen*, ii. 8 (1590).

More (*Margareta*), the heroine and feigned authoress of *Household of Sir Thomas More*, by Miss Manning (1851).

More of More Hall, a legendary hero, who armed himself with armor full of spikes, and, concealing himself in the cave where the dragon of Wantley dwelt, slew the monster by kicking it in the mouth, where alone it was mortal.

⁎⁎ In the burlesque of H. Carey, entitled *The Dragon of Wantley*, the hero is called "Moore of Moore Hall," and he is made to be in love with Gubbins's daughter, Margery, of Roth'ram Green (1696-1743).

Morecraft, at first a miser, but after losing most of his money he became a spendthrift.—Beaumont and Fletcher, *The Scornful Lady* (1616).

⁎⁎ "Luke," in Massinger's *City Madam*, is the exact opposite. He was at first a poor spendthrift, but coming into a fortune he turned miser.

Morell (*Sir Charles*), the pseudonym of the Rev. James Ridley, affixed to some of the early editions of *The Tales of the Genii*, from 1764.

More´love (*Lord*), in love with Lady Betty Modish, who torments him almost to madness by an assumed indifference, and rouses his jealousy by coquetting with Lord Foppington. By the advice of Sir Charles Easy, Lord Morelove pays the lady in her own coin, assumes an indifference to her, and flirts with Lady Grave´airs. This brings Lady Betty to her senses, and all ends happily.—Colley Cibber, *The Careless Husband* (1704).

Morë´no (*Don Antonio*), a gentleman of Barcelona, who entertained Don Quixote with mock-heroic hospitality.—Cervantes, *Don Quixote*, II. iv. 10 (1615).

Morfin (*Mr.*), a cheerful bachelor, in the office of Mr. Dombey, merchant. He calls himself "a creature of habit," has a great respect for the head of the house, and befriends John Carker when he falls into disgrace by robbing his employer. Mr. Morfin is a musical amateur, and finds in his violoncello a solace for all cares and worries. He marries Harriet Carker, the sister of John and James.—C. Dickens, *Dombey and Son* (1846).

Morgan (*le Fay*), one of the sisters of King Arthur (pt. i. 18); the others were Margawse, Elain, and Anne (Bellicent was his half-sister). Morgan calls herself "queen of the land of Gore" (pt. i. 103). She was the wife of King Vrience (pt. i. 63), the mother of Sir Ew´ain (pt. i. 73), and lived in the castle of La Belle Regard (pt. ii. 122).

On one occasion, Morgan le Fay stole her brother's sword, "Excalibur," with its scabbard, and sent them to Sir Accolon, of Gaul, her paramour, that he might kill her brother Arthur in mortal combat. If this villany had succeeded, Morgan intended to murder her husband, marry Sir Accolon, and "devise to make him king of Britain;" but Sir Accolon, during the combat, dropped the sword, and Arthur, snatching it up, would have slain him had he not craved mercy and confessed the treasonable design (pt. i. 70). After this, Morgan stole the scabbard and threw it into the lake (pt. i. 73). Lastly, she tried to murder her brother by means of a poisoned robe; but Arthur told the messenger to try it on, that he might see it, and when he did so he dropped down dead, "being burnt to a coal" (pt. i. 75).—Sir T. Malory, *History of Prince Arthur* (1470).

W. Morris, in his *Earthly Paradise* ("August"), makes Morgan la Fée the bride of Ogier, the Dane, after his earthly career was ended.

Morgan, a feigned name adopted by Belarius, a banished lord.—Shakespeare, *Cymbeline* (1605).

Morgan, one of the soldiers of Prince Gwenwyn of Powys-land.—Sir W. Scott, *The Betrothed* (time, Henry II.).

Morgane (2 *syl.*), a fay, to whose charge Zephyr committed young Passelyon and his cousin, Bennucq. Passelyon fell in love with the fay's daughter, and the adventures of these young lovers are related in the romance of *Perceforest*, iii.

Morgante (3 *syl.*), a ferocious giant, converted to Christianity by Orlando. After performing the most wonderful feats, he died at last from the bite of a crab.—Pulci, *Morgante Maggiore* (1488).

He [*Don Quixote*] spoke favorably of Morgante, who, though of gigantic race, was most gentle in his manners.—Cervantes, *Don Quixote*, I. i. 1 (1605).

Morgause or MARGAWSE, wife of King Lot. Their four sons were Gaw´ain, Agravain, Ga´heris, and Gareth (ch. 36); but Morgause had another son by

Prince Arthur, named Mordred. Her son Gaheris, having caught his mother in adultery with Sir Lamorake, cut off her head.

Morgia´na, the female slave, first of Cassim, and then of Ali Baba, "crafty, cunning, and fruitful in inventions." When the thief marked the door of her master's house with white chalk in order to recognize it, Morgiana marked several other doors in the same manner; next day she observed a red mark on the door, and made a similar one on others, as before. A few nights afterwards, a merchant with thirty-eight oil-jars begged a night's lodging; and as Morgiana wanted oil for a lamp, she went to get some from one of the leather jars. "Is it time?" asked a voice. "Not yet," replied Morgiana, and going to the others, she discovered that a man was concealed in thirty-seven of the jars. From the last jar she took oil, which she made boiling hot, and with it killed the thirty-seven thieves. When the captain discovered that all his men were dead, he decamped without a moment's delay. Soon afterwards, he settled in the city as a merchant, and got invited by Ali Baba to supper, but refused to eat salt. This excited the suspicion of Morgiana, who detected in the pretended merchant the captain of the forty thieves. She danced awhile for his amusement, playfully sported with his dagger, and suddenly plunged it into his heart. When Ali Baba knew who it was that she had slain, he not only gave the damsel her liberty, but also married her to his own son.—*Arabian Nights* ("Ali Baba, or the Forty Thieves").

Morglay, the sword of Sir Bevis, of Hamptoun, *i.e.* Southampton, given to him by his wife, Josian, daughter of the king of Armenia.—Drayton, *Polyolboin*, ii. (1612).

You talk of Morglay, Excalibur [*Arthur's sword*], and Durindana [*Orlando's sword*], or so. Tut! I lend no credit to that is fabled of 'em.—Ben Jonson, *Every Man in His Humor*, iii. 1 (1598).

Morgue la Faye, a *fée* who watched over the birth of Ogier, the Dane, and after he had finished his earthly career, restored him to perpetual youth, and took him to live with her in everlasting love in the isle and castle of Av´alon.—*Ogier, le Danois* (a romance).

Mor´ice (*Gil* or *Child*), the natural son of Lady Barnard, "brought forth in her father's house wi' mickle sin and shame." One day, Gil Morice sent Willie to the baron's hall, with a request that Lady Barnard would go at once to Greenwood to see the child. Lord Barnard, fancying the "child" to be some paramour, forbade his wife to leave the hall, and went himself to Greenwood, where he slew Gil Morice, and sent his head to Lady Barnard. On his return, the lady told her lord he had slain her son, and added, "Wi' the same spear, oh, pierce my heart, and put me out o' pain!" But the baron repented of his hasty deed, and cried, "I'll lament for Gil Morice, as gin he were mine ain."—Percy, *Reliques, etc.*, III. i.

✳ This tale suggested to Home the plot of his tragedy called *Douglas*.

Mor'land, in *Lend Me Five Shillings*, by J. M. Morton (1838).

Morland (Henry), "the heir-at-law" of Baron Duberly. It was generally supposed that he had perished at sea; but he was cast on Cape Breton, and afterwards returned to England, and married Caroline Dormer, an orphan.—G. Colman, *The Heir-at-Law* (1797).

Mr. Beverley behaved like a father to me [B. *Webster*], and engaged me as a walking gentleman for his London theatre, where I made my first appearance as "Henry Morland," in *The Heir-at-Law*, which, to avoid legal proceedings, he called *The Lord's Warming-pan*.—Peter Paterson.

Morley (Mrs.), the name under which Queen Anne corresponded with Mrs. Freeman (*The Duchess of Marlborough*).

Morna, daughter of Cormac, king of Ireland. She was in love with Câthba, youngest son of Torman. Duchômar, out of jealousy, slew his rival, and then asked Morna to be his bride. She replied, "Thou art dark to me, O, Duchômar, and cruel is thine arm to Morna." She then begged him for his sword, and when "he gave it to her she thrust it into his heart." Duchômar fell, and begged the maid to pull out the sword that he might die, but when she did so, he seized it from her and plunged it into her side. Whereupon Cuthullin said:

"Peace to the souls of the heroes! Their deeds were great in fight. Let them ride around me in clouds. Let them show their features in war. My soul shall then be firm in danger, mine arm like the thunder of heaven. But be thou on a moonbeam, O, Morna, near the window of my rest, when my thoughts are at peace, when the din of war is past."—Ossian, *Fingal*, i.

Morna, wife of Compal, and mother of Fingal. Her father was Thaddu, and her brother Clessammor.—Ossian.

Mornay, the old seneschal, at Earl Herbert's tower at Peronne.—Sir W. Scott, *Quentin Durward* (time, Edward IV.).

Morning Star of the Reformation, John Wycliffe (1324-1384).

Morocco or MAROCCUS, the performing horse, generally called "Bankes's Horse." Among other exploits, we are told that "it went up to the top of St. Paul's." Both horse and man were burnt alive at Rome, by order of the pope, as magicians.—Don Zara del Fogo, 114 (1660).

✳ Among the entries at Stationers' Hall is the following:—*Nov. 14, 1595: A Ballad showing the Strange Qualities of a Young Nagg called Morocco*.

In 1595 was published the pamphlet *Maroccus Extaticus*, or *Bankes's Horse in a Trance*.

Morocco Men, agents of lottery assurances. In 1796, The great State lottery employed 7500 morocco men. Their business was to go from house to house among the customers of the assurances, or to attend in the back parlors of public-houses, where the customers came to meet them.

Morolt (*Dennis*), the old squire of Sir Raymond Berenger.—Sir W. Scott, *The Betrothed* (time, Henry II.).

Morose (2 *syl.*), a miserly old hunks, who hates to hear any voice but his own. His nephew, Sir Dauphine, wants to wring out of him a third of his property, and proceeds thus: He gets a lad to personate "a silent woman," and the phenomenon so delights the old man, that he consents to a marriage. No sooner is the ceremony over, than the boy-wife assumes the character of a virago of loud and ceaseless tongue. Morose, driven half-mad, promises to give his nephew a third of his income if he will take this intolerable plague off his hands. The trick being revealed, Morose retires into private life, and leaves his nephew master of the situation.—Ben Jonson, *The Silent Woman* (1609).

("Wasp" in *Bartholomew Fair*, "Corbaccio" in *The Fox*, and "Ananias" in *The Alchemist*.)

Moroug, the monkey mistaken for the devil. A woman of Cambalu died, and Moroug, wishing to personate her, slipped into her bed, and dressed himself in her night-clothes, while the body was carried to the cemetery. When the funeral party returned, and began the usual lamentations for the dead, pug stretched his night-capped head out of the bed, and began moaning and grimacing most hideously. All the mourners thought it was the devil, and scampered out as fast they could run. The priests assembled, and resolved to exorcise Satan; but pug, noting their terror, flew on the chief of the bonzes, and bit his nose and ears most viciously. All the others fled in disorder; and when pug had satisfied his humor, he escaped out of the window. After a while, the bonzes returned, with a goodly company well armed, when the chief bonze told them how he had fought with Satan, and prevailed against him. So he was canonized, and made a saint in the calendar for ever.—T. S. Gueulette, *Chinese Tales* ("The Ape Moroug," 1723).

Morrel or **Morell**, a goat-herd, who invites Thomalin, a shepherd, to come to the higher grounds, and leave the low-lying lands. He tells Thomalin that many hills have been canonized, as St. Michael's Mount, St. Bridget's Bower in Kent, and so on; then there was Mount Sinah and Mount Parnass, where the Muses dwelt. Thomalin replies, "The lowlands are safer, and hills are not for shepherds." He then illustrates his remark by the tale of shepherd

Algrind, who sat, like Morrel, on a hill, when an eagle, taking his white head for a stone, let a shell-fish fall on it, and cracked his skull.—Spenser, *Shepheardes Calendar*, vii.

[Æschylus was killed by a tortoise dropped on his head by an eagle].

(This is an allegory of the high and low church parties. Morel is an anagram of Elmer or Aylmer, bishop of London, who "sat on a hill," and was the leader of the high-church party. Algrind is Grindal, archbishop of Canterbury, head of the low-church party, who in 1578 was sequestrated for writing a letter to the queen on the subject of puritanism. Thomalin represents the puritans. This could not have been written before 1578, unless the reference to Algrind was added in some later edition).

Morris, a domestic of the earl of Derby.—Sir W. Scott, *Peveril of the Peak* (time, Charles II).

Morris (*Mr.*), the timid fellow-traveller of Frank Osbaldistone, who carried the portmanteau. Osbaldistone says, concerning him, "Of all the propensities which teach mankind to torment themselves, that of causeless fear is the most irritating, busy, painful, pitiable."—Sir W. Scott, *Rob Roy* (time, George I.).

Morris (*Peter*), the pseudonym of John G. Lockhart, in *Peter's Letters to His Kinsfolk* (1819).

Morris (*Dinah*). Beautiful gospeller, who marries Adam Bede, after the latter recovers from his infatuation for pretty *Hetty Sorrel*. Hetty is seduced by the young squire, murders her baby, and is condemned to die for the crime. Dinah visits the doomed girl in prison, wins her to a confession and repentance, and accompanies her in the gallows-cart. They are at the scaffold when a reprieve arrives.—George Eliot, *Adam Bede*.

Morris-Dance, a comic representation of every grade of society. The characters were dressed partly in Spanish and partly in English costume. Thus, the huge sleeves were Spanish, but the laced stomacher English. Hobby-horse represented the king and all the knightly order; Maid Marian, the queen; the friar, the clergy generally; the fool, the court jester. The other characters represented a franklin or private gentleman, a churl or farmer, and the lower grades were represented by a clown. The Spanish costume is to show the origin of the dance.

A representation of a morris-dance may still be seen at Betley, in Staffordshire, in a window placed in the house of George Tollet, Esq., in about 1620.

Morrison (*Hugh*), a Lowland drover, the friend of Robin Oig.—Sir W. Scott, *The Two Drovers* (time, George III.).

Mortality (*Old*), a religious itinerant who frequented country churchyards and the graves of covenanters. He was first discovered in the burial ground at Gandercleugh, clearing the moss from the gray tombstones, renewing with his chisel the half-defaced inscriptions, and repairing the decorations of the tombs.—Sir W. Scott, *Old Mortality* (time, Charles II.).

*** "Old Mortality" is said to be meant for Robert Patterson.

Morta´ra, the boy who died from being covered all over with gold-leaf by Leo XII., to adorn a pageant.

Mortcloke (*Mr.*), the undertaker at the funeral of Mrs. Margaret Bertram of Singleside.—Sir W. Scott, *Guy Mannering* (time, George II.).

Morte d'Arthur, a compilation of Arthurian tales, called on the title-page *The History of Prince Arthur*, compiled from the French by Sir Thomas Malory, and printed by William Caxton in 1470. It is divided into three parts. The first part contains the birth of King Arthur, the establishment of the Round Table, the romance of Balin and Balan, and the beautiful allegory of Gareth and Linet´. The second part is mainly the romance of Sir Tristram. The third part is the romance of Sir Launcelot, the quest of the Holy Graal, and the death of Arthur, Guenever, Tristram, Lamorake, and Launcelot.

*** The difference of style in the third part is very striking. The end of ch. 44, pt. i., is manifestly the close of a romance. The separate romances are not marked by any formal indication; but, in the modern editions, the whole is divided into chapters, and these are provided with brief abstracts of their contents.

This book was finished the ninth year of the reign of King Edward IV. by Sir Thomas Malory, knight. Thus endeth this noble and joyous book, entitled *La Morte d'Arthur*, notwithstanding it treateth of the birth, life and acts of the said King Arthur, and of his noble knights of the Round Table ... and the achieving of the Holy Sancgreall, and in the end the dolorous death and departing out of the world of them all.—Concluding paragraph.

Morte d'Arthur, by Tennyson. The poet follows closely the story of the death of Arthur, as told by Malory. The king is borne off the field by Sir Bedivere. Arthur orders the knight to throw his sword Excalibur into the mere. Twice the knight disobeyed the command, intending to save the sword; but the dying king detected the fraud, and insisted on being obeyed. Sir Bedivere then cast the sword into the mere, and an arm, clothed in white samite, caught it by the hilt, brandished it three times, and drew it into the mere. Sir Bedivere then carried the dying king to a barge, in which were three queens, who conveyed him to the island-valley of Avil´ion, "where falls not hail, or rain, or any snow, nor ever wind blows loudly." Here was he taken to be healed of his grievous wound; but whether he lived or died we are not told.

In his "Idylls of the King," Tennyson has taken the stories as told by Malory, and has turned them into his own melodious verse; yet, while adhering to the substance of each tale, he has in minor matters taken such liberties as have been allowed to poets since the earliest times. Shakespeare, in his "Julius Cæsar," makes a like use of Sir Thomas North's translation of Plutarch; the speech of Mark Antony over the body of Cæsar, to cite the most striking instance among many, is almost a literal transcription of North's version, but subjected to the laws of verse.

Mortemar (*Alberick of*), an exiled nobleman, *alias* Theodorick, the hermit of Engaddi, the enthusiast.—Sir W. Scott, *The Talisman* (time, Richard I.).

Mor´timer (*Mr.*), executor of Lord Abberville, and uncle of Frances Tyrrell. "He sheathed a soft heart in a rough case." Externally, Mr. Mortimer seemed unsympathetic, brusque and rugged; but in reality he was most benevolent, delicate and tender-hearted. "He did a thousand noble acts without the credit of a single one." In fact, his tongue belied his heart, and his heart his tongue.—Cumberland, *The Fashionable Lover* (1780).

Mortimer (*Sir Edward*), a most benevolent man, oppressed with some secret sorrow. In fact, he knew himself to be a murderer. The case was this: Being in a county assembly, the uncle of Lady Helen insulted him, struck him down, and kicked him. Sir Edward rode home to send a challenge to the ruffian; but, meeting him on the road drunk, he murdered him, was tried for the crime, but was honorably acquitted. He wrote a statement of the case, and kept the papers connected with it in an iron chest. One day Wilford, his secretary, whose curiosity had been aroused, saw the chest unlocked, and was just about to take out the documents when Sir Edward entered, and threatened to shoot him; but he relented, made Wilford swear secrecy, and then told him the whole story. The young man, unable to live under the jealous eyes of Sir Edward, ran away; but Sir Edward dogged him, and at length arrested him on the charge of robbery. The charge broke down, Wilford was acquitted, Sir Edward confessed himself a murderer, and died.—G. Colman, *The Iron Chest* (1796).

Mortimer Lightwood, solicitor employed in the "Harmon murder" case. He was the great friend of Eugene Wrayburn, barrister-at-law, and it was the ambition of his life to imitate the *nonchalance* and other eccentricities of his friend. At one time he was a great admirer of Bella Wilfer. Mr. Veneering called him "one of his oldest friends;" but Mortimer was never in the merchant's house but once in his life, and resolved never to enter it again.—C. Dickens, *Our Mutual Friend* (1864).

Morten (*Sir*), a spectre who appears at King Olaf's feast, in the guise of a one-eyed old man, and carouses with the guests until bed-time. When the morning breaks, he has departed, and no trace of him is to be found.

"King Olaf crossed himself and said—
'I know that Odin the Great is dead;
Sure is the triumph of our Faith,
This one-eyed stranger was his wraith.'
Dead rides Sir Morten of Fogelsang."
H. W. Longfellow, *The Wraith of Odin*.

Morton, a retainer of the earl of Northumberland.—Shakespeare, 2 *Henry IV*. (1508).

Morton (Henry), a leader in the covenanters' army with Balfour. While abroad, he is Major-general Melville. Henry Morton marries Miss Edith Bellenden.

Old Ralph Morton of Milnwood, uncle of Henry Morton.

Colonel Silas Morton of Milnwood, father of Henry Morton.—Sir W. Scott, *Old Mortality* (time, Charles II.).

Morton (The earl of), in the service of Mary queen of Scots, and a member of the privy council of Scotland.—Sir W. Scott, *The Monastery* and *The Abbot* (time, Elizabeth).

Morton (The Rev. Mr.) the Presbyterian pastor of Cairnvreckan village.—Sir W. Scott, *Waverley* (time, George II.).

Mortsheugh (*Johnie*), the old sexton of Wolf's Hope village.—Sir W. Scott, *The Bride of Lammermoor* (time, William III.).

Morvi′dus, son of Danius by his concubine, Tangustĕla. In his reign, there "came from the Irish coasts a most cruel monster, which devoured the people continually, but as soon as Morvidus heard thereof, he ventured to encounter it alone. When all his darts were spent, the monster rushed upon him, and swallowed him up like a small fish."—Geoffrey of Monmouth, *British History*, iii. 15 (1142).

Mosby, an unmitigated villain. He seduced Alicia, the wife of Arden of Feversham. Thrice he tried to murder Arden, but was baffled, and then frightened Alicia into conniving at a most villainous scheme of murder. Pretending friendship, Mosby hired two ruffians to murder Arden while he was playing a game of draughts. The villains, who were concealed in an adjacent room, were to rush on their victim when Mosby said, "Now I take you." The whole gang was apprehended and executed.—*Arden of Feversham* (1592), altered by George Lillo (1739).

Mosca, the knavish confederate of Vol′pone (2 *syl.*), the rich Venetian "fox."—Ben Jonson, *Volpone* or *The Fox* (1605).

If your mother, in hopes to ruin me, should consent to marry my pretended uncle, he might, like "Mosca" in *The Fox*, stand upon terms.—W. Congreve, *The Way of the World*, ii. 1. (1700).

Mo′ses, the Jew money-lender in Sheridan's comedy, *The School for Scandal* (1777).

Moses' Clothes. The *Korân* says: "God cleared Moses from the scandal which was rumored against him" (ch. xxxiii.). The scandal was that his body was not properly formed, and therefore he would never bathe in the presence of others. One day, he went to bathe, and laid his clothes on a stone, but the stone ran away with them into the camp. Moses went after it as fast as he could run, but the Israelites saw his naked body, and perceived the untruthfulness of the common scandal.—Sale, *Al Korân*, xxxiii. notes.

Moses' Horns. The Vulgate gives *quod cornuta esset facies sua*, for what our version has translated "he wist not *that the skin of his face shone*." The Hebrew word used means both a "horn" and an "irradiation." Michael Angelo followed the Vulgate.

Moses' Rod.

While Moses was living with Re'uël [*Jethro*], the Midianite, he noticed a staff in the garden, and he took it to be his walking-stick. This staff was Joseph's, and Re'uel carried it away when he fled from Egypt. This same staff Adam carried with him out of Eden. Noah inherited it, and gave it to Shem. It passed into the hands of Abraham, and Abraham left it to Isaac; and when Jacob fled from his brother's anger into Mesopotamia, he carried it in his hand, and gave it at death to his son Joseph.—*The Talmud*, vi.

Moses Slow of Speech. The tradition is this: One day, Pharaoh was carrying Moses in his arms, when the child plucked the royal beard so roughly that the king, in a passion, ordered him to be put to death. Queen Asia said to her husband, the child was only a babe, and was so young he could not discern between a ruby and a live coal. Pharaoh put it to the test, and the child clapped into his mouth the burning coal, thinking it something good to eat. Pharaoh's anger was appeased, but the child burnt its tongue so severely that ever after it was "slow of speech."—Shalshel, *Hakkabala*, 11.

Moses Slow of Speech. The account given in the *Talmud* is somewhat different. It is therein stated that Pharaoh was sitting one day with Moses on his lap, when the child took the crown from the king's head and placed it on his own. The "wise men" of Egypt persuaded Pharaoh that this act was treasonable, and that the child should be put to death. Jithro [*sic*] the priest of Midian, said it was the act of a child who knew no better. "Let two plates," said he, "be set before the child, one containing gold and the other live coals, and you will presently see that he will choose the coals in preference to the gold." The advice of Jithro being followed, the boy Moses snatched at the coals, and putting one of them into his mouth, burnt his tongue so severely that ever after he was "heavy of speech."—*The Talmud*, vi.

Moses Pennell. Waif rescued from a wrecked vessel, and adopted by old Captain Pennell and his wife. He is, in time, discovered to belong to a noble Cuban family.—Harriet Beecher Stowe, *The Pearl of Orr's Island.*

Most Christian King (*Le Roy Tres-Chretien*). The king of France is so called by others, either with or without his proper name; but he never styles himself so in any letter, grant, or rescript.

In St. Remigius or Remy's Testament, King Clovis is called *Christianissimus Ludovicus.*—Flodoard, *Historia Remensis*, i. 18 (A.D. 940).

Motallab (*Abd al*), one of the four husbands of Zesbet, the mother of Mahomet. He was not to know her as a wife till he had seen Mahomet in his pre-existing state. Mahomet appeared to him as an old man, and told him he had chosen Zesbet, for her virtue and beauty, to be his mother.—Comte de Caylus, *Oriental Tales* ("History of Abd al Motallab," 1743).

Mo′tar ("*One doomed* or *devoted to sacrifice*"). So Prince Assad was called, when he fell into the hands of the old fire-worshipper, and was destined by him to be sacrificed on the fiery mountain.—*Arabian Nights* ("Amgiad and Assad").

Moth, page to Don Adriano de Arma′do, the fantastic Spaniard. He is cunning and versatile, facetious and playful.—Shakespeare, *Love's Labor's Lost* (1594).

Moth, one of the fairies.—Shakespeare, *Midsummer Night's Dream* (1592).

Moths and Candles. The moths fell in love with the night-fly; and the night-fly, to get rid of their importunity, maliciously bade them to go and fetch fire for her adornment. The blind lovers flew to the first flame to obtain the love-token, and few escaped injury or death.—Kæmpfer, *Account of Japan*, vii. (1727).

Mother Ann, Ann Lee, the "spiritual mother" of the Shakers (1731-1784).

*** Mother Ann is regarded by the Shakers as the female form, and Jesus as the male form, of the Messiah.

Mother Bunch, a celebrated ale-wife in Dekker's *Satiromaster* (1602).

*** In 1604 was published *Pasquil's Jests, mixed with Mother Bunch's Merriments.* In 1760 was published, in two parts, *Mother Bunch's Closet Newly Broke Open, etc.*, by a "Lover of Mirth and Hater of Treason."

Mother Bunch's *Fairy Tales* are known in every nursery.

Mother Carey's Chickens. The fish-fags of Paris in the first Great Revolution were so called, because, like the "stormy petrel," whenever they appeared in force in the streets of Paris, they always foreboded a tumult or political storm.

Mother Carey's Goose, the great black petrel or gigantic fulmar of the Pacific Ocean.

Mother Douglas, a noted crimp, who lived at the north-east corner of Covent Garden. Her house was superbly furnished. She died 1761.

* Foote introduces her in *The Minor*, as "Mrs. Cole" (1760); and Hogarth in his picture called "The March to Finchley."

Mother Goose, in French *Contes de Ma Mère l'Oye*, by Charles Perrault (1697).

* There are ten stories in this book, seven of which are from the *Pentamerone*.

Mother Goose, according to a new exploded story, was a native of Boston, and the author of the nursery rhymes that bear her name. She used to sing her rhymes to her grandson, and Thomas Fleet, her brother-in-law, published the first edition of these rhymes, entitled *Songs for the Nursery*, or *Mother Goose's Melodies*, in 1719.

* Dibdin wrote a pantomime entitled *Mother Goose*.

Mother Hubbard, an old lady, whose whole time and attention were taken up by her dog, who was most willful; but the dame never lost her temper, or forgot her politeness. After running about all day to supply Master Doggie,

The dame made a curtsey, the dog made a bow;
The dame said, "Your servant!" the dog said, "Bow, wow!"
A Nursery Tale in Rhyme.

Mother Hubberd, the supposed narrator of a tale called *The Fox and the Ape*, related to the poet Spenser to beguile the weary hours of sickness. Several persons told him tales, but

Amongst the rest a good old woman was
Hight Mother Hubberd, who did far surpass
The rest in honest mirth that seemed her well;
She, when her turn was come her tale to tell,
Told of a strange adventure that betided
Betwixt a fox and ape by him misguided;
The which, for that my sense it greatly pleased ...
I'll write it as she the same did say.
Spenser.

Mother Hubberd's Tale. A fox and an ape determined to travel about the world as *chevaliers de l'industrie*. First, Ape dressed as a broken-down soldier, and Fox as his servant. A farmer agreed to take them for his shepherds; but they devoured all his lambs and then decamped. They next "went in for holy orders." Reynard contrived to get a living given him, and appointed the ape as his clerk; but they soon made the parish too hot to hold them, and again sheered off. They next tried their fortune at court; the ape set himself up as a foreigner of distinction with Fox for his groom. They played the part of rakes, but being found to be desperate rogues, had to flee with all despatch, and seek another field of action. As they journeyed on, they saw a lion sleeping, and Master Fox persuaded his companion to steal the crown, sceptre and royal robes. The ape, arrayed in these, assumed to be king, and Fox was his prime minister; but so ill did they govern, that Jupiter interfered, the lion was restored, and the ape was docked of his tail and had his ears cropt.

Since which, all apes but half their ears have left,
And of their tails are utterly bereft.
So Mother Hubberd her discourse did end.
Spenser, *Mother Hubberd's Tale.*

Mother Shipton, T. Evan Preece, of South Wales, a prophetess, whose predictions (generally in rhymes) were at one time in everybody's mouth in South Wales, especially in Glamorganshire.

⁎ She predicted the death of Wolsey, Lord Percy, and others. Her prophecies are still extant, and contain the announcement that "the end of the world shall come in eighteen hundred and eighty-one."

Mother of the People (*The*), Marguerite of France, *La Mère des Peuples*, daughter of François I. (1523-1574).

Mould (*Mr.*), undertaker. His face had a queer attempt at melancholy, sadly at variance with a smirk of satisfaction which might be read between the lines. Though his calling was not a lively one, it did not depress his spirits, as in the bosom of his family he was the most cheery of men, and to him the "tap, tap" of coffin-making was as sweet and exhilarating as the tapping of a woodpecker.—C. Dickens, *Martin Chuzzlewit* (1844).

Mouldy (*Ralph*), "a good-limbed fellow, young, strong, and of good friends." Ralph was pricked for a recruit in Sir John Falstaff's regiment. He promised Bardolph forty shillings "to stand his friend." Sir John being told this, sent Mouldy home, and when Justice Shallow remonstrated, saying that Ralph "was the likeliest man of the lot," Falstaff replied, "Will you tell me, Master Shallow, how to choose a man? Care I for the limb, the thews, the stature, bulk, and big assemblance of a man? Give me the spirit, Master Shallow."—Shakespeare, 2 *Henry IV*. act iii. sc. 2 (1598).

Moullahs, Mohammedan lawyers, from which are selected the judges.

Mountain *(The)*, a name given in the French revolution to a faction which sat on the benches most elevated in the Hall of Assembly. The Girondins sat in the centre or lowest part of the hall, and were nicknamed the "plain." The "mountain" for a long time was the dominant part; it utterly overthrew the "plain" on August 31, 1793, but was in turn overthrown at the fall of Robespierre (9 Thermidor ii. or July 27, 1794).

Mountain (The Old Man of the), the imaum Hassan ben Sabbah el Homari. The sheik Al Jebal was so called. He was the prince of the Assassins.

*** In Rymer's *Fœdera* (vol. i.), Dr. Clarke, the editor, has added two letters of this sheik; but the doctor must be responsible for their genuineness.

Mountain Brutus *(The)*, William Tell (1282-1350).

Mountain of Flowers, the site of the palace of Violenta, the mother fairy who brought up the young princess afterwards metamorphosed into "The White Cat."—Comtesse D'Aunoy, *Fairy Tales* ("The White Cat," 1682).

Mountain of Miseries. Jupiter gave permission for all men to bring their grievances to a certain plain, and to exchange them with any others that had been cast off. Fancy helped them; but though the heap was so enormous, not one single *vice* was to be found amongst the rubbish. Old women threw away their wrinkles, and young ones their mole-spots; some cast on the heap poverty; many their red noses and bad teeth; but no one his crimes. Now came the choice. A galley-slave picked up gout, poverty picked up sickness, care picked up pain, snub noses picked up long ones, and so on. Soon all were bewailing the change they had made; and Jupiter sent Patience to tell them they might, if they liked, resume their old grievances again. Every one gladly accepted the permission, and Patience helped them to take up their own bundle and bear it without murmuring.—Addison, *The Spectator* (1711, 1712, 1714).

Mourning. In Colman's *Heir-at-Law* (1796), every character is in mourning: the Dowlases as relatives of the deceased Lord Duberly; Henry Morland as heir of Lord Duberly; Steadfast as the chief friend of the family; Dr. Pangloss as a clergyman; Caroline Dormer for her father recently buried; Zekiel and Cicely Homespun for the same reason; Kenrick for his deceased master.—James Smith, *Memoirs* (1840).

Mourning Bride *(The)*, a drama by W. Congreve (1697). "The mourning bride" is Alme´ria, daughter of Manuel, king of Grana´da, and her husband was Alphonso, prince of Valentia. On the day of their espousals they were shipwrecked, and each thought the other had perished; but they met together in the court of Granada, where Alphonso was taken captive under the assumed name of Osmyn. Osmyn, having effected his escape, marched to Granada, at the head of an army, found the king dead, and "the mourning bride" became his joyful wife.

Mouse-Tower (*The*), on the Rhine. It was here that Bishop Hatto was devoured by mice. (See HATTO.)

*** *Mauth* is a toll or custom house, and the mauth or toll-house for collecting duty on corn being very unpopular, gave rise to the tradition.

Moussa, Moses.

Mowbray (*Mr. John*), lord of the manor of St. Ronan's.

Clara Mowbray, sister of John Mowbray. She was betrothed to Frank Tyrrel, but married Valentine Bulmer.—Sir W. Scott, *St. Ronan's Well* (time, George III.).

Mowbray (*Sir Miles*), a dogmatical, self-willed old man, who fancied he could read character, and had a natural instinct for doing the right thing; but he would have been much wiser if he had paid more heed to the proverb, "Mind your own business and not another's."

Frederick Mowbray, his eldest son, a young man of fine principle, and greatly liked. His "first love" was Clara Middleton, who, being poor, married the rich Lord Ruby. His lordship soon died, leaving all his substance to his widow, who bestowed it, with herself, on Frederick Mowbray, her first and only love.

David Mowbray, younger brother of Frederick. He was in the navy, and was a fine, open-hearted, frank and honest British tar.

Lydia Mowbray, sister of Frederick and David, and the wife of Mr. Wrangle.—R. Cumberland, *First Love* (1796).

Mow´cher (*Miss*), a benevolent little dwarf, patronized by Steerforth. She is full of humor and comic vulgarity. Her chief occupation is that of hair-dressing.—C. Dickens, *David Copperfield* (1849).

Mowis, the bridegroom of snow, who wooed and won a beautiful bride, but at dawn melted in the sun. The bride hunted for him night and day, but never saw him more.—*Indian Legend*.

Mowis, the bridegroom of snow, who won and wedded a maiden,
But, when the morning came, arose and passed from the wigwam,
Fading and melting away, and dissolving into the sunshine,
Till she beheld him no more, tho' she followed far into the forest.
Longfellow, *Evangeline*, ii. 4 (1849).

Moxon (*Mr.*), clergyman at Agawam (Mass.). Sincere in his bigotry, pitiable in the superstition that darkens his life, honestly persuaded that he and his are the victims of witchcraft, and that duty forces him to punish those who have afflicted the Lord's saints.—Josiah Gilbert Holland, *The Bay Path* (1857).

Mozaide (2 *syl.*), the Moor who befriended Vasco de Gama when he first landed on the Indian continent.

The Moor attends Mozaide, whose zealous care
To Gama's eyes revealed each treacherous snare.
Camoens, *Lusiad*, ix. (1569).

Mozart (*The English*), Sir Henry Bishop (1780-1855).

Mozart (*The Italian*), Cherubini, of Florence (1760-1842).

Much, the miller's son, the bailiff or "acater" of Robin Hood. (See MIDGE.)

Robyn stode in Bernysdale,
And lened hym to a tree;
And by hym stode Lytell Johan,
A good yeman was he;
And also dyde good Scathelock,
And Much, the miller's sone.
Ritson, *Robin Hood Ballads*, i. 1 (1594).

Much, the miller's son, in the morris-dance. His feat was to bang, with an inflated bladder, the heads of gaping spectators. He represented the fool or jester.

Much Ado about Nothing, a comedy by Shakespeare (1600). Hero, the daughter of Leonato, is engaged to be married to Claudio of Aragon; but Don John, out of hatred to his brother, Leonato, determines to mar the happiness of the lovers. Accordingly, he bribes the waiting-maid of Hero to dress in her mistress's clothes, and to talk with his man by night from the chamber balcony. The villain tells Claudio that Hero has made an assignation with him, and invites him to witness it. Claudio is fully persuaded that the woman he sees is Hero, and when next day she presents herself at the altar, he rejects her with scorn. The priest feels assured there is some mistake, so he takes Hero apart, and gives out that she is dead. Then Don John takes to flight, the waiting-woman confesses, Claudio repents, and, by way of amendment (as Hero is dead) promises to marry her cousin, but this cousin turns out to be Hero herself.

*** A similar tale is told by Ariosto in his *Orlando Furioso*, v. (1516).

Another occurs in the *Faëry Queen*, by Spenser, bk. ii. 4, 38, etc. (1590).

George Turbervil's *Geneura* (1576) is still more like Shakespeare's tale. Belleforest and Bandello have also similar tales (see *Hist.*, xviii.).

Mucklebacket (*Saunders*), the old fisherman at Musselcrag.

Old Elspeth Mucklebacket, mother of Saunders, and formerly servant to Lady Glenallan.

Maggie Mucklebacket, wife of Saunders.

Steenie Mucklebacket, eldest son of Saunders. He is drowned.

Little Jennie Mucklebacket, Saunders's child.—Sir W. Scott, *The Antiquary* (time, George III.).

Mucklethrift (*Bailie*), ironmonger and brazier of Kippletringan, in Scotland.—Sir W. Scott, *Guy Mannering* (time, George II.).

Mucklewrath (*Habukkuk*), a fanatic preacher.—Sir W. Scott, *Old Mortality* (time, Charles II.).

Mucklewrath (John), smith at Cairnvreckan village.

Dame Mucklewrath, wife of John. A terrible virago.—Sir W. Scott, *Waverley* (time, George II.).

Muckworm (*Sir Penurious*), the miserly old uncle and guardian of Arbella. He wants her to marry Squire Sapskull, a raw Yorkshire tike; but she loves Gaylove, a young barrister, and, of course, Muckworm is outwitted.—Carey, *The Honest Yorkshireman* (1736).

Mudarra, son of Gonçolo Bustos de Salas de Lara, who murdered his uncle Rodri´go, while hunting, to avenge the death of his seven half-brothers. The tale is, that Rodrigo Velasquez invited his seven nephews to a feast, when a fray took place in which a Moor was slain; the aunt, who was a Moorish lady, demanded vengeance, whereupon the seven boys were allured into a ravine and cruelly murdered. Mudarra was the son of the same father as "the seven sons of Lara," but not of the same mother.—*Romance of the Eleventh Century*.

Muddle, the carpenter under Captain Savage and Lieutenant O'Brien.—Captain Marryat, *Peter Simple* (1833).

Muddlewick (*Triptolemus*), in *Charles XII.*, an historical drama by J. R. Planché (1826).

Mudjekee´wis, the father of Hiawatha, and subsequently potentate of the winds. He gave all the winds but one to his children to rule; the one he reserved was the west wind, which he himself ruled over. The dominion of the winds was given to Mudjekeewis, because he slew the great bear called the Mishê-Mokwa.

Thus was slain the Mishê-Mokwa …
"Honor be to Mudjekeewis!

Henceforth he shall be the west wind.
And hereafter, e'en for ever,
Shall he hold supreme dominion,
Over all the winds of heaven."
Longfellow, *Hiawatha*, ii. (1855).

Mug (*Matthew*), a caricature of the duke of Newcastle.—S. Foote, *The Mayor of Garratt* (1763).

Mugello, the giant slain by Averardo de Medici, a commander under Charlemagne. This giant wielded a mace from which hung three balls, which the Medici adopted as their device.

*** They have been adopted by pawnbrokers as a symbol of their trade.

Muggins (*Dr.*), a sapient physician, who had the art "to suit his physic to his patients' taste;" so when King Artaxaminous felt a little seedy after a night's debauch, the doctor prescribed to his majesty "to take a morning whet."—W. B. Rhodes, *Bombastes Furioso* (1790).

Muhldenau, the minister of Mariendorpt, and father of Meeta and Adolpha. When Adolpha was an infant, she was lost in the siege of Magdeburg; and Muhldenau, having reason to suppose that the child was not killed went to Prague in search of her. Here Muhldenau was seized as a spy, and condemned to death. Meeta, hearing of his capture, walked to Prague to beg him off, and was introduced to the governor's supposed daughter, who, in reality, was Meeta's sister, Adolpha. Rupert Roselheim, who was betrothed to Meeta, stormed the prison and released Muhldenau.—S. Knowles, *The Maid of Mariendorpt* (1838).

Mulatto, a half-caste. Strictly speaking, *Zambo* is the issue of an Indian and a Negress; *Mulatto*, of a White man and a Negress; *Terzeron*, of a White man and a Mulatto woman; *Quadroon*, of a Terzeron and a White.

Mul'ciber, Vulcan, who was blacksmith, architect, and god of fire.

In Ausonian land
Men called him Mulciber; and how he fell
From heaven, they fabled, thrown by angry Jove
Sheer o'er the crystal battlements; from morn
To noon he fell, from noon to dewy eve,
A Summer's day; and with the setting sun
Dropt from the Zenith like a falling star,
On Lemnos, the Ægean isle.
Milton, *Paradise Lost*, 739, etc. (1665).

Muley Bugentuf, king of Morocco, a blood-and-thunder hero. He is the chief character of a tragedy of the same name, by Thomas de la Fuenta.

In the first act, the king of Morocco, by way of recreation, shot a hundred Moorish slaves with arrows; in the second, he beheaded thirty Portuguese officers, prisoners of war; and in the third and last act, Muley, mad with his wives, set fire with his own hand to a detached palace, in which they were shut up, and reduced them all to ashes.... This conflagration, accompanied with a thousand shrieks, closed the piece in a very diverting manner.—Lesage, *Gil Blas*, ii. 9 (1715).

Mull Sack. John Cottington, in the time of the Commonwealth, was so called, from his favorite beverage. John Cottington emptied the pockets of Oliver Cromwell when lord protector; stripped Charles II. of £1500; and stole a watch and chain from Lady Fairfax.

*** Mull sack is spiced sherry negus.

Mulla's Bard, Spenser, author of the *Faëry Queen*. The Mulla, a tributary of the Blackwater, in Ireland, flowed close by the spot where the poet's house stood. He was born and died in London (1553-1599).

... it irks me while I write,
As erst the bard of Mulla's silver stream,
Oft as he told of deadly dolorous plight
Sighed as he sung, and did in tears indite.
Shenstone, *The Schoolmistress* (1758).

Mulla. Thomas Campbell, in his poem on the *Spanish Parrot*, calls the island of Mull, "Mulla's Shore."

Mullet (*Professor*), the "most remarkable man" of North America. He denounced his own father for voting on the wrong side at an election for president, and wrote thunderbolts in the form of pamphlets, under the signature of "Suturb" or Brutus reversed.—C. Dickens, *Martin Chuzzlewit* (1844).

Mullins (*Rev. Peter*). A minister of the gospel, who holds so hard to the belief that the laborer is worthy of his hire, that he can see nothing but the hire.

"How am I to know whether my services are acceptable unless every year there is some voluntary testimonial concerning them? It seems to me that I must have such a testimonial. I find myself looking forward to it."—Josiah Gilbert Holland, *Arthur Bonnicastle* (1873).

Mul′mutine Laws, the code of Dunvallo Mulmutius, sixteenth king of the Britons (about B.C. 400). This code was translated by Gildas from British into Latin, and by Alfred into English. The Mulmutine laws obtained in this country till the Conquest.—Holinshed, *History of England, etc.*, iii. 1 (1577).

Mulmutius made our laws,
Who was the first of Britain which did put
His brows within a golden crown, and call'd
Himself a king.
Shakespeare, *Cymbeline*, act iii. sc. 1 (1605).

Mulmutius (*Dunwallo*), son of Cloten, king of Cornwall. "He excelled all the kings of Britain in valor and gracefulness of person." In a battle fought against the allied Welsh and Scotch armies, Mulmutius tried the very scheme which Virgil (*Æneid*, ii.) says was attempted by Æneas and his companions—that is, they dressed in the clothes and bore the arms of the enemy slain, and thus disguised, committed very great slaughter. Mulmutius, in his disguise, killed both the Cambrian and Albanian kings, and put the allied army to thorough rout.—Geoffrey, *British History*, ii. 17.

Mulmutius this land in such estate maintained
As his great Belsire Brute.
Drayton, *Polyolbion*, viii. (1612).

Mulvaney (*Terence*). Rollicking, epigrammatic, harum-scarum Irish trooper, in the Indian service, whose adventures and sayings are narrated in *Soldiers Three*, *The Courting of Dinah Shadd*, etc., by Rudyard Kipling.

Multon (*Sir Thomas de*), of Gilsland. He is Lord de Vaux, a crusader, and master of the horse to King Richard I.—Sir. W. Scott, *The Talisman* (time, Richard I.).

Mumblazen (*Master Michael*), the old herald, a dependant of Sir Hugh Robsart.—Sir W. Scott, *Kenilworth* (time, Elizabeth).

Mumbo Jumbo, an African bogie, hideous and malignant, the terror of women and children.

Mumps (*Tib*), keeper of the "Mumps' Ha' ale-hous'," on the road to Charlie's Hope farm.—Sir W. Scott, *Guy Mannering* (time, George II.).

Munchau′sen (*The Baron*), a hero of most marvellous adventures.—Rudolf Erich Raspe (a German, but storekeeper of the Dolcoath mines, in Cornwall, 1792).

⁎ The name is said to refer to Hieronymus Karl Friedrich von Münchhausen, a German officer in the Russian army, noted for his marvellous stories (1720-1797). It is also supposed to be an implied satire on the traveller's tales of Baron de Tott, in his *Mémoires sur les Turcs et Tartares* (1784), and those of James Bruce, "The African Traveller," in his *Travels to Discover the Sources of the Nile* (1790).

Munchausen (*The Baron*). The French Baron Munchausen is represented by M. de Crac, the hero of a French operetta.

Mu'nera, daughter of Pollentê, the Saracen, to whom he gave all the spoils he could lay his hands on. Munera was beautiful and rich exceedingly; but Talus, having chopped off her golden hands and silver feet, tossed her into the moat.—Spenser, *Faëry Queen*, v. 2 (1596).

Mungo, a black slave of Don Diego.

Dear heart, what a terrible life am I led!
A dog has a better dat's sheltered and fed ...
Mungo here, Mungo dere,
Mungo everywhere ...
Me wish to the Lord me was dead.
I. Bickerstaff, *The Padlock* (1768).

Münster (*Baroness*). American woman married to a German prince, who wants to get rid of her. She comes to America with her brother to visit relatives, and is bored by everything, and forever threatening to write to the reigning prince to recall her to Germany.—Henry James, Jr., *The Europeans* (1878).

Murat (*The Russian*), Michael Miloradowitch (1770-1820).

Murdstone (*Edward*), the second husband of Mrs. Copperfield. His character was "firmness," that is, an unbending self-will, which rendered the young life of David intolerably wretched.

Jane Murdstone, sister of Edward, as hard and heartless as her brother. Jane Murdstone became the companion of Dora Spenlow, and told Mr. Spenlow of David's love for Dora, hoping to annoy David. At the death of Mr. Spenlow, Jane returned to live with her brother.—Dickens, *David Copperfield* (1849).

Murray or **Moray** (*The bonnie earl of*), James Stewart, the "Good Regent," a natural son of James V. of Scotland, by Margaret, daughter of John, Lord Erskine. He joined the reform party in 1556, and went to France in 1561, to invite Mary queen of Scots to come and reside in her kingdom. He was an accomplice in the murder of Rizzio, and during the queen's imprisonment was appointed regent. According to an ancient ballad, this bonny earl "was the queen's love," *i.e.* Queen Anne of Denmark, daughter of Frederick II., and wife of James I. of England. It is said that James, being jealous of the handsome earl, instigated the earl of Huntly to murder him (1531-1570).

Introduced by Sir W. Scott in *The Monastery* and *The Abbot* (time, Elizabeth).

Murray (*John*), of Broughton, secretary to Charles Edward, the Young Pretender. He turned king's evidence, and revealed to Government all the circumstances which gave rise to the rebellion, and the persons most active in its organization.

If crimes like these hereafter are forgiven,
Judas and Murray both may go to heaven.
Jacobite Relics, ii. 374.

Musæus, the poet (B.C. 1410), author of the elegant tale of *Leander and Hero*. Virgil places him in the Elysian fields attended by a vast multitude of ghosts, Musæus being taller by a head than any of them (*Æneid*, vi. 677).

Swarm ... as the infernal spirits
On sweet Musæus when he came to hell.
C. Marlowe, *Dr. Faustus* (1590).

Muscadins of Paris, Paris exquisites, who aped the London cockneys in the first French Revolution. Their dress was top-boots with thick soles, knee-breeches, a dress-coat with long tails and high stiff collar, and a thick cudgel called a *constitution*. It was thought John Bull-like to assume a huskiness of voice, a discourtesy of manners, and a swaggering vulgarity of speech and behavior.

Cockneys of London! Muscadins of Paris!
Byron, *Don Juan*, viii. 124 (1824).

Mus'carol, king of flies, and father of Clarion, the most beautiful of the race.—Spenser, *Muiopotmos, or The Butterfly's Fate* (1590).

Muse (*The Tenth*), Marie Lejars de Gournay, a French writer (1566-1645).

Antoinette Deshoulieres; also called "The French Callĭŏpê." Her best work is an allegory called *Les Moutons* (1633-1694).

Mdlle. Scudéri was preposterously so called (1607-1701).

Also Delphine Gray, afterwards Mde. Emile de Girardin. Her *nom de plume* was "viconte de Launay." Béranger sang of "the beauty of her shoulders," and Châteaubriand, of "the charms of her smile" (1804-1855).

Muse-Mother, Mnemos'ynê, goddess of memory, and mother of the Muses.

Memory,
That sweet Muse-mother.
E. B. Browning, *Prometheus Bound* (1850).

Muses (*Symbols of the*).

CAL′LIOPE [*Kăl′.ly.ŏ.py*], the epic Muse: a tablet and stylus, sometimes a scroll.

CLIO, Muse of history: a scroll or open chest of books.

ER′ATO, Muse of love ditties: a lyre.

EUTER′PÊ, Muse of lyric poetry: a flute.

MELPOM′ENÊ, Muse of tragedy: a tragic mask, the club of Hercules, or a sword. She wears the cothurnus, and her head is wreathed with vine leaves.

POL′YHYM′NIA, Muse of sacred poetry: sits pensive, but has no attribute, because deity is not to be represented by any visible symbol.

TERPSIC′HORÊ [*Terp.sick′.o.ry*], Muse of choral song and dance: a lyre and the plectrum.

THALI′A, Muse of comedy and idyllic poetry: a comic mask, a shepherd's staff, or a wreath of ivy.

URAN′IA, Muse of astronomy: carries a staff pointing to a globe.

Museum (*A Walking*), Longīnus, author of a work on *The Sublime* (213-273).

Musgrave (*Sir Richard*), the English champion who fought with Sir William Deloraine, the Scotch champion, to decide by combat whether young Scott, the heir of Branksome Hall, should become the page of King Edward, or be delivered up to his mother. In the combat, Sir Richard was slain, and the boy was delivered over to his mother.—Sir W. Scott, *Lay of the Last Minstrel* (1805).

Musgrave (*Sir Miles*), an officer in the king's service under the earl of Montrose.—Sir W. Scott, *Legend of Montrose* (time, Charles I.).

Music. Amphion is said to have built the walls of Thebes by the music of his lyre. Ilium and the capital of Arthur's kingdom were also built to divine music. The city of Jericho was destroyed by music (*Joshua* vi. 20).

They were building still, seeing the city was built
To music.
Tennyson.

Music and Men of Genius. Hume, Dr. Johnson, Sir W. Scott, Robert Peel and Lord Byron had no ear for music, and neither vocal nor instrumental music gave them the slightest pleasure. To the poet Rogers it gave actual discomfort. Even the harmonious Pope preferred the harsh dissonance of a street organ to Handel's oratorios.

Music (*Father of*), Giovanni Battista Pietro Aloisio da Palestri′na (1529-1594).

Music (*Father of Greek*), Terpander (fl. B.C. 676).

Music's First Martyr. Menaphon says that when he was in Thessaly he saw a youth challenge the birds in music; and a nightingale took up the challenge. For a time the contest was uncertain; but then the youth, "in a rapture," played so cunningly that the bird, despairing, "down dropped upon his lute, and brake her heart."

⁎ This beautiful tale, by Strada (in Latin) has been translated in rhyme by R. Crashaw. Versions have been given by Ambrose Philips, and others; but none can compare with the exquisite relation of John Ford, in his drama entitled *The Lover's Melancholy* (1628).

Musical Small-Coal Man, Thos. Britton, who used to sell small coals and keep a musical club (1654-1714).

Musicians (*Prince of*), Giovanni Battista Pietro Aloisio da Palestri´na (1529-1594).

Musidora, the *dame du cœur* of Damon. Damon thought her coyness was scorn; but one day he caught her bathing, and his delicacy on the occasion so enchanted her that she at once accepted his proffered love.—Thomson, *Seasons* ("Summer," 1727).

Musido´rus, a hero, whose exploits are told by Sir Philip Sidney, in his *Arcadia* (1581).

Musketeer, a soldier armed with a musket, but specially applied to a company of gentlemen who were a mounted guard in the service of the king of France from 1661.

They formed two companies, the *grey* and the *black*; so called from the color of their hair. Both were clad in scarlet, and hence their quarters were called the *Maison rouge*. In peace they followed the king in the chase, to protect him; in war they fought either on foot or horseback. They were suppressed in 1791; restored in 1814, but only for a few months; and after the restoration of Louis XVIII. we hear no more of them. Many Scotch gentlemen enrolled themselves among these dandy soldiers, who went to war with curled hair, white gloves, and perfumed like milliners.

⁎ A. Dumas has a novel called *The Three Musketeers* (1844), the first of a series; the second is *Twenty Years Afterwards*; and the third, *Viconte de Bragelonne*.

Muslin, the talkative, impertinent, intriguing *suivante* of Mrs. Lovemore. Mistress Muslin is sweet upon William, the footman, and loves cards.—A. Murphy, *The Way to Keep Him* (1760).

Mus´tafa, a poor tailor of China, father of Aladdin, killed by illness brought on by the idle vagabondism of his son.—*Arabian Nights* ("Aladdin and the Wonderful Lamp").

Mutton, a courtezan, sometimes called a "laced mutton." "Mutton Lane," in Clerkenwell, was so called because it was a suburra or quarter for harlots. The courtezan was called a "Mutton" even in the reign of Henry III., for Bracton speaks of them as *oves*.—*De Legibus*, etc., ii. (1569).

Mutton-Eating King (*The*), Charles II. of England (1630, 1659-1685).

Here lies our mutton-eating king,
Whose word no man relies on;
He never *said* a foolish thing,
And never *did* a wise on'.
Earl of Rochester.

Mutual Friend (*Our*), a novel by Charles Dickens (1864). The "mutual friend" is Mr. Boffin, "the golden dustman," who was the mutual friend of John Harmon and of Bella Wilfer. The tale is this: John Harmon was supposed to have been murdered by Julius Handford; but it was Ratford, who was murdered by Rogue Riderhood, and the mistake arose from a resemblance between the two persons. By his father's will, John Harmon was to marry Bella Wilfer; but John Harmon knew not the person destined by his father for his wife, and made up his mind to dislike her. After his supposed murder, he assumed the name of John Rokesmith, and became the secretary of Mr. Boffin, "the golden dustman," residuary legatee of old John Harmon, by which he became possessor of £100,000. Boffin knew Rokesmith, but concealed his knowledge for a time. At Boffin's house, John Harmon (as Rokesmith) met Bella Wilfer, and fell in love with her. Mr. Boffin, in order to test Bella's love, pretended to be angry with Rokesmith for presuming to love Bella; and, as Bella married him, he cast them both off "for a time," to live on John's earnings. A baby was born, and then the husband took the young mother to a beautiful house, and told her he was John Harmon, that the house was their house, that he was the possessor of £100,000 through the disinterested conduct of their "mutual friend," Mr. Boffin; and the young couple lived happily with Mr. and Mrs. Boffin, in wealth and luxury.

Mutusa-ili, Babylonian sage and unsuspected Jew, high in repute for wisdom and prophetic powers.—Elizabeth Stuart Phelps and Herbert D. Ward, *The Master of the Magicians* (1890).

My Book (*Dr.*). Dr. John Aberne´thy (1765-1830) was so called because he used to say to his patients, "Read my book" (*On Surgical Observations*).

My Little All.

I was twice burnt out, and lost my little all both times.—Sheridan, *The Critic*, i. 1 (1779).

Myrebeau (*Le sieure de*), one of the committee of the states of Burgundy.—Sir W. Scott, *Anne of Geierstein* (time, Edward IV.).

Myro, a statuary of Eleu´thĕræ, who carved a cow so true to nature that even bulls mistook it for a living animal. (See HORSE PAINTED.)

E'en Myro's statues, which for art surpass
All others, once were but a shapeless mass.
Ovid, *Art of Love*, iii.

Myrra, an Ionian slave, and the beloved concubine of Sardanapa´lus, the Assyrian king. She roused him from his indolence to resist Arba´cês, the Mede, who aspired to his throne, and when she found his cause hopeless, induced him to mount a funeral pile, which she fired with her own hand, and then, springing into the flames, she perished with the tyrant.—Byron, *Sardanapalus* (1819).

Myrtle (*Mrs. Lerviah*), sentimental Christian, who finds Magdalens and poor, ill-clad, homeless girls "so depressing," but begs Nixy Trent, the only one who ever entered her house, "to consider that there is hope for us all in the way of salvation which our Lord has marked out for sinners." After which crumb of ghostly consolation she proceeds to turn Nixy out of the house.—Elizabeth Stuart Phelps, *Hedged In* (1870).

Mysie, the female attendant of Lady Margaret Bellenden, of the Tower of Tillietudlem.—Sir W. Scott, *Old Mortality* (time, Charles II.).

Mysie, the old housekeeper at Wolf's Crag Tower.—Sir W. Scott, *Bride of Lammermoor* (time, William III.).

Mysis, the scolding wife of Sile´no, and mother of Daph´nê and Nysa. It is to Mysis that Apollo sings that popular song, "Pray, Goody, please to moderate the rancour of your tongue" (act i. 3).—Kane O'Hara, *Midas* (1764).

Mysterious Husband (*The*), a tragedy by Cumberland (1783). Lord Davenant was a bigamist. His first wife was Marianne Dormer, whom he forsook in three months to marry Louisa Travers. Marianne, supposing her husband to be dead, married Lord Davenant's son. Miss Dormer's brother was the betrothed of the second Lady Davenant before her marriage with his lordship. She was told that he had proved faithless and had married another. The report of Lord Davenant's death and the marriage of Captain Dormer were both false. When the villainy of Lord Davenant could be concealed no longer, he destroyed himself.

AT, the fairy that addressed Orpheus, in the infernal regions, and offered him for food a roasted ant, a flea's thigh, butterflies' brains, some sucking mites, a rainbow tart etc., to be washed down with dew-drops and beer made from seven barleycorns—a very heady liquor.—King, *Orpheus and Eurydice* (1730-1805).

Nab-man (*The*), a sheriff's officer.

Old Dornton has sent the nab-man after him at last.—*Guy Mannering*, ii. 3.

*** This is the dramatized version of Sir W. Scott's novel, by Terry (1816).

Nacien, the holy hermit who introduced Galahad to the "Siege Perilous," the only vacant seat in the Round Table. This seat was reserved for the knight who was destined to achieve the quest of the Holy Graal. Nacien told the king and his knights that no one but a virgin knight could achieve that quest.—Sir T. Malory, *History of Prince Arthur*, iii. (1470).

Nadab, in Dryden's satire of *Absalom and Achitophel*, is meant for Lord Howard, a profligate, who laid claim to great piety. As Nadab offered incense with strange fire and was slain, so Lord Howard, it is said, mixed the consecrated wafer with some roast apples and sugar.—Pt. i. (1681).

Nadgett, a man employed by Montague Tigg (manager of the "Anglo-Bengalee Company") to make private inquiries. He was a dried-up, shrivelled old man. Where he lived and how he lived, nobody knew; but he was always to be seen waiting for some one who never appeared; and he would glide along apparently taking no notice of any one.—C. Dickens, *Martin Chuzzlewit* (1844).

Nag's Head Consecration, a scandal perpetuated by Pennant, on the dogma of "apostolic succession." The "high-church clergy" assert that the ceremony called holy orders has been transmitted without interruption from the apostles. Thus, the apostles laid hands on certain persons, who (say they) became ministers of the gospel; these persons "ordained" others in the same manner; and the succession has never been broken. Pennant says, at the Reformation the bishops came to a fix. There was only one bishop, viz., Anthony Kitchen, of Llandaff, and Bonner would not allow him to perform the ceremony. In this predicament, the fourteen candidates for episcopal ordination rummaged up Story, a deposed bishop, and got him to "lay hands" on Parker, as archbishop of Canterbury. As it would have been profanation for Story to do this in a cathedral or church, the ceremony was performed in a tavern called the Nag's Head, corner of Friday Street, Cheapside. Strype refutes this scandalous tale in his *Life of Archbishop Parker*, and so does Dr. Hook; but it will never be stamped out.

Naggleton (*Mr.* and *Mrs.*), types of a nagging husband and wife. They are for ever jangling at trifles and willful misunderstandings.—*Punch* (1864-5).

Naked Bear (*The*). *Hush! the naked bear will hear you!* a threat and reproof to unruly children in North America. The naked bear, says the legend, was larger and more ferocious than any of the species. It was quite naked, save and except one spot on its back, where was a tuft of white hair.—Heckewelder, *Transactions of the American Phil. Soc.*, iv. 260.

Thus the wrinkled old Nokomis
Nursed the little Hiawatha,
Rocked him in his linden cradle,
Stilled his fretful wail by saying
"Hush! the naked bear will get thee!"
Longfellow, *Hiawatha*, iii. (1855).

Nakir´, **Nekir**, or **Nakeer**. (See MONKER AND NAKIR.)

Nala, a legendary king of India, noted for his love of Damayanti, and his subsequent misfortunes. This legendary king has been the subject of numerous poems.

⁎ Dean Milman has translated into English the episode from the *Mahâbhârata*, and W. Yates has translated the Nalodaya of the great Sanskrit poem.

Nama, a daughter of man, beloved by the angel Zaraph. Her wish was to love intensely and to love holily, but as she fixed her love on a seraph, and not on God, she was doomed to abide on earth, "unchanged in heart and frame," so long as the earth endureth; but at the great consummation both Nama and her seraph will be received into those courts of love, where "love never dieth."—Moore, *Loves of the Angels*, ii. (1822).

Namby (*Major*), a retired officer, living in the suburbs of London. He had been twice married; his first wife had four children, and his second wife three. Major Namby, though he lived in a row, always transacted his domestic affairs by bawling out his orders from the front garden, to the annoyance of his neighbors. He used to stalk half-way down the garden path, with his head high in the air, his chest stuck out, and flourishing his military cane. Suddenly he would stop, stamp with one foot, knock up the hinder brim of his hat, begin to scratch the nape of his neck, wait a moment, then wheel round, look at the first-floor window, and roar out, "Matilda!" (the name of his wife) "don't do so-and-so;" or "Matilda! do so-and-so." Then he would bellow to the servants to buy this, or not to let the children eat that, and so on.—Wilkie Collins, *Pray Employ Major Namby* (a sketch).

Names of Terror. The following amongst others, have been employed as bogie-names to frighten children with:—

ATTILA was a bogie-name to the Romans.

BO or BOH, son of Odin, was a fierce Gothic captain. His name was used by his soldiers when they would fight or surprise the enemy.—Sir William Temple.

※ Warton tells us that the Dutch scared their children with the name of Boh.

BONAPARTE, at the close of the eighteenth and beginning of the nineteenth centuries, was a name of terror in Europe.

CORVI′NUS (*Mathias*), the Hungarian, was a scare-name to the Turks.

LILIS or LILITH was a bogie-name used by the ancient Jews to unruly children. The rabbinical writers tell us that Lilith was Adam's wife before the creation of Eve. She refused to submit to him, and became a horrible night-spectre, especially hostile to young children.

LUNSFORD, a name employed to frighten children in England. Sir Thomas Lunsford, governor of the Tower, was a man of most vindictive temper, and the dread of everyone.

Made children with your tones to run for't,
As bad as Bloody-bones or Lunsford.
S. Butler, *Hudibras*, iii. 2, line 1112, (1678).

NARSES (2 *syl.*) was the name used by Assyrian mothers to scare their children with.

The name of Narses was the formidable sound with which the Assyrian mothers were accustomed to terrify their infants.—Gibbon, *Decline and Fall of the Roman Empire*, viii. 219 (1776-88).

RAWHEAD and BLOODY-BONES were at one time bogie-names to children.

Servants awe children and keep them in subjection by telling them of Rawhead and Bloody-bones.—Locke.

RICHARD I., "Cœur de Lion." This name, says Camden (*Remains*), was employed by the Saracens as a "name of dread and terror."

His tremendous name was employed by the Syrian mothers to silence their infants; and if a horse suddenly started from the way, his rider was wont to exclaim, "Dost thou think King Richard is in the bush?"—Gibbon, *Decline and Fall of the Roman Empire*, xi. 146 (1776-88).

SEBASTIAN (*Don*), a name of terror once used by the Moors.

Nor shall Sebastian's formidable name
Be longer used to still the crying babe.
Dryden, *Don Sebastian* (1690).

TALBOT (*John*), a name used in France *in terrorem* to unruly children.

They in France to feare their young children crye, "The Talbot commeth!"—Hall, *Chronicles* (1545).

Here (said they) is the terror of the French,
The scarecrow that affrights our children so.
Shakespeare, 1 *Henry VI*. act. i. sc. 4 (1589).

Is this the Talbot so much feared abroad,
That with his name the mothers still their babes?
Shakespeare, 1 *Henry VI*. act iv. sc. 5 (1589).

TAMERLANE, a name used by the Persians *in terrorem*.

TARQUIN, a name of terror in Roman nurseries.

The nurse to still her child, will tell my story,
And fright her crying babe with Tarquin's name.
Shakespeare, *Rape of Lucrece* (1594).

(See also NAKED BEAR.)

Namo, duke of Bavaria, and one of Charlemagne's twelve paladins.—Ariosto, *Orlando Furioso* (1516).

Namou'na, an enchantress. Though first of created beings, she is still as young and beautiful as ever.—*Persian Mythology*.

Namous, the envoy of Mahomet in paradise.

Nancy, eldest daughter of an English country family, in straitened circumstances. Nancy is a romp and untamed, but sound-hearted, and loves her brothers and sister tenderly. To advance their interests she marries Sir Roger Tempest, who is much her senior. In time, and after many misunderstandings, she learns to love him, and "they live happily together ever after."—Rhoda Broughton, *Nancy*.

Nancy, servant to Mrs. Pattypan. A pretty little flirt, who coquets with Tim Tartlet and young Whimsey, and helps Charlotte Whimsey in her "love affairs."—James Cobb, *The First Floor* (1756-1818).

Nancy, a poor misguided girl, who really loves the villain Bill Sykes (1 *syl.*). In spite of her surroundings, she has still some good feelings, and tries to prevent a burglary planned by Fagin and his associates. Bill Sykes, in a fit of passion, strikes her twice upon the face with the butt-end of a pistol, and she falls dead at his feet.—C. Dickens, *Oliver Twist* (1837).

Nancy, the sailor's fancy. At half-past four he parted from her; at eight next morn he bade her adieu. Next day a storm arose, and when it lulled the enemy appeared; but when the fight was hottest, the jolly tar "put up a prayer for Nancy." Dibdin, *Sea Songs* ("'Twas post meridian half-past four," 1790).

Nancy (Miss), Mrs. Anna Oldfield, a celebrated actress, buried in Westminster Abbey. She died in 1730, and lay in state, attended by two noblemen. Mrs. Oldfield was buried in a "very fine Brussels lace head-dress, a new pair of kid gloves, and a robe with lace ruffles and a lace collar." (See NARCISSA.)

Nancy Dawson, a famous actress, who took London by storm. Her father was a poster in Clare Market (1728-1767).

Her easy mien, her shape so neat,
She foots, she trips, she looks so sweet;
I die for Nancy Dawson.

Nancy of the Vale, a village maiden, who preferred Strephon to the gay lordlings who sought her hand in marriage.—Shenstone, *A Ballad* (1554).

Nannic, deformed brother of Guenn, and her darling. He is versed in all manner of auguries and much feared and consulted by the peasants on this account.—Blanche Willis Howard, *Guenn*.

Nannie, Miss Fleming, daughter of a farmer in the parish of Tarbolton, in Ayrshire. Immortalized by R. Burns.

Nannie (Little).

"This world, whose brightest day
Seems to us so dreary,
Nannie found all bright and gay,
Love-alight and cheery,
Stayed a little while to play
And went home unweary."
Elizabeth Akers Allen, *Poems* (1866).

Nan´tolet, father of Rosalura and Lillia-Bianca.—Beaumont and Fletcher, *The Wild-Goose Chase* (1652).

Napoleon I., called by the Germans "Kaiser Kläs" (*q.v.*).

"M" is curiously coupled with the history of Napoleon I. and III. (See M.)

The following is a curious play on the word Napoleon.

Napoleôn   apoleôn   poleôn   oleôn   leôn   eôn   ôn

Napoleon   Apollyon   cities   destroying   a lion   going about   } being.

That is:

Napoleon Apollyon is [*being*] a lion going about destroying cities.

Chauvinism, Napoleon idolatry. Chauvvin is a blind idolater of Napoleon I., in Scribe's drama entitled *Soldat Laboureur*.

Napoleon III. *His nicknames.*

ARENENBERG (*Comte d'*). So he called himself after his escape from the fortress of Ham.

BADINGUET, the name of the man he shot in his Boulogne escapade.

BOUSTRAPA, a compound of Bou[logne], Stra[sbourg] and Pa[ris], the places of his noted escapades.

GROSBEC. So called from the rather unusual size of his nose.

MAN OF DECEMBER. So called because December was his month of glory. Thus, he was elected president December 11, 1848; made his *coup d'état* December 2, 1851; and was created emperor December 2, 1852.

MAN OF SEDAN. So called because at Sedan he surrendered his sword to the king of Prussia (September, 1870).

RATIPOLE, same as the west of England RANTIPOLE, a harum-scarum, half idiot, half madcap.

THE LITTLE. Victor Hugo gave him this title; but the hatred of Hugo to Napoleon was monomania.

VERHUEL, the name of his supposed father.

Number 2. The second of the month was Louis Napoleon's day. It was also one of the days of his uncle, the other being the fifteenth.

The *coup d'état* was December 2; he was made emperor December 2, 1852; the Franco-Prussian war opened at Saarbrück, August 2, 1870; he surrendered his sword to William of Prussia, September 2, 1870.

Napoleon I. was crowned December 2, 1804; and the victory of Austerlitz was December 2, 1805.

Numerical Curiosities. 1. 1869, the last year of Napoleon's glory; the next year was that of his downfall. As a matter of curiosity, it may be observed that if the day of his birth, or the day of the empress's birth, or the date of the capitulation of Paris, be added to that of the coronation of Napoleon III., the result always points to 1869. Thus, he was crowned 1852; he was born 1808; the Empress Eugénie was born 1826: the capitulation of Paris was 1871. Whence:

1852	1852	1852 coronation
1	1	1

8 —		8 —		8 —	
0	birth of Napoleon.	2	birth of Eugénie.	7	capitulation of Paris.
8		6		1	
1869		1869		1869	

2. 1870, the year of his downfall. By adding the numerical values of the birth date either of Napoleon or Eugénie to the date of the marriage, we get their fatal year of 1870. Thus, Napoleon was born 1808; Eugénie, 1826; married, 1853.

1853		1853	year of marriage.
1		1	
8	birth of Napoleon.	8	birth of Eugénie.
0		2	
8		6	
1870		1870	

2. *Empereur.* The votes for the president to be emperor were 7,119,791; those against him were 1,119,000. If now the numbers 711979r/1119 be written on a piece of paper, and held up to the light, the reverse side will show the word *empereur.* (The dash is the dividing mark, and forms the long stroke of the "p.")

Napoleon and Talleyrand. Napoleon I. one day entered a roadside inn, and called for breakfast. There was nothing in the house but eggs and cider (which Napoleon detested). "What shall we do?" said the emperor to Talleyrand. In answer to this, the *grand chambellan* improvised the rhymes following:—

Le bon roi Dagobert
Aimait le bon vin au dessert.
Le grand St. Eloi
Lui dit, "O mon roi,
Le droit réuni
L'a bien renchéri."
"Eh bien!" lui dit le roi ...

But he could get no further. Whereupon Napoleon himself instantly capped the line thus:

"Je boirai du cidre avec toi."
Chapus, *Dieppe, etc.* (1853).

Our royal master, Dagobert,
Good wine loved at his dessert.
But St. Eloi
Once said, "Mon roi,
We here prepare
No dainty fare."
"Well," cried the king, "so let it be,
Cider to-day we'll drink with thee."

Napoleon of the Drama. Alfred Bunn, lessee of Drury Lane Theatre (1819-1826) was so called; and so was Robert William Elliston, his predecessor (1774-1826, died 1831).

Napoleon of Mexico, the emperor Augusto Iturbidê (1784-1824).

Napoleon of Oratory, W. E. Gladstone (1809-).

Napoleon of Peace, Louis Philippe of France (1773, reigned 1830-1848, died 1850).

Narcissa, meant for Elizabeth Lee, the step-daughter of Dr. Young. In Night ii. the poet says she was clandestinely buried at Montpelier, because she was a Protestant.—Dr. Young, *Night Thoughts* (1742-6).

Narcissa, Mrs. Oldfield, the actress, who insisted on being rouged and dressed in Brussels lace when she was "laid out." (See NANCY.)

"Odious! In woolen? 'Twould a saint provoke!"
Were the last words that poor Narcissa spoke.
"No, let a charming chintz and Brussels lace
Wrap my cold limbs and shade my lifeless face;
One would not, sure, be frightful when one's dead!
And, Betty, give this cheek a little red."
Pope, *Moral Essays*, i. (1731).

Narcisse, an airy young Creole. He has boundless faith in himself, and a Micawberish confidence in the future. He would like to be called "Papillon," the butterfly; "'Cause thass my natu'e! I gatheth honey eve'y day fum eve'y opening floweh, as the bahd of Avon wemawked."—George W. Cable, *Dr. Sevier* (1883).

Narcissus, a flower. According to Grecian fable, Narcissus fell in love with his own reflection in a fountain, and, having pined away because he could not kiss it, was changed into the flower which bears his name.—Ovid, *Metamorphoses*, iii. 346, etc.

Echo was in love with Narcissus, and died of grief because he would not return her love.

Narcissus fair,
As o'er the fabled fountain hanging still.
Thomson, *Seasons* ("Spring," 1728).

⁎ Glück, in 1779, produced an opera called *Echo et Narcisse*.

Narren-Schiff (*"The ship of fools"*), a satirical poem, in German, by Brandt (1491), lashing the follies and vices of the period. Brandt makes knowledge of one's self the beginning of wisdom; maintains the equality of man; and speaks of life as a brief passage only. The book at one time enjoyed unbounded popularity.

Narses (2 *syl.*), a Roman general against the Goths; the terror of children.

The name of Narses was the formidable sound with which the Assyrian mothers were accustomed to terrify their infants.—Gibbon, *Decline and Fall of the Roman Empire*, viii. 219 (1776-88).

Narses, a domestic slave of Alexius Comnēnus, emperor of Greece.—Sir W. Scott, *Count Robert of Paris* (time, Rufus).

Naso, Ovid, the Roman poet, whose full name was Publius Ovidius Naso. (*Naso* means "nose.") Hence the pun of Holofernes:

And why Naso, but for smelling out the odoriferous flowers of fancy?—Shakespeare, *Love's Labor's Lost*, act iv. sc. 2 (1594).

Nathan the Wise, a prudent and wealthy old Jew who lives near Jerusalem in the time of Saladin. The play is a species of argument for religious toleration.—G. E. Lessing, *Nathan der Weise* (1778).

Nathaniel (*Sir*), the grotesque curate of Holofernês.—Shakespeare, *Love's Labor's Lost* (1594).

Nathos, one of the three sons of Usnoth, lord of Etha (in Argyllshire), made commander of the Irish army at the death of Cuthullin. For a time he propped up the fortune of the youthful Cormac, but the rebel Cairbar increased in strength and found means to murder the young king. The army under Nathos then deserted to the usurper, and Nathos, with his two brothers, was obliged to quit Ireland. Dar´-Thula, the daughter of Colla, went with them to avoid Cairbar, who persisted in offering her his love. The wind drove the vessel back to Ulster, where Cairbar lay encamped, and the three young men, being overpowered, were slain. As for Dar-Thula, she was pierced with an arrow, and died also.—Ossian, *Dar-Thula*.

Nation of Gentlemen. The Scotch were so called by George IV., when he visited Scotland in 1822.

Nation of Shopkeepers. The English were so called by Napoleon I.

National Assembly. (1) The French deputies which met in the year 1789. The states-general was convened, but the clergy and nobles refused to sit in the same chamber with the commons, so the commons or deputies of the *tiers état* withdrew, constituted themselves into a deliberative body, and assumed the name of the *Assemblée Nationale*. (2) The democratic French parliament of 1848, consisting of 900 members elected by manhood suffrage, was so called also.

National Convention, the French parliament of 1792. It consisted of 721 members, but was reduced, first to 500, then to 300. It succeeded the National Assembly.

Natty Bumpo, called "Leather-stocking." He appears in five of F. Cooper's novels: (1) *The Deerslayer*; (2) *The Pathfinder*; (3) "Hawkeye" in *The Last of the Mohicans*; (4) "Natty Bumpo," in *The Pioneer*; and (5) "The Trapper," in *The Prairie*, in which he dies.

Nausic'aa (4 *syl.*), daughter of Alcinous, king of the Phœa'cians, who conducted Ulysses to the court of her father when he was shipwrecked on the coast.

Navigation (*The Father of*), Don Henrique, duke of Viseo, the greatest man that Portugal has produced (1394-1460).

Navigation (*The Father of British Inland*), Francis Egerton, duke of Bridgewater (1736-1803).

Neæra, a name used by Horace, Virgil, Tibullus, and Milton as a synonym of sweetheart.

To sport with Amaryllis in the shade,
Or with the tangles of Neæra's hair.
Milton, *Lycidas* (1638).

Neal'liny (4 *syl.*), a suttee, the young widow of Ar'valan, son of Keha'ma.—Southey, *Curse of Kehama*, i. 11 (1809).

Nebuchadnezzar [*Ne-boch-ad-ne-Tzar*], in Russian, means "there is no God but the Czar."—M. D., *Notes and Queries* (21st July, 1877).

Neck. Calig'ula, the Roman emperor used to say, "Oh that the Roman people had but one neck, that I might cut it off at a blow!"

I love the sex, and sometimes would reverse
The tyrant's wish, that, "mankind only had

One neck, which he with one fell stroke might pierce."
Byron, *Don Juan*, vi. 27 (1824).

Neck or Nothing, a farce by Garrick (1766). Mr. Stockwell promises to give his daughter in marriage to the son of Sir Harry Harlowe, of Dorsetshire, with a *dot* of £10,000; but it so happens that the young man is privately married. The two servants of Mr. Belford and Sir Harry Harlowe try to get possession of the money, by passing off Martin (Belford's servant) as Sir Harry's son; but it so happens that Belford is in love with Miss Stockwell, and hearing of the plot through Jenny, the young lady's-maid, arrests the two servants as vagabonds. Old Stockwell gladly consents to his marriage with Nancy, and thinks himself well out of the terrible scrape.

Nectaba′nus, the dwarf at the cell of the hermit of Engaddi. Sir W. Scott, *The Talisman* (time, Richard I.).

Nectar, the beverage of the gods. It was white as cream, for when Hebê spilt some of it, the white arch of heaven, called the Milky Way, was made. The food of the gods was *ambrosia*.

Ned (*Lying*), "the chimney-sweeper of Savoy," that is, the duke of Savoy, who joined the allied army against France in the war of the Spanish Succession.—Dr. Arbuthnot, *History of John Bull* (1712).

Negro′ni, a princess, the friend of Lucrezia di Borgia. She invited the notables who had insulted the Borgia to a banquet, and killed them with poisoned wine.—Donizetti, *Lucrezia di Borgia* (an opera, 1834).

Ne′gus, sovereign of Abyssinia. Erco′co, or Erquico, on the Red Sea, marks the north-east boundary of this empire.

The empire of Negus to his utmost port,
Ercoco.
Milton, *Paradise Lost*, xi. 397 (1665).

Nehemiah Holdenough, a Presbyterian preacher.—Sir W. Scott, *Woodstock* (time, commonwealth).

Neilson (*Mr. Christopher*), a surgeon at Glasgow.—Sir W. Scott, *Rob Roy* (time, George I.).

Neim′heid (2 *syl.*) employed four architects to build him a palace in Ireland; and, that they might not build another like it or superior to it for some other monarch, had them all secretly murdered.—O'Halloran, *History of Ireland*.

** A similar story is told of Nômanal-Aôuar, king of Hirah, who employed Senna′mar to build him a palace. When finished, he cast the architect headlong from the highest tower, to prevent his building another to rival it.—D'Herbelot, *Bibliothèque Oriental* (1697).

Nekayah, sister of Rasselas, prince of Abyssinia. She escapes with her brother from the "happy valley," and wanders about with him to find what condition or rank of life is the most happy. After roaming for a time, and finding no condition of life free from its drawbacks, the brother and sister resolved to return to the "happy valley."—Dr. Johnson, *Rasselas* (1759).

Nell, the meek and obedient wife of Jobson; taught by the strap to know who was lord and master. Lady Loverule was the imperious, headstrong bride of Sir John Loverule. The two women by a magical hocus-pocus, were changed for a time, without any of the four knowing it. Lady Loverule was placed with Jobson, who soon brought down her turbulent temper with the strap, and when she was reduced to submission, the two women were restored again to their respective husbands.—C. Coffey, *The Devil to Pay* (1731).

Nell (*Little*), or NELLY TRENT, a sweet, innocent, loving child of 14 summers, brought up by her old miserly grandfather, who gambled away all his money. Her days were monotonous and without youthful companionship, her evenings gloomy and solitary; there were no child-sympathies in her dreary home, but dejection, despondence akin to madness, watchfulness, suspicion, and imbecility. The grandfather being wholly ruined by gaming, the two went forth as beggars, and ultimately settled down in a cottage adjoining a country churchyard. Here Nell died, and the old grandfather soon afterwards was found dead upon her grave.—C. Dickens, *The Old Curiosity Shop* (1840).

Nelly, the servant-girl of Mrs. Dinmont.—Sir W. Scott, *Guy Mannering* (time, George II.).

Nelson's Ship, the *Victory*.

Now from the fleet of the foemen past
Ahead of the *Victory*,
A four-decked ship, with a flagless mast,
An Anak of the sea.
His gaze on the ship Lord Nelson cast:
"Oh, oh! my old friend!" quoth he.
"Since again we have met, we must all be glad
To pay our respects to the *Trinidad*."
So, full on the bow of the giant foe,
Our gallant *Victory* runs;
Thro' the dark'ning smoke the thunder broke
O'er her deck from a hundred guns.
Lord Lytton, *Ode*, iii. 9 (1839).

Nem´ean Lion, a lion of Argŏlis, slain by Hercŭlês.

In this word Shakespeare has preserved the correct accent: "As hardy as the Nem´ean lion's nerve" (*Hamlet*, act i. sc. 5); but Spenser incorrectly throws the accent on the second syllable, which is *e* short: "Into the great Neme´an's lion's grove" (*Faëry Queen*, v. 1).

Ere Nemĕa's beast resigned his shaggy spoils.
Statius, *The Thebaid*, i.

Nem´esis, the Greek personification of retribution, or that punishment for sin which sooner or later overtakes the offender.

... and some great Nemesis
Break from a darkened future.
Tennyson, *The Princess*, (1847).

Ne´mo, the name by which Captain Hawdon was known at Krook's. He had once won the love of the future Lady Dedlock, by whom he had a child called Esther Summerson; but he was compelled to copy law-writings for daily bread, and died a miserable death from an overdose of opium.—C. Dickens, *Bleak House* (1852).

Nepen´the (3 *syl.*) or NEPENTHES, a care-dispelling drug, which Polydamna, wife of Tho´nis, king of Egypt, gave to Helen (daughter of Jove and Leda). A drink containing this drug "changed grief to mirth, melancholy to joyfulness, and hatred to love." The water of Ardenne had the opposite effects. Homer mentions the drug nepenthê in his *Odyssey*, iv. 228.

That nepenthês which the wife of Thone,
In Egypt gave to Jove-born Helena.
Milton, *Comus*, (1634).

Nepenthê is a drink of sovereign grace.
Devisèd by the gods for to assuage
Heart's grief, and bitter gall away to chase
Which stirs up anger and contentious rage;
Instead thereof sweet peace and quietage
It doth establish in the troubled mind ...
And such as drink, eternal happiness do find.
Spencer, *Faëry Queen*, iv. 2 (1596).

Nep´omuk or **Nep´omuck** (*St. John*), canon of Prague. He was thrown from a bridge in 1381, and drowned by order of King Wenceslaus, because he refused to betray the secrets confided to him by the queen in the holy rite of confession. The spot whence he was cast into the Moldau is still marked by a cross with five stars on the parapet, indicative of the miraculous flames seen flickering over the dead body for three days. Nepomuk was canonized in 1729, and became the patron saint of bridges. His statue in stone usually occupies such a position on bridges as it does in Prague.

Like St. John Nep´omuck in stone, Looking down into the stream.
Longfellow, *The Golden Legend* (1851).

*** The word is often accented on the second syllable.

Neptune (*Old Father*), the ocean or sea-god.

Nerestan, son of Gui Lusignan D'Outremer, king of Jerusalem, and brother of Zara. Nerestan was sent on his parole to France, to obtain ransom for certain Christians, who had fallen into the hands of the Saracens. When Osman, the sultan, was informed of his relationship to Zara, he ordered all Christian captives to be at once liberated "without money and without price."—A. Hill, *Zara* (adapted from Voltaire's tragedy).

Nereus (2 *syl.*), father of the water-nymphs. A very old prophetic god of great kindliness. The scalp, chin and breast of Nereus were covered with seaweed instead of hair.

By hoary Nêreus' wrinkled look.
Milton, *Comus*, (1634).

Neri´nê, Doto, and **Nysê**, the three nereids who guarded the fleet of Vasco da Gama. When the treacherous pilot had run Vasco's ship upon a sunken rock, these three sea-nymphs lifted up the prow and turned it round.

The lovely Nysê and Nerinê spring
With all the vehemence and speed of wing.
Camoens, *Lusiad*, ii. (1569).

Nerissa, the clever confidential waiting-woman of *Portia*, the Venetian heiress. Nerissa is the counterfeit of her mistress, with a fair share of the lady's elegance and wit. She marries *Gratiano*, a friend of the merchant *Antonio*.—Shakespeare, *The Merchant of Venice* (1698).

Nero of the North, Christian II. of Denmark (1480, reigned 1534-1558, died 1559).

Nesle (*Blondel de*), the favorite minstrel of Richard Cœur de Lion [Nesle = *Neel*].—Sir W. Scott, *The Talisman* (time, Richard I.).

Nessus's Shirt. Nessos (in Latin *Nessus*), the centaur, carried the wife of Herculês over a river, and, attempting to run away with her, was shot by Herculês. As the centaur was dying, he told Deïani´ra (5 *syl.*), that if she steeped in his blood her husband's shirt, she would secure his love forever. This she did, but when Herculês put the shirt on, his body suffered such agony, that he rushed to Mount Œta, collected together a pile of wood, set it on fire, and rushing into the midst of the flames, was burnt to death.

When Creūsa (3 *syl.*), the daughter of King Creon, was about to be married to Jason, Medēa sent her a splendid wedding robe; but when Creusa put it on, she was burnt to death by it in excruciating pain.

Morgan le Fay, hoping to kill King Arthur, sent him a superb royal robe. Arthur told the messenger to try it on, that he might see its effect; but no sooner had the messenger done so, than he dropped down dead, "burnt to mere coal."—Sir T. Malory, *History of Prince Arthur*, i. 75 (1470).

Nestor (*A*), a wise old man. Nestor of Pylos, was the oldest and most experienced of all the Greek chieftains who went to the siege of Troy.—Homer, *Iliad*.

Nestor of the Chemical Revolution. Dr. Black is so called by Lavoisier (1728-1799).

Nestor of Europe, Leopold, king of Belgium (1790, 1831-1865).

Neu′ha, a native of Toobouai, one of the Society Islands. It was at Toobouai that the mutineers of the *Bounty* landed, and Torquil married Neuha. When a vessel was sent to capture the mutineers, Neuha conducted Torquil to a secret cave, where they lay *perdu* till all danger was over, when they returned to their island home.—Byron, *The Island*. (The character of Neuha is given in canto ii. 7.)

Nevers (*Comte de*), to whom Valenti′na (daughter of the governor of the Louvre) was affianced, and whom she married in a fit of jealousy. The count having been shot in the Bartholomew slaughter, Valentina married Raoul [*Rawl*] her first love, but both were killed by a party of musketeers commanded by the governor of the Louvre.—Meyerbeer, *Les Huguenots* (opera, 1836).

⁎ The duke [not *count*] de Nevers, being asked by the governor of the Louvre to join in the Bartholomew Massacre, replied that his family contained a long list of warriors, but not one assassin.

Neville (*Major*), an assumed name of Lord Geraldin, son of the earl of Geraldin. He first appears as Mr. William Lovell.

Mr. Geraldin Neville, uncle to Lord Geraldin.—Sir W. Scott, *The Antiquary* (time, George III.).

Neville (*Miss*), the friend and *confidante* of Miss Hardcastle. A handsome, coquettish girl, destined by Mrs. Hardcastle for her son Tony Lumpkin, but Tony did not care for her, and she dearly loved Mr. Hastings; so Hastings and Tony plotted together to outwit madam, and of course won the day.—O. Goldsmith, *She Stoops to Conquer* (1773).

Neville (Sir Henry), chamberlain of Richard Cœur de Lion.—Sir W. Scott, *The Talisman* (time, Richard I.).

New Atlantis *(The)*, an imaginary island in the middle of the Atlantic. Bacon in his allegorical fiction so called, supposes himself wrecked on this island, where he finds an association for the cultivation of natural science, and the promotion of arts.—Lord Bacon, *The New Atlantis* (1626).

*** Called the *New* Atlantis to distinguish it from Plato's Atlantis, an imaginary island of fabulous charms.

New Inn *(The)*, or THE LIGHT HEART, a comedy by Ben Jonson (1628).

New Way to Pay Old Debts, a drama by Philip Massinger (1625). Wellborn, the nephew of Sir Giles Overreach, having run through his fortune and got into debt, induces Lady Allworth, out of respect and gratitude to his father, to give him countenance. This induces Sir Giles to suppose that his nephew is about to marry the wealthy dowager. Feeling convinced that he will then be able to swindle him out of all the dowager's property, as he had ousted him out of his paternal estates, Sir Giles pays his nephew's debts, and supplies him liberally with ready money, to bring about the marriage as soon as possible. Having paid Wellborn's debts, the overreaching old man is compelled, through the treachery of his clerk, to restore the estates also, for the deeds of conveyance are found to be only blank sheets of parchment, the writing having been erased by some chemical acids.

New Zealander, It was Macaulay who said the time might come when some "New Zealand artist shall, in the midst of a vast solitude, take his stand on a broken arch of London bridge to sketch the ruins of St. Paul's."

*** Shelley was before Macaulay in the same conceit.—See *Dedication of Peter Bell the Third*.

Newcastle *(The duchess of)*, in the court of Charles II.).—Sir W. Scott, *Peveril of the Peak* (time, Charles II.).

Newcastle (The marquis of), a royalist in the service of Charles I.—Sir W. Scott, *Legend of Montrose* (time, Charles I.).

Newcastle Apothecary *(The)*, Mr. Bolus, of Newcastle, used to write his prescriptions in rhyme. A bottle bearing the couplet, "When taken to be well shaken," was sent to a patient, and when Bolus called next day to inquire about its effect, John told the apothecary his master was dead. The fact is, John had shaken the *sick man* instead of the bottle, and had shaken the life out of him.—G. Colman, Jr.

Newcome (*Clemency*), about 30 years old, with a plump and cheerful face, but twisted into a tightness that made it comical. Her gait was very homely, her limbs seemed all odd ones; her shoes were so self-willed that they never wanted to go where her feet went. She wore blue stockings, a printed gown of hideous pattern and many colors, and a white apron. Her sleeves were short, her elbows always grazed, her cap anywhere but in the right place; but she was scrupulously clean, and "maintained a kind of dislocated tidiness." She carried in her pocket "a handkerchief, a piece of wax-candle, an apple, an orange, a lucky penny, a cramp-bone, a padlock, a pair of scissors, a handful of loose beads, several balls of worsted and cotton, a needle-case, a collection of curl-papers, a biscuit, a thimble, a nutmeg-grater, and a few miscellaneous articles." Clemency Newcome married Benjamin Britain, her fellow-servant at Dr. Jeddler's, and opened a country inn called the Nutmeg-Grater, a cozy, well-to-do place as any one could wish to see, and there were few married people so well matched as Clemency and Ben Britain.—C. Dickens, *The Battle of Life* (1846).

Newcome (*Colonel*), a widower, distinguished for the moral beauty of his life. He loses his money and enters the Charter House.

Clive Newcome, his son. He is in love with Ethel Newcome, his cousin, whom he marries as his second wife.—Thackeray, *The Newcomes* (1855).

Newcome (*Johnny*), any raw youth when he first enters the army or navy.

Newman Noggs. Ralph Nickleby's clerk, but Ralph's nephew's friend and secret coadjutor.—Charles Dickens, *Nicholas Nickleby*.

Newland (*Abraham*), one of the governors of the Bank of England, to whom, in the early part of the nineteenth century, all Bank of England notes were made payable. A bank-note was called an "Abraham Newland;" and hence the popular song, "I've often heard say, sham Ab'ram you may, but must not sham Abraham Newland."

Trees are notes issued from the bank of nature, and as current as those payable to Abraham Newland.—G. Colman, *The Poor Gentleman*, i. 2 (1802).

Newman. An intelligent American who has made a fortune as a manufacturer, yet kept his head steady. He sees life with clear, sometimes with amused eyes.

"In America," Newman reflected, "lads of twenty-five and thirty have old heads and young hearts, or at least, young morals; abroad they have young heads and very aged hearts, morals the most grizzled and wrinkled."—Henry James Jr., *The Americans* (1877).

Newton.

Newton ... declared, with all his grand discoveries recent,
That he himself felt only "like a youth
Picking up shells by the great ocean, truth."
Byron, *Don Juan*, vii. 5 (1824).

Newton discovered the prismatic colors of light, and explained the phenomenon by the emission theory.

Nature and Nature's laws lay hid in night.
God said, "Let Newton be," and all was light.

Pope, *Epitaph, intended for Newton's Monument in Westminster Abbey* (1727).

Newton is called by Campbell "The Priest of Nature."—*Pleasures of Hope*, i. (1799).

Newton and the Apple. It is said that Newton was standing in the garden of Mrs. Conduitt, of Woolsthorpe, in the year 1665, when an apple fell from a tree and set him thinking. From this incident he ultimately developed his theory of gravitation.

Nibelung, a mythical king of Nibelungeland (*Norway*). He had twelve paladins, all giants. Siegfried [*Sege.freed*], prince of the Netherlands, slew the giants, and made Nibelungeland tributary.—*Nibelungen Lied*, iii. (1210).

Nibelungen Hoard, a mythical mass of gold and precious stones which Siegfried [*Sege.freed*], prince of the Netherlands, took from Nibelungeland and gave to his wife as a dowry. The hoard filled thirty-six wagons. After the murder of Siegfried, Hagan seized the hoard, and, for concealment, sank it in the "Rhine at Lockham," intending to recover it at a future period, but Hagan was assassinated, and the hoard was lost for ever.—*Nibelungen Lied*, xix.

Nibelungen Lied [*Ne.by-lung.'nleed*], the German *Iliad* (1210). It is divided into two parts, and thirty-two lieds or cantos. The first part ends with the death of Siegfried, and the second part with the death of Kriemhild.

Siegfried, the youngest of the kings of the Netherlands, went to Worms, to crave the hand of Kriemhild in marriage. While he was staying with Günther, king of Burgundy (the lady's brother), he assisted him to obtain in marriage Brunhild, queen of Issland, who announced publicly that he only should be her husband who could beat her in hurling a spear, throwing a huge stone, and in leaping. Siegfried, who possessed a cloak of invisibility, aided Günther in these three contests, and Brunhild became his wife. In return for these services, Günther gave Siegfried his sister Kriemhild, in marriage. After a time, the bride and bridegroom went to visit Günther, when the two ladies disputed about the relative merits of their respective husbands, and Kriemhild, to exalt Siegfried, boasted that Günther owed to him his victories and his wife. Brunhild, in great anger, now employed Hagan to murder Siegfried, and this he did by stabbing him in the back while he was drinking from a brook.

Thirteen years elapsed, and the widow married Etzel, king of the Huns. After a time, she invited Brunhild and Hagan to a visit. Hagan, in this visit, killed Etzel's young son, and Kriemhild was like a fury. A battle ensued, in which Günther and Hagan were made prisoners, and Kriemhild cut off both their heads with her own hand. Hildebrand, horrified at this act of blood, slew Kriemhild; and so the poem ends.—Authors unknown (but the story pieced together by the minnesingers).

. The *Völsunga Saga* is the Icelandic version of the *Nibelungen Lied*. This saga has been translated into English by William Morris.

The *Nibelungen Lied* has been ascribed to Heinrich von Ofterdingen, a minnesinger; but it certainly existed before that epoch, if not as a complete whole, in separate lays, and all that Heinrich von Ofterdingen could have done was to collect the floating lays, connect them, and form them into a complete story.

F. A. Wolf, in 1795, wrote a learned book to prove that Homer did for the *Iliad* and *Odyssey* what Ofterdingen did for the *Nibelungen Lied*.

Richard Wagner composed a series of operas founded on the Nibelungen Lied.

Nibelungen Nôt, the second part of the *Nibelungen Lied*, containing the marriage of Kriemhild with Etzel, the visit of the Burgundians to the court of the Hun, and the death of Günther, Hagan, Kriemhild, and others. This part contains eighty-three four-line stanzas more than the first part. The number of lines in the two parts is 9836; so that the poem is almost as long as Milton's *Paradise Lost*.

Nibelungers, whoever possessed the Nibelungen hoard. When it was in Norway, the Norwegians were so called: when Siegfried [*Sege.freed*] got the possession of it, the Netherlanders were so called; and when the hoard was removed to Burgundy, the Burgundians were the Nibelungers.

Nic. Frog, the Dutch as a nation; as the English are called John Bull.—Dr. Arbuthnot, *History of John Bull* (1712).

Nica′nor, "the Protospathaire," a Greek general.—Sir W. Scott, *Count Robert of Paris* (time, Rufus).

Nice (*Sir Courtley*), the chief character and title of a drama by Croune (1685).

Nicholas, a poor scholar, who boarded with John, a rich old miserly carpenter. The poor scholar fell in love with Alison, his landlord's young wife, who joined him in duping the foolish old carpenter. Nicholas told John that such a rain would fall on the ensuing Monday as would drown every one in "less than an hour;" and he persuaded the old fool to provide three large tubs, one for himself, one for his wife, and the other for his lodger. In these tubs, said Nicholas, they would be saved; and when the flood abated, they would then be lords and masters of the whole earth. A few hours before the time of the "flood," the old carpenter went to the top chamber of his house to repeat his *pater nosters*. He fell asleep over his prayers, and was roused by the cry of "Water! water! Help! help!" Supposing the rain had come, he jumped into his tub, and was let down by Nicholas and Alison into the street. A crowd soon assembled, were delighted at the joke, and pronounced the old man an idiot and fool.—Chaucer, *Canterbury Tales* ("The Miller's Tale," 1388).

Nicholas, the barber of the village in which Don Quixote lived.—Cervantes, *Don Quixote*, I. (1605).

Nicholas (Brother), a monk at St. Mary's Convent.—Sir W. Scott, *The Monastery* (time, Elizabeth).

Nicholas (St.), patron saint of boys, parish clerks, sailors, thieves, and of Aberdeen, Russia, etc.

Nicholas (St.). The legend is, that an angel told him a father was so poor he was about to raise money by the prostitution of his three daughters. On hearing this St. Nicholas threw in at the cottage window three bags of money, sufficient to portion each of the three damsels.

The gift
Of Nicholas, which on the maidens he
Bounteous bestowed, to save their youthful prime
Unblemished.
Dantê, *Purgatory*, xx. (1308).

Nicholas of the Tower *(The)*, the duke of Exeter, constable of the Tower.

Nicholas's Clerks, highwaymen; so called by a pun on the phrase *Old Nick* and *St. Nicholas* who presided over scholars.

St. Nicholas's Clerks, scholars; so called because St. Nicholas was the patron of scholars. The statutes of Paul's School require the scholars to attend divine service on St. Nicholas's Day.—Knight, *Life of Dean Colet*, 362 (1726).

Nicholas Minturn, hero of novel of that name, by Josiah Gilbert Holland (1876).

Nickleby *(Nicholas)*, the chief character and title of a novel by C. Dickens (1838). He is the son of a poor country gentleman, and has to make his own way in the world. He first goes as usher to Mr. Squeers, schoolmaster at Dotheboys Hall, in Yorkshire; but leaves in disgust with the tyranny of Squeers and his wife, especially to a poor boy named Smike. Smike runs away from the school to follow Nicholas, and remains his humble follower till death. At Portsmouth, Nicholas joins the theatrical company of Mr. Crummles, but leaves the profession for other adventures. He falls in with the brothers Cheeryble, who make him their clerk; and in this post he rises to become a merchant, and ultimately marries Madeline Bray.

Mrs. Nickleby, mother of Nicholas, and a widow. She is an enormous talker, fond of telling long stories with no connection. Mrs. Nickleby is a weak, vain woman, who imagines an idiot neighbor is in love with her because he tosses cabbages and other articles over the garden wall. In conversation, Mrs. Nickleby rides off from the main point at every word suggestive of some new idea. As a specimen of her sequence of ideas, take the following example: "The name began with 'B' and ended with 'g,' I am sure. Perhaps it was Waters" (p. 198).

*** "The original of 'Mrs. Nickleby,'" says John Foster, "was the mother of Charles Dickens."—*Life of Dickens*, iii. 8.

Kate Nickleby, sister of Nicholas; beautiful, pure-minded, and loving. Kate works hard to assist in the expenses of housekeeping, but shuns every attempt of Ralph and others to allure her from the path of virgin innocence. She ultimately marries Frank, the nephew of the Cheeryble brothers.

Ralph Nickleby, of Golden Square (London), uncle to Nicholas and Kate. A hard, grasping money-broker, with no ambition but the love of saving, no spirit beyond the thirst of gold, and no principle except that of fleecing every one who comes into his power. This villain is the father of Smike, and ultimately hangs himself, because he loses money, and sees his schemes one after another burst into thin air.—C. Dickens, *Nicholas Nickleby*, (1838).

Nicneven, a gigantic, malignant hag of Scotch superstition.

*** Dunbar, the Scotch poet, describes her in his *Flyting of Dunbar and Kennedy* (1508).

Nicode´mus, one of the servants of General Harrison.—Sir W. Scott, *Woodstock* (time, Commonwealth).

Nicole (2 *syl.*), a female servant of M. Jourdain, who sees the folly of her master, and exposes it in a natural and amusing manner.—Molière, *Le Bourgeois Gentlehomme* (1670).

Night or **Nox**. So Tennyson calls Sir Peread, the Black Knight of the Black Lands, one of the four brothers who kept the passages to Castle Perilous.—

Tennyson, *Idylls of the King* ("Gareth and Lynette"); Sir T. Malory, *History of Prince Arthur*, i. 126 (1470).

Nightingale (*The Italian*), Angelica Catala´ni; also called "The Queen of Song" (1782-1849).

Nightingale (The Swedish), Jenny Lind, afterwards Mde. Goldschmidt. She appeared in London 1847, and retired from public life in 1851 (1821-1887).

Nightingale and the Lutist. The tale is, that a lute-master challenged a nightingale in song. The bird, after sustaining the contest for some time, feeling itself outdone, fell on the lute, and died broken-hearted.

*** This tale is from the Latin of Strada, translated by Richard Crashaw, and called *Music's Duel* (1650). It is most beautifully told by John Ford, in his drama entitled *The Lover's Melancholy*, where Men´aphon is supposed to tell it to Ame´thus (1628).

Nightingale and the Thorn.

As it fell upon a day
In the merry month of May,
Sitting in a pleasant shade
Which a grove of myrtles made—
Beasts did leap, and birds did sing,
Trees did grow, and plants did spring,
Everything did banish moan,
Save the nightingale alone;
She, poor bird, as all forlorn,
Leaned her breast up-till a thorn.
Richard Barnfield, *Address to the Nightingale* (1594).

So Philomel, perched on an aspen sprig,
Weeps all the night her lost virginity,
And sings her sad tale to the merry twig,
That dances at such joyful mysery.
Never lets sweet rest invade her eye;
But leaning on a thorn her dainty chest,
For fear soft sleep should steal into her breast,
Expresses in her song grief not to be expressed.
Giles Fletcher, *Christ's Triumph over Death* (1610).

The nightingale that sings with the deep thorn,
Which fable places in her breast.
Byron, *Don Juan*, vi. 87 (1824).

Nightmare of Europe (*The*), Napoleon Bonaparte (1769, reigned 1804-1814, died 1821).

Nightshade (*Deadly*). We are told that the berries of this plant so intoxicated the soldiers of Sweno, the Danish king, that they became an easy prey to the Scotch, who cut them to pieces.

※ Called "deadly," not from its poisonous qualities, but because it was used at one time for blackening the eyes in mourning.

Nimrod, pseudonym of Charles James Apperley, author of *The Chase, The Road, The Turf* (1852), etc.

Nim′ue, a "damsel of the lake," who cajoled Merlin in his dotage to tell her the secret "whereby he could be rendered powerless;" and then, like Delilah, she overpowered him, by "confining him under a stone."

Then after these quests, Merlin fell in a dotage on ... one of the damsels of the lake, hight Nimue, and Merlin would let her have no rest, but always he would be with her in every place. And she made him good cheer till she learned of him what she desired.... And Merlin shewed to her in a rock, whereas was a great wonder ... which went under a stone. So by her subtle craft, she made Merlin go under that stone ... and he never came out, for all the craft that he could do.—Sir T. Malory, *History of Prince Arthur*, i. 60 (1470).

It is not unlikely that this name is a clerical error for Nineve or Ninive. It occurs only once in the three volumes. (See NINIVE.)

※ Tennyson makes Vivien the seductive betrayer of Merlin, and says she enclosed him "in the four walls of a hollow tower;" but the *History* says "Nimue put him under the stone" (pt. i. 60).

Nino-Thoma, daughter of Tor-Thoma (chief of one of the Scandinavian islands). She eloped with Uthal (son of Larthmor, a petty king of Berrathon, a neighboring island); but Uthal soon tired of her, and, having fixed his affections on another, confined her in a desert island. Uthal, who had also dethroned his father, was slain in single combat by Ossian, who had come to restore the deposed monarch to his throne. When Nina-Thoma heard of her husband's death, she languished and died, "for though most cruelly entreated, her love for Uthal was not abated."—Ossian, *Berrathon*.

Nine. "It is by nines that Eastern presents are given, when they would extend their magificence to the highest degree." Thus, when Dakiānos wished to ingratiate himself with the shah,

He caused himself to be preceded by nine superb camels. The first was loaded with nine suits of gold adorned with jewels; the second bore nine sabres, the hilts and scabbards of which were adorned with diamonds; upon the third camel were nine suits of armor; the fourth had nine suits of house furniture; the fifth had nine cases full of sapphires; the sixth had nine cases full of rubies; the seventh nine cases full of emeralds; the eighth had nine cases full of amethysts; and the ninth had nine cases full of diamonds.—Comte de Caylus, *Oriental Tales* ("Dakianos and the Seven Sleepers," 1743).

Nine Gods (*The*) of the Etruscans: Juno, Minerva, and Tin´ia (*the three chief*). The other six were Vulcan, Mars, Saturn, Herculês, Summa´nus, and Vedius. (See NOVENSILES.)

Lars Por´sĕna of Clusium
By the nine gods he swore
That the great house of Tarquin
Should suffer wrong no more.
By the nine gods he swore it,
And named a trysting day ...
To summon his array.
Lord Macaulay, *Lays of Ancient Rome* ("Horatius," i., 1842).

Nine Orders of Angels (*The*): (1) Seraphim, (2) Cherubim (*in the first circle*); (3) Thrones, (4) Dominions (*in the second circle*); (5) Virtues, (6) Powers, (7) Principalities, (8) Archangels, (9) Angels (*in the third circle*).

In heaven above
The effulgent bands in triple circles move.
Tasso, *Jerusalem Delivered*, xi. 13 (1575).

Novem vero angelorum ordines dicimus; ... scimus (1) Angelos, (2) Archangelos, (3) Virtues, (4) Potestates, (5) Principatus, (6) Dominationes, (7) Thronos, (8) Cherubim, (9) Seraphim.—Gregory, *Homily*, 34 (A.D. 381).

Nine Worthies (*The*). Three were *pagans*: Hector, Alexander, and Julius Cæsar. Three were *Jews*: Joshua, David, and Judas Maccabæus. Three were *Christians*: Arthur, Charlemagne, and Godfrey of Bouillon.

Nine. Worthies (privy councillors to William III.). Four were *Whigs*: Devonshire, Dorset, Monmouth, and Edward Russell. Five were *Tories*: Caermarthen, Pembroke, Nottingham, Marlborough, and Lowther.

Nine Worthies of London (*The*): Sir William Walworth, Sir Henry Pritchard, Sir William Sevenoke, Sir Thomas White, Sir John Bonham, Christopher Croker, Sir John Hawkwood, Sir Hugh Caverley, and Sir Henry Maleverer.

⁎ The chronicles of these nine worthies are written in prose and verse by Richard Johnson (1592), author of *The Seven Champions of Christendom*.

Nineve (2 *syl.*), the Lady of the Lake, in Arthurian romance.

Then the Lady of the Lake, that was always friendly unto King Arthur, understood by her subtle craft that he was like to have been destroyed; and so the Lady of the Lake, that hight Nineve, came into the forest to seek Sir Launcelot du Lake.—Sir T. Malory, *History of Prince Arthur*, ii. 57 (1470).

⁎ This name occurs three times in the *Morte d'Arthur*—once as "Nimue," once as "Nineve," and once as "Ninive." Probably "Nimue" (*q.v.*) is a clerical error.

Ninon de Lenclos, a beautiful Parisian, rich, *spirituelle*, and an atheist, who abandoned herself to epicurean indulgence, and preserved her charms to a very advanced age. Ninon de Lenclos renounced marriage, and had numberless lovers. Her house was the rendezvous of all the most illustrious persons of the period, as Molière, St. Evremont, Fontenelle, Voltaire, and so on (1615-1705).

Niobe [*Ne´.oby*], the beau-ideal of grief. After losing her twelve children, she was changed into a stone, which wept continually.

⁎ The group of "Niobe and her Children" in Florence, discovered at Rome in 1583, is now arranged in the Uffizii Gallery.

She followed my poor father's body,
Like Niobê, all tears.
Shakespeare, *Hamlet*, act i. sc. 2 (1596).

Niobe of Nations (*The*). Rome is so called by Byron.—*Childe Harold*, iv. 79 (1817).

Nipper (*Susan*), generally called "Spitfire," from her snappish disposition. She was the nurse of Florence Dombey, to whom she was much attached. Susan Nipper married Mr. Toots (after he had got over his infatuation for Florence).

Nippotate (4 *syl.*), "a live lion stuffed with straw," exhibited in a raree-show. This proved to be the body of a tame hedgehog exhibited by Old Harry, a notorious character in London at the beginning of the eighteenth century (died 1710).

Of monsters stranger than can be expressed,
There's Nippotatê lies amongst the rest.
Sutton Nicholls.

Niquee [*Ne´.kay*], the sister of Anasterax, with whom she lived in incest. The fairy Zorphee was her godmother, and enchanted her, in order to break off this connection.—Vasco de Lobeira, *Amadis de Gaul* (thirteenth century).

Nisroch [*Niz´.rok*], "of principalities the prince." A god of the Assyrians. In the book of *Kings* the Septuagint calls him "Meserach," and in *Isaiah* "Nasarach." Josephus calls him "Araskês." One of the rebel angels in Milton's *Paradise Lost*. He says:

Sense of pleasure we may well
Spare out of life, perhaps, and not repine,
But live content, which is the calmest life;
But pain is perfect misery, the worst
Of evils, and, excessive, overturns
All patience.
Milton, *Paradise Lost*, (1665).

Nit, one of the attendants of Queen Mab.

Hop, and Mop, and Drap so clear,
Pip, and Trip, and Skip, that were
To Mab their sovereign dear—
Her special maids of honor.
Fib, and Tib, and Pinck, and Pin,
Tick, and Quick, and Jil, and Jin,
Tit, and Nit, and Wap, and Win—
The train that wait upon her.
Drayton, *Nymphidia* (1563-1631).

Nitchs, daughter of Amases, king of Egypt. She was sent to Persia to become the wife of Cambyses.—Georg Ebers, *An Egyptian Princess*.

Nixon (*Christal*), agent to Mr. Edward Redgauntlet, the Jacobite.—Sir W. Scott, *Redgauntlet* (time, George III.).

Nixon (*Martha*), the old nurse of the earl of Oxford.—Sir W. Scott, *Anne of Geierstein* (time, Edward IV.).

No One (*Cæsar or*). Julius Cæsar said, "Aut Cæsar aut nullus." And again, "I would sooner be first in a village than second at Rome."

Milton makes Satan say, "Better to reign in hell than serve in heaven."

Jonathan Wild used to say, "I'd rather stand on the top of a dunghill than at the bottom of a hill in paradise."

Tennyson says, "All in all or not at all."—*Idylls* ("Vivien").

"Six thrice or three dice" (aces were called *dice*, and did not count).

No Song no Supper, a musical drama by Prince Hoare, F.S.A. (1790). Crop, the farmer, has married a second wife called Dorothy, who has an amiable weakness for a rascally lawyer named Endless. During the absence of her husband, Dorothy provides a supper for Endless, consisting of roast lamb and a cake; but just as the lawyer sits down to it, Crop, with Margaretta, knocks at the door. Endless is concealed in a sack, and the supper is carried away. Presently Robin, the sweetheart of Margaretta, arrives, and Crop regrets there is nothing but bread and cheese to offer him. Margaretta now volunteers a song, the first verse of which tells Crop there is roast lamb in the house, which is accordingly produced; the second verse tells him there is a cake, which is produced also; and the third verse tells him that Endless is concealed in a sack. Had there been no song there would have been no supper, but the song produced the roast lamb and new cake.

Noah's Wife, Wâïla (3 *syl.*), who endeavored to persuade the people that her husband was distraught.

The wife of Noah [*Wâïla*] and the wife of Lot [*Wâhela*] were both unbelievers ... and deceived their husbands ... and it shall be said to them at the last day, "Enter ye into hell fire."—Sale, *Al Korân*, lxvi.

Nobbs, the horse of "Dr. Dove of Doncaster."—Southey, *The Doctor* (1834).

Noble (*The*), Charles III. of Navarre (1361, 1387-1425).

Soliman, *Tchelibi*, the Turk (died 1410).

*** Khosrou or Chosroës I. was called "The Noble Soul" (*, 531-579).

Nodel, the lion, in the beast-epic called *Reynard the Fox*. Nodel, the lion, represents the regal element of Germany; Isengrin, the wolf, represents the baronial element; and Reynard, the fox, the Church element (1498).

Noel (*Eusebe*), schoolmaster of Bout du Monde. "His clothes are old and worn, and his manner vacant."—E. Stirling, *The Gold Mine*, or *Miller of Grenoble*, act i. sc. 2 (1854).

Noggs (*Newman*), Ralph Nickleby's clerk. A tall man of middle age, with two goggle eyes (one of which was fixed), a rubicund nose, a cadavarous face, and a suit of clothes decidedly the worse for wear. He had the gift of distorting and cracking his finger-joints. This kind-hearted, dilapidated fellow "kept his hunter and hounds once," but ran through his fortune. He discovered a plot of old Ralph, which he confided to the Cheeryble brothers, who frustrated it, and then provided for Newman.—C. Dickens, *Nicholas Nickleby* (1838).

Noko'mis, mother of Weno'nah, and grandmother of Hiawatha. Nokomis was the daughter of the Moon. While she was swinging one day, some of her companions, out of jealousy, cut the ropes, and she fell to earth in a meadow. The same night her first child, a daughter, was born, and was named Wenonah.

There among the ferns and mosses ...
Fair Nokomis bore a daughter,
And she called her name Wenonah.
Longfellow, *Hiawatha*, iii. (1855).

Non Mi Ricordo, the usual answer of the Italian courier and other Italian witnesses when on examination at the trial of Queen Caroline (the wife of George IV.), in 1820.

"Lord Flint," in *Such Things Are*, by Mrs. Inchbald (1786), when asked a question he wished to evade, used to reply, "My people know, no doubt, but I cannot recollect."

"Pierre Choppard," in *The Courier of Lyons*, by Edward Stirling (1852), when asked an ugly question, always answered "I'll ask my wife, my memory's so slippery."

The North American society called the "Know Nothings," founded in 1853, used to reply to every question about their order, "I know nothing about it."

Nona´cris' Stream, the river Styx, in Arcadia. Cassander says he has in a phial some of this "horrid spring," one drop of which, mixed with wine, would act as a deadly poison. To this Polyperchon replies:

I know its power, for I have seen it tried.
Pains of all sorts thro' every nerve and artery
At once it scatters,—burns at once and freezes—
Till, by extremity of torture forced,
The soul consents to leave her joyless home.
N. Lee, *Alexander the Great*, iv. i (1678).

Nonentity (*Dr.*), a metaphysician, and thought by most people to be a profound scholar. He generally spreads himself before the fire, sucks his pipe, talks little, drinks much, and is reckoned very good company. You may know him by his long grey wig, and the blue handkerchief round his neck.

Dr. Nonentity, I am told, writes indexes to perfection, makes essays, and reviews any work with a single day's warning.—Goldsmith, *A Citizen of the World*, xxix. (1759).

Norbert (*Father*), Pierre Parisot Norbert, the French missionary (1697-1769).

Norland (*Lord*), father of Lady Eleanor Irwin, and guardian of Lady Ramble (Miss Maria Wooburn). He disinherited his daughter for marrying against his will, and left her to starve, but subsequently relented, and relieved her wants and those of her young husband.—Inchbald, *Every One has His Fault* (1794).

Norma, a vestal who had been seduced, and discovers her paramour trying to seduce a sister vestal. In despair, she contemplates the murder of her baseborn children.—Bellini, *Norma* (1831); libretto, by Romani.

Norman, forester of Sir William Ashton, lord-keeper of Scotland.—Sir W. Scott, *Bride of Lammermoor* (time, William III.).

Norman, a "sea-captain," in love with Violet, the ward of Lady Arundel. It turns out that this Norman is her ladyship's son by her first husband, and heir to the title and estates; but Lady Arundel, having married a second husband, had a son named Percy, whom she wished to make her heir. Norman's father was murdered, and Norman, who was born three days afterwards, was brought up by Onslow, a village priest. At the age of 14 he went to sea, and became captain of a man-of-war. Ten years later he returned to Arundel, and though at first his mother ignored him, and Percy flouted him, his noble and generous conduct disarmed hostility, and he not only reconciled his half-brother, but won his mother's affection, and married Violet, his heart's "sweet sweeting."—Lord Lytton, *The Sea-Captain* (1839).

Norm-nan-Ord or Norman of the Hammer, one of the eight sons of Torquil of the Oak.—Sir W. Scott, *Fair Maid of Perth* (time, Henry IV.).

Normandy (*The Gem of*), Emma, daughter of Richard I. (died 1052).

Norna of the Fitful Head, "The Reimkennar." Her real name was, Ulla Troil, but after her seduction by Basil Mertoun (Vaughan), and the birth of a son named Clement Cleveland (the future pirate), she changed her name. Towards the end of the novel, Norna gradually recovered her senses. She was the aunt of Minna and Brenda Troil.—Sir W. Scott, *The Pirate* (time, William III.).

[*One*] cannot fail to trace in Norna—the victim of remorse and insanity, and the dupe of her own imposture, her mind too flooded with all the wild literature and extravagant superstitions of the north—something distinct from the Dumfriesshire gypsy, whose pretensions to supernatural powers are not beyond those of a Norwood prophetess.—*The Pirate* (introduction, 1821).

Norris, a family to whom Martin Chuzzlewit was introduced while he was in America. They were friends of Mr. Bevan, rabid abolitionists, and yet hankering after titles as the gilt of the gingerbread of life.—C. Dickens, *Martin Chuzzlewit* (1844).

Norris (*Black*), a dark, surly man, and a wrecker. He wanted to marry Marian, "the daughter" of Robert (also a wrecker); but Marian was betrothed to Edward, a young sailor. Robert, being taken up for murder, was condemned to death; but Norris told Marian he would save his life if she would promise to marry him. Marian consented, but was saved by the arrest of Black Norris for murder.—S. Knowles, *The Daughter* (1836).

North (*Christopher*), pseudonym of John Wilson, professor of moral philosophy, Edinburgh, editor of *Blackwood's Magazine*, in which appeared the "Noctes Ambrosianæ" (1805-1861).

North (*Lord*), one of the judges in the State trial of Geoffrey Peveril, Julian, and the dwarf, for being concerned in the popish plot.—Sir W. Scott, *Peveril of the Peak* (time, Charles II).

North Britain (*The*), a radical periodical, conducted by John Wilkes. The celebrated number of this serial was No. 45, in which the ministers are charged "with putting a lie in the king's mouth."

Northamptonshire Poet (*The*), John Clare (1793-1864).

Northern Harlot (*The*), Elizabeth Petrowna, empress of Russia; also called "The Infamous" (1709-1761).

Northern Wagoner, a group of seven stars called variously Charles's Wain, or Wagon, *i.e.* churl's wain; Ursa Major, The Great Bear, and The Dipper. Four make the wagon, or the dipper, three form the shaft, or the handle. Two are called Pointers because they point to the Pole-star.

By this the northern wagoner has set
His sevenfold team behind the steadfast star
That was in ocean waves yet never wet,
But firm is fixed, and sendeth light from far
To all that on the wide deep wandering are.
Spenser, *Faëry Queen*, I. ii. 1 (1590).

Norval (*Old*), a shepherd, who brings up Lady Randolph's son (Douglas) as his own. He was hidden at birth in a basket, because Sir Malcolm (her father) hated Douglas, whom she had privately married. The child being found by old Norval, was brought up as his own, but the old man discovered that the foundling was "Sir Malcolm's heir and Douglas's son." When 18 years old, the foster-son saved the life of Lord Randolph. Lady Randolph took great interest in the young man, and when old Norval told her his tale, she instantly perceived that the young hero was in fact her own son.

Young Norval, the infant exposed and brought up by the old shepherd as his own son. He turned out to be Sir Malcolm's heir. His mother was Lady Randolph, and his father Lord Douglas, her first husband. Young Norval, having saved the life of Lord Randolph, was given by him a commission in the army. Glenalvon, the heir-presumptive of Lord Randolph, hated the new favorite, and persuaded his lordship that the young man was too familiar with Lady Randolph. Being waylaid, Norval was attacked, slew Glenalvon, but was in turn slain by Lord Randolph. After the death of Norval, Lord Randolph discovered that he had killed the son of his wife by a former marriage. The mother, in her distraction, threw herself headlong from a lofty precipice, and Lord Randolph went to the war then raging between Denmark and Scotland.—J Home, *Douglas* (1757).

(This was a favorite character with John Kemble, 1757-1823.)

Norway (*The Fair Maid of*), Margaret, granddaughter of Alexander III. of Scotland. She died (1290) of sea-sickness on her passage from Norway to Scotland. Her father was Eric II., king of Norway, and her mother was Margaret, only daughter of Alexander III.

Nose (*Golden*), Tycho Brahê, the Danish astronomer. Having lost his nose in a duel with one Passberg, he adopted a golden one, and attached it to his face by a cement which he carried about with him.

Nosebag (*Mrs.*), wife of a lieutenant in the dragoons. She is the inquisitive travelling companion of Waverley when he travels by stage to London.—Sir W. Scott, *Waverley* (time, George II.).

Nosey (*Play up!*) This exclamation was common in our theatres in the days of Macklin, etc. M. Nozay was the leader of the orchestra in Covent Garden Theatre.

** Some persons affirm that "Old Nosey" was Cervetto, the violoncello player at Drury Lane (1753), and say that he was so called from his long nose.

Napoleon III., was nicknamed *Grosbec* ("Nosey").

Nosnot-Bocai [*Bo´.ky*], prince of purgatory.

Sir, I last night received command
To see you out of Fairy-land.
Into the realm of Nosnot-Bocai.
King, *Orpheus and Eurydice*.

Nostrada′mus (*Michael*), an astrologer of the sixteenth century, who published an annual *Almanac* and a *Recueil of Prophecies*, in verse (1503-1566).

Nostrada′mus of Portugal, Gonçalo Annês Bandarra, a poet-cobbler, whose career was stopped, in 1556, by the Inquisition.

Nottingham (*The countess of*), a quondam sweetheart of the earl of Essex, and his worst enemy, when she heard that he had married the countess of Rutland. The queen sent her to the Tower to ask Essex if he had no petition to make, and the earl requested her to take back a ring, which the queen had given him as a pledge of mercy in time of need. As the countess out of jealousy forbore to deliver it, the earl was executed.—Henry Jones, *The Earl of Essex* (1745).

Nottingham Lambs, (*The*), the Nottingham roughs.

Nottingham Poet (*The*), Philip James Bailey, the author of *Festus*, etc. (1816-).

No´tus, the south wind; *Afer* is the south-west wind.

Notus and Afer, black with thundrous clouds.
Milton, *Paradise Lost*, (1665).

Noukhail, the angel of day and night.

The day and night are trusted to my care. I hold the day in my right hand and the night in my left; and I maintain the just equilibrium between them, for if either were to overbalance the other, the universe would either be consumed by the heat of the sun, or would perish with the cold of darkness.—Comte de Caylus, *Oriental Tales* ("History of Abdal Motallab," 1743).

Nouman (*Sidi*), an Arab who married Aminê, a very beautiful woman, who ate her rice with a bodkin. Sidi, wishing to know how his wife could support life and health without more food than she partook of in his presence, watched her narrowly, and discovered that she was a ghoul, who went by stealth every night and feasted on the fresh-buried dead. When Sidi made this discovery, Aminê changed him into a dog. After he was restored to his normal shape, he changed Aminê into a mare, which every day he rode almost to death.—*Arabian Nights* ("History of Sidi Nouman").

Your majesty knows that ghouls of either sex are demons which wander about the fields. They commonly inhabit ruinous buildings, whence they issue suddenly on unwary travellers, whom they kill and devour. If they fail to meet with travellers, they go by night into burying grounds, and dig up dead bodies, on which they feed.—"History of Sidi Nouman."

Nouredeen, son of Khacan (vizier of Zinebi, king of Balsora). He got possession of the "beautiful Persian" purchased for the king. At his father's death he soon squandered away his patrimony in the wildest extravagance, and fled with his beautiful slave to Bagdad. Here he encountered Haroun-al-Raschid in disguise, and so pleased the caliph, that he was placed in the number of those courtiers most intimate with his majesty, who also bestowed on him so plentiful a fortune, that he lived with the "beautiful Persian" in affluence all the rest of his life.—*Arabian Nights* ("Nouredeen and the Beautiful Persian").

Nour´eddin´ Ali, younger son of the vizier of Egypt. "He was possessed of as much merit as can fall to the lot of man." Having quarrelled with his elder brother, he travelled to Baso´ra, where he married the vizier's daughter, and succeeded his father-in-law in office. A son was born to him in due time, and on the very same day the wife of his elder brother had a daughter. Noureddin died when his son was barely twenty, and unmarried.—*Arabian Nights* ("Noureddin Ali," etc.).

Nourgehan's Bracelet. Nourgehan, emperor of the Moguls, had a bracelet which had the property of discovering poison, even at a considerable distance. When poison was anywhere near the wearer, the stones of the bracelet seemed agitated, and the agitation increased as the poison approached them.—Comte de Caylus, *Oriental Tales* ("The Four Talismans," 1743).

Nour´jahad, a sleeper, like Rip Van Winkle, Epimen´idês, etc. (See SLEEPERS.)

Nourjeham ("*light of the world*"). So the Sultana Nourmahal was subsequently called.—T. Moore, *Lalla Rookh* ("The Light of the Haram," 1817).

Nourmahal´ (*The sultana*), *i.e.* "Light of the Haram," afterwards called *Nourjeham* ("light of the world"). She was for a season estranged from the sultan, till he gave a grand banquet, at which she appeared in disguise as a lute-player and singer. The sultan was so enchanted with her performance, that he exclaimed, "If Nourmahal had so played and sung, I could forgive her all;" whereupon the sultana threw off her mask, and Selim "caught her to his heart."—T. Moore, *Lalla Rookh* ("The Light of the Haram," 1817).

Nouron´ihar, daughter of the Emir Fakreddin; a laughing, beautiful girl, full of fun and pretty mischief, dotingly fond of Gulchenrouz, her cousin, a boy of 13. She married the Caliph Vathek, with whom she descended into the abyss of Eblis, whence she never after returned to the light of day.

The trick she played Bababalouk was this: Vathek, the caliph, was on a visit to Fakreddin, the emir´, and Bababalouk, his chief eunuch, intruded into the bathroom, where Nouronihar and her damsels were bathing. Nouronihar induced the old eunuch to rest himself on the swing, when the girls set it going with all their might. The cords broke, the eunuch fell into the bath, and the girls made off with their lamps, and left the meddlesome old fool to flounder about till morning, when assistance came, but not before he was half dead.—W. Beckford, *Vathek* (1784).

Nouroun´nihar, niece of a sultan of India, who had three sons, all in love with her. The sultan said he would give her to him who, in twelve months, gave him the most valuable present. The three princes met in a certain inn at the expiration of the time, when one prince looked through a tube, which showed Nourounnihar at the point of death; another of the brothers transported all three instantaneously on a magic carpet to the princess's chamber; and the third brother gave her an apple to smell of which effected an instant cure. It was impossible to decide which of these presents was the most valuable; so the sultan said he should have her who shot an arrow to the greatest distance. The eldest (Houssian) shot first; Ali overshot the arrow of his eldest brother; but that of the youngest brother (Ahmed) could nowhere be found. So the award was given to Ahmed.—*Arabian Nights* ("Ahmed and Pari-Banou").

Novel (*Father of the English*). Henry Fielding is so called by Sir W. Scott (1707-1754).

Noven´siles (4 *syl.*), the nine Sabine gods, viz.: Herculês, Romulus, Esculapius, Bacchus, Æneas, Vesta, Santa, Fortuna and Fidês or Faith. (See NINE GODS of the Etruscans.)

Novit (*Mr. Nichil*), the lawyer of the old laird of Dumbiedikes.—Sir W. Scott, *Heart of Midlothian* (time, George II.).

Novius, the usurer, famous for the loudness of his voice.

... at hic si plaustra ducenta
Concurrantque foro tria funera magna sonabit
Cornua quod vincatque tubas.
Horace, *Satires*, i. 6.

These people seem to be of the race of Novius, that Roman banker, whose voice exceeded the noise of carmen.—Lesage, *Gil Blas*, vii. 13 (1735).

Now-now (*Old Anthony*), an itinerant fiddler. The character is a skit on Anthony Munday, the dramatist.—Chettle, *Kindheart's Dream* (1592).

Nuath (2 *syl.*), father of Lathmon and Oith´ona (*q.v.*).—Ossian, *Oithona*.

Nubbles (*Mrs.*), a poor widow woman, who was much given to going to Little Bethel.

Christopher or *Kit Nubbles*, her son, the servant in attendance on little Nell, whom he adored. After the death of little Nell, Kit married Barbara, a fellow-servant.—C. Dickens, *The Old Curiosity Shop* (1840).

Nugent Dubourg, twin brother of Oscar Dubourg, somewhat conceited, who patronizes his brother, and would like to marry his brother's betrothed, Lucilla Finch, blind and an heiress. Her sight is restored by an operation, and Nugent places himself where her eyes will first fall upon him, instead of on his disfigured brother. Beginning with this, he personates Oscar until Lucilla again loses her sight. He then yields her to his brother, joins an Arctic exploring expedition, and perishes in the Polar regions.—Wilkie Collins, *Poor Miss Finch*.

Numa Roumestan, French deputy from the South of France. Audacious, gay and unprincipled, he possesses all the qualities that render him "the joy of the street, the sorrow of the home."—Alphonse Daudet, *Numa Roumestan*.

Number Nip, the name of the gnome king of the Giant Mountains.—Musæus, *Popular Tales* (1782).

⁎ Musæus was a German, uncle of Kotzebue (died 1788).

Nuncanou (*Aurore and Clotilde*). Beautiful Creoles, mother and daughter, in George W. Cable's novel, *The Grandissimes*.

Nun's Tale (*The*), the tale of the cock and the fox. One day, dan Russell, the fox, came into the poultry-yard, and told Master Chanticlere, he could not resist the pleasure of hearing him sing, for his voice was so divinely ravishing. The cock, pleased with this flattery, shut his eyes, and began to crow most lustily; whereupon dan Russell seized him by the throat, and ran off with him. When they got to the wood, the cock said to the fox, "I would recommend you to eat me at once, I think I can hear your pursuers." "I am going to do so," said the fox; but when he opened his mouth to reply, off flew the cock into a tree, and while the fox was deliberating how he might regain his prey, up came the farmer and his men with scythes, flails, and pitchforks, with which they despatched the fox without mercy.—Chaucer, *Canterbury Tales* (1388).

⁎ This fable is one of those by Marie, of France, called *Don Coc and Don Werpil*.

Nun's Tale (*The Second*). This is the tale about Maxime and the martyrs, Valerian and Tiburcê. The prefect ordered Maxime (2 *syl.*) to put Valerian and Tiburcê to death, because they refused to worship the image of Jupiter; but Maxime showed kindness to the two Christians, took them home, became converted, and was baptized. When Valerian and Tiburcê were put to death, Maxime declared that he saw angels come and carry them up to heaven, whereupon the prefect caused him to be beaten to death with whips of lead.—Chaucer, *Canterbury Tales* (1388).

⁎ This tale is very similar to that of St. Cecilia, in the *Legenda Aurea*. See also *Acts* xvi. 25-34.

Nupkins, mayor of Ipswich, a man who has a most excellent opinion of himself, but who, in all magisterial matters, really depends almost entirely on Jinks, his half-starved clerk.—C. Dickens, *The Pickwick Papers* (1836).

Nurse (*Rebecca*). Accused of witchcraft and acquitted by the court. "And suddenly, after all the afflicted out of court made a hideous outcry ... one of the judges expressed himself not satisfied, another, as he was going off the bench, said they would have her indicted anew."

At the second trial she was condemned, and she was executed with the rest.

"The testimonials of her Christian behavior, both in the course of her life and at her death, and her extraordinary care in educating her children, and setting them a good example, etc., under the hands of so many, are so numerous that for brevity they are here omitted."—Robert Calef, *More Wonders of the Invisible World* (1700).

Nut-Brown Maid (*The*), the maid wooed by the "banished man." The "banished man" describes to her the hardships she would have to undergo if she married him; but finding that she accounted these hardships as nothing compared with his love, he revealed himself to be an earl's son, with large hereditary estates in Westmoreland, and married her.—Percy, *Reliques*, II.

This ballad is based on the legendary history of Lord Henry Clifford, called "The Shepherd Lord." It was modernized by Prior, who called his version of the story *Henry and Emma*. The oldest form of the ballad extant is contained in Arnolde's *Chronicle* (1502).

Nydia. Greek flower-girl, blind and friendless. Glaucus is kind to, and protects her, finally purchases her of her brutal master. She loves him passionately and hopelessly, saves his life and that of his betrothed at the destruction of Pompeii; embarks with them in a skiff bound for a safer harbor, and while all are asleep, springs overboard and drowns herself.—E. L. Bulwer, *Last Days of Pompeii* (1834).

Nym, corporal in the army under Captain Sir John Falstaff, introduced in *The Merry Wives of Windsor* and in *Henry V.*, but not in *Henry IV.* It seems that Lieutenant Peto had died, and given a step to the officers under him. Thus, Ensign Pistol becomes lieutenant, Corporal Bardolph becomes ensign, and Nym takes the place of Bardolph. He is an arrant rogue, and both he and Bardolph are hanged *(Henry V.)*. The word means to "pilfer."

It would be difficult to give any other reply save that of Corporal Nym—it was the author's humor or caprice.—Sir W. Scott.

Nymphid'ia, a mock-heroic by Drayton. The fairy Pigwiggen is so gallant to Queen Mab as to arouse the jealousy of King Oberon. One day, coming home and finding his queen absent, Oberon vows vengeance on the gallant, and sends Puck to ascertain the whereabouts of Mab and Pigwiggen. In the mean time, Nymphidia gives the queen warning, and the queen, with all her maids of honor, creep into a hollow nut for concealment. Puck, coming up, sets foot in the enchanted circle which Nymphidia had charmed, and, after stumbling about for a time, tumbles into a ditch. Pigwiggen, seconded by Tomalin, encounters Oberon, seconded by Tom Thum, and the fight is "both fast and furious." Queen Mab, in alarm, craves the interference of Proserpine, who first envelopes the combatants in a thick smoke, which compels them to desist, and then gives them a draught "to assuage their thirst." The draught was from the river Lethê; and immediately the combatants had tasted it, they forgot not only the cause of the quarrel, but even that they had quarrelled at all.—M. Drayton, *Nymphidia* (1593).

Nysa, daughter of Silēno and Mys′is, and sister of Daphnê. Justice Mi′das is in love with her; but she loves Apollo, her father's guest.—Kane O'Hara, *Midas* (1764).

Nysê, Doto, and Neri′nê, the three nereids who went before the fleet of Vasco da Gama. When the treacherous pilot steered the ship of Vasco towards a sunken rock, these three sea-nymphs lifted up the prow and turned it round.—Camoens, *Lusiad*, ii. (1569).

(*OUR LADY OF*). The Virgin Mary is so called in some old Roman rituals, from the ejaculation at the beginning of the seven anthems preceding the *Magnificat*, as: "O, when will the day arrive...?" "O, when shall I see...?" "O, when...?" and so on.

Oakly (*Major*), brother to Mr. Oakly, and uncle to Charles. He assists his brother in curing his "jealous wife."

Mr. Oakly, husband of the "jealous wife." A very amiable man, but deficient in that strength of mind which is needed to cure the idiosyncrasy of his wife; so he obtains the assistance of his brother, the major.

Mrs. Oakly, "the jealous wife" of Mr. Oakly. A woman of such suspicious temper, that every remark of her husband is distorted into a proof of his infidelity. She watches him like a tiger, and makes both her own and her husband's life utterly wretched.

Charles Oakly, nephew of the major. A fine, noble-spirited young fellow, who would never stand by and see a woman insulted; but a desperate debauchee and drunkard. He aspires to the love of Harriot Russet, whose influence over him is sufficiently powerful to reclaim him.—George Colman, *The Jealous Wife* (1761).

Oates (*Dr. Titus*), the champion of the popish plot.

Forth came the notorious Dr. Oates, rustling in the full silken canonicals of priesthood, for ... he affected no small dignity of exterior decoration and deportment.... His exterior was portentous. A fleece of white periwig showed a most uncouth visage, of great length, having the mouth ... placed in the very centre of the countenance, and exhibiting to the astonished spectator as much chin below as there was nose and brow above it. His pronunciation was after a conceited fashion of his own, in which he accented the vowels in a manner altogether peculiar to himself.—Sir W. Scott, *Peveril of the Peak* (time, Charles II.).

Oaths.

JOHN PERROT, a natural son of Henry VIII., was the first to employ the profane oath of *God's Wounds*, which Queen ELIZABETH adopted, but the ladies of her court minced and softened it into *zounds* and *zouterkins*.

WILLIAM the CONQUEROR swore by *the Splendor of God*.

WILLIAM RUFUS, by *St. Luke's face*.

King JOHN, by *God's Tooth*.

HENRY VIII., by *God's Wounds*.

CHARLES II., by *Ods fish* [God's Flesh].

LOUIS XI. of France, by *God's Easter*.

CHARLES VIII. of France, by *God's Light*.

LOUIS XII., by *The Devil take me (Diable m'emporte)*.

The Chevalier BAYARD by *God's Holyday*.

FRANCOIS I. used for asseveration, *On the word of a gentleman*.

HENRY III. of England, when he confirmed "Magna Charta," used the expression, *On the word of a gentleman, a king and a knight*.

Earl of ANGUS (reign of Queen Mary), when incensed, used to say, *By the might of God*, but at other times his oath was *By St. Bride of Douglas*.—Godscroft, 275.

ST. WINFRED or BONI'FACE used to swear by *St. Peter's tomb*.

In the reign of Charles II. fancy oaths were the fashion. (For specimens, see FOPPINGTON.)

The most common oath of the ancient Romans was *By Herculês!* for men; and *By Castor!* for women; *By Pollux!* for both.

Viri per *Herculem*, mulieres per *Castorem*, utrique per *Pollucem* jurare soliti.—Gellius, *Noctes Atticæ*, ii. 6.

Obad'don, the angel of death. This is not the same angel as Abbad'ona, one of the fallen angels, and once the friend of Ab'diel (bk. vi.).

My name is Ephod Obaddon or Sevenfold Revenge. I am an angel of destruction. It was I who destroyed the first-born of Egypt. It was I who slew the army of Sennacherib.—Klopstock, *The Messiah*, xiii. (1771).

Obadi'ah, "the foolish fat scullion" in Sterne's novel of *Tristram Shandy* (1759).

Obadiah, clerk to Justice Day. A nincompoop, fond of drinking, but with just a shade more brains than Abel Day, who is "a thorough ass" (act i. 1).—T. Knight, *The Honest Thieves* (died 1820).

This farce is a mere *réchauffé* of *The Committee* (1670), a comedy by the Hon. Sir R. Howard, the names and much of the conversation being identical. Colonel Blunt is called in the farce "Captain Manly."

Obadiah Prim, a canting, knavish hypocrite; one of the four guardians of Anne Lovely, the heiress. Colonel Feignwell personates Simon Pure, and obtains the Quaker's consent to his marriage with Anne Lovely.—Mrs. Centlivre, *A Bold Stroke for a Wife* (1717).

Obermann, the impersonation of high moral worth without talent, and the tortures endured by the consciousness of this defect.—Etienne Pivert de Sen´ancour, *Obermann* (1804).

Oberon, king of the fairies, quarrelled with his wife, Titania, about a "changeling" which Oběron wanted for a page, but Titania refused to give up. Oberon, in revenge, anointed her eyes in sleep with the extract of "Love in Idleness," the effect of which was to make the sleeper in love with the first object beheld on waking. Titania happened to see a country bumpkin, whom Puck had dressed up with an ass's head. Oberon came upon her while she was fondling the clown, sprinkled on her an antidote, and she was so ashamed of her folly that she readily consented to give up the boy to her spouse for his page.—Shakespeare, *Midsummer Night's Dream* (1592).

Oberon, the Fay, king of Mommur, a humpty dwarf, three feet high, of angelic face. He told Sir Huon that the lady of the Hidden Isle (*Cephalonia*) married Neptanēbus, king of Egypt, by whom she had a son named Alexander "the Great." Seven hundred years later she had another son, Oberon, by Julius Cæsar, who stopped in Cephalonia on his way to Thessaly. At the birth of Oberon the fairies bestowed their gifts on him. One was insight into men's thoughts, and another was the power of transporting himself instantaneously to any place. At death he made Huon his successor, and was borne to paradise.—*Huon de Bordeaux* (a romance).

Oberthal (*Count*), lord of Dordrecht, near the Meuse. When Bertha, one of his vassals, asked permission to marry John of Leyden, the count withheld his consent, as he designed to make Bertha his mistress. This drove John into rebellion, and he joined the anabaptists. The count was taken prisoner by Gio´na, a discarded servant, but was liberated by John. When John was crowned prophet-king the count entered the banquet-hall to arrest him, and perished with him in the flames of the burning palace.—Meyerbeer, *Le Prophète* (opera, 1849).

Obi. Among the negroes of the West Indies "Obi" is the name of a magical power, supposed to affect men with all the curses of an "evil eye."

Obi-Woman (*An*), an African sorceress, a worshipper of Mumbo Jumbo.

Obi´dah, a young man who meets with various adventures and misfortunes allegorical of human life.—Dr. Johnson, *The Rambler* (1750-2).

Obid´icut, the fiend of lust, and one of the five which possessed "poor Tom."—Shakespeare, *King Lear*, act iv. sc. 1 (1605).

O'Brallaghan (*Sir Callaghan*), "a wild Irish soldier in the Prussian army. His military humor makes one fancy he was not only born in a siege, but that Bellōna had been his nurse, Mars his schoolmaster and the Furies his playfellows." He is the successful suitor of Charlotte Goodchild.—Macklin, *Love-à-la-mode* (1759).

O'Brien, the Irish lieutenant under Captain Savage.—Captain Marryat, *Peter Simple* (1833).

Observant Friars, those friars who observe the rule of St. Francis; to abjure books, land, house and chapel, to live on alms, dress in rags, feed on scraps and sleep anywhere.

Obstinate, an inhabitant of the City of Destruction, who advised Christian to return to his family, and not run on a wild-goose chase.—Bunyan, *Pilgrim's Progress*, i. (1678).

Occasion, the mother of Furor; an ugly, wrinkled old hag, lame of one foot. Her head was bald behind, but in front she had a few hoary locks. Sir Guyon seized her, gagged her and bound her.—Spenser, *Faëry Queen*, ii. 4 (1590).

Ochiltree (*Old Edie*), a king's bedesman or blue-gown. Edie is a garrulous, kind-hearted, wandering beggar, who assures Mr. Lovel that the supposed ruin of a Roman camp is no such thing. The old bedesman delighted "to daunder down the burnsides and green shaws." He is a well-drawn character.—Sir W. Scott, *The Antiquary* (time, George III.).

Ocnus (*The Rope of*), profitless labor. Ocnus is represented as twisting with unwearied diligence a rope, which an ass eats as fast as it is made. The allegory signifies that Ocnus worked hard to earn money, which his wife spent by her extravagance.

Octave (2 *syl.*), the son of Argante (2 *syl.*). During the absence of his father, Octave fell in love with Hyacinthe, daughter of Géronte, and married her, supposing her to be the daughter of Signor Pandolphe, of Tarentum. His father wanted him to marry the daughter of his friend Géronte, but Octave would not listen to it. It turned out, however, that the daughter of Pandolphe and the daughter of Géronte were one and the same person, for Géronte had assumed the name of Pandolphe while he lived in Tarentum, and his wife and daughter stayed behind after the father went to live at Naples.—Molière, *Les Fourberies de Scapin* (1671).

. In the English version, called *The Cheats of Scapin*, by Thomas Otway, Octave is called "Octavian," Argante is called "Thrifty," Hyacinthe is called "Clara," and Géronte is "Gripe."

Octavian, the lover of Floranthê. He goes mad because he imagines Floranthê loves another; but Roque, a blunt, kind-hearted old man, assures him that Doña Floranthê is true to him, and induces him to return home.—Colman, the younger, *The Mountaineers* (1793).

Octavian, the English form of "Octave" (2 *syl.*), in Otway's *Cheats of Scapin*. (See OCTAVE.)

Octa´vio, the supposed husband of Jacintha. This Jacintha was at one time contracted to Don Henrique, but Violante (4 *syl.*), passed for Don Henrique's wife.—Beaumont and Fletcher, *The Spanish Curate* (1622).

Octavio, the betrothed of Donna Clara.—Jephson, *Two Strings to your Bow* (1792).

Octer, a sea-captain in the reign of King Alfred, who traversed the Norwegian mountains, and sailed to the Dwina in the north of Russia.

The Saxon swaying all, in Alfred's powerful reign,
Our English Octer put a fleet to sea again.
Drayton, *Polyolbion*, xix. (1622).

O'Cutter (*Captain*), a ridiculous Irish captain, befriended by Lady Freelove and Lord Trinket. He speaks with a great brogue, and interlards his speech with sea terms.—George Colman, *The Jealous Wife* (1761).

Oc´ypus, son of Podalirius and Astasia, noted for his strength, agility and beauty. Ocypus used to jeer at the gout, and the goddess of that disease caused him to suffer from it for ever.—Lucian.

Odalisque, in Turkey, one of the female slaves in the sultan's harem (*odalik*, Arabic, "a chamber companion," *oda*, "a chamber").

He went forth with the lovely odalisques.
Byron, *Don Juan*, vi. 29 (1824).

Ode (*Prince of the*), Pierre de Ronsard (1534-1585).

Odoar, the venerable abbot of St. Felix, who sheltered King Roderick after his dethronement.—Southey, *Roderick, Last of the Goths*, iv. (1814).

*** Southey sometimes makes the word Odoar´ [O´.dor], and sometimes O´doar (3 *syl.*), *e.g.*:

Odoar´, the venerable abbot sat (2 *syl.*)....
Odoar´ and Urban eyed him while he spake....
The Lady Adosinda O´doar cried (3 *syl.*)....
Tell him in O´doar's name the hour has come!

O'Doh´erty (*Sir Morgan*), a pseudonym of W. Maginn, LL.D., in *Blackwood's Magazine* (1819-1842).

O'Donohue's White Horses. The boatmen of Killarney, so call those waves which, on a windy day, come crested with foam. The spirit of O'Donohue is supposed to glide over the lake of Killarney every May-day on his favorite white horse, to the sound of unearthly music.

Odori´co, a Biscayan, to whom Zerbi´no commits Isabella. He proves a traitor, and tries to defile her, but is interrupted in his base endeavor. Almonio defies him to single combat, and he is delivered bound to Zerbino, who condemns him, in punishment, to attend on Gabrina for twelve months, as her squire. He accepts the charge, but hangs Gabrina on an elm, and is himself hung by Almonio to the same tree.—Ariosto, *Orlando Furioso* (1516).

Odors for Food. Plutarch, Pliny, and divers other ancients tell us of a nation in India that lived only upon pleasing odors. Democ´ritos lived for several days together on the mere effluvia of hot bread.—Dr. John Wilkins (1614-1672).

O'Dowd (*Cornelius*), the pseudonym of Charles James Lever, in *Blackwood's Magazine* (1809-1872).

Odyssey. Homer's epic, recording the adventures of Odysseus (*Ulysses*) in his voyage home from Troy.

Book I. The poem opens in the island of Calypso, with a complaint against Neptune and Calypso for preventing the return of Odysseus (3 *syl.*) to Ithaca.

II. Telemachus, the son of Odysseus, starts in search of his father, accompanied by Pallas, in the guise of Mentor.

III. Goes to Pylos, to consult old Nestor, and

IV. Is sent by him to Sparta; where he is told by Menelāus that Odysseus is detained in the island of Calypso.

V. In the mean time, Odysseus leaves the island, and, being shipwrecked, is cast on the shore of Phæācia.

VI. Where Nausicāa, the king's daughter, finds him asleep, and

VII. Takes him to the court of her father, Alcinöos, who

VIII. Entertains him hospitably.

IX. At a banquet, Odysseus relates his adventures since he started from Troy. Tells about the Lotus-eaters and the Cyclops, with his adventures in the cave of Polyphēmos. He tells how

X. The wind-god gave him the winds in a bag. In the island of Circê, he says, his crew were changed to swine, but Mercury gave him a herb called Mōly, which disenchanted them.

XI. He tells the king how he descended into Hadês;

XII. Gives an account of the syrens; of Scylla and Charybdis; and of his being cast on the island of Calypso.

XIII. Alcinoos gives Odysseus a ship which conveys him to Ithăca, where he assumes the disguise of a beggar,

XIV. And is lodged in the house of Eumœos, a faithful old domestic.

XV. Telemachus, having returned to Ithaca, is lodged in the same house,

XVI. And becomes known to his father.

XVII. Odysseus goes to his palace, is recognized by his dog, Argos; but

XVIII. The beggar Iros insults him, and Odysseus breaks his jaw-bone.

XIX. While bathing, the returned monarch is recognized by a scar on his leg;

XX. And when he enters his palace, becomes an eye-witness to the disorders of the court, and to the way in which

XXI. Penelopê is pestered by suitors. To excuse herself, Penelopê tells her suitors he only shall be her husband who can bend Odysseus's bow. None can do so but the stranger, who bends it with ease. Concealment is no longer possible or desirable;

XXII. He falls on the suitors hip and thigh;

XXIII. Is recognized by his wife.

XXIV. Visits his old father, Laertês; and the poem ends.

Œa′grian Harpist (*The*), Orpheus, son of Œa′gros and Cal′liōpê.

... can no lesse
Tame the fierce walkers of the wilderness,
Than that Œagrian harpist, for whose lay
Tigers with hunger pined and left their prey.
Wm. Browne, *Brittania's Pastorals*, v. (1613).

Œ′dipos (in Latin *Œdipus*), son of Laïus and Jocasta. The most mournful tale of classic story.

⁎ This tale has furnished the subject matter of several tragedies. In Greek we have *Œdipus Tyrannus* and *Œdipus at Colōnus*, by Sopho′oclês. In French, *Œdipe*, by Corneille (1659); *Œdipe*, by Voltaire (1718); *Œdipe chez Admète*, by J. F. Ducis (1778); *Œdipe Roi* and *Œdipe à Colone*, by Chénier; etc. In English, *Œdipus*, by Dryden and Lee.

Œno′ne (3 *syl.*), a nymph of Mount Ida, who had the gift of prophecy, and told her husband, Paris, that his voyage to Greece would involve him and his country (Troy) in ruin. When the dead body of old Priam's son was laid at her feet, she stabbed herself.

Hither came at noon
Mournful Œnōnê, wandering forlorn
Of Paris, once her playmate on the hills [*Ida*]
Tennyson, *Œnone*.

⁎ Kalkbrenner, in 1804, made this the subject of an opera.

Œno′pian, father of Mer′opê, to whom the giant Orīon made advances. Œnopian, unwilling to give his daughter to him, put out the giant's eyes in a drunken fit.

Orion ...
Reeled as of yore beside the sea,
When blinded by Œnopian.
Longfellow, *The Occultation of Orion*.

Œte′an Knight (*The*). Her′culês is so called, because he burnt himself to death on Mount Œta or Œtæa, in Thessaly.

So also did that great Œtean knight
For his love's sake his lion's skin undight.
Spenser, *Faëry Queen*, v. 8 (1596).

Offa, king of Mercia, was the son of Thingferth, and the eleventh in descent from Woden. Thus: Woden (1) his son Wihtlæg, (2) his son Wærmund, (3) Offa I., (4) Angeltheow, (5) Eomær, (6) Icel, (7) Pybba, (8) Osmod, (9) Enwulf, (10) Thingferth, (11) Offa, whose son was Egfert, who died within a year of his father. His daughter, Eadburga, married Bertric, king of the West Saxons; and after the death of her husband, she went to the court of King Charlemagne. Offa reigned thirty-nine years (755-794).

O'Flaherty (*Dennis*), called "Major O'Flaherty." A soldier, says he, is "no livery for a knave," and Ireland is "not the country of dishonor." The major pays court to old Lady Rusport, but when he detects her dishonest purposes in bribing her lawyer to make away with Sir Oliver's will, and cheating Charles Dudley of his fortune, he not only abandons his suit, but exposes her dishonesty.—Cumberland, *The West Indian* (1771).

Og, king of Basan. Thus saith the rabbis:

The height of his stature was 23,033 cubits [*nearly six miles*]. He used to drink water from the clouds, and toast fish by holding them before the orb of the sun. He asked Noah to take him into the ark, but Noah would not. When the flood was at its deepest, it did not reach to the knees of this giant. Og lived 3000 years, and then he was slain by the hand of Moses.

Moses was himself ten cubits in stature [*fifteen feet*], and he took a spear ten cubits long, and threw it ten cubits high, and yet it only reached the heel of Og.... When dead, his body reached as far as the river Nile, in Egypt.

Og's mother was Enac, a daughter of Adam. Her fingers were two cubits long [*one yard*], and on each finger she had two sharp nails. She was devoured by wild beasts.—Maracci.

In the satire of *Absalom and Achitophel*, by Dryden and Tate, Thomas Shadwell, who was a very large man, is called "Og."

O´gier, the Dane, one of the paladins of the Charlemagne epoch. When 100 years old, Morgue, the fay, took him to the island of Av´alon, "hard by the terrestrial paradise;" gave him a ring which restored him to ripe manhood, a crown which made him forget his past life, and introduced him to King Arthur. Two hundred years afterwards, she sent him to defend France from the paynims, who had invaded it; and having routed the invaders, he returned to Avalon again.—*Ogier, le Danois* (a romance).

In a pack of French cards, Ogier, the Dane, is knave of spades. His exploits are related in the *Chansons de Geste*; he is introduced by Ariosto in *Orlando Furioso*, and by Morris in his *Earthly Paradise* ("August").

Ogier's Swords, Curtāna ("the cutter") and Sauvagine.

Ogier's Horse, Papillon.

Ogle (*Miss*), friend of Mrs. Racket; she is very jealous of young girls, and even of Mrs. Racket, because she was some six years her junior.—Mrs. Cowley, *The Belle's Stratagem* (1780).

O´gleby (*Lord*), an old fop, vain to excess, but good-natured withal, and quite the slave of the fair sex, were they but young and fair. At the age of 70, his lordship fancied himself an Adonis, notwithstanding his qualms and his rheumatism. He required a great deal of "brushing, oiling, screwing, and winding up before he appeared in public," but when fully made up, was game for the part of "lover, rake, or fine gentleman." Lord Ogleby made his bow to Fanny Sterling, and promised to make her a countess; but the young lady had been privately married to Lovewell for four months.—Colman and Garrick, *The Clandestine Marriage* (1766).

O'gri, giants who fed on human flesh.

O'Groat (*John*), with his two brothers, Malcolm and Gavin, settled in Caithness in the reign of James IV. The families lived together in harmony for a time, and met once a year at John's house. On one occasion a dispute arose about precedency—who was to take the head of the table, and who was to go out first. The old man said he would settle the question at the next annual muster; accordingly he made as many doors to his house as there were families, and placed his guests at a round table.

Oig M'Combich (*Robin*), or M'Gregor, a Highland drover, who quarrels with Harry Wakefield, an English drover, about a pasture-field, and stabs him. Being tried at Carlisle for murder, Robin is condemned to death.—Sir W. Scott, *The Two Drovers* (time, George III.).

Oina-Morul, daughter of Mal-Orchol, king of Fuärfed (a Scandinavian Island). Ton-Thormod asked her in marriage, and being refused by the father, made war upon him. Fingal sent his son Ossian to the aid of Mal-Orchol, and he took Ton-Thormod prisoner. The king now offered Ossian his daughter to wife, but the warrior-bard discovered that the lady had given her heart to Ton-Thormod; whereupon he resigned his claim, and brought about a happy reconciliation.—Ossian, *Oina-Morul*.

Oith'ona, daughter of Nuäth, betrothed to Gaul, son of Morni, and the day of their marriage was fixed; but before the time arrived, Fingal sent for Gaul to aid him in an expedition against the Britons. Gaul promised Oithona, if he survived, to return by a certain day. Lathmon, the brother of Oithona, was called away from home at the same time, to attend his father on an expedition; so the damsel was left alone in Dunlathmon. It was now that Dunrommath, lord of Uthal (one of the Orkneys) came and carried her off by force to Trom'athon, a desert island, where he concealed her in a cave. Gaul returned on the day appointed, heard of the rape, sailed for Trom'athon, and found the lady, who told him her tale of woe; but scarcely had she ended when Dunrommath entered the cave with his followers. Gaul instantly fell on him, and slew him. While the battle was raging, Oithona, arrayed as a warrior, rushed into the thickest of the fight, and was slain. When Gaul had cut off the head of Dunrommath, he saw what he thought a youth dying of a wound, and taking off the helmet, perceived it was Oithona. She died, and Gaul returned disconsolate to Dunlathmon.—Ossian, *Oithona*.

Okba, one of the sorcerers in the caves of Dom-Daniel "under the roots of the ocean." It was decreed by fate that one of the race of Hodei'rah (3 *syl.*), would be fatal to the sorcerers; so Okba was sent forth to kill the whole race, both root and branch. He succeeded in cutting off eight of them, but Thal´aba contrived to escape. Abdaldar was sent to hunt down the survivor, but was himself killed by a simoom.

"Curse on thee, Okba!" Khawla cried....
"Okba, wert thou weak of heart?
Okba, wert thou blind of eye?
Thy fate and ours were on the lot ...
Thou hast let slip the reins of Destiny.
Curse thee, curse thee, Okba!"
Southey, *Thalaba, the Destroyer*, ii. 7 (1797).

O'Kean (*Lieutenant*), a quondam admirer of Mrs. Margaret Bertram, of Singleside.—Sir W. Scott, *Guy Mannering* (time, George II.).

Olave, brother of Norma, and grandfather of Minna and Brenda Troil.—Sir W. Scott, *The Pirate* (time, William III.).

Old Bags. John Scott, Lord Eldon; so called because he carried home with him in sundry bags the cases pending his judgment (1751-1838).

Old Bona Fide (2 *syl.*), Louis XIV. (1638, 1643-1715).

Old Curiosity Shop (*The*), a tale by C. Dickens (1840). An old man, having run through his fortune, opened a curiosity shop in order to earn a living, and brought up a granddaughter, named Nell [Trent], 14 years of age. The child was the darling of the old man, but, deluding himself with the hope of making a fortune by gaming, he lost everything, and went forth, with the child, a beggar. Their wanderings and adventures are recounted till they reach a quiet country village, where the old clergyman gives them a cottage to live in. Here Nell soon dies, and the grandfather is found dead upon her grave. The main character, next to Nell, is that of a lad named Kit [Nubbles], employed in the curiosity shop, who adored Nell as "an angel." This boy gets in the service of Mr. Garland, a genial, benevolent, well-to-do man in the suburbs of London; but Quilp hates the lad, and induces Brass, a solicitor of Bevis Marks, to put a £5 bank-note in the boy's hat, and then accuse him of theft. Kit is tried, and condemned to transportation, but the villainy being exposed by a girl-of-all-work, nicknamed "The Marchioness," Kit is liberated and restored to his place, and Quilp drowns himself.

Old Cutty Soames (1 *syl.*), the fairy of the mine.

Old Fox (*The*), Marshal Soult; so called from his strategic abilities and never-failing resources (1769-1851).

Old Glory, Sir Francis Burdett; so called by the radicals, because at one time he was their leader. In his later years Sir Francis joined the tories (1770-1844).

Old Grog, Admiral Edward Vernon; so called from his wearing a grogram coat in foul weather (1684-1757).

Old Harry, the devil. The Hebrew *seirim* ("hairy ones") is translated "devils" in *Lev.* xvii. 7, probably meaning "he-goats."

Old Hickory. General Andrew Jackson was so called in 1813. He was first called "Tough," then "Tough as Hickory," then "Hickory," and lastly "Old Hickory."

Old Humphrey, the pseudonym of George Mogridge, of London (died 1854).

Old Maid (*The*), a farce by Murphy (1761). Miss Harlow is the "old maid," aged 45, living with her brother and his bride, a beautiful young woman of 23. A young man of fortune, having seen them at Ranelagh, falls in love with the younger lady; and, inquiring their names, is told they are "Mrs. and Miss Harlow." He takes it for granted that the elder lady is the mother, and the younger the daughter, so asks permission to pay his addresses to "Miss Harlow." The request is granted, but it turns out that the young man meant Mrs. Harlow; and the worst of the matter is that the elder spinster was engaged to be married to Captain Cape, but turned him off for the younger man; and, when the mistake was discovered, was left like the last rose of summer to "pine on the stem," for neither felt inclined to pluck and wear the flower.

Old Maids, a comedy by S. Knowles (1841). The "old maids" are Lady Blanche and Lady Anne, two young ladies who resolved to die old maids. Their resolutions, however, are but ropes of sand, for Lady Blanche falls in love with Colonel Blount, and Lady Anne with Sir Philip Brilliant.

Old Man (*An*), Sir Francis Bond Head, Bart., who published his *Bubbles from the Brunnen of Nassau* under this signature.

Old Man Eloquent (*The*), Isoc´ratês, the orator. The defeat of the Athenians at Cheronæ´a had such an effect on his spirits that he languished and died within four days, in the 99th year of his age.

... that dishonest victory
At Cheronæa, fatal to liberty,
Killed with report that Old Man Eloquent.
Milton, *Sonnet*, ix.

The same *sobriquet* was freely applied to John Quincy Adams.

Old Man of the Mountains, Hussan-ben-Sabah, sheik al Jebal; also called subah of Nishapour, the founder of the band (1090). Two letters are inserted in Rymer's *Fœdera* by Dr. Adam Clarke, the editor, said to be written by this sheik.

Aloaddin, "prince of the Assassins" (thirteenth century).

Old Man of the Sea *(The)*, a monster which contrived to get on the back of Sindbad the sailor, and refused to dismount. Sindbad at length made him drunk, and then shook him off.—*Arabian Nights* ("Sindbad the Sailor," fifth voyage).

Old Man of the Sea (The), Phorcus. He had three daughters, with only one eye and one tooth between 'em.—*Greek Mythology*.

Old Manor-House *(The)*, a novel by Charlotte Smith. Mrs. Rayland is the lady of the manor (1793).

Old Moll, the beautiful daughter of John Overie or Audery (contracted into Overs) a miserly ferryman. "Old Moll" is a standing toast with the parish officers of St. Mary Overs'.

Old Mortality, the best of Scott's historical novels (1716). Morton is the best of his young heroes, and serves as an excellent foil to the fanatical and gloomy Burley. The two classes of actors, viz., the brave and dissolute cavaliers, and the resolute, oppressed covenanters, are drawn in bold relief. The most striking incidents are the terrible encounter with Burley in his rocky fastness; the dejection and anxiety of Morton on his return from Holland; and the rural comfort of Cuddie Headrigg's cottage on the banks of the Clyde, with its thin blue smoke among the trees, "showing that the evening meal was being made ready."

Old Mortality always appeared to me the "Marmion" of Scott's novels.—Chambers, *English Literature*, ii. 587.

Old Mortality, an itinerant antiquary, whose craze is to clean the moss from gravestones, and keep their letters and effigies in good condition.—Sir W. Scott, *Old Mortality* (time, Charles II.).

*** The prototype of "Old Mortality" was Robert Patterson.

Old Noll, Oliver Cromwell (1590-1658).

Old Noll's Fiddler, Sir Roger Lestrange, who played the base-viol at the musical parties held at John Hingston's house, where Oliver Cromwell was a constant guest.

Old Rowley, Charles II., so called from his favorite race-horse (1630, 1660-1685).

Old Stone. Henry Stone, statuary and painter (died 1653).

Oldboy (*Colonel*), a manly retired officer, fond of his glass, and not averse to a little spice of the Lothario spirit.

Lady Mary Oldboy, daughter of Lord Jessamy, and wife of the colonel. A sickly nonentity, "ever complaining, ever having something the matter with her head, back, or legs." Afraid of the slightest breath of wind, jarred by a loud voice, and incapable of the least exertion.

Diana Oldboy, daughter of the colonel. She marries Harman.

Jessamy, son of the colonel and Lady Mary. An insufferable prig.—Bickerstaff, *Lionel and Clarissa*.

Oldbuck (*Jonathan*), the antiquary, devoted to the study and accumulation of old coins and medals, etc. He is sarcastic, irritable, and a woman-hater; but kind-hearted, faithful to his friends, and a humorist.—Sir W. Scott, *The Antiquary* (time, George III.).

An excellent temper, with a slight degree of subacid humor; learning, wit, and drollery, the more poignant that they were a little marked by the peculiarities of an old bachelor; a soundness of thought, rendered more forcible by an occasional quaintness of expression—these were the qualities in which the creature of my imagintion resembled my benevolent and excellent friend.—Sir W. Scott.

The merit of *The Antiquary* as a novel rests on the inimitable delineation of Oldbuck, that model of black-letter and Roman-camp antiquaries, whose oddities and conversation are rich and racy as any of the old crusted port that John of the Girnel might have held in his monastic cellars.—Chambers, *English Literature*, ii. 586.

Oldcastle (*Sir John*), a drama by Anthony Munday (1600). This play appeared with the name of Shakespeare on the title-page.

Old Sledge. Game of cards that, played at the "Settlemint"—(a group of log huts) among the Tennessee mountains, has a fatal fascination for Josiah Tait, who loses to a former suitor of the woman he has married everything he owns. The property is restored through the unexpected magnanimity of the winner, and the playing of Old Sledge becomes a lost art at the "Settlemint."—Charles Egbert Craddock, *In the Tennessee Mountains* (1884).

Oldworth, of Oldworth Oaks, a wealthy squire, liberally educated, very hospitable, benevolent, humorous, and whimsical. He brings up Maria, "the maid of the Oaks" as his ward, but she is his daughter and heiress.—J Burgoyne, *The Maid of the Oaks* (1779).

Ole 'Stracted, a superannuated negro, formerly a slave, whose fancy is to wait in a hut on the old plantation for his master's return. He was "sold South" forty years before, and his young master promised to go down next summer and buy him back. The poor fellow has saved in these years twelve hundred dollars to pay for his freedom. Unknown to himself or to them, his son and daughter-in-law minister to him in his last moments. He has put on his clean shirt, sure that "young marster" will come to-day. Rising to his feet he cries out:

"Heah de one you lookin' for, Marster! Mymy—heah's Little Ephrum!"

And with a smile on his face he sank back into his son's arms.—Thomas Nelson Page, *In Ole Virginia* (1887).

Olifant, the horn of Roland or Orlando. This horn and the sword "Durinda´na" were buried with the hero. Turpin tells us in his *Chronicle* that Charlemagne heard the blare of this horn at a distance of eight miles.

Olifant (Basil), a kinsman of Lady Margaret Bellenden, of the Tower of Tillietudlem.—Sir W. Scott, *Old Mortality* (time, Charles II.).

Olifaunt (*Lord Nigel*), of Glenvarloch. On going to court to present a petition to James I. he aroused the dislike of the duke of Buckingham. Lord Dalgarno gave him the cut direct, and Nigel struck him, but was obliged to seek refuge in Alsatia. After various adventures he married Margaret Ramsay, the watchmaker's daughter, and obtained the title-deeds of his estates.—Sir W. Scott, *The Fortunes of Nigel* (time, James I.).

Olim´pia, the wife of Bireno, uncompromising in love, and relentless in hate.—Ariosto, *Orlando Furioso* (1516).

Olimpia, a proud Roman lady of high rank. When Rome was sacked by Bourbon, she flew for refuge to the high altar of St. Peter's, where she clung to a golden cross. On the advance of certain soldiers in the army of Bourbon to seize her, she cast the huge cross from its stand, and as it fell it crushed to death the foremost soldier. Others then attempted to seize her, when Arnold dispersed them and rescued the lady; but the proud beauty would not allow the foe of her country to touch her, and flung herself from the high altar on the pavement. Apparently lifeless, she was borne off; but whether she recovered or not we are not informed, as the drama was never finished.—Byron, *The Deformed Transformed* (1821).

Olindo, the lover of Sophronia. Aladine, king of Jerusalem, at the advice of his magicians, stole an image of the Virgin, and set it up as a palladium in the chief mosque. During the night it was carried off, and the king, unable to discover the thief, ordered all his Christian subjects to be put to death. To prevent this massacre, Sophronia delivered up herself as the perpetrator of the deed, and Olindo, hearing thereof, went to the king and declared Sophronia innocent, as he himself had stolen the image. The king commanded both to be put to death, but, by the intercession of Clorinda, they were both set free.—Tasso, *Jerusalem Delivered*, ii. (1575).

Oliphant or **Ollyphant**, the twin-brother of Argan´tê, the giantess. Their father was Typhæus, and their mother Earth.—Spenser, *Faëry Queen*, iii. 7, 11 (1590).

Olive Litchfield, young woman married to an elderly man, whose fatherly kindness wins her grateful esteem. With her knowledge and sanction he leaves the bulk of his property to charitable objects, thereby disappointing her rapacious relatives. She is quite willing, as a widow, to marry the man her mother dismissed in order to wed her to a millionaire, but James Merion, the cured suitor, prefers a fresh love.—Ellen Olney Kirk, *A Daughter of Eve*.

Olive Tree (*The*), emblem of Athens, in memory of the famous dispute between Minerva (the patron goddess of Athens) and Neptune. Both deities wished to found a city on the same spot; and, referring the matter to Jove, the king of gods and men decreed that the privilege should be granted to whichever would bestow the most useful gift on the future inhabitants. Neptune struck the earth with his trident, and forth came a war-horse; Minerva produced an olive tree, emblem of peace; and Jove gave the verdict in favor of Minerva.

Olive Carraze, beautiful quadroon, virtuous and accomplished, whose mother, *Madame Delphine*, swears Olive is not her child, that she may secure the girl's legal marriage with a white man who loves her honorably. On the afternoon of the marriage-day, when the wedded pair have taken their departure, Madame Delphine seeks her confessor, owns the perjury, receives absolution, and falls dead in the confessional.—George W. Cable, *Madame Delphine* (1879).

Oliver, the elder son of Sir Rowland de Bois [*Bwor*], left in charge of his younger brother, Orlando, whom he hated and tried indirectly to murder. Orlando, finding it impossible to live in his brother's house, fled to the forest of Arden, where he joined the society of the banished duke. One morning he saw a man sleeping, and a serpent and lioness bent on making him their prey. He slew both the serpent and lioness, and then found that the sleeper was his brother Oliver. Oliver's disposition from this moment underwent a complete change, and he loved his brother as much as he had before hated him. In the forest the two brothers met Rosalind and Celia. The former, who was the daughter of the banished duke, married Orlando; and the latter, who was the daughter of the usurping duke, married Oliver.—Shakespeare, *As You Like It* (1598).

Oliver and Rowland, the two chief paladins of Charlemagne. Shakespeare makes the duke of Alençon say:

Froissart, a countryman of ours, records,
England all Olivers and Rowlands bred
During the time Edward the Third did reign.
1 *Henry VI*. act i. sc. 2 (1589).

Oliver's Horse, Ferrant d'Espagne.

Oliver's Sword, Haute-claire.

Oliver le Dain or *Oliver le Diable*, court barber, and favorite minister of Louis XI. Introduced by Sir W. Scott in *Quentin Durward* and *Anne of Geierstein* (time, Edward IV.).

Oliver Floyd, a dashing lawyer, with iron-gray hair, and separated from his wife. His guardianly attention to Carol Lester set village and town gossip to talking.—Charlotte Dunning, *Upon a Cast* (1885).

Oliv´ia, a rich countess, whose love was sought by Orsino, duke of Illyria; but having lost her brother, Olivia lived for a time in entire seclusion, and in no wise reciprocated the duke's love; in consequence of which Viola nicknamed her "Fair Cruelty." Strange as it may seem, Olivia fell desperately in love with Viola, who was dressed as the duke's page, and sent her a ring. Mistaking Sebastian (Viola's brother) for Viola, she married him out of hand.—Shakespeare, *Twelfth Night* (1614).

Never were Shakespeare's words more finely given than by Miss M. Tree [1802-1862] in the speech to "Olivia," beginning, "Make me a willow cabin at thy gate."—Talfourd (1821).

Olivia, a female Tartuffe (2 *syl.*), and consummate hypocrite of most unblushing effrontery.—Wycherly, *The Plain Dealer* (1677).

The duc de Montausier was the prototype of Wycherly's "Mr. Manly," the "plain dealer," and of Molière's "Misanthrope."

Olivia, daughter of Sir James Woodville, left in charge of a mercenary wretch, who, to secure to himself her fortune, shut her up in a convent in Paris. She was rescued by Leontine Croaker, brought to England, and became his bride.—Goldsmith, *The Good-natured Man* (1768).

Olivia, the tool of Ludovico. She loved Vicentio, but Vicentio was plighted to Evadne, sister of Colonna. Ludovico induced Evadne to substitute the king's miniature for that of Vicentio, which she was accustomed to wear. When Vicentio returned, and found Evadne with the king's miniature, he believed what Ludovico had told him that she was the king's wanton, and he cast her off. Olivia repented of her duplicity, and explained it all to Vicentio, whereby a reconciliation took place, and Vicentio married his troth-plighted lady, "more sinned against than sinning."—Shiel, *Evadne* or *The Statue* (1820).

Olivia, "the rose of Aragon," was the daughter of Ruphi´no, a peasant, and bride of Prince Alonzo of Aragon. The king refused to recognize the marriage, and, sending his son to the army, compelled the cortez to pass an act of divorce. This brought to a head a general revolt. The king was dethroned, and Almagro made regent. Almagro tried to make Olivia marry him; ordered her father to the rack, and her brother to death. Meanwhile the prince returned at the head of his army, made himself master of the city, put down the revolt, and had his marriage duly recognized. Almagro took poison and died.—S. Knowles, *The Rose of Aragon* (1842).

Olivia [PRIMROSE], the elder daughter of the vicar of Wakefield. She was a sort of a Hebê in beauty, open, sprightly, and commanding. Olivia Primrose "wished for many lovers," and eloped with Squire Thornhill. Her father went in search of her, and on his return homeward, stopped at a roadside inn, called the Harrow, and there found her turned out of the house by the landlady. It was ultimately discovered that she was legally married to the squire.—Goldsmith, *Vicar of Wakefield* (1765).

Olivia, young girl who hearkens to *The Talking Oak* in Tennyson's poem of that name (1842).

Olivia de Zenuga, daughter of Don Cæsar. She fixed her heart on having Julio de Melessina for her husband, and so behaved to all other suitors as to drive them away. Thus to Don Garcia, she pretended to be a termagant; to Don Vincentio, who was music-mad, she professed to love a Jew's-harp above every other instrument. At last Julio appeared, and her "bold stroke" obtained as its reward "the husband of her choice."—Mrs. Cowley, *A Bold Stroke for a Husband* (1782).

Olla, bard of Cairbar. These bards acted as heralds.—Ossian.

Ol´lapod (*Cornet*), at the Galen's Head. An eccentric country apothecary, "a jumble of physic and shooting." Dr. Ollapod is very fond of "wit," and when he has said what he thinks a smart thing he calls attention to it, with "He! he! he!" and some such expression as "Do you take, good sir! do you take?" But when another says a smart thing, he titters, and cries, "That's well! that's very well! Thank you, good sir, I owe you one!" He is a regular rattle; details all the scandal of the village; boasts of his achievements or misadventures; is very mercenary, and wholly without principle.—G. Colman, *The Poor Gentleman* (1802).

⁎ This character is evidently a copy of Dibdin's "Doctor Pother" in *The Farmer's Wife* (1780).

Ol'lomand, an enchanter, who persuaded Ahu´bal, the rebellious brother of Misnar, sultan of Delhi, to try by bribery to corrupt the troops of the sultan. By an unlimited supply of gold, he soon made himself master of the southern provinces and Misnar marched to give him battle. Ollomand, with 5000 men, went in advance and concealed his company in a forest; but Misnar, apprised thereof by spies, set fire to the forest, and Ollomand was shot by the discharge of his own cannons, fired spontaneously by the flames: "For enchantment has no power except over those who are first deceived by the enchanter."—Sir C. Morell [J. Ridley], *Tales of the Genii* ("The Enchanter's Tale," vi., 1751).

Oluf (*Sir*), a bridegroom who rode late to collect guests to his wedding. On his ride, the daughter of the erl king met him and invited him to dance a measure, but Sir Oluf declined. She then offered him a pair of gold spurs, a silk doublet, and a heap of gold, if he would dance with her: and when he refused to do so, she struck him "with an elf-stroke." On the morrow, when all the bridal party was assembled, Sir Oluf was found dead in a wood.—*A Danish Legend* (Herder).

Olympia, countess of Holland and wife of Bire´no. Being deserted by Bireno, she was bound naked to a rock by pirates, but was delivered by Orlando, who took her to Ireland, where she married King Oberto (bks. iv., v.).—Ariosto, *Orlando Furioso* (1516).

Olympia, sister to the grand-duke of Muscovia.—Beaumont and Fletcher, *The Loyal Subject* (1618).

Omawhaws [*Om´.a.waws*] or **Omahas**, an Indian tribe of Dakota.

O, chief of the mighty Omahaws!
Longfellow, *To the Driving Cloud*.

Ombre´lia, the rival of Smilinda, for the love of Sharper; "strong as the footman, as the master sweet."—Pope, *Eclogues* ("The Basset Table," 1715).

O'Neal (*Shan*), leader of the Irish insurgents in 1567. Shan O'Neal was notorious for profligacy.

O'Malley (*Charles*). Dashing Irishman in Charles James Lever's novel *Charles O'Malley*.

O'More (*Rory*). Hero of a novel of same name and the lover of Katharine O'Bawn, in the popular song, Rory O'More. Novel and song are by Samuel Lover.

Onei´za (3 *syl.*), daughter of Moath, a well-to-do Bedouin, in love with Thal´aba, "the destroyer" of sorcerers. Thalaba, being raised to the office of vizier, married Oneiza, but she died on the bridal night.—Southey, *Thalaba, the Destroyer*, ii., vii. (1797).

Oneida Warrior *(The)*, Outalissi *(q.v.)*.—Campbell, *Gertrude of Wyoming* (1809).

Only *(The)*, Johann Paul Friedrich Richter, called by the Germans *Der Einzige*, from the unique character of his writings.

⁎ The Italians call Bernardo Accolti, an Italian poet of the sixteenth century, "Aretino the Only," or *L'Unico Aretino*.

Open, Ses´ame! (3 *syl.*) the magic words which caused the cave door of the "forty thieves" to open of itself. "Shut Sesamê!" were the words which caused it to shut. Sesame is a grain, and hence Cassim, when he forgot the word, cried, "Open, Wheat!" "Open, Rye!" "Open, Barley!" but the door obeyed no sound but "Open, Sesamê!"—*Arabian Nights* ("Ali Baba or The Forty Thieves").

Ophelia, the young, beautiful, and pious daughter of Polo´nius, lord chamberlain to the king of Denmark. Hamlet fell in love with her, but her father forbade her holding word or speech with the Prince, and she obeyed so strictly that her treatment of him, with his other wrongs, drove him to upbraid and neglect her. Ophelia was so wrought upon by his conduct that her mind gave way. In her madness, attempting to hang a wreath of flowers on a willow by a brook, a branch broke, and she was drowned.—*Hamlet* (1596).

Tate Wilkinson, speaking of Mrs. Cibber (Dr. Arne's daughter, 1710-1766), says: "Her features, figure and singing, made her the best 'Ophelia' that ever appeared either before or since."

Ophiuchus [*Of´.i.ū´.kus*], the constellation *Serpentarius*. Ophiuchus is a man who holds a serpent (Greek *Ophis*) in his hands. The constellation is situated to the south of *Herculês*; and the principal star, called "Ras Alhague," is in the man's head. (*Ras Alhague*) is from the Arabic, *rás-al-hawwá*, "the serpent-charmer's head.")

Satan stood
Unterrified, and like a comet burned,
That fires the length of Ophiuchus huge,
In the Arctic sky.
Milton, *Paradise Lost*, ii. 709, etc. (1665).

Opium-Eater *(The English)*, Thomas de Quincey, who published *Confessions of an English Opium-Eater* (1845).

O. P. Q., Robert Merry (1755-1798); object of Gifford's satire in *Baviad* and *Mæviad*, and of Byron's in his *English Bards and Scotch Reviewers*. He marries Miss Brunton, the actress.

And Merry's metaphors appear anew,
Chained to the signature of O. P. Q.
Byron, *English Bards and Scotch Reviewers* (1809).

Oracle of the Church (*The*), St. Bernard (1091-1153).

Oracle of the Holy Bottle (*The*), an oracle sought for by Rabelais, to solve the knotty point "whether Panurge (2 *syl.*) should marry or not." The question had been put to sibyl and poet, monk and fool, philosopher and witch, but none could answer it. The oracle was ultimately found in Lantern-land.

This, of course, is a satire on the celibacy of the clergy and the withholding of the cup from the laity. Shall the clergy marry or not?—that was the moot point; and the "Bottle of Tent Wine," or the clergy, who kept the bottle to themselves, alone could solve it. The oracle and priestess of the bottle were both called *Bacbuc* (Hebrew for "bottle").—Rabelais, *Pantag'ruel*, iv., v. (1545).

Oracle (*Sir*), name used in Merchant of Venice to express conceited, pugnacious man.

... I am Sir Oracle,
And when I ope my lips, let no dog bark!"

Orange (*Prince of*), a title given to the heir-apparent of the king of Holland. "Orange" is a petty principality in the territory of Avignon, in the possession of the Nassau family.

Orania, the lady-love of Am'adis of Gaul.—Lobeira, *Amadis of Gaul* (fourteenth century).

Orator Henley, the Rev. John Henley, who for about thirty years delivered lectures on theological, political, and literary subjects (1692-1756).

*** Hogarth has introduced him into several of his pictures; and Pope says of him:

Imbround with native bronze, lo! Henley stands,
Tuning his voice, and balancing his hands,
How fluent nonsense trickles from his tongue!
How sweet the periods, neither said nor sung!...

Oh, great restorer of the good old stage,
Preacher at once and zany of thy age!
Oh, worthy thou of Egypt's wise abodes;

A decent priest where monkeys were the gods!
The Dunciad (1742).

Orator Hunt, the great demagogue in the time of the Wellington and Peel administration. Henry Hunt, M.P., used to wear a gray hat, and these hats were for the time a badge of democratic principles, and called "radical hats" (1773-1835).

Orbaneja, the painter of Ube´da, who painted so preposterously that he inscribed under his objects what he meant them for.

Orbaneja would paint a cock so wretchedly designed that he was obliged to inscribe under it, "This is a cock."—Cervantes, *Don Quixote*, II. i. 3 (1615).

Orbilius, the schoolmaster who taught Horace. The poet calls him "the flogger" (*plagōsus*).—*Ep.* ii. 71.

⁎ *The Orbilian Stick* is a birch rod or cane.

Ordigale, the otter in the beast-epic of *Reynard the Fox*, i. (1498).

Ordovi´ces (4 *syl.*), people of Ordovicia, that is, Flintshire, Denbighshire, Merionetshire, Montgomeryshire, Carnarvonshire and Anglesey. (In Latin the *i* is short: *Ordovĭcês*.)

The Ordovīces now which North Wales people be.
Drayton, *Polyolbion*, xvi. (1613).

Or´dovies (3 *syl.*), the inhabitants of North Wales. (In Latin North Wales is called *Ordovic´ia*.)

Beneath his [*Agricola's*] fatal sword the Ordovies to fall
(Inhabiting the west), those people last of all
... withstood.
Drayton, *Polyolbion*, viii. (1612).

Or´ead (3 *syl.*), a mountain-nymph. Tennyson calls "Maud" an *oread*, because her hall and garden were on a hill.

I see my Oreäd coming down.
Maud, I. xvi. 1 (1855).

Oreäd. Echo is so called.

Ore´ades (4 *syl.*) or **O´reads** (3 *syl.*), mountain-nymphs.

Ye Cambrian [*Welsh*] shepherds then, whom these our mountains please,
And ye our fellow-nymphs, ye light Oreädês.
Drayton, *Polyolbion*, ix. (1612).

Orel´io, the favorite horse of King Roderick, the last of the Goths.

'Twas Orelio
On which he rode, Roderick's own battle-horse,
Who from his master's hand had wont to feed,
And with a glad docility obey
His voice familiar.
Southey, *Roderick, etc.*, xxv. (1814).

Ores′tes (3 *syl.*), son of Agamemnon, betrothed to Hermi′onê (4 *syl.*), daughter of Menela′us (4 *syl.*), king of Sparta. At the downfall of Troy Menelāus promised Hermionê in marriage to Pyrrhus, king of Epīrus, but Pyrrhus fell in love with Androm′achê, the widow of Hector, and his captive. An embassy, led by Orestês, was sent to Epirus to demand that the son of Andromachê should be put to death, lest, as he grew up, he might seek to avenge his father's death. Pyrrhus refused to comply. In this embassage Orestês met Hermionê again, and found her pride and jealousy aroused to fury by the slight offered her. She goaded Orestês to avenge her insults, and the ambassadors fell on Pyrrhus and murdered him. Hermionê, when she saw the dead body of the king borne along, stabbed herself, and Orestês went raving mad.—Ambrose Philips, *The Distressed Mother* (1712).

Orfeo and Heuro′dis, the tale of Orpheus and Eurydĭcê, with the Gothic machinery of elves and fairies.

₊ Glück has an opera called *Orfeo*; the libretto, by Calzabigi, based on a dramatic piece by Poliziano (1764).

Orgari′ta, "the orphan of the Frozen Sea," heroine of a drama. (See MARTHA.)—Stirling, *The Orphan of the Frozen Sea* (1856).

Or′gilus, the betrothed lover of Penthe′a, by the consent of her father; but, at the death of her father, her brother, Ith′oclês, compelled her to marry Bass′anês, whom she hated. Ithoclês was about to marry the princess of Sparta, but a little before the event was to take place Penthea starved herself to death, and Orgilus was condemned to death for murdering Ithoclês.—John Ford, *The Broken Heart* (1633).

Orgoglio [*Or.gole′.yo*], a hideous giant, as tall as three men, son of Earth and Wind. Finding the Red Cross Knight at the fountain of Idleness he beats him with a club, and makes him his slave. Una informs Arthur of it, and Arthur liberates the knight and slays the giant (*Rev.* xiii. 5, 7, with *Dan.* vii. 21, 22).—Spenser, *Faëry Queen*, i. (1590).

₊ Arthur first cut off Orgoglio's *left arm*, *i. e.* Bohemia was cut off first from the Church of Rome; then he cut off the giant's *right leg*, *i. e.* England.

Orgon, brother-in-law of Tartuffe (2 *syl.*). His credulity and faith in Tartuffe, like that of his mother, can scarcely be shaken even by the evidence of his senses. He hopes against hope, and fights every inch of ground in defence of the religious hypocrite.—Molière, *Tartuffe* (1664).

Oria´na, daughter of Lisuarte, king of England, and spouse of Am´adis of Gaul (bk. ii. 6). The general plot of this series of romances bears on this marriage, and tells of the thousand and one obstacles from rivals, giants, sorcerers and so on, which had to be overcome before the consummation could be effected. It is in this unity of plot that the Amadis series differs from its predecessors—the Arthurian romances, and those of the paladins of Charlemagne, which are detached adventures, each complete in itself, and not bearing to any common focus.—*Amadis de Gaul* (fourteenth century).

*** Queen Elizabeth is called "the peerless Oriana," especially in the madrigals entitled *The Triumphs of Oriana* (1601). Ben Jonson applies the name to the queen of James I. (*Oriens Anna*).

Oriana, the nursling of a lioness, with whom Esplandian fell in love, and for whom he underwent all his perils and exploits. She was the gentlest, fairest, and most faithful of her sex.—Lobeira, *Amadis de Gaul* (fourteenth century).

Orian´a, the fair, brilliant, and witty "chaser" of the "wild goose" Mirabel, to whom she is betrothed, and whose wife she ultimately becomes.—Beaumont and Fletcher, *The Wild-Goose Chase* (1652).

Oriana, the ward of old Mirabel, and bound by contract to her guardian's son whom she loves; but young Mirabel shilly-shallies, till he gets into trouble with Lamorce (3 *syl.*), and is in danger of being murdered, when Oriana, dressed as a page, rescues him. He then declared that his "inconstancy has had a lesson," and he marries the lady.—G. Farquhar, *The Inconstant* (1702).

Oriana, in Tennyson's ballad so called, "stood on the castle wall," to see her spouse, a Norland chief, fight. A foeman went between "the chief, and the wall," and discharged an arrow, which, glancing aside, pierced the lady's heart and killed her. The ballad is the lamentation of the spouse on the death of his bride (1830).

O´riande (3 *syl.*), a fay who lived at Rosefleur, and was brought up by Maugis d'Aygremont. When her *protégé* grew up, she loved him, "d'un si grand amour, qu'elle doute fort qu'il ne se departe d'avecques elle."—*Romance de Maujis d'Aygremont et de Vivian son Frère*.

O´riel, a fairy, whose empire lay along the banks of the Thames, when King Oberon held his court in Kensington Gardens.—Tickell, *Kensington Gardens* (1686-1740).

Orient (*The*). In *The New Priest of Conception Bay*, Fanny Dare sings to little Mary Barré how the good ship *Orient* was wrecked.

"Woe for the brave ship Orient!
Woe for the old ship Orient!
For in the broad, broad light
With the land in sight,—
Where the waters bubbled white,—
One great, sharp shriek!—one shudder of affright!
And——
down went the brave old ship, the Orient!"
Robert Lowell, *The New Priest of Conception Bay* (1858).

Oriflamme, the banner of St. Denis. When the counts of Vexin became possessed of the abbey, the banner passed into their hands, and when, in 1082, Philippe I. united Vexin to the crown, the oriflamme or sacred banner belonged to the king. In 1119 it was first used as a national banner. It consists of a crimson silk flag, mounted on a gilt staff (*un glaive tout doré où est attaché une banière vermeille*). The loose end is cut into three wavy vandykes, to represent tongues of flame, and a silk tassel is hung at each cleft. In war the display of this standard indicates that no quarter will be given. The English standard of no quarter was the "burning dragon."

Raoul de Presle says it was used in the time of Charlemagne, being the gift of the patriarch of Jerusalem. We are told that all infidels were blinded who looked upon it. Froissart says it was displayed at the battle of Rosbecq, in the reign of Charles VI., and "no sooner was it unfurled than the fog cleared away, and the sun shone on the French alone."

I have not reared the Oriflamme of death.
... me it behooves
To spare the fallen foe.
Southey, *Joan of Arc*, viii. 621, etc. (1837).

Origilla, the lady-love of Gryphon, brother of Aquilant; but the faithless fair one took up with Martāno, a most impudent boaster and a coward. Being at Damascus during a tournament in which Gryphon was the victor, Martano stole the armor of Gryphon, arrayed himself in it, took the prizes, and then decamped with the lady. Aquilant happened to see them, bound them, and took them back to Damascus, where Martano was hanged, and the lady kept in bondage for the judgment of Lucīna.—Ariosto, *Orlando Furioso* (1516).

Orillo, a magician and robber, who lived at the mouth of the Nile. He was the son of an imp and fairy. When any one of his limbs was lopped off, he had the power of restoring it; and when his head was cut off, he could take it up and replace it. When Astolpho encountered this magician, he was informed that his life lay in one particular hair; so instead of seeking to maim his adversary, Astolpho cut off the magic hair, and the magician fell lifeless at his feet.—Ariosto, *Orlando Furioso* (1516).

Orinda, "the incomparable," Mrs. Katherine Philipps, who lived in the reign of Charles II., and died of small-pox.

⁎ Her praises were sung by Cowley, Dryden, and others.

We allowed you beauty, and we did submit ...
Ah, cruel sex, will you depose us too in wit?
Orinda does in that too reign.
Cowley, *On Orinda's Poems* (1647).

Ori′on, a giant of great beauty, and a famous hunter, who cleared the island of Chios of wild beasts. While in the island, Orion fell in love with Merŏpê, daughter of king Œnop′ion; but one day, in a drunken fit, having offered her violence, the king put out the giant's eyes, and drove him from the island. Orion was told if he would travel eastward, and expose his sockets to the rising sun, he would recover his sight. Guided by the sound of a Cyclop's hammer, he reached Lemnos, where Vulcan gave him a guide to the abode of the sun. In due time, his sight returned to him, and at death he was made a constellation. The lion's skin was an emblem of the wild beasts which he slew in Chios, and the club was the instrument he employed for the purpose.

He [*Orion*]
Reeled as of yore beside the sea,
When, blinded by Œnopion,
He sought the blacksmith at his forge,
And, climbing up the mountain gorge,
Fixed his blank eyes upon the sun.
Longfellow, *The Occultation of Orion.*

Orion and the Blacksmith. The reference is to the blacksmith mentioned in the preceding article, whom Orion took on his back to act as guide to the place where the rising sun might be best seen.

Orion's Dogs were Arctophŏnus ("the bear-killer") and Ptoophăgos ("the glutton of Ptoon," in Bœōtia).

Orion's Wife, Sidê.

Orion. After Orion has set in the west, *Aurīga* (the Charioteer) and *Gem′ini* (Castor and Pollux) are still visible. Hence Tennyson says:

... the Charioteer
And starry Gemini hang like glorious crowns
Over Orion's grave low down in the west.
Maud, III. vi. 1 (1855).

Orion, a seraph, the guardian angel of Simon Peter.—Klopstock, *The Messiah,* iii. (1748).

Orith´yia or **Orith´ya**, daughter of Erectheus, carried off by Boreas to Thrace.

Such, dalliance as alone the North wind hath with her,
Orithya not enjoyed, from Thrace when he her took,
And in his saily plumes the trembling virgin shook.
Drayton, *Polyolbion*, x. (1612).

Phineas Fletcher calls the word "Orithy´a."

None knew mild zephyr's from cold Eurus' mouth,
Nor Orithya's lover's violence [*North wind*].
Purple Island, i. (1633).

Orlando, the younger son of Sir Rowland de Bois [*Bwor*]. At the death of his father, he was left under the care of his elder brother, Oliver, who was charged to treat him well; but Oliver hated him, wholly neglected his education, and even tried by many indirect means to kill him. At length, Orlando fled to the forest of Arden´, where he met Rosalind and Celia in disguise. They had met before at a wrestling match, when Orlando and Rosalind fell in love with each other. The acquaintance was renewed in the forest, and ere many days had passed the two ladies resumed their proper characters, and both were married, Rosalind to Orlando, and Celia to Oliver, the elder brother.—Shakespeare, *As You Like It* (1598).

Orlando (in French ROLAND, *q.v.*), one of the paladins of Charlemagne, whose nephew he was. Orlando was confiding and loyal, of great stature, and possessed unusual strength. He accompanied his uncle into Spain, but on his return was waylaid in the valley of Roncesvallês (in the Pyrenees) by the traitor Ganelon, and perished with all his army, A.D. 778. His adventures are related in Turpin's *Chronique;* in the *Chanson de Roland*, attributed to Théroulde. He is the hero of Bojardo's epic, *Orlando Innamorato*; and of Ariosto's continuation called *Orlando Furioso* ("Orlando mad"). Robert Greene, in 1594, produced a drama which he called *The History of Orlando*. Rhode's farce of *Bombastês Furioso* (1790) is a burlesque of Ariosto's *Orlando Furioso*.

Orlando's Ivory Horn, Olifant, once the property of Alexander the Great. Its bray could be heard for twenty miles.

Orlando's Horse, Brigliadoro ("golden bridal").

Orlando's Sword, Durinda´na or Durandana, which once belonged to Hector, is "preserved at Rocamadour, in France; and his spear is still shown in the cathedral of Pa´via, in Italy."

Orlando was of middling stature, broad-shouldered, crooked-legged, brown-visaged, red-bearded, and had much hair on his body. He talked but little, and had a very surly aspect, although he was perfectly good-humored.—Cervantes, *Don Quixote*, II. i. 1 (1615).

Orlando's Vulnerable Part. Orlando was invulnerable except in the sole of his foot, and even there nothing could wound him but the point of a large pin; so that when Bernardo del Carpio assailed him at Roncesvallês, he took him in his arms and squeezed him to death, in imitation of Herculês, who squeezed to death the giant Antæ´us (3 *syl.*).—Cervantes, *Don Quixote*, II. ii. 13 (1615).

Orlando Furioso, a continuation of Bojardo's story, with the same hero. Bojardo leaves Orlando in love with Angelica, whom he fetched from Cathay and brought to Paris. Here, says Ariosto, Rinaldo falls in love with her, and, to prevent mischief, the king placed the coquette under the charge of Namus; but she contrived to escape her keeper, and fled to the island of Ebūda, where Rogēro found her exposed to a sea-monster, and liberated her. In the mean time, Orlando went in search of his lady, was decoyed into the enchanted castle of Atlantês, but was liberated by Angelica, who again succeeded in effecting her escape to Paris. Here she arrived just after a great battle between the Christians and pagans, and, finding Medōra, a Moor, wounded, took care of him, fell in love with him, and eloped with him to Cathay. When Orlando found himself jilted, he was driven mad with jealousy and rage, or rather his wits were taken from him for three months by way of punishment, and deposited in the moon. Astolpho went to the moon in Elijah's chariot, and St. John gave him "the lost wits" in an urn. On reaching France Astolpho bound the madman, then, holding the urn to his nose, the wits returned to their nidus, and the hero was himself again. After this, the siege was continued, and the Christians were wholly successful. (See ORLANDO INNAMORATO.)—Ariosto, *Orlando Furioso* (1516).

⁎ This romance in verse extends to forty-six cantos. Hoole, in his translation, has compressed the forty-six cantos into twenty-four books; but Rose has retained the original number. The adventures of Orlando, under the French form "Roland," are related by Turpin in his *Chronicle*, and by Théroulde in his *Chanson de Roland*.

⁎ The true hero of Ariosto's romance is Rogēro, and not Orlando. It is with Rogero's victory over Rodomont that the poem ends. The concluding lines are:

Then at full stretch he [*Rogero*] raised his arm above
The furious Rodomont, and the weapon drove
Thrice in his gaping throat—so ends the strife,
And leaves secure Rogero's fame and life.

Orlando Innamora´to, or *Orlando in love*, in three books, by Count Bojardo, of Scandiano, in Italy (1495). Bojardo supposes Charlemagne to be warring against the Saracens in France, under the walls of Paris. He represents the city to be besieged by two infidel hosts—one under Agramantê, emperor of Africa, and the other under Gradasso, king of Sirica´na. His hero is Orlando, whom he supposes (though married at the time to Aldebella) to be in love with Angelica, a fascinating coquette from Cathay, whom Orlando had brought to France. (See ORLANDO FURIOSO.)

⁎ Berni of Tuscany, in 1538, published a burlesque in verse on the same subject.

Orleans, a most passionate innamorato, in love with Agripy´na.—Thomas Dekker, *Old Fortunatus* (1600).

Orleans talks "pure Biron and Romeo;" he is almost as poetical as they, quite as philosophical, only a little madder.—C. Lamb.

("Biron," in Shakespeare's *Love's Labor's Lost*; "Romeo," in his *Romeo and Juliet*.)

Orleans (Gaston, duke of), brother of Louis XIII. He heads a conspiracy to assassinate Richelieu and dethrone the king. If the plot had been successful, Gaston was to have been made regent; but the conspiracy was discovered, and the duke was thwarted in his ambitious plans.—Lord Lytton, *Richelieu* (1839).

Orleans (Louis, duc d'), to whom the Princess Joan (daughter of Louis XI.) is affianced.—Sir W. Scott, *Quentin Durward* (time, Edward IV.).

Orlick (*Dolge*), usually called "Old Orlick," though not above five and twenty, journeyman to Joe Gargery, blacksmith. Obstinate, morose, broad-shouldered, loose-limbed, swarthy, of great strength, never in a hurry, and always slouching. Being jealous of Pip, he allured him to a hut in the marshes, bound him to a ladder, and was about to kill him, when, being alarmed by approaching steps, he fled. Subsequently, he broke into Mr. Pumblechook's house, was arrested, and confined in the county jail. This surly, ill-conditioned brute was in love with Biddy, but Biddy married Joe Gargery.—C. Dickens, *Great Expectations* (1860).

Orloff Diamond (*The*), the third largest cut diamond in the world, set in the top of the Russian sceptre. The weight of this magnificent diamond is 194 carats, and its size is that of a pigeon's egg. It was once one of the eyes of the idol Sheringham, in the temple of Brahma; came into the hands of the Shah Nadir; was stolen by a French grenadier and sold to an English sea-captain for £2000; the captain sold it to a Jew for £12,000; it next passed into the hands of Shafras; and in 1775, Catherine II. of Russia gave for it £90,000. (See DIAMONDS.)

Or'mandine (3 *syl.*), the necromancer who threw St. David into an enchanted sleep for seven years, from which he was reclaimed by St. George.—R. Johnson, *The Seven Champions of Christendom*, i. 9 (1617).

Orme (*Victor*), a poor gentleman in love with Elsie.—Wybert Reeve, *Parted*.

Ormond (*The duke of*), a privy councillor of Charles II.—Sir W. Scott, *Peveril of the Peak* (time, Charles II.).

Ormston (*Jock*), a sheriff's officer at Fairport.—Sir W. Scott, *The Antiquary* (time, George III.).

Ornithol'ogy (*The Father of*), George Edwards (1693-1773).

Oroma'zes (4 *syl.*), the principle of good in Persian mythology. Same as Yezad (*q.v.*).

Oroonda'tes (5 *syl.*), only son of a Scythian king, whose love for Statīra (widow of Alexander the Great) led him into numerous dangers and difficulties, which, however, he surmounted.—La Calprenède, *Cassandra* (a romance).

Oroono'ko (*Prince*), son and heir of the king of Angola, and general of the forces. He was decoyed by Captain Driver aboard his ship; his suite of twenty men were made drunk with rum; the ship weighed anchor; and the prince, with all his men, were sold as slaves in one of the West Indian Islands. Here Oroonoko met Imoin'da (3 *syl.*), his wife, from whom he had been separated, and whom he thought was dead. He headed a rising of the slaves, and the lieutenant-governor tried to seduce Imoinda. The result was that Imoinda killed herself, and Oroonoko (3 *syl.*) slew first the lieutenant-governor and then himself. Mrs. Aphra Behn became acquainted with the prince at Surinam, and made the story of his life the basis of a novel, which Thomas Southern dramatized (1696).

Orozem'bo, a brave and dauntless old Peruvian. When captured and brought before the Spanish invaders, Orozembo openly defied them, and refused to give any answer to their questions (act i. 1).—Sheridan, *Pizarro* (altered from Kotzebue, 1799).

Orpas, once archbishop at Sev'ille. At the overthrow of the Gothic kingdom in Spain, Orpas joined the Moors and turned Moslem. Of all the renegades "the foulest and the falsest wretch was he that e'er renounced his baptism." He wished to marry Florinda, daughter of Count Julian, in order to secure "her wide domains;" but Florinda loathed him. In the Moorish council Orpas advised Abulcacem to cut off Count Julian, "whose power but served him for fresh treachery; false to Roderick first, and to the caliph now." This advice was acted on; but, as the villain left the tent, Abulcacem muttered to himself, "Look for a like reward thyself; that restless head of wickedness in the grave will brood no treason."—Southey, *Roderick, etc.*, xx., xxii. (1814).

Orphan of China, a drama by Murphy. Zaphimri, the sole survivor of the royal race of China, was committed in infancy to Zamti, the mandarin, that he might escape from the hand of Ti´murkan´, the Tartar conqueror. Zamti brought up Zaphimri as his son, and sent Hamet, his real son, to Corea, where he was placed under the charge of Morat. Twenty years afterwards, Hamet led a band of insurgents against Timurkan, was seized, and ordered to be put to death under the notion that he was "the orphan of China." Zaphimri, hearing thereof, went to the Tartar and declared that he, not Hamet, was the real prince; whereupon Timurkan ordered Zamti and his wife, Mandānê, with Hamet and Zaphimri, to be seized. Zamti and Mandanê were ordered to the torture, to wring from them the truth. In the interim, a party of insurgent Chinese rushed into the palace, killed the king, and established "the orphan of China" on the throne of his fathers (1759).

Orphan of the Frozen Sea, Martha, the daughter of Ralph de Lascours (captain of the *Uran´ia*) and his wife, Louise. The crew having rebelled, the three, with their servant, Bar´abas, were cast adrift in a boat, which ran on an iceberg in the Frozen Sea. Ralph thought it was a small island, but the iceberg broke up, both Ralph and his wife were drowned, but Barabas and Martha escaped. Martha was taken by an Indian tribe, which brought her up and named her Orgari´ta ("withered wheat"), from her white complexion. In Mexico she met with her sister, Diana, and her grandmother, Mde. de Theringe (2 *syl.*), and probably married Horace de Brienne.—E. Stirling, *Orphan of the Frozen Sea* (1856).

Orphan of the Temple, Marie Thérèse Charlotte, duchess d'Angoulême, daughter of Louis XVI.; so called from the Temple, where she was imprisoned. She was called "The Modern Antig´onê" by her uncle, Louis XVIII.

Orphant Annie. A bound girl, who is credited by *l'enfant terrible* of the household with the goblin-lore he lavishes upon a visitor, this being the moral:

"You better mind yer parents and yer teachers fond and dear,
An' churish 'em 'at loves you an' dry the orphant's tear,
An' he'p the poor an' needy ones 'at clusters all about,
Er the gobble-uns 'll git you
Ef you
Don't
Watch

Out!"
James Whitcomb Riley, *The Boss Girl and Other Sketches* (1886).

Orpheus. (For a parallel fable, see WAINAMOINEN.)

Orpheus and Eurydice (4 *syl.*), Glück's best opera (*Orfeo*). Libretto by Calzabigi, who also wrote for Glück the libretto of *Alceste* (1767). King produced an English version of *Orpheus and Eurydice*.

*** The tale is introduced by Pope in his *St. Cecilia's Ode*.

Of Orpheus now no more let poets tell,
To bright Cecilia greater power is given;
His numbers raised a shade from hell,
Hers lift the soul to heaven.
Pope, *St. Cecilia's Day* (1709).

Orpheus of Highwaymen, John Gay, author of *The Beggar's Opera* (1688-1732).

Orpheus of the Green Isle (*The*), Furlough O'Carolan, poet and musician (1670-1738).

Or'raca (*Queen*), wife of Affonso II. The legend says that five friars of Morocco, went to her, and said, "Three things we prophesy to you: (1) we five shall all suffer martyrdom; (2) our bodies will be brought to Coimbra; and (3) which ever see our relics the first, you or the king, will die the same day." When their bodies were brought to Coimba, the king told Queen Orraca she must join the procession with him. She pleaded illness, but Affonso replied the relics would cure her; so they started on their journey. As they were going, the queen told the king to speed on before, as she could not travel so fast; so he speeded on with his retinue, and started a boar on the road. "Follow him!" cried the king, and they went after the boar and killed it. In the mean time, the queen reached the procession, fully expecting her husband had joined it long ago; but lo! she beheld him riding up with great speed. That night the king was aroused at midnight with the intelligence that the queen was dead.—Southey, *Queen Orraca* (1838); Francisco Manoel da Esperança, *Historia Sarafica* (eighteenth century).

Orrock (*Puggie*), a sheriff's officer at Fairport.—Sir W. Scott, *The Antiquary* (time, George III.).

Orsin, one of the leaders of the rabble rout that attacked Hudibras at the bear-baiting.—S. Butler, *Hudibras* (1663).

Orsi'ni (*Maffio*), a young Italian nobleman, whose life was saved by Genna'ro at the battle of Rim'ini. Orsini became the fast friend of Gennaro, but both were poisoned by the Princess Neg′roni at a banquet.—Donizetti, *Lucrezia di Borgia* (opera, 1834).

Orsi′no, duke of Illyria, who sought the love of Olivia, a rich countess; but Olivia gave no encouragement to his suit, and the duke moped and pined, leaving manly sports for music and other effeminate employments. Viola entered the duke's service as a page, and soon became a great favorite. When Olivia married Sebastian (Viola's brother), and the sex of Viola became known, the duke married her, and made her duchess of Illyria.—Shakespeare, *Twelfth Night* (1614).

Orson, twin brother of Valentine, and son of Bellisant. The twin-brothers were born in a wood near Orleans, and Orson was carried off by a bear, which suckled him with its cubs. When he grew up he became the terror of France, and was called "The Wild Man of the Forest." Ultimately, he was reclaimed by his brother Valentine, overthrew the Green Knight, and married Fezon, daughter of the duke of Savary, in Aquitane.—*Valentine and Orson* (fifteenth century).

Orson and Ellen. Young Orson was a comely young farmer from Taunton, stout as an oak, and very fond of the lasses, but he hated matrimony, and used to say, "the man who can buy milk is a fool to keep a cow." While still a lad, Orson made love to Ellen, a rustic maiden; but, in the fickleness of youth, forsook her for a richer lass, and Ellen left the village, wandered far away, and became waiting maid to old Boniface, the innkeeper. One day Orson happened to stop at this very inn, and Ellen waited on him. Five years had passed since they had seen each other, and at first neither knew the other. When, however, the facts were known, Orson made Ellen his wife, and their marriage feast was given by Boniface himself.—Peter Pindar [Dr. Wolcot], *Orson and Ellen* (1809).

Ortel′lius (*Abraham*), a Dutch geographer, who published in 1570, his *Theatrum Orbis Terræ*, or *Universal Geography* (1527-1598).

I more could tell to prove the place our own,
Than by his spacious maps are by Ortellius shown.
Drayton, *Polyolbion*, vi. (1612).

Ortheris, cockney companion of Mulvaney. He suffers violently from homesickness in India.—Rudyard Kipling, *Soldiers Three*.

Orthodoxy. When Lord Sandwich said, "he did not know the difference between orthodoxy and heterodoxy," Warburton, bishop of Gloucester, replied, "Orthodoxy, my lord, is *my* doxy, and heterodoxy is *another man's* doxy."

Orthodoxy (The Father of), Athanasius (296-373).

Orthrus, the two-headed dog of Euryt´ion, the herdsman of Geryon´eo. It was the progeny of Typha´on and Echidna.

With his two-headed dogge that Orthrus hight,
Orthrus begotten by great Typhaon
And foule Echidna in the house of Night.
Spenser, *Faëry Queen*, v., 10 (1596).

Ortwine (2 *syl.*), knight of Metz, sister's son of Sir Hagan of Trony, a Burgundian.—*The Nibelungen Lied* (eleventh century).

Or´ville (*Lord*), the amiable and devoted lover of Evelina, whom he ultimately marries.—Miss Burney, *Evelina* (1778).

Osbaldistone (*Mr.*), a London merchant.

Frank Osbaldistone, his son, in love with Diana Vernon, whom he marries.

Sir Hildebrand Osbaldistone, of Osbaldistone Hall, uncle of Frank, his heir.

His Sons were: Percival, "the sot;" Thorncliffe, "the bully;" John, "the gamekeeper;" Richard, "the horse-jockey;" Wilfred, "the fool;" and Rashleigh, "the scholar," a perfidious villain killed by Rob Roy.—Sir W. Scott, Rob Roy (time, George I.).

Rob Roy Macgregor was dramatized by Pocock.

Osborne (*Mr.*), a hard, money-loving, purse-proud, wealthy London merchant, whose only gospel was that "according to Mammon." He was a widower, and his heart of hearts was to see his son, Captain George, marry a rich mulatto. While his neighbor, Sedley, was prosperous, old Sedley encouraged the love-making of George and Miss Sedley; but when old Sedley failed, and George dared to marry the bankrupt's daughter, to whom he was engaged, the old merchant disinherited him. Captain George fell on the field of Waterloo, but the heart of old Osborne would not relent, and he allowed the widow to starve in abject poverty. He adopted, however, the widow's son George, and brought him up in absurd luxury and indulgence. A more detestable cad than old Sedley cannot be imagined.

Maria and *Jane Osborne*, daughters of the merchant, and of the same mould. Maria married Frederick Bullock, a banker's son.

Captain George Osborne, son of the merchant; selfish, vain, extravagant, and self-indulgent. He was engaged to Amelia Sedley, while her father was in prosperity, and Captain Dobbin induced him to marry her after the father was made a bankrupt. Happily, George fell on the field of Waterloo, or one would never vouch for his conjugal fidelity.—Thackeray, *Vanity Fair* (1848).

Oscar, son of Ossian and grandson of Fingal. He was engaged to Malvi′na, daughter of Toscar, but before the day of marriage arrived, he was slain in Ulster, fighting against Cairbar, who had treacherously invited him to a banquet and then slew him, A.D. 296. Oscar is represented as most brave, warm-hearted, and impetuous, most submissive to his father, tender to Malvina, and a universal favorite.

Oscar Roused from Sleep. "Caolt took up a huge stone and hurled it on the hero's head. The hill for three miles round shook with the reverberation of the blow, and the stone, rebounding, rolled out of sight. Whereupon Oscar awoke, and told Caolt to reserve his blows for his enemies."

Gun thog Caoilte a chlach nach gàn,
Agus a n' aighai' chiean gun bhuail;
Tri mil an tulloch gun chri.
Gaelic Romances.

Oscar Dubourg. Amiable, affectionate young fellow, betrothed to blind Lucilla Finch. To cure the epilepsy attendant upon an injury to his head, he takes nitrate of silver, concealing the discoloration of his complexion caused by the drug from the knowledge of his betrothed, who has a nervous horror of ugliness and deformity. When she regains her sight, he leaves her because he dares not disclose the truth that she has mistaken his brother for himself, and does not enter her presence until her sight again leaves her.—Wilkie Collins, *Poor Miss Finch.*

Os′ewald (3 *syl.*), the reeve, of "the carpenteres craft," an old man.—Chaucer, *Canterbury Tales* (1388).

Oseway (*Dame*), the ewe, in the beast-epic of *Reynard the Fox* (1498).

O'Shanter (*Tam*), a farmer, who, returning home from Ayr very late and well-soaked with liquor, had to pass the kirk of Alloway. Seeing it was illuminated, he peeped in, and saw there the witches and devils dancing, while old Clootie was blowing the bagpipes. Tam got so excited that he roared out to one of the dancers, "Weel done, Cutty Sark!" In a moment all was dark. Tam now spurred his "grey mare Meg" to the top of her speed, while all the fiends chased after him. The river Doon was near, and Tam just reached the middle of the bridge when one of the witches, whom he called Cutty Sark, reached him; but it was too late—he had passed the *middle* of the stream, and was out of the power of the crew. Not so his mare's tail—that had not yet passed the magic line, and Cutty Sark, clinging thereto, dragged it off with an infernal wrench.—R. Burns, *Tam O'Shanter.*

Osi′ris, judge of the dead, brother and husband of Isis. Osiris is identical with Adonis and Thammuz. All three represent the sun, six months above the equator, and six months below it. Adonis passed six months with

Aphroditê in heaven, and six months with Persephŏnê in hell. So Osiris in heaven was the beloved of Isis, but in the land of darkness was embraced by Nepthys.

Osiris, the sun; Isis, the moon.

They [*the priests*] wore rich mitres shaped like the moon,
To show that Isis doth the moon portend,
Like as Osiris signifies the sun.
Spenser, *Faëry Queen*, v. 7 (1596).

Osman, sultan of the East, the great conqueror of the Christians, a man of most magnanimous mind and of noble generosity. He loved Zara, a young Christian captive, and was by her beloved with equal ardor and sincerity. Zara was the daughter of Lusignan d'Outremer, a Christian king of Jerusalem; she was taken prisoner by Osman's father, with her elder brother, Nerestan, then four years old. After twenty years' captivity, Nerestan was sent to France for ransom, and on his return presented himself before the sultan, who fancied he perceived a sort of intimacy between the young man and Zara, which excited his suspicion and jealousy. A letter, begging that Zara would meet him in a "secret passage" of the seraglio, fell into the sultan's hands, and confirmed his suspicions. Zara went to the rendezvous, where Osman met her and stabbed her to the heart. Nerestan was soon brought before him, and told him he had murdered his sister, and all he wanted of her was to tell her of the death of her father, and to bring her his dying benediction. Stung with remorse, Osman liberated all his Christian captives, and then stabbed himself.—Aaron Hill, *Zara* (1735).

*** This tragedy is an English adaptation of Voltaire's *Zaïre* (1733).

Osmand, a necromancer, who, by enchantment, raised up an army to resist the Christians. Six of the champions were enchanted by Osmand, but St. George restored them. Osmand tore off his hair, in which lay his spirit of enchantment, bit his tongue in two, disembowelled himself, cut off his arms, and died.—R. Johnson, *Seven Champions of Christendom*, i. 19 (1617).

Osmond, an old Varangian guard.—Sir W. Scott, *Count Robert of Paris* (time, Rufus).

Osmond (Gilbert), the incarnation of polished selfishness. He deserts one woman, who has sacrificed everything for him, and marries Isabel Archer for her money; eyes his only child as he might a pretty puppet, and sends her back to her convent upon finding that she will not increase his social consequence by marrying an English nobleman.—Henry James, Jr., *Portrait of a Lady* (1881).

Osmyn, *alias* ALPHONSO, son of Anselmo, king of Valentia, and husband of Alme´ria, daughter of Manuel, king of Grana´da. Supposed to have been lost at sea, but in reality cast on the African coast, and tended by Queen Zara, who falls in love with him. Both are taken captive by Manuel, and brought to Granada. Here Manuel falls in love with Zara, but Zara retains her passionate love for Alphonso. Alphonso makes his escape, returns at the head of an army to Granada, finds both the king and Zara dead, but Almeria, being still alive, becomes his acknowledged bride.—W. Congreve, *The Mourning Bride* (1697).

Osric, a court fop, contemptible for his affectation and finical dandyism. He is made umpire by King Claudius, when Laertês and Hamlet "play" with rapiers in "friendly" combat.—Shakespeare, *Hamlet* (1596).

Osse´o, son of the Evening Star, whose wife was O´weenee. In the Northland there were once ten sisters of surpassing beauty; nine married beautiful young husbands, but the youngest, named Oweenee, fixed her affections on Osseo, who was "old, poor and ugly," but "most beautiful within." All being invited to a feast, the nine set upon their youngest sister, taunting her for having married Osseo; but forthwith Osseo leaped into a fallen oak, and was transformed into a most handsome young man, his wife to a very old woman, "wrinkled and ugly," but his love changed not. Soon another change occurred; Oweenee resumed her former beauty, and all the sisters and their husbands were changed to birds, who were kept in cages about Osseo's wigwam. In due time a son was born, and one day he shot an arrow at one of the caged birds, and forthwith the nine, with their husbands, were changed to pygmies.

From the story of Osseo
Let [*us*] learn the fate of jesters.
Longfellow, *Hiawatha*, xii. (1855).

Ossian, the warrior-bard. He was son of Fingal (king of Morven) and his first wife, Ros-crana (daughter of Cormac, king of Ireland).

His wife was Evir-Allen, daughter of Branno (a native of Ireland); and his son was Oscar.

Oswald, steward to Goneril, daughter of King Lear.—Shakespeare, *King Lear* (1605).

Oswald, the cup-bearer to Cedric, the Saxon, of Rotherwood.—Sir W. Scott, *Ivanhoe* (time, Richard I.).

Oswald (Prince), being jealous of Gondibert, his rival for the love of Rhodalind (the heiress of Aribert, king of Lombardy), headed a faction against him. A battle was imminent, but it was determined to decide the quarrel by four combatants on each side. In this combat Oswald was slain by Grondibert.—Sir W. Davenant, *Gondibert*, i. (died 1668).

Othel′lo, the Moor, commander of the Venetian army. Iago was his ensign or ancient. Desdemona, the daughter of Brabantio, the senator, fell in love with the Moor, and he married her; but Iago, by his artful villainy, insinuated to him such a tissue of circumstantial evidence of Desdemona's love for Cassio, that Othello's jealousy being aroused, he smothered her with a pillow, and then killed himself.—Shakespeare, *Othello* (1611).

⁎ The story of this tragedy is taken from the novelletti of Giovanni Giraldi Cinthio (died 1573).

Addison says of Thomas Betterton (1635-1710): "The wonderful agony which he appeared in when he examined the circumstance of the handkerchief in the part of 'Othello,' and the mixture of love that intruded on his mind at the innocent answers of 'Desdemona,' ... were the perfection of acting." Donaldson, in his *Recollections*, says that Spranger Barry (1719-1777) was the beau-ideal of an "Othello;" and C. Leslie, in his *Autobiography*, says the same of Edmund Kean (1787-1833).

Otho, the lord at whose board Count Lara was recognized by Sir Ezzelin. A duel was arranged for the next day, and the contending parties were to meet in Lord Otho's hall. When the time of meeting arrived, Lara presented himself, but no Sir Ezzelin put in his appearance; whereupon Otho, vouching for the knight's honor, fought with the count, and was wounded. On recovering from his wound, Lord Otho became the inveterate enemy of Lara, and accused him openly of having made away with Sir Ezzelin. Lara made himself very popular, and headed a rebellion; but Lord Otho opposed the rebels, and shot him.—Byron, *Lara* (1814).

Otnit, a legendary emperor of Lombardy, who gains the daughter of the soldan for wife, by the help of Elberich, the dwarf.—*The Heldenbuch* (twelfth century).

Otranto (*Tancred, prince of*), a crusader.

Ernest of Otranto, page of the prince of Otranto.—Sir W. Scott, *Count Robert of Paris* (time, Rufus).

Otranto (The Castle of), a romance by Horace Walpole (1769).

O'Trigger (*Sir Lucius*), a fortune-hunting Irishman, ready to fight every one, on any matter, at any time.—Sheridan, *The Rivals* (1775).

Otta′vio (*Don*), the lover of Donna Anna, whom he was about to make his wife, when Don Giovanni seduced her and killed her father (the commandant of the city) in a duel.—Mozart, *Don Giovanni* (opera, 1787).

Otto, duke of Normandy, the victim of Rollo, called "The Bloody Brother."—Beaumont and Fletcher, *The Bloody Brother* (1639).

Ot´uel (*Sir*), a haughty and presumptuous Saracen, miraculously converted. He was a nephew of Ferragus or Ferracute, and married a daughter of Charlemagne.

Ouida, an infantile corruption of Louisa. The full name is Louise de la Ramée, authoress of *Under Two Flags* (1867), and many other novels.

Outalissi, eagle of the Indian tribe of Onei´da, the death-enemies of the Hurons. When the Hurons attacked the fort under the command of Waldegrave (2 *syl.*), a general massacre was made, in which Waldegrave and his wife was slain. But Mrs. Waldegrave, before she died, committed her boy, Henry, to the charge of Outalissi, and told him to place the child in the hands of Albert of Wy´oming, her friend. This Outalissi did. After a lapse of fifteen years, one Brandt, at the head of a mixed army of British and Indians, attacked Oneida, and a general massacre was made; but Outalissi, wounded, escaped to Wyoming, just in time to give warning of the approach of Brandt. Scarcely was this done, when Brandt arrived. Albert and his daughter, Gertrude, were both shot, and the whole settlement was extirpated.—Campbell, *Gertrude of Wyoming* (1809).

Outis (Greek for "nobody"), a name assumed by Odysseus (*Ulysses*) in the cave of Polypheme (3 *syl.*). When the monster roared with pain from the loss of his eye, his brother giants demanded who was hurting him. "Outis" (*Nobody*), thundered out Polypheme, and his companions left him.—Homer, *Odyssey*.

Outram (*Lance*), park-keeper to Sir Geoffrey Peveril.—Sir W. Scott, *Peveril of the Peak* (time, Charles II.).

Overdees (*Rowley*), a highwayman.—Sir W. Scott, *Guy Mannering* (time, George II.).

O´verdo (*Justice*), in Ben Jonson's *Bartholomew Fair* (1614).

Overdone (*Mistress*), a bawd.—Shakespeare, *Measure for Measure* (1603).

Overreach (*Sir Giles*), Wellborn's uncle. An unscrupulous, hard-hearted rascal, grasping and proud. He ruined the estates both of Wellborn and Allworth, and by overreaching grew enormously rich. His ambition was to see his daughter Margaret marry a peer; but the overreacher was overreached. Thinking Wellborn was about to marry the rich dowager Allworth, he not only paid all his debts, but supplied his present wants most liberally, under the delusion "if she prove his, all that is her's is mine." Having thus done, he finds that Lady Allworth does not marry Wellborn, but Lord Lovell. In regard to Margaret, fancying she was sure to marry Lord Lovell, he gives his full consent to her marriage; but finds she returns from church not Lady Lovell, but Mrs. Allworth.—Massinger, *A New Way to Pay Old Debts* (1628).

⁎ The prototype of "Sir Giles Overreach" was Sir Giles Mompesson, a usurer outlawed for his misdeeds.

Overs (*John*), a ferryman who used to ferry passengers from Southwark to the City, and accumulated a considerable hoard of money by his savings. On one occasion, to save the expenses of board, he simulated death, expecting his servants would fast till he was buried; but they broke into his larder and cellar and held riot. When the old miser could bear it no longer he started up and belabored his servants right and left; but one of them struck the old man with an oar and killed him.

Mary Overs, the beautiful daughter of the ferryman. Her lover, hastening to town, was thrown from his horse, and died. She then became a nun, and founded the church of St. Mary Overs on the site of her father's house.

Overton (*Colonel*), one of Cromwell's officers.—Sir W. Scott, *Woodstock* (time, Commonwealth).

Ovid (*The French*), Du Bellay; also called "The Father of Grace and Elegance" (1524-1560).

Ovid and Corinna. Ovid disguises, under the name of Corinna, the daughter of Augustus, named Julia, noted for her beauty, talent and licentiousness. Some say that Corinna was Livia, the wife of Augustus.—*Amor.*, i. 5.

So was her heavenly body comely raised
On two faire columnes; those that Ovid praised
In Julia's borrowed name.

O'wain (*Sir*), the Irish knight of King Stephen's court, who passed through St. Patrick's purgatory by way of penance.—Henry of Saltrey, *The Descent of Owain* (1153).

O'weenee, the youngest of ten sisters, all of surpassing beauty. She married Osseo, who was "old, poor, and ugly," but "most beautiful within." (See OSSEO.)—Longfellow, *Hiawatha*, xii. (1855).

Owen (*Sam*), groom of Darsie Latimer, *i.e.* Sir Arthur Darsie Redgauntlet.—Sir W. Scott, *Redgauntlet* (time, George III.).

Owen, confidential clerk of Mr. Osbaldistone, senior.—Sir W. Scott, *Rob Roy* (time, George I.).

Owen (*Sir*), passed in dream through St. Patrick's purgatory. He passed the convent gate, and the warden placed him in a coffin. When the priests had sung over him the service of the dead, they placed the coffin in a cave, and Sir Owen made his descent. He came first to an ice desert, and received three warnings to retreat, but the warnings were not heeded, and a mountain of ice fell on him. "Lord, Thou canst save!" he cried, as the ice fell, and the solid mountain became like dust, and did Sir Owen no harm. He next came to a lake of fire, and a demon pushed him in. "Lord, Thou canst save!" he cried, and angels carried him to paradise. He woke with ecstacy, and found himself lying before the cavern's mouth.—R. Southey, *St. Patrick's Purgatory* (from the *Fabliaux* of M. le Grand.

Owen Meredith, Robert Bulwer Lytton, afterwards Lord Lytton, son of the poet and novelist (1831-1892).

Owl (*The*), sacred to Minerva, was the emblem of Athens.

Owls hoot in Bb and Gb, or in F♯ and Ab.—Rev. G. White, *Natural History of Selborne*, xlv. (1789).

Owl a Baker's Daughter (*The*). Our Lord once went into a baker's shop to ask for bread. The mistress instantly put a cake in the oven for Him, but the daughter, thinking it to be too large, reduced it to half the size. The dough, however, swelled to an enormous bulk, and the daughter cried out, "Heugh! heugh! heugh!" and was transformed into an owl.

Well, God 'ield you! They say the owl was a baker's daughter.—Shakespeare, *Hamlet* (1596).

Ox (*The Dumb*), St. Thomas Aqui´nas; so named by his fellow-students on account of his taciturnity (1224-1274).

An ox once spoke as learned men deliver.—Beaumont and Fletcher, *Rule a Wife and Have a Wife*, iii. 1 (1640).

Ox. The black ox hath trod on his foot, he has married and is hen-pecked; calamity has befallen him. The black ox was sacrificed to the infernals, and was consequently held accursed. When Tusser says the best way to thrive is to get married, the objector says:

Why, then, do folk this proverb put,
"The black ox near trod on thy foot,"
If that way were to thrive?
Wiving and Thriving, lvii. (1557).

The black oxe had not trode on his or her foote;
But ere his branch of blesse could reach any roote,
The flowers so faded that in fifteen weekes
A man might copy the change in the cheekes

Both of the poore wretch and his wife.
Heywood (1646).

Oxford (*John, earl of*), an exiled Lancastrian. He appears with his son Arthur as a travelling merchant, under the name of Philipson.

⁎ *The son of the merchant Philipson* is Sir Arthur de Vere.

The countess of Oxford, wife of the earl.—Sir W. Scott, *Anne of Geierstein* (time, Edward IV.).

Oxford (*The young earl of*), in the court of Queen Elizabeth.—Sir W. Scott, *Kenilworth* (time, Elizabeth).

Ozair (2 *syl.*), a prophet. One day, riding on an ass by the ruins of Jerusalem, after its destruction by the Chaldeans, he doubted in his mind whether God could raise the city up again. Whereupon God caused him to die, and he remained dead a hundred years, but was then restored to life. He found the basket of figs and cruse of wine as fresh as when he died, but his ass was a mass of bones. While he still looked, the dry bones came together, received life, and the resuscitated ass began to bray. The prophet no longer doubted the power of God to raise up Jerusalem from its ruins.—*Al Korân*, ii. (Sale's notes).

⁎ This legend is based on *Neh.* ii. 12-20.

PLACENTICUS, the Dominican, wrote a poem of 253 Latin hexameters, called *Pugna Porcorum*, every word of which begins with the letter *p* (died 1548). It begins thus:

Plaudite, Porcelli, porcorum pigra propago
Progreditur ... etc.

There was one composed in honor of Charles le Chauve, every word of which began with *c*.

The best known alliterative poem in English is the following:—

An Austrian army, awfully arrayed,
Boldly by battery besieged Belgrade.
Cossack commanders, cannonading, come,
Dealing destruction's devastating doom;
Every endeavor engineers essay
For fame, for fortune, forming furious fray.
Gaunt gunners grapple, giving gashes good;
Heaves high his head heroic hardihood.
Ibraham, Islam, Ismael, imps in ill,
Jostle John, Jarovlitz, Jem, Joe, Jack, Jill;
Kick kindling Kutusoff, kings' kinsmen kill;

Labor low levels loftiest, longest lines;
Men march 'mid moles, 'mid mounds, 'mid murderous mines.
Now nightfall's nigh, now needful nature nods,
Opposed, opposing, overcoming odds.
Poor peasants, partly purchased, partly pressed,
Quite quaking, "Quarter! Quarter!" quickly quest.
Reason returns, recalls redundant rage,
Saves sinking soldiers, softens signiors sage.
Truce, Turkey, truce! truce, treacherous Tartar train!
Unwise, unjust, unmerciful Ukraine!
Vanish, vile vengeance! vanish, victory vain!
Wisdom walls war—wails warring words. What were
Xerxes, Xantippê, Ximenês, Xavier?
Yet Yassy's youth, ye yield your youthful yest
Zealously, zanies, zealously, zeal's zest.
From H. Southgate, *Many Thoughts on Many Things*.

Tusser has a poem of twelve lines, in rhyme, every word of which begins with *t*. The subject is on *Thriftiness* (died 1580).

P's (*The Five*), William Oxberry, printer, poet, publisher, publican and player (1784-1824).

Pache (*J. Nicolas*), a Swiss by birth. He was minister of war in 1792, and maire de Paris 1793. Pache hated the Girondists, and at the fall of Danton, was imprisoned. After his liberation, he retired to Thym-le-Moutiers (in the Ardennes), and died in obscurity (1740-1823).

Swiss Pache sits sleek-headed, frugal, the wonder of his own ally for humility of mind.... Sit there, Tartuffe, till wanted.—Carlyle.

Pacific (*The*), Amadeus VIII., count of Savoy (1383, 1391-1439, abdicated, and died 1451).

Frederick III., emperor of Germany (1415, 1440-1493).

Olaus III. of Norway (*, 1030-1093).

Pac'olet, a dwarf, "full of great sense and subtle ingenuity." He had an enchanted horse, made of wood, with which he carried off Valentine, Orson and Clerimond from the dungeon of Ferrăgus. This horse is often alluded to. "To ride Pacolet's horse" is a phrase for *going very fast.—Valentine and Orson*, fifteenth century).

Pacolet, a familiar spirit.—Steele, *The Tatler* (1709).

Pacolet, or NICK STRUMPFER, the dwarf servant of Norna "of the Fitful Head."—Sir W. Scott, *The Pirate* (time William III.).

Pacomo (*St.*), an Egyptian, who lived in the fourth century. It is said that he could walk among serpents unhurt; and when he had occasion to cross the Nile, he was carried on the back of a crocodile.

The hermit fell on his knees before an image of St. Pacomo, which was glued to the wall.—Lesage, *Gil Blas*, iv. 9 (1724).

Paddington (*Harry*), one of Macheath's gang of thieves. Peachum describes him as a "poor, petty-larceny rascal, without the least genius. That fellow," he says, "though he were to live for six months, would never come to the gallows with credit" (act i. 1).—Gay, *The Beggar's Opera* (1727).

Paddy, an Irishman. A corruption of *Padhrig*, Irish for Patrick.

Padlock (*The*), a comic opera by Bickerstaff. Don Diego (2 *syl.*), a wealthy lord of 60, saw a country maiden named Leonora, to whom he took a fancy, and arranged with the parents to take her home with him and place her under the charge of a duenna for three months, to see if her temper was as sweet as her face was pretty; and then either "to return her to them spotless, or make her his lawful wife." At the expiration of the time, the don went to arrange with the parents for the wedding, and locked up his house, giving the keys to Ursula, the duenna. To make assurance doubly sure, he put a padlock on the outer door, and took the key with him. Leander, a young student, smitten with the damsel, laughed at locksmiths and duennas, and, having gained admission into the house, was detected by Don Diego, who returned unexpectedly. The old don, being a man of sense, perceived that Leander was a more suitable bridegroom than himself, so he not only sanctioned the alliance, but gave Leonora a handsome wedding dowry (1768).

Pæan, the physician of the immortals.

Pæa´na, daughter of Corflambo, "fair as ever yet saw living eye," but "too loose of life and eke too light." Pæana fell in love with Amĭas, a captive in her father's dungeon; but Amias had no heart to give away. When Placĭdae was brought captive before Pæana, she mistook him for Amias, and married him. The poet adds, that she thenceforth so reformed her ways "that all men much admired the change, and spake her praise."—Spenser, *Faëry Queen*, iv. 9 (1596).

Pagan, a fay who loved the Princess Imis; but Imis rejected his suit, as she loved her cousin, Philax. Pagan, out of revenge, shut them up in a superb crystal palace, which contained every delight except that of leaving it. In the course of a few years, Imis and Philax longed as much for a separation as, at one time, they wished to be united.—Comtesse D'Aunoy, *Fairy Tales* ("Palace of Revenge," 1682).

Page (*Mr.*), a gentleman living at Windsor. When Sir John Falstaff made love to Mrs. Page, Page himself assumed the name of Brooke, to outwit the knight. Sir John told the supposed Brooke his whole "course of wooing," and how nicely he was bamboozling the husband. On one occasion, he says, "I was carried out in a buck-basket of dirty linen before the very eyes of Page, and the deluded husband did not know it." Of course, Sir John is thoroughly outwitted and played upon, being made the butt of the whole village.

Mrs. Page, wife of Mr. Page of Windsor. When Sir John Falstaff made love to her, she joined with Mrs. Ford to dupe him and punish him.

Anne Page, daughter of the above, in love with Fenton. Slender calls her "the sweet Anne Page."

William Page, Anne's brother, a schoolboy.—Shakespeare, *Merry Wives of Windsor* (1595).

Page (*Sir Francis*), called "The Hanging Judge" (1661-1741).

Slander and poison dread from Delia's rage;
Hard words or hanging if your judge be Page.
Pope.

Page (*Ruth*). A dainty little miss, bright, happy and imaginative, called sometimes "Teenty-Taunty." Her head is full of fairy-lore, and when she tumbles into the water one day, she dreams in her swoon of Fairy-Land and the wonders thereof, of a bunch of forget-me-nots she was to keep alive if she would have her mother live, and so many other marvellous things, that her distressed father opines that "the poor child would be rational enough, if she had not read so many fairy-books."—John Neal, *Goody Gracious and the Forget-me-not* (183-).

Paget (*The Lady*), one of the ladies of the bedchamber in Queen Elizabeth's court.—Sir W. Scott, *Kenilworth* (time, Elizabeth).

Paine (*Squire*). "Hard-headed, hard fe'tured Yankee," whose conversion to humanity and Christianity is effected by Roxanna Keep.

She "drilled the hole, an' put in the powder of the Word, an' tamped it down with some pretty stiff facts ... but *the Lord fired the blast Himself*."—Rose Terry Cooke, *Somebody's Neighbors* (1881).

Painter of Nature. Remi Belleau, one of the Pleiad poets, is so called (1528-1577).

The Shepheardes Calendar, by Spenser, is largely borrowed from Belleau's *Song of April*.

Painter of the Graces. Andrea Appiani (1754-1817).

Painters.

A Bee. Quentin Matsys, the Dutch painter, painted a bee so well that the artist Mandyn thought it a real bee, and proceeded to brush it away with his handkerchief (1450-1529).

A Cow. Myro carved a cow so true to nature that bulls mistook it for a living animal (B.C. 431).

A Curtain. Parrhasios painted a curtain so admirably that even Zeuxis, the artist, mistook it for real drapery (B.C. 400).

A Fly. George Alexander Stevens says, in his *Lectures on Heads*:

I have heard of a connoisseur who was one day in an auction-room where there was an inimitable piece of painting of fruits and flowers. The connoisseur would not give his opinion of the picture till he had first examined the catalogue; and, finding it was done by an Englishman, he pulled out his eye-glass. "Oh, sir," says he, "those English fellows have no more idea of genius than a Dutch skipper has of dancing a cotillion. The dog has spoiled a fine piece of canvas; he is worse than a Harp Alley signpost dauber. There's no keeping, no perspective, no foreground. Why, there now, the fellow has actually attempted to paint a fly upon that rosebud. Why, it is no more like a fly than I am like—;" but, as he approached his finger to the picture, the fly flew away (1772)

Grapes. Zeuxis (2 *syl.*) a Grecian painter, painted some grapes so well that birds came and pecked at them, thinking them real grapes (B.C. 400).

A Horse. Apellês painted Alexander's horse Bucephalos so true to life that some mares came up to the canvas neighing, under the supposition that it was a real animal (about B.C. 334).

A Man. Velasquez painted a Spanish admiral so true to life that when King Felipe IV. entered the studio he mistook the painting for the man, and began reproving the supposed officer for neglecting his duty in wasting his time in the studio, when he ought to have been with his fleet (1590-1660).

Accidental effects in painting.

Apellês, being at a loss to paint the foam of Alexander's horse, dashed his brush at the picture in a fit of annoyance, and did by accident what his skill had failed to do (about B.C. 334).

The same tale is told of Protog´enês, who dashed his brush at a picture, and thus produced "the foam of a dog's mouth," which he had long been trying in vain to represent (about B.C. 332).

Painters (Prince of). Parrhasios and Apellês are both so called (fourth century B.C.).

Painters' Characteristics.

ANGELO (*Michael*): an iron frame, strongly developed muscles, and an anatomical display of the human figure. The Æschylos of painters (1474-1564).

CARRACCI: eclectic artists, who picked out and pieced together parts taken from Correggio, Raphael, Titian and other great artists. If Michael Angelo is the Æschylos of artists, and Raphael the Sophoclês, the Carracci may be called the Euripidês of painters. I know not why in England the name is spelt with only one *r*.

CORREGGIO: known by his wonderful foreshortenings, his magnificent light and shade. He is, however, very monotonous (1494-1534).

CROME (*John*): an old woman in a red cloak walking up an avenue of trees (1769-1821).

DAVID: noted for his stiff, dry, pedantic, "highly classic" style, according to the interpretation of the phrase by the French in the first Revolution (1748-1825).

DOLCE (*Cario*): famous for his Madonnas, which were all finished with most extraordinary delicacy (1616-1686).

DOMENICHI'NO: famed for his frescoes, correct in design and fresh in coloring (1581-1614).

GUIDO: his specialty is a pallid or bluish-complexioned saint, with saucer or uplifted eyes (1574-1642).

HOLBEIN: characterized by bold relief, exquisite finish, force of conception, delicacy of tone, and dark background (1498-1554).

LORRAINE (*Claude*): a Greek temple on a hill, with sunny and highly finished classic scenery. Aerial perspective (1600-1682).

MURILLO: a brown-faced Madonna (1618-1682).

OMMEGANCK: sheep (1775-1826).

PERUGINO (*Pietro*): known by his narrow, contracted figures and scrimpy drapery (1446-1524).

POUSSIN: famous for his classic style. Reynolds says: "No works of any modern have so much the air of antique painting as those of Poussin" (1593-1665).

POUSSIN *(Gaspar)*: a landscape painter, the very opposite of Claude Lorraine. He seems to have drawn his inspiration from Hervey's *Meditations Among the Tombs,* Blair's *Grave,* Young's *Night Thoughts,* and Burton's *Anatomy of Melancholy* (1613-1675).

RAPHAEL: the Sophoclês of painters. Angelo's figures are all gigantesque and ideal, like those of Æschylos. Raphael's are perfect human beings (1483-1520).

REYNOLDS: a portrait-painter. He presents his portraits in *bal masqué*, not always suggestive either of the rank or character of the person represented. There is about the same analogy between Watteau and Reynolds as between Claude Lorraine and Gaspar Poussin (1723-1792).

ROSA *(Salvator)*: dark, inscrutable pictures, relieved by dabs of palette-knife. He is fond of savage scenery, broken rocks, wild caverns, blasted heaths, and so on (1615-1673).

RUBENS: patches of vermillion dabbed about the human figure, wholly out of harmony with the rest of the coloring (1577-1640).

STEEN *(Jan)*: an old woman peeling vegetables, with another old woman looking at her (1636-1679).

TINTORETTI: full of wild fantastical inventions. He is called "The Lightning of the Pencil" (1512-1594).

TITIAN: noted for his broad shades of divers gradations (1477-1576).

VERONESE *(Paul)*: noted for his great want of historical correctness and elegance of design; but he abounds in spirited banquets, sumptuous edifices, brilliant aerial spectres, magnificent robes, gaud, and jewelry (1530-1588).

WATTEAU: noted for his *fêtes galantes,* fancy-ball costumes, and generally gala-day figures (1684-1721).

Paix des Dames *(La)*, the treaty of peace concluded at Cambray in 1529, between François I. of France and Karl V., emperor of Germany. So called because it was mainly negotiated by Louise of Savoy (mother of the French king), and Margaret, the emperor's aunt.

Palabras Carinosas.

"Good-night! I have to say good-night
To such a host of peerless things!
Good-night unto the fragile hand
All queenly with its weight of rings;
Good-night to fond uplifted eyes,
Good-night to chestnut braids of hair,

Good-night unto the perfect mouth
And all the sweetness nestled there,—
The snowy hand detains me,—then
I'll have to say Good-night again!"
Thomas Bailey Aldrich, *Poems*, 1858-84.

Paladore, a Briton in the service of the king of Lombardy. One day, in a boar-hunt, the boar turned on the Princess Sophia, and, having gored her horse to death, was about to attack the lady, but was slain by the young Briton. Between these two young people a strong attachment sprang up; but the Duke Bire′no, by an artifice of false impersonation, induced Paladore to believe that the princess was a wanton, and had the audacity to accuse her as such to the senate. In Lombardy, the punishment for this offence was death, and the princess was ordered to execution. Paladore, having learned the truth, accused the duke of villainy. They fought, and Bireno fell. The princess, being cleared of the charge, married Paladore.—Robert Jephson, *The Law of Lombardy* (1779).

Palame′des (4 *syl.*), son of Nauplios, was, according to Suidas, the inventor of dice. (See ALEA.)

Palamedes (*Sir*), a Saracen, who adored Isolde, the wife of King Mark of Cornwall. Sir Tristram also loved the same lady, who was his aunt. The two "lovers" fought, and Sir Palamedês, being overcome, was compelled to turn Christian. He was baptized, and Sir Tristram stood his sponsor at the font.— Thomas of Erceldoune, called "The Rhymer," *Sir Tristram* (thirteenth century).

Palame′des of Lombardy, one of the allies of the Christian army in the first crusade. He was shot by Corinda with an arrow (bk. xi.).—Tasso, *Jerusalem Delivered* (1575).

Palamon and Arcite (2 *syl.*), two young Theban knights, who fell into the hands of Duke Theseus (2 *syl.*), and were by him confined in a dungeon at Athens. Here they saw the duke's sister-in-law, Emily, with whom both fell in love. When released from captivity, the two knights told to the duke their tale of love; and the duke promised that whichever proved the victor in single combat, should have Emily for his prize. Arcite prayed to Mars "for victory," and Palamon to Venus that he might "obtain the lady," and both their prayers were granted. Arcite won the victory, according to his prayer, but, being thrown from his horse, died; so Palamon, after all, "won the lady," though he did not win the battle.—Chaucer, *Canterbury Tales* ("The Knight's Tale," 1388).

This tale is taken from the *Le Teseide* of Boccaccio.

The Black Horse, a drama by John Fletcher, is the same tale. Richard Edwards has a comedy called *Palæmon and Arcyte* (1566).

Pale (*The*), or THE ENGLISH PALE, a part of Ireland, including Dublin, Meath, Carlow, Kilkenny and Louth.

Pale Faces. So the American Indians call the European settlers.

Pale′mon, son of a rich merchant. He fell in love with Anna, daughter of Albert, master of one of his father's ships. The purse-proud merchant, indignant at this, tried every means to induce his son to abandon such a "mean connection," but without avail; so at last he sent him in the *Britannia* (Albert's ship) "in charge of the merchandise." The ship was wrecked near Cape Colonna, in Attica; and although Palēmon escaped, his ribs were so broken that he died almost as soon as he reached the shore.

A gallant youth, Palemon was his name,
Charged with the commerce hither also came;
A father's stern resentment doomed to prove,
He came, the victim of unhappy love.
Falconer, *The Shipwreck*, i. 2 (1756).

Pale′mon and Lavinia, a poetic version of Boaz and Ruth. "The lovely young Lavinia" went to glean in the fields of young Palemon, "the pride of swains;" and Palemon, falling in love with the beautiful gleaner, both wooed and won her.—Thomson, *The Seasons* ("Autumn," 1730).

Pales (2 *syl.*), god of shepherds and their flocks.—*Roman Mythology.*

Pomōna loves the orchard;
And Liber loves the vine;
And Palês loves the straw-built shed,
Warm with the breath of kine.
Lord Macaulay, *Lays of Ancient Rome* ("Prophecy of Capys," 1842).

Pal′inode (3 *syl.*), a shepherd in Spenser's *Eclogues*. In ecl. v. Palinode represents the Catholic priest. He invites Piers (who represents the Protestant clergy) to join in the fun and pleasures of May. Piers then warns the young man of the vanities of the world, and tells him of the great degeneracy of pastoral life, at one time simple and frugal, but now discontented and licentious. He concludes with the fable of the kid and her dam. The fable is this: A mother-goat, going abroad for the day, told her kid to keep at home, and not to open the door to strangers. She had not been gone long when up came a fox, with head bound from "headache," and foot bound from "gout," and carrying a ped of trinkets. The fox told the kid a most piteous tale, and showed her a little mirror. The kid, out of pity and vanity, opened the door; but while stooping over the ped to pick up a little bell, the fox clapped down the lid and carried her off.

In ecl. vii. Palinode is referred to by the shepherd Thomalin, as "lording it over God's heritage," feeding the sheep with chaff, and keeping for himself the grains.—Spenser, *Shepheardes Calendar* (1572).

Palinode (3 *syl.*), a poem in recantation of a calumny. Stesich´oros wrote a bitter satire against Helen, for which her brothers, Castor and Pollux, plucked out his eyes. When, however, the poet recanted, his sight was restored to him again.

The bard who libelled Helen in his song,
Recanted after, and redressed the wrong.
Ovid, *Art of Love*, iii.

Horace's *Ode*, xvi. i. is a palinode. Samuel Butler has a palinode, in which he recanted what he said in a previous poem of the Hon. Edward Howard. Dr. Watts recanted in a poem the *praise* he had previously bestowed on Queen Anne.

Palinu´rus, the pilot of Æne´as. Palinurus, sleeping at the helm, fell into the sea and was drowned. The name is employed as a generic word for a steersman or pilot, and sometimes for a chief minister. Thus, Prince Bismarck might have been called the palinurus of William, emperor of Germany and king of Prussia.

More had she spoke, but yawned. All nature nods ...
E'en Palinurus nodded at the helm.
Pope, *The Dunciad*, iv. 614 (1742).

Palisse (*La*), a sort of M. Prudhomme; a pompous utterer of truisms and moral platitudes.

Palissy (*Bernard, the potter*), succeeded, after innumerable efforts and privations, in inventing the art of enamelling stone ware. He was arrested and confined in the Bastille for Huguenot principles, and died there in 1589.

Palla´dio (*Andrea*), the Italian classical architect (1518-1580).

The English Palladio, Inigo Jones (1573-1653).

Palla´dium.

Of Ceylon, the deláda or tooth of Buddha, preserved in the Malegawa temple at Kandy. Natives guard it with great jealousy, from a belief that whoever possesses it acquires the right to govern Ceylon. When, in 1815, the English obtained possession of the tooth, the Ceylonese submitted to them without resistance.

Of Eden Hall, a drinking-glass, in the possession of Sir Christopher Musgrave, Bart., of Edenhall, Cumberland.

Of Jerusalem. Aladine, king of Jerusalem, stole an image of the Virgin, and set it up in a mosque, that she might no longer protect the Christians, but become the palladium of Jerusalem. The image was rescued by Sophronia, and the city taken by the crusaders.

Of Meg´ara, a golden hair of King Nisus. Scylla promised to deliver the city into the hands of Minos, and cut off the talismanic lock of her father's head while he was asleep.

Of Rome, the ancīle or sacred buckler which Numa said fell from heaven, and was guarded by priests called Salii.

Of Scotland, the great stone of Scone, near Perth, which was removed by Edward I. to Westminster, and is still there, preserved in the coronation chair.

Of Troy, a colossal wooden statue of Pallas Minerva, which "fell from heaven." It was carried off by the Greeks, by whom the city was taken, and burned to the ground.

Pallet, a painter, in Smollett's novel of *Peregrine Pickle* (1751).

The absurdities of Pallet are painted an inch thick, and by no human possibility could such an accumulation of comic disasters have befallen the characters of the tale.

Pal´merin of England, the hero and title of a romance in chivalry. There is also an inferior one entitled *Palmerin d'Oliva*.

The next two books were *Palmerin d'Ol´iva* and *Palmerin of England*. "The former," said the curé, "shall be torn in pieces and burnt to the last ember; but *Palmerin of England* shall be preserved as a relique of antiquity, and placed in such a chest as Alexander found amongst the spoils of Darius, and in which he kept the writings of Homer. This same book is valuable for two things: first, for its own especial excellency, and next because it is the production of a Portuguese monarch, famous for his literary talents. The adventures of the castle of Miraguarda therein, are finely imagined, the style of composition is natural and elegant, and the utmost decorum is preserved throughout."—Cervantes, *Don Quixote*, I. i. 6 (1605).

Palmi´ra, daughter of Alcānor, chief of Mecca. She and her brother, Zaphna, were taken captives in infancy, and brought up by Mahomet. As they grew in years they fell in love with each other, not knowing their relationship; but when Mahomet laid siege to Mecca, Zaphna was appointed to assassinate Alcanor, and was himself afterwards killed by poison. Mahomet then proposed marriage to Palmira, but to prevent such an alliance, she killed herself.—James Miller, *Mahomet, the Impostor* (1740).

Pal'myrene (*The*), Zenobia, queen of Palmyra, who claimed the title of "Queen of the East." She was defeated by Aurelian, and taken prisoner (A.D. 273). Longinus lived at her court, and was put to death on the capture of Zenobia.

The Palmyrene that fought Aurelian.
Tennyson, *The Princess*, ii. (1847).

Pal'omides (*Sir*), son and heir of Sir Astlabor. His brothers were Sir Safire and Sir Segwar'idês. He is always called the Saracen, meaning "unchristened." Next to the three great knights (Sir Launcelot, Sir Tristram, and Sir Lamorake), he was the strongest and bravest of the fellowship of the Round Table. Like Sir Tristram, he was in love with La Belle Isond, wife of King Mark, of Cornwall; but the lady favored the love of Sir Tristram, and only despised that of the Saracen knight. After his combat with Sir Tristram, Sir Palomides consented to be baptized by the bishop of Carlisle (pt. iii. 28).

He was well made, cleanly and bigly, and neither too young nor too old. And though he was not christened, yet he believed in the best manners, and was faithful and true of his promise, and also well conditioned. He made a vow that he would never be christened unto the time that he achieved the beast Glatisaint.... And also he avowed never to take full christendom unto the time that he had done seven battles within the lists.—Sir T. Malory, *History of Prince Arthur*, ii. 149 (1470).

Pam, Henry John Temple, viscount Palmerston (1784-1865).

Pam'ela. Lady Edward Fitzgerald is so called (*-1831).

Pam'ela [ANDREWS], a simple, unsophisticated country girl, the daughter of two aged parents, and maid-servant of a rich young squire, called B, who tries to seduce her. She resists every temptation, and at length marries the young squire, and reforms him. Pamela is very pure and modest, bears her afflictions with much meekness, and is a model of maidenly prudence and rectitude. The story is told in a series of letters which Pamela sends to her parents.—S. Richardson, *Pamela*, or *Virtue Rewarded* (1740).

The pure and modest character of the English maiden [*Pamela*] is so well maintained, ... her sorrows and afflictions are borne with so much meekness; her little intervals of hope ... break in on her troubles so much like the specks of blue sky through a cloudy atmosphere—that the whole recollection is soothing, tranquilizing, and doubtless edifying.—Sir W. Scott.

Pamela is a work of much humbler pretensions than *Clarissa Harlowe*.... A simple country girl whom her master attempts to seduce, and afterwards marries.... The wardrobe of poor Pamela, her gown of sad-colored stuff, and her round-eared caps; her various attempts at escape, and the conveyance of her letters; the hateful character of Mrs. Jewkes, and the fluctuating passions of her master before the better part of his nature obtains ascendancy—these are all touched with the hand of a master.—Chambers, *English Literature*, ii. 161.

Pamina and Tam´ino, the two lovers who were guided by "the magic flute" through all worldly dangers to the knowledge of divine truth (or the mysteries of Iris).—Mosart, *Die Zauberflöte* (1790).

Pamphlet (*Mr.*), a penny-a-liner. His great wish was "to be taken up for sedition." He writes on both sides, for as he says, he has "two hands, *ambo dexter.*"

"Time has been," he says, "when I could turn a penny by an earthquake, or live upon a jail distemper, or dine upon a bloody murder; but now that's all over—nothing will do now but roasting a minister, or telling the people they are ruined. The people of England are never so happy as when you tell them they are ruined."—Murphy, *The Upholsterer*, ii. 1 (1758).

Pan, Nature personified, especially the vital crescent power of nature.

Universal Pan.
Knit with the Graces and the Hours in dance,
Led on the eternal spring.
Milton, *Paradise Lost*, iv. 266, etc. (1665).

Pan, in Spenser's ecl. iv., is Henry VIII., and "Syrinx" is Anne Boleyn. In ecl. v. "Pan" stands for Jesus Christ in one passage, and for God the Father in another.—Spenser, *Shepheardes Calendar* (1572).

Pan (*The Great*), François M. A. de Voltaire; also called "The Dictator of Letters" (1694-1778).

Pancaste (3 *syl.*), or CAMPASPE, one of the concubines of Alexander the Great. Apellés fell in love with her while he was employed in painting the king of Macedon, and Alexander, out of regard to the artist, gave her to him for a wife. Apellês selected for his "Venus Rising from the Sea" (usually called "Venus Anadyomênê") this beautiful Athenian woman, together with Phrynê, another courtezan.

** Phrynê was also the academy figure for the "Cnidian Venus" of Praxitĕlês.

Pancks, a quick, short, eager, dark man, with too much "way." He dressed in black and rusty iron grey; had jet-black beads for eyes, a scrubby little black chin, wiry black hair striking out from his head in prongs like hair-pins, and a complexion that was very dingy by nature, or very dirty by art, or a compound of both. He had dirty hands, and dirty, broken nails, and looked as if he had been in the coals. He snorted and sniffed, and puffed and blew, and was generally in a perspiration. It was Mr. Pancks who "moled out" the secret that Mr. Dorrit, imprisoned for debt in the Marshalsea prison, was heir-at-law to a great estate, which had long lain unclaimed, and was extremely rich (ch. xxxv.). Mr. Pancks also induced Clennam to invest in Merdle's bank shares, and demonstrated by figures the profit he would realize; but the bank being a bubble the shares were worthless.—C. Dickens, *Little Dorrit* (1857).

Pancrace, a doctor of the Aristotelian school. He maintained that it was improper to speak of the "*form* of a hat," because form "est la disposition extérieure des corps qui sont animés," and therefore we should say the "*figure* of a hat," because figure "est la disposition extérieure des corps qui sont inanimés;" and because his adversary could not agree, he called him "un ignorant, un ignorantissime, ignorantifiant, et ignorantifiè" (sc. viii.).— Molière, *Le Mariage Forcé* (1664).

Pancras (*The earl of*), one of the skillful companions of Barlow, the famous archer; another was called the "Marquis of Islington;" while Barlow himself was mirthfully created by Henry VIII., "Duke of Shoreditch."

Pancras (*St.*), patron saint of children, martyred by Diocletian at the age of 14 (A.D. 304).

Pan´darus, the Lycian, one of the allies of Priam in the Trojan war. He is drawn under two widely different characters: In classic story he is depicted as an admirable archer, slain by Diomed, and honored as a hero-god in his own country; but in mediæval romance he is represented as a despicable pimp, insomuch that the word *pander* is derived from his name. Chaucer, in his *Troïlus and Cresseide*, and Shakespeare, in his drama of *Troilus and Cressida*, represent him as procuring for Troilus the good graces of Cressid, and in *Much Ado About Nothing*, it is said that Troilus "was the first employer of pandars."

Pandemo´nium, "the high capital of Satan and his peers." Here the infernal parliament was held, and to this council Satan convened the fallen angels to consult with him upon the best method of encompassing the "fall of man." Satan ultimately undertook to visit the new world; and, in the disguise of a serpent, he tempted Eve to eat of the forbidden fruit.—Milton, *Paradise Lost*, ii. (1665).

Pandi´on, king of Athens, father of Procnê and Philome´la.

None take pity on thy pain;
Senseless trees, they cannot hear thee;
Ruthless bears, they will not cheer thee;

King Pandion he is dead;
All thy friends are lapped in lead.
Richard Barnfield, *Address to the Nightingale* (1594).

Pandolf (*Sir Harry*), the teller of whole strings of stories, which he repeats at every gathering. He has also a stock of *bon-mots*. "Madam," said he, "I have lost by you to-day." "How so, Sir Harry!" replies the lady. "Why, madam," rejoins the baronet, "I have lost an excellent appetite." "This is the thirty-third time that Sir Harry hath been thus arch."

We are constantly, after supper, entertained with the Glastonbury Thorn. When we have wondered at that a little, "Father," saith the son, "let us have the Spirit in the Wood." After that, "Now tell us how you served the robber." "Alack!" saith Sir Harry, with a smile, "I have almost forgotten that; but it is a pleasant conceit, to be sure;" and accordingly he tells that and twenty more in the same order over and over again.—Richard Steele.

Pandolfe (2 *syl.*), father of Lélie.—Molière, *L'Etourdi* (1653).

Pando′ra, the "all-gifted woman." So called because all the gods bestowed some gift on her to enhance her charms. Jove sent her to Prometheus for a wife, but Hermês gave her in marriage to his brother, Epime′theus (4 *syl.*). It is said that Pandora enticed the curiosity of Epimetheus to open a box in her possession, from which flew out all the ills that flesh is heir to. Luckily the lid was closed in time to prevent the escape of Hope.

More lovely than Pandora, whom the gods
Endowed with all their gifts, ... to the unwiser son
Of Japhet brought by Hermês, she ensnared
Mankind with her fair looks, to be avenged
On him [*Promētheus*] who had stole Jove's ... fire.
Milton, *Paradise Lost*, iv. 714, etc. (1665).

⁎ "Unwiser son" is a Latinism, and means "not so wise as he should have been;" so *audacior, timidior, vehementior, iracundior*, etc.

Pandos′to, or *The Triumph of Time*, a tale by Robert Greene (1588), the quarry of the plot of *The Winter's Tale* by Shakespeare.

Panel (*The*), by J. Kemble, is a modified version of Bickerstaff's comedy *'Tis Well 'tis no Worse*. It contains the popular quotation:

Perhaps it was right to dissemble your love;
But why do you kick me downstairs?

Pangloss (*Dr. Peter*), an LL.D. and A.S.S. He began life as a muffin-maker in Milk Alley. Daniel Dowlas, when he was raised from the chandler's shop in Gosport to the peerage, employed the doctor "to larn him to talk English;"

and subsequently made him tutor to his son Dick, with a salary of £300 a year. Dr. Pangloss was a literary prig of ponderous pomposity. He talked of a "locomotive morning," of one's "sponsorial and patronymic appellations," and so on; was especially fond of quotations, to all of which he assigned the author, as "Lend me your ears. Shakespeare. Hem!" or "*Verbum sat.* Horace. Hem!" He also indulged in an affected "He! he!"—G. Colman, *The Heir-at-Law* (1797).

A.S.S. stands for *Artium Societatis Socius* ("Fellow of the Society of Arts").

Pangloss, an optimist philosopher. (The word means "All Tongue.")—Voltaire, *Candide*.

Panjam, a male idol of the Oroungou tribes of Africa; his wife is Alēka, and his priests are called *panjans*. Panjam is the special protector of kings and governments.

Panjandrum (*The Grand*), and village potentate or Brummagem magnate. The word occurs in S. Foote's farrago of nonsense, which he wrote to test the memory of old Macklin, who said in a lecture "he had brought his own memory to such perfection that he could learn anything by rote on once hearing it."

He was the Great Panjandrum of the place.—Percy Fitzgerald.

⁎ The squire of a village is the Grand Panjandrum, and the small gentry the Picninnies, Joblillies, and Garyulies.

Foote's nonsense lines are these:

So she went into the garden to cut a cabbage leaf to make an apple pie; and at the same time a great she-bear, coming up the street, pops its head into the shop. "What! no soap?" So he died, and she very imprudently married the barber! and there were present the Picninnies, and the Joblillies, and the Garyulies, and the Grand Panjandrum himself, with the little round button at top, and they all fell to playing the game of catch as catch can, till the gunpowder ran out at the heel of their boots.—S. Foote, *The Quarterly Review*, xcv. 516, 517 (1854).

Pan′ope (3 *syl.*), one of the nereids. Her "sisters" are the sea-nymphs. Panopê was invoked by sailors in storms.

Sleek Panope with all her sisters played.
Milton, *Lycidas*, 95 (1638).

Pansy Osmund, daughter of Mr. Osmund and Madame Merle, but ignorant who her mother is. After her father's second marriage, the girl, who has been brought up by the nuns, is extremely fond of her step-mother, and when she grows under her fostering care into a lovely woman, becomes attached to

Edward Rosier, a man of small fortune. Her father, cold and hard as stone, decrees that she shall marry an English lord, and upon her refusal, sends her back to the convent.—Henry James, Jr., *Portrait of a Lady* (1881).

Pantag′ruel′, king of the Dipsodes (2 *syl.*), son of Gargantua, and last of the race of giants. His mother, Badebec, died in giving him birth. His paternal grandfather was named Grangousier. Pantagruel was a lineal descendant of Fierabras, the Titans, Goliath, Polypheme (3 *syl.*), and all the other giants traceable to Chalbrook, who lived in that extraordinary period noted for its "week of three Thursdays." The word is a hybrid, compounded of the Greek *panta* ("all"), and the Hagarene word *gruel* ("thirsty"). His immortal achievement was his "quest of the oracle of the Holy Bottle."—Rabelais, *Gargantua and Pantagruel*, ii. (1533).

Pantagruel's Course of Study. Pantagruel's father, Gargantua, said in a letter to his son:

"I intend and insist that you learn all languages perfectly; first of all Greek, in Quintillian's method; then Latin, then Hebrew, then Arabic and Chaldee. I wish you to form your style of Greek on the model of Plato, and of Latin on that of Cicero. Let there be no history you have not at your finger's ends, and study thoroughly cosmography and geography. Of liberal arts, such as geometry, mathematics and music, I gave you a taste when not above five years old, and I would have you now master them fully. Study astronomy, but not divination and judicial astrology, which I consider mere vanities. As for civil law, I would have thee know the *digests* by heart. You should also have a perfect knowledge of the works of Nature, so that there is no sea, river, or smallest stream, which you do not know for what fish it is noted, whence it proceeds, and whither it directs its course; all fowls of the air, all shrubs and trees, whether forest or orchard, all herbs and flowers, all metals and stones should be mastered by you. Fail not at the same time most carefully to peruse the Talmudists and Cabalists, and be sure by frequent anatomies to gain a perfect knowledge of that other world called the microcosm, which is man. Master all these in your young days, and let nothing be superficial; as you grow into manhood, you must learn chivalry, warfare, and field manœuvres."—Rabelais, *Pantagruel*, ii. 8 (1533).

Pantag′ruel's Tongue. It formed shelter for a whole army. His throat and mouth contained whole cities.

Then did they [*the army*] put themselves in close order, and stood as near to each other as they could, and Pantagruel put out his tongue half-way, and covered them all, as a hen doth her chickens.—Rabelais, *Pantagruel*, ii. 32 (1533).

Pantagruelian Lawsuit (*The*). This was between Lord Busqueue and Lord Suckfist, who pleaded their own cases. The writs, etc., were as much as four asses could carry. After the plaintiff had stated his case, and the defendant had made his reply, Pantagruel gave judgment, and the two suitors were both satisfied, for no one understood a word of the pleadings, or the tenor of the verdict.—Rabelais, *Pantagruel*, ii. (1533).

Pantaloon. In the Italian comedy, *Il Pantalo´ne* is a thin, emaciated, old man, and the only character that acts in slippers.

The sixth age shifts
Into the lean and slippered Pantaloon.
Shakespeare, *As You Like It*, act ii. sc. 7 (1600).

Panther (*The*), symbol of pleasure. When Dantê began the ascent of fame, this beast met him, and tried to stop his further progress.

Scarce the ascent
Began, when lo! a panther, nimble, light,
And covered with a speckled skin, appeared,
... and strove to check my onward going.
Dantê, *Hell*, i. (1300).

Panther (The Spotted), the Church of England. The "milk-white doe" is the Church of Rome.

The panther, sure the noblest next the hind,
The fairest creature of the spotted kind;
Oh, could her inborn stains be washed away,
She were too good to be a beast of prey.
Dryden, *The Hind and the Panther*, i. (1687).

Panthino, servant of Antonio (the father of Protheus, one of the two heroes of the play).—Shakespeare, *Two Gentlemen of Verona* (1594).

Panton, a celebrated punster in the reign of Charles II.

And Panton, waging harmless war with words.
Dryden, *MacFlecknoe*, (1682).

Panurge, a young man, handsome and of good stature, but in very ragged apparel when Pantag´ruel first met him on the road leading from Charenton Bridge. Pantagruel, pleased with his person, and moved with pity at his distress, accosted him, when Panurge replied, first in German, then in Arabic, then in Italian, then in Biscayan, then in Bas-Breton, then in Low Dutch, then in Spanish. Finding that Pantagruel knew none of these languages, Panurge tried Danish, Hebrew, Greek, Latin, with no better success. "Friend," said the prince, "can you speak French?" "Right well," answered

Panurge, "for I was born in Touraine, the garden of France." Pantagruel then asked him if he would join his suite, which Panurge most gladly consented to do, and became the fast friend of Pantagruel. His great *forte* was practical jokes. Rabelais describes him as of middle stature, with an aquiline nose, very handsome, and always moneyless. Pantagruel made him governor of Salmygondin.—Rabelais, *Pantagruel*, iii. 2 (1545).

Panza (*Sancho*), of Adzpetia, the squire of Don Quixote de la Mancha; "a little squat fellow, with a tun belly and spindle shanks" (pt. I. ii. 1). He rides an ass called Dapple. His sound common sense is an excellent foil to the knight's craze. Sancho is very fond of eating and drinking, is always asking the knight when he is to be put in possession of the island he promised. He salts his speech with most pertinent proverbs, and even with wit of a racy, though sometimes of rather a vulgar savor.—Cervantes, *Don Quixote* (1605).

*** The wife of Sancho is called "Joan Panza" in pt. I., and "Teresa Panza" in pt. II. "My father's name," she says to Sancho, "was Cascajo, and I, by being your wife, am now called Teresa Panza, though by right I should be called Teresa Cascajo" (pt. II. i. 5).

Paolo (2 *syl.*), the cardinal brother of Count Guido Franceschi´ni, who advised his bankrupt brother to marry an heiress, in order to repair his fortune.

When brother Paolo's energetic shake
Should do the relics justice.
R. Browning, *The Ring and the Book*, ii. 409.

Paper King (*The*), John Law, projector of the Mississippi Bubble (1671-1729).

The basis of Law's project was the idea that paper money may be multiplied to any extent, provided there be security in fixed stock.—Rich.

Paphian Mimp, a certain plie of the lips, considered needful for "the highly genteel." Lady Emily told Miss Alscrip, "the heiress," that it was acquired by placing one's self before a looking-glass, and repeating continually the words "nimini pimini;" "when the lips cannot fail to take the right plie."—General Burgoyne, *The Heiress*, iii. 2 (1781).

(C. Dickens has made Mrs. General tell Amy Dorrit that the pretty plie is given to the lips by pronouncing the words "papa, potatoes, poultry, prunes and prism.")

Papillon, a broken-down critic, who earned four shillings a week for reviews of translations "without knowing one syllable of the original," and of "books which he had never read." He then turned French valet, and got well paid. He then fell into the service of Jack Wilding, and was valet, French marquis, or anything else to suit the whims of that young scapegrace.—S. Foote, *The Liar* (1761).

Papy′ra, goddess of printing and literature; so called from papyrus, a substance once used for books, before the invention of paper.

Till to astonished realms Papyra taught
To paint in mystic colors sound and thought.
With Wisdom's voice to print the page sublime,
And mark in adamant the steps of Time.
Darwin, *Loves of the Plants*, ii. (1781).

Paracelsus is said to have kept a small devil prisoner in the pommel of his sword. He favored metallic substances for medicines, while Galen preferred herbs. His full name was Philippus Aure′olus Theophrastus Paracelsus, but his family name was Bombastus (1493-1541).

Paracelsus, at the age of 20, thinks *knowledge* the *summum bonum*, and, at the advice of his two friends, Festus and Michal, retires to a seat of learning in quest thereof. Eight years later, being dissatisfied, he falls in with Aprile, an Italian poet, and resolves to seek the *summum bonum* in love. Again he fails, and finally determines "to know and to enjoy."—R. Browning, *Paracelsus*.

Par′adine (3 *syl.*), son of Astolpho, and brother of Dargonet, both rivals for the love of Laura. In the combat provoked by Prince Oswald against Gondibert, which was decided by four combatants on each side, Hugo "the Little" slew both the brothers.—Sir. Wm. Davenant, *Gondibert*, i. (died 1668).

Paradisa′ica (*"the fruit of paradise"*). So the banana is called. The Mohammedans aver that the "forbidden fruit" was the banana or Indian fig, and cite in confirmation of this opinion that our first parents used fig leaves for their covering after their fall.

Paradise, in thirty-three cantos, by Dantê (1311). Paradise is separated from Purgatory by the river Lethê; and Dantê was conducted through nine of the spheres by Beatrice, who left him in the sphere of "unbodied light," under the charge of St. Bernard (canto xxxi.). The entire region is divided into ten spheres, each of which is appropriated to its proper order. The first seven spheres are the seven planets, viz. (1) the Moon, for angels, (2) Mercury, for archangels, (3) Venus, for virtues, (4) the Sun, for powers, (5) Mars, for principalities, (6) Jupiter, for dominions, (7) Saturn, for thrones. The eighth sphere is that of the fixed stars for the cherubim; the ninth is the *primum mobilê* for the seraphim; and the tenth is the empyre′an for the Virgin Mary and the triune deity. Beatrice, with Rachel, Sarah, Judith, Rebecca and Ruth, St. Augustin, St. Francis, St. Benedict, and others, were enthroned in Venus, the sphere of the virtues. The empyrean, he says, is a sphere of "unbodied light," "bright effluence of bright essence, uncreate." This is what the Jews called "the heaven of the heavens."

Paradise was placed in the legendary maps of the Middle Ages, in Ceylon; but Mahomet placed it "in the seventh heaven." The Arabs have a tradition that when our first parents were cast out of the garden, Adam fell in the isle of Ceylon, and Eve in Joddah (the port of Mecca).—*Al Korân*, ii.

Paradise and the Pe´ri. A peri was told she would be admitted into heaven if she would bring thither the gift most acceptable to the Almighty. She first brought a drop of a young patriot's blood, shed on his country's behalf; but the gates would not open for such an offering. She next took thither the last sigh of a damsel who had died nursing her betrothed, who had been stricken by the plague; but the gates would not open for such an offering. She then carried up the repentant tear of an old man converted by the prayers of a little child. All heaven rejoiced, the gates were flung open, and the peri was received with a joyous welcome.—T. Moore, *Lalla Rookh* ("Second Tale," 1817).

Paradise Lost. Satan and his crew, still suffering from their violent expulsion out of heaven, are roused by Satan's telling them about a "new creation;" and he calls a general council to deliberate upon their future operations (bk. i.). The council meet in the Pandemonium hall, and it is resolved that Satan shall go on a voyage of discovery to this "new world" (bk. ii.). The Almighty sees Satan, and confers with His Son about man. He foretells the Fall, and arranges the scheme of man's redemption. Meantime, Satan enters the orb of the sun, and there learns the route to the "new world" (bk. iii.). On entering Paradise, he overhears Adam and Eve talking of the one prohibition (bk. iv.). Raphael is now sent down to warn Adam of his danger, and he tells him who Satan is (bk. v.); describes the war in heaven, and expulsion of the rebel angels (bk. vi.). The angel visitant goes on to tell Adam why and how this world was made (bk. vii.); and Adam tells Raphael his own experience (bk. viii.) After the departure of Raphael, Satan enters into a serpent, and, seeing Eve alone, speaks to her. Eve is astonished to hear the serpent talk, but is informed that it had tasted of "the tree of knowledge," and had become instantly endowed with both speech and wisdom. Curiosity induces Eve to taste the same fruit, and she persuades Adam to taste it also (bk. ix.). Satan now returns to hell, to tell of his success (bk. x.). Michael is sent to expel Adam and Eve from the garden (bk. xi.); and the poem concludes with the expulsion, and Eve's lamentation (bk. xii.).—Milton (1665).

Paradise Lost was first published by Matthias Walker, of St. Dunstan's. He gave for it £5 down; on the sale of 1300 copies, he gave another £5. On the next two impressions, he gave other like sums. For the four editions, he therefore paid £20. The agreement between Walker and Milton is preserved in the British Museum.

It must be remembered that the wages of an ordinary workman was at that time about 3*d.* a day, and now we give 3*s.*; so that the price given was equal to about £250, according to the present value of money. Goldsmith tells us that the clergyman of his "deserted village" was "passing rich" with £40 a year = £500 present value of money.

Paradise Regained, in four books. The subject is the Temptation. Eve, being tempted, *lost* paradise; Christ, being tempted, *regained* it.

Book I. Satan presents himself as an old peasant, and, entering into conversation with Jesus, advises Him to satisfy His hunger by miraculously converting stones into bread. Jesus gives the tempter to know that He recognizes him, and refuses to follow his suggestion.

II. Satan reports progress to his ministers, and asks advice. He returns to the wilderness, and offers Jesus wealth, as the means of acquiring power; but the suggestion is again rejected.

III. Satan shows Jesus several of the kingdoms of Asia, and points out to Him their military power. He advises Him to seek alliance with the Parthians, and promises his aid. He says by such alliance He might shake off the Roman yoke, and raise the kingdom of David to first-class power. Jesus rejects the counsel, and tells the tempter that the Jews were for the present under a cloud for their sins, but that the time would come when God would put forth His hand on their behalf.

IV. Satan shows Jesus Rome, with all its greatness, and says, "I can easily dethrone Tiberius, and seat Thee on the imperial throne." He then shows Him Athens, and says, "I will make Thee master of their wisdom and high state of civilization, if Thou wilt fall down and worship me." "Get thee behind Me, Satan!" was the indignant answer; and Satan, finding all his endeavors useless, tells Jesus of the sufferings prepared for Him, takes Him back to the wilderness, and leaves Him there; but angels come and minister unto Him.—Milton (1671).

Paraguay (*A Tale of*), by Southey, in four cantos (1814). The small-pox, having broken out amongst the Guarānis, carried off the whole tribe except Quiāra and his wife, Monněma, who then migrated from the fatal spot to the Mondai woods. Here a son (Yerūti) and afterwards a daughter (Mooma) were born; but before the birth of the latter, the father was eaten by a jagŭar. When the children were of a youthful age, a Jesuit priest induced the three to come and live at St. Joăchin (3 *syl.*); so they left the wild woods for a city life. Here, in a few months, the mother flagged and died. The daughter next drooped, and soon followed her mother to the grave. The son, now the only remaining one of the entire race, begged to be baptized, received the rite, cried, "Ye are come for me! I am ready;" and died also.

Par´cinus, a young prince, in love with his cousin, Irolit´a, but beloved by Az´ira. The fairy Danamo was Azira's mother, and resolved to make Irolita marry the fairy Brutus; but Parcinus, aided by the fairy Favorable, surmounted all obstacles, married Irolita, and made Brutus marry Azira.

Parcinus had a noble air, a delicate shape, a fine head of hair admirably white.... He did everything well, danced and sang to perfection, and gained all the prizes at tournaments, whenever he contended for them.—Comtesse D'Aunoy, *Fairy Tales* ("Perfect Love," 1682).

Par´dalo, the demon-steed given to Iniguez Guerra, by his gobelin mother, that he might ride to Tolēdo and liberate his father, Don Diego Lopez, lord of Biscay, who had fallen into the hands of the Moors.—*Spanish Story*.

Par´diggle (*Mrs.*) a formidable lady, who conveyed to one the idea "of wanting a great deal more room." Like Mrs. Jellyby, she devoted herself to the concerns of Africa, and made her family of small boys contribute all their pocket money to the cause of the Borrioboola Gha mission.—C. Dickens, *Bleak House* (1853).

Pardoner's Tale (*The*), in Chaucer's *Canterbury Tales*, is "Death and the Rioters." Three rioters agree to hunt down Death, and kill him. An old man directs them to a tree in a lane, where, as he said, he had just left him. On reaching the spot, they find a rich treasure, and cast lots to decide who is to go and buy food. The lot falls on the youngest; and the other two, during his absence, agree to kill him on his return. The rascal sent to buy food poisons the wine, in order to secure to himself the whole treasure. Now comes the catastrophe: The two set on the third and slay him, but die soon after of the poisoned wine; so the three rioters *find death* under the tree, as the old man said, paltering in a double sense (1388).

Parian Verse, ill-natured satire; so called from Archil´ochus, a native of Paros.

Pari-Ba´nou, a fairy who gave Prince Ahmed a tent, which would fold into so small a compass that a lady might carry it about as a toy, but, when spread, it would cover a whole army.—*Arabian Nights* ("Prince Ahmed and Pari-Banu").

Paridel is a name employed in the *Dunciad* for an idle libertine—rich, young, and at leisure. The model is Sir Paridel, in the *Faëry Queen*.

Thee, too, my Paridel, she marked thee there,
Stretched on the rack of a too-easy chair,
And heard thy everlasting yawn confess
The pains and penalties of idleness.
Pope, *The Dunciad*, iv. 341 (1742).

Paridel (Sir), descendant of Paris, whose son was Parius, who settled in Paros, and left his kingdom to his son, Par´idas, from whom Paridel descended. Having gained the hospitality of Malbecco, Sir Paridel eloped with his wife, Dame Hel´inore (3 *syl.*), but soon quitted her, leaving her to go whither she would. "So had he served many another one" (bk. iii. 10). In bk. iv. 1 Sir Paridel is discomfited by Sir Scudamore.—Spenser, *Faëry Queen*, iii. 10; iv. 1 (1590, 1596).

*** "Sir Paridel" is meant for Charles Nevil, sixth and last of the Nevils, earls of Westmoreland. He joined the Northumberland rebellion of 1569 for the restoration of Mary queen of Scots; and when the plot failed, made his escape to the Continent, where he lived in poverty and obscurity. The earl was quite a Lothario, whose delight was to win the love of women, and then to abandon them.

Paris, a son of Priam and Hecŭba, noted for his beauty. He married Œnōnê, daughter of Cebren, the river-god. Subsequently, during a visit to Menelāus, king of Sparta, he eloped with Queen Helen, and this brought about the Trojan war. Being wounded by an arrow from the bow of Philoctētês, he sent for his wife, who hastened to him with remedies; but it was too late—he died of his wound, and Œnonê hung herself.—Homer, *Iliad*.

Paris was appointed to decide which of the three goddesses (Juno, Pallas or Minerva) was the fairest fair, and to which should be awarded the golden apple thrown "to the most beautiful." The three goddesses tried by bribes to obtain the verdict: Juno promised him dominion if he would decide in her favor; Minerva promised him wisdom; but Venus said she would find him the most beautiful of women for wife if he allotted to her the apple. Paris handed the apple to Venus.

Not Cytherea from a fairer swain
Received her apple on the Trojan plain.
Falconer, *The Shipwreck*, i. 3 (1756).

Paris, a young nobleman, kinsman of Prince Es´calus of Verona, and the unsuccessful suitor of his cousin, Juliet.—Shakespeare, *Romeo and Juliet* (1598).

Paris (Notre Dame de), by Victor Hugo (1831). (See ESMERALDA and QUASIMODO.)

Parisina, wife of Azo, chief of Ferrara. She had been betrothed before her marriage to Hugo, a natural son of Azo, and after Azo took her for his bride, the attachment of Parisina and Hugo continued and had freer scope for indulgence. One night Azo heard Parisina in sleep confess her love for Hugo, whereupon he had his son beheaded, and, though he spared the life of Parisina, no one ever knew what became of her.—Byron, *Parisina* (1816).

Such is Byron's version; but history says Niccolo III. of Ferrara (Byron's "Azo") had for his second wife Parisina Malatesta, who showed great aversion to Ugo, a natural son of Niccolo, whom he greatly loved. One day, with the hope of lessening this strong aversion, he sent Ugo to escort her on a journey, and the two fell in love with each other. After their return the affection of Parisina and Ugo continued unabated, and a servant, named Zoe´se (3 *syl.*), having told the marquis of their criminal intimacy, he had the two guilty ones brought to open trial. They were both condemned to death; Ugo was beheaded first, then Parisina. Some time after, Niccolo married a third wife, and had several children.—Frizzi, *History of Ferrara*.

Parisme´nos, the hero of the second part of *Parismus* (*q.v.*). This part contains the adventurous travels of Parismenos, his deeds of chivalry, and love for the Princess Angelica, "the Lady of the Golden Tower."—Emanuel Foord, *Parismenos* (1598).

Paris´mus, a valiant and renowned prince of Bohemia, the hero of a romance so called. This "history" contains an account of his battles against the Persians, his love for Laurana, daughter of the king of Thessaly, and his strange adventures in the Desolate Island. The second part contains the exploits and love affairs of Parisme´nos.—Emanuel Foord, *Parismus* (1598).

Pariza´de (4 *syl.*), daughter of Khrosrou-schah, sultan of Persia, and sister of Bahman and Perviz. These three, in infancy, were sent adrift, each at the time of birth, through the jealousy of their two maternal aunts, who went to nurse the sultana in her confinement; but they were drawn out of the canal by the superintendent of the sultan's gardens, who brought them up. Parizadê rivalled her brothers in horsemanship, archery, running and literature. One day, a devotee who had been kindly entreated by Parizadê, told her the house she lived in wanted three things to make it perfect: (1) *the talking bird*, (2) *the singing tree*, and (3) *the golden-colored water*. Her two brothers went to obtain these treasures, but failed. Parizadê then went, and succeeded. The sultan paid them a visit, and the talking bird revealed to him the story of their birth and bringing up. When the sultan heard the infamous tale, he commanded the two sisters to be put to death, and Parizadê, with her two brothers, were then proclaimed the lawful children of the sultan.—*Arabian Nights* ("The Two Sisters," the last story).

⁎⁎⁎ The story of *Cherry and Fairstar*, by the Comtesse D'Aunoy, is an imitation of this tale; and introduces the "green bird," the "singing apple," and the "dancing water."

Parkes (*Mr.*). A clergyman "of simplicity and sincerity, fully in earnest to do the Lord's work and do it with all his might." He suggests to his congregation when the Week of Prayer comes around that they "make a Week of Practice instead." The result is told in *The Deacon's Week*.—Rose Terry Cooke (1886).

Parley (*Peter*), Samuel Griswold Goodrich, an American. Above seven millions of his books were in circulation in 1859 (1793-1860).

⁎⁎⁎ Several piracies of this popular name have appeared. Thus, S. Kettell, of America, pirated the name in order to sell under false colors; Darton and Co. issued a Peter Parley's *Annual* (1841-1855); Simkins, a Peter Parley's *Life of Paul* (1845); Bogue, a Peter Parley's *Visit to London*, etc. (1844); Tegg, several works under the same name; Hodson, a Peter Parley's *Bible Geography* (1839); Clements, a Peter Parley's *Child's First Step* (1839). None of which works were by Goodrich, the real "Peter Parley."

William Martin was the writer of Darton's "Peter Parley series." George Mogridge wrote several tales under the name of Peter Parley. How far such "false pretences" are justifiable, public opinion, must decide.

Parliament (*The Black*), a parliament held by Henry VIII. in Bridewell.

(For Addled parliament, Barebone's parliament, the Devil's parliament, the Drunken parliament, the Good parliament, the Long parliament, the Mad parliament, the Pensioner parliament, the Rump parliament, the Running parliament, the Unmerciful parliament, the Useless parliament, the Wonder-making parliament, the parliament of Dunces, see *Dictionary of Phrase and Fable*, 657.)

Parnelle (*Mde.*), the mother of M. Orgon, and an ultra-admirer of Tartuffe, whom she looks on as a saint. In the adaptation of Molière's comedy by Isaac Bickerstaff, Mde. Parnelle is called "old Lady Lambert;" her son, "Sir John Lambert;" and Tartuffe, "Dr. Cantwell."—Molière, *Tartuffe* (1664); Bickerstaff, *The Hypocrite* (1768).

⁎⁎⁎ *The Nonjuror*, by Cibber (1706), was the quarry of Bickerstaff's play.

Parody (*Father of*), Hippo′nax of Ephesus (sixth century B.C.).

Parol′les (3 *syl.*), a boastful, cowardly follower of Bertram, count of Rousillon. His utterances are racy enough, but our contempt for the man smothers our mirth, and we cannot laugh. In one scene the bully is taken blindfolded among his old acquaintances, whom he is led to suppose are his enemies, and he villifies their characters to their faces in most admired foolery.—Shakespeare, *All's Well that Ends Well* (1598).

He [*Dr. Parr*] was a mere Parolles in a pedagogue's wig.—*Noctes Ambrosianæ*.

(For similar tongue-doughty heroes, see BASILISCO, BESSUS, BLUFF, BOBADIL, BOROUGHCLIFF, BRAZEN, FLASH, PISTOL, PYRGO, POLINICES, SCARAMOUCH, THRASO, VINCENT DE LA ROSA, etc.)

Parpaillons (*King of the*), the father of Gargamelle, "a jolly pug and well-mouthed wench," who married Grangousier "in the vigor of his age," and became the mother of Gargantua.—Rabelais, *Gargantua*, i. 3 (1533).

Parr (*Old*). Thomas Parr, we are told, lived in the reign of ten sovereigns. He married his second wife when he was 120 years old, and had a child by her. He was a husbandman, born at Salop, in 1483, and died 1635, aged 152.

Parricide (*The Beautiful*), Beatrice Cenci, who is said to have murdered her father for the incestuous brutality with which he had treated her (died 1599).

Shelley has a tragedy on the subject, called *The Cenci* (1819).

Parsley Peel, the first Sir Robert Peel. So called from the great quantity of printed calico with the parsley-leaf pattern manufactured by him (1750-1830).

Parson Adams, a simple-minded country clergyman of the eighteenth century. At the age of 50 he was provided with a handsome income of £23 a year (nearly £300 of our money).—Fielding, *Joseph Andrews* (1742).

Timothy Burrell, Esq., in 1715, bequeathed to his nephew Timothy, the sum of £20 a year, to be paid during his residence at the university, and to be continued to him till he obtained some preferment worth at least £30 a year.—*Sussex Archæological Collections*, iii. 172.

Parson Bate, a stalwart choleric, sporting parson, editor of the *Morning Post* in the latter half of the eighteenth century. He was afterwards Sir Henry Bate Dudley, Bart.

When Sir Henry Bate Dudley was appointed an Irish dean, a young lady of Dublin said, "Och! how I long to see our dane! They say ... he fights like an angel."—*Cassell's Magazine* ("London Legends," iii.)

Parson Collins, shrewd backwoodsman, ready for fight or prayer. He suffers at the hands of desperadoes, but is dauntless, and always gets the better of his partner in a trade. His white mule Ma'y Jane, is the only creature that outwits him, and that only at fence-corners.—Octave Thanet, *Expiation* (1890).

Parson Runo (*A*), a simple-minded clergyman, wholly unacquainted with the world; a Dr. Primrose, in fact. It is a Russian household phrase, having its origin in the singular simplicity of the Lutheran clergy of the Isle of Runo.

Parson Trulliber, a fat clergyman, slothful, ignorant, and intensely bigoted.—Fielding, *Joseph Andrews* (1742).

Parsons (*Walter*), the giant porter of King James I. (died 1622).—Fuller, *Worthies* (1662).

Parsons' Kaiser (*The*), Karl IV., of Germany, who was set up by Pope Clement VI., while Ludwig IV. was still on the throne. The Germans called the pope's *protégé* "*pfaffen kaiser*."

Parthe′nia, the mistress of Argălus.—Sir Philip Sidney, *Arcadia* (1580).

Parthenia, Maidenly Chastity personified. Parthenia is sister of Agnei′a (3 *syl.*), or wifely chastity, the spouse of Encra′tês, or temperance. Her attendant is Er′ythre, or modesty. (Greek, *parthĕnia*, "maidenhood.")—Phineas Fletcher, *The Purple Island*, x. (1633).

Parthen′ope (4 *syl.*), one of the three syrens. She was buried at Naples. Naples itself was anciently called Parthenopê, which name was changed to *Neap′olis* ("the new city") by a colony of Cumæans.

By dead Parthenope's dear tomb.
Milton, *Comus*, 879 (1634).

Loitering by the sea
That laves the passionate shores of soft Parthenopê.
Lord Lytton, *Ode*, iii. 2 (1839).

(The three syrens were Parthenopê, Ligēa, and Leucos′ia, not *Leucoth′ea, q.v.*)

Parthenope (4 *syl.*), the damsel beloved by Prince Volscius.—Duke of Buckingham, *The Rehearsal* (1671).

Parthen′ope of Naples, Sannazora, the Neapolitan poet called "The Christian Virgil." Most of his poems were published under the assumed name of *Actius Sincerus* (1458-1530).

At last the Muses ... scattered ...
Their blooming wreaths from fair Valclusa's bowers [*Petrarch*]
To Arno [*Dante and Boccaccio*] ... and the shore
Of soft Parthenope.
Akenside, *Pleasures of Imagination*, ii. (1744).

Partington (*Mrs.*), an old lady of amusing affectations and ridiculous blunders of speech. Sheridan's "*Mrs. Malaprop*" and Smollett's "*Tabitha Bramble*" are similar characters.—B. P. Shillaber (an American humorist).

I do not mean to be disrespectful; but the attempt of the lords to stop the progress of reform reminds me very forcibly of the great storm of Sidmouth, and the conduct of the excellent Mrs. Partington on that occasion. In the winter of 1824, there set in a great flood upon that town; the tide rose to an incredible height; the waves rushed in upon the houses; and everything was threatened with destruction. In the midst of this sublime storm, Dame Partington, who lived upon the beach, was seen at the door of her house with mop and pattens, trundling her mop, squeezing out the sea-water, and vigorously pushing away the Atlantic Ocean. The Atlantic was roused, Mrs. Partington's spirit was up; but I need not tell you that the contest was unequal. The Atlantic beat Mrs. Partington. She was excellent at a slop or puddle, but should never have meddled with a tempest.—Sydney Smith (speech at Taunton, 1831).

Partlet, the hen, in "The Nun's Priest's Tale," and in the famous beast-epic of *Reynard the Fox* (1498).—Chaucer, *Canterbury Tales* (1388).

Sister Partlet with her hooded head, the cloistered community of nuns; the Roman Catholic clergy being the "barn-door fowls."—Dryden, *Hind and Panther* (1687).

Partridge. Talus was changed into a partridge.

Partridge, cobbler, quack, astrologer, and almanac-maker (died 1708). Dean Swift wrote an elegy on him.

Here five feet deep, lies on his back,
A cobbler, starmonger, and quack,
Who, to the stars in pure gold will,
Does to his best look upward still,
Weep all you customers that use
His pills, his almanacs, or shoes.

Partridge, the attendant of Tom Jones, as Strap, is of Smollett's "Roderick Random." Faithful, shrewd, and of child-like simplicity. He is half-barber and half-schoolmaster. His excitement in the play-house when he went to see Garrick in "Hamlet" is charming.—Fielding, *The History of Tom Jones* (1749).

The humor of Smollett, although genuine and hearty, is coarse and vulgar. He was superficial where Fielding showed deep insight; but he had a rude conception of generosity of which Fielding seems incapable. It is owing to this that "Strap" is superior to "Partridge."—Hazlitt, *Comic Writers*.

Parvenue. One of the O'Neals, being told that Barrett of Castlemone had only been 400 years in Ireland, replied, "I hate the upstart, which can only look back to yesterday."

Parviz ("*victorious*"), surname of Khosrou II. of Persia. He kept 15,000 female musicians, 6000 household officers, 20,500 saddle-mules, 960 elephants, 200 slaves to scatter perfumes when he went abroad, and 1000 sekabers to water the roads before him. His horse, Shibdiz, was called "the Persian Bucephălus."

The reigns of Khosrou I. and II. were the golden period of Persian history.

Parzival, the hero and title of a metrical romance, by Wolfram v. Eschenbach. Parzival was brought up by a widowed mother, in solitude, but when grown to manhood, two wandering knights persuaded him to go to the court of King Arthur. His mother, hoping to deter him, consented to his going if he would wear the dress of a common jester. This he did, but soon achieved such noble deeds that Arthur made him a knight of the Round Table. Sir Parzival went in quest of the Holy Graal, which was kept in a magnificent castle called Graalburg, in Spain, built by the royal priest Titurel. He reached the castle, but having neglected certain conditions, was shut out, and, on his return, the priestess of Graalburg insisted on his being expelled the court and degraded from knighthood. Parzival then led a new life of abstinence and self-abnegation, and a wise hermit became his instructor. At length he reached such a state of purity and sanctity that the priestess of Graalburg declared him worthy to become lord of the castle (1205).

_{*} This, of course, is an allegory of a Christian giving up everything in order to be admitted a priest and king in the city of God, and becoming a fool in order to learn true wisdom (see 1 *Cor.* iii. 18).

Pasquin, a Roman cobbler of the latter half of the fifteenth century, whose shop stood in the neighborhood of the Braschi palace near the Piazza Navoni. He was noted for his caustic remarks and bitter sayings. After his death, a mutilated statue near the shop was called by his name, and made the repository of all the bitter epigrams and satirical verses of the city; hence called *pasquinades* (3 *syl.*).

Passamonte (*Gines de*), the galley-slave set free by Don Quixote. He returned the favor by stealing Sancho's wallet and ass. Subsequently he reappeared as a puppet-showman.—Cervantes, *Don Quixote*.

Passatore (*Il*), a title assumed by Belli'no, an Italian bandit chief who died 1851.

Passel'yon, a young foundling brought up by Morgan la Fée. He was detected in an intrigue with Morgan's daughter. The adventures of this amorous youth are related in the romance called *Perceforest*, iii.

Passe Rose, fair orphan girl, warm of heart and single of purpose. Ingenuous as a babe, and made strong by love. Her adventures are the theme of the novel bearing her name.—Arthur Sherburne Hardy, *Passe Rose* (1889).

Passetreul, the name of Sir Tristram's horse.

Passe-tyme of Plesure, an allegorical poem in forty-six capitulos and in seven-line stanzas, by Stephen Hawes (1506) The poet supposes that while Graunde Amoure was walking in a meadow he encountered Fame, "enuyroned with tongues of fyre," who told him about La bell Pucell, a ladye fair, living in the Tower of Musike, and then departed, leaving him under the charge of Gouernaunce and Grace, who conducted him to the Tower of Doctrine. Countenaunce, the portress, showed him over the tower, and Lady Science sent him to Gramer. Afterwards he was sent to Logyke, Rethorike, Inuention, Arismetrike and Musike. In the Tower of Musike he met La bell Pucell, pleaded his love, and was kindly entreated; but they were obliged to part for the time being, while Graunde Amoure continued his "passe-tyme of plesure." On quitting La bell Pucell he went to Geometrye and then to Dame Astronomy. Then, leaving the Tower of Science, he entered that of Chyualry. Here Mynerue introduced him to Kyng Melyzyus, after which he went to the temple of Venus, who sent a letter on his behalf to La bell Pucell. Meanwhile the giant False Report (or Godfrey Gobilyue) met him, and put him to great distress in the house of Correction, but Perceueraunce at length conducted him to the manor-house of Dame Comfort. After sundry trials Graunde Amoure married La bell Pucell, and, after many a long day of happiness and love, was arrested by Age, who took him before Policye and Auarice. Death in time came for him, and Remembraunce wrote his epitaph.

Pastor Fi′do (*Il*), a pastoral by Giovanni Battista Guari′ni of Ferrara (1585).

Pastoral Romance (*The Father of*), Honoré d'Urfé (1567-1625).

Pastorella, the fair shepherdess (bk. vi. 9), beloved by Corydon, but "neither for him nor any other did she care a whit." She was a foundling, brought up by the shepherd Melibee. When Sir Calidore (3 *syl.*) was the shepherd's guest, he fell in love with the fair foundling, who returned his love. During the absence of Sir Calidore in a hunting expedition, Pastorella, with Melibee and Corydon, were carried off by brigands. Melibee was killed, Corydon effected his escape, and Pastorella was wounded. Sir Calidore went to rescue his shepherdess, killed the brigand chief, and brought back the captive in safety (bk. vi. 11). He took her to Belgard Castle, and it turned out that the beautiful foundling was the daughter of Lady Claribel and Sir Bellamour (bk, vi. 12).— Spenser, *Faëry Queen*, vi. 9-12 (1596).

"Pastorella" is meant for Frances Walsingham, daughter of Sir Francis Walsingham, whom Sir Philip Sidney ("Sir Calidore") married. After Sidney's death the widow married the earl of Essex (the queen's favorite). Sir Philip being the author of a romance called *Arcadia* suggested to the poet the name Pastorella.

Patch, the clever, intriguing waiting-woman of Isabinda, daughter of Sir Jealous Traffick. As she was handing a love-letter in cipher to her mistress, she let it fall, and Sir Jealous picked it up. He could not read it, but insisted on knowing what it meant. "O," cried the ready wit, "it is a charm for the toothache!" and the suspicions of Sir Jealous were diverted (act iv. 2).—Mrs. Centlivre, *The Busy Body* (1709).

Patch (*Clause*), king of the beggars. He died in 1730, and was succeeded by Bampfylde Moore Carew.

Patche (1 *syl.*), Cardinal Wolsey's jester. When the cardinal felt his favor giving way, he sent Patche as a gift to the king, and Henry VIII. considered the gift a most acceptable one.

We call one Patche or Cowlson, whom we see to do a thing foolishly, because these two in their time were notable fools.—Wilson, *Art of Rhetorique* (1553).

Patelin (2 *syl.*), the hero of an ancient French comedy. He contrives to obtain on credit six ells of cloth from William Josseaume, by artfully praising the tradesman's father. Any subtle, crafty fellow, who entices by flattery and insinuating arts, is called a Patelin.—P. Blanchet, *L'Avocat Patelin* (1459-1519).

On lui attribue, mais à tort, la farce de *L'Avocat Patelin*, qui est plus ancienne que lui.—Bouillet, *Dictionary Universel d'Histoire, etc.*, art. "Blanchet."

Consider, sir, I pray you, how the noble Patelin, having a mind to extol to the third heavens, the father of William Josseaume, said no more than this: he did lend his goods freely to those who were desirous of them.—Rabelais, *Pantagruel*, iii. 4 (1545).

Pater Patrum. St. Gregory, of Nyssa is so called by the council of Nice (332-395).

Paterson (*Paté*), serving-boy to Bryce Snailsfoot, the pedlar.—Sir W. Scott, *The Pirate* (time, William III.).

Pathfinder (*The*), Natty Bumpo; also called "The Deerslayer," "The Hawk-eye," and "The Trapper."—Fenimore Cooper, (five novels called *The Pathfinder, The Pioneers, The Deerslayer, The Last of the Mohicans,* and *The Prairie*).

Pathfinder of the Rocky Mountains. (*The*), Major-General John Charles Fremont, who conducted four exploring expeditions across the Rocky Mountains in 1842.

Patient Griselda or **Grisildis**, the wife of Wautier, marquis of Salucês. Boccaccio says she was a poor country lass, who became the wife of Gualtiere, marquis of Saluzzo. She was robbed of her children by her husband, reduced to abject poverty, divorced, and commanded to assist in the marriage of her husband with another woman; but she bore every affront patiently, and without complaint.—Chaucer, *Canterbury Tales* ("The Clerk's Tale," 1388); Boccaccio, *Decameron*, x. 10 (1352).

Patience Strong. Delightful old maid, who, after passing most of her life in a quiet New England township, goes abroad and tells her experiences in *Sights and Insights*.—A. D. T. Whitney (1860).

She is also the central figure in a quiet story of domestic life, entitled *Patience Strong's Outings* (1858).

Patin, brother of the emperor of Rome. He fights with Am´adis of Gaul, and has his horse killed under him.—Vasco de Lobeira, *Amadis de Gaul* (thirteenth century).

Patison, licensed jester to Sir Thos. More. Hans Holbein has introduced this jester in his famous picture of the lord chancellor.

Patriarch of Dorchester, John White, of Dorchester, a puritan divine (1574-1648).

Patriarchs (*The Last of the*). So *Christopher Casby*, of Bleeding-heart Yard was called. "So grey, so slow, so quiet, so impassionate, so very bumpy in the head, that patriarch was the word for him." Painters implored him to be a model for some patriarch they designed to paint. Philanthropists looked on him as famous capital for a platform. He had once been town agent in the Circumlocution Office, and was well-to-do.

His face had a bloom on it like ripe wall-fruit, and his blue eyes seemed to be the eyes of wisdom and virtue. His whole face teemed with the look of benignity. Nobody could say where the wisdom was, or where the virtue was, or where the benignity was, but they seemed to be somewhere about him.... He wore a long wide-skirted bottle-green coat, and a bottle-green pair of trousers, and a bottle-green waistcoat. The patriarchs were not dressed in bottle-green broadcloth, and yet his clothes looked patriarchal.—C. Dickens, *Little Dorrit* (1857).

Patrick, an old domestic at Shaw's Castle.—Sir W. Scott, *St. Ronan's Well* (time, George III.).

Patrick (*St.*), the tutelar saint of Ireland. Born at Kirk Patrick, near Dumbarton. His baptismal name was "Succeath" ("valor in war"), changed by Milcho, to whom he was sold as a slave into "Cotharig" (four families or four masters, to whom he had been sold). It was Pope Celestine who changed the name to "Patricius," when he sent him to convert the Irish.

Certainly the most marvellous of all the miracles ascribed to the saints is that recorded of St. Patrick. "He swam across the Shannon with his head in his mouth!"

Saint Patrick and King O'Neil. One day, the saint set the end of his crozier on the foot of O'Neil, king of Ulster, and, leaning heavily on it, hurt the king's foot severely; but the royal convert showed no indication of pain or annoyance whatsoever.

A similar anecdote is told of St. Areed, who went to show the king of Abyssinia a musical instrument he had invented. His majesty rested the head of his spear on the saint's foot, and leaned with both his hands on the spear while he listened to the music. St. Areed, though his great toe was severely pierced, showed no sign of pain, but went on playing as if nothing was the matter.

St. Patrick and the Serpent. St Patrick cleared Ireland of vermin. One old serpent resisted, but St. Patrick overcame it by cunning. He made a box, and invited the serpent to enter in. The serpent insisted it was too small; and so high the contention grew that the serpent got into the box to prove that he was right, whereupon St. Patrick slammed down the lid, and cast the box into the sea.

This tradition is marvellously like an incident of the *Arabian Nights' Entertainments.* A fisherman had drawn up a box or vase in his net, and on breaking it open a genius issued therefrom, and threatened the fisherman with immediate destruction because he had been enclosed so long. Said the fisherman to the genius, "I wish to know whether you really were in that vase." "I certainly was," said the genius. "I cannot believe it," replied the fisherman, "for the vase could not contain even one of your feet." Then the genius, to prove his assertion, changed into smoke, and entered into the vase, saying, "Now, incredulous fisherman, dost thou believe me?" But the fisherman clapped the leaden cover on the vase, and told the genius that he was about to throw the box into the sea, and that he would build a house on the spot to warn others not to fish up so wicked a genius.—*Arabian Nights* ("The Fisherman," one of the early tales).

*** St. Patrick, I fear, had read the *Arabian Nights,* and stole a leaf from the fisherman's book.

St. Patrick a Gentleman.

Oh, St. Patrick was a gentleman,
Who came of dacent people ...

This song was written by Messrs. Bennet and Toleken, of Cork, and was first sung by them at a masquerade in 1814. It was afterwards lengthened for Webbe, the comedian, who made it popular.

Patriot King (*The*), Henry St. John, Viscount Bolingbroke (1678-1751). He hired Mallet to traduce Pope after his decease, because the poet refused to give up certain copies of a work which the statesman wished to have destroyed.

Write as if St. John's soul could still inspire,
And do from hate what Mallet did for hire.
Byron, *English Bards and Scotch Reviewers* (1809).

Patriot of Humanity. So Byron calls Henry Grattan (1750-1820).—*Don Juan* (preface to canto vi., etc., 1824).

Patron (*The*), a farce by S. Foote (1764). The patron is Sir Thomas Lofty, called by his friends, "sharp-judging Adriel, the Muse's friend, himself a Muse," but by those who loved him less, "the modern Midas." Books without number were dedicated to him, and the writers addressed him as the "British Pollio, Atticus, the Mæcenas of England, protector of arts, paragon of poets, arbiter of taste, and sworn appraiser of Apollo and the Muses." The plot is very simple: Sir Thomas Lofty has written a play called *Robinson Crusoe*, and gets Richard Bever to stand godfather to it. The play is damned past redemption, and to soothe Bever, Sir Thomas allows him to marry his niece, Juliet.

Horace Walpole, earl of Orford, is the original of "Sir Thomas Lofty" (1717-1797).

Patten, according to Gay, is so called from Patty, the pretty daughter of a Lincolnshire farmer, with whom the village blacksmith fell in love. To save her from wet feet when she went to milk the cows, he mounted her clogs on an iron eke.

The patten now supports each frugal dame,
Which from the blue-eyed Patty takes its name.
Gay, *Trivia*, i. (1712).

(Of course, the word is the French *patin*, "a skate or high-heeled shoe," from the Greek, *patein*, "to walk.")

Pattieson (*Mr. Peter*), in the introduction of *The Heart of Midlothian*, by Sir W. Scott, and again in the introduction of *The Bride of Lammermoor*. He is a hypothetical assistant teacher at Gandercleuch, and the feigned author of *The Tales of My Landlord*, which Sir Walter Scott pretends were published by Jedediah Cleishbotham, after the death of Pattieson.

Patton (*Mrs.*). Tailoress and talker, otherwise known as "the Widow Jim," who has all genealogy and relationship at her tongue's end. "She chatters all day as the swallows chatter, and you do not tire of her."—Sarah Orne Jewett, *Deephaven* (1877).

Patterson (*Elizabeth*). One of the most remarkable women of this century. The beautiful daughter of a Baltimore merchant prince, she captivated Jerome Bonaparte, (then a minor, and dependent on his brother), who was visiting America. In the face of parental opposition, she married him Dec. 24, 1803. Napoleon (First Consul) promptly repudiated the marriage, ordered his brother home, and forbade all French vessels to receive as a passenger, "*the young person* with whom Citizen Joseph has connected himself." In October, 1804, the young couple sailed for France in the ship *Philadelphia*, but were blown ashore at Lewes, Del. In March, 1805, they embarked again, reaching Lisbon, April 2. Napoleon (now emperor) refused to allow them to enter France, but sent to know "what he could do for *Miss Patterson*." She replied that "Madame Bonaparte demanded her rights as one of the imperial family." The contest was unequal. She was sent back to America, and the marriage declared null and void. Her son, Jerome, was born in England, July 7, 1805. She was never allowed to see her husband again, yet her ambitious projects for "Bo," as she called her son, were unremitting until the downfall of the Bonarparte family. After this, she aimed to ally him with the English nobility, a design thwarted by his love-match with a lovely Baltimorean. She was an able financier, and became one of the richest women in Baltimore. Retaining her mind and many traces of her extraordinary beauty to the last, she died, April 3, 1879, at the age of ninety-four.

"By the laws of justice and of the Church she was a queen, although she was never allowed to reign.... There was about her the brilliancy of courts and palaces, the enchantment of a love-story, the suffering of a victim of despotic power."—Eugene Dìdier, *Life and Letters of Madame Bonaparte* (1879).

Patty, "the maid of the mill," daughter of Fairfield, the miller. She was brought up by the mother of Lord Aimworth, and was promised by her father in marriage to Farmer Giles; but she refused to marry him, and became the bride of Lord Aimworth. Patty was very clever, very pretty, very ingenuous, and loved his lordship to adoration.—Bickerstaff, *The Maid of the Mill* (1765).

Pattypan (*Mrs.*), a widow who keeps lodgings, and makes love to Tim Tartlet, to whom she is ultimately engaged.

By all accounts, she is just as loving now as she was thirty years ago.—James Cobb, *The First Floor*, i. 2 (1756-1818).

Patullo (*Mrs.*), waiting-woman to Lady Ashton.—Sir W. Scott, *Bride of Lammermoor* (time, William III.).

Pau-Puk-Keewis, a cunning mischief-maker, who taught the North American Indians the game of hazard, and stripped them, by his winnings, of all their possessions. In a mad freak Pau-Puk-Keewis entered the wigwam of Hiawatha and threw everything into confusion; so Hiawatha resolved to slay him. Pau-Puk-Keewis, taking to flight, prayed the beavers to make him a beaver ten times their own size. This they did; but when the other beavers made their escape, at the arrival of Hiawatha, Pau-Puk-Keewis was hindered from getting away by his great size; and Hiawatha slew him. His spirit, escaping, flew upwards, and prayed the storm-fools to make him a "brant" ten times their own size. This was done, and he was told never to look downwards, or he would lose his life. When Hiawatha arrived, the "brant" could not forbear looking at him; and immediately he fell to earth, and Hiawatha transformed him into an eagle.

Now in winter, when the snowflakes
Whirl in eddies round the lodges,...
"There," they cry, "comes Pau-Puk-Keewis;
He is dancing thro' the village,
He is gathering in his harvest."
Longfellow, *Hiawatha*, xvii. (1855).

Paul, the love-child of Margaret, who retired to Port Louis, in the Mauritius, to bury herself, and bring up her only child. Hither came Mde. de la Tour, a widow, and was confined of a daughter, whom she named Virginia. Between these neighbors a mutual friendship arose, and the two children became playmates. As they grew in years their fondness for each other developed into love. When Virginia was 15, her mother's aunt adopted her, and begged she might be sent to France to finish her education. She was above two years in France; and as she refused to marry a count of the "aunt's" providing, she was disinherited and sent back to her mother. When within a cable's length of the island a hurricane dashed the ship to pieces, and the dead body of Virginia was thrown upon the shore. Paul drooped from grief, and within two months followed her to the grave.—Bernardin de St. Pierre, *Paul et Virgine* (1788).

In Cobb's dramatic version, Paul's mother (Margaret) is made a faithful domestic of Virginia's parents. Virginia's mother dies, and commits her infant daughter to the care of Dominique, a faithful old negro servant, and Paul and Virginia are brought up in the belief that they are brother and sister. When Virginia is 15 years old, her aunt, Leonora de Guzman, adopts her, and sends Don Antonio de Guardes to bring her to Spain and make her his bride. She is taken by force on board ship; but scarcely has the ship started, when a hurricane dashes it on rocks, and it is wrecked. Alhambra, a runaway slave whom Paul and Virginia had befriended, rescues Virginia, who is brought to shore and married to Paul; but Antonio is drowned (1756-1818).

Paul (Father), Paul Sarpi (1552-1628).

Paul (St.). The very sword which cut off the head of this apostle is preserved at the convent of La Lisla, near Tolēdo, in Spain. If any one doubts the fact he may, for a gratuity, see a "copper sword, twenty-five inches long and three and a half broad, on one side of which is the word MUCRO ('a sword'), and on the other PAULUS ... CAPITE." Can anything be more convincing?

Paul (The Second St.). St Remi or *Remigius*, "The Great Apostle of the French." He was made bishop of Rheims when only 22 years old. It was St Remi who baptized Clovis, and told him that henceforth he must worship what he hitherto had hated, and abjure what he had hitherto adored (439-535).

. The cruse employed by St. Remi in the baptism of Clovis was used through the French monarchy in the anointing of all the kings.

Paul Pry, an idle, inquisitive, meddlesome fellow, who has no occupation of his own, and is forever poking his nose into other people's affairs. He always comes in with the apology, "I hope I don't intrude."—John Poole, *Paul Pry*.

Thomas Hill, familiarly called "Tommy Hill," was the original of this character, and also of "Gilbert Gurney," by Theodore Hook. Planché says of Thomas Hill:

His *specialité* was the accurate information he could impart on all the petty details of the domestic economy of his friends, the contents of their wardrobes, their pantries, the number of pots of preserves in their store-closets, and of the table-napkins in their linen-presses, the dates of their births and marriages, the amounts of their tradesmen's bills, and whether paid weekly or quarterly. He had been on the press, and was connected with the *Morning Chronicle*. He used to drive Mathews crazy by ferreting out his whereabouts when he left London, and popping the information into some paper.—*Recollections*, i. 131-2.

Paul Rushleigh, son of a wealthy manufacturer, and in love from boyhood with Faith Gartney. She can give him only sisterly affection in return, but her refusal makes a man of the boy. Ten years afterwards, as General Rushleigh, a noble, high-minded patriot, he meets Margaret Regis and marries her.— A. D. T. Whitney, *Sights and Insights* (1876).

Pauletti (*the Lady Erminia*), ward of Master George Heriot, the king's goldsmith.—Sir W. Scott, *The Fortunes of Nigel* (time, James I.).

Pauli´na, the noble-spirited wife of Antig´onus, a Sicilian lord, and the kind friend of Queen Hermi´onê. When Hermionê gave birth in prison to a daughter, Paulina undertook to present it to King Leontês, hoping that his heart would be softened at the sight of his infant daughter; but he commanded the child to be cast out on a desert shore, and left there to perish. The child was drifted to the "coast" of Bohemia, and brought up by a shepherd, who called it Perdĭta. Florizel, the son of king Polixĕnês, fell in love with her, and fled with her to Sicily, to escape the vengeance of the angry king. The fugitives being introduced to Leontês, it was soon discovered that Perdita was the king's daughter, and Polixenês consented to the union he had before forbidden. Paulina now invited Leontês and the rest to inspect a famous statue of Hermionê, and the statue turned out to be the living queen herself.—Shakespeare, *The Winter's Tale* (1604).

Pauline, "The Beauty of Lyons," daughter of M. Deschappelles, a Lyonese merchant; "as pretty as Venus, and as proud as Juno." Pauline rejected the suits of Beauseant, Glavis and Claude Melnotte; and the three rejected lovers combined on vengeance. To this end, Claude, who was a gardener's son, pretended to be the Prince Como, and Pauline married him, but was indignant when she discovered the trick which had been played upon her. Claude left her, and entered the French army, where in two years and a half he rose to the rank of colonel. Returning to Lyons, he found his father-in-law on the eve of bankruptcy, and Pauline about to be sold to Beauseant for money to satisfy the creditors. Being convinced that Pauline really loved him, Claude paid the money required, and claimed the lady as his loving and grateful wife.—Lord L. B. Lytton, *The Lady of Lyons* (1838).

Pauline (Mademoiselle) or MONNA PAULA, the attendant of Lady Erminia Pauletti, the goldsmith's ward.—Sir W. Scott, *The Fortunes of Nigel* (time, James I.).

Pauline Pavlovna, heroine of T. B. Aldrich's drama of that name (1890).

Pauli´nus of York, christened 10,000 men, besides women and their children in one single day in the Swale. (Altogether some 50,000 souls, *i.e.* 104 every minute, 6,250 every hour, supposing he worked eight hours without stopping.)

When the Saxons first received the Christian faith,
Paulinus of old York, the zealous bishop then,
In Swale's abundant stream christened ten thousand men,
With women and their babes, a number more besides,
Upon one happy day.
Drayton, *Polyolbion*, xxviii. (1622).

Paulo, the cardinal and brother of Count Guido Franceschi´ni. He advised the count to repair his bankrupt fortune by marrying an heiress.—R. Browning, *The Ring and the Book*.

Paupiah, the Hindû steward of the British governor of Madras.—Sir W. Scott, *The Surgeon's Daughter* (time, George II.).

Pausa´nias (*The British*), William Camden (1551-1623). Pausanias was a traveller and geographer in the 2d century A.D., who wrote an Itinerary of Greece. Camden wrote in Latin his "Brittania," a survey of the British Isles.

Pauvre Jacques. When Marie Antoinette had her artificial Swiss village in the "Little Trianon," a Swiss girl was brought over to heighten the illusion. She was observed to pine, and was heard to sigh out, *pauvre Jacques*! This little romance pleased the queen, who sent for Jacques, and gave the pair a wedding portion; while the Marchioness de Travanet wrote the song called *Pauvre Jacques*, which created at the time quite a sensation. The first and last verses run thus:

Pauvre Jacques, quand j'etais près de toi,
Je ne sentais pas ma misère;
Mais à présent que tu vis loin de moi,
Je manque de tout sur la terre.

Poor Jack, while I was near to thee,
Tho' poor, my bliss was unalloyed;
But now thou dwell'st so far from me,
The world appears a lonesome void.

Pa´via (*Battle of*). Francis I. of France is said to have written to his mother these words, after the loss of this battle: "Madame, tout est perdu hors l'honneur;" but what he really wrote was: "Madame ... de toutes choses ne m'est demeuré pas que l'honneur et la vie."

And with a noble siege revolted Pavia took.
Drayton, *Polyolbion*, xviii. (1613).

Pavillon (*Meinheer Hermann*), the syndic at Liège [*Le-aje*].

Mother Mabel Pavillon, wife of Meinheer Hermann.

Trudchen or *Gertrude Pavillon*, their daughter, betrothed to Hans Glover.—Sir W. Scott, *Quentin Durward* (time, Edward IV.).

Pawkins (*Major*), a huge, heavy man, "one of the most remarkable of the age." He was a great politician and great patriot, but generally under a cloud, wholly owing to his distinguished genius for bold speculations, not to say "swindling schemes." His creed was "to run a moist pen slick through everything, and start afresh."—C. Dickens, *Martin Chuzzlewit* (1844).

Pawnbrokers' Balls. The gilded balls, the sign of pawnbrokers, are the pills on the shield of the Medici family. Its founder, Cosmo, named after Saint Cosmo, the patron of physicians, joined the guild of the doctors (*Medici*), as every Florentine enrolled himself in one of these charitable societies. The Medici family became great money-lenders, and their shield with the "balls" or "pills" was placed over the doors of their agents.

Paynim Harper (*The*), referred to by Tennyson in the *Last Tournament*, was Orpheus.

Swine, goats, asses, rams and geese
Troop'd round a Paynim harper once ...
Then were swine, goats, asses, geese
The wiser fools, seeing thy Paynim bard
Had such a mastery of his mystery
That he could harp his wife up out of hell.
Tennyson, *The Last Tournament* (1859).

Peace (*Prince of the*), Don Manuel Godoy, born at Badajoz. So called because he concluded the "peace of Basle" between the French and Spanish nations in 1795 (1767-1851).

Peace (*The Father of*), Andrea Doria (1469-1560).

Peace (*The Surest Way to*). Fox, afterwards bishop of Hereford, said to Henry VIII., *The surest way to peace is a constant preparation for war*. The Romans had the axiom, *Si vis pacem, para bellum*. It was said of Edgar, surnamed "the Peaceful," king of England, that he preserved peace in those turbulent times "by being always prepared for war" (reigned 959-975.)

Peace Thirlmore, ambitious daughter of a scholarly recluse near New Haven. She marries a clever student, who becomes a sensational preacher, then farmer, then an army officer. His wife passes through many stages of belief and emotion, emerging at last into the sunshine.—W. M. Baker, *His Majesty, Myself* (1879).

Peace at any Price. Mézeray says of Louis XII., that he had such detestation of war that he rather chose to lose his duchy of Milan than burden his subjects with a war-tax.—*Histoire de France* (1643).

Peace of Antal´cidas, the peace concluded by Antalcidas, the Spartan, and Artaxerxes (B.C. 387).

Peace of God, a peace enforced by the clergy on the barons of Christendom, to prevent the perpetual feuds between baron and baron (1035).

Peach´um, a pimp, patron of a gang of thieves, and receiver of their stolen goods. His house is the resort of thieves, pickpockets, and villains of all sorts.

He betrays his comrades when it is for his own benefit, and even procures the arrest of Captain Macheath.

Mrs. Peachum, wife of Peachum. She recommends her daughter Polly to be "somewhat nice in her deviations from virtue."

Polly Peachum, daughter of Peachum. (See POLLY.)—J. Gay, *The Beggar's Opera* (1727).

Pearl (*Little*), illegitimate child of Hester Prynne and Arthur Dimmesdale. A piquant, tricksy sprite, as naughty as she is bewitching—a creature of fire and air, more elfish than human, at once her mother's torment and her treasure.—Nathaniel Hawthorne, *The Scarlet Letter* (1850).

Pearl. It is said that Cleopatra swallowed a pearl of more value than the whole of the banquet she had provided in honor of Antony. This she did when she drank to his health. The same sort of extravagant folly is told of Æsopus, son of Clodius Æsopus, the actor (Horace, *Satire*, ii. 3).

A similar act of vanity and folly is ascribed to Sir Thomas Gresham, when Queen Elizabeth dined at the City banquet, after her visit to the Royal Exchange.

Here £15,000 at one clap goes
Instead of sugar; Gresham drinks the pearl
Unto his queen and mistress.
Thomas Heywood.

Pearson (*Captain Gilbert*), officer in attendance on Cromwell.—Sir W. Scott, *Woodstock* (time, Commonwealth).

Peasant-Bard (*The*), Robert Burns (1859-1796).

Peasant-Painter of Sweden, Hörberg. His chief paintings are altar-pieces.

The altar-piece painted by Hörberg.
Longfellow, *The Children of the Lord's Supper*.

Peasant Poet of Northamptonshire, John Clare (1793-1864).

Peasant of the Danube (*The*), Louis Legendre, a member of the French National Convention (1755-1797); called in French *Le Paysan du Danube*, from his "éloquence sauvage."

Peau de Chagrin, a story by Balzac. The hero becomes possessed of a magical wild ass's skin, which yields him the means of gratifying every wish; but for every wish thus gratified, the skin shrank somewhat, and at last vanished, having been wished entirely away. Life is a *peau d'âne*, for every vital act diminishes its force, and when all its force is gone, life is gone (1834).

Peckhams (*The*), *Silas Peckham*, "a thorough Yankee, born on a windy part of the coast, and reared chiefly on salt-fish; keeps a young ladies' school exactly as he would have kept a hundred head of cattle—for the simple, unadorned purpose of making just as much money in just as few years as can be safely done."

Mrs. Peckham's specialty is "to look after the feathering, cackling, roosting, rising, and general behavior of these hundred chicks. An honest, ignorant woman, she could not have passed an examination in the youngest class."—Oliver Wendell Holmes *Elsie Venner* (1861).

Peck'sniff, "architect and land surveyor," at Salisbury. He talks homilies even in drunkenness, prates about the beauty of charity, and duty of forgiveness, but is altogether a canting humbug, and is ultimately so reduced in position that he becomes a "drunken, begging, squalid, letter-writing man," out at elbows, and almost shoeless. Pecksniff's specialty is the "sleek, smiling abominations of hypocrisy."

If ever man combined within himself all the mild qualities of the lamb with a considerable touch of the dove, and not a dash of the crocodile, or the least possible suggestion of the very mildest seasoning of the serpent, that man was Mr. Pecksniff, "the messenger of peace."

Charity and *Mercy Pecksniff*, the two daughters of the "architect and land surveyor." Charity is thin, ill-natured, and a shrew, eventually jilted by a weak young man, who really loves her sister. Mercy Pecksniff, usually called "Merry," is pretty and true-hearted; though flippant and foolish as a girl, she becomes greatly toned down by the troubles of her married life.—C. Dickens, *Martin Chuzzlewit* (1843).

Peculiar, negro slave, endowed with talent, ambitious of an opportunity to develop and use these, but hopeless of gaining it, until emancipated by the Civil War between the United States and the Southern Confederacy.—Epes Sargent, *Peculiar*.

Pedant, an old fellow set up to personate Vincentio in Shakespeare's comedy called *The Taming of the Shrew* (1695).

Pèdre (*Don*), a Sicilian nobleman, who has a Greek slave of great beauty, named Isidore (3 *syl.*). This slave is loved by Adraste (2 *syl.*), a French gentleman, who gains access to the house under the guise of a portrait-painter. He next sends his slave, Zaïda, to complain to the Sicilian of ill-treatment, and Don Pèdre volunteers to intercede on her behalf. At this moment Adraste comes up, and demands that Zaïde be given up to deserved chastisement. Pedrè pleads for her, Adraste appears to be pacified, and Pedrè calls for Zaïde to come forth. Isidore, in the veil of Zaïde, comes out, and Pedrè says, "There, take her home, and use her well." "I will do so," says

Adraste, and leads off the Greek slave.—Molière, *Le Sicilien ou L'Amour Peintre* (1667).

Pedrillo, the tutor of Don Juan. After the shipwreck, the men in the boat, being wholly without provisions, cast lots to know which should be killed as food for the rest, and the lot fell on Pedrillo, but those who feasted on him most ravenously went mad.

His tutor, the licentiate Pedrillo,
Who several languages did understand.
Byron, *Don Juan*, ii. 25; see 76-79 (1819).

Pedro, "the pilgrim," a noble gentleman servant to Alinda (daughter of Lord Alphonso).—Beaumont and Fletcher, *The Pilgrim* (1621).

Pedro (Don), prince of Aragon.—Shakespeare, *Much Ado about Nothing* (1600).

Pedro (Don), father of Leonora.—R. Jephson, *Two Strings to your Bow* (1792).

Pedro (Don), a Portuguese nobleman, father of Donna Violante.—Mrs. Centlivre, *The Wonder* (1714).

Pedro (Dr.), whose full name was Dr. Pedro Rezio de Aguero, court physician in the island of Barataria. He carried a whalebone rod in his hand, and whenever any dish of food was set before Sancho Panza, the governor, he touched it with his wand, that it might be instantly removed, as unfit for the governor to eat. Partridges were "forbidden by Hippoc´ratês," olla podridas were "most pernicious," rabbits were "a sharp-haired diet," veal might not be touched, but "a few wafers, and a thin slice or two of quince," might not be harmful.

The governor, being served with some beef hashed with onions, ... fell to with more avidity than if he had been set down to Milan godwits, Roman pheasants, Sorrento veal, Moron partridges, or green geese of Lavajos; and turning to Dr. Pedro, he said, "Look you, signor doctor, I want no danties, ... for I have always been used to beef, bacon, pork, turnips and onions."—Cervantes, *Don Quixote*, II. iii. 10, 12 (1615).

Peebles (*Peter*), the pauper litigant. He is vain, litigious, hard-hearted, and credulous; a liar, a drunkard, and a pauper. His "ganging plea" is worthy of Hogarth.—Sir W. Scott, *Redgauntlet* (time, George III.).

Peecher (*Miss*), a schoolmistress, in the flat country where Kent and Surrey meet. "Small, shining, neat, methodical, and buxom was Miss Peecher; cherry-cheeked and tuneful of voice. A little pincushion, a little hussie, a little book, a little work-box, a little set of tables and weights and measures, and a little woman all in one. She could write a little essay on any subject exactly a slate long, and strictly according to rule. If Mr. Bradley Headstone had proposed marriage to her, she would certainly have replied 'yes,' for she loved him;" but Mr. Headstone did not love Miss Peecher—he loved Lizzie Hexam, and had no love to spare for any other woman.—C. Dickens, *Our Mutual Friend*, ii. 1 (1864).

Peel-the-Causeway (*Old*), a smuggler. Sir W. Scott, *Redgauntlet* (time, George III.).

Peeler (*Sir*), any crop which greatly impoverishes the ground. To *peel* is to impoverish soil, as "oats, rye, barley, and grey wheat," but not peas (xxxiii. 51).

Wheat doth not well,
Nor after Sir Peeler he loveth to dwell.
T. Tusser, *Five Hundred Points of Good Husbandry*, xviii. 12 (1557).

Peelers, the constabulary of Ireland, appointed under the Peace Preservation Act of 1814, proposed by Sir Robert Peel. The name was subsequently given to the new police of England, who are also called "Bobbies" from Sir Robert Peel.

Peep-o'-Day Boys, Irish insurgents of 1784, who prowled about at daybreak, searching for arms.

Peeping Tom of Coventry. Lady Godiva earnestly besought her husband (Leofric, earl of Mercia) to relieve the men of Coventry of their grievous oppressions. Leofric, annoyed at her importunity, told her he would do so when she had ridden on horseback, naked, through the town. The countess took him at his word, rode naked through the town, and Leofric was obliged to grant the men of Coventry a charter of freedom.—Dugdale.

Rapin says that the countess commanded all persons to keep within doors and away from windows during her ride. One man, named Tom of Coventry, took a peep of the lady on horseback, but it cost him his life.

*** Tennyson, in his *Godiva*, has reproduced this story.

Peerage of the Saints. In the preamble of the statutes instituting the Order of St. Michael, founded by Louis XI in 1469, the archangel is styled "my lord," and created a knight. The apostles had been already ennobled and knighted. We read of "the Earl Peter," "Count Paul," "the Baron Stephen," and so on. Thus, in the introduction of a sermon upon St. Stephen's Day, we have these lines:

Entendes toutes a chest sermon,
Et clair et lai tules environ;
Contes vous vueille la pation
De St. Estieul le baron.

Peerce (1 *syl.*), a generic name for a farmer or ploughman. Piers the plowman is the name assumed by Robert or William Langland, in a historico-satirical poem so called.

And yet, my priests, pray you to God for Peerce ...
And if you have a "pater noster" spare,
Then you shal pray for saylers.
G. Gascoigne, *The Steele Glas* (died 1577).

Peery (*Paul*), landlord of the Ship, Dover.

Mrs. Peery, Paul's wife.—G. Colman, *Ways and Means* (1788).

Peerybingle (*John*), a carrier, "lumbering, slow, and honest; heavy, but light of spirit; rough upon the surface, but gentle at the core; dull without, but quick within; stolid, but so good. O, Mother Nature, give thy children the true poetry of heart that hid itself in this poor carrier's breast, and we can bear to have them talking prose all their life long!"

Mrs. [Mary] Peerybingle, called by her husband "Dot." She was a little chubby, cheery, young wife, very fond of her husband, and very proud of her baby; a good housewife, who delighted in making the house snug and cozy for John, when he came home after his day's work. She called him "a dear old darling of a dunce," or "her little goosie." She sheltered Edward Plummer in her cottage for a time, and got into trouble; but the marriage of Edward with May Fielding cleared up the mystery, and John loved his little Dot more fondly than ever.—C. Dickens, *The Cricket on the Hearth* (1845).

Peg. *Drink to your peg*. King Edgar ordered "that pegs should be fastened into drinking-horns at stated distances and whoever drank beyond his peg at one draught should be obnoxious to a severe punishment."

I had lately a peg-tankard in my hand. It had on the inside a row of eight pins, one above another, from bottom to top. It held two quarts, so that there was a gill of liquor between peg and peg. Whoever drank short of his pin or beyond it, was obliged to drink to the next, and so on till the tankard was drained to the bottom.—Sharpe, *History of the Kings of England*.

Peg-a-Ramsey, the heroine of an old song. Percy says it was an indecent ballad. Shakespeare alludes to it in his *Twelfth Night*, act ii. sc. 3 (1614).

James I. had been much struck with the beauty and embarrassment of the pretty Peg-a-Ramsey? as he called her.—Sir W. Scott.

Peg'asus, the winged horse of the Muses. It was caught by Bellerophon, who mounted thereon, and destroyed the Chimæra; but when he attempted to ascend to heaven, he was thrown from the horse, and Pegasus mounted alone to the skies, where it became the constellation of the same name.

To break Pegasus's neck, to write halting poetry.

Some, free from rhyme or reason, rule or check,
Break Priscian's head, and Pegasus's neck.
Pope, *The Dunciad*, iii. 161 (1728).

₊ To "break Priscian's head," is to write ungrammatically. Priscian was a great grammarian of the fifth century.

Pegg (*Catharine*), one of the mistresses of Charles II. She was the daughter of Thomas Pegg, Esq., of Yeldersay, in Derbyshire.

Peggot´ty (*Clara*), servant of Mrs. Copperfield, and the faithful old nurse of David Copperfield. Her name "Clara" was tabooed, because it was the name of Mrs. Copperfield. Clara Peggotty married Barkis, the carrier.

Being very plump, whenever she made any little exertion after she was dressed, some of the buttons on the back of her gown flew off.—Ch. ii.

Dan'el Peggotty, brother of David Copperfield's nurse. Dan'el was a Yarmouth fisherman. His nephew, Ham Peggotty, and his brother-in-law's child, "little Em'ly," lived with him. Dan'el himself was a bachelor, and Mrs. Gummidge (widow of his late partner) kept house for him. Dan'el Peggotty was most tender-hearted, and loved little Em'ly with all his heart.

Ham Peggotty, nephew of Dan'el Peggotty, of Yarmouth, and son of Joe, Dan'el's brother. Ham was in love with little Em'ly, daughter of Tom (Dan's brother-in-law), but Steerforth stepped in between them, and stole Em'ly away. Ham Peggotty is represented as the very beau-ideal of an uneducated, simple-minded, honest, and warm-hearted fisherman. He was drowned in his attempt to rescue Steerforth from the sea.

Em'ly Peggotty, daughter of Dan's brother-in-law, Tom. She was engaged to Ham Peggotty; but being fascinated with Steerforth, ran off with him. She was afterwards reclaimed, and emigrated to Australia with Dan'el and Mrs. Gummidge.—C. Dickens, *David Copperfield* (1849).

Peggy, grandchild of the old widow Maclure, a covenanter.—Sir W. Scott, *Old Mortality* (time, Charles II.).

Peggy, the laundry-maid of Colonel Mannering, at Woodburne.—Sir W. Scott, *Guy Mannering* (time, George II.).

Peggy (*Shippen*). A love-letter from Benedict Arnold to this young lady is extant in which after telling her that he has presumed to write to her papa and has requested his sanction to his addresses, Arnold goes on to protest.

"May I perish if I would give you one moment's inquietude, to purchase the greatest possible felicity to myself. Whatever my fate may be, my most ardent wish is for your happiness, and my latest breath will be to implore the blessing of heaven on the idol and only wish of my soul." September 26, 1778.

Peggy [Thrift], the orphan daughter of Sir Thomas Thrift, of Hampshire, and the ward of Moody, who brings her up in seclusion in the country. When Moody is 50, and Peggy 19, the guardian tries to marry her, but "the country girl" outwits him, and marries Belville, a young man of more suitable age. Peggy calls her guardian "Bud." She is very simple but sharp, ingenuous but crafty, lively and girlish.—*The Country Girl* (Garrick altered from Wycherly's *Country Wife*, 1675).

Peggy. Dream-wife about whom cluster the imaginations of the bachelor over the fire of green wood.

"Smoke always goes before blaze, and doubt before decision."—Ik. Marvel (Donald G. Mitchell), *Reveries of a Bachelor* (1850).

Pegler (*Mrs.*), mother of Josiah Boundderby, Esq., banker and mill-owner, called "The Bully of Humility." The son allows the old woman £30 a year to keep out of sight.—C. Dickens. *Hard Times* (1854).

Peg Woffington, celebrated English actress, *intriguante*, but kind of heart. Sir Charles Vane is one of her lovers, but after the appearance of his simple-hearted wife upon the scene, the actress dismisses her admirer, and induces him to return to domestic life.—Charles Reade, *Peg Woffington*.

Pek´uah, the attendant of Princess Nekayah, of the "happy valley." She accompanied the princess in her wanderings, but refused to enter the great pyramid, and, while the princess was exploring the chambers, was carried off by some Arabs. She was afterwards ransomed for 200 ounces of gold.—Dr. Johnson, *Rasselas* (1759).

Pelay´o (*Prince*), son of Favil´a, founder of the Spanish monarchy after the overthrow of Roderick, last of the Gothic kings. He united, in his own person, the royal lines of Spain and of the Goths.

In him the old Iberian blood,
Of royal and remotest ancestry
From undisputed source, flowed undefiled ...
He, too, of Chindasuintho's regal line
Sole remnant now, drew after him the love
Of all true Goths.
Southey, *Roderick, etc.*, viii. (1814).

Pelham, the hero of a novel by Lord Lytton, entitled *Pelham, or The Adventures of a Gentleman* (1828).

Pelham (M.), one of the many *aliases* of Sir R. Phillips, under which he published *The Parent's and Tutor's First Catechism*. In the preface he calls the writer *authoress*. Some of his other names are Rev. David Blair, Rev. C. C. Clarke, Rev. J. Goldsmith.

Pel'ian Spear (*The*), the lance of Achillês which wounded and cured Te'lephos. So called from Peleus, the father of Achillês.

Such was the cure the Arcadian hero found—
The Pelian spear that wounded, made him sound.
Ovid, *Remedy of Love*.

Peli'des (3 *syl.*), Achillês, son of Peleus (2 *syl.*), chief of the Greek warriors at the siege of Troy.—Homer, *Iliad*.

When, like Pelidês, bold beyond control,
Homer raised high to heaven the loud impetuous song.
Beattie, *The Minstrel* (1773-4).

Pe'lion ("*mud-sprung*"), one of the frog chieftains.

A spear at Pelion, Troglodytês cast
The missive spear within the bosom past
Death's sable shades the fainting frog surround,
And life's red tide runs ebbing from the wound.
Parnell, *Battle of the Frogs and Mice*, iii. (about 1712).

Pell (*Solomon*), an attorney in the Insolvent Debtors' court. He has the very highest opinions of his own merits, and by his aid Tony Weller contrives to get his son Sam sent to the Fleet for debt, that he may be near Mr. Pickwick to protect and wait upon him.—C. Dickens, *The Pickwick Papers* (1836).

Pelleas (*Sir*), lord of many isles, and noted for his great muscular strength. He fell in love with Lady Ettard, but the lady did not return his love. Sir Gaw'ain promised to advocate his cause with the lady, but played him false. Sir Pelleas caught them in unseemly dalliance with each other, but forbore to kill them. By the power of enchantment, the lady was made to dote on Sir Pelleas; but the knight would have nothing to say to her, so she pined and died. After the Lady Ettard played him false, the Damsel of the Lake "rejoiced him, and they loved together during their whole lives."—Sir T. Malory, *History of Prince Arthur*, i. 79-82 (1470).

⁎ Sir Pelleas must not be confounded with Sir Pelles (*q.v.*).

Pellegrin, the pseudonym of de la Motte Fouqué (1777-1843).

Pelles (*Sir*), of Corbin Castle, "king of the foragn land and nigh cousin of Joseph of Arimathy." He was father of Sir Eliazar, and of the Lady Elaine, who fell in love with Sir Launcelot, by whom she became the mother of Sir Galahad, "who achieved the quest of the Holy Graal." This Elaine was not the "lily maid of Astolat."

While Sir Launcelot was visiting King Pelles, a glimpse of the Holy Graal was vouchsafed them:

For when they went into the castle to take their repast ... there came a dove to the window, and in her bill was a little censer of gold, and there withall was such a savour as though all the spicery of the world had been there ... and a damsel, passing fair, bare a vessel of gold between her hands, and thereto the king kneeled devoutly and said his prayers.... "Oh, mercy!" said Sir Launcelot, "what may this mean?" ... "This," said the king, "is the Holy Sancgreall which ye have seen."—Sir T. Malory, *History of Prince Arthur*, iii. 2 (1470).

Pellinore (*Sir*), king of the isles and knight of the Round Table (pt. i. 57). He was a good man of power, was called "The Knight with the Stranger Beast," and slew King Lot of Orkney, but was himself slain ten years afterwards by Sir Gawain, one of Lot's sons (pt. i. 35). Sir Pellinore (3 *syl.*) had, by the wife of Aries, the cowherd, a son named Sir Tor, who was the first knight of the Round Table created by King Arthur (pt. i. 47, 48); one daughter, Elein, by the Lady of Rule (pt. iii. 10); and three sons in lawful wedlock; Sir Aglouale (sometimes called Aglavale, probably a clerical error), Sir Lamorake Dornar (also called Sir Lamorake de Galis), and Sir Percivale de Gralis (pt. ii. 108). The widow succeeded to the throne (pt. iii. 10).—Sir T. Malory, *History of Prince Arthur* (1470).

Milton calls the name "Pellenore" (2 *syl.*).

Fair damsels, met in forests wide
By knights of Logres, or of Lyones,
Lancelot, or Pelleas, or Pellenore.
Milton.

Pelob´ates (4 *syl.*), one of the frog champions. The word means "mud-wader." In the battle he flings a heap of mud against Psycarpax, the Hector of the mice, and half blinds him; but the warrior mouse heaves a stone "whose bulk would need ten degenerate mice of modern days to lift," and the mass, falling on the "mud-wader," breaks his leg.—Parnell, *Battle of the Frogs and Mice*, iii. (about 1712).

Pel´ops' Shoulder, ivory. The tale is that Demēter ate the shoulder of Pelops when it was served up by Tan´talos for food. The gods restored Pelops to life by putting the dismembered body into a caldron, but found that it lacked a shoulder; whereupon Demeter supplied him with an ivory shoulder, and all his descendants bore this distinctive mark.

N.B.—It will be remembered that Pythag´oras had a *golden thigh*.

Your forehead high,
And smooth as Pelop's shoulder.
John Fletcher, *The Faithful Shepherdess*, ii. 1 (1610).

Pelos, father of Physigna´thos, king of the frogs. The word means "mud."—Parnell, *Battle of the Frogs and Mice* (about 1712).

Pembroke (*The earl of*), uncle to Sir Aymer de Valence.—Sir W. Scott, *Castle Dangerous* (time, Henry I.).

Pembroke (*the Rev. Mr.*), chaplain at Waverley Honor.—Sir W. Scott, *Waverley* (time, George II.).

Pen, Philemon Holland, translator-general of the classics. Of him was the epigram written:

Holland, with his translations doth so fill us,
He will not let *Suetonius* be *Tranquillus*.

(The point of which is, of course, that the name of the Roman historian was *C. Suetonius Tranquillus*.)

Many of these translations were written from beginning to end with one pen, and hence he himself wrote:

With one sole pen I writ this book,
Made of a grey goose-quill;
A pen it was when it I took,
And a pen I leave it still.

Pendennis (*Arthur*), pseudonym of W. M. Thackeray in *The Newcomes* (1854).

Pendennis, a novel by Thackeray (1849), in which much of his own history and experience is recorded with a novelist's license. *Pendennis* stands in relation to Thackeray as *David Copperfield* to Charles Dickens.

Arthur Pendennis, a young man of ardent feelings and lively intellect, but conceited and selfish. He has a keen sense of honor, and a capacity for loving, but altogether he is not an attractive character.

Laura Pendennis. This is one of the best of Thackeray's characters.

Major Pendennis, a tuft-hunter, who fawns on his patrons for the sake of wedging himself into their society.—*History of Pendennis*, published originally in monthly parts, beginning in 1849.

Pendrag′on, probably a title meaning "chief leader in war." *Dragon* is Welsh for a "leader in war," and *pen* for "head" or "chief." The title was given to Uther, brother of Constans, and father of Prince Arthur. Like the word "Pharaoh," it is used as a proper name without the article.—Geoffrey of Monmouth, *Chron.*, vi. (1142).

Once I read,
That stout Pendragon in his litter, sick,
Came to the field, and vanquished his foes.
Shakespeare, 1 *Henry VI.* act iii. sc. 2 (1589).

Penel′ope's Web, a work that never progresses. Penelopê, the wife of Ulysses, being importuned by several suitors during her husband's long absence, made reply that she could not marry again, even if Ulysses were dead, till she had finished weaving a shroud for her aged father-in-law. Every night she pulled out what she had woven during the day, and thus the shroud made no progress towards completion.—*Greek Mythology*.

The French say of a work "never ending, still beginning," *c'est l'ouvrage de Pénélope*.

Penelope Lapham, vivacious, but not pretty daughter of Silas Lapham. Her wit wins the love her sister's beauty could not capture. Penelope's unintentional conquest brings painful perplexity to herself, with anguish to her sister. Still she yields finally to Irene's magnanimity and her suitor's persuasions, and weds Tom Corey.—W. D. Howells, *The Rise of Silas Lapham* (1887).

Penel′ophon, the beggar loved by King Cophetua. Shakespeare calls the name Zenelophon in *Love's Labor's Lost*, act iv. sc. 1 (1594).—Percy, *Reliques*, I. ii. 6 (1765).

Penelva (*The Exploits and Adventures of*), part of the series called *Le Roman des Romans*, pertaining to "Am′adis of Gaul." This part was added by an anonymous Portuguese (fifteenth century).

Penfeather (*Lady Penelope*), the Lady Patroness at the Spa.—Sir W. Scott, *St. Ronan's Well* (time, George III.).

Pengwern (*The Torch of*), prince Gwenwyn of Powys-land.—Sir W. Scott, *The Betrothed* (time, Henry II.).

Pengwinion (*Mr.*), from Cornwall; a Jacobite conspirator with Mr. Redgauntlet.—Sir W. Scott, *Redgauntlet* (time, George III.).

Peninsular War (*The*), the war carried on by Sir Arthur Wellesley against Napoleon in Portugal and Spain (1808-1814).

Southey wrote a *History of the Peninsular War* (1822-32).

Penitents of Love (*Fraternity of the*), an institution established in Languedoc, in the thirteenth century, consisting of knights and esquires, dames and damsels, whose object was to prove the excess of their love by bearing, with invincible constancy, the extremes of heat and cold. They passed the greater part of the day abroad, wandering about from castle to castle, wherever they were summoned by the inviolable duties of love and gallantry; so that many of these devotees perished by the inclemency of the weather, and received the crown of martyrdom to their profession.—See Warton, *History of English Poetry* (1781).

Pen'lake (*Richard*), a cheerful man, both frank and free, but married to Rebecca, a terrible shrew. Rebecca knew if she once sat in St. Michael's chair (on St. Michael's Mount, in Cornwall), that she would rule her husband ever after; so she was very desirous of going to the mount. It so happened that Richard fell sick, and both vowed to give six marks to St. Michael if he recovered. Richard did recover, and they visited the shrine; but while Richard was making the offering, Rebecca ran to seat herself in St. Michael's chair; but no sooner had she done so, than she fell from the chair, and was killed in the fall.—Southey, *St. Michael's Chair* (a ballad, 1798).

Penniless (*The*), Maximilian I., emperor of Germany (1459, 1493-1519).

Penniman (*Wolfert*). Young captain of the Mayga in *Outward Bound*.—W. T. Adams (Oliver Optic).

Penny (*Jock*), a highwayman.—Sir W. Scott, *Guy Mannering* (time, George II.).

Penruddock (*Roderick*), a "philosopher," or rather a recluse, who spent his time in reading. By nature gentle, kind-hearted, and generous, but soured by wrongs. Woodville, his trusted friend, although he knew that Arabella was betrothed to Roderick, induced her father to give his daughter to himself, the richer man; and Roderick's life was blasted. Woodville had a son, who reduced himself to positive indigence by gambling. Sir George Penruddock was the chief creditor. Sir George dying, all his property came to his cousin, Roderick, who now had ample means to glut his revenge on his treacherous friend; but his heart softened. First, he settled all "the obligations, bonds, and mortgages, covering the whole Woodville property," on Henry Woodville, that he might marry Emily Tempest; and next, he restored to Mrs. Woodville "her settlement, which in her husband's desperate necessity, she had resigned to him;" lastly, he sold all his own estates, and retired again to a country cottage to his books and solitude.—Cumberland, *The Wheel of Fortune* (1779).

Pentap'oliff, "with the naked arm," king of the Garaman'teans, who always went to battle with his right arm bare. Alifanfaron, emperor of Trap'oban, wished to marry his daughter, but, being refused, resolved to urge his suit by the sword. When Don Quixote saw two flocks of sheep coming along the road in opposite directions, he told Sancho Panza they were the armies of these two puissant monarchs met in array against each other.—Cervantes, *Don Quixote*, I. iii. 4 (1605).

Pentecôte Vivante (*La*), Cardinal Mezzofanti, who was the master of fifty or fifty-eight languages (1774-1849).

Penthe´a, sister of Ith´oclês, betrothed to Or´gilus by the consent of her father. At the death of her father, Ithoclês compelled her to marry Bass´anes, whom she hated, and she starved herself to death.—John Ford, *The Broken Heart* (1633).

Penthesile´a, queen of the Amazons, slain by Achilles. S. Butler calls the name "Penthes´ilê."

And laid about in fight more busily
Than th' Amazonian dame Penthesile.
S. Butler, *Hudibras*.

Pen´theus (3 *syl.*), a king of Thebes, who tried to abolish the orgies of Bacchus, but was driven mad by the offended god. In his madness he climbed into a tree to witness the rites, and being descried was torn to pieces by the Bacchantes.

As when wild Pentheus, grown mad with fear,
Whole troops of hellish hags about him spies.
Giles Fletcher, *Christ's Triumph over Death* (1610).

Pentheus (2 *syl.*), a king of Thebes, resisted the introduction of the worship of Dyoni´sos (*Bacchus*) into his kingdom, in consequence of which the Bacchantes pulled his palace to the ground, and Pentheus, driven from the throne, was torn to pieces on Mount Cithæron by his own mother and her two sisters.

He the fate [*may sing*]
Of sober Pentheus.
Akenside, *Hymn to the Naiads* (1767).

Pentweazel (*Alderman*), a rich city merchant of Blowbladder Street. He is wholly submissive to his wife, whom he always addresses as "Chuck."

Mrs. Pentweazel, the alderman's wife, very ignorant, very vain, and very conceitedly humble. She was a Griskin by birth, and "all her family by the mother's side were famous for their eyes." She had an aunt among the beauties of Windsor, "a perdigious fine woman. She had but one eye, but that was a piercer, and got her three husbands. We was called the gimlet family." Mrs. Pentweazel says her first likeness was done after "Venus de Medicis, the sister of Mary de Medicis."

Sukey Pentweazel, daughter of the alderman, recently married to Mr. Deputy Dripping, of Candlewick Yard.

Carel Pentweazel, a schoolboy, who had been under Dr. Jerks, near Doncaster, for two years and a quarter, and had learnt all *As in Præsenti* by heart. The terms of this school were £10 a year for food, books, board, clothes and tuition.—Foote, *Taste* (1753).

People (*Man of the*), Charles James Fox (1749-1806).

Pepin (*William*), a White Friar and most famous preacher at the beginning of the sixteenth century. His sermons, in eight volumes quarto, formed the grand repertory of the preachers of those times.

Pepita, Spanish beauty of whom the poet sings:

I, who dwell over the way
Watch where Pepita is hid,
Safe from the glare of the day,
Like an eye under its lid;
Over and over I say—
Name like the song of a bird,
Melody shut in a word—
"Pepita!"
Frank Dempster Sherman, *Madrigals and Catches* (1887).

Pepperpot (*Sir Peter*), a West Indian epicure, immensely rich, conceited and irritable.—Foote, *The Patron* (1764).

Peppers. (See WHITE HORSE OF THE PEPPERS.)

Peps (*Dr Parker*), a court physician who attended the first Mrs. Dombey on her death-bed. Dr. Peps always gave his patients (by mistake, of course), a title, to impress them with the idea that his practice was exclusively confined to the upper ten thousand.—C. Dickens, *Dombey and Son* (1846).

Perceforest (*King*), the hero of a prose romance "in Greek." The MS. is said to have been found by Count William of Hainault in a cabinet at "Burtimer" Abbey, on the Humber; and in the same cabinet was deposited a crown, which the count sent to King Edward. The MS. was turned into Latin by St. Landelain, and thence into French under the title of *La Tres Elegante Deliceux Melliflue et Tres Plaisante Hystoire du Tres Noble Roy Perceforest* (printed at Paris in 1528).

(Of course, this pretended discovery is only an invention. An analysis of the romance is given in Dunlop's *History of fiction*.)

He was called "Perceforest," because he dared to *pierce*, almost alone, an enchanted *forest*, where women and children were most evilly treated. Charles IX., of France, was especially fond of this romance.

Perch, messenger in the house of Mr. Dombey, merchant, whom he adored, and plainly showed by his manner to the great man: "You are the light of my eyes," "You are the breath of my soul."—C. Dickens, *Dombey and Son* (1846).

Perche Notary (*A*), a lawyer who sets people together by the ears, one who makes more quarrels than contracts. The French proverb is, *Notaire du Perche, qui passe plus d'échalliers que de contrat.*

Le Perche, qui se trouve partagé entre les départements de l'Orne et d'Eure-et-Loir, est un contrée fort boisée, dans laquelle la plupart des champs sont entourés de haies dans lesquelles sont ménagées certaines ouvertures propres à donner passage aux piétons seulement, et que l'on nomme *échalliers*.—Hilaire le Gai.

Percinet, a fairy prince, in love with Graciosa. The prince succeeds in thwarting the malicious designs of Grognon, the step-mother of the lovely princess.—*Percinet and Graciosa* (a fairy tale).

Percival (*Sir*), the third son of Sir Pellinore, king of Wales. His brothers were Sir Aglavale and Sir Lamorake Dornar, usually called Sir Lamorake de Galis (*Wales*). Sir Tor was his half-brother. Sir Percival caught a sight of the Holy Graal after his combat with Sir Ector de Maris (brother of Sir Launcelot), and both were miraculously healed by it. Crétien de Troyes wrote the *Roman de Perceval* (before 1200), and Menessier produced the same story in a metrical form. (See PARZIVAL.)

Sir Percivale had a glimmering of the Sancgreall and of the maiden that bare it, for he was perfect and clean. And forthwith they were both as whole of limb and hide as ever they were in their life days. "O, mercy!" said Sir Percival, "what may this mean?" ... "I wot well," said Sir Ector ... "it is the holy vessel, wherein is a part of the holy blood of our blessed Saviour; but it may not be seen but by a perfect man."—Pt. iii. 14.

Sir Percival was with Sir Bors and Sir Galahad, when the visible Saviour went into the consecrated wafer which was given to them by the bishop. This is called the achievement of the quest of the Holy Graal (pt. iii. 101, 102.—Sir T. Malory, *History of Prince Arthur* (1470).

Percival Glyde (*Sir*). Rascally husband of *Laura Fairlie*. To possess himself of her fortune, he incarcerates her in an insane asylum, gives out that she is dead, and uses the corpse of her half-sister to confirm the rumor.—Wilkie Collins, *The Woman in White*.

Percy Arundel (*Lord Ashdale*), son of Lady Arundel, by her second husband. A hot, fiery youth, proud and overbearing. When grown to manhood, a "sea-captain" named Norman, made love to Violet, Lord Ashdale's cousin. The young "Hotspur" was indignant and somewhat jealous, but discovered that Norman was the son of Lady Arundel by her first husband, and the heir to the title and estates. In the end, Norman agreed to divide the property equally, but claimed Violet for his bride.—Lord Lytton, *The Sea-Captain* (1839).

Per′dita, the daughter of the Queen Hermionê, born in prison. Her father, King Leontês, commanded the infant to be cast on a desert shore, and left to perish there. Being put to sea, the vessel was driven by a storm to the "coast" of Bohemia, and the infant child was brought up by a shepherd, who called its name Perdĭta. Flor′izel, the son of the Bohemian king, fell in love with Perdita, and courted her under the assumed name of Doriclês; but the king, having tracked his son to the shepherd's hut, told Perdita that if she did not at once discontinue this foolery, he would command her and the shepherd too to be put to death. Florizel and Perdita now fled from Bohemia to Sicily, and being introduced to the king, it was soon discovered that Perdita was Leontês's daughter. The Bohemian king, having tracked his son to Sicily, arrived just in time to hear the news, and gave his joyful consent to the union which he had before forbidden.—Shakespeare, *The Winter's Tale* (1604).

Perdita, Mrs. Mary Robinson (born Darby), the victim of George IV., while prince of Wales. She first attracted his notice while acting the part of "Perdĭta," and the prince called himself "Florizel." George, prince of Wales, settled a pension for life on her, £500 a year for herself, and £200 a year for her daughter. She caught cold one winter, and losing the use of her limbs, could neither walk nor stand (1758-1799, not 1800 as is given usually).

Perdrix, toujours Perdrix! Walpole tells us that the confessor of one of the French kings, having reproved the monarch for his conjugal infidelities, was asked what dish he liked best. The confessor replied, "Partridges;" and the king had partridges served to him every day, till the confessor got quite sick of them. "Perdrix, toujours perdrix!" he would exclaim, as the dish was set before him. After a time, the king visited him, and hoped his favorite dish had been supplied him. "Mais oui," he replied, "toujours perdrix, toujours perdrix!" "Ah, ah!" said the amorous monarch, "and one mistress is all very well, but not *perdrix, toujours perdrix!*"—See *Notes and Queries*, 337, October 23, 1869).

The story is at least as old as the *Cent Nouvelles Nouvelles*, compiled between 1450-1461, for the amusement of the dauphin of France, afterwards Louis XI. (*Notes and Queries*, November 27, 1869).

⁎ Farquhar parodies the French expression into "Soup for breakfast, soup for dinner, soup for supper, and soup for breakfast again."—Farquhar, *The Inconstant*, iv. 2 (1702).

Père Duchesne (*Le*), Jacques René Hébert; so called from the *Père Duchesne*, a newspaper of which he was the editor (1755-1794).

Pereard (*Sir*), the Black Knight of the Black Lands. Called by Tennyson "Night" or "Nox." He was one of the four brothers who kept the passages to Castle Perilous, and was overthrown by Sir Gareth.—Sir T. Malory, *History of Prince Arthur*, i. 126 (1470); Tennyson, *Idylls* ("Gareth and Lynette").

Peredur (*Sir*), son of Evrawe, called "Sir Peredur of the Long Spear," one of the knights of the Round Table. He was for many years called "The Dumb Youth," from a vow he made to speak to no Christian till Angharad of the Golden Hand loved him better than she loved any other man. His great achievements were: (1) the conquest of the Black Oppressor, "who oppressed every one and did justice to no one;" (2) killing the Addanc of the Lake, a monster that devoured daily some of the sons of the king of Tortures. This exploit he was enabled to achieve by means of a stone which kept him invisible; (3) slaying the three hundred heroes privileged to sit round the countess of the Achievements; on the death of these men the seat next the countess was freely given to him; (4) the achievement of the Mount of Mourning, where was a serpent with a stone in its tail which would give inexhaustible wealth to its possessor; Sir Peredur killed the serpent, but gave the stone to his companion, Earl Etlym of the east country. These exploits over, Sir Peredur lived fourteen years with the Empress Cristinobyl the Great.

Sir Peredur is the Welsh name for Sir Percival of Wales.—*The Mabinogion* (from the Red Book of Hergest, twelfth century).

Per′egrine (3 *syl.*), a sentimental prig, who talks by the book. At the age of 15 he runs away from home, and Job Thornberry lends him ten guineas, "the first earnings of his trade as a brazier." After thirty years absence, Peregrine returns just as the old brazier is made a bankrupt "through the treachery of a friend." He tells the bankrupt that his loan of ten guineas has by honest trade grown to 10,000, and these he returns to Thornberry as his own by right. It turns out that Peregrine is the eldest brother of Sir Simon Rochdale, J. P., and when Sir Simon refuses justice to the old brazier Peregrine asserts his right to the estate, etc. At the same time, he hears that the ship he thought was wrecked has come safe into port, and has thus brought him £100,000.— G. Colman, junior, *John Bull* (1805).

Peregrine Pickle, the hero and title of a novel by Smollett (1751). Peregrine Pickle is a savage, ungrateful spendthrift, fond of practical jokes, and suffering with evil temper the misfortunes brought on himself by his own wilfulness.

Peregri′nus Proteus, a cynic philosopher, born at Parium, on the Hellespont. After a youth spent in debauchery and crimes, he turned Christian, and, to obliterate the memory of his youthful ill practices, divided his inheritance among the people. Ultimately he burned himself to death in public at the Olympic games, A.D. 165. Lucan has held up this immolation to ridicule in his *Death of Peregrinus*; and C. M. Wieland has an historic romance in German entitled *Peregrinus Proteus* (1733-1813).

Per′es (*Gil*), a canon, and the eldest brother of Gil Blas' mother. Gil was a little punchy man, three feet and a half high, with his head sunk between his shoulders. He lived well, and brought up his nephew and godchild, Gil Blas. "In so doing, Perês taught himself also to read his breviary without stumbling." He was the most illiterate canon of the whole chapter.—Lesage, *Gil Blas*, i. (1715).

Perez (*Michael*), the "copper captain," a brave Spanish soldier, duped into marrying Estifania, a servant of intrigue, who passed herself off as a lady of property. Being reduced to great extremities, Estifania pawned the clothes and valuables of her husband; but these "valuables" were but of little worth—a jewel which sparkled as the "light of a dark lanthorn," a "chain of whitings' eyes" for pearls, and as for his clothes, she tauntingly says to her husband:

Put these and them [*his jewels*] on, and you're a man of copper,
A copper, copper captain.
Beaumont and Fletcher, *Rule a Wife and Have a Wife* (1640).

Peri, (plu., **Peris**), gentle, fairy-like beings of Eastern mythology, offspring of the fallen angels, and constituting a race of beings between angels and men. They direct with a wand the pure-minded the way to heaven, and dwell in Shadu′kiam′ and Am′bre-abad, two cities subject to Eblis.

Are the peries coming down from their spheres?
W. Beckford, *Vathek* (1786).

Pe′richole (*La*), the heroine of Offenbach's comic opera (*opera bouffe*) of that name. She was originally a street-singer of Lima, the capital of Peru, but became the mistress of the viceroy. She was not a native of Lima and offended the Creole ladies by calling them, in her bad Spanish, *pericholas*, "flaunting, bedizened creatures," and they, in retaliation, called her "La Périchole," *i.e.*, "the flaunting one *par excellence*."

Pericles, the Athenian who raised himself to royal supremacy (died B.C. 429). On his death-bed he overheard his friends recalling his various merits, and told them they had forgotten his greatest praise, viz., that no Athenian through his administration had had to put on mourning, *i.e.* he had caused no one to be put to death.

Perī′cles was a famous man of warre ...
Yet at his death he rather did rejoice
In clemencie.... "Be still," quoth he, "you grave Athenians"
(Who whisperèd and told his valiant acts);
"You have forgot my greatest glorie got:
For yet by me nor mine occasion
Was never sene a mourning garment worn."
G. Gascoigne, *The Steele Glas* (died 1577).

Per′icles, prince of Tyre, a voluntary exile, in order to avert the calamities which Anti′ochus, emperor of Greece, vowed against the Tyrians. Pericles, in his wanderings, first came to Tarsus, which he relieved from famine, but was obliged to quit the city to avoid the persecution of Antiochus. He was then shipwrecked, and cast on the shore of Pentap′olis, where he distinguished himself in the public games, and being introduced to the king, fell in love with the Princess Thaïs′a, and married her. At the death of Antiochus, he returned to Tyre; but his wife, supposed to be dead in giving birth to a daughter (Marina), was thrown into the sea. Periclês entrusted his infant child to Cleon (governor of Tarsus), and his wife, Dionysia, who brought her up excellently well till she became a young woman, when Dionysia employed a man to murder her; and when Periclês came to see her, he was shown a splendid sepulchre which had been raised to her honor. On his return home, the ship stopped at Metalinê, and Marina was introduced to Periclês to divert his melancholy. She told him the tale of her life, and he discovered that she was his daughter. Marina was now betrothed to Lysim′achus, governor of Metalinê; and the party, going to the shrine of Diana of Ephesus to return thanks to the goddess, discovered the priestess to be Thaïsa, the wife of Periclês, and mother of Marina.—Shakespeare, *Pericles, Prince of Tyre* (1608).

*** This is the story of *Ismene and Ismenias* by Eustathius. The tale was known to Gower by the translation of Godfrey Viterbo.

Perigort (*Cardinal*). Previous to the battle of Poitiers, he endeavors to negotiate terms with the French king, but the only terms he can obtain, he tells Prince Edward, are:

That to the castles, towns, and plunder ta'en,
And offered now by you to be restored,
Your royal person with a hundred knights
Are to be added prisoners at discretion.
Shirley, *Edward the Black Prince*, iv. 2 (1640).

Peri´got (the *t* pronounced, so as to rhyme with *not*), a shepherd in love with Am´oret; but the shepherdess Amaryllis also loves him, and, by the aid of the Sullen Shepherd, gets transformed into the exact likeness of the modest Amoret. By her wanton conduct she disgusts Perigot, who casts her off; and by and by, meeting Amoret, whom he believes to be the same person, rejects her with scorn, and even wounds her with intent to kill. Ultimately the truth is discovered by Clor´in, "the faithful shepherdess," and the lovers, being reconciled, are married to each other.—John Fletcher, *The Faithful Shepherdess* (1610).

Periklym´enos, son of Neleus (2 *syl.*). He had the power of changing his form into a bird, beast, reptile, or insect. As a bee, he perched on the chariot of Heraklês (*Herculês*), and was killed.

Peril´los, of Athens, made a brazen bull for Phal´aris, tyrant of Agrigentum, intended for the execution of criminals. They were to be shut up in the bull, and the metal of the bull was to be made red hot. The cries of the victims inside were so reverberated as to resemble the roarings of a gigantic bull. Phalaris made the first experiment by shutting up the inventor himself in his own bull.

What's a protector?
A tragic actor, Cæsar in a clown;
He's a brass farthing stamped with a crown;
A bladder blown with other breaths puffed full;
Not a Perillus, but a Perillus' bull.
John Cleveland, *A Definition of a Protector* (died 1650).

Perilous Castle. The castle of Lord Douglas was so called in the reign of Edward I., because the good Lord Douglas destroyed several English garrisons stationed there, and vowed to be revenged on any one who dared to take possession of it. Sir W. Scott calls it "Castle Dangerous" in his novel so entitled.

⁎ In the story of Gareth and Linet, the castle in which Lionês was held prisoner by Sir Ironside, the Red Knight of the Red Lands, was called Castle Perilous. The passages to the castle were held by four knights, all of whom Sir Gareth overthrew; lastly he conquered Sir Ironside, liberated the lady, and married her.—Sir T. Malory, *History of Prince Arthur*, i. 120-153 (1470).

Perimo´nes (*Sir*), the Red Knight, one of the four brothers who kept the passages to Castle Perilous. He was overthrown by Sir Gareth. Tennyson calls him "Noonday Sun" or "Meridies."—Sir T. Malory, *History of Prince Arthur*, i. 129 (1470); Tennyson, *Idylls* ("Gareth and Lynette").

Per′ion, king of Gaul, father of Am′adis of Gaul. His "exploits and adventures" form part of the series called *Le Roman des Romans*. This part was added by Juan Diaz (fifteenth century).

*** It is generally thought that "Gaul" in this romance is the same as *Galis*, that is "Wales."

Perissa, the personification of extravagance, step-sister of Elissa (*meanness*) and of Medi′na (*the golden mean*); but they never agreed in any single thing. Perissa's suitor is Sir Huddibras, a man "more huge in strength than wise in works." (Greek, *perissos*, "extravagant," *perissotês*, "excess.").—Spenser, *Faëry Queen*, ii. 2 (1590).

Per′iwinkle (*Mr.*), one of the four guardians of Anne Lovely, the heiress. He is a silly, half-witted virtuoso, positive and surly; fond of everything antique and foreign; and wears clothes of the last century. Mr. Periwinkle dotes upon travellers, and believes more of Sir John Mandeville than he does of the Bible. Colonel Feignwell, to obtain his consent to his marriage with Mr. Periwinkle's ward, disguised himself as an Egyptian, and passed himself off as a great traveller. His dress, he said, "belonged to the famous Claudius Ptolemēus, who lived in the year 135." One of his curiosities was *poluflosboio*, "part of those waves which bore Cleopatra's vessel, when she went to meet Antony." Another was the *moros musphonon*, or girdle of invisibility. His trick, however, miscarried, and he then personated Pillage, the steward of Periwinkle's father, and obtained Periwinkle's signature to the marriage by a fluke.—Mrs. Centlivre, *A Bold Stroke For a Wife* (1717).

Perker (*Mr.*), the lawyer employed for the defence in the famous suit of "Bardell *v.* Pickwick" for the breach of promise.—C. Dickens, *The Pickwick Papers* (1836).

Perkin Warbeck, an historic play or "chronicle history," by John Ford (1635).

Perley Kelso. A woman with "a weakness for an occupation, who suffers passions of superfluous life. At the Cape she rebelled because Providence did not create her a bluefisher. In Paris, she would make muslin flowers, and learn the *métier* to-morrow."—Elizabeth Stuart Phelps, *The Silent Partner* (1871).

Pernelle (*Madame*), mother of Orgon; a regular vixen, who interrupts every one, without waiting to hear what was to have been said to her.—Molière, *Tartuffe* (1664).

Peronella, a pretty country lass, who changes places with an old decrepit queen. Peronella rejoices for a time in the idolatry paid to her rank, but gladly resumes her beauty, youth, and rags.—*A Fairy Tale*.

Perrette and her Milk-Pail. Perrette, carrying her milk-pail well-poised upon her head, began to speculate on its value. She would sell the milk and buy eggs; she would set the eggs and rear chickens; the chickens she would sell and buy a pig; this she would fatten and change for a cow and calf, and would it not be delightful to see the little calf skip and play? So saying, she gave a skip, let the milk-pail fall, and all the milk ran to waste. "Le lait tombe. Adieu, veau, vache, cochon, couvée," and poor Perrette "va s'excuser à son mari, en grand danger d'etre battue."

Quel esprit ne bat la campagne?
Qui ne fait château en Espagne?
Picrochole [*q.v.*], Pyrrhus, la laitière, enfin tous,
Autant les sages que les fous....
Quelque accident fait-il que je rentre en moi-même;
Je suis Gros-Jean comme devant.
Lafontaine, *Fables* ("La Laitière et le Po tau Lait," 1668).

(Dodsley has this fable, and makes his milkmaid speculate on the gown she would buy with her money. It should be green, and all the young fellows would ask her to dance, but she would toss her head at them all—but ah! in tossing her head, she tossed over her milk-pail.)

⁎ Echephron, an old soldier, related this fable to the advisers of King Picrochole, when they persuaded the king to go to war: A shoemaker bought a ha'p'orth of milk; this he intended to make into butter, and with the money thus obtained he would buy a cow. The cow in due time would have a calf, the calf was to be sold, and the man when he became a nabob would marry a princess; only the jug fell, the milk was spilt, and the dreamer went supperless to bed.—Rabelais, *Gargantua*, i. 33 (1533).

In a similar day-dream, Alnaschar invested all his money in a basket of glassware, which he intended to sell, and buy other wares, till by barter he became a princely merchant, when he should marry the vizier's daughter. Being offended with his wife, he became so excited that he kicked out his foot, smashed all his wares, and found himself penniless.—*Arabian Nights* ("The Barber's Fifth Brother").

Perrin, a peasant, the son of Thibaut.—Molière, *Le Médecin Malgré Lui* (1666).

Persaunt of India (*Sir*), the Blue Knight, called by Tennyson "Morning Star," or "Phosphŏrus." One of the four brothers who kept the passages to Castle Perilous. Overthrown by Sir Gareth.—Sir T. Malory, *History of Prince Arthur*, i. 131 (1470); Tennyson, *Idylls*.

"Then, at his call, 'O, daughters of the Dawn,
And servants of the Morning Star, approach,
Arm me,' from out the silken curtain-folds

Bare-footed and bare-headed three fair girls
In gilt and rosy raiment came; their feet
In dewy grasses glisten'd; and the hair
All over glanced with dewdrop or with gem,
Like sparkles in the stone Avanturine.
These arm'd him in blue arms, and gave a shield,
Blue also, and thereon the morning star."
Tennyson, *Gareth and Lynette*.

Perseus [*Per.suce*], a famous Argive hero, whose exploits resemble those of Herculês, and hence he was called "The Argive Herculês."

Benvenuto Cellini made a bronze statue of Perseus, which is in the Loggia dei Lanzi, in Florence.

Perseus's Horse, a ship. Perseus having cut off Medusa's head, made the ship *Pegasé*, the swiftest ship hitherto known, and generally called "Perseus's flying horse."

The thick-ribbed bark thro' liquid mountains cut ...
Like Perseus' horse.
Shakespeare, *Troilus and Cressida*, act i. sc. 3 (1602).

Persian Creed (*The*). Zoroaster supposes there are two gods or spirit-principles—one good and the other evil. The good is Yezad, and the evil, Ahriman.

Perth (*The Fair Maid of*), Catharine, or Katie Glover, "universally acknowledged to be the most beautiful young woman of the city or its vicinity." Catharine was the daughter of Simon Glover (the glover of Perth), and married Henry Smith, the armorer.—Sir W. Scott, *Fair Maid of Perth* (time, Henry IV.).

Pertinax (*Sir*). (See MACSYCOPHANT.)

Pertolope (*Sir*), the Green Knight. One of the four brothers who kept the passages to Castle Perilous. He was overthrown by Sir Gareth. Tennyson calls him "Evening Star," or "Hesperus."—Sir T. Malory, *History of Prince Arthur*, i. 127 (1470); Tennyson, *Idylls*.

"For there, beyond a bridge of treble bow,
All in a rose-red from the west, and all
Naked it seem'd, and glowing in the broad,
Deep-dimpled current underneath, the knight
That named himself the Star of Evening, stood,
And Gareth, 'Wherefore waits the madman there
Naked in open dayshine?' 'Nay,' she cried,
'Not naked, only wrapt in harden'd skins

That fit him like his own; and so ye cleave
His armor off him, these will turn the blade.'"
Tennyson, *Gareth and Lynette.*

Perviz (*Prince*), son of the Sultan Khrosru-schar of Persia. At birth he was taken away by the sultana's sisters, and set adrift on a canal, but was rescued and brought up by the superintendent of the sultan's gardens. When grown to manhood, "the talking-bird" told the sultan that Pervis was his son, and the young prince, with his brother and sister, were restored to their rank and position in the empire of Persia.—*Arabian Nights* ("The Two Sisters").

Prince Perviz's String of Pearls. When Prince Perviz went on his exploits, he gave his sister, Parizādê, a string of pearls, saying, "So long as these pearls move readily on the string, you will know that I am alive and well; but if they stick fast and will not move, it will signify that I am dead."—*Arabian Nights* ("The Two Sisters").

⁎⁎* Birtha's emerald ring, and Prince Bahman's knife gave similar warning. (See BIRTHA and BAHMAN.)

Pescec'ola, a famous diver, whose English name was *Fish* (Italian, *Pesce* = fish). He dived in the pool of Charybdis and returned. King Frederick then threw a golden cup into the pool; Pescecola dived for it, and was drowned.

Schiller, in *The Diver*, tells the story, but gives the diver no name.

Pest (*Mr.*), a barrister.—Sir W. Scott, *Redgauntlet* (time, George III.).

Pet, a fair girl, with rich brown hair hanging free in natural ringlets. A lovely girl, with a free, frank face, and most wonderful eyes—so large, so soft, so bright, and set to perfection in her kind, good face. She was round, and fresh, and dimpled, and spoilt, most charmingly timid, most bewitchingly self-willed. She was the daughter of Mr. Meagles, and married Henry Gowan.— C. Dickens, *Little Dorrit* (1857).

Pétaud (*King*), king of the beggars.

"It is an old saying," replied the Abbé Huet, "Petaud being derived from the Latin *peto*, 'I beg.'"—*Asylum Christi*, ii.

The court of King Pétaud, a disorderly assembly, a place of utter confusion, a bear-garden.

On n'y respecte rien, chacun y parle haut,
Et c'est tout justement le cour du roi Pétaud.
Molière *Tartuffe*, i. 1 (1664).

Le cour du roi Pétaud, où chacun est maitre.—*French Proverb.*

Petella, the waiting-woman of Rosalura and Lillia-Bianca, the two daughters of Nantolet.—Beaumont and Fletcher, *The Wild-goose Chase* (1652).

Peter, the stupid son of Solomon, butler of the Count Wintersen. He grotesquely parrots in an abridged form whatever his father says. Thus: *Sol.* "we are acquainted with the reverence due to exalted personages." *Pet.* "Yes, we are acquainted with exalted personages." Again: *Sol.* "Extremely sorry it is not in my power to entertain your lordship." *Pet.* "Extremely sorry." *Sol.* "Your lordship's most obedient, humble, and devoted servant." *Pet.* "Devoted servant."—Benjamin Thompson, *The Stranger* (1797).

Peter, the pseudonym of John Gibson Lockhart, in a work entitled *Peter's Letters to his Kinsfolk* (1819).

Peter (Lord), the pope of Rome.—Dean Swift, *Tale of a Tub* (1704).

Peter Botte, a steep, almost perpendicular "mountain" in the Mauritius, more than 2800 feet in height. It is so called from Peter Botte, a Dutch sailor, who scaled it and fixed a flag on its summit, but lost his life in coming down.

Peter Parley, the *nom de plume* of Samuel G. Goodrich, an American, whose books for children had an enormous circulation in the middle of the nineteenth century (1793-1860).

The name was pirated by numerous persons. Darton and Co., Simkins, Bogue, Tegg, Hodson, Clements, etc., brought out books under the name, but not written by S. G. Goodrich.

Peter Peebles, a litigious, hard-hearted drunkard, noted for his lawsuit.—Sir W. Scott, *Redgauntlet* (time, George III.).

Peter Pindar, the pseudonym of Dr. John Wolcot, of Dodbrooke, Devonshire (1738-1819).

Peter Plymley's Letters, attributed to the Rev. Sydney Smith (1769-1845).

Peter Porcupine, William Cobbett, when he was a tory. He brought out *Peter Porcupine's Gazette*, *The Porcupine Papers*, etc. (1762-1835).

Peter Wilkins, the hero of a tale of adventures, by Robert Pultock, of Clifford's Inn. His "flying woman" (gawreys) suggested to Southey the "glendoveer" in *The Curse of Kehama*.

Peter of Provence and the Fair Magalo´na, the chief characters of a French romance so called. Peter comes into possession of Merlin's wooden horse.

Peter the Great of Egypt, Mehemet Ali (1768-1848.

Peter the Hermit, a gentleman of Amiens, who renounced the military life for the religious. He preached up the first crusade, and put himself at the head of 100,000 men, all of whom, except a few stragglers, perished at Nicea.

He is introduced by Tasso in *Jerusalem Delivered* (1575); and by Sir W. Scott in *Count Robert of Paris*, a novel laid in the time of Rufus. A statue was erected to him at Amiens in 1854.

Peter, the Wild Boy, a savage discovered in November, 1725, in the forest of Hertswold, Hanover. He walked on all fours, climbed trees like a monkey, ate grass and other herbage. Efforts were made to reclaim him, but without success. He died February, 1785.

Peter's Gate (*St.*), the gate of purgatory, guarded by an angel stationed there by St. Peter. Virgil conducted Dantê through hell and purgatory, and Beatrice was his guide through the planetary spheres. Dantê says to the Mantuan bard:

... lead me,
That I St. Peter's gate may view ...
Onward he moved, I close his steps pursued.
Dantê, *Hell*, i. (1300).

Peterborough, in Northamptonshire; so called from Peada (son of Pendar, king of Mercia), who founded here a monastery in the seventh century. In 1541 the monastery (then a mitred abbey) was converted by Henry VIII. into a cathedral and bishop's see. Before Peada's time, Peterborough was a village called Medhamsted.—See Drayton, *Polyolbion*, xxiii. (1622).

Peters (*Dr.*), benevolent, eccentric physician, who is a sympathetic fellow-sinner to the most depraved of his patients, going through it all "with a grimly humorous hope that some good, in some unseen direction, may come of it." The waif, *Midge*, committed by fate to his guardianship, steals his heart, and finally wrings it to bleeding by marrying another man.—H. C. Bunner, *The Midge* (1886).

Peterson, a Swede, who deserts from Gustavus Vasa to Christian II., king of Denmark.—H. Brooke, *Gustavus Vasa* (1730).

Petit André, executioner.—Sir W. Scott, *Quentin Durward* (time, Edward IV.).

Petit Perroquet, a king's gardener, with whom the king's daughter fell in love. It so happened that a prince was courting the lady, and, being jealous of Petit Perroquet, said to the king that the young man boasted he could bring hither Tartaro's horse. Now Tartaro was a huge giant and a cannibal. Petit Perroquet, however, made himself master of the horse. The prince next told the king that the young gardener boasted he could get possession of the giant's diamond. This he also contrived to make himself master of. The prince then told the king that the young man boasted he could bring hither the giant himself; and the way he accomplished the feat was to cover himself first, with honey, and then with feathers and horns. Thus disguised, he told the giant, to get into the coach he was driving, and he drove him to the king's court, and then married the princess.—Rev. W. Webster, *Basque Legends* (1877).

Pe´to, lieutenant of "Captain" Sir John Falstaff's regiment. Pistol was his ensign or ancient, and Bardolph his corporal.—Shakespeare, 1 and 2 *Henry IV.* (1597-8).

Petow´ker (*Miss Henrietta*), of the Theatre Royal, Drury Lane. She marries Mr. Lillyvick, the collector of water-rates, but elopes with an officer.—C. Dickens, *Nicholas Nickleby* (1838).

Petrarch (*The English*). Sir Philip Sidney (1554-1586) is so called by Sir Walter Raleigh.

Petrarch and Laura. Laura was a lady of Avignon, the wife of Hugues de Sade, *née* Laura de Noves, the mistress of the poet Petrarch. (See LAURA AND PETRARCH.)

Petrarch of Spain, Garcilaso de la Vega, born at Toledo (1530-1568, or, according to others, 1503-1536).

Petro´nius (*C.* or *T.*), a kind of Roman "beau Brummell" in the court of Nero. He was a great voluptuary and profligate, whom Nero appointed *Arbiter Elegantiæ*, and considered nothing *comme il faut* till it had received the sanction of this dictator-in-chief of the imperial pleasures. Tigellinus accused him of treason, and Petronius committed suicide by opening his veins (A.D. 66).

Behold the new Petronius of the day,
The arbiter of pleasure and of play.
Byron, *English Bards and Scotch Reviewers* (1809).

Petruccio = *Pe.truch´.e.o*, governor of Bologna.—Beaumont and Fletcher, *The Chances* (1620).

Petru´chio, a gentleman of Vero´na who undertakes to tame the haughty Katharina, called "the Shrew." He marries her, and, without the least personal chastisement, reduces her to lamb-like submission. Being a fine compound of bodily and mental vigor, with plenty of wit, spirit, and good-nature, he rules his subordinates dictatorially, and shows he will have his own way, whatever the consequences.—Shakespeare, *Taming of the Shrew* (1594).

Beaumont and Fletcher wrote a comedy called *The Tamer Tamed*, in which Petruchio is supposed to marry a second wife, by whom he is hen-pecked (1647).

Pet′ulant, an "odd sort of small wit," "without manners or breeding." In controversy he would bluntly contradict, and he never spoke the truth. When in his "club," in order to be thought a man of intrigue, he would steal out quietly, and then in disguise return and call for himself, or leave a letter for himself. He not unfrequently mistook impudence and malice for wit, and looked upon a modest blush in woman as a mark of "guilt or ill-breeding."— W. Congreve, *The Way of the World* (1700).

Peu-à-Peu. So George IV. called Prince Leopold. Stein, speaking of the prince's vacillating conduct in reference to the throne of Greece, says of him, "He has no color," *i.e.* no fixed plan of his own, but is blown about by every wind.

Peveril (*William*), natural son of William the Conqueror, and ancestor of Peveril of the Peak.

Sir Geoffrey Peveril, a cavalier, called "Peveril of the Peak."

Lady Margaret Peveril, wife of Sir Geoffrey.

Julian Peveril, son of Sir Geoffrey; in love with Alice Bridgenorth. He was named by the author after Julian Young, son of the famous actor.—Sir W. Scott, *Peveril of the Peak* (time, Charles II.).

"Whom is he called after!" said Scott. "It is a fancy name," said Young: "in memoriam of his mother, Julia Ann." "Well, it is a capital name for a novel, I must say," he replied. In the very next novel by the author of *Waverley*, the hero's name is "Julian." I allude, of course, to *Peveril of the Peak*.—J. Young, *Memoirs*, 91.

Peveril of the Peak, the hero of Sir W. Scott's novel of that name (1823).

Peyton (*Dunwoodie*), fine young fellow, major in the American army, and in love with Frances Wharton. Yet, when forced to choose between marrying her at once or doing his duty in keeping her brother under arrest, he plays the man of honor and true soldier. After many vicissitudes he becomes the husband of Frances.

Peyton (*Miss Jeannette*), sister-in-law to Mr. Wharton, relative of Major Dunwoodie, and affectionate guardian of her nieces. A warm friend of Dr. Sitgreaves, the American surgeon.—James Fennimore Cooper, *The Spy*.

Phædra, daughter of Minos, and wife of Theseus. (See PHEDRE.)

Phædra, waiting-woman of Alcmē´na (wife of Amphit´ryon). A type of venality of the lowest and grossest kind. Phædra is betrothed to Judge Gripus, a stupid magistrate, ready to sell justice to the highest bidder. Neither Phædra nor Gripus forms any part of the *dramatis personæ* of Molière's *Amphitryon* (1668).—Dryden, *Amphitryon* (1690).

Phædria, the impersonation of wantonness. She is handmaid of the enchantress Acrasia, and sails about Idle Lake in a gondola. Seeing Sir Guyon, she ferries him across the lake to the floating island, where he is set upon by Cymoch´les. Phædria interposes, and ferries Sir Guyon (the Knight Temperance) over the lake again.—Spenser, *Faëry Queen*, ii. (1590).

Pha´eton (3 *syl.*), son, of Helĭos and Clymēnê. He obtained leave to drive his father's sun-car for one day, but was overthrown, and nearly set the world on fire. Jove or Zeus (1 *syl.*) struck him with a thunderbolt for his presumption, and cast him into the river Po.

Phal´aris, tyrant of Agrigentum, in Sicily. When Perillos, the brass-founder of Athens, brought to him a brazen bull, and told the tyrant it was intended for the punishment of criminals, Phalăris inquired into its merits. Perillos said the victim was to be enclosed in the bull, and roasted alive, by making the figure red hot. Certain tubes were so constructed as to make the groans of the victim resemble the bellowings of a mad bull. The tyrant much commended the ingenuity, and ordered the invention to be tried on Perillos himself.

Letters of Phalaris, certain apocryphal letters ascribed to Phalaris, the tyrant, and published at Oxford, in 1718, by Charles Boyle. There was an edition in 1777 by Walckenaer; another in 1823, by G. H. Schæfer, with notes by Boyle and others. Bentley maintained that the letters were forgeries, and no doubt Bentley was right.

Phallas, the horse of Heraclius (Greek, *phalios*, "a grey horse.").

Pha´on, a young man who loved Claribel, but being told that she was unfaithful to him, watched her. He saw, as he thought, Claribel holding an assignation with some one he supposed to be a groom. Returning home, he encountered Claribel herself, and "with wrathfull hand he slew her innocent." On the trial for murder, "the lady" was proved to be Claribel's servant. Phaon would have slain her also, but while he was in pursuit of her he was attacked by Furor.—Spenser, *Faëry Queen*, ii. 4, 28, etc. (1590).

*** Shakespeare's *Much Ado about Nothing* is a similar story. Both are taken from a novel by Belleforest, copied from one by Bandello. Ariosto, in his *Orlando Furioso*, has introduced a similar story (bk. v.), and Turbervil's *Geneura* is the same tale.

Pharamond, king of the Franks, who visited, *incognito*, the court of King Arthur, to obtain by his exploits a place among the knights of the Round Table. He was the son of Marcomir, and father of Clodion.

Calprenède has an heroic romance so called, which (like his *Cleopatra and Cassandra*) is a *Roman de Longue Haleine* (1612-1666).

Pharamond, prince of Spain, in the drama called *Philaster*, or *Love Lies a-bleeding*, by Beaumont and Fletcher (date uncertain, probably about 1662).

Pharaoh, the titular name of all the Egyptian kings till the time of Solomon, as the Roman emperors took the titular name of Cæsar. After Solomon's time, the titular name Pharaoh never occurs alone, but only as a forename, as Pharaoh Necho, Pharaoh Hophra, Pharaoh Shishak. After the division of Alexander's kingdom, the kings of Egypt were all called Ptolemy, generally with some distinctive after-name, as Ptolemy Philadelphos, Ptolemy Euergetês, Ptolemy Philopător, etc.—Selden, *Titles of Honor*, v. 50 (1614).

Pharaohs before Solomon (mentioned in the Old Testament):

1. Pharaoh contemporary with Abraham (*Gen.* xii. 15). This may be Osirtesen I. (dynasty xii.).

2. The *good* Pharaoh who advanced Joseph (*Gen.* xli.). This was, perhaps, Apōphis (one of the Hyksos).

3. The Pharaoh who "knew not Joseph" (*Exod.* i. 8). This may be Amen´ophis I. (dynasty xviii.). The king, at the flight of Moses, I think, was Thothmes II.

4. The Pharaoh drowned in the Red Sea. As this was at least eighty years after the persecutions began, probably this was another king. Some say it was Menephthes, son of Ram´eses II., but it seems quite impossible to reconcile the account in *Exodus* with any extant historical account of Egypt (*Exod.* xiv. 28). Was it Thothmes III.?

5. The Pharaoh who protected Hadad (1 *Kings* xi. 19).

6. The Pharaoh whose daughter Solomon married (1 *Kings* iii. 1; ix. 16). I think this was Psusennes I. (dynasty xxi.).

Pharaohs after Solomon's time (mentioned in the Old Testament):

1. Pharaoh Shishak, who warred against Rehoboam (1 *Kings* xiv. 25, 26; 2 *Chron.* xii. 2).

2. The Pharaoh called "So" king of Egypt, with whom Hoshea made an alliance (2 *Kings* xvii. 4).

3. The Pharaoh who made a league with Hezekiah against Sennacherib. He is called Tirhākah (2 *Kings*, xviii. 21; xix. 9).

4. Pharaoh Necho, who warred against Josiah (2 *Kings* xxiii. 29, etc.).

5. Pharaoh Hophra, the ally of Zedekiah. Said to be Pharaoh Apries, who was strangled, B.C. 569-525 (*Jer.* xliv. 30).

⁎ Bunsen's solution of the Egyptian dynasties cannot possibly be correct.

Pharaohs noted in romance:

1. Cheops, or Suphis I., who built the great pyramid (dynasty iv.).

2. Cephrenês, or Suphis II., his brother, who built the second pyramid.

3. Mencherês, his successor, who built the most beautiful, though not the largest, of the pyramids.

4. Memnon, or A-menophis III., whose musical statue is so celebrated (dynasty xviii.).

5. Sethos I. the Great, whose tomb was discovered by Belzoni (dynasty xix.).

6. Sethos II., called "Proteus," who detained Helen and Paris in Egypt (dynasty xix.).

7. Phuōris or Thuōris, who sent aid to Priam in the siege of Troy.

8. Rampsinītus or Rameses Nēter, the miser, mentioned by Herodotus (dynasty xx.).

9. Osorthon IV. (or Osorkon), the Egyptian Herculês (dynasty xxiii.).

Pharaoh's Daughter. The daughter of Pharaoh, who brought up Moses, was Bathia.

Pharaoh's Wife, Asia, daughter of Mozâhem. Her husband cruelly tormented her because she believed in Moses. He fastened her hands and feet to four stakes, and laid a millstone on her as she lay in the hot sun with her face upwards; but angels shaded off the sun with their wings, and God took her, without dying, into Paradise.—Sale, *Al Korân*, lxvi. note.

Among women, four have been perfect; Asia, wife of Pharaoh; Mary, daughter of Imràn; Khadîjah, daughter of Khowailed, Mahomet's first wife; and Fâtima, Mahomet's daughter.—Attributed to Mahomet.

⁎ There is considerable doubt respecting the Pharaoh meant—whether the Pharaoh, whose daughter adopted Moses, or the Pharaoh who was drowned in the Red Sea. The tale suits the latter king far better than it does the first.

Pharsa′lia (*The*), a Latin epic in ten books, by Lucan, the subject being the fall and death of Pompey. It opens with the passage of Cæsar across the Rubĭcon. This river formed the boundary of his province, and his crossing it was virtually a declaration of war (bk. i.). Pompey is appointed by the senate general of the army to oppose him (bk. v.). Cæsar retreats to Thessaly; Pompey follows (bk. vi.), and both prepare for war. Pompey, being routed in the battle of Pharsalia, flees (bk. vii.), and seeking protection in Egypt, is met by Achillas, the Egyptian general, who murders him, cuts off his head, and casts his body into the sea (bk. viii.). Cato leads the residue of Pompey's army to Cyrēnê, in Africa (bk. ix.); and Cæsar, in pursuit of Pompey, landing at Alexandria, is hospitably entertained by Cleopatra (bk. x.). While here, he tarries in luxurious dalliance, the palace is besieged by Egyptians, and Cæsar with difficulty escapes to Pharos. He is closely pursued, hemmed in on all sides, and leaps into the sea. With his imperial robe held between his teeth, his commentaries in his left hand, and his sword in his right, he buffets the waves. A thousand javelins are hurled at him, but touch him not. He swims for empire, he swims for life; 'tis Cæsar and his fortunes that the waves bear on. He reaches his fleet; is received by his soldiers with thundering applause. The stars in their courses fought for Cæsar. The sea-gods were with him, and Egypt with her host was a by-word and a scorn.

⁎ Bk. ix. contains the account of the African serpents, by far the most celebrated passage of the whole poem. The following is a pretty close translation of the passage in question. It would have occupied too much room to give their onslaught also:—

Here all the serpent deadly brood appears;
First the dull Asp its swelling neck uprears;
The huge Hemor′rhoïs, vampire of the blood;
Chersy′ders, that pollute both field and flood;
The Water-serpent, tyrant of the lake;
The hooded Cobra; and the Plantain snake;
Here with distended jaws the Prester strays;
And Seps, whose bite both flesh and bone decays;
The Amphisbæna with its double head,
One on the neck, and one of tail instead;
The horned Cerastês; and the Hammodyte,
Whose sandy hue might balk the keenest sight;
A feverish thirst betrays the Dipsas' sting;
The Scytăla, its slough that casts in spring;
The Natrix here the crystal streams pollutes;
Swift thro' the air the venomed Javelin shoots;
Here the Parēas, moving on its tail,
Marks in the sand its progress by its trail;

The speckled Cenchris darts its devious way,
Its skin with spots as Theban marble gay;
The hissing Sibīla; and Basilisk,
With whom no living thing its life would risk,
Where'er it moves none else would dare remain,
Tyrant alike and terror of the plain.
E. C. B.

In this battle Pompey had 45,000 legionaries, 7000 horse, and a large number of auxiliaries. Cæsar had 22,000 legionaries, and 1000 horse. Pompey's battle cry was *Herculês invictus!* That of Cæsar was *Venus victrix!* Cæsar won the battle.

Phebe (2 *syl.*), a shepherdess beloved by the shepherd Silvius. While Rosalind was in boy's clothes, Phebe fell in love with the stranger, and made a proposal of marriage; but when Rosalind appeared in her true character, and gave her hand to Orlando, Phebe was content to accept her old love, Silvius.— Shakespeare, *As You Like It* (1600).

Phedre (or PHÆDRA), daughter of Minos, king of Crete, and wife of Theseus. She conceived a criminal love for Hippolytos, her step-son, and, being repulsed by him, accused him to her husband of attempting to dishonor her. Hippolytos was put to death, and Phædra, wrung with remorse, strangled herself.

This has been made the subject of tragedy by Eurip´idês in Greek, Sen´eca in Latin, Racine in French (1677). "Phèdre" was the great part of Mdlle. Rachel; she first appeared in this character in 1838.

(Pradon, under the patronage of the duchess de Bouillon and the duc de Nevers, produced, in 1677, his tragedy of *Phèdre* in opposition to that of Racine. The duke even tried to hiss down Racine's play, but the public judgment was more powerful than the duke; and, while it pronounced decidedly for Racine's *chef d'œuvre*, it had no tolerance for Pradon's production.)

Phelis "the Fair," the wife of Sir Guy, earl of Warwick.

Phid´ias (*The French*), (1) Jean Goujon; also called "The Correggio of Sculptors." He was slain in the St. Bartholomew Massacre (1510-1572). (2) J. B. Pigalle (1714-1785).

Phil (*Little*), the lad of John Davies, the old fisherman.—Sir W. Scott, *Redgauntlet* (time, George III.).

Philaminte (3 *syl.*), wife of Chrysale, the bourgeois, and mother of Armande, Henrietta, Ariste, and Bélise.—Molière, *Les Femmes Savantes* (1672).

Philan'der, of Holland, was a guest at the house of Arge'o, baron of Servia, and the baron's wife, Gabri'na, fell in love with him. Philander fled the house, and Gabrina told her husband he had abused her, and had fled out of fear of him. He was pursued, overtaken, and cast into a dungeon. One day Gabrina visited him there and asked him to defend her against a wicked knight. This he undertook to do, and Gabrina posted him in a place where he could make his attack. Philander slew the knight, but discovered that it was Argeo. Gabrina now declared she would give him up to justice unless he married her; and Philander, to save his life, did so. But in a very short time the infamous woman tired of her toy, and cut him off by poison.—Ariosto, *Orlando Furioso* (1516).

Philander, a dawdling lover; so called from Philander, the Dutch knight mentioned above, who was wooed by Gabrina. To "philander" is to hang about a woman in a half-hearted way; to toy.

Yes, I'll baste you together, you and your Philander.—W. Congreve, *The Way of the World* (1700).

Philander, prince of Cyprus, passionately in love with the Princess Ero'ta.—Beaumont and Fletcher, *The Laws of Candy* (1647).

Philanthropist (*The*), John Howard (1726-1790).

Philario, an Italian, at whose house Posthumus made his silly wager with Iachimo. (See POSTHUMUS.)—Shakespeare, *Cymbeline* (1605).

Philario, an Italian improvisatore, who remained faithful to Fazio even in disgrace.—Dean Milman, *Fazio* (1815).

Philaster (*Prince*), heir to the crown of Messi'na. Euphra'sia, who was in love with Philaster, disguised herself as a boy, and, assuming for the nonce the name of Bellario, entered the prince's service. Philaster, who was in love with the Princess Arethu'sa, transferred Bellario to her service, and then grew jealous of Arethusa's love for the young page.—Beaumont and Fletcher, *Philaster*, or *Love Lies a-bleeding* (? 1622).

There is considerable resemblance between Euphrasia and "Viola" in *Twelfth Night* (Shakespeare, 1614).

Philax, cousin of the Princess Imis. The fay Pagan shut them up in the "Palace of Revenge," a superb crystal palace, containing every delight except the power of leaving it. In the course of a few years Imis and Philax longed as much for a separation as at one time they had wished for a union.—Comtesse D'Aunoy, *Fairy Tales* ("Palace of Revenge," 1682).

Phile'mon (3 *syl.*), an aged rustic who, with his wife, Baucis, hospitably received Jupiter and Mercury, after every one else had refused to receive them. The gods sent an inundation to destroy the inhospitable people, but saved Baucis and Philemon, and converted their cottage into a magnificent temple. At their own request the aged couple died on the same day, and were changed into two trees, which stood before the temple.—*Greek Mythology.*

Philinte (2 *syl.*), friend of Alceste (2 *syl.*)—Molière, *Le Misanthrope* (1666).

Philip, father of William Swidger. His favorite expression was, "Lord, keep my memory green. I am 87."—C. Dickens, *The Haunted Man* (1848).

Philip, the butler of Mr. Peregrine Lovel; a hypocritical, rascally servant, who pretends to be most careful of his master's property, but who in reality wastes it most recklessly, and enriches himself with it most unblushingly. Being found out, he is summarily dismissed.—Rev. J. Townley, *High Life Below Stairs* (1759).

Philip (Father), sacristan of St. Mary's.—Sir W. Scott, *The Monastery* (time, Elizabeth).

Philip Augustus, king of France, introduced by Sir W. Scott in *The Talisman* (time, Richard I.).

Philip Nolan, officer in U. S. Navy, condemned by president of court martial for complicity with Aaron Burr, and for swearing at the United States, "never to hear the name of the United States again." He is passed from one man-of-war to another, never allowed to converse upon national affairs, to see a U. S. newspaper or read a history of the United States, until homesick and heartsick, after an exile of fifty-five years, he dies, praying for the country that had disowned him.—Edward Everett Hale, *The Man Without a Country* (1863).

Philip Nye, brought up for the Anglican Church, but became a Presbyterian, and afterwards an independent. He was noted for the cut of his beard.

This reverend brother, like a goat,
Did wear a tail upon his throat.
But set in such a curious frame,
As if 'twere wrought in filograin,
And cut so even, as if 't had been
Drawn with a pen upon his chin.
S. Butler, *On Philip Nye's Thanksgiving Beard* (1652).

Philip Ogden, lover and hero in Blanche Willis Howard's *One Summer.* He is nearly blinded by the point of Leigh's umbrella at their first meeting, and after an idyllic courtship they are wedded (1875).

Philip Quarl, a castaway-sailor, who becomes a hermit. His "man Friday" is a chimpanzee.—*Philip Quarl* (1727).

Philip's Four Daughters. We are told, in *Acts* xxi. 9, that Philip, the deacon or evangelist, had four daughters which did prophesy.

Helen, the mother of great Constantine,
Nor yet St. Philip's daughters, were like thee [*Joan of Arc*].
Shakespeare, 1 *Henry VI.* act i. sc. 2 (1589).

Philippe, a parched and haggard wretch, infirm and bent beneath a pile of years, yet shrewd and cunning, greedy of gold, malicious, and looked upon by the common people as an imp of darkness. It was this old villain who told Thancmar that the provost of Bruges was the son of a serf on Thancmar's estates.—S. Knowles, *The Provost of Bruges* (1836).

Philippe Egalité, (4 *syl.*), Louis Philippe, duc d'Orléans (1747-1793).

Philipson (*The elder*), John, earl of Oxford, an exiled Lancastrian, who goes to France disguised as a merchant.

Arthur Philipson, Sir Arthur de Vere, son of the earl of Oxford, whom he accompanies to the court of King René of Provence.—Sir W. Scott, *Anne of Geierstein* (time, Edward IV.).

Phil′isides (3 *syl.*), Sir Philip Sidney (1554-1586).

It was the harp of Phil′isides, now dead....
And now in heaven a sign it doth appear,
The Harp well known beside the Northern Bear.
Spenser, *The Ruins of Time* (1591).

⁎ *Phili[p] Sid[ney]*, with the Greek termination, makes *Phili-sides*. Bishop Hall calls the word *Phil-is′-ides*: "Which sweet Philis′ides fetched of late from France."

Philistines, a title complacently bestowed, in England and America, by the advance-guard in literature and art, on the Conservatives. The French equivalent is "les bourgeois."

Demonstrative and offensive whiskers, which are the special inheritance of the British Philistines.—Mrs. Oliphant, *Phœbe, Junr.*, i. 2.

Phillips (*Jessie*), the title and chief character of a novel by Mrs. Trollope, the object being an attack on the new poor-law system (1843).

Phillis, a drama written in Spanish, by Lupercio Leonardo, of Argensola.—Cervantes, *Don Quixote* (1605-15).

Phillis, a pastoral name for a maiden.

Where Corydon and Thyrsis met,
Are at their savory dinner set,

Of herbs and other country messes,
Which the neat-handed Phillis dresses.
Milton, *L'Allegro* (1638).

Phillis, "the Exigent," asked "Damon thirty sheep for a kiss;" next day, she promised him thirty kisses for a sheep;" the third day, she would have given "thirty sheep for a kiss;" and the fourth day, Damon bestowed his kisses for nothing on Lizette.—C. Rivière Dufresny, *La Coquette de Village* (1715).

Philo, a Pharisee, one of the Jewish sanhedrim, who hated Caiaphas, the high priest, for being a Sadducee. Philo made a vow in the judgment hall, that he would take no rest till Jesus was numbered with the dead. In bk. xiii. he commits suicide, and his soul is carried to hell by Obaddon, the angel of death.—Klopstock, *The Messiah*, iv. (1771).

Philoc´lea, one of the heroines in Sir Philip Sidney's "Arcadia." It has been sought to identify her with Lady Penelopê Devereux, with whom Sidney was thought to be in love.

Philocte´tes (4 *syl.*) one of the Argonauts, who was wounded in the foot while on his way to Troy. An oracle declared to the Greeks that Troy could not be taken "without the arrows of Herculês," and as Herculês at death had given them to Philoctētês, the Greek chiefs sent for him, and he repaired to Troy in the tenth and last year of the siege.

All dogs have their day, even rabid ones. Sorrowful, incurable *Philoctetês* Marat, without whom Troy cannot be taken.—Carlyle.

Philomel, daughter of Pandīon, king of Attica. She was converted into a nightingale.

Philosopher (*The*), Marcus Aurelius Antoninus, the Roman emperor, was so called by Justin Martyr (121, 161-180).

Leo VI., emperor of the East (866, 886-911).

Porphyry, the Neoplatonist (223-304).

Alfred or Alured, surnamed "Anglicus," was also called "The Philosopher" (died 1270).

Philosopher of China, Confucius (B.C. 551-479).

Philosopher of Ferney, Voltaire, who lived at Ferney, near Geneva, for the last twenty years of his life (1694-1778).

Philosopher of Malmesbury, Thomas Hobbs, author of *Leviathan*. He was born at Malmesbury (1588-1679).

Philosopher of Persia (*The*), Abou Ebn Sina, of Shiraz (died 1037).

Philosopher of Sans Souci, Frederick the Great of Prussia (1712, 1740-1786).

∗∗∗ Frederick, elector of Saxony, was called "The Wise" (1463, 1544-1554).

Philosopher of Wimbledon (*The*), John Horne Tooke, author of the *Diversions of Purley*. He lived at Wimbledon, near London (1736-1812).

(For the philosophers of the different Greek sects, as the Cynic, Cyrenaic, Eleac, Eleatic, Epicurean, Haraclitian, Ionic, Italic, Megaric, Peripatetic, Sceptic, Socratic, Stoic, etc., see *Dictionary of Phrase and Fable*, 680-1.)

Philosophers (*The five English*): (1) Roger Bacon, author of *Opus Majus* (1214-1292; (2) Sir Francis Bacon, author of *Novum Organum* (1561-1626); (3) the Hon. Robert Boyle (1627-1691; (4) John Locke, author of a treatise on the *Human Understanding and Innate Ideas* (1632-1704); (5) Sir Isaac Newton, author of *Princip'ia* (1641-1727).

Philosophy (*The Father of*), (1) Albrecht von Haller, of Berne (1708-1777). (2) Roger Bacon is also so called (1214-1292).

Philosophy (*The Father of Inductive*), Francis Bacon [*Lord Verulam*] (1561-1626).

Philosophy (*The Father of Roman*), Cicero, the orator (B.C.) 106-43).

Philosophy (*The Nursing Mother of*). Mde. de Boufflers was so called by Marie Antoinette.

Phil′ostrate (3 *syl.*), master of the revels to Theseus (2 *syl.*) king of Athens.—Shakespeare, *Midsummer Night's Dream* (1592).

Philo′tas, son of Parmenio, and commander of the Macedonian cavalry. He was charged with plotting against Alexander the Great. Being put to the rack, he confessed his guilt, and was stoned to death.

The king may doom to me a thousand tortures,
Ply me with fire, and rack me like Philotas,
Ere I will stoop to idolize his pride.
N. Lee, *Alexander the Great*, i. 1 (1678).

Philot′ime (4 *syl.*, "*love of glory*"), daughter of Mammon, whom the money-god offers to Sir Guyon for a wife; but the knight declines the honor, saying he is bound by love-vows to another.—Spenser, *Faëry Queen*, ii. 7 (1590).

Philot′imus, Ambition personified. (Greek, *Philo-tīmus*, "ambitious, covetous of honor.")—Phineas Fletcher, *The Purple Island*, viii. (1633).

Philotimus, steward of the house in the suite of Gargantua.—Rabelais, *Gargantua*, i. 18 (1533).

Philpot (*Senior*), an avaricious old hunks, and father of George Philpot. The old city merchant cannot speak a sentence without bringing in something about money. "He wears square-toed shoes with little tiny buckles, a brown coat with small brass buttons.... His face is all shrivelled and pinched with care, and he shakes his head like a mandarin upon a chimney-piece" (act i. 1).

When I was very young, I performed the part of "Old Philpot," at Brighton, with great success, and next evening I was introduced into a club-room full of company. On hearing my name announced, one of the gentlemen laid down his pipe, and taking up his glass, said, "Here's to your health, young gentleman, and to your father's, too. I had the pleasure of seeing him last night in the part of 'Philpot,' and a very nice, clever old gentleman he is. I hope, young sir, you may one day be as good an actor as your worthy father."—Munden.

George Philpot. The profligate son of old Philpot, destined for Maria Wilding, but the betrothal is broken off, and Maria marries Beaufort. George wants to pass for a dashing young blade, but is made the dupe of every one. "Bubbled at play; duped by a girl to whom he paid his addresses; cudgelled by a rake; laughed at by his cronies; snubbed by his father, and despised by every one."—Murphy, *The Citizen* (1757 or 1761).

Philtra, a lady of large fortune, betrothed to Bracĭdas; but, seeing the fortune of Amĭdas daily increasing, and that of Bracidas getting smaller and smaller, she forsook the declining fortune of her first lover, and attached herself to the more prosperous younger brother.—Spenser, *Faëry Queen*, v. 4 (1596).

Phineus [*Fi´.nuce*], a blind soothsayer, who was tormented by the harpies. Whenever a meal was set before him, the harpies came and carried it off, but the Argonauts delivered him from these pests in return for his information respecting the route they were to take in order to obtain the golden fleece. (See TIRESIAS.)

Tiresias and Phineus, prophets old.
Milton, *Paradise Lost*, iii. 36 (1665).

Phiz, the pseudonym of Hablot K. Browne, who illustrated the *Pickwick Papers* (1836), *Nicholas Nickleby*, and most of Charles Dickens's works of fiction. He also illustrated the Abbotsford edition of the *Waverley Novels*.

Phleg´rian Size, gigantic. Phlegra, or the Phlegræ´an plain, in Macedon, is where the giants attacked the gods, and were defeated by Hercŭlés. Drayton makes the diphthong *æ* a short *i*:

Whose only love surprised those of the Phlegrian size,
The Titanois, that once against high heaven durst rise.
Polyolbion, vi. (1612).

Phobbs. Captain and Mrs. Phobbs, with Mrs. Major Phobbs, a widow, sister-in-law to the captain, in *Lend Me Five Shillings*, by J. M. Morton.

Pho′cion, husband of Euphra′sia, "the Grecian daughter."—A. Murphy, *The Grecian Daughter* (1772).

Pho′cyas, general of the Syrian army in the siege of Damascus. Phocyas was in love with Eudo′cia, daughter of Eu′menês, the governor, but when he asked the governor's consent, Eumenês sternly refused to give it. After gaining several battles, Phocyas fell into the hands of the Arabs, and consented to join their army to revenge himself on Eumenês. The Arabs triumphed, and Eudocia was taken captive, but she refused to wed a traitor. Ultimately, Phocyas died, and Eudocia entered a convent.—John Hughes, *Siege of Damascus* (1720).

Phœbe, village girl seduced and afterward married by Barry Crittenden. He takes her to the cottage allotted him by his father, and introduces her to his mother and sisters. She tries diligently to adapt herself to her new sphere until she becomes jealous of a woman whom she imagines Barry once fancied, and now loves. Phœbe flees secretly to her mother's cottage, taking her child with her, and refuses to return to her husband, until accident reveals the causelessness of her jealousy.—Miriam Coles Harris, *Phœbe* (1884).

Phœbus, the sun-god. **Phœbe** (2 *syl.*), the moon-goddess.—*Greek Mythology*.

Phœbus's Son. Pha′ëton obtained permission of his father to drive the sun-car for one day, but, unable to guide the horses, they left their usual track, the car was overturned, and both heaven and earth were threatened with destruction. Jupiter struck Phaeton with his thunderbolt, and he fell headlong into the Po.

... like Phœbus fayrest childe,
That did presume his father's fiery wayne,
And flaming mouths of steeds unwonted wilde,
Thro' highest heaven with weaker hand to rayne; ...
He leaves the welkin way most beaten playne,
And, wrapt with whirling wheels, inflamed the skyen
With fire not made to burne, but fayrely for to shyne.
Spenser, *Faëry Queen*, i. 4, 10 (1590).

Phœbus. Gaston de Foix was so called, from his great beauty (1488-1512).

Phœbus (*Captain*), the betrothed of Fleur de Marie. He also entertains a base love for Esmeralda, the beautiful gypsy girl.—Victor Hugo, *Notre Dame de Paris* (1831).

Phœnix (*The*), is said to live 500 (or 1,000) years, when it makes a nest of spices, burns itself to ashes, and comes forth with renewed life for another similar period. There never was but one phœnix.

The bird of Arabye ... Can never dye,
And yet there is none, But only one,
A phœnix ... Plinni showeth al In his *Story Natural*,
What he doth finde Of the phœnix kinde.
J. Skelton, *Philip Sparow* (time, Henry VIII.).

Phœnix Tree, the raisin, an Arabian tree. Floro says: "There never was but one, and upon it the phœnix sits."—*Dictionary* (1598).

Pliny thinks the tree on which the phœnix was supposed to perch is the date tree (called in Greek *phoinix*), adding that "the bird died with the tree, and revived of itself as the tree revived."—*Nat. Hist.*, xiii. 4.

Now I will believe
That there are unicorns; that in Arabia
There is one tree, the phœnix' throne; one phœnix
At this hour reigning there.
Shakespeare, *The Tempest*, act iii. sc. 3 (1609).

Phorcus, "the old man of the sea." He had three daughters, with only one eye and one tooth between 'em.—*Greek Mythology*.

This is not "the old man of the sea" mentioned in the *Arabian Nights* ("Sindbad the Sailor").

Phor′mio, a parasite, who is "all things to all men."—Terence, *Phormio*.

Phosphor, the light-bringer or morning star; also called *Hespĕrus*, and by Homer and Hesiod *Heôs-phŏros*.

Bright Phosphor, fresher for the night,
Sweet Hesper-Phosphor, double name.
Tennyson, *In Memoriam*, cxxi. (1850).

Phos′phorus, a knight called by Tennyson "Morning Star," but, in the *History of Prince Arthur*, "Sir Persaunt of India, or the Blue Knight." One of the four brothers who kept the passages to Castle Perilous.—Tennyson, *Idylls* ("Gareth and Lynette"); Sir T. Malory, *History of Prince Arthur*, i. 131 (1470).

*** It is evidently a blunder to call the *Blue* Knight "Morning Star," and the *Green* Knight "Evening Star." In the old romance, the combat with the

"Green Knight," is at dawn, and with the "Blue Knight" at nightfall. The error arose from not bearing in mind that our forefathers began the day with the preceding eve, and ended it at sunset.

Phraortes (3 *syl.*), a Greek admiral.—Sir W. Scott, *Count Robert of Paris* (time, Rufus).

Phry´ne (2 *syl.*), an Athenian courtezan of surpassing beauty. Apellês's celebrated picture of "Venus Anadyomenê" was drawn from Phrynê, who entered the sea with hair dishevelled for a model. The "Cnidian Venus" of Praxitĕlês was also taken from the same model.

Some say Campaspê was the academy figure of the "Venus Anadyomenê." Pope has a poem called *Phryne*.

Phyllis, a Thracian, who fell in love with Demoph´oön. After some months of mutual affection, Demophoon was obliged to sail for Athens, but promised to return within a month. When a month had elapsed, and Demophoon did not put in an appearance, Phyllis so mourned for him that she was changed into an almond tree, hence called by the Greeks *Phylia*. In time, Demophoon returned, and, being told the fate of Phyllis, ran to embrace the tree, which though bare and leafless at the time, was instantly covered with leaves, hence called *Phylla* by the Greeks.

Let Demophoon tell
Why Phyllis by a fate untimely fell.
Ovid, *Art of Love*, iii.

Phyllis, a country girl in Virgil's third and fifth *Eclogues*. Hence a rustic maiden. Also spelt Phillis (*q.v.*).

Phyllis, in Spenser's eclogue, *Colin Clout's Come Home Again*, is Lady Carey, wife of Sir George Carey (afterwards Lord Hunsdon, 1596). Lady Carey was Elizabeth, the second of the six daughters of Sir John Spenser, of Althorpe, ancestor of the noble houses of Spenser and Marlborough.

No less praiseworthy are the sisters three,
The honor of the noble family
Of which I, meanest, boast myself to be, ...
Phyllis, Charyllis, and sweet Amaryllis:
Phyllis the fair is eldest of the three.
Spenser, *Colin Clout's Come Home Again* (1594).

Phyllis and Brunetta, rival beauties. Phyllis procured for a certain festival some marvellous fabric of gold brocade in order to eclipse her rival, but Brunetta dressed the slave who bore her train, in a robe of the same material and cut in precisely the same fashion, while she herself wore simple black. Phyllis died of mortification.—*The Spectator* (1711, 1712, 1714).

Phynnodderee, a Manx spirit, similar to the Scotch brownie. Phynnodderee is an outlawed fairy, who absented himself from Fairy-court on the great *levée* day of the harvest moon. Instead of paying his respects to King Oberon, he remained in the glen of Rushen, dancing with a pretty Manx maid whom he was courting.

Physic a Farce is (*His*). Sir John Hill began his career as an apothecary in St. Martin's Lane, London; became author, and amongst other things wrote farces. Grarrick said of him:

For physic and farces, his equal there scarce is:
His farces are physic, his physic a farce is.

Physician (*The Beloved*), St. Luke, the evangelist (*Col.* iv. 14).

Physicians (*The prince of*), Avicenna, the Arabian (980-1037).

Physigna'thos, king of the frogs, and son of Pelus ("mud"). Being wounded in the battle of the frogs and mice by Troxartas, the mouse king, he flees ingloriously to a pool, "and half in anguish of the flight, expires" (bk. iii. 112). The word means "puffed chaps."

Great Physignathos I from Pelus' race,
Begot in fair Hydromedê's embrace.
Parnell, *Battle of the Frogs and Mice*, i. (about 1712).

Pibrac (*Seigneur de*), poet and diplomatist, author of *Cinquante Quatrains* (1574). Gorgibus bids his daughter to study Pibrac instead of trashy novels and poetry.

Lisez-moi, comme il faut, au lieu de ces sornettes,
Les *Quatrains* de Pibrac, et les doctes *Tablettes*
Du conseiller Matthieu; l'ouvrage est de valeur, ...
La Guide des pécheurs est encore un bon livre.
Molière, *Sganarelle*, i. 1 (1660).

(Pierre Matthieu, poet and historian, wrote *Quatrains de la Vanité du Monde*, 1629.)

Picanninies (4 *syl.*), little children; the small fry of a village.—*West Indian Negroes*.

There were at the marriage the picanninies and the Joblilies, but not the Grand Panjandrum.—Yonge.

Pic'atrix, the pseudonym of a Spanish monk; author of a book on demonology.

When I was a student ... that same Rev. Picatrix ... was wont to tell us that devils did naturally fear the bright flashes of swords as much as he feared the splendor of the sun.—Rabelais, *Pantag'ruel*, iii. 23 (1545).

Picciola, flower that, springing up in the court-yard of his prison, cheers and elevates the lonely life of the prisoner whom X. B. Saintine makes the hero of his charming tale, *Picciola* (1837).

Piccolino, an opera by Mons. Guiraud (1875); libretto by MM. Sardou and Nuittier. This opera was first introduced to an English audience in 1879. The tale is this: Marthé, an orphan girl adopted by a Swiss pastor, is in love with Frédéric Auvray, a young artist, who "loved and left his love." Marthé plods through the snow from Switzerland to Rome to find her young artist, but, for greater security, puts on boy's clothes, and assumes the name of Piccolino. She sees Frédéric, who knows her not; but, struck with her beauty, makes a drawing of her. Marthé discovers that the faithless Frédéric is paying his addresses to Elena (sister of the Duke Strozzi). She tells the lady her love-tale; and Frédéric, deserted by Elena, forbids Piccolino (Marthé) to come into his presence again. The poor Swiss wanderer throws herself into the Tiber, but is rescued. Frédéric repents, and the curtain falls on a reconciliation and approaching marriage.

Pickel-Herringe (5 *syl.*), a popular name among the Dutch for a buffoon; a corruption of *pickle-härin* ("a hairy sprite"), answering to Ben Jonson's *Puck-hairy*.

Pickle (*Peregrine*), a savage, ungrateful spendthrift, fond of practical jokes, delighting in tormenting others; but suffering with ill temper the misfortunes which result from his own wilfulness. His ingratitude to his uncle, and his arrogance to Hatchway and Pipes, are simply hateful.—T. Smollett, *The Adventures of Peregrine Pickle* (1751).

Pickwick (*Samuel*), the chief character of *The Pickwick Papers*, a novel by C. Dickens. He is general chairman of the Pickwick Club. A most verdant, benevolent elderly gentleman, who, as member of a club instituted "for the purpose of investigating the source of the Hampstead ponds," travels about with three members of the club, to whom he acts as guardian and adviser. The adventures they encounter form the subject of the *Posthumous Papers of the Pickwick Club* (1836).

The original of Seymour's picture of "Pickwick" was a Mr. John Foster (*not* the biographer of Dickens, but a friend of Mr. Chapman's, the publisher). He lived at Richmond, and was "a fat old beau," noted for his "drab tights and black gaiters."

Pickwickian Sense (*In a*), an insult whitewashed. Mr. Pickwick accused Mr. Blotton of acting in "a vile and calumnious manner;" whereupon Mr. Blotton retorted by calling Mr. Pickwick "a humbug," But it finally was made to appear that both had used the offensive words only in a parliamentary sense, and that each entertained for the other "the highest regard and esteem." So the difficulty was easily adjusted, and both were satisfied.

Lawyers and politicians daily abuse each other in a Pickwickian sense.—Bowditch.

Pic′rochole, king of Lernê, noted for his choleric temper, his thirst for empire, and his vast but ill-digested projects.—Rabelais, *Gargantua*, i. (1533).

Supposed to be a satire on Charles V. of Spain.

Picrochole's Counsellors. The duke of Smalltrash, the earl of Swashbuckler, and Captain Durtaille, advised King Picrochole to leave a small garrison at home, and to divide his army into two parts—to send one south, and the other north. The former was to take Portugal, Spain, Italy, Germany (but was to spare the life of Barbarossa), to take the islands of the Mediterranean, the Morea, the Holy Land, and all Lesser Asia. The northern army was to take Belgium, Denmark, Prussia, Poland, Russia, Norway, Sweden, sail across the Sandy Sea, and meet the other half at Constantinople, when king Picrochole was to divide the nations amongst his great captains. Echephron said he had heard about a pitcher of milk which was to make its possessor a nabob, and give him for wife a sultan's daughter; only the poor fellow broke his pitcher, and had to go supperless to bed. (See BOBADIL.)—Rabelais, *Pantagruel*, i. 33 (1533).

A shoemaker bought a ha'p'orth of milk; with this he intended to make butter, the butter was to buy a cow, the cow was to have a calf, the calf was to be sold, and the man to become a nabob; only the poor dreamer cracked the jug, and spilt the milk and had to go supperless to bed.—*Pantagruel*, i. 33.

Picts, the Caledonians or inhabitants of Albin, *i.e.* northern Scotland. The Scots came from Scotia, north of Ireland, and established themselves under Kenneth M'Alpin in 843.

The etymology of "Picts" from the Latin *picti* ("painted men") is about equal to Stevens's etymology of the word "brethren" from *tabernacle* "because we breathe-therein.

Picture (*The*), a drama by Massinger (1629). The story of this play (like that of the *Twelfth Night*, by Shakespeare) is taken from the novelette of Bandello, of Piedmont, who died 1555.

Pi′cus, a soothsayer and augur; husband of Canens. In his prophetic art he made use of a woodpecker (*picus*), a prophetic bird sacred to Mars. Circé fell in love with him, and as he did not requite her advances, she changed him into a woodpecker, whereby he still retained his prophetic power.

"There is Picus," said Maryx. "What a strange thing is tradition! Perhaps it was in this very forest that Circê, gathering her herbs, saw the bold friend of Mars on his fiery courser, and tried to bewitch him, and, failing, metamorphosed him so. What, I wonder, ever first wedded that story to the woodpecker?"—Ouida, *Ariadnê*, i. 11.

Pied Horses, Motassem had 130,000 *pied horses*, which he employed to carry earth to the plain of Catoul; and having raised a mound of sufficient height to command a view of the whole neighborhood, he built thereon the royal city of Shamarah´.—Khondemyr, *Khelassat al Akhbar* (1495).

The Hill of the Pied Horses, the site of the palace of Alkoremmi, built by Motassem, and enlarged by Vathek.

Pied Piper of Hamelin (3 *syl.*), a piper named Bunting, from his dress. He undertook, for a certain sum of money, to free the town of Hamelin, in Brunswick, of the rats which infested it; but when he had drowned all the rats in the river Weser, the townsmen refused to pay the sum agreed upon. The piper, in revenge, collected together all the children of Hamelin, and enticed them by his piping into a cavern in the side of the mountain Koppenberg, which instantly closed upon them, and 130 went down alive into the pit (June 26, 1284). The street through which Bunting conducted his victims was Bungen, and from that day to this no music is ever allowed to be played in this particular street.—Verstegan, *Restitution of Decayed Intelligence* (1634).

Robert Browning has a poem entitled *The Pied Piper*.

Erichius, in his *Exodus Hamelensis*, maintains the truth of this legend; but Martin Schoock, in his *Fabula Hamelensis*, contends that it is a mere myth.

"Don't forget to pay the piper" is still a household expression in common use.

*** The same tale is told of the fiddler of Brandenberg. The children were led to the Marienberg, which opened upon them and swallowed them up.

*** When Lorch was infested with ants, a hermit led the multitudinous insects by his pipe into a lake, where they perished. As the inhabitants refused to pay the stipulated price, he led their pigs the same dance, and they, too, perished in the lake.

Next year, a charcoal-burner cleared the same place of crickets; and when the price agreed upon was withheld, he led the sheep of the inhabitants into the lake.

The third year came a plague of rats, which an old man of the mountain piped away and destroyed. Being refused his reward, he piped the children of Lorch into the Tannenberg.

⁂ About 200 years ago, the people of Ispahan were tormented with rats, when a little dwarf named Giouf, not above two feet high, promised, on the payment of a certain sum of money, to free the city of all its vermin in an hour. The terms were agreed to, and Giouf, by tabor and pipe, attracted every rat and mouse to follow him to the river Zenderou, where they were all drowned. Next day, the dwarf demanded the money; but the people gave him several bad coins, which they refused to change. Next day, they saw with horror an old black woman, fifty feet high, standing in the market-place with a whip in her hand. She was the genie Mergian Banou, the mother of the dwarf. For four days she strangled daily fifteen of the principal women, and on the fifth day led forty others to a magic tower, into which she drove them, and they were never after seen by mortal eye.—T. S. Gueulette, *Chinese Tales* ("History of Prince Kader-Bilah," 1723).

⁂ The syrens of classic story had, by their weird spirit-music, a similar irresistible influence.

(Weird music is called Alpleich or Elfenseigen.

Pierre [*Peer*], a blunt, bold, outspoken man, who heads a conspiracy to murder the Venetian senators, and induces Jaffier to join the gang. Jaffier (in order to save his wife's father, Priuli), reveals the plot, under promise of free pardon; but the senators break their pledge, and order the conspirators to torture and death. Jaffier, being free, because he had turned "king's evidence" stabs Pierre, to prevent his being broken on the wheel, and then kills himself.—T. Otway, *Venice Preserved* (1682).

Pierre, a very inquisitive servant of M. Darlemont, who long suspects his master has played falsely with his ward, Julio, count of Harancour.—Thomas Holcroft, *The Deaf and Dumb* (1785).

Pierre Alphonse (*Rabbi Moïse Sephardi*), a Spanish Jew converted to Christianity in 1062.

All stories that recorded are
By Pierre Alfonse he knew by heart.
Longfellow, *The Wayside Inn* (prelude).

Pierre du Coignet or **Coignères**, an advocate-general in the reign of Philippe de Valois, who stoutly opposed the encroachments of the Church. The monks, in revenge, nicknamed those grotesque figures in stone (called "gargoyles"), *pierres du coignet*. At Notre Dame de Paris there were at one time gargoyles used for extinguishing torches, and the smoke added not a little to their ugliness.

You may associate them with Master Pierre du Coignet, ... which perform the office of extinguishers.—Rabelais, *Gargantua and Pantagruel* (1533-45).

Pierrot [*Pe´-er-ro*], a character in French pantomime, representing a man in stature and a child in mind. He is generally the tallest and thinnest man in the company, and appears with his face and hair thickly covered with flour. He wears a white gown, with very long sleeves, and a row of big buttons down the front. The word means "Little Peter."

Piers and Palinode, two shepherds in Spenser's fifth eclogue, representing the Protestant and the Catholic priest.

Piers or Percy again appears in ecl. x. with Cuddy, a poetic shepherd. This noble eclogue has for its subject "poetry." Cuddy complains that poetry has no patronage or encouragement, although it comes by inspiration. He says no one would be so qualified as Colin to sing divine poetry, if his mind were not so depressed by disappointed love.—Spenser, *The Shepheardes Calendar* (1579).

Pie´tro (2 *syl.*), the putative father of Pompilia. This paternity was a fraud to oust the heirs of certain property which would otherwise fall to them.—R. Browning, *The Ring and the Book*, ii. 580.

Pig. Phædrus tells a tale of a popular actor who imitated the squeak of a pig. A peasant said to the audience that he would himself next night challenge and beat the actor. When the night arrived, the audience unanimously gave judgment in favor of the actor, saying that his squeak was by far the better imitation; but the peasant presented to them a real pig, and said, "Behold, what excellent judges are ye!"

Pigal (*Mons. de*), the dancing-master who teaches Alice Bridgenorth.—Sir W. Scott, *Peveril of the Peak* (time, Charles II.).

Pigeon and Dove (*The*). Prince Constantio was changed into a pigeon, and the Princess Constantia into a dove, because they loved, but were always crossed in love. Constantio found that Constantia was sold by his mother for a slave, and in order to follow her, he was converted into a pigeon. Constantia was seized by a giant, and in order to escape him was changed into a dove. Cupid then took them to Paphos, and they became "examples of a tender and sincere passion; and ever since have been the emblems of love and constancy."—Comtesse D'Aunoy, *Fairy Tales* ("The Pigeon and Dove," 1682).

Pigmy, a dwarf. (See PYGMY.)

Pigott Diamond (*The*), brought from India by Lord Pigott. It weighs 82-1/4 carats. In 1818 it came into the hands of Messrs. Rundell and Bridge.

Pigrogrom´itus, a name alluded to by Sir Andrew Ague-cheek.

In sooth thou wast in very gracious fooling last night when thou spokest of Pigrogromitus, of the Vapian passing the equinoctial of Queubus. 'Twas very good, i' faith.—Shakespeare, *Twelfth Night*, act ii. sc. 3 (1614).

Pigwig´gen, a fairy knight, whose amours with Queen Mab, and furious combat with Oberon, form the subject of Drayton's *Nymphidia* (1593).

Pike (*Gideon*), valet to old Major Bellenden.—Sir W. Scott, *Old Mortality* (time, Charles II.).

Pila´tus (*Mount*), in Switzerland. The legend is that Pontius Pilate, being banished to Gaul by the Emperor Tiberius, wandered to this mount, and flung himself into a black lake at the summit of the hill, being unable to endure the torture of conscience for having given up the Lord to crucifixion.

Pilgrim Fathers. They were 102 puritans (English, Scotch, and Dutch), who went, in December, 1620, in a ship called the *Mayflower*, to North America, and colonized Maine, New Hampshire, Vermont, Massachusetts, and Connecticut. These states they called "New England." New Plymouth (near Boston) was the second colony planted by the English in the New World.

Men in the middle of life, austere and grave in deportment....
God had sifted three kingdoms to find the wheat for this planting.
Longfellow, *Courtship of Miles Standish*, iv. (1858).

Pilgrim—Palmer. *Pilgrims* had dwellings, *palmers* had none. *Pilgrims* went at their own charge, *palmers* professed willing poverty, and lived on charity. *Pilgrims* might return to a secular life, *palmers* could not. *Pilgrims* might hold titles and follow trades, *palmers* were wholly "religious" men.

Pilgrim to Compostella. Some pilgrims on their way to Compostella, stopped at a hospice in La Calzāda. The daughter of the innkeeper solicited a young Frenchman to spend the night with her, but he refused; so she put in his wallet a silver cup, and when he was on the road, she accused him to the alcaydê of theft. As the property was found in his possession, the alcaydê ordered him to be hung. His parents went on their way to Compostella, and returned after eight days, but what was their amazement to find their son alive on the gibbet, and uninjured. They went instantly to tell the alcaydê; but the magistrate replied, "Woman, you are mad! I would just as soon believe these pullets, which I am about to eat, are alive, as that a man who has been gibbeted eight days is not dead." No sooner had he spoken than the two pullets actually rose up alive. The alcaydê was frightened out of his wits, and was about to rush out of doors, when the heads and feathers of the birds came scampering in to complete the resuscitation. The cock and hen were taken in grand procession to St. James's Church of Compostella, where they lived seven years, and the hen hatched two eggs, a cock and a hen, which lived just seven years, and did the same. This has continued to this day, and pilgrims receive feathers from these birds as holy relics; but no matter how many feathers are given away, the plumage of the sacred fowls is never deficient.

⁎ This legend is also seriously related by Bishop Patrick, *Parable of the Pilgrims*, xxxv. 430-4. Udal ap Rhys repeats it in his *Tour through Spain and Portugal*, 35-8. It is inserted in the *Acta Sanctorum*, vi. 45. Pope Calixtus II. mentions it among the miracles of Santiago.

Pilgrim (*A Passionate*), American who visits England, as one seeks the home he has loved throughout a tedious exile. It is like the return of a weary child to his mother's arms, as night comes on. He lingers upon each feature of the landscape as upon the face of his beloved, and counts the rest of the world but "a garish" place.—Henry James, Jr., *A Passionate Pilgrim*.

Pilgrim's Progress (*The*), by John Bunyan. Pt. i., 1670; pt. ii., 1684. This is supposed to be a dream, and to allegorize the life of a Christian, from his conversion to his death. His doubts are giants, his sins a pack, his Bible a chart, his minister, Evangelist, his conversion a flight from the City of Destruction, his struggle with besetting sins a fight with Apollyon, his death a toilsome passage over a deep stream, and so on.

The second part is Christiana and her family led by Greatheart through the same road, to join Christian who had gone before.

Pillar of the Doctors (*La Colonne des Docteurs*), William de Champeaux (*-1121).

Pilot (*The*), an important character and the title of a nautical burletta by E. Fitzball, based on the novel so called by J. Fenimore Cooper, of New York. "The pilot" turns out to be the brother of Colonel Howard, of America. He happened to be in the same vessel which was taking out the colonel's wife and only son. The vessel was wrecked, but "the pilot" (whose name was John Howard) saved the infant boy, and sent him to England to be brought up, under the name of Barnstable. When young Barnstable was a lieutenant in the British navy, Colonel Howard seized him as a spy, and commanded him to be hung to the yardarm of an American frigate, called the *Alacrity*. At this crisis, "the pilot" informed the colonel that Barnstable was his own son, and the father arrived just in time to save him from death.

Pilpay', the Indian Æsop. His compilation was in Sanskrit, and entitled *Pantschatantra*.

It was rumored he could say ...
All the "Fables" of Pilpay.
Longfellow, *The Wayside Inn* (prelude).

Pilum´nus, the patron god of bakers and millers, because he was the first person who ever ground corn.

Then there was Pilumnus, who was the first to make cheese, and became the god of bakers.—Ouida, *Ariadnê*, i. 40.

Pinabello, son of Anselmo (king of Maganza). Marphi´sa overthrew him, and told him he could not wipe out the disgrace till he had unhorsed a thousand dames and a thousand knights. Pinabello was slain by Brad´amant.—Ariosto, *Orlando Furioso* (1516).

Pinac, the lively, spirited fellow-traveller of Mirabel, "the wild goose." He is in love with the sprightly Lillia-Bianca, a daughter of Nantolet.—Beaumont and Fletcher, *The Wild Goose Chase* (1652).

Pinch, a schoolmaster and conjuror, who tries to exorcise Antiph´olus (act iv. sc. 4).—Shakespeare, *Comedy of Errors* (1593).

Pinch (Tom), clerk to Mr. Pecksniff "architect and land surveyor." Simple as a child, green as a salad, and honest as truth itself. Very fond of story-books, but far more so of the organ. It was the seventh heaven to him to pull out the stops for the organist's assistant at Salisbury Cathedral; but when allowed, after service, to finger the notes himself, he lived in a dreamland of unmitigated happiness. Being dismissed from Pecksniff's office, Tom was appointed librarian to the Temple Library, and his new catalogue was a perfect model of workmanship.

Ruth Pinch, a true-hearted, pretty girl, who adores her brother, Tom, and is the sunshine of his existence. She marries John Westlock.—C. Dickens, *Martin Chuzzlewit* (1844).

Pinchbeck. Sham doctor and matrimonial agent in John Brougham's play, *Playing With Fire*.

Pinchbeck (Lady), with whom Don Juan placed Leila to be brought up.

Olden she was—but had been very young;
Virtuous she was—and had been, I believe ...
She merely now was amiable and witty.
Byron, *Don Juan*, xii. 43, 47 (1824).

Pinchwife (*Mr.*), the town husband of a raw country girl, wholly unpractised in the ways of the world, and whom he watches with ceaseless anxiety.

Lady Drogheda ... watched her town husband assiduously as Mr. Pinchwife watched his country wife.—Macaulay.

Mrs. Pinchwife, the counterpart of Molière's "Agnes," in his comedy entitled *L'école des Femmes*. Mrs. Pinchwife is a young woman wholly unsophisticated in affairs of the heart.—Wycherly, *The Country Wife* (1675).

⁎ Garrick altered Wycherly's comedy to *The Country Girl*.

Pindar *(Peter)*, the pseudonym of Dr. John Wolcot (1738-1819).

Pindar (The British), Thomas Gray (1716-1771). On his monument in Westminster Abbey is inscribed these lines:

No more the Grecian muse unrivalled reigns;
To Britain let the nations homage pay:
She felt a Homer's fire in Milton's strains,
A Pindar's rapture in the lyre of Gray.

Pindar (The French), (1) Jean Dorat (1507-1588); (2) Ponce Denis Lebrun (1719-1807).

Pindar (The Italian), Gabriello Chiabrera (1552-1637).

Pindar of England. Cowley was preposterously called by the duke of Buckingham "The Pindar, Horace and Virgil of England." Posterity has not endorsed this absurd eulogium (1618-1667).

Pindar of Wakefield *(The)*, George-a-Green, pinner of the town of Wakefield—that is, keeper of the public pound for the confinement of estrays.—*The History of George-a-Green, Pindar of the Town of Wakefield* (time, Elizabeth).

Pindo′rus and Aride′us, the two heralds of the Christian army in the siege of Jerusalem.—Tasso, *Jerusalem Delivered* (1575).

Pine-Bender *(The)*, Sinis, the Corinthian robber who used to fasten his victims to two pine trees bent towards the earth, and leave them to be torn to pieces by the rebound.

Pingree *(Nancy)*, called "Old Lady Pingree" because of her pride and black lace turban. She lives by herself in the lower part of the old Pingree house, and is so poor that to give an egg to the lodgers above stairs is an act of self-denying generosity. She has money and burial-clothes laid away for her funeral, yet when the neighbor upstairs dies, Nancy "lends" it to the daughter to keep her mother out of the Potter's field. A sudden rise in property brings Nancy a few hundreds, and enables her to face death with calm certainty of an independent burial in the Pingree lot.—Mary E. Wilkins, *A Humble Romance, and Other Stories* (1887).

Pinkerton (*Miss*), a most majestic lady, tall as a grenadier, and most proper. Miss Pinkerton kept an academy for young ladies on Chiswick Mall. She was "the Semiramis of Hammersmith, the friend of Dr. Johnson, and the correspondent of Mrs. Chapone." This very distinguished lady "had a Roman nose, and wore a solemn turban." Amelia Sedley was educated at Chiswick Mall academy, and Rebecca Sharp was a pupil-teacher there.—Thackeray, *Vanity Fair*, i. (1848).

Pinnit (*Orson*), keeper of the bears.—Sir W. Scott, *Kenilworth* (time, Elizabeth).

Pinto (*Ferdinand Mendez*), a Portuguese traveller, whose "voyages" were at one time wholly discredited, but have since been verified (1509-1583).

Ferdinand Mendez Pinto was but a type of thee, thou liar of the first magnitude.—W. Congreve, *Love for Love* (1695).

Pious (*The*), Ernst I., founder of the house of Gotha (1601-1674).

Robert, son of Hugues Capet (971, 996-1031).

Eric IX. of Sweden (*, 1155-1161).

Pip, the hero of Dickens's novel called *Great Expectations*. His family name was Pirrip, and his Christian name Philip. He was enriched by a convict named Abel Magwitch; and was brought up by Joe Gargery, a smith, whose wife was a woman of thunder and lightning, storm and tempest. Magwitch, having made his escape to Australia, became a sheep farmer, grew very rich, and deposited £500 a year with Mr. Jaggers, a lawyer, for the education of Pip, and to make a gentleman of him. Ultimately, Pip married Estella, the daughter of Magwitch, but adopted from infancy by Miss Havisham, a rich banker's daughter. His friend, Herbert Pocket, used to call him "Handel."—C. Dickens, *Great Expectations* (1860).

Pipchin (*Mrs.*), an exceedingly "well-connected lady," living at Brighton, where she kept an establishment for the training of *enfants*. Her "respectability" chiefly consisted in the circumstance of her husband having broken his heart in pumping water out of some Peruvian mines (that is, in having invested in these mines and been let in). Mrs. Pipchin was an ill-favored old woman, with mottled cheeks and grey eyes. She was given to buttered toast and sweetbreads, but kept her *enfants* on the plainest possible fare.—C. Dickens, *Dombey and Son* (1846).

Piper (*Tom*), one of the characters in a morris-dance.

So have I seen
Tom Piper stand upon our village green,

Backed with the May-pole.
William Browne, *Shepherd's Pipe* (1614).

Piper (Paddy, the), an Irish piper, supposed to have been eaten by a cow. Going along one night during the "troubles," he knocked his head against the body of a dead man dangling from a tree. The sight of the "iligant" boots was too great a temptation: and as they refused to come off without the legs, Paddy took them too, and sought shelter for the night in a cowshed. The moon rose, and Paddy, mistaking the moon-light for the dawn, started for the fair, having drawn on the boots and left the "legs" behind. At daybreak, some of the piper's friends went in search of him, and found, to their horror, that the cow, as they supposed, had devoured him with the exception of his legs—clothes, bags, and all. They were horror-struck, and of course the cow was condemned to be sold; but while driving her to the fair, they were attracted by the strains of a piper coming towards them. The cow startled, made a bolt, with a view, as it was supposed, of making a meal on another piper. "Help, help!" they shouted; when Paddy himself ran to their aid. The mystery was soon explained over a drop of the "cratur," and the cow was taken home again.—S. Lover, *Legends and Stories of Ireland* (1834).

Piper of Hamelin (*The Pied*), Bunting, who first charmed the rats of Hamelin into the Weser, and then allured the children (to the number of 130) to Koppenberg Hill, which opened upon them. (See PIED PIPER OF HAMELIN.)

Piperman, the factotum of Chalomel, chemist and druggist. He was "so handy" that he was never at his post; and being "so handy," he took ten times the trouble of doing anything that another would need to bestow. For the self-same reason, he stumbled and blundered about, muddled and marred everything he touched, and being a Jack-of-all-trades was master of none.

There has been an accident because I am so handy. I went to the dairy at a bound, came back at other, and fell down in the open street, where I spilt the milk. I tried to bale it up—no go. Then I ran back or ran home, I forget which, and left the money somewhere; and then, in fact, I have been four times to and fro, because I am so handy.—J. R. Ware, *Piperman's Predicament.*

Pipes (*Tom*), a retired boatswain's mate, living with Commodore Trunnion to keep the servants in order. Tom Pipes is noted for his taciturnity.—Tobias Smollett, *The Adventures of Peregrine Pickle* (1751).

The incident of Tom Pipes concealing in his shoe his master's letter to Emilia was suggested by Ovid.

Cum possit solea chartas celare ligatas,
Et vincto blandas sub pede ferre notas.
Art of Love.

Pippa. Peasant maid who sings in tripping through the streets on the morning of her holiday. The song reaches the windows of those who sorrow, doubt and sin, and thus influences other lives than her own.—Robert Browning, *Pippa Passes* (1842).

Pirate *(The)*, a novel by Sir W. Scott (1821). In this novel we are introduced to the wild sea scenery of the Shetlands; the primitive manners of the old udaller, Magnus Troil, and his fair daughters Minna and Brenda; lovely pictures, drawn with nice discrimination, and most interesting.

* A udaller is one who holds his lands on allodial tenure.

Pirner *(John)*, a fisherman at Old St. Ronan's.—Sir W. Scott, *St. Ronan's Well* (time, George III.).

Pisa. The banner of Pisa is a cross on a crimson field, said to have been brought from heaven by Michael the archangel, and delivered by him to St. Efeso, the patron saint of that city.

Pisanio, servant of Posthu´mus. Being sent to murder Imogen, the wife of Posthumus, he persuades her to escape to Milford Haven in boy's clothes, and sends a bloody napkin to Posthumus, to make him believe that she has been murdered. Ultimately, Imogen becomes reconciled to her husband. (See POSTHUMUS.)—Shakespeare, *Cymbeline* (1605).

Pisis´tratos, of Athens, being asked by his wife to punish with death a young man who had dared to kiss their daughter, replied, "How shall we requite those who wish us evil, if we condemn to death those who love us?" This anecdote is referred to by Dantê, in his *Purgatory*, xv.—Valerius Maximus, *Memorable Acts and Sayings*, v.

Pisis´tratos and His Two Sons. The history of Pisistratos and his two sons is repeated in that of Cosmo de Medici, of Florence, and his two grandsons. It would be difficult to find a more striking parallel, whether we regard the characters or the incidents of the two families.

Pisistratos was a great favorite of the Athenian populace; so was Cosmo de Medici with the populace of Florence. Pisistratos was banished, but, being recalled by the people, was raised to sovereign power in the republic of Athens; so Cosmo was banished, but, being recalled by the people, was raised to supreme power in the republic of Florence. Pisistratos was just and merciful, a great patron of literature, and spent large sums of money in beautifying Athens with architecture; the same may be said of Cosmo de Medici. To Pisistratos we owe the poems of Homer in a connected form; and to Cosmo we owe the best literature of Europe, for he spent fortunes in the copying of valuable MSS. The two sons of Pisistratos were Hipparchos and Hippias; and the two grandsons of Cosmo were Guiliano and Lorenzo.

Two of the most honored citizens of Athens (Harmodios and Aristogīton) conspired against the sons of Pisistratos—Hipparchos was assassinated, but Hippias escaped; so Francesco Pazzi and the archbishop of Pisa conspired against the grandsons of Cosmo—Guiliano was assassinated, but Lorenzo escaped. In both cases it was the elder brother who fell, and the younger who escaped. Hippias quelled the tumult, and succeeded in placing himself at the head of Athens; so did Lorenzo in Florence.

Pistol, in *The Merry Wives of Windsor* and the two parts of *Henry IV.*, is the ancient or ensign of Captain Sir John Falstaff. Peto is his lieutenant, and Bardolph his corporal. Peto being removed, (probably killed), we find in *Henry V.*, Pistol is lieutenant, Bardolph ancient, and Nym corporal. Pistol is also introduced as married to Mistress Nell Quickly, hostess of the tavern in Eastcheap. Both Pistol and his wife die before the play is over; so does Sir John Falstaff; Bardolph and Nym are both hanged. Pistol is a model bully, wholly unprincipled, and utterly despicable; but he treats his wife kindly, and she is certainly fond of him.—Shakespeare.

Pistris, the sea-monster sent to devour Androm´eda. It had a dragon's head and a fish's tail.—Aratus, *Commentaries*.

Pithyrian [*Pi.thirry.an*], a pagan of Antioch. He had one daughter, named Mara´na, who was a Christian. A young dragon of most formidable character infested the city of Antioch, and demanded a virgin to be sent out daily for its meal. The Antioch´eans cast lots for the first victim, and the lot fell on Marana, who was led forth in grand procession as the victim of the dragon. Pithyrian, in distraction, rushed into a Christian church, and fell before an image which attracted his attention, at the base of which was the real arm of a saint. The sacristan handed the holy relic to Pithyrian, who kissed it, and then restored it to the sacristan; but the servitor did not observe that a thumb was missing. Off ran Pithyrian with the thumb, and joined his daughter. On came the dragon, with tail erect, wings extended, and mouth wide open, when Pithyrian threw into the gaping jaws the "sacred thumb." Down fell the tail, the wings drooped, the jaws were locked, and up rose the dragon into the air to the height of three miles, when it blew up into a myriad pieces. So the lady was rescued, Antioch delivered; and the relic, minus a thumb, testifies the fact of this wonderful miracle.—Southey, *The Young Dragon* (Spanish legend).

Pitt Diamond (*The*), the sixth largest cut diamond in the world. It weighed 410 carats uncut, and 136-3/4 carats cut. It once belonged to Mr. Pitt, grandfather of the famous earl of Chatham. The duke of Orleans, regent of France, bought it for £135,000, whence it is often called "The Regent." The French republic sold it to Treskon, a merchant of Berlin. Napoleon I. bought it to ornament his sword. It now belongs to the king of Prussia. (See DIAMONDS.)

Pizarro, a Spanish adventurer, who made war on Atali´ba, inca of Peru. Elvi´ra, mistress of Pizarro, vainly endeavored to soften his cruel heart. Before the battle, Alonzo, the husband of Cora, confided his wife and child to Rolla, the beloved friend of the inca. The Peruvians were on the point of being routed, when Rolla came to the rescue, and redeemed the day; but Alonzo was made a prisoner of war. Rolla, thinking Alonzo to be dead, proposed to Cora; but she declined his suit, and having heard that her husband had fallen into the hands of the Spaniards, she implored Rolla to set him free. Accordingly, he entered the prison where Alonzo was confined, and changed clothes with him, but Elvira liberated him on condition that he would kill Pizarro. Rolla found his enemy sleeping in his tent, spared his life, and made him his friend. The infant child of Cora being lost, Rolla recovered it, and was so severely wounded in this heroic act that he died. Pizarro was slain in combat by Alonzo; Elvira retired to a convent; and the play ends with a grand funeral march, in which the dead body of Rolla is borne to the tomb.—Sheridan, *Pizarro* (1814).

(Sheridan's drama of *Pizarro* is taken from that of Kotzebue, but there are several alterations: Thus, Sheridan makes Pizarro killed by Alonzo, which is a departure both from Kotzebue and also from historic truth. Pizarro lived to conquer Peru, and was assassinated in his palace at Lima, by the son of his friend, Almagro.)

Pizarro, "the ready tool of fell Velasquez' crimes."—R. Jephson, *Braganza* (1775).

Pizarro, the governor of the State prison, in which Fernando Florestan was confined. Fernando's young wife, in boy's attire, and under the name of Fidelio, became the servant of Pizarro, who, resolving to murder Fernando, sent Fidelio and Rocco (the jailer) to dig his grave. Pizarro was just about to deal the fatal blow, when the minister of state arrived, and commanded the prisoner to be set free.—Beethoven, *Fidelio* (1791).

Place´bo, one of the brothers of January, the old baron of Lombardy. When January held a family conclave to know whether he should marry, Placebo told him "to please himself, and do as he liked."—Chaucer, *Canterbury Tales* ("The Merchant's Tale," 1388).

Placid (*Mr.*), a hen-pecked husband, who is roused at last to be somewhat more manly, but could never be better than "a boiled rabbit without oyster sauce." (See PLIANT.)

Mrs. Placid, the lady paramount of the house, who looked quite aghast if her husband expressed a wish of his own, or attempted to do an independent act.—Inchbald, *Every One Has His Fault* (1794).

Plac´idas, the exact fac-simile of his friend, Amias. Having heard of his friend's captivity, he went to release him, and being detected in the garden, was mistaken by Corflambo's dwarf for Amias. The dwarf went and told Pæa´na (the daughter of Corflambo, "fair as ever yet saw living eye, but too loose of life and eke of love too light"). Placidas was seized and brought before the lady, who loved Amias, but her love was not requited. When Placidas stood before her, she thought he was Amias, and great was her delight to find her love returned. She married Placidas, reformed her ways, "and all men much admired the change, and spake her praise."—Spenser, *Faëry Queen*, iv. 8, 9 (1596).

Plagiary (*Sir Fretful*), a playwright, whose dramas are mere plagiarisms from "the refuse of obscure volumes." He pretends to be rather pleased with criticism, but is sorely irritated thereby. Richard Cumberland (1732-1811), noted for his vanity and irritability, was the model of this character.—Sheridan, *The Critic*, i. 1 (1779).

Herrick, who had no occasion to steal, has taken this image from Suckling, and spoilt it in the theft. Like Sir Fretful Plagiary, Herrick had not skill to steal with taste.—R. Chambers, *English Literature*, i. 134.

William Parsons [1736-1795] was the original "Sir Fretful Plagiary," and from his delineation most of our modern actors have borrowed their idea.—*Life of Sheridan*.

Plaids et Gieux sous l'Ormel, a society formed by the troubadours of Picardy in the latter half of the twelfth century. It consisted of knights and ladies of the highest rank, exercised and approved in courtesy, who assumed an absolute judicial power in matters of the most delicate nature; trying with the most consummate ceremony, all causes in love brought before their tribunals.

This was similar to the "Court of Love," established about the same time, by the troubadours of Provence.—*Universal Magazine* (March, 1792).

Plain (*The*), the level floor of the National Convention of France, occupied by the Girondists, or moderate republicans.

The red republicans occupied the higher seats, called "the mountain." By a figure of speech, the Girondist party was called "the plain," and the red republican party "the mountain."

Plain and Perspicuous Doctor (*The*), Walter Burleigh (1275-1357).

Plain Dealer (*The*), a comedy by William Wycherly (1677).

The countess of Drogheda ... inquired for the *Plain Dealer*. "Madam," said Mr. Fairbeard, ... "there he is," pushing Mr. Wycherly towards her.—Cibber, *Lives of the Poets*, iii. 252.

(Wycherly married the countess in 1680. She died soon afterwards, leaving him the whole of her fortune.)

Plantagenet (*Lady Edith*), a kinswoman of Richard I. She marries the prince royal of Scotland (called Sir Kenneth, knight of the Leopard, or David, earl of Huntingdon).—Sir W. Scott, *The Talisman* (time, Richard I.).

Plato. The mistress of this philosopher was Archianassa; of Aristotle, Hepyllis; and of Epicurus, Leontium. (See LOVERS.)

Plato (*The German*), Friedrich Heinrich Jacobi (1743-1819).

Plato (*The Jewish*), Philo Judæus (fl. 30-40).

Plato (*The Puritan*), John Howe (1630-1706).

Plato and the Bees. It is said that when Plato was an infant, bees settled on his lips while he was asleep, indicating that he would become famous for his "honeyed words." The same story is told of Sophoclês also.

And as when Plato did i' the cradle thrive,
Bees to his lips brought honey from the hive;
So to this boy [*Dor'idon*] they came—I know not whether
They brought or from his lips did honey gather.
W. Browne, *Brittania's Pastorals*, ii. (1613).

Plato and Homer. Plato greatly admired Homer, but excluded him from his ideal republic.

Plato, 'tis true, great Homer doth commend,
Yet from his common-weal did him exile.
Lord Brooke, *Inquisition upon Fame, etc.* (1554-1628).

Plato and Poets.

Plato, anticipating the Reviewers,
From his "republic," banished without pity
The poets.
Longfellow, *The Poet's Tale*.

Platonic Puritan (*The*), John Howe, the puritan divine (1630-1706).

Plausible (*Counsellor*) and Serjeant Eitherside, two pleaders in *The Man of the World*, by C. Macklin (1764).

Pleasant (*Mrs.*) in *The Parson's Wedding*, by Tom Killigrew (1664).

Pleasures of Hope, a poem in two parts by Thomas Campbell (1799). It opens with a comparison between the beauty of scenery, and the ideal enchantments of fancy, in which hope is never absent, but can sustain the seaman on his watch, the soldier on his march, and Byron in his perilous adventures. The hope of a mother, the hope of a prisoner, the hope of the wanderer, the grand hope of the patriot, the hope of regenerating uncivilized nations, extending liberty, and ameliorating the condition of the poor. Pt. ii. speaks of the hope of love, and the hope of a future state, concluding with the episode of Conrad and Ellenore. Conrad was a felon, transported to New South Wales, but, though "a martyr to his crimes, was true to his daughter." Soon, he says, he shall return to the dust from which he was taken;

But not, my child, with life's precarious fire,
The immortal ties of Nature shall expire;
These shall resist the triumph of decay,
When time is o'er, and worlds have passed away.
Cold in the dust this perished heart may lie,
But that which warmed it once shall never die—
That spark, unburied in its mortal frame,
With living light, eternal, and the same,
Shall beam on Joy's interminable years,
Unveiled by darkness, unassuaged by tears.
Pt. ii.

Pleasures of Imagination, a poem in three books, by Akenside (1744). All the pleasures of imagination arise from the perception of greatness, wonderfulness, or beauty. The beauty of greatness—witness the pleasures of mountain scenery, of astronomy, of infinity. The pleasure of what is wonderful—witness the delight of novelty, of the revelations of science, of tales of fancy. The pleasure of beauty, which is always connected with truth—the beauty of color, shape, and so on, in natural objects; the beauty of mind and the moral faculties. Bk. ii. contemplates accidental pleasures arising from contrivance and design, emotion and passion, such as sorrow, pity, terror, and indignation. Bk. iii. Morbid imagination the parent of vice; the benefits of a well-trained imagination.

Pleasures of Memory, a poem in two parts, by Samuel Rogers (1793). The first part is restricted to the pleasure of memory afforded by the five senses, as that arising from visiting celebrated places, and that afforded by pictures. Pt. ii. goes into the pleasures of the mind, as imagination and memory of past griefs and dangers. The poem concludes with the supposition that in the life to come this faculty will be greatly enlarged. The episode is this: Florio, a young sportsman, accidentally met Julia in a grot, and followed her home, when her father, a rich squire, welcomed him as his guest, and talked with delight of his younger days, when hawk and hound were his joy of joys. Florio took Julia for a sail on the lake, but the vessel was capsized, and, though Julia was saved from the water, she died on being brought to shore. It was Florio's delight to haunt the places which Julia frequented.

Her charm around the enchantress Memory threw,
A charm that soothes the mind and sweetens too.
Pt. ii.

Pleiads (*The*), a cluster of seven stars in the constellation *Taurus*, and applied to a cluster of seven celebrated contemporaries. The stars were the seven daughters of Atlas: Maïa, Electra, Taygĕtê, (4 *syl.*), Asterŏpê, Merŏpê, Alcyŏnê and Celēno.

The Pleiad of Alexandria consisted of Callimachos, Apollonios Rhodios, Arātos, Homer the Younger, Lycophron, Nicander, and Theocrĭtos. All of Alexandria, in the time of Ptolemy Philadelphos.

The Pleiad of Charlemagne consisted of Alcuin, called "Albīnus;" Angilbert, called "Homer;" Adelard, called "Augustine;" Riculfe, called "Damætas;" Varnefrid; Eginhard; and Charlemagne himself, who was called "David."

The First French Pleiad (sixteenth century): Ronsard, Joachim du Bellay, Antoine de Baïf, Remi-Belleau, Jodelle, Ponthus de Thiard, and the seventh is either Dorat or Amadis de Jamyn. All under Henri III.

The Second French Pleiad (seventeenth century): Rapin, Commire, Larue, Santeuil, Ménage, Dupérier, and Petit.

We have also our English clusters. There were those born in the second half of the sixteenth century: Spenser (1553), Drayton (1563), Shakespeare and Marlowe (1564), Ben Jonson (1574), Fletcher (1576), Massinger (1585), Beaumont (Fletcher's colleague) and Ford (1586). Besides these there were Tusser (1515), Raleigh (1552), Sir Philip Sidney (1554), Phineas Fletcher (1584), Herbert (1593), and several others.

Another cluster came a century later: Prior (1664), Swift (1667), Addison and Congreve (1672), Rowe (1673), Farquhar (1678), Young (1684), Gay and Pope (1688), Macklin (1690).

These were born in the latter half of the eighteenth century: Sheridan (1751), Crabbe (1754), Burns (1759), Rogers (1763), Wordsworth (1770), Scott (1771), Coleridge (1772), Southey (1774), Campbell (1777), Moore (1779), Byron (1788), Shelley and Keble (1792), and Keats (1796).

Butler (1600), Milton (1608), and Dryden (1630) came between the first and second clusters. Thomson (1700), Gray (1717), Collins (1720), Akenside

(1721), Goldsmith (1728), and Cowper (1731), between the second and the third.

Pleonec´tes (4 *syl.*), Covetousness personified, in *The Purple Island*, by Phineas Fletcher (1633). "His gold his god" ... he "much fears to keep, much more to lose his lusting." Fully described in canto viii. (Greek, *pleonektês*, "covetous.")

Pleydell (*Mr. Paulus*), an advocate in Edinburgh, shrewd and witty. He was at one time the sheriff at Ellangowan.

Mr. Counsellor Pleydell was a lively, sharp-looking gentleman, with a professional shrewdness in his eye, and, generally speaking, a professional formality in his manner; but this he could slip off on a Saturday evening, when ... he joined in the ancient pastime of High Jinks.—Sir W. Scott, *Guy Mannering*, xxxix. (time, George II.).

Pliable, a neighbor of Christian, whom he accompanied as far as the "Slough of Despond," when he turned back.—Bunyan, *Pilgrim's Progress*, i. (1678).

Pliant (*Sir Paul*), a hen-pecked husband, who dares not even touch a letter addressed to himself till my lady has read it first. His perpetual oath is "Gadsbud!" He is such a dolt that he would not believe his own eyes and ears, if they bore testimony against his wife's fidelity and continency. (See PLACID.)

Lady Pliant, second wife of Sir Paul. "She's handsome, and knows it; is very silly, and thinks herself wise; has a choleric old husband" very fond of her, but whom she rules with spirit, and snubs "afore folk." My lady says, "If one has once sworn, it is most unchristian, inhuman, and obscene that one should break it." Her conduct with Mr. Careless is most reprehensible.—Congreve, *The Double Dealer* (1694).

Pliny (*The German*), or "Modern Pliny," Konrad von Gesner of Zurich, who wrote *Historia Animalium*, etc. (1516-1565).

Pliny of the East, Zakarija ibn Muhammed, surnamed "Kazwînî," from Kazwîn, the place of his birth. He is so called by De Sacy (1200-1283).

Plon-Plon, Prince Napoleon Joseph Charles Bonaparte, son of Jerome Bonaparte by his second wife (the Princess Frederica Catherine of Würtemberg). Plon-Plon is a euphonic corruption of *Craint-Plomb* ("fear-bullet"), a nickname given to the prince in the Crimēan war (1854-6).

Plornish, plasterer, Bleeding-heart Yard. He was a smooth-cheeked, fresh-colored, sandy-whiskered man of 30. Long in the legs, yielding at the knees, foolish in the face, flannel-jacketed and lime-whitened. He generally chimed in conversation by echoing the words of the person speaking. Thus, if Mrs.

Plornish said to a visitor, "Miss Dorrit dursn't let him know;" he would chime in, "Dursn't let him know." "Me and Plornish says, 'Ho! Miss Dorrit;'" Plornish repeated, after his wife, "Ho! Miss Dorrit." "Can you employ Miss Dorrit?" Plornish repeated as an echo, "Employ Miss Dorrit?" (See PETER.)

Mrs. Plornish, the plasterer's wife. A young woman, somewhat slatternly in herself and her belongings, and dragged by care and poverty already into wrinkles. She generally began her sentences with, "Well, not to deceive you." Thus: "Is Mr. Plornish at home?" "Well, sir, not to deceive you, he's gone to look for a job." "Well, not to deceive you, ma'am, I take it kindly of you."— C. Dickens, *Little Dorrit* (1857).

Plotting Parlor (*The*). At Whittington, near Scarsdale, in Derbyshire, is a farmhouse where the earl of Devonshire (Cavendish), the earl of Danby (Osborne), and Baron Delamer (Booth), concerted the Revolution. The room in which they met is called "The Plotting Parlor."

Where Scarsdale's cliffs the swelling pastures bound,
... there let the farmer hail
The sacred orchard which embowers his gate,
And shew to strangers, passing down the vale,
Where Cav'ndish, Booth, and Osborne sate
When, bursting from their country's chain, ...
They planned for freedom this her noblest reign.
Akenside, *Ode* XVIII. v. 3 (1767).

Plotwell (*Mrs.*), in Mrs. Centlivre's drama, *The Beau's Duel* (1703).

Plough of Cincinnatus. The Roman patriot of this name, when sought by the ambassadors sent to entreat him to assume command of state and army, was found ploughing his field. Leaving the plough in the furrow, he accompanied them to Rome, and after a victorious campaign returned to his little farm.

Plousina, called Hebê, endowed by the fairy Anguilletta with the gifts of wit, beauty, and wealth. Hebê still felt she lacked something, and the fairy told her it was love. Presently came to her father's court a young prince named Atimir, the two fell in love with each other, and the day of their marriage was fixed. In the interval, Atimir fell in love with Hebê's elder sister Iberia; and Hebê, in her grief, was sent to the Peaceable Island, where she fell in love with the ruling prince, and married him. After a time, Atimir and Iberia, with Hebê and her husband, met at the palace of the ladies' father, when the love between Atimir and Hebê revived. A duel was fought between the young princes, in which Atimir was slain, and the prince of the Peaceable Islands was severely wounded. Hebê, coming up, threw herself on Atimir's sword, and the dead bodies of Atimir and Hebê were transformed into two trees called "charms."—Countess D'Aunoy, *Fairy Tales* ("Anguilletta," 1682).

Plowman (*Piers*), the dreamer, who, falling asleep on the Malvern Hills, Worcestershire, saw in a vision pictures of the corruptions of society, and particularly of the avarice and wantonness of the clergy. This supposed vision is formed into a poetical satire of great vigor, fancy, and humor. It is divided into twenty parts, each part being called a *passus*, or separate vision.—William [or Robert] Langland, *The Vision of Piers the Plowman* (1362).

Plumdamas (*Mr. Peter*), grocer.—Sir W. Scott, *Heart of Midlothian* (time, George II.).

Plume (*Captain*), a gentleman and an officer. He is in love with Sylvia, a wealthy heiress, and, when he marries her, gives up his commission.—G. Farquhar, *The Recruiting Officer* (1705).

Plummer (*Caleb*), a little old toy-maker, in the employ of Gruff and Tackleton, toy merchants. He was spare, gray-haired, and very poor. It was his pride "to go as close to Natur' in his toys as he could for the money." Caleb Plummer had a blind daughter, who assisted him in his toy-making, and whom he brought up under the belief that he himself was young, handsome, and well off, and that the house they lived in was sumptuously furnished and quite magnificent. Every calamity he smoothed over, every unkind remark of their snarling employer he called a merry jest; so that the poor blind girl lived in a castle of the air, "a bright little world of her own." When merry or puzzled, Caleb used to sing something about "a sparkling bowl."

Bertha Plummer, the blind daughter of the toy-maker, who fancied her poor old father was a young fop, that the sack he threw across his shoulders was a handsome blue great-coat, and that their wooden house was a palace. She was in love with Tackleton, the toy merchant, whom she thought to be a handsome young prince; and when she heard that he was about to marry May Fielding, she drooped and was like to die. She was then disillusioned, heard the real facts, and said, "Why, oh, why did you deceive me thus? Why did you fill my heart so full, and then come like death, and tear away the objects of my love?" However, her love for her father was not lessened, and she declared that the knowledge of the truth was "sight restored." "It is my sight," she cried. "Hitherto I have been blind, but now my eyes are open. I never knew my father before, and might have died without ever having known him truly."

Edward Plummer, son of the toy-maker, and brother of the blind girl. He was engaged from boyhood to May Fielding, went to South America, and returned to marry her; but, hearing of her engagement to Tackleton, the toy merchant, he assumed the disguise of a deaf old man, to ascertain whether she loved Tackleton or not. Being satisfied that her heart was still his own, he married her, and Tackleton made them a present of the wedding-cake which he had ordered for himself.—C. Dickens, *The Cricket on the Hearth* (1845).

Plush (*John*), any gorgeous footman, conspicuous for his plush breeches and rainbow colors.

Plutarch (*The Modern*), Vayer, born at Paris. His name in full was Francis Vayer de la Mothe (1586-1672).

Pluto, the god of Hadês.

Brothers, be of good cheer, for this night we shall sup with Pluto.—Leonidas, *To the Three Hundred at Thermopylæ*.

Plutus, the god of wealth.—*Classic Mythology*.

Within a heart, dearer than Plutus' mine.
Shakespeare, *Julius Cæsar*, act iv. sc. 3 (1607).

Po (*Tom*), a ghost. (Welsh, *bo*, "a hobgoblin.")

He now would pass for spirit Po.
S. Butler, *Hudibras*, iii. 1 (1678).

Pocahontas, daughter of Powhatan, an Indian chief of Virginia, who rescued Captain John Smith when her father was on the point of killing him. She subsequently married John Rolfe, and was baptized under the name of Rebecca (1595-1617).—*Old and New London*, ii. 481 (1876).

The Indian Princess is the heroine of John Brougham's drama, *Po-ca-hon-tas, or the Gentle Savage*.

Pochet (*Madame*), the French "Mrs. Gamp."—Henri Monnier.

Pochi Dana'ri ("*the pennyless*"). So the Italians call Maximilian I., emperor of Germany (1459, 1493-1519).

Pocket (*Mr. Matthew*), a real scholar, educated at Harrow, and an honor-man at Cambridge, but, having married young, he had to take up the calling of "grinder" and literary fag for a living. Mr. Pocket, when annoyed, used to run his two hands into his hair, and seemed as if he intended to lift himself by it. His house was a hopeless muddle, the best meals and chief expense being in the kitchen. Pip was placed under the charge of this gentleman.

Mrs. Pocket (*Belinda*), daughter of a City knight, brought up to be an ornamental nonentity, helpless, shiftless, and useless. She was the mother of eight children, whom she allowed to "tumble up" as best they could, under the charge of her maid, Flopson. Her husband, who was a poor gentleman, found life a very uphill work.

Herbert Pocket, son of Mr. Matthew Pocket, and an insurer of ships. He was a frank, easy young man, lithe and brisk, but not muscular. There was nothing mean or secretive about him. He was wonderfully hopeful, but had not the stuff to push his way into wealth. He was tall, slim, and pale; had a languor which showed itself even in his briskness; was most amiable, cheerful, and communicative. He called Pip "Handel," because Pip had been a blacksmith, and Handel composed a piece of music entitled *The Harmonious Blacksmith*. Pip helped him to a partnership in an agency business.

Sarah Pocket, sister of Matthew Pocket, a little dry, brown, corrugated old woman, with a small face that might have been made of walnut-shell, and a large mouth, like a cat's without the whiskers.—C. Dickens, *Great Expectations* (1860).

Podgers (*The*), lickspittles of the great.—J. Hollingshead, *The Birthplace of Podgers*.

Podsnap (*Mr.*), "a too, too smiling large man, with a fatal freshness on him." Mr. Podsnap has "two little light-colored wiry wings, one on either side of his else bald head, looking as like his hair-brushes as his hair." On his forehead are generally "little red beads," and he wears "a large allowance of crumpled shirt-collar up behind."

Mrs. Podsnap, a "fine woman for Professor Owen: quantity of bone, neck, and nostrils like a rocking-horse, hard features, and majestic head-dress in which Podsnap has hung golden offerings."

Georgiana Podsnap, daughter of the above; called by her father "the young person." She is a harmless, inoffensive girl, "always trying to hide her elbows." Georgiana adores Mrs. Lammle, and when Mr. Lammle tries to marry the girl to Mr. Fledgeby, Mrs. Lammle induces Mr. Twemlow to speak to the father and warn him of the connection.

Poe (*Edgar Allen*). Poe's parents were actors, and in 1885, the actors of America erected a monument to the memory of the unhappy poet. The poem read at the dedication of the memorial was by *William Winter*.

"His music dies not, nor can ever die,
Blown 'round the world by every wandering wind,
The comet, lessening in the midnight sky,
Still leaves its trail of glory far behind."

Poem in Marble (*A*), the Taj, a mausoleum of white marble, raised in Agra, by Shah Jehan, to his favorite, Shahrina Moomtaz-i-Mahul, who died in childbirth of her eighth child. It is also called "The Marble Queen of Sorrow."

Poet (*The Quaker*), Bernard Barton (1784-1849).

Poet Sire of Italy, Dantê Alighieri (1265-1321).

Poet Squab. John Dryden was so called by the earl of Rochester, on account of his corpulence (1631-1701).

Poet of France (*The*), Pierre Ronsard (1524-1585).

Poet of Poets, Percy Bysshe Shelley (1792-1822).

Poet of the Poor, the Rev. George Crabbe (1754-1832).

Poets (*The prince of*). Edmund Spenser is so called on his monument in Westminster Abbey (1553-1598).

Prince of Spanish Poets. So Cervantês calls Garcilaso de la Vega (1503-1536).

Poets of England.

Addison, Beaumont, Elizabeth Barrett Browning, Robert Browning, Burns, Butler, Byron, Campbell, Chatterton, Chaucer, Coleridge, Collins, Congreve, Cowley, Cowper, Crabbe, Drayton, Dryden, Fletcher, Ford, Gay, Goldsmith, Gray, Mrs. Hemans, Herbert, Herrick, Hood, Ben Jonson, Keats, Keble, Landor, Marlowe, Marvel, Massinger, Milton, Moore, Otway, Pope, Prior, Rogers, Rowe, Scott, Shakespeare, Shelley, Shenstone, Southey, Spenser, Thomson, Waller, Wordsworth, Young. With many others of less celebrity.

Poets' Corner, in the south transept of Westminster Abbey. No one knows who christened the corner thus. With poets are divines, philosophers, actors, novelists, architects and critics.

The "corner" contains a bust, statue, tablet, or monument, to five of our first-rate poets: viz., Chaucer (1400), Dryden (1700), Milton (1674), Shakespeare (1616), and Spenser (1598); and some seventeen of second or third class merit, as Addison, Beaumont (none to Fletcher), S. Butler, Campbell, Cowley, Cumberland, Drayton, Gay, Gray, Goldsmith, Ben Jonson, Macaulay, Prior, Rowe, Sheridan, Thomson and Wordsworth.

⁎ Dryden's monument was erected by Sheffield, duke of Buckingham. Wordsworth's statue was erected by a public subscription.

Poetry (*The Father of*), Orpheus (2 *syl.*) of Thrace.

Father of Dutch Poetry, Jakob Maerlant; also called "The Father of Flemish Poetry" (1235-1300).

Father of English Poetry, Geoffrey Chaucer (1328-1400).

Father of Epic Poetry, Homer.

He compares Richardson to Homer, and predicts for his memory the same honors which are rendered to the Father of Epic Poetry.—Sir W. Scott.

Poetry—Prose. Pope advised Wycherly "to convert his poetry into prose."

Poganuc, small Puritan town in New England as it was 100 years ago.— Harriet Beecher Stowe, *Poganuc People* (1876).

Po´gram (*Elijah*), one of the "master minds" of America, and a member of Congress. He was possessed with the idea that there was a settled opposition in the British mind against the institutions of his "free and enlightened country."—C. Dickens, *Martin Chuzzlewit* (1844).

Poinder (*George*), a city officer.—Sir W. Scott, *Heart of Midlothian* (time, George II.).

Poins, a companion of Sir John Falstaff.—Shakespeare, 1 and 2 *Henry IV*. (1597, 1598).

The chronicles of that day contain accounts of many a mad prank which [*Lord Warwick, Addison's step-son*] played ... [*like*] the lawless freaks of the madcap prince and Poins.—Thackeray.

Poison. It is said that Mithridātês VI., surnamed "the Great," had so fortified his constitution that poisons had no baneful effect on him (B.C. 131, 120-63).

Poison of Khaïbar. By this is meant the poison put into a leg of mutton by Zaïnab, a Jewess, to kill Mahomet while he was in the citadel of Kha´ïbar. Mahomet partook of the mutton, and suffered from the poison all through life.

Poisoners (*Secret*).

1. *Of Ancient Rome*: Locusta, employed by Agrippi´na to poison her husband, the Emperor Claudius. Nero employed the same woman to poison Britannicus and others.

2. *Of English History*: the countess of Somerset, who poisoned Sir Thomas Overbury in the Tower of London. She also poisoned others.

Villiers, duke of Buckingham, it is said poisoned King James I.

3. *Of France*: Lavoisin and Lavigoreux, French midwives and fortune-tellers.

Catherine de Medicis is said to have poisoned the mother of Henri IV. with a pair of wedding-gloves, and several others with poisoned fans.

The marquise de Brinvilliers, a young profligate Frenchwoman, was taught the art of secret poisoning by Sainte-Croix, who learnt it in Italy.—*World of Wonders*, vii. 203.

4. *Of Italy*: Pope Alexander VI. and his children, Cæsar and Lucrezia [Borgia] were noted poisoners; so were Hieronyma Spara and Tofa´na.

Polexan´dre, an heroic romance by Gomberville (1632).

Policy (*Mrs.*), housekeeper at Holyrood Palace. She appears in the introduction.—Sir W. Scott, *Fair Maid of Perth* (time, Henry IV.).

Pol´idore (3 *syl.*), father of Valère.—Molière, *Le Dépit Amoureux* (1654).

Polinesso, duke of Albany, who falsely accused Geneura of incontinency, and was slain in single combat by Ariodantês.—Ariosto, *Orlando Furioso* (1516).

Polish Jew (*The*), also called THE BELLS, a melodrama by J. R. Ware, brought prominently into note by the acting of Henry Irving at the Lyceum. Mathis, a miller in a small German town, is visited on Christmas Eve by a Polish Jew, who comes through the snow in a sledge. After rest and refreshment he leaves for Nantzig, "four leagues off." Mathis follows him, kills him with an axe, and burns the body in a lime-kiln. He then pays his debts, becomes a prosperous and respected man, and is made burgomaster. On the wedding night of his only child, Annette, he dies of apoplexy, of which he had ample warning by the constant sound of sledge-bells in his ears. In his dream he supposes himself put into a mesmeric sleep in open court, when he confesses everything and is executed (1874).

Polixène, the name assumed by Madelon Gorgibus, a shopkeeper's daughter, as far more romantic and genteel than her baptismal name. Her cousin, Cathos, called herself Aminte (2 *syl.*).

Polix´enes (4 *syl.*), king of Bohemia, schoolfellow and old companion of Leontês, king of Sicily. While on a visit to the Sicilian king, Leontês grew jealous of him, and commanded Camillo to poison him; but Camillo only warned him of his danger, and fled with him to Bohemia. Polixenês's son, Flor´izel, fell in love with Perdĭta, the supposed daughter of a shepherd; but the king threatened Perdita and the shepherd with death unless this foolish suit were given up. Florizel and Perdita now fled to Sicily, where they were introduced to King Leontês, and it was soon discovered that Perdita was his lost daughter. Polixenês, having tracked the fugitives to Sicily, learned that Perdita was the king's daughter, and joyfully consented to the union he had before forbidden.—Shakespeare, *The Winter's Tale* (1604).

Poll Pineapple, the bumboat woman, once sailed in seaman's clothes with Lieutenant Belaye (2 *syl.*), in the *Hot Cross-Bun*. Jack tars generally greet each other with "Messmate, ho! what cheer?" but the greeting on the *Hot Cross-Bun* was always, "How do you do, my dear?" and never was any oath more naughty than "Dear me!" One day, Lieutenant Belaye came on board and said to his crew, "Here, messmates, is my wife, for I have just come from church." Whereupon they all fainted; and it was found the crew consisted of young women only, who had dressed like sailors to follow the fate of Lieutenant Belaye.—S. Gilbert, *The Bab Ballads* ("The Bumboat Woman's Story").

Pollente (3 *syl.*), a Saracen, lord of the Perilous Bridge. When his groom, Guizor, demands the "passage-penny" of Sir Artegal, the knight gives him a "stunning blow," saying, "Lo! knave, there's my hire;" and the groom falls down dead. Pollentê then comes rushing up at full speed, and both he and Sir Artegal fall into the river, fighting most desperately. At length Sir Artegal prevails, and the dead body of the Saracen is carried down "the blood-stained stream."—Spenser, *Faëry Queen*, v. 2 (1596).

Upton conjectures that "Pollente" is intended for Charles IX. of France, and his groom, "Guizor" (he says), means the duke of Guise, noted for the part he took in the St. Bartholomew Massacre.

Polly, daughter of Peachum. A pretty girl, who really loved Captain Macheath, married him, and remained faithful even when he disclaimed her. When the reprieve arrived, "the captain" confessed his marriage, and vowed to abide by Polly for the rest of his life.—J. Gay, *The Beggar's Opera* (1727).

Polly (Cousin), "a small, bright-eyed lady of indefatigable activity in sacrificing herself for the good of others.... In her trig person she embodied the several functions of housekeeper, nurse, confidante, missionary, parish-clerk, queen of the poultry-yard, and genealogist."—Constance Cary Harrison, *Flower de Hundred* (1890).

Polly, the idolized pet of "the Colonel," her grandfather. He will not let "Bob" marry her, but when the two elope together and present themselves as man and wife, on Christmas Day, and Polly's face "like a dew-bathed flower" is pressed to his, he yields and takes both to his big heart.—Thomas Nelson Page, *In Ole Virginia* (1887).

Polo′nius, a garralous old chamberlain, of Denmark, and father of Laer′tês and Ophelia; conceited, politic, and a courtier. Polonius conceals himself, to overhear what Hamlet says to his mother, and, making some unavoidable noise, startles the prince, who, thinking it is the king concealed, rushes blindly on the intruder, and kills him; but finds too late he has killed the chamberlain, and not Claudius, as he hoped and expected.—Shakespeare, *Hamlet* (1596).

Polonius is a man bred in courts, exercised in business, stored with observations, confident of his knowledge, proud of his eloquence, and declining to dotage.—Dr. Johnson.

It was the great part of William Mynitt (1710-1763).

Soon after Munden retired from the stage, an admirer met him in Covent Garden. It was a wet day, and each carried an umbrella. The gentleman's was an expensive silk one, and Joe's an old gingham. "So you have left the stage, ... and 'Polonius,' 'Jemmy Jumps,' 'Old Dornton,' and a dozen others have left the world with you? I wish you'd give me some trifle by way of memorial, Munden!" "Trifle, sir? I' faith, sir, I've got nothing. But, hold, yes, egad, suppose we exchange umbrellas."—*Theatrical Anecdotes*.

Polwarth (*Alick*), a servant of Waverley's.—Sir W. Scott, *Waverley* (time, George II.).

Polycle′tos (in Latin *Polycletus*), a statuary of Sicyon, who drew up a canon of the proportions of the several parts of the human body: as, twice round the thumb is once round the wrist; twice round the wrist is once round the neck; twice round the neck is once round the waist; once round the fist is the length of the foot; the two arms extended is the height of the body; six times the length of the foot, or eighteen thumbs, is also the height of the body.

Again, the thumb, the longest toe, and the nose should all be of the same length. The index finger should measure the breadth of the hand and foot, and twice the breadth should give the length. The hand, the foot, and the face should all be the same length. The nose should be one-third of the face; and, of course, the thumbs should be one-third the length of the hand. Gerard de Lairesse has given the exact measurements of every part of the human figure, according to the famous statues of "Antinöus, "Apollo Belvidere," "Herculês," and "Venus de'Medici."

Polycrates (4 *syl.*), tyrant of Samos. He was so fortunate in everything, that Am′asis, king of Egypt, advised him to part with something he highly prized. Whereupon, Polycrătês threw into the sea an engraved gem of extraordinary value. A few days afterwards, a fish was presented to the tyrant, in which this very gem was found. Amasis now renounced all friendship with him, as a man doomed by the gods; and not long after this, a satrap, having entrapped the too fortunate despot, put him to death by crucifixion. (See FISH AND THE RING.)—*Herodotus*, iii. 40.

Polyd′amas, a Thessalian athlete of enormous strength. He is said to have killed an angry lion, to have held by the heels a raging bull and thrown it helpless at his feet, to have stopped a chariot in full career, etc. One day, he attempted to sustain a falling rock, but was killed and buried by the huge mass.

Milo carried a bull, four years old, on his shoulders through the stadium at Olympia; he also arrested a chariot in full career. One day, tearing asunder a pine tree, the two parts, rebounding, caught his hands and held him fast, in which state he was devoured by wolves.

Polydore (3 *syl.*), the name by which Belarius called Prince Guiderius, while he lived in a cave in the Welsh mountains. His brother, Prince Arvirăgus, went by the name of Cadwal.—Shakespeare, *Cymbeline* (1605).

Polydore (3 *syl.*), brother of General Memnon, beloved by the Princess Calis, sister of Astorax, king of Paphos.—Beaumont and Fletcher, *The Mad Lover* (1618).

Polydore (Lord), son of Lord Acasto, and Castalio's younger brother. He entertained a base passion for his father's ward Monimia, "the orphan," and, making use of the signal ("three soft taps upon the chamber door") to be used by Castalio, to whom she was privately married, indulged his wanton love, Monimia supposing him to be her husband. When, next day, he discovered that Monimia was actually married to Castalio, he was horrified, and provoked a quarrel with his brother; but as soon as Castalio drew his sword, he ran upon it and was killed.—Thomas Otway, *The Orphan* (1680).

Polydore (3 *syl.*), a comrade of Ernest of Otranto (page of Prince Tancred).—Sir W. Scott, *Count Robert of Paris* (time, Rufus).

Polyglot (*Ignatius*), the master of seventeen languages, and tutor of Charles Eustace (aged 24). Very learned, very ignorant of human life; most strict as a disciplinarian, but tender-hearted as a girl. His pupil has married clandestinely, but Polyglot offers himself voluntarily to be the scapegoat of the young couple, and he brings them off triumphantly.—J. Poole, *The Scapegoat.*

Polyglott (*A Walking*), Cardinal Mezzofanti, who knew fifty-eight different languages (1774-1849).

Polyolbion (the "*greatly blessed*"), by Michael Drayton, in thirty parts, called "songs." It is a topographical description of England. Song i. The landing of Bruce. Song ii. Dorsetshire, and the adventures of Sir Bevis of Southampton. Song iii. Somerset. Song iv. Contention of the rivers of England and Wales respecting Lundy—to which country it belonged. Song v. Sabrina, as arbiter, decides that it is "allied alike both to Enggland and Wales;" Merlin and Milford Haven. Song vi. The salmon and beaver of Twy; the tale of Sabrina; the druids and bards. Song vii. Hereford. Song viii. Conquest of Britain by the Romans and by the Saxons. Song ix. Wales. Song x. Merlin's prophecies; Winifred's well; defence of the "tale of Brute" (1612). Song xi. Cheshire, the religious Saxon kings. Song xii. Shropshire and Staffordshire; the Saxon warrior kings; and Guy of Warwick. Song xiii. Warwick; Guy of Warwick concluded. Song xiv. Gloucestershire. Song xv. The marriage of Isis and Thame. Song xvi. The Roman roads and Saxon kingdoms. Song xvii. Surrey and Sussex; the sovereigns of England from William to Elizabeth. Song xviii. Kent; England's great generals and sea-captains (1613). Song xix. Essex and Suffolk; English navigators. Song xx. Norfolk. Song xxi. Cambridge and Ely. Song xxii. Buckinghamshire, and England's intestine battles. Song xxiii. Northamptonshire. Song xxiv. Rutlandshire; and the British saints. Song xxv. Lincolnshire. Song xxvi. Nottinghamshire, Leicestershire, Derbyshire; with the story of Robin Hood. Song xxvii. Lancashire and the Isle of Man. Song xxviii. Yorkshire. Song xxix. Northumberland. Song xxx. Cumberland (1622).

Pol′ypheme (3 *syl.*), a gigantic cyclops of Sicily, who fed on human flesh. When Ulysses, on his return from Troy, was driven to this Island, he and twelve of his companions were seized by Polypheme, and confined in his cave, that he might devour two daily for his dinner. Ulysses made the giant drunk, and, when he lay down to sleep, bored out his one eye. Roused by the pain, the monster tried to catch his tormentors; but Ulysses and his surviving companions made their escape by clinging to the bellies of the sheep and rams when they were let out to pasture (*Odyssey*, ix.).

There is a Basque legend told of the giant Tartaro, who caught a young man in his snares, and confined him in his cave for dessert. When, however, Tartaro fell asleep, the young man made the giant's spit red hot, bored out his one eye, and then made his escape by fixing the bell of the bell-ram round his neck, and a sheep-skin over his back. Tartaro seized the skin, and the man, leaving it behind, made off.—*Basque Legends*.

A very similar adventure forms the tale of Sindbad's third voyage, in the *Arabian Nights*. He was shipwrecked on a strange island, and entered, with his companions, a sort of palace. At nightfall, a one-eyed giant entered, and ate one of them for supper, and another for breakfast next morning. This went on for a day or two, when Sindbad bored out the giant's one eye with a charred olive stake. The giant tried in vain to catch his tormentors, but they ran to their rafts; and Sindbad, with two others, contrived to escape.

*** Homer was translated into Syriac by Theophilus Edessenes in the caliphate of Hárun-ur-Ráshid (A.D. 786-809).

Polypheme and Galatea. Polypheme loved Galatēa, the sea-nymph; but Galatea had fixed her affections on Acis, a Sicilian shepherd. The giant, in his jealousy, hurled a huge rock at his rival, and crushed him to death.

The tale of Polypheme is from Homer's *Odyssey*, ix. It is also given by Ovid in his *Metamorphoses*, xiv. Euripidês introduces the monster in his *Cyclops*; and the tragedy of Acis and Galatea is the subject of Handel's famous opera so called.

(In Greek the monster is called *Polyphêmos*, and in Latin *Polyphēmus*.)

Polyphe'mus of Literature, Dr. Samuel Johnson (1709-1784).

Polypho'nus (*"big voiced"*), the Kapăneus and most boastful of the frog heroes. He was slain by the mouse Artophăgus ("the bread-nibbler").

But great Artophagus avenged the slain, ...
And Polyphōnus died, a frog renowned
For boastful speech and turbulence of sound.
Parnell, *Battle of the Frogs and Mice*, iii. (about 1712).

Polyx'ena, a magnanimous and most noble woman, wife of Charles Emmanuel, king of Sardinia (who succeeded to the crown in 1730).—R. Browning, *King Victor and King Charles, etc.*

Pomegranate Seed. When Perseph'onê was in Hadês, whither Pluto had carried her, the god, foreknowing that Jupiter would demand her release, gathered a pomegranate, and said to her, "Love, eat with me, this parting day, of the pomegranate seed;" and she ate. Demēter, in the mean time, implored Zeus (*Jupiter*) to demand Persephonê's release; and the king of Olympus promised she should be set at liberty, if she had not eaten anything during her detention in Hadês. As, however, she had eaten pomegranate seeds, her return was impossible.

Low laughs the dark king on his throne—
"I gave her of pomegranate seeds" ...

And chant the maids of Enna still—
"O fateful flower beside the rill,
The daffodil, the daffodil." (See DAFFODIL.)
Jean Ingelow, *Persephone*.

Pomoma. The incomparable maid-of-work, custodian, novelist, comedienne, tragedienne, and presiding genius of Rudder Grange. Her *chef d'œuvre* is the expedient of posting the premises *"To be Sold for Taxes,"* to keep away peddlers of trees, etc., in her employers' absence.—Frank Stockton, *Rudder Grange* (1879).

Pompey, a clown; servant to Mrs. Overdone (a bawd).—Shakespeare, *Measure for Measure* (1603).

Pompey the Great, was killed by Achillas and Septimius, the moment the Egyptian fishing-boat reached the coast. Plutarch tells us they threw his head into the sea. Others say his head was sent to Cæsar, who turned from it with horror, and shed a flood of tears. Shakespeare makes him killed by "savage islanders" (2 *Henry VI.* act iv. sc. 1, 1598).

Pompil′ia, a foundling, the putative daughter of Pietro (2 *syl.*). She married Count Guido Franceschini, who treated her so brutally that she made her escape under the protection of a young priest named Caponsacchi. Pompilia subsequently gave birth to a son, but was slain by her husband.

The babe had been a find i' the filth-heap, sir,
Catch from the kennel. There was found at Rome,
Down in the deepest of our social dregs,
A woman who professed the wanton's trade ...
She sold this babe eight months before its birth
To our Violante (3 *syl.*), Pietro's honest spouse, ...
Partly to please old Pietro,
Partly to cheat the rightful heirs, agape
For that same principal of the usufruct,
It vexed him he must die and leave behind.
R. Browning, *The Ring and the Book*, ii, 557, etc.

Ponce de Léon, the navigator who went in search of the *Fontaine de Jouvence*, "qui fit rajovenir la gent." He sailed in two ships on this "voyage of discoveries," in the sixteenth century.

Like Ponce de Léon, he wants to go off to the Antipodês in search of that *Fontaine de Jouvence* which was fabled to give a man back his youth.—*Véra*, 130.

Pongo, a cross between "a land-tiger and a sea-shark." This terrible monster devastated Sicily, but was slain by the three sons of St. George.—R. Johnson, *The Seven Champions, etc.* (1617).

Ponoc′rates (4 *syl.*), the tutor of Gargantua.—Rabelais, *Gargantua* (1533).

Pontius Pilate's Body-Guard, the 1st Foot Regiment. In Picardy the French officers wanted to make out that they were the seniors, and, to carry their point, vaunted that they were on duty on the night of the Crucifixion. The colonel of the 1st Foot replied, "If we had been on guard we should not have slept at our posts" (see *Matt.* xxviii. 13).

Pontoys (*Stephen*), a veteran in Sir Hugo de Lacy's troop.—Sir W. Scott, *The Betrothed* (time, Henry II.).

Pony (*Mr. Garland's*), Whisker (*q.v.*).

Poole (1 *syl.*), in Dorsetshire; once "a young and lusty sea-born lass," courted by Great Albion, who had by her three children, Brunksey, Fursey and [St.] Hellen. Thetis was indignant that one of her virgin train should be guilty of such indiscretion; and, to protect his children from her fury, Albion placed them in the bosom of Poole, and then threw his arms around them.—M. Drayton, *Polyolbion*, ii. (1612).

Poor (*Father of the*), Bernard Gilpin. (1517-1583).

Poor Gentleman (*The*), a comedy by George Colman, the younger (1802). "The poor gentleman" is Lieutenant Worthington, discharged from the army on half-pay because his arm had been crushed by a shell in storming Gibraltar. On his half-pay he had to support himself, his daughter Emily, an old corporal and a maiden sister-in-law. Having put his name to a bill for £500, his friend died without effecting an insurance, and the lieutenant was called upon for payment. Imprisonment would have followed if Sir Robert Bramble had not most generously paid the money. With this piece of good fortune came another—the marriage of his daughter Emily to Frederick Bramble, nephew and heir of the rich baronet.

Poor Richard, the pseudonym of Benjamin Franklin, under which he issued a series of almanacs, which he made the medium of teaching thrift, temperance, order, cleanliness, chastity, forgiveness, and so on. The maxims or precepts of these almanacs generally end with the words, "as poor Richard says" (begun in 1732).

Poor Robin, the pseudonym of Robert Herrick, the poet, under which he issued a series of almanacs (begun in 1661).

Pope (*to drink like a*). Benedict XII. was an enormous eater, and such a huge wine-drinker that he gave rise to the Bacchanalian expression, *Bibāmus papaliter*.

Pope Changing His Name. Peter Hogsmouth, or, as he is sometimes called, Peter di Porca, was the first pope to change his name. He called himself Sergius II. (844-847). Some say he thought it arrogant to be called Peter II.

Pope-Fig-Lands, Protestant countries. The Gaillardets, being shown the pope's image, said, "A fig for the pope!" whereupon their whole island was put to the sword, and the name changed to Pope-fig-land, the people being called "Pope-figs."—Rabelais, *Pantag'ruel*, iv. 45 (1545).

The allusion is to the kingdom of Navarre, once Protestant; but in 1512 it was subjected to Ferdinand, the Catholic.

Pope-Figs, Protestants. The name was given to the Gaillardets for saying "A fig for the pope!"

They were made tributaries and slaves to the Papimans for saying "A fig for the pope's image!" and never after did the poor wretches prosper, but every year the devil was at their doors, and they were plagued with hail, storms, famine, and all manner of woes, in punishment of this sin of their forefathers.—Rabelais, *Pantagruel*, iv. 45 (1545).

Pope Joan, between Leo IV. and Benedict III., and called John [VIII.]. The subject of this scandalous story was an English girl, educated at Cologne, who left her home in man's disguise with her lover (the monk Folda), and went to Athens, where she studied law. She went to Rome and studied theology, earning so great a reputation that, at the death of Leo IV., she was chosen his successor. Her sex was discovered by the birth of a child, while she was going to the Lateran Basilica, between the Coliseum and the church of St. Clement. Pope Joan died, and was buried, without honors, after a pontificate of two years and five months (853-855).—Marianus Scotus (who died 1086).

The story is given most fully by Martinus Polonus, confessor to Gregory X., and the tale was generally believed till the Reformation. There is a German miracle-play on the subject, called *The Canonization of Pope Joan* (1480). David Blondel, a Calvinist divine, has written a book to confute the tale.

The following note contains the chief points of interest:—

Anastasius, the librarian, is the first to mention such a pope, A.D. 886, or thirty years after the death of Joan.

Marianus Scotus, in his *Chronicle*, says she reigned two years, five months and four days (853-855). Scotus died 1086.

Sigebert de Gemblours, in his *Chronicle*, repeats the same story (1112).

Otto of Friesingen and Gotfried of Viterbo both mention her in their histories.

Martin Polonus gives a very full account of the matter. He says she went by the name of John Anglus, and was born at Metz, of English parents. While she was pope, she was prematurely delivered of a child in the street "between the Coliseum and St. Clement's Church."

William Ocham alludes to the story.

Thomas de Elmham repeats it (1422).

John Huss tells us her baptismal name was not Joan, but Agnes.

Others insist that her name was Gilberta.

In the *Annalés Augustani* (1135), we are told her papal name was John VIII., and that she it was who conscrated Louis II., of France.

Arguments in favor of the allegation are given by Spanheim, *Exercit. de Papa Fæmina*, ii. 577; in Lenfant, *Historie de la Papesse Jeanne*.

Arguments against the allegation are given by Allatius or Allatus, *Confutatio Fabulæ de Johanna Papissa*; and in Lequien, *Oriens Christianus*, iii. 777.

Arguments on both sides are given in Cunningham's translation of *Geiseler, Lehrbuch*, ii. 21, 22; and in La Bayle's *Dictionnaire*, iii., art. "Papisse."

⁎ Gibbon says, "Two Protestants, Blondel and Bayle, have annihilated the female pope;" but the expression is certainly too strong, and even Mosheim is more than half inclined to believe there really was such a person.

Pope of Philosophy, Aristotle (B.C. 384-322).

Popes (*Titles assumed by*). "Universal Bishop," prior to Gregory the Great. Gregory the Great adopted the style of "Servus Servorum" (591).

Martin IV. was addressed as "the lamb of God which takest away the sins of the world," to which was added, "Grant us thy peace!" (1281).

Leo X. was styled, by the council of Lateran, "Divine Majesty," "Husband of the Church," "Prince of the Apostles," "The Key of all the Universe," "The Pastor, the Physician, and a God possessed of all power both in heaven and on earth" (1513).

Paul V. styled himself "Monarch of Christendom," "Supporter of the Papal Omnipotence," "Vice-God," "Lord God the Pope" (1605).

Others, after Paul, "Master of the World," "Pope the Universal Father," "Judge in the place of God," "Vicegerent of the Most High."—Brady, *Clavis Calendaria*, 247 (1839).

The pope assumes supreme dominion, not only over spiritual but also over temporal affairs, styling himself "Head of the Catholic or Universal Church, Sole Arbiter of its rights, and Sovereign Father of all the Kings of the Earth." From these titles, he wears a triple crown, one as High Priest, one as emperor, and the third as king. He also bears keys, to denote his privilege of opening the gates of heaven to all true believers.—Brady, 250-1.

⁎ For the first five centuries the bishops of Rome wore a bonnet, like other ecclesiastics. Pope Hormisdas placed on his bonnet the crown sent him by Clovis; Boniface VIII. added a second crown during his struggles with Philip the Fair; and John XXII. assumed the third crown.

Popish Plot, a supposed Roman Catholic conspiracy to massacre the Protestants, burn London, and murder the king (Charles II.). This fiction was concocted by one Titus Oates, who made a "good thing" by his schemes; but being at last found out, was pilloried, whipped, and imprisoned (1678-9).

Poppy (*Ned*), a prosy old anecdote teller, with a marvellous tendency to digression.

Poquelin (*Jean-ah*), a wealthy Creole living in seclusion in an old house, attended only by a deaf-mute negro. The secrecy and mystery of his life excite all sorts of ugly rumors, and he is mobbed by a crowd of mischievous boys and loafers, receiving injuries that cause his death. The story that his house is haunted keeps intruders from the doors, but they venture near enough on the day of his funeral, to see the coffin brought out by the mute negro, and laid on a cart, and that the solitary mourner is Poquelin's brother, long supposed to be dead. He is a *leper*, for whom the elder brother has cared secretly all these years, not permitting the knowledge of his existence to get abroad, lest the unfortunate man should be removed forcibly, and sent to what is the only asylum for him now that his guardian is dead—the abhorrent *Terre aux Lepreux*.—George W. Cable, *Old Creole Days* (1879).

Porch (*The*). The Stoics were so called, because their founder gave his lectures in the Athenian *stoa*, or *porch*, called "Pœ´cilê."

The successors of Socrătês formed ... the Academy, the Porch, the Garden.—Professor Seeley, *Ecce Homo*.

George Herbert has a poem called *The Church Porch* (six-line stanzas). It may be considered introductory to his poem entitled *The Church* (Sapphic verse and sundry other metres).

Porcius, son of Cato, of Utĭca (in Africa), and brother of Marcus. Both brothers were in love with Lucia; but the hot-headed, impulsive Marcus, being slain in battle, the sage and temperate Porcius was without a rival.—J. Addison, *Cato* (1713).

When Sheridan reproduced *Cato*, Wignell, who acted "Porcius," omitted the prologue, and began at once with the lines, "The dawn is overcast, the morning lowers...." "The prologue! the prologue!" shouted the audience; and Wignell went on in the same tone, as if continuing his speech:

Ladies and gentleman, there has not been
A prologue spoken to this play for years—
And heavily on clouds brings on the day,
The great, th' important day, big with the fate
Of Cato and of Rome.
History of the Stage.

Porcupine (*Peter*). William Cobbett, the politician, published *The Rushlight* under this pseudonym in 1860.

Pornei´us (3 *syl.*), Fornication personified; one of the four sons of Anag´nus (*inchastity*), his brothers being Mæ´chus (*adultery*), Acath´arus, and Asel´gês (*lasciviousness*). He began the battle of Mansoul by encountering Parthen´ia (*maidenly chastity*), but "the martial maid" slew him with her spear. (Greek, *porneia*, "fornication.").

> In maids his joy; now by a maid defied,
> His life he lost and all his former pride.
> With women would he live, now by a woman died.
> Phineas Fletcher, *The Purple Island*, xi. (1633).

Porphyrius, in Dryden's drama of *Tyrannic Love*.

Valeria, daughter of Maximin, having killed herself for the love of Porphyrus, was on one occasion being carried off by the bearers, when she started up and boxed one of the bearers on the ears, saying to him:

> Hold! are you mad, you damned confounded dog?
> I am to rise and speak the epilogue.

W. C. Russell, *Representative Actors*, 456.

Porphyro-Genitus ("*born in the Porphyra*"), the title given to the kings of the Eastern empire, from the apartments called Porphyra, set apart for the empresses during confinement.

There he found Irene, the empress, in travail, in a house anciently appointed for the empresses during childbirth. They call that house "Porphyra," whence the name of the Porphyro-geniti came into the world.—See Selden, *Titles of Honor*, v. 61 (1614).

Porrex, younger son of Gorboduc, a legendary king of Britain. He drove his elder brother, Ferrex, from the kingdom, and, when Ferrex returned with a large army, defeated and slew him. Porrex was murdered while "slumbering on his careful bed," by his own mother, who stabbed him to the heart with a knife."—Thomas Norton and Thomas Sackville, *Gorboduc* (a tragedy, 1561-2).

Por´sena, a legendary king of Etruria, who made war on Rome to restore Tarquin to the throne.

Lord Macaulay has made this the subject of one of his *Lays of Ancient Rome* (1842).

Port´amour, Cupid's sheriff's officer, who summoned offending lovers to "Love's Judgment Hall."—Spenser, *Faëry Queen*, vi. 7 (1596).

Porteous (*Captain John*), an officer of the city guard. He is hanged by the mob (1736).

Mrs. Porteous, wife of the captain.—Sir W. Scott, *The Heart of Midlothian* (time, George II.)

Porter (*Sir Joseph*), K. C. B. The admiral who "stuck close to his desk, and never went to sea." His reward was the appointment as "ruler of the Queen's navee."—W. S. Gilbert, *Pinafore*.

Portia, the wife of Pontius Pilate, in Klopstock's *Messiah*.

Portia, wife of Marcus Brutus. Valerius Maximus says: "She, being determined to kill herself, took hot burning coals into her mouth, and kept her lips closed till she was suffocated by the smoke."

With this she fell distract,
And, her attendants absent, swallowed fire.
Shakespeare, *Julius Cæsar*, act iv. sc. 3 (1607).

Portia, a rich heiress, in love with Bassa´nio; but her choice of a husband was restricted by her father's will to the following condition: Her suitors were to select from three caskets, one of gold, one of silver, and one of lead, and he who selected the casket which contained Portia's picture, was to claim her as his wife. Bassanio chose the lead, and being successful, became the espoused husband. It so happened that Bassanio had borrowed 3,000 ducats, and Antonio, a Venetian merchant, was his security. The money was borrowed of Shylock, a Jew, on these conditions: If the loan was repaid within three months, only the principal would be required; if not, the Jew should be at liberty to claim a pound of flesh from Antonio's body. The loan was not repaid, and the Jew demanded the forfeiture. Portia, in the dress of a law doctor, conducted the defence, and saved Antonio by reminding the Jew that a pound of *flesh* gave him no drop of blood, and that he must cut neither more nor less than an exact pound, otherwise his life would be forfeited. As it would be plainly impossible to fulfill these conditions, the Jew gave up his claim, and Antonio was saved.—Shakespeare, *Merchant of Venice* (1598).

Portsmouth (*The duchess of*), "La Belle Louise de Querouaille," one of the mistresses of Charles II.—Sir W. Scott, *Perveril of the Peak* (time, Charles II.).

Portuguese Cid (*The*), Nunez Alvarez Pereria (1360-1431).

Portuguese Horace (*The*), Antonio Ferreira (1528-1569).

"**Posson Jone**," a gigantic parson from "up the river" who has "been to Mobile on business for Bethesdy Church." His sojourn in New Orleans on his way home is marked by divers adventures. He is beguiled into a gambling den, drugged and made drunk. While intoxicated, he visits a circus and has a scene with the showman and his tiger; he is locked up and awakes in his senses and penitent. His simplicity of self-condemnation, his humility and fortitude move his tempter to restore the $500 of church-money he has "borrowed" from the confiding victim whose transport of pious gratitude overwhelms the world-hardened man with shame and inspires him to new resolves.—George W. Cable, "*Posson Jone*" (1879).

Posthu′mus [LEONATUS] married Imogen, daughter of Cymbeline, king of Britain, and was banished the kingdom for life. He went to Italy, and there, in the house of Philario, bet a diamond ring with Iachimo that nothing could seduce the fidelity of Imogen. Iachimo accepted the bet, concealed himself in a chest in Imogen's chamber, made himself master of certain details and also of a bracelet, and with these vouchers claimed the ring. Posthūmus now ordered his servant, Pisanio, to inveigle Imogen to Milford Haven under the promise of meeting her husband, and to murder her on the road; but Pisanio told Imogen to assume boy's apparel, and enter the service of the Roman general in Britain, as a page. A battle being fought, the Roman general, Iachimo, and Imogen were among the captives; and Posthumus, having done great service in the battle on Cymbeline's behalf, was pardoned. The Roman general prayed that the supposed page might be set at liberty, and the king told her she might also claim a boon, whereupon she asked that Iachimo should state how he became possessed of the ring he was wearing. The whole villainy being thus exposed, Imogen's innocence was fully established, and she was re-united to her husband.—Shakespeare, *Cymbeline* (1605).

Potage (*Jean*), the French "Jack Pudding;" similar to the Italian "Macaroni," the Dutch "Pickel-herringe," and the German "Hanswurst." Clumsy, gormandizing clowns, fond of practical jokes, especially such as stealing eatables and drinkables.

Pother (*Doctor*), an apothecary, "city register, and walking story-book." He had a story *à propos* of every remark made and of every incident; but as he mixed two or three together, his stories were pointless and quite unintelligible. "I know a monstrous good story on that point He! he! he" "I tell you a famous good story about that, you must know. He! he! he!..." "I could have told a capital story, but there was no one to listen to it. He! he! he!" This is the style of his chattering ... "speaking professionally—for anatomy, chemistry, pharmacy, phlebotomy, oxygen, hydrogen, caloric, carbonic, atmospheric, galvanic. Ha! ha! ha! Can tell you a prodigiously laughable story on the subject. Went last summer to a watering-place—lady of fashion—feel pulse—not lady, but lap-dog—talk Latin—prescribed galvanism—out jumped Pompey plump into a batter pudding, and lay like a toad in a hole. Ha! ha! ha!"—Dibdin, *The Farmer's Wife* (1780).

*** Colman's "Ollapod" (1802) was evidently copied from Dibdin's "Doctor Pother."

Potiphar (*Mr.*), freshly-made man intensely uncomfortable in his plated harness. His ideas of art are grounded upon a dim picture in his wife's drawing-room, called by him "Giddo's Shay Doover."

Mrs. Potiphar, shoddy of shoddys. Purse-proud, affected, pretentious and ambitious, and even less fit for her position than her husband for his.—George William Curtis, *Potiphar Papers* (1853).

Potiphar's Wife, Zoleikha or Zuleika; but some call her Raïl.—Sale, *Al Korân*, xii. note.

Pott (*Mr.*), the librarian at the Spa.

Mrs. Pott, the librarian's wife.—Sir W. Scott, *St. Roman's Well* (time, George III.).

Potteries (*Father of the*), Josiah Wedgewood (1730-1795).

Pounce (*Mr. Peter*), in *The Adventures of Joseph Andrews*, by Fielding (1742).

Poundtext (*Peter*), an "indulged pastor" in the covenanters' army.—Sir W. Scott, *Old Mortality* (time, Charles II.).

Pourceaugnac [*Poor-sone-yak*], the hero of a comedy so called. He is a pompous country gentleman, who comes to Paris to marry Julie, daughter of Oronte (2 *syl.*); but Julie loves Eraste (2 *syl.*), and this young man plays off so many tricks, and devises so many mystifications upon M. de Pourceaugnac, that he is fain to give up his suit.—Molière, *M. de Pourceaugnac* (1669).

Poussin (*The British*), Richard Cooper (*-1806).

Poussin (*Gaspar*). So Gaspar Dughet, the French painter, is called (1613-1675).

Powell (*Mary*), the first wife of John Milton.

Powheid (*Lazarus*), the old sexton in Douglas.—Sir W. Scott, *Castle Dangerous* (time, Henry I.).

Poyning's Law, a statute to establish the English jurisdiction in Ireland. The parliament that passed it was summoned in the reign of Henry VII. by Sir Edward Poynings, governor of Ireland (1495).

Poyser (*Mrs.*), shrewd, capable and ready-tongued wife of a British yeoman, and aunt of Hetty Sorrel.—George Eliot, *Adam Bede*.

P. P., "Clerk of the Parish," the feigned signature of Dr. Arbuthnot, subscribed to a volume of *Memoirs* in ridicule of Burnet's *History of My Own Times*.

Those who were placed around the dinner-table had those feelings of awe with which *P. P., Clerk of the Parish*, was oppressed when he first uplifted the psalm in presence of ... the wise Mr. Justice Freeman, the good Lady Jones, and the great Sir Thomas Truby.—Sir W. Scott.

Pragmatic Sanction. The word *pragmaticus* means "relating to State affairs," and the word *sanctio* means "an ordinance" or "decree." The four most famous statutes so called are:

1. *The Pragmatic Sanction of St. Louis* (1268), which forbade the court of Rome to levy taxes or collect subscriptions in France without the express permission of the king. It also gave French subjects the right of appealing, in certain cases, from the ecclesiastical to the civil courts of the realm.

2. *The Pragmatic Sanction of Bourges,* passed by Charles VII. of France, in 1438. By this ordinance the power of the people in France was limited and defined. The authority of the National Council was declared superior to that of the pope. The French clergy were forbidden to appeal to Rome on any point affecting the secular condition of the nation; and the Roman pontiff was wholly forbidden to appropriate to himself any vacant living, or to appoint to any bishopric or parish church in France.

3. *The Pragmatic Sanction of Kaiser Karl VI. of Germany* (in 1713), which settled the empire on his daughter, the Archduchess Maria Theresa, wife of François de Loraine. Maria Theresa ascended the throne in 1740, and a European war was the result.

4. *The Pragmatic Sanction of Charles III. of Spain* (1767). This was to suppress the Jesuits of Spain.

What is meant emphatically by *The Pragmatic Sanction* is the third of these ordinances, viz., settling the line of succession in Germany on the house of Austria.

Pramnian Mixture *(The),* any intoxicating draught; so called from the Pramnian grape, from which it was made. Circê gave Ulysses "Pramnian wine" impregnated with drugs, in order to prevent his escape from the island.

And for my drink prepared
The Pramnian mixture in a golden cup,
Impregnating (on my destruction bent)
With noxious herbs the draught.
Homer, *Odyssey,* x. (Cowper's trans.).

Prasildo, a Babylonish nobleman, who falls in love with Tisbi´na, wife of his friend Iroldo. He is overheard by Tisbina threatening to kill himself, and, in order to divert him from his guilty passion she promises to return his love on condition of his performing certain adventures which she thinks to be impossible. However, Prasildo performs them all, and then Tisbina and Iroldo, finding no excuse, take poison to avoid the alternative. Prasildo resolves to do the same, but is told by the apothecary that the "poison" he had supplied was a harmless drink. Prasildo tells his friend, Iroldo quits the country, and Tisbina marries Prasildo. Time passes on and Prasildo hears that his friend's life is in danger, whereupon he starts forth to rescue him at the hazard of his own life.—Bojardo, *Orlando Innamorato* (1495).

Prasu´tagus or **Præsu´tagus**, husband of Bonduica or Boadicēa, queen of the Icēni.—Richard of Cirencester, *History*, xxx. (fourteenth century).

Me, the wife of rich Prasutagus; me the lover of liberty.—
Me, they seized, and me they tortured!
Tennyson, *Boadicea*.

Prate´fast (*Peter*), who "in all his life spake no word in waste." His wife was Maude, and his eldest son, Sym Sadle Gander, who married Betres (daughter of Davy Dronken Nole, of Kent, and his wife, Al´yson).—Stephen Hawes, *The Passe-tyme of Plesure*, xxix. (1515).

Prattle (*Mr.*), medical practitioner, a voluble gossip, who retails all the news and scandal of the neighborhood. He knows everybody, everybody's affairs, and everybody's intentions.—G. Colman, Sr, *The Deuce is in Him* (1762).

Pre-Adamite Kings, Soliman Raad, Soliman Daki, and Soliman de Gian ben Gian. The last named, having chained up the dives (1 *syl.*) in the dark caverns of Pâf, became so presumptuous as to dispute the Supreme Power. All these kings maintained great state [before the existence of that contemptible being denominated by us "The Father of Mankind"]; but none can be compared with the eminence of Soliman ben Daoud.

Pre-Adamite Throne (*The*). It was Vathek's ambition to gain the pre-Adamite throne. After long search, he was shown it at last in the abyss of Eblis; but being there, return was impossible, and he remained a prisoner without hope forever.

They reached at length the hall [*Argenk*] of great extent, and covered with a lofty dome.... A funereal gloom prevailed over it. Here, upon two beds of incorruptible cedar, lay recumbent the fleshless forms of the pre-Adamite kings, who had once been monarchs of the whole earth.... At their feet were inscribed the events of their several reigns, their power, their pride, and their crimes. [*This was the pre-Adamite throne, the ambition of the Caliph Vathek.*]—W. Beckford, *Vathek* (1784).

Preacher (*The*) Solomon, the son of David, author of *The Preacher* (i. e. *Ecclesiastes*).

Thus saith the Preacher, "Nought beneath the sun
Is new;" yet still from change to change we run.
Byron.

Preacher (The Glorious), St. Chrys´ostom (347-407). The name means "Golden mouth."

Preacher (The Little), Samuel de Marets, Protestant controversialist (1599-1663).

Preacher (The Unfair). Dr. Isaac Barrow was so called by Charles II., because his sermons were so exhaustive that they left nothing more to be said on the subject, which was "unfair" to those that came after him.

Preachers *(The King of)*, Louis Bourdaloue (1632-1704).

Précieuses Ridicules *(Les)*, a comedy by Molière, in ridicule of the "*precieuses*," as they were styled, forming the coterie of the Hotel de Rambouillet in the seventeenth century. The *soirées* held in this hotel were a great improvement on the licentious assemblies of the period; but many imitators made the thing ridiculous, because they wanted the same presiding talent and good taste.

The two girls of Molière's comedy are Madelon and Cathos, the daughter and niece of Gorgibus, a bourgeois. They change their names to Polixène and Aminte, which they think more genteel, and look on the affectations of two flunkies as far more *distingué* than the simple, gentlemanly manners of their masters. However, they are cured of their folly, and no harm comes of it (1659).

Preciosa, the heroine of Longfellow's *Spanish Student*, in love with Victorian, the student.

Precocious Genius.

JOHANN PHILIP BARATIER, a German, at the age of five years, knew Greek, Latin, and French, besides his native German. At nine he knew Hebrew and Chaldaic, and could translate German into Latin. At thirteen he could translate Hebrew into French, or French into Hebrew (1721-1740).

*** The life of this boy was written by Formey. His name is enrolled in all biographical dictionaries.

CHRISTIAN HENRY HEINECKEN, at one year old, knew the chief events of the Pentatauch!! at thirteen months he knew the history of the Old Testament!! at fourteen months he knew the history of the New Testament!! at two and a half years he could answer any ordinary question of history or geography; and at three years old knew French and Latin as well as his native German (1721-1725).

⁂ The life of this boy was written by Schœneich, his teacher. His name is duly noticed in biographical dictionaries.

Pressæus (*"eater of garlic"*), the youngest of the frog chieftains.

The pious ardor young Pressæus brings,
Betwixt the fortunes of contending kings;
Lank, harmless frog! with forces hardly grown,
He darts the reed in combats not his own,
Which, faintly tinkling on Troxartas' shield,
Hangs at the point and drops upon the field.
Parnell, *Battle of the Frogs and Mice*, iii. (about 1712).

Prest, a nickname given by Swift to the duchess of Shrewsbury, who was a foreigner.

Prester John, a corruption of *Belul Gian*, meaning "precious stone." Gian (pronounced *zjon*) has been corrupted into John, and Belul, translated into "precious;" in Latin *Johannes preciosus* ("precious John") corrupted into "Presbyter Joannes." The kings of Ethiopia or Abyssinia, from a gemmed ring given to Queen Saba, whose son by Solomon was king of Ethiopia, and was called Melech, with the "precious stone," or Melech *Gian-Belul*.

Æthiopes regem suum, quem nos vulgo "Prete Gianni" corrupte dicimus, quatour appellant nominibus, quorum primum est "Belul Giad," hoc est *lapis preciosus*. Ductum est autem hoc nomen ab *annulo Salomonis* quem ille filio ex regina Saba, ut putant genito, dono dedisse, quove omnes postea reges usos fuisse descriptor.... Cum vero eum coronant, appellant "Neghuz." Postremo cum vertice capitis in coronæ modum abraso, ungitur a patriarcha, vocant "Masih," hoc est *unctum*. Hæc autem regiæ dignitatis nomina omnibus communia sunt.—Quoted by Selden, from a little annal of the Ethiopian kings (1552), in his *Titles of Honor*, v. 65 (1614).

⁂ As this title was like the Egyptian *Pharaoh*, and belonged to whole lines of kings, it will explain the enormous diversity of time allotted by different writers to "Prester John."

Marco Polo says that Prester John was slain in battle by Jenghiz Khan; and Gregory Bar-Hebræus says, "God forsook him because he had taken to himself a wife of the Zinish nation, called Quarakhata.

Bishop Jordānus, in his description of the world, sets down Abyssinia as the kingdom of Prester John. Abyssinia used to be called "Middle India."

Otto of Freisingen is the first author to mention him. This Otto wrote a chronicle to the date 1156. He says that John was of the family of the Magi, and ruled over the country of these Wise Men. Otto tells us that Prester John had "a sceptre of emeralds."

Maimonĭdês, about the same time (twelfth century), mentions him, but calls him "Prester-Cuan."

Before 1241 a letter was addressed by "Prester John" to Manuel Comnēnus, emperor of Constantinople. It is preserved in the *Chronicle* of Albericus Trium Fontium, who gives for its date 1165.

Mandeville calls Prester John a lineal descendant of Ogier, the Dane. He tells us that Ogier, with fifteen others, penetrated into the north of India, and divided the land amongst his followers. John was made sovereign of Teneduc, and was called "Prester" because he converted the natives to the Christian faith.

Another tradition says that Prester John had seventy kings for his vassals, and was seen by his subjects only three times in a year.

In *Orlando Furioso*, Prester John is called by his subjects "Senāpus, king of Ethiopia." He was blind, and though the richest monarch of the world, he pined with famine, because harpies flew off with his food by way of punishment for wanting to add paradise to his empire. The plague, says the poet, was to cease "when a stranger appeared on a flying griffin." This stranger was Astolpho, who drove the harpies to Cocy´tus. Prester John, in return for this service, sent 100,000 Nubians to the aid of Charlemagne. Astolpho supplied this contingent with horses by throwing stones into the air, and made transport-ships to convey them to France by casting leaves into the sea. After the death of Agramant, the Nubians were sent home, and then the horses became stones again, and the ships became leaves (bks. xvii.-xix.).

Pretender (*The Young*), Prince Charles Edward Stuart, son of James Francis Edward Stuart (called "The *Old* Pretender"). James Francis was the son of James II., and Charles Edward was the king's grandson.—Sir W. Scott, *Waverley* (time, George II.).

Charles Edward was defeated at Cullōden in 1746, and escaped to the Continent.

God bless the king—I mean the "Faith's defender;"
God bless—no harm in blessing—the Pretender.
Who that Pretender is, and who is king,
God bless us all! that's quite another thing.
Ascribed by Sir W. Scott to John Byrom (in *Redgauntlet*).

The mistress of Charles Edward Stuart was Miss Walkingshaw.

Prettyman (*Prince*), in love with Cloris. He is sometimes a fisherman, and sometimes a prince.—Duke of Buckingham, *The Rehearsal* (1671).

⁎ "Prince Prettyman" is said to be a parody on "Leonidas" in Dryden's *Marriage-à-la-mode*.

Pri′amus (*Sir*), a knight of the Round Table. He possessed a phial, full of four waters that came from paradise. These waters instantly healed any wounds which were touched by them.

"My father," says Sir Priamus, "is lineally descended of Alexander and of Hector by right line. Duke Josuê and Machabæus were of our lineage. I am right inheritor of Alexandria, and Affrike of all the out isles."

And Priamus took from his page a phial, full of four waters that came out of paradise; and with certain balm nointed he their wounds, and washed them with that water, and within an hour after they were both as whole as ever they were.—Sir T. Malory, *History of Prince Arthur*, i. 97 (1470).

Price (*Matilda*), a miller's daughter; a pretty, coquettish young woman, who marries John Browdie, a hearty Yorkshire corn-factor.—C. Dickens, *Nicholas Nickleby* (1838).

Pride (*Sir*), first a drayman, then a colonel in the parliamentary army.—S. Butler, *Hudibras* (1663-78).

Pride of Humility. Antisthênês, the Cynic, affected a very ragged coat; but Socrătês said to him, "Antisthenês, I can see your vanity peering through the holes of your coat."

Pride's Purge, a violent invasion of parliamentary rights by Colonel Pride, in 1649. At the head of two regiments of soldiers he surrounded the House of Commons, seized forty-one of the members and shut out 160 others. None were allowed into the House but those most friendly to Cromwell. This fag-end went by the name of "the Rump."

Pridwin or PRIWEN, Prince Arthur's shield.

Arthur placed a golden helmet upon his head, on which was engraven the figure of a dragon; and on his shoulders his shield, called Priwen, upon which the picture of the blessed Mary, mother of God, was painted; then, girding on his Caliburn, which was an excellent sword, made in the isle of Avallon; he took in his right hand his lance, Ron, which was hard, broad, and fit for slaughter.—Geoffrey, *British History*, ix. 4 (1142).

Priest of Nature, Sir Isaac Newton (1642-1727).

Lo! Newton, priest of nature, shines afar,
Scans the wide world, and numbers every star.
Campbell, *Pleasures of Hope*, i. (1799).

Prig, a knavish beggar.—Beaumont and Fletcher, *The Beggars' Bush* (1622).

Prig (Betsey), an old monthly nurse, "the frequent pardner" of Mrs. Gamp; equally ignorant, equally vulgar, equally selfish, and brutal to her patients.

"Betsey," said Mrs. Gamp, filling her own glass, and passing the teapot [*of gin*], "I will now propoge a toast: 'My frequent pardner, Betsey Prig.'" "Which, altering the name to Sairah Gamp, I drink," said Mrs. Prig, "with love and tenderness."—C. Dickens, *Martin Chuzzlewit*, xlix. (1843).

Prim′er (*Peter*), a pedantic country schoolmaster, who believes himself to be the wisest of pedagogues.—Samuel Foote, *The Mayor of Garratt* (1763).

Primitive Fathers (*The*). The five apostolic fathers contemporary with the apostles (viz., Clement of Rome, Barnăbas, Hermas, Ignatius and Polycarp), and the nine following, who all lived in the first three centuries:—Justin, Theoph′ilus of Antioch, Irenæus, Clement of Alexandria, Cyprian of Carthage, Orĭgen, Gregory "Thaumatur′gus," Dionysius of Alexandria and Tertullian.

⁎⁎* For the "Fathers" of the fourth and fifth centuries see GREEK CHURCH, LATIN CHURCH.

Primrose (*The Rev. Dr. Charles*), a clergyman rich in heavenly wisdom, but poor indeed in all worldly knowledge. Amiable, charitable, devout, but not without his literary vanity, especially on the Whistonian theory about second marriages. One admires his virtuous indignation against the "washes," which he deliberately demolished with the poker. In his prosperity his chief "adventures were by the fireside, and all his migrations were from the blue bed to the brown."

Mrs. [*Deborah*] *Primrose*, the doctor's wife, full of motherly vanity, and desirous to appear *genteel*. She could read without much spelling, prided herself on her housewifery, especially on her gooseberry wine, and was really proud of her excellent husband.

(She was painted as "Venus," and the vicar, in gown and bands, was presenting to her his book on "second marriages," but when complete the picture was found to be too large for the house.)

George Primrose, son of the vicar. He went to Amsterdam to teach the Dutch English, but never once called to mind that he himself must know something of Dutch before this could be done. He becomes Captain Primrose, and marries Miss Wilmot, an heiress.

(Goldsmith himself went to teach the French English under the same circumstances.)

Moses Primrose, younger son of the vicar, noted for his greenness and pedantry. Being sent to sell a good horse at a fair, he bartered it for a gross of green spectacles, with copper rims and shagreen cases, of no more value than Hodge's razors (ch. xii.).

Olivia Primrose, the eldest daughter of the doctor. Pretty, enthusiastic, a sort of Hebê in beauty. "She wished for many lovers," and eloped with Squire Thornhill. Her father found her at a roadside inn called the Harrow, where she was on the point of being turned out of the house. Subsequently, she was found to be legally married to the squire.

Sophia Primrose, the second daughter of Dr. Primrose. She was "soft, modest, and alluring." Not like her sister, desirous of winning all, but fixing her whole heart upon one. Being thrown from her horse into a deep stream, she was rescued by Mr. Burchell (*alias* Sir William Thornhill), and being abducted, was again rescued by him. She married him at last.—Goldsmith, *Vicar of Wakefield* (1766).

Prince of Alchemy, Rudolph II., kaiser of Germany; also called "The German Trismegistus" (1552, 1576-1612).

Prince of Angels, Michael.

So spake the prince of angels. To whom thus
The Adversary [i.e. *Satan*].
Milton, *Paradise Lost*, vi. 281 (1665).

Prince of Celestial Armies, Michael, the archangel.

Go, Michael, of celestial armies prince.
Milton, *Paradise Lost*, vi. 44 (1665).

Prince of Darkness, Satan (*Eph*. vi 12).

Whom thus the prince of darkness answered glad:
"Fair daughter,
High proof ye now have given to be the race
Of Satan (I glory in the name)."
Milton, *Paradise Lost*, x, 383 (1665).

Prince of Hell, Satan.

And with them comes a third of regal port,
But faded splendor wan; who by his gait
And fierce demeanor seems the prince of Hell.
Milton, *Paradise Lost*, iv. 868 (1665).

Prince of Life, a title given to Christ (*Acts* iii. 15).

Prince of Peace, a title given to the Messiah (*Isaiah* ix. 6).

Prince of Peace, Don Manuel Godoy, of Badajoz. So called because he concluded the "peace of Basle" in 1795, between France and Spain (1757-1851).

Prince of the Air, Satan.

... Jesus, son of Mary, second Eve,
Saw Satan fall, like lightning, down from heaven,
Prince of the air.
Milton, *Paradise Lost*, x. 185 (1665).

Prince of the Devils, Satan (*Matt.* xii. 24).

Prince of the Kings of the Earth, a title given to Christ (*Rev.* i. 5).

Prince of the Power of the Air, Satan (*Eph.* ii. 2).

Prince of this World, Satan (*John* xiv. 30).

Princes. It was Prince Bismarck, the German Chancellor, who said to a courtly attendant, "Let princes be princes, and mind your own business."

Prince's Peers, a term of contempt applied to peers of low birth. The phrase arose in the reign of Charles VII., of France, when his son Louis (afterwards Louis XI.) created a host of riff-raff peers, such as tradesmen, farmers, and mechanics, in order to degrade the aristocracy, and thus weaken its influence in the state.

Printed Books. The first book produced in England, was printed in England in 1477, by William Caxton, in the Almonry, at Westminster, and was entitled *The Dictes and Sayings of the Philosophers*.

The Rev. T. Wilson says: "The press at Oxford existed ten years before there was any press in Europe, except those of Haarlem and Mentz." The person who set up the Oxford press was Corsellis, and his first printed book bore the date of 1468. The colophon of it ran thus: "Explicit exposicio Sancti Jeronimi in simbolo apostolorum ad papam laurēcium. Impressa Oxonii Et finita Anno Domini Mcccclxviij., xvij. die Decembris." The book is a small quarto of forty-two leaves, and was first noticed in 1664 by Richard Atkins in his *Origin and Growth of Printing*. Dr. Conyers Middleton, in 1735, charged Atkins with forgery. In 1812, S. W. Singer defended the book. Dr. Cotton took the subject up in his *Typographical Gazetteer* (first and second series).

Prior (*Matthew*). The monument to this poet in Westminster Abbey was by Rysbrack; executed by order of Louis XIV.

Priory (*Lord*), an old-fashioned husband, who actually thinks that a wife should "love, honor, and obey" her husband; nay, more, that "forsaking all others, she should cleave to him so long as they both should live."

Lady Priory, an old-fashioned wife, but young and beautiful. She was, however, so very old-fashioned that she went to bed at ten and rose at six; dressed in a cap and gown of her own making; respected and loved her husband; discouraged flirtation; and when assailed by any improper advances, instead of showing temper or conceited airs, quietly and tranquilly seated herself to some modest household duty till the assailant felt the irresistible power of modesty and virtue.—Mrs. Inchbald, *Wives as They Were and Maids as They Are* (1797).

Priscian, a great grammarian of the fifth century. The Latin phrase, *Diminuĕre Prisciani caput* ("to break Priscian's head"), means to "violate the rules of grammar." (See PEGASUS.)

Some, free from rhyme or reason, rule or check,
Break Priscian's head, and Pegasus's neck.
Pope, *The Dunciad*, iii. 161 (1728).

Quakers (that like to lanterns, bear
Their light within them) will not swear
And hold no sin so deeply red
As that of breaking Priscian's head.
Butler, *Hudibras*, II. ii. 219, etc. (1664).

Priscilla, daughter of a noble lord. She fell in love with Sir Aladine, a poor knight.—Spenser, *Faëry Queen*, vi. 1 (1596).

Priscilla, the beautiful puritan in love with John Alden. When Miles Standish, a bluff old soldier, in the middle of life, wished to marry her, he asked John Alden to go and plead his cause; but the puritan maiden replied archly, "Why don't you speak for yourself, John?" Upon this hint, John did speak for himself, and Priscilla listened to his suit.—Longfellow, *The Courtship of Miles Standish* (1858).

Priscilla. Fragile, pretty, simple girl, whom Hollingsworth and Coverdale love, instead of falling victims to the superb Zenobia. She is thin-blooded and weak-limbed, and her very helplessness charms the strong men, who suppose themselves proof against love of the ordinary kind.—Nathaniel Hawthorne, *The Blithedale Romance* (1852).

Prison Life Endeared. The following are examples of prisoners who, from long habit, have grown attached to prison life:—

Comte de Lorge was confined for thirty years in the Bastile, and when liberated (July 14, 1789) declared that freedom had no joys for him. After imploring in vain to be allowed to return to his dungeon, he lingered for six weeks and pined to death.

Goldsmith says, when Chinvang the Chaste, ascended the throne of China, he commanded the prisons to be thrown open. Among the prisoners was a venerable man of 85 years of age, who implored that he might be suffered to return to his cell. For sixty-three years he had lived in its gloom and solitude, which he preferred to the glare of the sun and the bustle of a city.—*A Citizen of the World* lxxiii. (1759).

Mr. Cogan once visited a prisoner of state in the King's Bench prison, who told him he had grown to like the subdued light and extreme solitude of his cell; he even liked the spots and patches on the wall, the hardness of his bed, the regularity, and the freedom from all the cares and worries of active life. He did not wish to be released, and felt sure he should never be so happy in any other place.

A woman of Leyden, on the expiration of a long imprisonment, applied for permission to return to her cell, and added, if the request was refused as a favor, she would commit some offence which should give her a title to her old quarters.

A prisoner condemned to death had his sentence commuted to seven years' close confinement on a bed of nails. After the expiration of five years, he declared, if ever he were released, he should adopt from choice what habit had rendered so agreeable to him.

Prisoner of Chillon, Françoise de Bonnivard, a Frenchman, who resided at Geneva, and made himself obnoxious to Charles III., duc de Savoie, who incarcerated him for six years in a dungeon of the Château de Chillon, at the east end of the lake of Geneva. The prisoner was ultimately released by the Bernese, who were at war with Savoy.

Byron has founded on this incident his poem entitled *The Prisoner of Chillon*, but has added two brothers, whom he supposes to be imprisoned with Françoise, and who die of hunger, suffering, and confinement. In fact, the poet mixes up Dantê's tale about Count Ugolino with that of Françoise de Bonnivard, and has produced a powerful and affecting story, but it is not historic.

Prisoner of State (*The*), Ernest de Fridberg. E. Sterling has a drama so called. (For the plot, see ERNEST DE FRIDBERG.)

Pritchard (*William*), commander of H.M. sloop, the *Shark*.—Sir W. Scott, *Guy Mannering* (time, George II.).

Priu'li, a senator of Venice, of unbending pride. His daughter had been saved from the Adriatic by Jaffier, and gratitude led to love. As it was quite hopeless to expect Priuli to consent to the match, Belvidera eloped in the night, and married Jaffier. Priuli now discarded them both. Jaffier joined

Pierre's conspiracy to murder the Venetian senators, but in order to save his father-in-law, revealed to him the plot under the promise of a general free pardon. The promise was broken, and all the conspirators except Jaffier were condemned to death by torture. Jaffier stabbed Pierre, to save him from the wheel, and then killed himself. Belvidera went mad and died. Priuli lived on, a broken-down old man, sick of life, and begging to be left alone in some "place that's fit for mourning." "There, all leave me:

Sparing no tears when you this tale relate,
But bid all cruel fathers dread my fate."
T. Otway, *Venice Preserved*, v. the end (1682).

Privolvans, the antagonists of the Subvolvans.

These silly, ranting Privolvans
Have every summer their campaigns,
And muster like the warlike sons
Of Rawhead and of Bloody-bones.
S. Butler, *The Elephant in the Moon*, v. 85 (1754).

Probe (1 *syl.*), a priggish surgeon, who magnifies mole-hill ailments into mountain maladies, in order to enhance his skill and increase his charges. Thus, when Lord Foppington received a small flesh-wound in the arm from a foil, Probe drew a long face, frightened his lordship greatly, and pretended the consequences might be serious; but when Lord Foppington promised him £500 for a cure, he set his patient on his legs the next day.—Sheridan, *A Trip to Scarborough* (1777).

Procida (*John of*), a tragedy by S. Knowles (1840). John of Procida was an Italian gentleman of the thirteenth century, a skillful physician, high in favor with King Fernando II., Conrad, Manfred, and Conrad´ine. The French invaded the island, put the last two monarchs to the sword, usurped the sovereignty, and made Charles d'Anjou king. The cruelty, licentiousness, and extortion of the French being quite unbearable, provoked a general rising of the Sicilians, and in one night (*Sicilian Vespers*, March 30, 1282), every Frenchman, Frenchwoman, and French child in the whole island was ruthlessly butchered. Procïda lost his only son Fernando, who had just married Isoline (3 *syl.*), the daughter of the French governor of Messina. Isoline died broken-hearted, and her father, the governor, was amongst the slain. The crown was given to John of Procida.

Procris, the wife of Cephălos. Out of jealousy she crept into a wood to act as a spy upon her husband. Cephalos, hearing something move, discharged an arrow in the direction of the rustling, thinking it to be caused by some wild beast, and shot Procris. Jupiter, in pity, turned Procris into a star.— *Greek and Latin Mythology*.

The unerring dart of Procris. Diana gave Procris a dart which never missed its aim, and after being discharged returned back to the shooter.

Procrus′tes (3 *syl.*), a highwayman of Attica, who used to place travellers on a bed; if they were too short he stretched them out till they fitted it, if too long he lopped off the redundant part. *Greek Mythology.*

Critic, more cruel than Procrustes old,
Who to his iron bed by torture fits
Their nobler parts, the souls of suffering wits.
Mallet, *Verbal Criticism* (1734).

Proctor's Dogs or *Bull-Dogs*, the two "runners" or officials who accompany a university proctor in his rounds, to give chase to recalcitrant gownsmen.

And he had breathed the proctor's dogs [*was a member of Oxford or Cambridge University*].
Tennyson, prologue of *The Princess* (1830).

Prodigal (*The*), Albert VI. duke of Austria (1418, 1439-1463).

Prodigy of France (*The*). Guillaume Budé was so called by Erasmus (1467-1540).

Prodigy of Learning (*The*). Samuel Hahnemann, the German, was so called by J. P. Richter (1755-1843).

Professor (*The*). The most important member of the party gathered about the social board in O. W. Holmes's *Autocrat of the Breakfast-Table* (1858).

Profound (*The*), Richard Middleton, an English scholastic divine (*-1304).

Profound Doctor (*The*), Thomas Bradwardine, a schoolman. Also called "The Solid Docter" (*-1349).

Ægidius de Columna, a Sicilian schoolman, was called "The Most Profound Doctor" (*-1316).

Progne (2 *syl.*), daughter of Pandīon, and sister of Philomēla. Prognê was changed into a swallow, and Philomela into a nightingale.—*Greek Mythology.*

As Prognê or as Philomela mourns ...
So Bradamant laments her absent knight.
Ariosto, *Orlando Furioso*, xxiii. (1516).

Prome′thean Unguent (*The*), made from the extract of a herb on which some of the blood of Promētheus (3 *syl.*), had fallen. Medea gave Jason some of this unguent, which rendered his body proof against fire and warlike instruments.

Prome´theus (3 *syl.*) taught man the use of fire, and instructed him in architecture, astronomy, mathematics, writing, rearing cattle, navigation, medicine, the art of prophecy, working metal, and, indeed, every art known to man. The word means "forethought," and forethought is the father of invention. The tale is that he made man of clay, and, in order to endow his clay with life, stole fire from heaven and brought it to earth in a hollow tube. Zeus, in punishment, chained him to a rock, and sent an eagle to consume his liver daily; during the night it grew again, and thus his torment was ceaseless, till Hercules shot the eagle, and unchained the captive.

Learn the while, in brief,
That all arts come to mortals from Prometheus.
E. B. Browning, *Prometheus Bound* (1850).

Truth shall restore the light by Nature given,
And, like Prometheus, bring the fire from heaven.
Campbell, *Pleasures of Hope*, i. (1700).

⁎ Percy B. Shelley has a classical drama entitled *Prometheus Unbound* (1819).

James Russell Lowell has a noble poem entitled *Prometheus*, beginning,—

"One after one the stars have risen and set,
Sparkling upon the hoarfrost on my chain."

Prompt, the servant of Mr. and Miss Blandish. General Burgoyne, *The Heiress* (1781).

Pronando (*Rast*). The early lover of Anne Douglas. He is handsome, weak, and attractive in disposition, a favorite with all his friends. His pliant character and good-natured vanity make him a prey to the whimsical fascinations of Tita, Anne's "little sister," whom he marries instead of his first betrothed.—Constance Fenimore Woolson, *Anne* (1882).

Pronouns. It was of Henry Mossop, tragedian (1729-1773), that Churchill wrote the two lines:

In monosyllables his thunders roll—
He, she, it, and we, ye, they, fright the soul;

because Mossop was fond of emphasizing his pronouns and little words.

Prophecy. Jourdain, the wizard, told the duke of Somerset, if he wished to live, to "avoid where castles mounted stand." The duke died in an ale-house called the Castle, in St. Alban's.

... underneath an ale-house' paltry sign,
The Castle, in St. Alban's, Sumerset

Hath made the wizard famous in his death.
Shakespeare, 2 *Henry VI.* act v. sc. 2 (1591).

Similar prophetic equivokes were told to Henry IV., Pope Sylvester II., and Cambysês (see JERUSALEM).

Aristomĕnês was told by the Delphic oracle to "flee for his life when he saw a goat drink from the river Neda." Consequently, all *goats* were driven from the banks of this river; but one day, Theŏclos observed that the branches of a fig tree bent into the stream, and it immediately flashed into his mind that the Messenian word for *fig tree* and *goat* was the same. The pun or equivoke will be better understood by an English reader if for *goat* we read *ewe*, and bear in mind that *yew* is to the ear the same word; thus:

When an *ewe* [*yew*] stops to drink of the "Severn," then fly,
And look not behind, for destruction is nigh.

Prophetess (*Thĕ*), Ayē´shah, the second and beloved wife of Mahomet. It does not mean that she prophesied, but, like *Sultana*, it is simply a title of honor. He was the *Prophet*, she the *Prophēta* or Madam Prophet.

Prose (*Father of English*), Wycliffe (1324-1384).

Prose (*Father of Greek*), Herodotus (B.C. 484-408).

Prose (*Father of Italian*), Boccaccio (1313-1375).

Pros´erpine (3 *syl.*), called *Proserpĭna* in Latin, and "Proser´pin" by Milton, was daughter of Ce´rês. She went to the field of Enna to amuse herself by gathering asphodels, and being tired, fell asleep. Dis, the god of Hell, then carried her off, and made her queen of the infernal reions. Cerês wandered for nine days over the world disconsolate, looking for her daughter, when Hec´ate (2 *syl.*) told her she had heard the girl's cries, but knew not who had carried her off. Both now went to Olympus, when the sun-god told them the true state of the case.

N.B.—This is an allegory of seed-corn.

Not that fair field
Of Enna, where Proser´pin, gathering flowers,
Herself a fairer flower, by gloomy Dis
Was gathered—which cost Cerês all that pain
To seek her thro' the world.
Milton, *Paradise Lost*, iv. 268 (1665).

Prosperity Robinson, Frederick Robinson, afterwards Viscount Goderich and earl of Ripon, chancellor of the exchequer in 1823. So called by Cobbett, from his boasting about the prosperity of the country just a little before the great commercial crisis of 1825.

Pros′pero, the banished duke of Milan, and father of Miranda. He was deposed by his brother, Antonio, who sent him to sea with Miranda in a "rotten carcass of a boat," which was borne to a desert island. Here Prospero practised magic. He liberated Ariel from the rift of a pine tree, where the witch Syc′orax had confined him for twelve years, and was served by that bright spirit with true gratitude. The only other inhabitant of the island was Calĭban, the witch's "welp." After a residence in the island of sixteen years, Prospero raised a tempest by magic to cause the shipwreck of the usurping duke and of Ferdinand, his brother's son. Ferdinand fell in love with his cousin, Miranda, and eventually married her.—Shakespeare, *The Tempest* (1609).

Still they kept limping to and fro,
Like Ariels round old Prospero,
Saying, "Dear master, let us go."
But still the old man answered, "No!"
T. Moore, *A Vision*.

Pross (*Miss*), a red-haired, ungainly creature, who lived with Lucie Manette, and dearly loved her. Miss Pross, although eccentric, was most faithful and unselfish.

Her character (dissociated from stature) was shortness.... It was characteristic of this lady that whenever her original proposition was questioned, she exaggerated it.—C. Dickens, *A Tale of Two Cities*, ii. 6 (1859).

Proterius of Cappadōcia, father of Cyra. (See SINNER SAVED.)

Protesila′os, husband of Laodamīa. Being slain at the siege of Troy, the dead body was sent home to his wife, who prayed that she might talk with him again, if only for three hours. Her prayer was granted, but when Protesilāos returned to death, Laodamia died also.—*Greek Mythology*.

In Fénelon's *Télémaque* "Protésilaos" is meant for Louvois, the French minister of state.

Protestant Duke (*The*), James, duke of Monmouth, a love-child of Charles II. So called because he renounced the Roman faith, in which he had been brought up, and became a Protestant (1619-1685).

Protestant Pope (*The*), Gian Vincenzo Ganganelli, Pope Clement XIV. So called from his enlightened policy, and for his bull suppressing the Jesuits (1705, 1769-1774).

Proteus [*Pro-tuce*], a sea-god who resided in the Carpathian Sea. He had the power of changing his form at will. Being a prophet also, Milton calls him "the Carpathian wizard."—*Greek Mythology*.

By hoary Nereus' wrinkled look,
And the Carpathian wizard's hook [*or trident*].
Milton, *Comus* (1634).

Periklym´enos, son of Neleus (2 *syl.*), had the power of changing his form into a bird, beast, reptile, or insect. As a bee he perched on the chariot of Heraklês (*Hercules*), and was killed.

Aristogīton, from being dipped in the Achelōus (4 *syl.*), received the power of changing his form at will.—Fénelon, *Télémaque*, xx. (1700).

The genii, both good and bad, of Eastern mythology, had the power of changing their form instantaneously. This is powerfully illustrated by the combat between the queen of Beauty and the son of Eblis. The genius first appeared as an enormous lion, but the queen of Beauty plucked out a hair which became a scythe, with which she cut the lion in pieces. The head of the lion now became a scorpion, and the princess changed herself into a serpent; but the scorpion instantly made itself an eagle, and went in pursuit of the serpent. The serpent, however, being vigilant, assumed the form of a white cat; the eagle in an instant changed to a wolf, and the cat, being hard pressed, changed into a worm; the wolf changed to a cock, and ran to pick up the worm, which, however, became a fish before the cock could pick it up. Not to be outwitted, the cock transformed itself into a pike to devour the fish, but the fish changed into a fire, and the son of Eblis was burnt to ashes before he could make another change.—*Arabian Nights* ("The Second Calender").

Proteus or *Protheus*, one of the two gentlemen of Verona. He is in love with Julia. His servant is Launce, and his father Anthonio or Antonio. The other gentleman is called Valentine, and his lady love is Silvia.—Shakespeare, *The Two Gentlemen of Verona* (1594).

Shakespeare calls the word *Pro-tĕ-us*. Malone, Dr. Johnson, etc., retain the *h* in both names, but the Globe edition omits them.

Protevangelon ("*first evangelist*"), a gospel falsely attributed to St. James the Less, first bishop of Jerusalem, noted for its minute details of the Virgin and Jesus Christ. Said to be the production of L. Carīnus, of the second century.

First of all we shall rehearse ...
The nativity of our Lord,
As written in the old record

Of the *Protevangelon*.
Longfellow, *The Golden Legend* (1851).

Protocol (*Mr. Peter*), the attorney in Edinburgh, employed by Mrs. Margaret Bertram, of Singleside.—Sir W. Scott, *Guy Mannering* (time, George II.).

Protosebastos (*The*), or SEBASTOCRATOR, the highest State officer in Greece.—Sir W. Scott, *Count Robert of Paris* (time, Rufus).

Protospathaire (*The*), or general of Alexius Comnēnus, emperor of Greece. His name is Nicanor.—Sir W. Scott, *Count Robert of Paris* (time, Rufus).

Proud (*The*). Tarquin II. of Rome, was called *Superbus* (reigned B.C. 535-510, died 496).

Otho IV., kaiser of Germany, was called "The Proud" (1175, 1209-1218).

Proud Duke (*The*), Charles Seymour, duke of Somerset. His children were not allowed to sit in his presence; and he spoke to his servants by signs only (*-1748).

Proudfute (*Oliver*), the boasting bonnet-maker at Perth.

Magdalen or *Maudie Proudfute*, Oliver's widow.—Sir W. Scott, *Fair Maid of Perth* (time, Henry IV.).

Proudie (*Dr.*), hen-pecked bishop of Barchester. A martinet in his diocese, a serf in his home.

Proudie (*Mrs.*), strong-willed, strong-voiced help-mate of the bishop. She lays down social, moral, religious and ecclesiastical laws with equal readiness and severity.—Anthony Trollope, *Framley Parsonage* and *Barchester Towers*.

Prout (*Father*), the pseudonym of Francis Mahoney, a humorous writer in *Fraser's Magazine*, etc. (1805-1866).

Provis, the name assumed by Abel Magwitch, Pip's benefactor. He was a convict, who had made a fortune, and whose chief desire was to make his protégé a gentleman.—C. Dickens, *Great Expectations* (1860).

Provoked Husband (*The*), a comedy by Cibber and Vanbrugh. The "provoked husband" is Lord Townly, justly annoyed at the conduct of his young wife, who wholly neglects her husband and her home duties for a life of gambling and dissipation. The husband seeing no hope of amendment, resolves on a separate maintenance; but then the lady's eyes are opened—she promises amendment, and is forgiven.

*** This comedy was Vanbrugh's *Journey to London*, left unfinished at his death. Cibber took it, completed it, and brought it out under the title of *The Provoked Husband* (1728).

Provoked Wife (*The*), Lady Brute, the wife of Sir John Brute, is, by his ill manners, brutality, and neglect, "provoked" to intrigue with one Constant. The intrigue is not of a very serious nature, since it is always interrupted before it makes head. At the conclusion, Sir John says:

Surly, I may be stubborn, I am not,
For I have both forgiven and forgot.
Sir J. Vanbrugh (1697).

Provost of Bruges (*The*), a tragedy based on "The Serf," in Leitch Ritchie's *Romance of History*. Published anonymously in 1836; the author is S. Knowles. The plot is this: Charles "the Good," earl of Flanders, made a law that a serf is always a serf till manumitted, and whoever marries a serf, becomes thereby a serf. Thus, if a prince married the daughter of a serf, the prince becomes a serf himself, and all his children were serfs. Bertulphe, the richest, wisest, and bravest man in Flanders, was provost of Bruges. His beautiful daughter, Constance, married Sir Bouchard, a knight of noble descent; but Bertulphe's father had been Thancmar's serf, and, according to the new law, Bertulphe, the provost, his daughter, Constance, and the knightly son-in-law were all the serfs of Thancmar. The provost killed the earl, and stabbed himself; Bouchard and Thancmar killed each other in fight; and Constance died demented.

Prowler (*Hugh*), any vagrant or highwayman.

For fear of Hugh Prowler, get home with the rest.
T. Tusser, *Five Hundred Points of Good Husbandry*, xxxiii. 25 (1557).

Prudence (*Mistress*), the lady attendant on Violet, ward of Lady Arundel. When Norman, "the sea-captain," made love to Violet, Mistress Prudence remonstrated, "What will the countess say if I allow myself to see a stranger speaking to her ward?" Norman clapped a guinea on her left eye, and asked, "What see you now?" "Why, nothing with my left eye," she answered, "but the right has still a morbid sensibility." "Poor thing!" said Norman; "this golden ointment soon will cure it. What see you now, my Prudence?" "Not a soul," she said.—Lord Lytton, *The Sea-Captain* (1839).

Prudhomme (*Joseph*), "pupil of Brard and Saint-Omer," caligraphist and sworn expert in the courts of law. Joseph Prudhomme is the synthesis of bourgeois imbecility; radiant, serene, and self-satisfied; letting fall from his fat lips "one weak, washy, everlasting flood" of puerile aphorisms and inane circumlocutions. He says, "The car of the state floats on a precipice." "This sword is the proudest day of my life."—Henri Monnier, *Grandeur et Décadence de Joseph Prudhomme* (1852).

Pruddoterie (*Madame de la*). Character in comedy of *George Dandin*, by Molière.

Prue (*Miss*), a schoolgirl still under the charge of a nurse, very precocious and very injudiciously brought up. Miss Prue is the daughter of Mr. Foresight, a mad astrologer, and Mrs. Foresight, a frail nonentity.—Congreve, *Love for Love* (1695).

Prue. Wife of "I"; a dreamer. "Prue makes everything think well, even to making the neighbors speak well of her."

Of himself Prue's husband says:

"How queer that a man who owns castles in Spain should be deputy bookkeeper at $900 per annum!"—George William Curtis, *Prue and I* (1856).

Prunes and Prisms, the words which give the lips the right plie of the highly aristocratic mouth, as Mrs. General tells Amy Dorrit.

"'Papa' gives a pretty form to the lips. 'Papa,' 'potatoes,' 'poultry,' 'prunes and prisms.' You will find it serviceable if you say to yourself on entering a room, 'Papa, potatoes, poultry, prunes and prisms.'"—C. Dickens, *Little Dorrit* (1855).

General Burgoyne, in *The Heiress*, makes Lady Emily tell Miss Alscrip that the magic words are "nimini pimini;" and that if she will stand before her mirror and pronounce these words repeatedly, she cannot fail to give her lips that happy plie which is known as the "Paphian mimp."—*The Heiress*, iii. 2 (1781).

Pru′sio, king of Alvarecchia, slain by Zerbi′no.—Ariosto, *Orlando Furioso* (1516).

Pry (*Paul*), one of those idle, meddling fellows, who, having no employment of their own, are perpetually interfering in the affairs of other people.—John Poole, *Paul Pry*.

Prydwen or PRIDWIN (*q.v.*), called in the *Mabinogion*, the ship of King Arthur. It was also the name of his shield. Taliessin speaks of it as a ship, and Robert of Gloucester as a shield.

Hys sseld that het Prydwen.
Myd ye suerd he was ygurd, that so strong was and kene;
Calybourne yt was ycluped, nas nour no such ye wene.
In ys right hond ys lance he nom, that ycluped was Ron.
I. 174.

Prynne (*Hester*). Handsome, haughty gentlewoman of English birth, married to a deformed scholar, whom she does not love. She comes alone to Boston, meets Arthur Dimmesdale, a young clergyman, and becomes his wife in all except in name. When her child is born she is condemned to stand in the pillory, holding it in her arms, to be reprimanded by officials, civic and clerical, and to wear, henceforward, upon her breast, the letter "A" in scarlet.

Her fate is more enviable than that of her undiscovered lover, whose vacillations of dread and despair and determination to reveal all but move Hester to deeper pity and stronger love. She is beside him when he dies in the effort to bare his bosom and show the cancerous *Scarlet Letter* that has grown into his flesh while she wore hers outwardly.—Nathaniel Hawthorne, *The Scarlet Letter* (1850).

Psalmist (*The*). King David is called "The Sweet Psalmist of Israel" (2 *Sam.* xxiii. 1). In the compilation called *Psalms*, in the Old Testament, seventy-three bear the name of David, twelve were composed by Asaph, eleven by the sons of Korah, and one (*Psalm* xc.) by Moses.

Psycarpax (*i. e. "granary-thief"*), son of Troxartas, king of the mice. The frog king offered to carry the young Psycarpax over a lake; but a water-hydra made its appearance, and the frog-king, to save himself, dived under water, whereby the mouse prince lost his life. This catastrophe brought about the fatal *Battle of the Frogs and Mice*. Translated from the Greek into English verse by Parnell (1679-1717).

Psyche [*Si´.ke*], a most beautiful maiden, with whom Cupid fell in love. The god told her she was never to seek to know who he was; but Psychê could not resist the curiosity of looking at him as he lay sleep. A drop of the hot oil from Psychê's lamp falling on the love-god, woke him, and he instantly took to flight. Psychê now wandered from place to place, persecuted by Venus; but after enduring ineffable troubles, Cupid came at last to her rescue, married her, and bestowed on her immortality.

This exquisite allegory is from the *Golden Ass* of Apulēios. Lafontaine has turned it into French verse. M. Laprade (born 1812) has rendered it into French most exquisitely. The English version, by Mrs. Tighe, in six cantos, is simply unreadable.

Pternog´lyphus (*"bacon-scooper"*), one of the mouse chieftains.—Parnell, *Battle of the Frogs and Mice*, iii. (about 1712).

Pternoph´agus (*"bacon-eater"*), one of the mouse chieftains.

But dire Pternophagus divides his way
Thro' breaking ranks, and leads the dreadful day.
No nibbling prince excelled in fierceness more,—
His parents fed him on the savage boar.
Parnell, *Battle of the Frogs and Mice*, iii. (about 1712).

Pternotractas (*"bacon-gnawer"*), father of "the meal-licker," Lycomĭlê (wife of Troxartas, "the bread-eater"). Psycarpas, the king of the mice, was son of Lycomĭlê, and grandson of Pternotractas.—Parnell, *Battle of the Frogs and Mice*, i. (about 1712).

Public Good (*The League of the*), a league between the dukes of Burgundy, Brittany, and other French princes against Louis XI.

Public′ola, of the *Despatch Newspaper*, was the *nom de plume* of Mr. Williams, a vigorous political writer.

Publius, the surviving son of Horatius after the combat between the three Horatian brothers against the three Curiatii of Alba. He entertained the Roman notion that "a patriot's soul can feel no ties but duty, and know no voice of kindred" if it conflicts with his country's weal. His sister was engaged to Caius Curiatius, one of the three Alban champions; and when she reproved him for "murdering" her betrothed, he slew her, for he loved Rome more than he loved friend, sister, brother, or the sacred name of father.—Whitehead, *The Roman Father* (1714).

Pucel. *La bel Pucel* lived in the tower of "Musyke." Graunde Amoure, sent thither by Fame to be instructed by the seven ladies of science, fell in love with her, and ultimately married her. After his death, Remembrance wrote his "epitaphy on his graue."—S. Hawes, *The Passe-tyme of Pleasure* (1506, printed 1515).

Pucelle (*La*), a surname given to Joan of Arc, the "Maid of Orleans" (1410-1431).

Puck, generally called Hobgoblin. Same as Robin Goodfellow. Shakespeare, in *Midsummer Night's Dream*, represents him as "a very Shetlander among the gossamer-winged, dainty-limbed fairies, strong enough to knock all their heads together, a rough, knurly-limbed, fawn-faced, shock-pated, mischievous little urchin."

He [*Oberon*] meeteth Puck, which most men call
Hobgoblin, and on him doth fall,
With words from phrenzy spoken.
"Hoh! hoh!" quoth Hob; "God save your grace...."
Drayton, *Nymphidia* (1593).

Pudding (*Jack*), a gormandizing clown. In French he is called *Jean Potage*; in Dutch, *Pickle-Herringe*; in Italian, *Macarōni*; in German, *John Sausage* (Hanswurst).

Puff, servant of Captain Loveit, and husband of Tag, of whom he stands in awe.—D. Garrick, *Miss in Her Teens* (1753).

Puff (*Mr.*), a man who had tried his hand on everything to get a living, and at last resorts to criticism. He says of himself, "I am a practitioner in panegyric, or to speak more plainly, a professor of the art of puffing."

"I open," says Puff, "with a clock striking, to beget an awful attention in the audience; it also marks the time, which is four o'clock in the morning, and saves a description of the rising sun, and a great deal about gilding the eastern hemisphere."—Sheridan, *The Critic*, i. 1 (1779).

"God forbid," says Mr. Puff, "that in a free country, all the fine words in the language should be engrossed by the highest characters of the piece."—Sir W. Scott, *The Drama*.

Puff, publisher. He says:

"Panegyric and praise! and what will that do with the public? Why, who will give money to be told that Mr. Such-a-one is a wiser and better man than himself? No, no! 'tis quite, and clean out of nature. A good, sousing satire, now, well powdered with personal pepper, and seasoned with the spirit of party, that demolishes a conspicuous character, and sinks him below our own level—there, there, we are pleased; there we chuckle and grin, and toss the half-crowns on the counter."—Foote, *The Patron* (1764).

Pug, a mischievous little goblin, called "Puck" by Shakespeare.—B. Jonson, *The Devil is an Ass* (1616).

Puggie-Orrock, a sheriff's officer at Fairport.—Sir W. Scott, *The Antiquary* (time, George III.).

Pul'ci (*L.*), poet of Florence (1432-1487), author of the heroï-comic poem called *Morganté Maggioré*, a mixture of the bizarre, the serious, and the comic, in ridicule of the romances of chivalry. This *Don Juan* class of poetry has since been called *Bernesque*, from Francesco Berni, of Tuscany, who greatly excelled in it.

Pulci was sire of the half-serious rhyme,
Who sang when chivalry was more quixotic,
And revelled in the fancies of the time,
True knights, chaste dames, huge giants, kings despotic.
Byron, *Don Juan*, iv. 6 (1820).

Pulia'no, leader of the Nasamo'ni. He was slain by Rinaldo.—Ariosto, *Orlando Furioso* (1516).

Pumblechook, uncle to Joe Gargery, the blacksmith. He was a well-to-do corn-chandler, and drove his own chaise-cart. A hard-breathing, middle-aged, slow man was uncle Pumblechook, with fishy eyes and sandy hair, inquisitively on end. He called Pip, in his facetious way, "six-pen'orth of h'pence;" but when Pip came into his fortune, Mr. Pumblechook was the most servile of the servile, and ended every sentence with, "May I, Mr. Pip?" *i.e.*, have the honor of shaking hands with you again.—C. Dickens, *Great Expectations* (1860).

Pumpernickel (*His Transparency*), a nickname by which the *Times* satirized the minor German princes.

Some ninety men and ten drummers constitute their whole embattled host on the parade-ground before their palace; and their whole revenue is supplied by a percentage on the tax levied on strangers at the Pumpernickel kursaal.—*Times*, July 18, 1866.

Pumpkin (*Sir Gilbert*), a country gentleman plagued with a ward (Miss Kitty Sprightly) and a set of servants all stage mad. He entertains Captain Charles Stanley, and Captain Harry Stukely at Strawberry Hall, when the former, under cover of acting, makes love to Kitty (an heiress), elopes with her, and marries her.

Miss Bridget Pumpkin, sister of Sir Gilbert, of Strawberry Hall. A Mrs. Malaprop. She says, "The Greeks, the Romans, and the Irish are barbarian nations who had plays;" but Sir Gilbert says, "they were all Jacobites." She speaks of "taking a degree at our principal adversity;" asks "if the Muses are a family living at Oxford," if so, she tells Captain Stukely, she will be delighted to "see them at Strawberry Hall, with any other of his friends." Miss Pumpkin hates "play acting," but does not object to love-making.—Jackman, *All the World's a Stage*.

Punch, derived from the Latin *Mimi*, through the Italian *Pullicenella*. It was originally intended as a characteristic representation. The tale is this: Punch, in a fit of jealousy, strangles his infant child, when Judy flies to her revenge. With a bludgeon she belabors her husband, till he becomes so exasperated that he snatches the bludgeon from her, knocks her brains out, and flings the dead body into the street. Here it attracts the notice of a police officer, who enters the house, and Punch flies to save his life. He is, however, arrested by an officer of the Inquisition, and is shut up in prison, from which he escapes by a golden key. The rest of the allegory shows the triumph of Punch over slander, in the shape of a dog, disease in the guise of a doctor death, and the devil.

Pantalone was a Venetian merchant; *Dottore* a Bolognese physician; *Spaviento* a Neapolitan braggadocio; *Pullicinella* a wag of Apulia; *Giangurgolo* and *Coviello* two clowns of Calabria; *Gelsomino* a Roman beau; *Beltrame* a Milanese simpleton; *Brighella* a Ferrarese pimp; and *Arlecchino* a blundering servant of Bergamo. Each was clad in an appropriate dress, had a characteristic mask, and spoke the dialect of the place he represented.

Besides these there were *Amorosos* or *Innamoratos*, with their servettas, or waiting-maids, as *Smeraldina*, *Columbina*, *Spilletta*, etc., who spoke Tuscan.—Walker, *On the Revival of the Drama in Italy*, 249.

Punch, the periodical. The first cover was designed by A. S. Henning; the present one by R. Doyle.

Pure (*Simon*), a Pennsylvanian Quaker. Being about to visit London to attend the quarterly meeting of his sect he brings with him a letter of introduction to Obadiah Prim, a rigid, stern Quaker, and the guardian of Anne Lovely, an heiress worth £30,000. Colonel Feignwell, availing himself of this letter of introduction, passes himself off as Simon Pure, and gets established as the accepted suitor of the heiress. Presently the real Simon Pure makes his appearance, and is treated as an impostor and swindler. The colonel hastens on the marriage arrangements, and has no sooner completed them than Master Simon re-appears, with witnesses to prove his identity; but it is too late, and Colonel Feignwell freely acknowledges the "bold stroke he has made for a wife."—Mrs. Centlivre, *A Bold Stroke for a Wife* (1717).

Purefoy (*Master*), former tutor of Dr. Anthony Rochecliffe, the plotting royalist.—Sir W. Scott, *Woodstock* (time, Commonwealth).

Purgatory, by Dantê, in thirty-three cantos (1308). Having emerged from Hell, Dantê saw in the southern hemisphere four stars, "ne'er seen before, save by our first parents." The stars were symbolical of the four cardinal virtues (prudence, justice, fortitude and temperance). Turning round, he observed old Cato, who said that a dame from Heaven had sent him to prepare the Tuscan poet for passing through Purgatory. Accordingly, with a slender reed, old Cato girded him, and from his face he washed "all sordid stain," restoring to his face "that hue which the dun shades of Hell had covered and concealed" (canto i.). Dantê then followed his guide, Virgil, to a huge mountain in mid-ocean antipodal to Judea, and began the ascent. A party of spirits were ferried over at the same time by an angel, amongst whom was Casella, a musician, one of Dantê's friends. The mountain, he tells us, is divided into terraces, and terminates in Earthly Paradise, which is separated from it by two rivers—Lethê and Eu′noe (3 *syl.*). The first eight cantos are occupied by the ascent, and then they come to the gate of Purgatory. This gate is approached by three stairs (faith, penitence and piety); the first stair is transparent white marble, as clear as crystal; the second is black and cracked; and the third is of blood-red porphyry (canto ix.). The porter marked on Dantê's forehead seven P's (*peccata*, "sins"), and told him he would lose one at every stage, till he reached the river which divided Purgatory from Paradise. Virgil continued his guide till they came to Lethê, when he left him during sleep (canto xxx.). Dantê was then dragged through the river Lethê, drank of the waters of Eunŏe, and met Beatrice, who conducted him till he arrived at the "sphere of unbodied light," when she resigned her office to St. Bernard.

Purgon, one of the doctors in Molière's comedy of *Le Malade Imaginaire*. When the patient's brother interfered, and sent the apothecary away with his clysters, Dr. Purgon got into a towering rage, and threatened to leave the house and never more visit it. He then said to the patient "Que vous tombiez dans la bradypepsie ... de la bradypepsie dans la dyspepsie ... de la dyspepsie dans l'apepsie ... de l'apepsie dans la lienterie ... de la lienterie dans la dyssenterie ... de la dyssenterie dans l'hydropisie ... et de l'hydropisie dans la privation de la vie."

Purita´ni (*I*), "the puritans," that is Elvi´ra, daughter of Lord Walton, also a puritan, affianced to Ar´turo (*Lord Arthur Talbot*) a cavalier. On the day of espousals, Arturo aids Enrichetta (*Henrietta, widow of Charles I.*), to escape; and Elvira, supposing that he is eloping, loses her reason. On his return, Arturo explains the facts to Elvira, and they vow nothing on earth shall part them more, when Arturo is arrested for treason, and led off to execution. At this crisis, a herald announces the defeat of the Stuarts, and Cromwell pardons all political offenders, whereupon Arturo is released, and marries Elvira.— Bellini's opera, *I Puritani* (1834).

Purley (*Diversions of*), a work on the analysis and etymology of English words, so called from Purley, where it was written by John Horne. In 1782 he assumed the name of Tooke, from Mr. Tooke, of Purley, in Surrey, with whom he often stayed, and who left him £8000 (vol. i, 1785; vol. ii., 1805).

Purple Island (*The*), the human body. It is the name of a poem in twelve cantos, by Phineas Fletcher (1633). Canto i. Introduction. Cantos ii.-v. An anatomical description of the human body, considered as an island kingdom. Cantos vi. The "intellectual" man. Cantos vii. The "natural man," with its affections and lusts. Canto viii. The world, the flesh, and the devil, as the enemies of man. Cantos ix., x. The friends of man who enable him to overcome these enemies. Cantos xi., xii. The battle of "Mansoul," the triumph, and the marriage of Eclecta. The whole is supposed to be sung to shepherds by Thirsil, a shepherd.

Pusil´lus, Feeble-mindedness personified in *The Purple Island*, by Phineas Fletcher (1633); "a weak, distrustful heart." Fully described in cantos viii. (Latin, *pusillus*, "pusillanimous.")

Puss-in-Boots, from Charles Perrault's tale *Le Chat Botté* (1697). Perrault borrowed the tale from the *Nights* of Straparola, an Italian. Straparola's *Nights* were translated into French in 1585, and Perrault's *Contes de Fées* were published in 1697. Ludwig Tieck, the German novelist, reproduced the same tale in his *Volksmärchen* (1795), called in German *Der Gestiefelte Kater*. The cat is marvellously accomplished, and by ready wit or ingenious tricks secures a fortune and royal wife for his master, a penniless young miller, who passes under the name of the marquis de Car´abas. In the Italian tale, puss is called "Constantine's cat."

Pwyll's Bag (*Prince*), a bag that it was impossible to fill.

Come thou in by thyself, clad in ragged garments, and holding a bag in thy hand, and ask nothing but a bagful of food, and I will cause that if all the meat and liquor that are in these seven cantreves were put into it, it would be no fuller than before.—*The Mabinogion* (Pwyll Prince of Dyved," twelfth century).

Pygma´lion, a sculptor of Cyprus. He resolved never to marry, but became enamored of his own ivory statue, which Venus endowed with life, and the sculptor married. Morris has a poem on the subject in his *Earthly Paradise* ("August"), and Gilbert a comedy.

Fell in loue with these,
As did Pygmalion with his carvèd tree.
Lord Brooke, *Treatie on Human Learning* (1554-1628).

⁎ Lord Brooke calls the statue "a carved tree." There is a vegetable ivory, no doubt, one of the palm species, and there is the *ebon tree*, the wood of which is black as jet. The former could not be known to Pygmalion, but the latter might, as Virgil speaks of it in his *Georgics*, ii. 117, "India nigrum fert ebenum." Probably Lord Brooke blundered from the resemblance between *ebor* ("ivory") and *ebon*, in Latin "ebenum."

Pygmy, a dwarf. The pygmies were a nation of dwarfs always at war with the cranes of Scythia. They were not above a foot high, and lived somewhere at the "end of the earth"—either in Thrace, Ethiopia, India, or the Upper Nile. The pygmy women were mothers at the age of three, and old women at eight. Their houses were built of egg-shells. They cut down a blade of wheat with an axe and hatchet, as we fell huge forest trees.

One day, they resolved to attack Herculês in his sleep, and went to work as in a siege. An army attacked each hand, and the archers attacked the feet. Herculês awoke, and with the paw of his lion-skin overwhelmed the whole host, and carried them captive to King Eurystheus.

Swift has availed himself of this Grecian fable in his *Gulliver's Travels* ("Lilliput," 1726).

Pyke and Pluck (*Messrs.*), the tools and toadies of Sir Mulberry Hawk. They laugh at all his jokes, snub all who attempt to rival their patron, and are ready to swear to anything Sir Mulberry wishes to have confirmed.—C. Dickens, *Nicholas Nickleby* (1838).

Pylades and Orestes, inseparable friends. Pyladês was a nephew of King Agamemnon, and Orestês was Agamemnon's son. The two cousins contracted a friendship which has become proverbial. Subsequently, Pyladês married Orestês's sister, Electra.

Lagrange-Chancel has a French drama entitled *Oreste et Pylade* (1695). Voltaire also (*Oreste*, 1750). The two characters are introduced into a host of plays, Greek, Italian, French, and English. (See ANDROMACHE.)

Pynchons (*The*). *Mr. Pynchon*, a "representative of the highest and noblest class" in the Massachusetts Colony; one of the first settlers in Agawam (Springfield, Mass.).

Mrs. Pynchon (a second wife), a woman of excellent sense, with thorough reverence for her husband.

Mary Pynchon, beautiful and winning girl, afterward wedded to Elizur Holyoke.

John Pynchon, a promising boy.—J. G. Holland, *The Bay Path* (1857).

Pyncheon (*Col.*). An old bachelor, possessed of great wealth, and of an eccentric and melancholy turn of mind, the owner and tenant of the old Pyncheon mansion. He dies suddenly, after a life of selfish devotion to his own interests, and is thus found when the house is opened in the morning.— Nathaniel Hawthorne, *The House of the Seven Gables* (1851).

Pyrac'mon, one of Vulcan's workmen in the smithy of Mount Etna. (Greek, *pûr akmôn*, "fire anvil.")

Far passing Bronteus or Pyracmon great,
The which in Lipari do day and night
Frame thunderbolts for Jove.
Spenser, *Faëry Queen*, iv. 5 (1596).

Pyramid. According to Diodo'rus Sic'ulus (*Hist.*, i.), and Pliny (*Nat. Hist.*, xxxvi. 12), there were 360,000 men employed for nearly twenty years upon one of the pyramids.

The largest pyramid was built by Cheops or Suphis, the next largest by Cephrēnês or Sen-Suphis, and the third by Menchērês, last king of the Fourth Egyptian dynasty, said to have lived before the birth of Abraham.

The Third Pyramid. Another tradition is that the third pyramid was built by Rhodŏpis or Rhodopê, the Greek courtezan. Rhodopis means the "rosy-cheeked."

The Rhodopê that built the pyramid.
Tennyson, *The Princess*, ii. (1830).

Pyr'amos (in Latin *Pyrămus*), the lover of Thisbê. Supposing Thisbê had been torn to pieces by a lion, Pyramos stabs himself in his unutterable grief "under a mulberry tree." Here Thisbê finds the dead body of her lover, and kills herself for grief on the same spot. Ever since then the juice of this fruit has been blood-stained.—*Greek Mythology*.

Shakespeare has introduced a burlesque of this pretty love story in his *Midsummer Night's Dream*, but Ovid has told the tale beautifully.

Pyrgo Polini'ces, an extravagant blusterer. (The word means "tower and town taker.")—Plautus, *Miles Gloriosus*.

If the modern reader knows nothing of Pyrgo Policinês and Thraso, Pistol and Parollês; if he is shut out from Nephelo-Coccygia, he may take refuge in Lilliput.—Macaulay.

⁂ "Thraso," a bully in Terence (*The Eunuch*); "Pistol," in the *Merry Wives of Windsor* and *2 Henry IV.*; "Parollês," in *All's Well that Ends Well*; "Nephelo-Coccygia," or cloud cuckoo-town, in Aristophanê's (*The Birds*); and "Lilliput," in Swift (*Gulliver's Travels*).

Py'rocles (3 *syl.*) and his brother, **Cy'moclês** (3 *syl.*) sons of Acratês (*incontinence*). The two brothers are about to strip Sir Guyon, when Prince Arthur comes up and slays both of them.—Spenser, *Faëry Queen*, ii. 8 (1590).

Pyroc'les and Musidorous, heroes, whose exploits are told by Sir Philip Sidney in his *Arcadia* (1581).

Pyr'rho, the founder of the sceptics or Pyrrhonian school of philosophy. He was a native of Elis, in Peloponne'sus, and died at the age of 90 (B.C. 285).

It is a pleasant voyage, perhaps, to float,
Like Pyrrho, on a sea of speculation.
Byron, *Don Juan*, ix. 18 (1824).

⁂ "Pyrrhonism" means absolute and unlimited infidelity.

Pythag'oras, the Greek philosopher, is said to have discovered the musical scale from hearing the sounds produced by a blacksmith hammering iron on his anvil.—See *Dictionary of Phrase and Fable*, 722.

As great Pythagoras of yore,
Standing beside the blacksmith's door.
And hearing the hammers, as he smote
The anvils with a different note ...
... formed the seven-chorded lyre.
Longfellow, *To a Child*.

Handel wrote an "air with variations" which he called *The Harmonious Blacksmith*, said to have been suggested by the sounds proceeding from a smithy, where he heard the village blacksmiths swinging their heavy sledges "with measured beat and slow."

Pyth´ias, a Syracusan soldier, noted for his friendship for Damon. When Damon was condemned to death by Dionysius, the new-made king of Syracuse, Pythias obtained for him a respite of six hours, to go and bid farewell to his wife and child. The condition of this respite was that Pythias should be bound, and even executed, if Damon did not return at the hour appointed. Damon returned in due time, and Dionysius was so struck with this proof of friendship, that he not only pardoned Damon, but even begged to be ranked among his friends. The day of execution was the day that Pythias was to have been married to Calanthê.—*Damon and Pythias*, a drama by R. Edwards (1571), and another by John Banim in 1825.

Python, a huge serpent engendered from the mud of the deluge, and slain by Apollo. In other words, pyto is the miasma or mist from the evaporation of the overflow, dried up by the sun. (Greek, *puthesthai*, "to rot;" because the serpent was left to rot in the sun.)

(OLD), the earl of March, afterwards duke of Queensberry, at the close of the last century and the beginning of this.

Quacks (*Noted*).

BECHIC, known for his "cough pills," consisting of *digitalis, white oxide of antimony* and *licorice*. Sometimes, but erroneously, called "Beecham's magic cough pills."

BOOKER (*John*), astrologer, etc. (1601-1667).

BOSSY (*Dr.*), a German by birth. He was well known in the beginning of the nineteenth century in Covent Garden, and in other parts of London.

BRODUM (eighteenth century). His "nervous cordial" consisted of *gentian root* infused in *gin*. Subsequently, a little *bark* was added.

CAGLIOSTRO, the prince of quacks. His proper name was Joseph Balsamo, and his father was Pietro Balsamo, of Palermo. He married Lorenza, the daughter of a girdle-maker of Rome, called himself the Count Alessandro di Cagliostro, and his wife the Countess Seraphina di Cagliostro. He professed to heal every disease, to abolish wrinkles, to predict future events, and was a great mesmerist. He styled himself "Grand Cophta, Prophet, and Thaumaturge." His "Egyptian pills" sold largely at 30*s.* a box (1743-1795). One of the famous novels of A. Dumas is *Joseph Balsamo* (1845).

He had a flat, snub face; dew-lapped, flat-nosed, greasy, and sensual. A forehead impudent, and two eyes which turned up most seraphically languishing. It was a model face for a quack.—Carlyle, *Life of Cagliostro*.

CASE (*Dr. John*), of Lime Regis, Dorsetshire. His name was Latinized into *Caseus*, and hence he was sometimes called Dr. Cheese. He was born in the reign of Charles II., and died in that of Anne. Dr. Case was the author of the *Angelic Guide*, a kind of *Zadkiel's Almanac*, and over his door was this couplet:

Within this place
Lives Dr. Case.

Legions of quacks shall join us in this place,
From great Kirlëus down to Dr. Case.
Garth, *Dispensary*, iii. (1699).

CLARKE, noted for his "world-famed blood-mixture" (end of the nineteenth century).

COCKLE (*James*), known for his anti-bilious pills, advertised as "the oldest patent medicine" (nineteenth century).

FRANKS (*Dr. Timothy*), who lived in Old Bailey, was the rival of Dr. Rock. Franks was a very tall man, while his rival was short and stout (1692-1763).

Dr. Franks, F.O.G.H., calls his rival "Dumplin' Dick,".... Sure the world is wide enough for two great personages. Men of science should leave controversy to the little world ... and then we might see Rock and Franks walking together, hand-in-hand, smiling, onward to immortality.—Goldsmith, *A Citizen of the World*, lxviii. (1759).

GRAHAM (*Dr.*), of the Temple of Health, first in the Adelphi, then in Pall Mall. He sold his "elixir of life" for £1000 a bottle, was noted for his mud baths, and for his "celestial bed," which assured a beautiful progeny. He died poor in 1784.

GRANT (*Dr.*), first a tinker, then a Baptist preacher in Southwark, then oculist to Queen Anne.

Her majesty sure was in a surprise,
Or else was very short-sighted,
When a tinker was sworn to look after her eyes,
And the mountebank tailor was knighted.
Grub Street Journal.

(The "mountebank tailor" was Dr. Read.)

HANCOCK (*Dr.*), whose panacea was cold water and stewed prunes.

*** Dr. Sandgrado prescribed hot water and stewed apples.—Lesage, *Gil Blas*.

Dr. Rezio, of Barataria, would allow Sancho Panza to eat only "a few wafers, and a thin slice or two of quince."—Cervantes, *Don Quixote*, II. iii. 10 (1615).

HANNES (*Dr.*), knighted by Queen Anne. He was born in Oxfordshire.

The queen, like heaven, shines equally on all,
Her favors now without distinction fall,
Great Read, and slender Hannes, both knighted, show
That none their honors shall to merit owe.
A Political Squib of the Period.

HOLLOWAY (*Professor*), noted for his ointment to cure all strumous affections, his digestive pills, and his enormous expenditure in advertising (nineteenth century). Holloway's ointment is an imitation of Albinolo's; being analyzed by order of the French law-courts, it was declared to consist of *butter*, *lard*, *wax* and *Venice turpentine*. His pills are made of *aloes*, *jalap*, *ginger* and *myrrh*.

KATERFELTO (*Dr.*), the influenza doctor. He was a tall man, dressed in a black gown and square cap, and was originally a common soldier in the Prussian service. In 1782 he exhibited in London his solar microscope, and created immense excitement by showing the infusoria of muddy water, etc. Dr. Katerfelto used to say that he was the greatest philosopher since the time of Sir Isaac Newton.

And Katerfelto, with his hair on end,
At his own wonders, wondering for his bread.
Cowper, *The Task* ("The Winter Evening," 1782).

LILLY (*William*), astrologer, born at Diseworth, in Leicestershire (1602-1681).

LONG (*St. John*), born at Newcastle, began life as an artist, but afterwards set up as a curer of consumption, rheumatism and gout. His profession brought him wealth, and he lived in Harley Street, Cavendish Square. St. John Long died himself of rapid consumption (1798-1834).

MAPP (*Mrs.*), bone-setter. She was born at Epsom, and at one time was very rich, but she died in great poverty at her lodgings in Seven Dials, 1737.

*** Hogarth has introduced her in his heraldic picture, "The Undertakers' Arms." She is the middle of the three figures at the top, and is holding a bone in her hand.

MOORE (*Mr. John*), of the Pestle and Mortar, Abchurch Lane, immortalized by his "worm-powder," and called the "Worm Doctor" (died 1733).

Vain is thy art, thy powder vain,
Since worms shall eat e'en thee.
Pope, *To Mr. John Moore* (1723).

MORISON (*Dr.*), famous for his pills (consisting of *aloes* and *cream of tartar*, equal parts). Professor Holloway, Dr. Morison, and Rowland, maker of hair-oil and tooth-powder, were the greatest advertisers of their generation.

PARTRIDGE, cobbler, astrologer, almanac-maker and quack (died 1708).

Weep, all you customers who use
His pills, his almanacs, or shoes.
Swift, *Elegy, etc.*

READ (*Sir William*), a tailor, who set up for oculist, and was knighted by Queen Anne. This quack was employed both by Queen Anne and George I. Sir William could not read. He professed to cure wens, wry-necks and hare-lips (died 1715).

... none their honors shall to merit owe—
That popish doctrine is exploded quite,
Or Ralph had been no duke, and Read no knight;
That none may virtue or their learning plead,
This hath no *grace*, and that can hardly *read*.
A Political Squib of the Period.

⁎ The "Ralph" referred to is Ralph Montagu, son of Edward Montagu, created viscount in 1682, and duke of Montagu in 1705 (died 1709).

ROCK (*Dr. Richard*), professed to cure every disease, at any stage thereof. According to his bills, "Be your disorder never so far gone, I can cure you." He was short in stature and fat, always wore a white, three-tailed wig, nicely combed and frizzed upon each cheek, carried a cane, and waddled in his gait (eighteenth century).

Dr. Rock, F.U.N., never wore a hat. He is usually drawn at the top of his own bills sitting in an armchair, holding a little bottle between his finger and thumb, and surrounded with rotten teeth, nippers, pills and gallipots.—Goldsmith, *A Citizen of the World*, lxviii. (1759).

SMITH (*Dr.*), who went about the country in the eighteenth century in his coach with four outriders. He dressed in black velvet, and cured any disease for sixpence. "His amusements on the stage were well worth the sixpence which he charged for his box of pills."

As I was sitting at the George Inn I saw a coach, with six bay horses, a calash and four, a chaise and four, enter the inn, in yellow livery turned up with red; and four gentlemen on horseback, in blue trimmed with silver. As yellow is the color given by the dukes in England, I went out to see what duke it was, but there was no coronet on the coach, only a plain coat-of-arms, with the motto ARGENTO LABORAT FABER [*Smith works for money*]. Upon inquiry I found this grand equipage belonged to a mountebank named Smith.—*A Tour through England* (1723).

SOLOMON (*Dr.*), eighteenth century. His "anti-impetigines" was simply a solution of *bichloride of mercury*, colored.

TAYLOR (*Dr. Chevalier John*). He called himself "Opthalminator, Pontificial, Imperial, and Royal." It is said that five of his horses were blind from experiments tried by him on their eyes (died 1767).

** Hogarth has introduced Dr. Taylor in his "Undertakers' Arms." He is one of the three figures at the top, to the left hand of the spectator.

UNBORN DOCTOR (*The*), of Moorfields. Not being born a doctor, he called himself "The Un-born Doctor."

WALKER (*Dr.*), one of the three great quacks of the eighteenth century, the others being Dr. Rock and Dr. Timothy Franks. Dr. Walker had an abhorrence of quacks, and was for ever cautioning the public not to trust them, but come at once to him, adding, "there is not such another medicine in the world as mine."

Not for himself but for his country he prepares his gallipot, and seals up his precious drops for any country or any town, so great is his zeal and philanthropy.—Goldsmith, *A Citizen of the World*, lxviii. (1759).

WARD (*Dr.*), a footman, famous for his "friars' balsam." He was called in to prescribe for George II., and died 1761. Dr. Ward had a claret stain on his left cheek, and in Hogarth's famous picture, "The Undertakers' Arms," the cheek is marked gules. He occupies the right hand side of the spectator, and forms one of the triumvirate, the others being Dr. Taylor and Mrs. Mapp.

Dr. Kirleüs and Dr. Tom Saffold are also known names.

Quackleben (*Dr. Quentin*), "the man of medicine," one of the committee at the Spa.—Sir W. Scott, *St. Ronan's Well* (time, George III.).

Quaint (*Timothy*), servant of Governor Heartall. Timothy is "an odd fish, that loves to swim in troubled waters." He says, "I never laugh at the governor's good humors, nor frown at his infirmities. I always keep a steady, sober phiz, fixed as the gentleman's on horseback at Charing Cross; and, in his worst of humors, when all is fire and faggots with him, if I turn round and coolly say, 'Lord, sir, has anything ruffled you?' he'll burst out into an immoderate fit of laughter, and exclaim, 'Curse that inflexible face of thine! Though you never suffer a smile to mantle on it, it is a figure of fun to the rest of the world."—Cherry, *The Soldier's Daughter* (1804).

Quaker Poet (*The*), Bernard Barton (1784-1849).

Quaker Widow. Gentle old dame who, on the afternoon of her husband's funeral, tells to a kindly visitor the simple story of her blameless life, its joys and sorrows, and of the light that comes at eventide.

"It is not right to wish for death;
The Lord disposes best.
His spirit comes to quiet hearts
And fits them for His rest.
And that He halved our little flock
Was merciful, I see;
For Benjamin has two in Heaven,
And two are left with me."
Bayard Taylor, *The Quaker Widow*.

Quale (*Mr.*), a philanthropist, noted for his bald, shining forehead. Mrs. Jellyby hopes her daughter, Caddy, will become Quale's wife.—Charles Dickens, *Bleak House* (1853).

Quarl (*Philip*), a sort of Robinson Crusoe, who had a chimpanzee for his "man Friday." The story consists of the adventures and sufferings of an English hermit named Philip Quarl (1727).

Quasimo′do, a foundling, hideously deformed, but of enormous muscular strength, adopted by Archdeacon Frollo. He is brought up in the cathedral of Notre Dame de Paris. One day, he sees Esmeralda, who had been dancing in the cathedral close, set upon by a mob as a witch, and he conceals her for a time in the church. When, at length, the beautiful gypsy girl is gibbeted, Quasimodo disappears mysteriously, but a skeleton corresponding to the deformed figure is found after a time in a hole under the gibbet.—Victor Hugo, *Notre Dame de Paris* (1831).

Quatre Filz Aymon (*Les*), the four sons of the duke of Dordona (*Dordogne*). Their names are Rinaldo, Guicciardo, Alardo, and Ricciardetto (*i.e.* Renaud, Guiscard, Alard, and Richard), and their adventures form the subject of an old French romance by Huon de Villeneuve (twelfth century).

Quaver, a singing-master, who says "if it were not for singing-masters, men and women might as well have been born dumb." He courts Lucy by promising to give her singing lessons.—Fielding, *The Virgin Unmasked*.

Queechy. Farmstead to which the Rossiters retired after the ruin of their fortunes in New York. Old-fashioned house and not productive land.—Susan Warner, *Queechy* (1852).

Queen (*The Starred Ethiop*), Cassiopēia, wife of Cepheus (2 *syl.*), king of Ethiopia. She boasted that she was fairer than the sea-nymphs, and the offended nereids complained of the insult to Neptune, who sent a sea-monster to ravage Ethiopia. At death, Cassiopeia was made a constellation of thirteen stars.

... that starred Ethiop queen that strove
To set her beauty's praise above
The sea-nymphs, and their powers offended.
Milton, *Il Penseroso*, 19 (1638).

Queen (The White), Mary queen of Scots, *La Reine Blanche*; so called by the French, because she dressed in white as mourning for her husband.

Queen Dick, Richard Cromwell (1626, 1658-1660, died 1712).

⁎⁎* *It happened in the reign of Queen Dick*, never, on the Greek kalends. This does not refer to Richard Cromwell, but to Queen "Outis." There never was a Queen Dick, except by way of joke.

Queen Sarah, Sarah Jennings, duchess of Marlborough (1660-1744).

Queen Anne only reigned while Queen Sarah governed.—*Temple Bar*, 208.

Queen Square Hermit, Jeremy Bentham, 1 Queen Square, London (1748-1832).

Queen of Hearts, Elizabeth Stuart, daughter of James I., the unfortunate queen of Bohemia (1596-1662).

Queen of Heaven, Ashtoreth ("the moon"). Horace calls the moon "the two-horned queen of the stars."

Some speak of the Virgin Mary as "the queen of heaven."

Queen of Queens. Cleopatra was so called by Mark Antony (B.C. 69-30).

Queen of Song, Angelica Catala'ni; also called "the Italian Nightingale" (1782-1849).

Queen of Sorrow, the marble tomb at Delhi called the Taj-Mahul, built by Shah Jehan for his wife, Moomtaz-i-Mahul.

Queen of Tears, Mary of Mo'dena, second wife of James II. of England (1658-1718).

Her eyes became eternal fountains of sorrow for that crown her own ill policy contributed to lose.—Noble, *Memoirs, etc.* (1784).

Queen of the East, Zenobia, queen of Palmy'ra (*, 266-273).

Queen of the South, Maqueda, or Balkis, queen of Sheba, or Saba.

The queen of the south ... came from the uttermost parts of the earth to hear the wisdom of Solomon.—*Matt.* xii. 42; see also 1 *Kings* x. 1.

⁎ According to tradition, the queen of the south had a son by Solomon, named Melech, who reigned in Ethiopia or Abyssinia, and added to his name the words Belul Gian ("precious stone"), alluding to a ring given to him by Solomon. Belul Gian translated into Latin, became *pretiosus Joannes*, which got corrupted into Prester John (*presbyter Johannes*), and has given rise to the fables of this "mythical king of Ethiopia."

Queen of the Swords. Minna Troil was so called, because the gentlemen, formed into two lines, held their swords so as to form an arch or roof under which Minna led the ladies of the party.—Sir W. Scott, *The Pirate* (time, William III.).

⁎ In 1877, W. Q. Orchardson, R. A., exhibited a picture in illustration of this incident.

Queen (*My*).

But thou thyself shall not come down
From that pure region far above,
But keep thy throne and wear thy crown,
Queen of my heart and queen of love!
A monarch in thy realm complete,
And I a monarch—at thy feet!
William Winter, *Wanderers* (1889).

Queens (*Four Daughters*). Raymond Ber´enger, count of Provence, had four daughters, all of whom married kings; Margaret married Louis IX. of France; Eleanor married Henry III. of England; Sancha married Henry's brother, Richard, king of the Romans; and Beatrice married Charles I. of Naples and Sicily.

Four daughters were there born
To Raymond Ber´enger, and every one
Became a queen.
Dantê, *Paradise*, vi. (1311).

Quentin (*Black*), groom of Sir John Ramorny.—Sir W. Scott, *Fair Maid of Perth* (time, Henry IV.).

Quentin Durward, a novel by Sir W. Scott (1823). A story of French history. The delineations of Louis XI., and Charles the Bold, of Burgundy, will stand comparison with any in the whole range of fiction or history.

Quern-Biter, the sword of Haco I. of Norway.

Quern-biter of Hacon the Good
Wherewith at a stroke he hewed

The millstone thro' and thro'.
Longfellow.

Querno (*Camillo*), of Apulia, was introduced to Pope Leo X., as a buffoon, but was promoted to the laurel. This laureate was called the "Antichrist of Wit."

Rome in her capitol saw Querno sit,
Throned on seven hills, the antichrist of wit.
Pope, *The Dunciad*, ii. (1728).

Querpo (*Shrill*), in Garth's *Dispensary*, is meant for Dr. Howe.

To this design shrill Querpo did agree,
A zealous member of the faculty,
His sire's pretended pious steps he treads,
And where the doctor fails, the saint succeeds.
Dispensary, iv. (1699).

Questing Beast (*The*), a monster called Glatisaunt, that made a noise called questing, "like thirty couple of hounds giving quest" or cry. King Pellinore (3 *syl.*) followed the beast for twelve months (pt. i. 17), and after his death Sir Palomidês gave it chase.

The questing beast had in shape and head like a serpent's head, and a body like a libard, buttocks like a lion, and footed like a hart; and in his body there was such a noise as it had been the noise of thirty couple of hounds questing, and such a noise that beast made wheresoever he went; and this beast evermore Sir Palomides followed.—Sir T. Malory, *History of Prince Arthur*, i. 17; ii. 53 (1470).

Quiara and Mon′nema, man and wife, the only persons who escaped the ravages of the small-pox plague which carried off all the rest of the Guara′ni race, in Paraguay. They left the fatal spot, settled in the Mondai woods, had one son, Yerūti, and one daughter, Mooma; but Quiāra was killed by a jagŭar before the latter was born.—Southey, *A Tale of Paraguay* (1814). (See MONNEMA and MOOMA.)

Quick (*Abel*), clerk to Surplus, the lawyer.—J. M. Morton, *A Regular Fix*.

Quick (*John*), called "The Retired Diocletian of Islington" (1748-1831).

Little Quick, the retired Diocletian of Islington, with his squeak like a Bart'lemew fiddle.—Charles Mathews.

Quickly (*Mistress*), servant-of-all-work, to Dr. Caius, a French physician. She says, "I wash, wring, brew, bake, scour, dress meat and drink, make the beds, and do all myself." She is the go-between of three suitors for "sweet Anne Page," and with perfect disinterestedness wishes all three to succeed, and does her best to forward the suit of all three, "but speciously of Master Fenton."—Shakespeare, *Merry Wives of Windsor* (1601).

Quickly (*Mistress Nell*), a hostess of a tavern in East-cheap, frequented by Harry, prince of Wales, Sir John Falstaff, and all their disreputable crew. In *Henry V*. Mistress Quickly is represented as having married Pistol, the "lieutenant of Captain Sir John's army." All three die before the end of the play. Her description of Sir John Falstaff's death (*Henry V*. act ii. sc. 3) is very graphic and true to nature. In 2 *Henry IV*. Mistress Quickly arrests Sir John for debt, but immediately she hears of his commission is quite willing to dismiss the bailiffs, and trust "the honey sweet" old knight again to any amount.—Shakespeare, 1 and 2 *Henry IV*. and *Henry V*.

Quid (*Mr.*), the tobacconist, a relative of Mrs. Margaret Bertram.—Sir W. Scott, *Guy Mannering* (time, George II.).

Quid Rides, the motto of Jacob Brandon, tobacco-broker, who lived at the close of the eighteenth century. It was suggested by Harry Calendon of Lloyd's coffee-house.

*** *Quid Ridês* (Latin) means "Why do you laugh?" *Quid rides*, *i.e.* "the tobacconist rides."

Quidnunc (*Abraham*), of St. Martin's-in-the-Fields, an upholsterer by trade, but bankrupt. His head "runs only on schemes for paying off the National Debt, the balance of power, the affairs of Europe, and the political news of the day."

*** The prototype of this town politician was the father of Dr. Arne (see *The Tatler*, No. 155).

Harriet Quidnunc, his daughter, rescued by Belmour from the flames of a burning house, and adored by him.

John Quidnunc, under the assumed name of Rovewell, having married a rich planter's widow, returns to England, pays his father's debts, and gives his sister to Mr. Belmour for wife.—Murphy, *The Upholsterer* (1758).

Quidnuncs, a name given to the ancient members of certain political clubs, who were constantly inquiring, "Quidnunc? What news?"

This the Great Mother dearer held than all
The clubs of Quidnuncs, or her own Guildhall.
Pope, *The Dunciad*, i. 269 (1728).

Quidnunkis, a monkey which climbed higher than its neighbors, and fell into a river. For a few moments the monkey-race stood panic-struck, but the stream flowed on, and in a minute or two the monkeys continued their gambols as if nothing had happened.—Gay, *The Quidnunkis* (a fable, 1726).

Quildrive (2 *syl.*), clerk to old Philpot "the citizen."—Murphy, *The Citizen* (1761).

Quilp (*Daniel*), a hideous dwarf, cunning, malicious, and a perfect master in tormenting. Of hard, forbidding features, with head and face large enough for a giant. His black eyes were restless, sly, and cunning; his mouth and chin bristly with a coarse, hard beard; his face never clean, but always distorted with a ghastly grin, which showed the few discolored fangs that supplied the place of teeth. His dress consisted of a large high-crowned hat, a worn-out dark suit, a pair of most capacious shoes, and a huge crumpled dirty white neck-cloth. Such hair as he had was a grizzled black, cut short but hanging about his ears in fringes. His hands were coarse and dirty; his fingernails crooked, long, and yellow. He lived on Tower Hill, collected rents, advanced money to seamen, and kept a sort of wharf, containing rusty anchors, huge iron rings, piles of rotten wood, and sheets of old copper, calling himself a ship-breaker. He was on the point of being arrested for felony, when he drowned himself.

He ate hard eggs, shell and all, for his breakfast, devoured gigantic prawns with their heads and tails on, chewed tobacco and water-cresses at the same time, drank scalding hot tea without winking, bit his fork and spoon till they bent again, and performed so many horrifying acts, that one might doubt if he were indeed human.—Ch. v.

Mrs. Quilp (*Betsy*), wife of the dwarf, a loving, young, timid, obedient, and pretty blue-eyed little woman, treated like a dog by her diabolical husband, whom she really loved but more greatly feared.—C. Dickens, *The Old Curiosity Shop* (1840).

Quinnailon (*Father*). Benevolent priest in Xerxes, a Western town. He succors the suffering of whatever creed and conditions, and shares his little all with the needy. When appointed bishop, he goes to Rome to beg for permission to decline the honor.

"I will fall at the feet of the Holy Father, and beseech him not to make a bishop out of a poor, simple old man who cannot bear so great a burden; but to let me come back and die among my dear people!"—Octave Thanet, *Quilters in the Sun* (1877).

Quinap′alus, the Mrs. Harris of "authorities in citations." If any one quotes from an hypothetical author, he gives Quinapalus as his authority.

What says Quinapalus: "Better a witty fool than a foolish wit."—Shakespeare, *Twelfth Night*, act. i. sc. 5 (1614).

Quinbus Flestrin (*the "man-mountain"*). So the Lilliputians called Gulliver (ch. ii.).—Swift, *Gulliver's Travels* ("Voyage to Lilliput," 1726).

Quince (*Peter*), a carpenter, who undertakes the management of the play called "Pyramus and Thisbê," in *Midsummer Night's Dream*. He speaks of "laughable tragedy," "lamentable comedy," "tragical mirth," and so on.—Shakespeare, *Midsummer Night's Dream* (1592).

Quino'nes (*Suero de*), in the reign of Juan II. He, with nine other cavaliers, held the bridge of Orbigo against all comers for thirty-six days, and in that time they overthrew seventy-eight knights of Spain and France.

Quintano'na, the duenna of Queen Guinever or Ginebra.—Cervantes, *Don Quixote*, II. ii. 6 (1615).

Quintessence (*Queen*), sovereign of Entélèchie, the country of speculative science visited by Pantag'ruel and his companions in their search for "the oracle of the Holy Bottle."—Rabelais, *Pantagruel*, v. 19 (1545).

Quin'tiquinies'tra (*Queen*), a much-dreaded, fighting giantess. It was one of the romances of Don Quixote's library condemned by the priest and barber of the village to be burnt.—Cervantes, *Don Quixote*, I. (1605).

Quintus Fixlein [*Fix.line*], the title and chief character of a romance by Jean Paul Friedrich Richter (1796).

Francia, like Quintus Fixlein, had perennial fireproof joys, namely, employments.—Carlyle.

Quiri'nus, Mars.

Now, by our sire Quirīnus,
It was a goodly sight
To see the thirty standards
Swept down the stream of flight.
Lord Macaulay, *Lays of Ancient Rome* ("Battle of the Lake Regillus," xxxvi., 1842).

Quitam (*Mr.*), the lawyer at the Black Bear inn at Darlington.—Sir W. Scott, *Rob Roy* (time, George I.).

∗∗* The first two words in an action on a penal statute are *Qui tam*. Thus, *Qui tam pro domina regina, quam pro seipso, sequitur*.

Quixa'da (*Gutierrè*), lord of Villagarcia. Don Quixote calls himself a descendant of this brave knight.—Cervantes, *Don Quixote*, I. (1605).

Quixote (*Don*), a gaunt country gentleman of La Mancha, about 50 years of age, gentle, and dignified, learned and high-minded; with strong imagination perverted by romance, and crazed with ideas of chivalry. He is the hero of a

Spanish romance by Cervantes. Don Quixote feels himself called on to become a knight-errant to defend the oppressed, and succor the injured. He engages for his squire Sancho Panza, a middle-aged, ignorant rustic, selfish, but full of good sense, a gourmand, attached to his master, shrewd and credulous. The knight goes forth on his adventures, thinks *wind-mills* to be giants, *flocks of sheep* to be armies, *inns* to be castles, and *galley-slaves* oppressed gentlemen; but the squire sees them in their true light. Ultimately, the knight is restored to his right mind, and dies like a peaceful Christian. The object of this romance was to laugh down the romances of chivalry of the Middle Ages.

(Quixote means "armor for the thighs," but Quixada means "lantern jaws." Don Quixote's favorite author was Feliciano de Sylva; his model knight was Am´adis de Gaul. The romance is in two parts, of four books each. Pt. I. was published in 1605, and pt. II. in 1615.)

The prototype of the knight was the duke of Lerma.

Don Quixote is a tall, meagre, lantern-jawed, hawk-nosed, long-limbed, grizzle-haired man, with a pair of large black whiskers, and he styles himself "The Knight of the Woeful Countenance."—Cervantes, *Don Quixote*, II. i. 14 (1615).

Don Quixote's Horse, Rosinantê (4 *syl.*), all skin and bone.

Quixote (The Female), or *Adventures of Arabella*, a novel by Mrs. Lennox (1752).

Quixote of the North (*The*), Charles XII. of Sweden; sometimes called "The Madman" (1682, 1697-1718).

Quodling (*The Rev. Mr.*), chaplain to the duke of Buckingham.—Sir W. Scott, *Peveril of the Peak* (time, Charles II.).

Quos Ego—, a threat intended but withheld; a sentence broken off. Eŏlus, angry with the winds and storms which had thrown the sea into commotion without his sanction, was going to say he would punish them severely for this act of insubordination; but having uttered the first two words, "Whom I——," he says no more, but proceeds to the business in hand.—Virgil, *Æneid*, i.

"Next Monday," said he, "you will be a 'substance,' and then——;" with which *quos ego* he went to the next boy.—Dasent, *Half a Life* (1850).

Quo´tem (*Caleb*), a parish clerk or Jack-of-all-trades.—G. Colman, *The Review, or The Ways of Windsor*.

I resolved like Caleb Quotem, to have a place at the review.—Washington Irving.

NEITHER Demosthĕnês nor Aristotle could pronounce the letter *r*.

R (*rogue*), vagabonds, etc., who were branded on the left shoulder with this letter.

They ... may be burned with a hot burning iron, of the breadth of a shilling, with a great Roman R on the left shoulder, which letter shall remain as a mark of a rogue.—Pyrnne, *Histriomastix*, or *The Player's Scourge*.

If I escape the halter with the letter R
Printed upon it.
Massinger, *A New Way to Pay Old Debts*, iv. 2 (1629).

Rab′agas, an advocate and editor of a journal called the *Carmagnole*. At the same office was published another radical paper, called the *Crapaud Volant*. Rabagas lived in the kingdom of Monaco, and was a demagogue leader of the deepest red; but was won over to the king's party by the tact of an American lady, who got him an invitation to dine at the palace, and made him chief minister of state. From this moment he became the most strenuous opponent of the "liberal" party.—M. Sardou, *Rabagas* (1872).

Rabbi Jehosha, wise teacher, whose good words are recorded in James Russell Lowell's poem "*What Rabbi Jehosha Said.*"

Rabbi Abron of Trent, a fictitious sage, and most wonderful linguist. "He knew the nature of all manner of herbs, beasts and minerals."—*Reynard the Fox*, xii. (1498).

Rabelais (*The English*). Dean Swift was so called by Voltaire (1667-1745).

Sterne (1713-1768) and Thomas Amory (1699-1788) have also been so called.

Rabelais (*The Modern*), William Maginn (1794-1842).

Rabelais of Germany, J. Fischart, called "Mentzer" (1550-1614).

Rabelais's Poison. Rabelais, being at a great distance from Paris, and without money to pay his hotel bill or his fare, made up three small packets of brick-dust. One he labelled "Poison for the king," another, "Poison for monsieur," and the third, "Poison for the dauphin." The landlord instantly informed against this "poisoner," and the secretary of state removed him at once to Paris. When, however, the joke was found out, it ended only in a laugh.—*Spectator* ("Art of Growing Rich").

Rab′ican or **Rabica′no**, the horse of Astolpho. Its sire was Wind and its dam Fire. It fed on human food. The word means "short tail."—Ariosto, *Orlando Furioso* (1516).

⁎ Argalia's horse is called by the same name in *Orlando Innamorato* (1495).

Rabisson, a vagabond tinker and knife-grinder. He was the only person who knew about "the gold-mine" left to the "miller of Grenoble." Rabisson was murdered for his secret by Eusebe Noel, the schoolmaster of Bout des Monde.—E. Stirling, *The Gold Mine*, or *Miller of Grenoble* (1854).

Rab´sheka (in the Bible RABSHAKEH), in the satire of *Absalom and Achitophel*, by Dryden and Tate, is meant for Sir Thomas Player (2 *Kings* xviii.).

Next him let railing Rabsheka have place—
So full of zeal, he has no need of grace.
Pt. ii. (1682).

Raby (*Aurora*), a rich young English orphan, Catholic in religion, of virgin modesty, "a rose with all its sweetest leaves yet folded." She was staying in the house of Lord and Lady Amundeville during the parliamentary vacation. Here Don Juan, "as Russian envoy," was also a guest, with several others. Aurora Raby is introduced in canto xv., and crops up here and there in the two remaining cantos; but, as the tale was never finished, it is not possible to divine what part the beautiful and innocent girl was designed by the poet to play. Probably Don Juan, having sowed his "wild oats," might become a not unfit match for the beautiful orphan.—Byron, *Don Juan* (1824).

Raby (*The Rose of*), the mother of Richard III. She was Cecily, daughter of Ralph Nevyll de Raby, first earl of Westmoreland. Her husband was Richard, duke of York, who was slain at the battle of Wakefield in 1460. She died 1495.

Rachael, a servant-girl at Lady Peveril's of the Peak.—Sir W. Scott, *Peveril of the Peak* (time, Charles II.).

Rachael (2 *syl*.), one of the "hands" in Bounderby's mill at Coketown. She loved Stephen Blackpool, and was greatly beloved by him in return; but Stephen was married to a worthless drunkard. After the death of Stephen, Rachael watched over the good-for-nothing young widow, and befriended her.—C. Dickens, *Hard Times* (1854).

Rachel Ffrench, beautiful daughter of Haworth's unworthy partner in the iron business. Haworth loves her, as does Murdoch, a young inventor who rises fast in Haworth's employ. She seems to vacillate between the two men, but really loves Murdoch, although pride will not let her avow it. When he is on the point of embarking to America, with an assured future, she confesses all, only to learn from him that "it is all over." Yet, in looking back at her "dark young face turned seaward" as his ship moves away, he mutters, "When I return it will be to you."—Frances Hodgson Burnett, *Haworth's* (1879).

Racine of Italy (*The*), Metastasio (1698-1782).

Racine of Music (*The*), Antonio Gaspare Sacchini, of Naples (1735-1786).

Racket (*Sir Charles*), a young man of fashion, who married the daughter of a wealthy London merchant. In the third week of the honeymoon Sir Charles paid his father-in-law a visit, and quarrelled with his bride about a game of whist. The lady affirmed that Sir Charles ought to have played a diamond instead of a club. Sir Charles grew furious, and resolved upon a divorce; but the quarrel was adjusted, and Sir Charles ended by saying, "You may be as wrong as you please, but I'll be cursed if I ever endeavor to set you right again."

Lady Racket, wife of Sir Charles, and elder daughter of Mr. Drugget.—Murphy, *Three Weeks after Marriage* (1776).

Racket (*Widow*), a sprightly, good-natured widow and woman of fashion.

A coquette, a wit, and a fine lady.—Mrs. Cowley, *The Belle's Stratagem*, ii. 1 (1780).

The "Widow Racket" was one of Mrs. Pope's best parts. Her usual manner of expressing piquant carelessness consisted in tossing her head from right to left, and striking the palm of one hand with the back of the other [1740-1797].—James Smith.

Rackrent (*Sir Condy*), in Miss Edgeworth's novel of *Castle Rackrent* (1802).

Raddle (*Mrs.*), keeper of the lodgings occupied by Bob Sawyer. The young medical practitioner invited Mr. Pickwick and his three friends to a convivial meeting; but the termagant Mrs. Raddle brought the meeting to an untimely end.—C. Dickens, *The Pickwick Papers* (1836).

Rad′egonde (*St.*) or ST. RADEGUND, queen of France (born 519, died 587). She was the daughter of Bertaire, king of Thuringia, and brought up a pagan. King Clotaire I. taught her the Christian religion, and married her in 538; but six years later she entered a nunnery, and lived in the greatest austerity.

There thou must walk in greatest gravity,
And seem as saintlike as St. Radegund.
Spenser, *Mother Hubbard's Tale* (1591).

Radigund or RADEGONE, the proud queen of the Amăzons. Being rejected by Bellodant "the Bold," she revenged herself by degrading all the men who fell into her power by dressing them like women, giving them woman's work to do, such as spinning, carding, sewing, etc., and feeding them on bread and water to effeminate them (canto 4). When she overthrew Sir Artegal in single combat, she imposed on him the condition of dressing in "woman's weeds," with a white apron, and to spend his time in spinning flax, instead of in deeds of arms. Radigund fell in love with the captive knight, and sent Clarinda as a go-between; but Clarinda tried to win him for herself, and told the queen he was inexorable (canto 5). At length Britomart arrived, cut off Radigund's head, and liberated the captive (canto 7).—Spenser, *Faëry Queen*, v. 4-7 (1596).

Rag and Famish (*The*), the Army and Navy Club; so christened by *Punch*. The *rag* refers to the flag, and the *famish* to the bad cuisine.

Ragged Regiment (*The*), the wan figures in Westminster Abbey, in a gallery over Islip's Chapel.

Railway King (*The*), George Hudson, of Yorkshire, chairman of the North Midland Company. In one day he cleared by speculation £100,000. It was the Rev. Sydney Smith who gave Hudson the title of "Railway king" (1800-1871).

Raine (*Old Roger*), the tapster, near the abode of Sir Geoffrey Peveril.

Dame Raine, old Roger's widow; afterwards Dame Chamberlain.—Sir W. Scott, *Peveril of the Peak* (time, Charles II.).

Rainy-Day Smith, John Thomas Smith, the antiquary (1766-1833).

Rajah of Mattan (*Borneo*), has a diamond which weighs 367 carats. The largest cut diamond in the world. It is considered to be a palladium. (See DIAMONDS.)

Rake (*Lord*), a nobleman of the old school, fond of debauch, street rows, knocking down Charlies, and seeing his guests drunk. His chief boon companions are Sir John Brute and Colonel Bully.—Vanbrugh, *The Provoked Wife* (1697).

Rakeland (*Lord*), a libertine, who makes love to married women, but takes care to keep himself free from the bonds of matrimony.—Mrs. Inchbald, *The Wedding Day* (1790).

Rak'she (2 *syl.*), a monster, which lived on serpents and dragons.

Raleigh (*Sir Walter*), introduced by Sir W. Scott in *Kenilworth*. The tradition of Sir Walter laying down his cloak on a miry spot for the queen to step on, and the queen commanding him to wear the "muddy cloak till her pleasure should be further known," is mentioned in ch. xv. (1821).

Raleigh (*Sir Walter*). Jealous of the earl of Essex, he plots with Lord Burleigh to compass his death.—Henry Jones, *The Earl of Essex* (1745).

Ralph, abbot of St. Augustine's, expended £43,000 on the repast given at his installation.

It was no unusual thing for powerful barons to provide 30,000 dishes at a wedding breakfast. The coronation dinner of Edward III., cost £40,000, equal to half a million of money now. The duke of Clarence, at his marriage, entertained 1000 guests, and furnished his table with 36 courses. Archbishop Neville had 1000 egrettes served at one banquet, and the whole species seems to have been extirpated.

After this it will be by no means difficult to understand why Apicius despaired of being able to make two ends meet, when he had reduced his enormous fortune to £80,000, and therefore hanged himself.

✱✱ After the winter of 1327 was over, the elder Spenser had left of the stores laid in by him the preceding November and salted down, "80 salted beeves, 500 bacons, and 600 muttons."

Ralph, son of Fairfield, the miller. An outlandish, ignorant booby, jealous of his sister, Patty, because she "could paint pictures and strum on the harpsicols." He was in love with Fanny, the gypsy, for which "feyther" was angry with him; but, "what argufies feyther's anger?" However, he treated Fanny like a brute, and she said of him, "He has a heart as hard as a parish officer. I don't doubt but he would stand by and see me whipped." When his sister married Lord Aimworth, Ralph said:

Captain Ralph my lord will dub me,
Soon I'll mount a huge cockade;
Mounseer shall powder, queue, and club me,—
'Gad! I'll be a roaring blade.
If Fan should offer then to snub me,
When in scarlet I'm arrayed;
Or my feyther 'temp to drub me—
Let him frown, but who's afraid?
Bickerstaff, *The Maid of the Mill* (1647).

Ralph or RALPHO, the squire of Hudibras. Fully described in bk. i. 457-644.— S. Butler, *Hudibras* (1663-78).

The prototype of "Ralph" was Isaac Robinson, a zealous butcher, in Morefields. Ralph represents the independent party, and Hudibras the Presbyterian.

✱✱ In regard to the pronunciation of this name, which, in 1878, was the subject of a long controversy in *Notes and Queries*, Butler says:

A squire he had whose name was Ralph,
That in th' adventure went his half: ...
And when we can, with metre safe,
We'll call him Ralpho, or plain Ra'ph.
Bk. 1. 456.

Ralph (*Rough*), the helper of Lance Outram, park-keeper at Sir Geoffrey Peveril's of the Peak.—Sir W. Scott, *Peveril of the Peak* (time, Charles II.).

Ralph (James), an American, who came to London and published a poem entitled *Night* (1725).

Silence, ye wolves! while Ralph to Cynthia howls,
Making night hideous; answer him ye owls.
Pope, *The Dunciad*, iii. 165 (1728).

Ralph [DE LASCOURS], captain of the *Uran´ia*, husband of Louise de Lascours. Ralph is the father of Diana and Martha, *alias* Orgari´ta. His crew having rebelled, Ralph, his wife, infant [Martha], and servant, Bar´abas, were put into a boat, and turned adrift. The boat ran on a huge iceberg, which Ralph supposed to be a small island. In time, the iceberg broke, when Ralph and his wife were drowned, but Martha and Barabas escaped. Martha was taken by an Indian tribe, who brought her up, and named her Orgarita ("withered corn"), because her skin was so white and fair.—E. Stirling, *Orphan of the Frozen Sea* (1856).

Ralph Roister Doister, by Nicholas Udall, the first English comedy, about 1534. It contains nine male and four female characters. Ralph is a vain, thoughtless, blustering fellow, who is in pursuit of a rich widow named Custance, but he is baffled in his intention.

Ramble (*Sir Robert*), a man of gallantry, treats his wife with such supreme indifference that she returns to her guardian, Lord Norland, and resumes her maiden name of Marie Wooburn. Subsequently, however, she returns to her husband.

Mrs. Ramble, wife of Sir Robert, and ward of Lord Norland.—Inchbald, *Every One Has His Fault* (1794).

Ram´iel (3 *syl.*), one of the "atheist crew" overthrown by Ab´diel. (The word means, according to Hume, "one who exalts himself against God.")—Milton, *Paradise Lost*, vi. 371 (1665).

Raminago´bris. Lafontaine, in his fables, gives this name to a cat. Rabelais, in his *Pantag´ruel*, iii. 21, satirizes under the same name Guillaume Crétin, a poet.

Rami´rez, a Spanish monk, and father confessor to Don Juan, duke of Braganza. He promised Velasquez, when he absolved the duke at bed-time, to give him a poisoned wafer prepared by the Carmelite Castruccio. This he was about to do, when he was interrupted, and the breaking out of the rebellion saved the duke from any similar attempt.—Robert Jephson, *Braganza* (1775).

Rami´ro (*King*) married Aldonza, who, being faithless, eloped with Alboa´zar, the Moorish king of Gaya. Ramiro came disguised as a traveller to Alboazar's castle, and asked a damsel for a draught of water, and when he lifted the pitcher to his mouth, he dropped in it his betrothal ring, which Aldonza saw and recognized. She told the damsel to bring the stranger to her apartment. Scarce had he arrived there when the Moorish king entered, and Ramiro hid himself in an alcove. "What would you do to Ramiro," asked Aldonza, "if you had him in your power?" "I would hew him limb from limb," said the Moor. "Then lo! Alboazar, he is now skulking in that alcove." With this, Ramiro was dragged forth, and the Moor said, "And how would you act if our lots were reversed?" Ramiro replied, "I would feast you well, send for my chief princes and counsellors, and set you before them and bid you blow your horn till you died." "Then be it so," said the Moor. But when Ramiro blew his horn, his "merry men" rushed into the castle, and the Moorish king, with Aldonza and all their children, princes, and counsellors, were put to the sword.—Southey, *Ramiro* (a ballad from the Portuguese, 1804).

Ramona, young Indian woman, who, in defiance of her duenna's fierce opposition, goes out into the wide world with gallant Alessandro. The struggles and disappointments of the wedded pair, and their oppression by Indian agents are told in Helen Hunt Jackson's novel, *Ramona*, (1884).

Ramorny (*Sir John*), a voluptuary, master of the horse to Prince Robert of Scotland.—Sir W. Scott, *Fair Maid of Perth* (time, Henry IV.).

Ramsay (*David*), the old watch-maker, near Temple Bar.

Margaret Ramsay, David's daughter. She marries Lord Nigel.—Sir W. Scott, *Fortunes of Nigel* (time, James I.).

Ramsbottom (*Mrs.*), a vile speller of the language. Theodore Hook's pseudonym in the *John Bull* newspaper, 1829.

*** Winifred Jenkins, the maid of Miss Tabitha Bramble (in Smollett's *Humphrey Clinker*, 1770), rivals Mrs. Ramsbottom in bad spelling.

Randal, the boatman at Lochleven Castle.—Sir W. Scott, *The Abbot* (time, Elizabeth).

Randolph (*Lord*), a Scotch nobleman, whose life was saved by young Norval. For this service, his lordship gave the youth a commission; but Glenalvon, the heir presumptive, hated the new favorite, and persuaded Lord Randolph that Norval was too familiar with his lady. Accordingly, Glenalvon and Lord Randolph waylaid the lad, who being attacked, slew Glenalvon in self-defence, but was himself slain by Lord Randolph. When the lad was killed, Lord Randolph learned that "Norval" was the son of Lady Randolph by Lord Douglas, her former husband. He was greatly vexed, and went to the war then raging between Scotland and Denmark, to drown his sorrow by activity and danger.

Lady Randolph, daughter of Sir Malcolm, was privately married to Lord Douglas, and when her first boy was born, she hid him in a basket, because there was a family feud between Malcolm and Douglas. Soon after this, Douglas was slain in battle, and the widow married Lord Randolph. The babe was found by old Norval, a shepherd, who brought it up as his own son. When 18 years old, the lad saved the life of Lord Randolph, and was given a commission in the army. Lady Randolph, hearing of the incident, discovered that young Norval was her own son, Douglas. Glenalvon, who hated the new favorite, persuaded Lord Randolph that the young man was too familiar with Lady Randolph, and being waylaid, a fight ensued, in which Norval slew Glenalvon, but was himself slain by Lord Randolph. Lord Randolph being informed that the young man was Lady Randolph's son, went to the wars to "drive away care;" and Lady Randolph, in her distraction, cast herself headlong from a steep precipice.—J. Home, *Douglas* (1757).

The voice of Mrs. Crawford [1734-1801], when thrown out by the vehemence of strong feeling, seemed to wither up the hearer; it was a flaming arrow, a lighting of passion. Such was the effect of her almost shriek to old Norval, "Was he alive?" It was like an electric shock, which drove the blood back to the heart, and produced a shudder of terror through the crowded theatre.—Boaden, *Life of Kemble*.

Random, a man of fortune with a scapegrace son. He is pale and puffy, with gout and a tearing cough. Random goes to France to recruit his health, and on his return to England, gets arrested for debt by mistake for his son. He raves and rages, threatens and vows vengeance, but finds his son on the point of marrying a daughter of Sir David Dunder of Dunder Hall, and forgets his evils in contemplation of this most desirable alliance.—G. Colman, *Ways and Means* (1788).

Random (Roderick), a young Scotch scapegrace, in quest of fortune. At one time he revels in prosperity, at another he is in utter destitution. Roderick is led into different countries (whose peculiarities are described), and falls into the society of wits, sharpers, courtiers, and harlots. Occasionally lavish, he is essentially mean; with a dash of humor, he is contemptibly revengeful; and, though generous minded when the whim jumps with his wishes, he is thoroughly selfish. His treatment of Strap is revolting to a generous mind. Strap lends him money in his necessity, but the heartless Roderick wastes the loan, treats Strap as a mere servant, fleeces him at dice, and cuffs him when the game is adverse.—T. Smollett, *Roderick Random* (1748).

Ranger, the madcap cousin of Clarinda, and the leading character in Hoadly's *Suspicious Husband* (1747).

Ran′tipole (3 *syl.*), a madcap. One of the nicknames given to Napoleon III. (See NAPOLEON III.)

Dick, be a little rantipolish,
Colman, *Heir-at-Law*, i. 2 (1797).

Raoul [*Rawl*], the old huntsman of Sir Raymond Berenger.—Sir W. Scott, *The Betrothed* (time, Henry II.).

Raoul di Nangis (*Sir*), the Huguenot in love with Valentina (daughter of the Comte de St. Bris, governor of the Louvre). Sir Raoul is offered the hand of Valentina in marriage, but rejects it because he fancies she is betrothed to the comte de Nevers. Nevers being slain in the Bartholomew Massacre, Raoul marries Valentina, but scarcely is the ceremony over when both are shot by the musketeers under the command of St. Bris.—Meyerbeer, *Les Huguenots* (opera, 1836).

Raphael (2 or 3 *syl.*), called by Milton, "The Sociable Spirit," and "The Affable Archangel." In the book of *Tobit* it was Raphael who travelled with Tobias into Media and back again; and it is the same angel that holds discourse with Adam through two books of *Paradise Lost*, v. and vi. (1665).

Raphael, the guardian angel of John the Beloved.

*** Longfellow calls Raphael "The Angel of the Sun," and says that he brings to man "the gift of faith."—*Golden Legend* ("Miracle-Play," iii., 1851).

Raphael (*The Flemish*), Frans Floris. His chief works are "St. Luke at His Easel," and the "Descent of the Fallen Angels," both in Antwerp Cathedral (1520-1570).

Raphael (*The French*), Eustace Lesueur (1617-1655).

Raphael of Cats (*The*), Godefroi Mind, a Swiss painter, famous for his cats (1768-1814).

Raphael of Holland (*The*), Martin van Hemskerck (1498-1574).

Raphael's Enchanter, La Fornarina, a baker's daughter. Her likeness appears in several of his paintings. (See FORNARINA.)

Rapier (*The*) was introduced by Rowland York in 1587.

He [*Rowland York*] was a Londoner, famous among the cutters in his time for bringing in a new kind of fight—to run the point of a rapier into a man's body ... before that time the use was with little bucklers, and with broadswords to strike and never thrust, and it was accounted unmanly to strike under the girdle.—Carleton, *Thankful Remembrance* (1625).

Rare Ben. Ben Jonson, the dramatist, was so called by Robert Herrick (1574-1637).

Raredrench (*Master*), apothecary.—Sir W. Scott, *Fortunes of Nigel* (time, James I.).

Rashleigh Osbaldistone, called "the scholar," an hypocritical and accomplished villain, killed by Rob Roy.—Sir W. Scott, *Rob Roy* (time, George I.).

⁎ Surely never gentleman was plagued with such a family as Sir Hildebrand Osbaldistone, of Osbaldistone Hall. (1) Percival, "the sot;" (2) Thorncliff, "the bully;" (3) John, "the gamekeeper;" (4) Richard, "the horse-jockey;" (5) Wilfred, "the fool;" (6) Rashleigh, "the scholar and knave."

Ras´selas, prince of Abyssina, fourth son of the emperor. According to the custom of the country, he was confined in a private paradise, with the rest of the royal family. This paradise was in the valley of Amhara, surrounded by high mountains. It had only one entrance, which was by a cavern under a rock concealed by woods, and closed by iron gates. He escaped with his sister, Nekayah, and Imlac, the poet, and wandered about to find out what condition or rank of life was the most happy. After careful investigation he found no lot without its drawbacks, and resolved to return to the "happy valley."—Dr. Johnson, *Rasselas* (1759).

Rats (*Devoured by*). Archbishop Hatto, Count Graaf, Bishop Widerolf of Strasburg, Bishop Adolph of Cologne, Freiherr von Güttingen were all devoured by rats. (See HATTO.)

Ratcliffe (*James*), a notorious thief.—Sir W. Scott, *Heart of Midlothian* (time, George II.).

Ratcliffe (*Mr. Hubert*), a friend of Sir Edward Mauley, "the Black Dwarf."—Sir W. Scott, *The Black Dwarf* (time, Anne).

Ratcliffe (*Mrs.*), the widow of "Don Carlos," who rescued Sheva at Cadiz from an *auto da fe*.

Charles Ratcliffe, clerk of Sir Stephen Bertram, discharged because he had a pretty sister, and Sir Stephen had a young son. Charles supported his widowed mother and his sister by his earnings. He rescued Sheva, the Jew, from a howling London mob, and was left the heir of the old man's property.

Miss [Eliza] Ratcliffe, sister of Charles, clandestinely married to Charles Bertram, and given £10,000 by the Jew to reconcile Sir Stephen Bertram to the alliance. She was handsome, virtuous and elegant, mild, modest and gentle.—Cumberland, *The Jew* (1776).

Rath´mor, chief of Clutha (*the Clyde*), and father of Calthon and Colmar. Dunthalmo, lord of Teutha, "came in his pride against him," and was overcome, whereupon his anger rose, and he went by night with his warriors and slew Rathmor in his own halls, where his feasts had so often been spread for strangers.—Ossian, *Calthon and Colmal*.

Rattlin (*Jack*), a famous naval character in Smollett's *Roderick Random*. Tom Bowling is in the same novel (1749).

Rattray (*Sir Runnion*), of Runnagullion; the duelling friend of Sir Mungo Malagrowther.—Sir W. Scott, *Fortunes of Nigel* (time, James I.).

Raucocan´ti, leader of a troupe of singers going to act in Sicily. The whole were captured by Lambro, the pirate, and sold in Turkey as slaves.

'Twould not become myself to dwell upon
My own merits, and, tho' young, I see, sir, you [*Don Juan*]
Have got a travelled air, which shews you one
To whom the opera is by no means new.
You've heard of Raucocanti—I'm that man ...
You was [*sic*] not last year at the fair of Lugo,
But next, when I'm engaged to sing there—do go.
Byron, *Don Juan*, iv. 88 (1820).

Raven (*Barnaby's*), Grip, a large bird of most impish disposition. Its usual phrases were: "I'm a devil!" "Never say die!" "Polly, put the kettle on!" He also uttered a cluck like cork-drawing, a barking like a dog, and a crowing like a cock. Barnaby Budge used to carry it about in a basket at his back. The bird drooped while it was in jail with his master, but after Barnaby's reprieve

It soon recovered its good looks, and became as glossy and sleek as ever ... but for a whole year it never indulged in any other sound than a grave and decorous croak.... One bright summer morning ... the bird advanced with fantastic steps to the door of the Maypole, and then cried "I'm a devil!" three or four times, with extraordinary rapture ... and from that time constantly practised and improved himself in the vulgar tongue.—C. Dickens, *Barnaby Rudge*, ii. (1841).

Raven (*The*), Edgar Allan Poe's poem bearing this caption is the best known of his works, and one of the most remarkable in the English language (1845).

Ravens of Owain (*The*). Owain had in his army 300 ravens, who were irresistible. It is thought that these ravens were warriors who bore this device on their shields.

A man who caused the birds to fly upon the host
Like the ravens of Owain, eager for prey.
Bleddynt Vardd, *Myvyrian Archaiology*, i. 365.

Ravens once White. One day a raven told Apollo that Coro´nis, a Thessalian nymph whom he passionately loved, was faithless. Apollo, in his rage, shot the nymph, but hated the raven, and "bade him prate in white plumes never more."—Ovid, *Metam.*, ii.

Ravenswood (*Allan, lord of*), a decayed Scotch nobleman of the royalist party.

Master Edgar Ravenswood, the son of Allan. In love with Lucy Ashton, daughter of Sir William Ashton, lord-keeper of Scotland. The lovers plight their troth at the "Mermaid's Fountain," but Lucy is compelled to marry Frank Hayston, laird of Bucklaw. The bride, in a fit of insanity, attempts to murder the bridegroom, and dies in convulsions. Bucklaw recovers, and goes abroad. Colonel Ashton appoints a hostile meeting with Edgar; but young Ravenswood, on his way to the place appointed, is lost in the quicksands of Kelpies Flow, in accordance with an ancient prophecy.—Sir W. Scott, *Bride of Lammermoor* (time, William III.).

*** In Donizetti's opera of *Lucia di Lammermoor*, Bucklaw dies of the wound inflicted by the bride, and Edgar, heart-broken, comes on the stage and kills himself.

The catastrophe in the *Bride of Lammermoor*, where [*Edgar*] Ravenswood is swallowed up by a quicksand, is singularly grand in romance, but would be inadmissible in a drama.—*Encyc. Brit.*, Art. "Romance."

Rawhead and Bloody-Bones, two bogies or bugbears, generally coupled together. In some cases the phrase is employed to designate one and the same "shadowy sprite."

Servants awe children ... by telling them of Rawhead and Bloody-bones.—Locke.

Ray. One of two brothers, divided by the civil war. Beltran is in the Southern army, Ray in the Northern. Both love the same woman whose heart is Beltran's. The brothers met in battle and Beltran falls. Ray is wounded and left for dead; recovers and makes his way homeward. There he lives—undergoing volcanic changes, now passionless lulls, and now rages and spasms of grief; "gradually out of them all he gathers his strength about him," and wins Vivia's hand.—Harriet Prescott Spofford, *Ray*.

Ray (*Will*), popular officer in a frontier brigade who steals through the deadly line of Cheyennes drawn about a handful of U. S. soldiers, and, followed by shots and yells, rides for his life and his comrades' lives to the nearest encampment of troops and brings succor to the devoted little band with the dawn of the day that, but for him, would have been the last on earth for those left behind.—Charles King, *Marion's Faith* (1886).

Rayland (*Mrs.*), the domineering lady of the *Old Manor-House*, by Charlotte Smith (1749-1806).

Mrs. Rayland is a sort of Queen Elizabeth in private life.—Sir W. Scott.

Raymond, count of Toulouse, the Nestor of the crusaders. He slays Aladine, king of Jerusalem, and plants the Christian standard on the tower of David.—Tasso, *Jerusalem Delivered*, xx. (1516).

*** Introduced by Sir W. Scott in *Count Robert of Paris*, a novel of the period of Rufus.

Raymond (Sir Charles), a country gentleman, the friend and neighbor of Sir Robert Belmont.

Colonel Raymond, son of Sir Charles, in love with Rosetta Belmont. Being diffident and modest, Rosetta delights in tormenting him, and he is jealous even of William Faddle "a fellow made up of knavery, noise and impudence."

Harriet Raymond, daughter of Sir Charles, whose mother died in giving her birth. She was committed to the care of a gouvernante, who changed her name to Fidelia, wrote to Sir Charles to say that she was dead, and sold her at the age of 12 to a villain named Villard. Charles Belmont, hearing her cries of distress, rescued her and took her home. The gouvernante at death confessed the truth, and Charles Belmont married her.—Edward Moore, *The Foundling* (1748).

Raz´eka, the giver of food, one of the four gods of the Adites (2 *syl.*).

We called on Razeka for food.
Southey, *Thalaba, the Destroyer*, i. 24 (1797).

Razor, a barber who could "think of nothing but old England." He was the friend and neighbor of Quidnunc, the upholsterer, who was equally crazy about the political state of the nation, and the affairs of Europe in general.—Murphy, *The Upholsterer* (1758).

Razor (To cut blocks with a). Oliver Goldsmith said of Edward Burke, the statesman.

Too deep for his hearers, he went on refining,
And thought of convincing, while they thought of dining:
Tho' equal to all things, to all things unfit;
Too nice for a statesman, too proud for a wit;
For a patriot too cool; for a drudge disobedient;
And too fond of the *right* to pursue the *expedient*.
In short, 'twas his fate, unemployed or in place, sir,
To eat mutton cold, and cut blocks with a razor.
Retaliation (1774.)

Read (*Sir William*), a tailor, who set up for oculist, and was knighted by Queen Anne. This quack was employed both by Queen Anne and George I.

Sir William could not read. He professed to cure wens, wry-necks, and hare-lips (died 1715).

None shall their rise to merit owe—
That popish doctrine is exploded quite,
Or Ralph had been no duke, and Read no knight.
A Political Squib of the Period.

*** The "Ralph" refered to is Ralph Montagu, created viscount in 1682, and duke of Montagu in 1705 (died 1709).

Ready-to-Halt, a pilgrim that journeyed to the Celestial City on crutches. He joined Mr. Greatheart's party, and was carried to heaven in a chariot of fire.—Bunyan, *Pilgrim's Progress*, ii. (1684).

Reason (*The goddess of*), in the French Revolution, some say, was the wife of Momoro, the printer; but Lamartine says it was Mdlle. Malliard, an actress.

Rebecca, leader of the Rebeccaïtes, a band of Welsh rioters, who, in 1843, made a raid upon toll-gates. The captain and his guard disguised themselves in female attire.

*** This name arose from a gross perversion of a text of Scripture: "And they blessed Rebekah, and said unto her, ... let thy seed possess the gate of those which hate them." (*Gen.* xxiv. 60).

Rebecca, daughter of Isaac, the Jew; meek, modest, and high-minded. She loves Ivanhoe, who has shown great kindness to her and to her father; and when Ivanhoe marries Rowena, both Rebecca and her father leave England for a foreign land.—Sir W. Scott, *Ivanhoe* (time, Richard I.).

Rebecca (*Mistress*), the favorite waiting-maid of Mrs. Margaret Bertram, of Singleside.—Sir W. Scott, *Guy Mannering* (time, George II.).

Record, noted for his superlatives, "most presumptuous," "most audacious," "most impatient," as:

Oh, you will, most audacious.... Look at him, most inquisitive.... Under lock and key, most noble.... I will, most dignified.—S. Birch, *The Adopted Child.*

Recruiting Officer (*The*), a comedy by G. Farquhar (1705). The "recruiting officer" is Sergeant Kite, his superior officer is Captain Plume, and the recruit is Sylvia, who assumes the military dress of her brother and the name of Jack Wilful, *alias* Pinch. Her father, Justice Balance, allows the name to pass the muster, and when the trick is discovered, to prevent scandal, the justice gives her in marriage to the captain.

Red Book of Hergest (*The*), a collection of children's tales in Welsh; so called from the name of the place where it was discovered. Each tale is called in Welsh a *Mabinogi*, and the entire collection is the *Mabinogion* (from *nab*, "a child"). The tales relate chiefly to Arthur and the early British kings. A translation in three vols., with notes, was published by Lady Charlotte Guest (1838-49).

Red-Cap (*Mother*), an old nurse at the Hungerford Stairs.—Sir W. Scott, *Fortunes of Nigel* (time, James I.).

Red-Cap (*Mother*). Madame Bufflon was so called, because her bonnet was deeply colored with her own blood in a street fight at the outbreak of the French Revolution.—W. Melville.

Red Cross Knight (*The*) represents St. George, the patron saint of England. His adventures, which occupy bk. i. of Spenser's *Faëry Queen*, symbolize the struggles and ultimate victory of holiness over sin (or protestantism over popery). Una comes on a white ass to the court of Gloriana, and craves that one of the knights would undertake to slay the dragon which kept her father and mother prisoners. The Red Cross Knight, arrayed in all the armor of God (*Eph.* vi. 11-17), undertakes the adventure, and goes, accompanied for a time, with Una; but, deluded by Archimago, he quits the lady, and the two meet with numerous adventures. At last, the knight, having slain the dragon, marries Una; and thus holiness is allied to the Oneness of Truth (1590).

Red Hand of Ulster.

Calverley, of Calverley, Yorkshire. Walter Calverley, Esq., in 1605, murdered two of his children, and attempted to murder his wife and a child "at nurse." This became the subject of *The Yorkshire Tragedy*. In consequence of these murders, the family is required to wear "the bloody hand."

The Holt family, of Lancashire, has a similar tradition connected with their coat armor.

Red Knight (*The*), Sir Perimo'nês, one of the four brothers who kept the passages leading to Castle Perilous. In the allegory of Gareth, this knight represents noon, and was the third brother. Night, the eldest born, was slain by Sir Gareth; the Green Knight, which represents the young day-spring, was overcome, but not slain; and the Red Knight, being overcome, was spared also. The reason is this: darkness is *slain*, but dawn is only *overcome* by the stronger light of noon, and noon decays into the evening twilight. Tennyson in his *Gareth and Lynette*, calls Sir Perimonês "Meridies," or "Noonday Sun." The Latin name is not consistent with a British tale.—Sir T. Malory, *History of Prince Arthur*, i. 129 (1470); Tennyson, *Idylls*.

Red Knight of the Red Lands (*The*), Sir Ironside. "He had the strength of seven men, and every day his strength went on increasing till noon." This knight kept the Lady Lionês captive in Castle Perilous. In the allegory of Sir

Gareth, Sir Ironside represents death, and the captive lady "the Bride," or Church triumphant. Sir Gareth combats with Night, Morn, Noon, and Evening, or fights the fight of faith, and then overcomes the last enemy, which is death, when he marries the lady, or is received into the Church, which is "the Lamb's Bride." Tennyson, in his *Gareth and Lynette*, makes the combat with the Red Knight ("Mors," or "Death") to be a single stroke; but the *History* says it is endured from morn to noon, and from noon to night—in fact, that man's whole life is a contest with moral and physical death.—Sir T. Malory, *History of Prince Arthur*, i. 134-137 (1470); Tennyson, *Idylls* ("Gareth and Lynette").

Red Pipe. The Great Spirit long ago called the Indians together, and, standing on the red pipe-stone rock, broke off a piece, which he made into a pipe, and smoked, letting the smoke exhale to the four quarters. He then told the Indians that the red pipe-stone was their flesh, and they must use the red pipe when they made peace; and that when they smoked it, the war-club and scalping-knife must not be touched. Having so spoken, the Great Spirit was received up into the clouds.—*Indian Mythology*.

The red pipe has blown its fumes of peace and war to the remotest corners of the continent. It visited every warrior, and passed through its reddened stem the irrevocable oath of war and desolation. Here, too, the peace-breathing calumet was born, and fringed with eagle's quills, which has shed its thrilling fumes over the land, and soothed the fury of the relentless savage.—Catlin, *Letters on ... the North Americans*, ii. 160.

Red Ridinghood (*Little*), a child with a red cloak, who went to carry cakes to her grandmother. A wolf placed itself in the grandmother's bed, and when the child remarked upon the size of its eyes, ears, and nose, replied it was the better to see, hear, and smell the little grandchild. "But, grandmamma," said the child, "what a great mouth you have got!" "The better to eat you up," was the reply, and the child was devoured by the wolf.

This nursery tale is, with slight variations, common to Sweden, Germany, and France. In Charles Perrault's *Contes des Fées* (1697) it is called "Le Petit Chaperon Rouge."

Red Swan (*The*). Odjibwa, hearing a strange noise, saw in the lake a most beautiful red swan. Pulling his bow, he took deliberate aim, without effect. He shot every arrow from his quiver with the same result; then, fetching from his father's medicine sack three poisoned arrows, he shot them also at the bird. The last of the three arrows passed through the swan's neck, whereupon the bird rose into the air and sailed away towards the setting sun.—Schoolcraft, *Algic Researches*, ii. 9 (1839).

Redgauntlet, a story told in a series of letters, about a conspiracy formed by Sir Edward Hugh Redgauntlet, on behalf of the "Young Pretender," Charles Edward, then above 40 years of age. The conspirators insist that the prince shall dismiss his mistress, Miss Walkingshaw, and, as he refuses to comply with this demand, they abandon their enterprise. Just as a brig is prepared for the prince's departure from the island, Colonel Campbell arrives with the military. He connives, however, at the affair, the conspirators disperse, the prince embarks, and Redgauntlet becomes the prior of a monastery abroad. This is one of the inferior novels, but is redeemed by the character of Peter Peebles.—Sir W. Scott, *Redgauntlet* (1824).

Redgauntlet embodies a great deal of Scott's own personal history and experience.—Chambers, *English Literature*, ii. 589.

Redgauntlet (Sir Alberick), an ancestor of the family.

Sir Edward Redgauntlet, son of Sir Alberick; killed by his father's horse.

Sir Robert Redgauntlet, an old tory, mentioned in Wandering Willie's tale.

Sir John Redgauntlet, son and successor of Sir Robert, mentioned in Wandering Willie's tale.

Sir Redwald Redgauntlet, son of Sir John.

Sir Henry Darsie Redgauntlet, son of Sir Redwald.

Lady Henry Darsie Redgauntlet, wife of Sir Henry Darsie.

Sir Arthur Darsie Redgauntlet, alias *Darsie Latimer*, son of Sir Henry and Lady Darsie.

Miss Lilias Redgauntlet, alias *Green-mantle*, sister of Sir Arthur. She marries Allan Fairford.

Sir Edward Hugh Redgauntlet, the Jacobite conspirator. He is uncle to Darsie Latimer, and is called "Laird of the Lochs," *alias* "Mr. Herries of Birrenswark," *alias* "Master Ingoldsby."—Sir W. Scott, *Redgauntlet* (time, George III.).

Redi (*Francis*), an Italian physician and lyric poet. He was first physician to the grand-duke of Tuscany (1626-1698).

Even Redi, tho' he chanted
Bacchus in the Tuscan valleys,
Never drank the wine he vaunted
In his dithyrambic sallies.
Longfellow, *Drinking Song*.

Redlaw (*Mr.*), the "haunted man." He was a professor of chemistry, who bargained with the spirit which haunted him to leave him, on condition of his imparting to others his own idiosyncrasies. From this moment the chemist carried with him the infection of sullenness, selfishness, discontent and ingratitude. On Christmas Day the infection ceased. Redlaw lost his morbid feelings, and all who suffered by his infection, being healed, were restored to love, mirth, benevolence and gratitude.—C. Dickens, *The Haunted Man* (1848).

Redmain (*Sir Magnus*), governor of the town of Berwick (fifteenth century).

He was remarkable for his long red beard, and was therefore called by the English "Magnus Red-beard," but by the Scotch, in derision, "Magnus Red-mane," as if his beard had been a horse-mane.—Godscroft, 178.

Redmond O'Neale, Rokeby's page, beloved by Rokeby's daughter, Matilda, whom he marries. He turns out to be Mortham's son and heir.—Sir W. Scott, *Rokeby* (1812).

Reece (*Captain*), R.N., of the *Mantelpiece*; adored by all his crew. They had feather-beds, warm slippers, hot-water cans, brown Windsor soap, and a valet to every four, for Captain Reece said, "It is my duty to make my men happy, and I will." Captain Reece had a daughter, ten female cousins, a niece and a ma, six sisters and an aunt or two, and, at the suggestion of William Lee, the coxswain, married these ladies to his crew—"It is my duty to make my men happy, and I will." Last of all, Captain Reece married the widowed mother of his coxswain, and they were all married on one day—"It was their duty, and they did it."—W. S. Gilbert, *The Bab Ballads* ("Captain Reece, R.N.").

Reeve's Tale (*The*). Symond Symkyn, a miller of Trompington, near Cambridge, used to serve "Soler Hall College," but was an arrant thief. Two scholars, Aleyn and John, undertook to see that a sack of corn sent to be ground was not tampered with; so one stood by the hopper, and one by the trough which received the flour. In the mean time the miller let their horse loose, and, when the young men went to catch it, purloined half a bushel of the flour, substituting meal instead. It was so late before the horse could be caught that the miller offered the two scholars a "shakedown" in his own chamber, but when they were in bed he began to belabor them unmercifully. A scuffle ensued, in which the miller, being tripped up, fell upon his wife. His wife, roused from her sleep, seized a stick, and, mistaking the bald pate of her husband for the night-cap of one of the young men, banged it so lustily that the man was almost stunned with the blows. In the mean time the two scholars made off without payment, taking with them the sack and also the half-bushel of flour, which had been made into cakes.—Chaucer, *Canterbury Tales* (1388).

⁂ Boccaccio has a similar story in his *Decameron*. It is also the subject of a *fabliau* entitled *De Gombert et des Deux Clers*. Chaucer borrowed his story from a *fabliau* given by Thomas Wright in his *Anecdota Literaria*, 15.

Reformation (*The*). It was in germ in the early Lollards, and was radiant in the works of Wycliffe.

It was present in the pulpit of Pierre de Bruys, in the pages of Arnoldo da Brescia, in the cell of Roger Bacon.

It was active in the field with Peter Revel, in the castle of Lord Cobham, in the pulpit with John Huss, in the camp with John Ziska, in the class-room of Pico di Mirandola, in the observatory of Abraham Zacuto, and the college of Antonio di Lebrija, and it burst into full light through Martin Luther.

Re′gan, second daughter of King Lear, and wife of the duke of Cornwall. Having received the half of her father's king- she refused to entertain him with his suite. On the death of her husband, she designed to marry Edmund, natural son of the earl of Gloster, and was poisoned by her elder sister, Goneril, out of jealousy. Regan, like Goneril, is proverbial for "filial ingratitude."—Shakespeare, *King Lear* (1605).

Regent Diamond (*The*). So called from the regent duke of Orleans. This diamond, the property of France, at first set in the crown, and then in the sword of state, was purchased in India by a governor of Madras, of whom the regent bought it for £80,000.

Regillus (*The Battle of Lake*). Regillus Lacus is about twenty miles east of Rome, between Gabii (north) and Lavīcum (south). The Romans had expelled Tarquin the Proud from the throne, because of the most scandalous conduct of his son Sextus, who had violated Lucretia, the wife of Collatinus. Thirty combined cities of Latium, with Sabines and Volscians, took the part of Tarquin, and marched towards Rome. The Romans met the allied army at the Lake Regillus, and here, on July 15, B.C. 499, they won the great battle which confirmed their republican constitution, and in which Tarquin, with his sons Sextus and Titus, was slain. While victory was still doubtful, Castor and Pollux, on their white horses, appeared to the Roman dictator, and fought for the Romans. The victory was complete, and ever after the Romans observed the anniversary of this battle with a grand procession and sacrifice. The procession started from the temple of Mars outside the city walls, entered by the Porta Capēna, traversed the chief streets of Rome, marched past the temple of Vesta in the Forum, and then to the opposite side of the "great square," where they had built a temple to Castor and Pollux in gratitude for the aid rendered by them in this battle. Here offerings were made, and sacrifice was offered to the Great Twin-Brothers, the sons of Leda. Macaulay has a lay, called *The Battle of the Lake Regillus*, on the subject.

Where, by the Lake Regillus,
Under the Porcian height,
All in the land of Tusculum,
Was fought the glorious fight.
Macaulay, *Lays of Ancient Rome* (1842).

A very parallel case occurs in the life of Mahomet. The Koreishites had armed to put down "the prophet;" but Mahomet met them in arms, and on January 13, 624, won the famous battle of Bedr. In the *Korân* (ch. iii.), he tells us that the angel Gabriel, on his horse, Haïzûm, appeared on the field with 3000 "angels," and won the battle for him.

In the conquest of Mexico, we are told that St. James appeared on his grey horse at the head of the Castilian adventurers, and led them on to victory. Bernal Diaz, who was in the battle, saw the grey horse, but fancies the rider was Francesco de Morla, though, he confesses, "it might be the glorious apostle St. James" for aught he knew.

Regimen of the School of Salerno, a collection of precepts in Latin verse, written by John of Milan, a poet of the eleventh century, for Robert, the duke of Normandy.

A volume universally known
As the "Regimen of the School of Salern."
Longfellow, *The Golden Legend* (1851).

Reginald Archer. A refined, debonnaire sensualist, courted by women and envied by men. He wooes and marries a gentle, pure heiress, and would, as her husband, break her heart were not the evil work cut short by his death at the hands of a man whose wife Reginald has lured from her allegiance to her lawful lord.—Anne Crane Seemuller, *Reginald Archer* (1865).

Region of Death, (*Marovsthulli*), Thurr, near Delhi, fatal, from some atmospheric influence, especially about sunset.

Regno (*The*), Naples.

Are our wiser heads leaning towards an alliance with the pope and the Regno?—George Eliot (Marian Evans).

Reg´ulus, a Roman general, who conquered the Carthaginians (B.C. 256), and compelled them to sue for peace. While negotiation was going on, the Carthaginians, joined by Xanthippos, the Lacedemonian, attacked the Romans at Tunis, and beat them, taking Regulus prisoner. The captive was sent to Rome to make terms of peace and demand exchange of prisoners, but he used all his influence with the senate to dissuade them from coming to terms with their foe. On his return to captivity, the Cathaginians cut off his eyelids and exposed him to the burning sun, then placed him in a barrel armed with nails, which was rolled up and down a hill till the man was dead.

⁎ This subject has furnished Pradon and Dorat with tragedies (*French*), and Metastasio, the Italian poet, with an opera called *Regolo* (1740).

"Regulus" was a favorite part of the French actor, François J. Talma.

Rehearsal (*The*), a farce by George Villiers, duke of Buckingham (1671). It was designed for a satire on the rhyming plays of the time. The chief character, Bayes (1 *syl.*), is meant for Dryden.

The name of George Villiers, duke of Buckingham, demands cordial mention by every writer on the stage. He lived in an age when plays were chiefly written in rhyme, which served as a vehicle for foaming sentiment clouded by hyperbolê.... The dramas of Lee and Settle ... are made up of blatant couplets that emptily thundered through five long acts. To explode an unnatural custom by ridiculing it, was Buckingham's design in *The Rehearsal*, but in doing this the gratification of private dislike was a greater stimulus than the wish to promote the public good.—W. C. Russell, *Representative Actors*.

Reichel (*Colonel*), in *Charles XII.*, by J. R. Planché (1826).

Rejected Addresses, parodies on Wordsworth, Cobbett, Southey, Scott, Coleridge, Crabbe, Byron, Theodore Hook, etc., by James and Horace Smith; the copyright after the sixteenth edition was purchased by John Murray, in 1819, for £131. The directors of Drury Lane Theatre had offered a premium for the best poetical address to be spoken at the opening of the new building, and the brothers Smith conceived the idea of publishing a number of poems supposed to have been written for the occasion and rejected by the directors (1812).

"I do not see why they should have been rejected," said a Leicestershire clergyman, "for I think some of them are very good."—James Smith.

Reksh, Sir Rustam's horse.

Relapse, (*The*), a comedy by Vanbrugh (1697). Reduced to three acts, and adapted to more modern times by Sheridan, under the title of *A Trip to Scarborough* (1777).

Rel'dresal, principal secretary for private affairs in the court of Lilliput, and great friend of Gulliver. When it was proposed to put the Man-mountain to death for high treason, Reldresal moved as an amendment, that the "traitor should have both his eyes put out, and be suffered to live that he might serve the nation."—Swift, *Gulliver's Travels* ("Voyage to Lilliput," 1726).

⁎ Probably the dean had the Bible story of Samson and the Philistines in his thoughts.

Relics. The following relics are worthy of note, if for no other reason, because of the immense number of pilgrims who are drawn to them from all parts of the world.

1. THE HOUSE OF THE VIRGIN. This is now to be seen at Loreto, a town on the Adriatic, near Ancona, whither it was miraculously transported through the air by angels in the year 1294. It had been originally brought from Nazareth to Dalmatia in 1291, but after resting there for three years was again lifted up and placed where it now stands. It is a small brick structure surrounded by a marble screen designed by Bramante and decorated with carvings and sculptures by a number of celebrated sculptors. The church in which the house stands was built over it to protect it shortly after its arrival.

2. THE HOLY COAT. This is the seamless coat worn by Jesus, and for which the soldiers drew lots at his crucifixion. It is described by John alone of the evangelists: "Now the coat was without seam, woven from the top throughout." John 19, 23. It is preserved at Treves in the cathedral, and is shown at long intervals to the faithful, attracting vast crowds of pilgrims from all parts of Europe and America. It was last shown in 1891. The village of Argenteuil, near Paris, disputes with Treves the possession of the true garment, insisting on its own superior claim, but the right of Treves is generally acknowledged by Catholics.

3. THE HOLY FACE. According to the legend, when Jesus was on His way to Calvary, one of the women standing by, whose name was Veronica, seeing Him sinking under the weight of the cross, gave Him her handkerchief to wipe the sweat from His face. When He returned it the impression of His face was left upon the cloth, and remains distinctly to be seen at the present day.

4. THE SAINTE CHAPELLE at Paris, one of the most beautiful Gothic buildings in Europe, was built as a shrine to contain the fragment of the true Cross and a thorn from the Crown of Thorns given by Louis IX. of France (Saint Louis). These relics have since been transferred to the Treasury of Notre Dame, at Paris. The church at Aachen (Aix-la-Chapelle) also contains a fragment of the true Cross. In various churches of Italy, pictures of the Virgin Mary said to have been painted by Saint Luke (a painter as well as a physician, and the patron saint of both professions) are preserved, but no one of them has any fame above the rest.

Remember, Thou Art Mortal! When a Roman conqueror entered the city in triumph, a slave was placed in the chariot to whisper from time to time into the ear of the conqueror, "Remember, thou art a man!"

Vespasian, the Roman emperor, had a slave who said to him daily as he left his chamber, "Remember, thou art a man!"

In the ancient Egyptian banquets it was customary during the feast to draw a mummy, in a car, round the banquet hall, while one uttered aloud, "To this estate you must come at last!"

When the sultan of Serendib (*i.e.* Ceylon) went abroad, his vizier cried aloud, "This is the great monarch, the tremendous sultan of the Indies ... greater than Solimo or the grand Mihragê!" An officer behind the monarch then exclaimed, "This monarch, though so great and powerful, must die, must die, must die!"—*Arabian Nights* ("Sindbad," sixth voyage).

Remois (2 *syl.*), the people of Rheims, in France.

Remond, a shepherd in *Britannia's Pastorals*, by William Browne (1613).

Remond, young Remond, that full well could sing,
And tune his pipe at Pan's birth carolling;
Who, for his nimble leaping, sweetest layes,
A laurell garland wore on holidayes;
In framing of whose hand Dame Nature swore,
There never was his like, nor should be more.
Pastoral, i.

Rem´ores, birds which retard the execution of a project.

"Remores" aves in auspicio dicuntur quæ acturum aliquid remorari compellunt.—Festus, *De VerborumSignificatione.*

Remus. (See ROMULUS AND REMUS.)

Remus (*Uncle*). Hero of many of Joel Chandler Harris's tales of negro-life. His fables of "Brer Rabbit," "Brer Bear," and the like are curious relics of African folk-lore (1886).

Re´naud, one of the paladins of Charlemagne, always described with the properties of a borderer, valiant, alert, ingenious, rapacious, and unscrupulous. Better known in the Italian form *Rinaldo* (*q.v.*).

Renault, a Frenchman, and one of the chief conspirators in which Pierre was concerned. When Jaffier joined the conspiracy, he gave his wife, Belvide´ra, as surety of his fidelity, and a dagger to be used against her if he proved unfaithful. Renault attempted the honor of the lady, and Jaffier took her back in order to protect her from such insults. The old villain died on the wheel, and no one pitied him.—T. Otway, *Venice Preserved* (1682).

René, the old king of Provence, father of Queen Margaret of Anjou (wife of Henry VI. of England). A minstrel-monarch, friend to the chase and tilt, poetry, and music. Thiebault says he gave in largesses to knights-errant and minstrels more than he received in revenue (ch. xxix.).—Sir W. Scott, *Anne of Geierstein* (time, Edward IV.).

René (2 *syl.*), the hero and title of a romance by Châteaubriand (1801). It was designed for an episode to his *Génie du Christianisme* (1802). René is a man of social inaction, conscious of possessing a superior genius, but his pride produces in him a morbid bitterness of spirit.

René [LEBLANC], notary public of Grand Pré, in Arcadia (*Nova Scotia*). Bent with age, but with long yellow hair flowing over his shoulders. He was the father of twenty children, and had a hundred grandchildren. When Acadia was ceded by the French to England, George II. confiscated the goods of the simple colonists, and drove them into exile. René went to Pennsylvania, where he died, and was buried.—Longfellow, *Evangeline* (1849).

Renton (*Dr.*). A Boston physician, whose best friend, dying, leaves a letter charging Renton, "*In the name of the Saviour, be true and tender to mankind.*" The doctor believes himself to be haunted by the ghost of this man, intent upon inforcing the admonition, and the needy and the afflicted profit by the hallucination.—William D. O'Connor, *The Ghost*.

Rentowel (*Mr. Jabesh*), a covenanting preacher.—Sir W. Scott, *Waverley* (time, George II.).

With vehemence of some pulpit-drumming Gowkthrapple, or "precious" Mr. Jabesh Rentowel.—Carlyle.

Renzo and Lucia, the hero and heroine of an Italian novel by Alessandro Manzoni, entitled *The Betrothed Lover* ("I Promessi Sposi"). This novel contains an account of the Bread Riot and plague of Milan. Cardinal Borro´meo is also introduced. There is an English translation (1827).

Republican Queen, (*The*), Sophie Charlotte, wife of Frederick I. of Prussia.

Resequenz, wily major-domo to the duke of Romagna, audacious, unscrupulous and treacherous.—William Waldorf Astor, *Valentino* (1886).

Resolute (*The*), John Florio, philologist (1545?-1625). Translated Montaigne's Essays and wrote a French and English Dictionary called a *World of Words*. One of the few autographs of Shakespeare is in a copy of Florio's Montaigne in the British Museum.

*** Florio is said to have been the prototype of Shakespeare's "Holofernês," in *Love's Labour's Lost*.

Resolute Doctor (*The*), John Baconthorpe (*-1346).

⁎ Guillaume Durandus de St. Pourçain was called "the Most Resolute Doctor (1267-1332).

Restless (*Sir John*), the suspicious husband of a suspicious wife.

Lady Restless, wife of Sir John. As she has a fixed idea that her husband is inconstant, she is always asking the servants, "Where is Sir John?" "Is Sir John returned?" "Which way did Sir John go?" "Has Sir John received any letters?" "Who has called?" etc.; and, whatever the answer, it is to her a confirmation of her surmises.—A. Murphy, *All in the Wrong* (1761).

Reuben Dixon, a village schoolmaster of "ragged lads."

'Mid noise, and dirt, and stench, and play, and prate,
He calmly cuts the pen or views the slate.
Crabbe, *Borough*, xxiv. (1810).

Reuben and Seth, servants of Nathan ben Israel, the Jew at Ashby, a friend of Isaac and Rebecca.—Sir W. Scott, *Ivanhoe* (time, Richard I.).

Reullu´ra (*i.e. "beautiful star"*), the wife of Aodh, one of the Culdees, or primitive clergy of Scotland, who preached the gospel of God in Io´na, an island south of Staffa. Here Ulvfa´gre, the Dane, landed, and, having put all who opposed him to death, seized Aodh, bound him in iron, carried him to the church, and demanded where the treasures were concealed. Just then appeared a mysterious figure all in white, who first unbound Aodh, and then taking the Dane by the arm, led him up to the statue of St. Columb, which immediately fell and crushed him to death. Then turning to the Norsemen, the same mysterious figure told them to "go back and take the bones of their chief with them;" adding, whoever lifted hand in the island again, should be a paralytic for life. The "saint" then transported the remnant of the islanders to Ireland; but when search was made for Reullura, her body was in the sea, and her soul in heaven.—Campbell, *Reullura*.

Reutha´mir, the principal man of Balclutha, a town belonging to the Britons on the river Clyde. His daughter, Moina, married Clessammor (Fingal's uncle on the mother's side). Reuthamir was killed by Combal (Fingal's father) when he attacked Balcutha and burned it to the ground.—Ossian, *Carthon*.

Reutner (*Karl*), young German, serving in the Federal army, finds, on the Gettysburg battle-field, a four-leafed clover, and waves it in the air. The gesture attracts a sharp-shooter, and Reutner falls insensible. He is taken from hospital to prison, and languishes for weeks, in delirium, all the while haunted by a vision of a woman, dark-eyed and beautiful, who brings him handfuls of four-leaved clover. When he reaches home, he recognizes her in Margaret Warren, a guest in his father's house. The betrothal-ring bears a four-leaved clover of green enamel, set in diamonds.—Helen Hunt Jackson, *A Four-Leaved Clover* (1886).

Rev′eller (*Lady*), cousin of Valeria, the blue-stocking. Lady Reveller is very fond of play, but ultimately gives it up, and is united to Lord Worthy.—Mrs. Centlivre, *The Basset Table* (1706).

Revenge (*The*), a tragedy by Edward Young (1721). (For the plot, see ZANGA.)

Revenge (*The*), the ship under the command of Sir Richard Grenville, anchored at Flores, in the Azores, when a fleet of fifty-three Spanish ships hove in sight. Lord Thomas Howard, with six men-of-war, sailed off; but Sir Richard stood his ground. He had only a hundred men, but with this crew and his one ship, he encountered the Spanish fleet. The fight was very obstinate. Some of the Spanish ships were sunk, and many shattered; but Sir Richard at length was wounded, and the surgeon shot while dressing the wound. "Sink the ship, master gunner!" cried Sir Richard; "sink the ship, and let her not fall into the hands of Spain!" But the crew were obliged to yield, and Sir Richard died. The Spaniards were amazed at Grenville's pluck, and gave him all honors, as they cast his body into the sea. *The Revenge* was then manned by Spaniards, but never reached the Spanish coast, for it was wrecked in a tempest, and went down with all hands aboard.—Tennyson, *The Revenge*, a ballad of the fleet (1878).

⁎ This sea-fight is the subject of one of Froude's essays.

Canon Kingsley has introduced it in *Westward Ho!* where he gives a description of Sir Richard Grenville.

Lord Bacon says the fight "was memorable even beyond credit, and to the height of heroic fable."

Mr. Arber published three interesting contemporary documents relating to *The Revenge*, by Sir Walter Raleigh.

Gervase Markham wrote a long poem on the subject (two hundred stanzas of eight lines each).

Revenge (*The Palace of*), a palace of crystal, provided with everything agreeable to life except the means of going out of it. The fairy Pagan made it, and when Imis rejected his suit because she loved Prince Philax, he shut them up in this palace out of revenge. At the end of a few years Pagan had his revenge, for Philax and Imis longed as eagerly for a separation as they had once done to be united.—Comtesse D'Aunoy, *Fairy Tales* ("Palace of Revenge," 1682).

Revenons à nos Moutons, let us return to the matter in hand. This phrase comes from an old French comedy of the fifteenth century, entitled *L'Avocat*

Patelin, by Blanchet. A clothier, giving evidence against a shepherd who had stolen some sheep, is for ever running from the subject to talk about some cloth of which Patelin, his lawyer, had defrauded him. The judge from time to time pulls him up by saying, "Well, well! and about the sheep?" "What about the sheep!" (See PATELIN.)

Revolutionary Songs. By far the most popular were:

1. *La Marseillaise*, both words and music by Rouget de Lisle (1792).

2. *Veillons au Salut de l'Empire*, by Adolphe S. Boy (1791). Music by Dalayra. Very strange that men whose whole purpose was to *destroy* the empire should go about singing "Let us guard it!"

3. *Ça Ira*, written to the tune of *Le Carillon National*, in 1789, while preparations were being made for the *Fête de la Féderation*. It was a great favorite with Marie Antoinette, who was for ever "strumming the tune on her harpsichord."

4. *Chant du Départ*, by Marie Joseph de Chénier (1794). Music by Méhul. This was the most popular next to the *Marseillaise*.

5. *La Carmagnole*. "Madame Veto avait promis de faire égorger tout Paris ..." (1792). Probably so called from Carmagnole, in Piedmont. The burden of this dancing song is:

Danson la Carmagnole,
Vive le son! Vive le son!
Danson la Carmagnole,
Vive le son du canon!

6. *La Vengeur*, a spirited story, in verse, about a ship so called. Lord Howe took six of the French ships, June 1, 1794; but *La Vengeur* was sunk by the crew, that it might not fall into the hands of the English, and went down while the crew shouted "Vive la République!" The story bears a strong resemblance to that of "The Revenge," Sir Richard Grenville's ship. See *ante*.

In the second Revolution we have:

1. *La Parisienne*, called "The *Marseillaise* of 1830," by Casimir Delavigne, the same year.

2. *La France a l'Horreur du Servage*, by Casimir Delavigne (1843).

3. *Le Champ de Bataille*, by Emile Debreaux (about 1830).

The chief political songs of Béranger are: *Adieux de Marie Stuart, La Cocarde Blanche, Jacques, La Déesse, Marquis de Carabas, Le Sacre de Charles le Simple, Le Senateur, Le Vieux Caporal*, and *Le Vilain*.

In the American Revolution the air of *Yankee Doodle* was sung to various sets of words, all derisive of the British and exhilarating to the Americans.

In the Civil War of the United States *The Star-Spangled Banner*, *Hail Columbia*, *Tramp! Tramp! Tramp!* and Julia Ward Howe's *Battle Hymn of the Republic* to the air of *John Brown's Body Lies Mouldering in the Ground* were favorites with the Federal troops.

Among the Confederates, *Dixie*, and *Maryland, My Maryland*, were most popular.

Rewcastle (*Old John*), a Jedburgh smuggler, and one of the Jacobite conspirators with the laird of Ellieslaw.—Sir W. Scott, *The Black Dwarf* (time, Anne).

Reynaldo, a servant to Polonius.—Shakespeare, *Hamlet* (1596).

Reynard the Fox, the hero of the beast-epic so called. This prose poem is a satire on the state of Germany in the Middle Ages. Reynard represents the Church; Isengrin, the wolf (his uncle), typifies the baronial element; and Nodel, the lion, stands for the regal power. The plot turns on the struggle for supremacy between Reynard and Isengrin. Reynard uses all his endeavors to victimize every one, especially his uncle, Isengrin, and generally succeeds.—*Reinecke Fuchs* (thierepos, 1498).

Reynardine (3 *syl.*), eldest son of Reynard the Fox. He assumed the names of Dr. Pedanto and Crabron.—*Reynard the Fox* (1498).

Reynold of Montalbon, one of Charlemagne's paladins.

Reynolds (*Sir Joshua*), is thus described by Goldsmith:

Here Reynolds is laid; and, to tell you my mind,
He has not left a wiser or better behind.
His pencil was striking, resistless and grand;
His manners were gentle, complying and bland ...
To coxcombs averse, yet most civilly steering,
When they judged without skill he was still hard of hearing;
When they talked of their Raphaels, Corregios, and stuff,
He shifted his trumpet, and only took snuff.
Retaliation (1774).

N.B.—Sir Joshua Reynolds was hard of hearing, and used an ear-trumpet.

Rez'io (*Dr.*) or "Pedro Rezio of Ague'ro," the doctor of Barata'ria, who forbade Sancho Panza to taste any of the meats set before him. Roast partridge was "forbidden by Hippoc'ratês." Podri'da was "the most pernicious food in the world." Rabbits were "a sharp-haired diet." Veal was "prejudicial to health." But, he said, the governor might eat "a few wafers, and a thin slice or two of quince."—Cervantes, *Don Quixote*, II. iii. 10 (1615).

Rhadaman´thus, son of Jupiter and Euro´pa. He reigned in the Cyclades with such partiality, that at death he was made one of the judges of the infernal regions.

And if departed souls must rise again ...
And bide the judgment of reward or pain ...
Then Rhadamanthus and stern Minos were
True types of justice while they livèd here.
Lord Brooke, *Monarchie*, i. (1554-1628).

Rhampsini´tos, king of Egypt, usually called Ram´esês III., the richest of the Egyptian monarchs, who amassed 72 millions sterling, which he secured in a treasury of stone. By an artifice of the builder, he was robbed every night.—*Herodotus*, ii. 121.

A parallel tale is told of Hyrieus [*Hy´.ri.uce*] of Hyrĭa. His two architects, Trophōnios and Agamēdês (brothers), built his treasure-vaults, but left one stone removable at pleasure. After great loss of treasure, Hyrieus spread a net, in which Agame´des was caught. To prevent recognition, Trophonios cut off his brother's head.—Pausanias, *Itinerary of Greece*, ix. 37, 3.

A similar tale is told of the treasure-vaults of Augĕas, king of Elis.

Rha´sis or Mohammed Aboubekr ibn Zakaria el Razi, a noted Arabian physician. He wrote a treatise on small-pox and measles, with some 200 other treatises (850-923).

Well, error has no end;
And Rhasis is a sage.
R. Browning, *Paracelsus*, iii.

Rhea's Child. Jupiter is so called by Pindar. He dethroned his father, Saturn.

The child
Of Rhea drove him [*Saturn*] from the upper sky.
Akenside, *Hymn to the Naiads* (1767).

Rheims (*The Jackdaw of*), The cardinal-archbishop of Rheims made a great feast, to which he invited all the joblillies of the neighborhood. There were abbots and prelates, knights and squires, and all who delighted to honor the great panjandrum of Rheims. The feast over, water was served, and his lordship's grace, drawing off his turquoise ring, laid it beside his plate, dipped his fingers into the golden bowl, and wiped them on his napkin; but when he looked to put on his ring, it was nowhere to be found. It was evidently gone. The floor was searched, the plates and dishes lifted up, the mugs and chalices, every possible and impossible place was poked into, but without avail. The ring must have been stolen. His grace was furious, and, in dignified indignation, calling for bell, book, and candle, banned the thief, both body and soul, this life and for ever. It was a terrible curse, but none of the guests seemed the worse for it—except, indeed, the jackdaw. The poor bird was a pitiable object, his head lobbed down, his wings draggled on the floor, his feathers were all ruffled, and with a ghost of a caw he prayed the company follow him; when lo! there was the ring, hidden in some sly corner by the jackdaw as a clever practical joke. His lordship's grace smiled benignantly, and instantly removed the curse; when lo! as if by magic, the bird became fat and sleek again, perky and impudent, wagging his tail, winking his eye, and cocking his head on one side, then up he hopped to his old place on the cardinal's chair. Never after this did he indulge in thievish tricks, but became so devout, so constant at feast and chapel, so well-behaved at matins and vespers, that when he died he died in the odor of sanctity, and was canonized, his name being changed to that of Jim Crow.—Barham, *Ingoldsby Legends* ("Jackdaw of Rheims," 1837).

Rheingold. The treasure given Siegfried by the dwarfs, and the cause of contention after his death.

Rhesus was on his march to aid the Trojans in their siege, and had nearly reached Troy, when he was attacked in the night by Ulysses and Diomed. In this surprise Rhesus and all his army were cut to pieces.—Homer, *Iliad*, x.

A parallel case was that of Sweno, the Dane, who was marching to join Godfrey and the crusaders, when he was attacked in the night by Solyman, and both Sweno and his army perished.—Tasso, *Jerusalem Delivered* (1575).

Rhiannon's Birds. The notes of these birds were so sweet that warriors remained spell-bound for eighty years together, listening to them. These birds are often alluded to by the Welsh bards. (Rhiannon was the wife of Prince Pwyll.)—*The Mabinogion*, 363 (twelfth century).

The snow-white bird which the monk Felix listened to, sang so enchantingly that he was spell-bound for a hundred years, listening to it.—Longfellow, *Golden Legend*.

Rhodalind, daughter of Aribert, king of Lombardy, in love with Duke Gondibert; but Gondibert preferred Birtha, a country girl, daughter of the sage, Astrăgon. While the duke is whispering sweet love-notes to Birtha, a page comes post-haste to announce to him that the king has proclaimed him his heir, and is about to give him his daughter in marriage. The duke gives Birtha an emerald ring, and says if he is false to her, the emerald will lose its lustre; then hastens to court, in obedience to the king's summons. Here the tale breaks off, and was never finished.—Sir Wm. Davenant, *Gondibert* (1605-1668).

Rhodian Venus (*The*). This was the "Venus" of Protog′enês mentioned by Pliny, *Natural History*, xxxv. 10.

When first the Rhodian's mimic art arrayed
The Queen of Beauty in her Cyprian shade,
The happy master mingled in his piece
Each look that charmed him in the fair of Greece.
Campbell, *Pleasures of Hope*, ii. (1799).

Prior (1664-1721) refers to the same painting in his fable of *Protogênes and Appellês*:

I hope, sir, you intend to stay
To see our Venus; 'tis the piece
The most renowned throughout all Greece.

Rhod′ope (3 *syl.*), or **Rhod′opis**, a celebrated Greek courtezan, who afterwards married Psammetichus, king of Egypt. It is said she built the third pyramid.—Pliny, *Nat. Hist.*, xxxvi. 12.

A statelier pyramis to her I'll rear,
Than Rhodope's.
Shakespeare, *Henry VI.* act i. sc. 6 (1589).

Rhombus, a schoolmaster who speaks "a leash of languages at once," puzzling himself and his hearers with a jargon like that of "Holofernês" in Shakespeare's *Love's Labor's Lost* (1594).—Sir Philip Sidney, *Pastoral Entertainment* (1587).

Rhombus, a spinning-wheel or rolling instrument used by the Roman witches for fetching the moon out of heaven.

Quæ nunc Thessalico lunam deducere rhombo [*sciet*].—Martial, *Epigrams*, ix. 30.

Rhone of Christian Eloquence (*The*), St. Hilary (300-367).

Rhone of Latin Eloquence (*The*). St. Hilary is so called by St. Jerome (300-367).

Rhongomyant, the lance of King Arthur.—*The Mabinogion* ("Kilhwch and Olwen," twelfth century).

Rhyming to Death. In 1 *Henry VI.* act i. sc. 1, Thomas Beaufort, duke of Exeter, speaking about the death of Henry V., says, "Must we think that the subtle-witted French conjurors and sorcerers, out of fear of him, 'by magic verses have contrived his end?'" The notion of killing by incantation was at one time very common.

Irishmen ... will not stick to affirme that they can rime either man or beast to death.—Reg. Scot, *Discoverie of Witchcraft* (1564).

Ribbon. The *yellow* ribbon, in France, indicates that the wearer has won a *médaille militaire* (instituted by Napoleon III.) as a minor decoration of the Legion of Honor.

The *red* ribbon marks a *chevalier* of the Legion of Honor. A *rosette* indicates a higher grade than that of *chevalier*.

Ribemont (3 *syl.*), the bravest and noblest of the French host in the battle of Poitiers. He alone dares confess that the English are a brave people. In the battle he is slain by Lord Audley.—Shirley, *Edward the Black Prince* (1640).

Ribemont (Count), in *The Siege of Calais*, by Colman.

Riccar'do, commander of Plymouth fortress, a Puritan to whom Lord Walton has promised his daughter, Elvira, in marriage. Riccardo learns that the lady is in love with Arthur Talbot, and when Arthur is taken prisoner by Cromwell's soldiers, Riccardo promises to use his efforts to obtain his pardon. This, however, is not needful, for Cromwell, feeling quite secure of his position, orders all the captives of war to be released. Riccardo is the Italian form of Sir Richard Forth.—Bellini, *I Puritani* (opera, 1834).

Ricciardetto, son of Aymon, and brother of Bradamante.—Ariosto, *Orlando Furioso* (1516).

Rice. *Eating rice with a bodkin.* Aminê, the beautiful wife of Sidi Nouman, ate rice with a bodkin, but she was a ghoul. (See AMINE.)

Richard, a fine, honest lad, by trade a smith. He marries, on New Year's Day, Meg, the daughter of Toby Veck.—C. Dickens, *The Chimes* (1844).

Richard (Squire), eldest son of Sir Francis Wronghead, of Bumper Hall. A country bumpkin, wholly ignorant of the world and of literature.—Vanbrugh and Cibber, *The Provoked Husband* (1727).

Robert Wetherilt [1708-1745] came to Drury Lane a boy, where he showed his rising genius in the part of "Squire Richard."—Chetwood, *History of the Stage*.

Richard (Prince), eldest son of King Henry II.—Sir W. Scott, *The Betrothed* (time, Henry II.).

Richard "Cœur de Lion," introduced in two novels by Sir W. Scott (*The Talisman* and *Ivanhoe*). In the latter he first appears as "The Black Knight," at the tournament, and is called *Le Noir Fainéant*, or "The Black Sluggard;" also "The Knight of the Fetter-lock."

Richard a Name of Terror. The name of Richard I., like that of Attila, Bonaparte, Corvīnus, Narses, Sebastian, Talbot, Tamerlane, and other great conquerors, was at one time employed *in terrorem* to disobedient children. (See NAMES OF TERROR.)

His tremendous name was employed by the Syrian mothers to silence their infants; and if a horse suddenly started from the way, his rider was wont to exclaim, "Dost thou think King Richard is in the bush?"—Gibbon, *Decline and Fall of the Roman Empire*, xi. 146 (1776-88).

The Daughters of Richard I. When Richard was in France, Fulco, a priest, told him he ought to beware how he bestowed his daughters in marriage. "I have no daughters," said the king. "Nay, nay," replied Fulco, "all the world knows that you have three—Pride, Covetousness and Lechery." "If these are my daughters," said the king, "I know well how to bestow them where they will be well cherished. My eldest I give to the Knights Templars, my second to the monks; and my third I cannot bestow better than on yourself, for I am sure she will never be divorced nor neglected."—Thomas Milles, *True Nobility* (1610).

The Horse of Richard I., Fennel.

Ah, Fennel, my noble horse, thou bleedest, thou art slain!—*Cœur de Lion and His Horse.*

The Troubadour of Richard I., Bertrand de Born.

Richard Pennyroyal, unhappy man whose weary indifference to his first wife heightens into aversion as she becomes insane. He is relieved when she drowns herself. His second wife, passionately beloved, is unfaithful to him, and loathes him as he drinks more and more to drown disappointment. His rival triumphs over him in a struggle for property, but Richard has his wife still. Straying one night toward the pool in which his first wife drowned herself, he comes upon the false wife and her lover, challenges the latter to a duel then and there, and is shot through the heart. His body is tossed into the pool and never discovered.—Julian Hawthorne, *Archibald Malmaison* (1878).

Richard II's Horse, Roan Barbary.—Shakespeare, *Richard II.* act v. sc. 5 (1597).

Richard III., a tragedy by Shakespeare (1597). At one time parts of Rowe's tragedy of *Jane Shore* were woven in the acting edition, and John Kemble introduced other clap-traps from Colley Cibber. The best actors of this part were David Garrick (1716-1779), Henry Mossop (1729-1773) and Edmund Kean (1787-1833).

Richard III. was only 19 years old at the opening of Shakespeare's play.—Sharon Turner.

The Horse of Richard III., White Surrey.—Shakespeare, *Richard III.* act v. sc. 3 (1597).

Richard's himself again! These words were interpolated by John Kemble from Colley Cibber.

Richards (*Allen*). He meets his lately betrothed in a parlor-car, and the dialogue that ensues ends in reconciliation and renewal of vows. They are alone, except when the porter enters from time to time, and a providential detention on the road prolongs the interview.—W. D. Howells, *The Parlor Car* (a farce, 1876).

Richelieu (*Armand*), cardinal and chief minister of France. The duke of Orleans (the king's brother), the count de Baradas (the king's favorite), and other noblemen, conspired to assassinate Richelieu, dethrone Louis XIII., and make Gaston, duke of Orleans, the regent. The plot was revealed to the cardinal by Marion de Lorme, in whose house the conspirators met. The conspirators were arrested, and several of them put to death, but Gaston, duke of Orleans, turned king's evidence, and was pardoned.—Lord Lytton, *Richelieu* (1839).

Richland (*Miss*), intended for Leontine Croaker, but she gives her hand in marriage to Mr. Honeywood, "the good-natured man," who promises to abandon his quixotic benevolence, and to make it his study in future "to reserve his pity for real distress, his friendship for true merit, and his love for her who first taught him what it is to be happy."—Goldsmith, *The Good-natured Man* (1768).

Richlings (*The*). Brave young couple who come to New Orleans to make a living. *John Richling* has forfeited the favor of a rich father by marrying the woman of his choice, but never regrets the action. From the outset ill-fortune pursues him. He is willing to work, but work is hard to get. He accepts various employments, more or less menial, and through no fault of his, loses one after another. Nothing is stable except *Mary's* love and *Dr. Sevier's* friendship. Just before the war poverty compels him to send Mary to her mother in Milwaukee. There her child is born. He remains in New Orleans, working hard, and steadily failing in health. For three years they are separated by war, the noble wife trying all the while to get to her husband. When she succeeds, it is to find him on his death-bed.

Mary becomes, under Dr. Sevier's direction a city-missionary. "The work ... seemed to keep John near. Almost, sometimes, he seemed to walk at her side in her errands of mercy, or to spread above her the arms of benediction."—George W. Cable, *Dr. Sevier* (1888).

Richmond (*The duchess of*) wife of Charles Stuart, in the court of Charles II. The line became extinct, and the title was given to the Lennox family.—Sir W. Scott, *Perveril of the Peak* (time, Charles II.).

Richmond (The earl of), Henry of Lancaster.—Sir W. Scott, *Anne of Geierstein* (time, Edward IV.).

Richmond Hill (*The Lass of*), Miss l'Anson, of Hill House, Richmond, Yorkshire. Words by M'Nally, music by James Hook, who married the young lady.

The Lass of Richmond Hill is one of the sweetest ballads in the language.—John Bell.

Richmond (*Kate*). New England girl, heroine of several sketches in Grace Greenwood's *Leaves*. "Aside from her beauty and unfailing cheerfulness, she has a clear, strong intellect, an admirable taste and an earnest truthfulness of character."—Grace Greenwood, *Greenwood Leaves* (1850).

Rickets (*Mabel*), the old nurse of Frank Osbaldistone.—Sir W. Scott, *Rob Roy* (time, George I.).

Riderhood (*Rogue*), the villain in Dickens's novel of *Our Mutual Friend* (1864).

Rides on the Tempest and Directs the Storm. Joseph Addison, speaking of the duke of Marlborough and his famous victories, says that he inspired the fainting squadrons, and stood unmoved in the shock of battle:

So when an angel by divine command,
With rising tempests shakes a guilty land,
Such as of late o'er pale Britannia past,
Calm and serene he drives the furious blast;
And, pleased th' Almighty's orders to perform,
Rides on the tempest and directs the storm.
The Campaign (1705).

Ridicule (*Father of*). François Rabelais is so styled by Sir Wm. Temple (1495-1553).

Ridolphus, one of the band of adventurers that joined the crusaders. He was slain by Argantês (bk. vii.)—Tasso, *Jerusalem Delivered* (1575).

Rienzi (*Nicolo Gabrïni*) or COLA DI RIENZI, last of the tribunes, who assumed the name of "Tribune of Liberty, Peace and Justice" (1313-1354).

⁎ Cola di Rienzi is the hero of a novel by Lord Bulwer Lytton, entitled *Rienzi*, or *The Last of the Tribunes* (1849).

Rienzi, an opera by Wagner (1841). It opens with a number of the Orsini breaking into Rienzi's house, in order to abduct his sister, Irēnê, but in this they are foiled by the arrival of the Colonna and his followers. The outrage provokes a general insurrection, and Rienzi is appointed leader. The nobles are worsted, and Rienzi becomes a senator; but the aristocracy hate him, and Paolo Orsini seeks to assassinate him, but without success. By the machinations of the German emperor and the Colonna, Rienzi is excommunicated and deserted by all his adherents. He is ultimately fired on by the populace and killed on the steps of the capitol.—Libretto by J. P. Jackson.

Rienzi (*The English*), William with the Long Beard, *alias* Fitzosbert (*-1196).

Rigaud (*Mons.*), a Belgian, 35 years of age, confined in a villainous prison at Marseilles, for murdering his wife. He has a hooked nose, handsome after its kind, but too high between the eyes, and his eyes, though sharp, were too near to one another. He was, however, a large, tall man, with thin lips, and a goodly quantity of dry hair shot with red. When he spoke, his moustache went up under his nose, and his nose came down over his moustache. After his liberation from prison, he first took the name of Lagnier, and then of Blandois, his name being Rigaud Lagnier Blandois.—Charles Dickens, *Little Dorrit* (1857).

Rigdum-Funnidos, a courtier in the palace of King Chrononhotonthologos. After the death of the king, the widowed queen is advised to marry again, and Rigdum Funnidos is proposed to her as "a very proper man." At this Aldiborontephoscophornio takes umbrage, and the queen says, "Well, gentlemen, to make matters easy, I'll have you both."— H. Carey, *Chrononhotonthologos* (1734).

⁎ John Ballantyne, the publisher, was so called by Sir W. Scott. He was "a quick, active, intrepid little fellow, full of fun and merriment ... all over quaintness and humorous mimicry."

Right-Hitting Brand, one of the companions of Robin Hood, mentioned by Mundy.

Rig′olette (3 *syl.*), a grisette and courtezan.—Eugène Sue, *Mysteries of Paris* (1842-3).

Rigoletto, an opera, describing the agony of a father obliged to witness the violation of his own daughter.—Verdi, *Rigoletto* (1852).

⁎ The libretto of this opera is borrowed from Victor Hugo's drama *Le Roi s'Amuse*.

Rimegap (*Joe*), one of the miners of Sir Geoffrey Perveril of the Peak.—Sir W. Scott, *Peveril of the Peak* (time, Charles II.).

Rimini (*Francesca di*), a woman of extraordinary beauty, daughter of the lord of Ravenna. She was married to Lanciotto Malatesta, signore of Rimini, a man of great bravery, but deformed. His brother, Paolo, was extremely handsome, and with him Francesca fell in love. Lanciotto, detecting them in criminal intercourse, killed them both (1389).

This tale forms one of the episodes of Dantê's *Inferno*; is the subject of a tragedy called *Francesca di Rimini*, by Silvio Pellico (1819); and Leigh Hunt, about the same time, published his *Story of Rimini*, in verse.

Rimmon, seventh in order of the hierarchy of Hell: (1) Satan, (2) Beëlzebub, (3) Moloch, (4) Chemos, (5) Thammuz, (6) Dagon, (7) Rimmon, whose chief temple was at Damascus (2 *Kings* v. 18).

Him [*Dagon*] followed Rimmon, whose delightful seat
Was fair Damascus on the fertile banks
Of A′bana and Pharpar, lucid streams.
Milton, *Paradise Lost*, i. 467, etc. (1665).

Rinaldo, son of the fourth Marquis d'Estê, cousin of Orlando, and nephew of Charlemagne. He was the rival of Orlando in his love for Angelica, but Angelica detested him. Rinaldo brought an auxiliary force of English and Scotch to Charlemagne, which "Silence" conducted safely into Paris.— Ariosto, *Orlando Furioso* (1516).

Rinaldo, the Achillês of the Christian army in the siege of Jerusalem. He was the son of Bertoldo and Sophia, but was brought up by Matilda. Rinaldo joined the crusaders at the age of 15. Being summoned to a public trial for the death of Gernando, he went into voluntary exile.—Tasso, *Jerusalem Delivered* (1575).

*** Pulci introduces the same character in his burlesque poem entitled *Morgantê Maggiorê*, which holds up to ridicule the romances of chivalry.

Rinaldo, steward to the countess of Rousillon—Shakespeare, *All's Well that Ends Well* (1598).

Rinaldo of Montalban, a knight who had the "honor" of being a public plunderer. His great exploit was stealing the golden idol of Mahomet.

In this same *Mirror of Knighthood* we meet with Rinaldo de Montalban and his companions, with the twelve peers of France, and Turpin, the historian.... Rinaldo had a broad face, and a pair of large rolling eyes; his complexion was ruddy, and his disposition choleric. He was, besides, naturally profligate, and a great encourager of vagrants.—Cervantes, *Don Quixote*, I. i. 1, 6 (1605).

Ring (*Dame Liŏnês's*), a ring given by Dame Lionês to Sir Gareth, during a tournament.

"That ring," said Dame Lionês, "increaseth my beauty much more than it is of itself; and this is the virtue of my ring: that which is green it will turn to red, and that which is red it will turn green; that which is blue it will turn white, and that which is white it will turn blue; and so with all other colors. Also, whoever beareth my ring can never lose blood."—Sir T. Malory, *History of Prince Arthur*, i. 146 (1470).

Ring (*Luned's*). This ring rendered the wearer invisible. Luned or Lynet gave it to Owain, one of King Arthur's knights. Consequently, when men were sent to kill him he was nowhere to be found, for he was invisible.

Take this ring, and put it on thy finger, with the stone inside thy hand; and close thy hand upon the stone; and as long as thou concealest it, it will conceal thee.—*The Mabinogion* ("Lady of the Fountain," twelfth century).

Ring (*The Steel*), made by Siedel-Beckir. This ring enabled the wearer to read the secrets of another's heart.—Comte de Caylus, *Oriental Tales* ("The Four Talismans," 1743).

Ring (*The Talking*), a ring given by Tartaro, the Basque Cyclops, to a girl whom he wished to marry. Immediately she put it on, it kept incessantly saying, "You there, and I here;" so, to get rid of the nuisance, she cut off her finger and threw both ring and finger into a pond.—Rev. W. Webster, *Basque Legends*, 4 (1876).

The same story appears in Campbell's *Popular Tales of the West Highlands*, i. 111, and in Grimm's tale of *The Robber and His Sons*. When the robber put on the ring, it incessantly cried out, "Here I am;" so he bit off his finger, and threw it from him.

Ring (*The Virgin's Wedding Ring*), kept in the Duomo of Perugia, under fourteen locks.

Ring and the Book (*The*), an idyllic epic, by Robert Browning, founded on a *cause célèbre* of Italian history in 1698. The case was this: Guido Franceschini, a Florentine count of shattered fortune, married Pompilia, thinking her to be an heiress. When the young bride discovered that she had been married for her money only, she told her husband she was no heiress at all, but was only the supposititious child of Pietro (2 *syl.*), supplied by one Violantê, for the sake of keeping in his hands certain entailed property. The count now treated Pompilia so brutally that she ran away from home, under the protection of Caponsacchi, a young priest, and being arrested at Rome, a legal separation took place. Pompilia sued for a divorce, but, pending the suit, gave birth to a son. The count now murdered Pietro, Violantê, and Pompilia, but being taken red-handed, was brought to trial, found guilty, and executed.

Ring the Bells Backwards (*To*), to ring a muffled peal, to lament. Thus, John Cleveland, wishing to show his abhorrence of the Scotch, says:

How! Providence! and yet a Scottish crew!...
Ring the bells backwards. I am all on fire;
Not all the buckets in a country quire
Shall quench my rage.
The Rebel Scot (1613-1659).

Ringdove (*The Swarthy*). The responses of the oracle of Dodōna, in Epīros, were made by old women called "pigeons," who derived their answers from the cooing of certain doves, the bubbling of a spring, a rustling of the sacred oak [or *beech*], and the tinkling of a gong or bell hung in the tree. The women were called pigeons by a play on the word *peliæ*, which means "old women" as well as "pigeons;" and as they came from Libya they were *swarthy*.

According to the fable, Zeus gave his daughter, Thēbê, two black doves endowed with the gift of human speech; one of them flew into Libya, and the other into Dodona. The former gave the responses in the temple of Ammon, and the latter in the oracle of Dodona.

... beach or lime,
Or that Thessalian growth,
In which the swarthy ringdove sat,
And mystic sentence spoke.
Tennyson.

Ringhorse (*Sir Robert*), a magistrate at Old St. Ronan's.—Sir W. Scott, *St. Ronan's Well* (time, George III.).

Ringwood, a young Templar.—Sir W. Scott, *Fortunes of Nigel* (time, James I.).

Rintherout (*Jenny*), a servant at Monkbarns to Mr. Jonathan Oldbuck, the antiquary.—Sir W. Scott, *The Antiquary* (time, George III.).

Riou (*Captain*), called by Nelson "The Gallant and the Good;" fell in the battle of the Baltic.

Brave hearts! to Britain's pride
Once so faithful and so true,
On the deck of fame that died,
With the gallant, good Riou.
Campbell, *Battle of the Baltic* (1777-1844).

Rip van Winkle slept twenty years in the Catskill Mountains, of North America. (See WINKLE.)

Epimenîdês, the Gnostic, slept for fifty-seven years.

Gyneth slept 500 years, by the enchantment of Merlin.

The seven sleepers slept for 250 years in Mount Celion.

St. David slept for seven years. (See ORMANDINE.)

(The following are not dead, but only sleep till the fulness of their respective times:—Elijah, Endymion, Merlin, King Arthur, Charlemagne, Frederick Barbarossa and his knights, the three Tells, Desmond of Kilmallock, Thomas of Erceldoune, Boabdil el Chico, Brian Boroimhe, Knez Lazar, King Sebastian of Portugal, Olaf Tryggvason, the French slain in the Sicilian Vespers, and one or two others.)

Riquet with the Tuft, the beau-ideal of ugliness, but with the power of bestowing wit and intelligence on the person he loved best. Riquet fell in love with a most beautiful woman, as stupid as he was ugly, but possessing the power of giving beauty to the person she loved best. The two married, whereupon Riquet gave his bride wit, and she bestowed on him beauty.—Charles Perrault, *Contes des Fées* ("Riquet à la Houppe," 1697).

*** This tale is borrowed from the *Nights* of Straparola. It is imitated by Mde. Villeneuve in her *Beauty and the Beast*.

Risingham (*Bertram*), the vassal of Philip of Mortham. Oswald Wycliffe induced him to shoot his lord at Marston Moor; and for this deed the vassal demanded all the gold and movables of his late master. Oswald, being a villain, tried to outwit Bertram, and even to murder him; but it turned out that Philip of Mortham, was not killed, neither was Oswald Wycliffe, his heir, for Redmond O'Neale (Rokeby's page) was found to be the son and heir of Philip of Mortham.—Sir W. Scott, *Rokeby* (1812).

Ritho or **Rython**, a giant who had made himself furs of the beards of kings killed by him. He sent to King Arthur, to meet him on Mount Aravius, or else to send his beard to him without delay. Arthur met him, slew him, and took "fur" as a spoil. Drayton says it was this Rython who carried off Helĕna, the niece of Duke Hoel; but Geoffrey of Monmouth says that King Arthur, having killed the Spanish giant, told his army "he had found none so great in strength *since* he killed the giant Ritho;" by which it seems that the Spanish giant and Ritho are different persons, although it must be confessed the scope of the chronicle seems to favor their identity.—Geoffrey, *British History*, x. 3 (1142).

As how great Rython's self he [*Arthur*] slew ...
Who ravished Howell's niece, young Helena, the fair.
Drayton, *Polyolbion*, iv. (1612).

Rival Queens (*The*), Stati'ra and Roxa'na. Statīra was the daughter of Darīus, and wife of Alexander the Great. Roxana was the daughter of Oxyartês, the Bactrian; her, also, Alexander married. Roxana stabbed Statira, and killed her.—N. Lee, *Alexander the Great*, or *The Rival Queens* (1678).

Rivals (*The*), a comedy by Sheridan (1775). The rivals are Bob Acres and Ensign Beverley (*alias* Captain Absolute), and Lydia Languish is the lady they contend for. Bob Acres tells Captain Absolute that Ensign Beverley is a booby; and if he could find him out, he'd teach him his place. He sends a challenge to the unknown, by Sir Lucius O'Trigger, but objects to forty yards, and thinks thirty-eight would suffice. When he finds that Ensign Beverley is Captain Absolute, he declines to quarrel with his friend; and when his second calls him a coward, he fires up and exclaims, "Coward! Mind, gentlemen, he calls me a 'coward,' coward by my valor!" and when dared by Sir Lucius, he replies, "I don't mind the word 'coward;' 'coward' may be said in a joke; but if he called me 'poltroon,' ods, daggers and balls——" "Well, sir, what then?" "Why," rejoined Bob Acres, "I should certainly think him very ill-bred." Of course, he resigns all claim to the lady's hand.

River of Juvenescence. Prester John, in his letter to Manuel Comnēnus, emperor of Constantinople, says there is a spring at the foot of Mount Olympus, which changes its flavor hour by hour, both night and day. Whoever tastes thrice of its waters, will never know fatigue or the infirmities of age.

River of Paradise, St. Bernard, abbot of Clairvaux (1091-1153).

Rivers Arise.... In this *Vacation Exercise*, George Rivers (son of Sir John Rivers of Westerham, in Kent), with nine other freshmen, took the part of the ten "Predicaments," while Milton himself performed the part of "Ens." Without a doubt, the pun suggested the idea in Milton's *Vacation Exercise* (1627):

Rivers arise; whether thou be the son
Of utmost Tweed, or Ouse, or gulpy Don,
Or Trent, who, like some earthborn giant, spreads
His thirty arms along the indented meads,
Or sullen Mole that runneth underneath,
Or Severn swift, guilty of maiden's death,
Or rocky Avon, or of sedgy Lee,
Or cooly Tyne, or ancient hallowed Dee,

Or Humber loud that keeps the Scythian's name,
Or Medway smooth, or royal towered Thame.

Rivulet Controversy (*The*) arose against Rev. T. T. Lynch, a Congregationalist, who, in 1853, had expressed neologian views in *The Rivulet*, a book of poems.

Rizzio (*David*), the private secretary of Marie Stuart, queen of the Scots, and reputed by her enemies to be her favored lover. He was murdered in her presence by a gang of conspirators, led by Henry Darnley, her husband. Poets and musicians have made lavish use of this episode in the life of the unhappy queen.

Road to Ruin, a comedy by Thomas Holcroft (1792). Harry Dornton and his friend, Jack Milford, are on "the road to ruin," by their extravagance. The former brings his father to the eve of bankruptcy; and the latter, having spent his private fortune, is cast into prison for debt. Sulky, a partner in the bank, comes forward to save Mr. Dornton from ruin; Harry advances £6000 to pay his friend's debts, and thus saves Milford from ruin; and the father restores the money advanced by Widow Warren to his son, to save Harry from the ruin of marrying a designing widow instead of Sophia Freelove, her innocent and charming daughter.

Roads (*The king of*), John Loudon Macadam, the improver of roads (1756-1836).

Roan Barbary, the charger of Richard II., which would eat from his master's hand.

Oh, how it yearned my heart when I beheld
In London streets, that coronation day,
When Bolingbroke rode on Roan Barbary!
That horse that thou so often hast bestrid;
That horse that I so carefully have dressed!
Shakespeare, *Richard II.* act v. sc. 5 (1597).

Rob Roy, published in 1818, excellent for its bold sketches of Highland scenery. The character of Bailie Nicol Jarvie is one of Scott's happiest conceptions; and the carrying of him to the wild mountains among outlaws and desperadoes is exquisitely comic. The hero, Frank Osbaldistone, is no hero at all. Dramatized by I. Pocock.

Rob Roy M'Gregor, *i.e.* "Robert the Red," whose surname was MacGregor. He was an outlaw who assumed the name of Campbell in 1662. He may be termed the Robin Hood of Scotland. The hero of the novel is Frank Osbaldistone, who gets into divers troubles, from which he is rescued by Rob Roy. The last service is to kill Rashleigh Osbaldistone, whereby Frank's great enemy is removed; and Frank then marries Diana Vernon.—Sir W. Scott, *Rob Roy* (time, George I.).

Rather beneath the middle size than above it, his limbs were formed upon the very strongest model that is consistent with agility.... Two points in his person interfered with the rules of symmetry: his shoulders were too broad ... and his arms (though round, sinewy and strong) were so very long as to be rather a deformity.—Ch. xxiii.

Rob Tally-ho, Esq., cousin of the Hon. Tom Dashall, the two blades whose rambles and adventures through the metropolis are related by Pierce Egan (1821-2).

Rob the Rambler, the comrade of Willie Steenson, the blind fiddler.—Sir W. Scott, *Redgauntlet* (time, George III.).

Robb (*Duncan*), the grocer near Ellangowan.—Sir W. Scott, *Guy Mannering* (time, George II.).

Robber (*Alexander's*). The pirate who told Alexander he was the greater robber of the two, was Dionĭdês. (See *Evenings at Home*, art. "Alexander and the Robber.") The tale is from Cicero:

Nam quum quæreretur ex eo, quo scelere impulsus mare haberet infestum uno myoparone: eodem, inquit, quo tu orbem terræ.—*De Repub.*, iii. 14 sc. 24.

Robber (*Edward the*). Edward IV. was so called by the Scotch.

Robert, father of Marian. He had been a wrecker, and still hankered after the old occupation. One night a storm arose, and Robert went to the coast to see what would fall into his hands. A body was washed ashore, and he rifled it. Marian followed, with the hope of restraining her father, and saw in the dusk some one strike a dagger into a prostrate body. She thought it was her father, and when Robert was on his trial he was condemned to death on his daughter's evidence. Black Norris, the real murderer, told her he would save her father if she would consent to be his wife; she consented, and Robert was acquitted. On the wedding day her lover, Edward, returned to claim her hand, Norris was seized as a murderer, and Marian was saved.—S. Knowles, *The Daughter* (1836).

Robert, a servant of Sir Arthur Wardour, at Knockwinnock Castle.—Sir W. Scott, *The Antiquary* (time, George III.).

Robert (*Mons.*), a neighbor of Sganarelle. Hearing the screams of Mde. Martine (Sganarelle's wife), he steps over to make peace between them, whereupon Madame calls him an impertinent fool, and says if she chooses to be beaten by her husband it is no affair of his; and Sganarelle says, "Je la veux battre, si je le veux; et ne la veux pas battre, si je ne le veux pas;" and beats M. Robert again.—Molière, *Le Médecin Malgré Lui* (1666).

Robert Kent. Weak, vicious husband of Margaret Kent. Causes trouble all his life and dies of yellow fever.—Ellen Olney Kirk, *The Story of Margaret Kent* (1886).

Robert Macaire, a bluff, free-living libertine. His accomplice is Bertrand, a simpleton and a villain.—Daumier, *L'Auberge des Adrets*.

Robert, duke of Albany, brother of Robert III. of Scotland.—Sir W. Scott, *Fair Maid of Perth* (time, Henry IV.)

Robert, duke of Normandy, sold his dominions to Rufus for 10,000 marks, to furnish him with ready money for the crusade, which he joined at the head of 1000 heavy-armed horse and 1000 light-armed Normans.—Tasso, *Jerusalem Delivered* (1575).

Robert III. of Scotland, introduced by Sir W. Scott in the *Fair Maid of Perth* (time, Henry IV.).

Robert le Diable, son of Bertha and Bertramo. Bertha was the daughter of Robert, duke of Normandy, and Bertramo was a fiend in the guise of a knight. The opera shows the struggle in Robert between the virtue inherited from his mother and the vice inherited from his father. His father allures him to gamble till he loses everything, and then claims his soul, but his foster-sister, Alice, counterplots the fiend, and rescues Robert by reading to him his mother's will.—Meyerbeer, *Roberto il Diavolo* (libretto by Scribe, 1831).

*** Robert le Diable was the hero of an old French metrical romance (thirteenth century). This romance in the next century was thrown into prose. There is a miracle-play on the same subject.

Robert of Paris (*Count*), one of the crusading princes. The chief hero of this novel is Hereward (3 *syl.*), one of the Varangian guard of the Emperor Alexius Comnēnus. He and the count fight a single combat with battle-axes; after which Hereward enlists under the count's banner, and marries Bertha, also called Agatha.—Sir W. Scott, *Count Robert of Paris* (time, Rufus).

Robert Penfold. Hero of Foul Play, by Charles Reade. He is foully wronged by Arthur Wardlaw, who forges his father's name on a note with Penfold's endorsement. Penfold is found guilty and imprisoned. After his release, he takes passage in the ship with Helen Rolleston, Wardlaw's betrothed. Penfold also loves her, but hopelessly. They are wrecked and cast upon an island in company, and for several months are the only residents. After their rescue and return home, the truth is made manifest, Robert is vindicated, and marries Helen. His aliases are James Seaton and John Hazel.

Robert the Devil, or **Robert the Magnificent**, Robert I., duke of Normandy, father of William "the Conqueror" (*, 1028-1035).

Robert François Damiens, who tried to assassinate Louis XV., was popularly so called (*, 1714-1757).

Robert of Lincoln. The saucy songster is an especial favorite with American poets. Bryant does not disdain to write a long poem that has him as the theme.

"Merrily singing on briar and reed,
Near to the nest of his little dame,
Over the mountain-side or mead,
Robert of Lincoln is telling his name:
'Bob-o'-link, bob-o'-link!
Spink, spank, spink!
Snug and safe is that nest of ours,
Hidden among the summer flowers,
Cha! cha! cha!'"
William Cullen Bryant, *Poems*.

Roberts, cash-keeper of Master George Heriot, the king's goldsmith.—Sir W. Scott, *Fortunes of Nigel* (time, James I.).

Roberts (John), a smuggler.—Sir W. Scott, *Redgauntlet* (time, George III.).

Robespierre's Weavers, the fish-fags and their rabble female followers of the very lowest class, partisans of Robespierre in the first French Revolution.

Robin, the page of Sir John Falstaff.—Shakespeare, *Merry Wives of Windsor* (1601).

Robin, servant of Captain Rovewell, whom he helps in his love adventure with Arethusa, daughter of Argus.—Carey, *Contrivances* (1715).

Robin, brother-in-law of Farmer Crop, of Cornwall. Having lost his property through the villainy of Lawyer Endless, he emigrates, and in three years returns. The ship is wrecked off the coast of Cornwall and Robin saves Frederick, the young squire. On landing, he meets his old sweetheart, Margaretta, at Crop's house, and the acquaintance is renewed by mutual consent.—P. Hoare, *No Song no Supper* (1790).

Robin, a young gardener, fond of the minor theatres, where he has picked up a taste for sentimental fustian, but all his rhapsodies bear upon his trade. Thus, when Wilhelmina asks why he wishes to dance with her, he replies:

Ask the plants why they love a shower; ask the sunflower why it loves the sun; ask the snowdrop why it is white; ask the violet why it is blue; ask the trees why they blossom; the cabbages why they grow. 'Tis all because they can't help it; no more can I help my love for you.—C. Didbin, *The Waterman*, i. (1774).

Robin (Old), butler to old Mr. Ralph Morton, of Milnwood.—Sir W. Scott, *Old Mortality* (time, Charles II.).

Robin Bluestring. Sir Robert Walpole was so called, in allusion to his blue ribbon as a knight of the garter (1676-1745).

Robin des Bois. Mysterious rover of the woods in *Freischütz*, also in Eugène Sue's novels—"a bug-a-boo!"

Robin Gray (*Auld*). The words of this song are by Lady Anne Lindsay, daughter of the earl of Balcarres; she was afterwards Lady Barnard. The song was written, in 1772, to an old Scotch tune called *The Bridegroom Grat when the Sun gaed Down*. (See GRAY.)

Robin Hood was born at Locksley, in Notts., in the reign of Henry II. (1160). His real name was Fitzooth, and it is commonly said that he was the earl of Huntingdon. Having outrun his fortune, and being outlawed, he lived as a freebooter in Barnsdale (Yorkshire), Sherwood (Notts.), and Plompton Park (Cumberland). His chief companions were Little John (whose name was *Nailor*), William Scadlock (or *Scarlet*), George Green, the pinder (or pound-keeper) of Wakefield, Much, a miller's son, and Tuck, a friar, with one woman, Maid Marian. His company at one time consisted of a hundred archers. He was bled to death in his old age by his sister, the Prioress of Kirkley's Nunnery, in Yorkshire, November 18, 1247, aged 87 years.

*** An excellent sketch of Robin Hood is given by Drayton in his *Polyolbion*, xxvi. Sir W. Scott introduces him in two novels—*Ivanhoe* and *The Talisman*. In the former he first appears as Locksley, the archer, at the tournament. He is also called "Dickon Bend-the-Bow."

The following dramatic pieces have the famous outlaw for the hero: *Robin Hood*, i. (1597), Munday; *Robin Hood*, ii. (1598), Chettle; *Robin Hood* (1741), an opera, by Dr. Arne and Burney; *Robin Hood* (1787), an opera by O'Keefe, music by Shield; *Robin Hood*, by Macnally (before 1820).

Major tells us that this famous robber took away the goods of rich men only; never killed any person except in self-defence; never plundered the poor, but charitably fed them; and adds, "he was the most humane and the prince of all robbers."—*Britanniæ Historia*, 128 (1740).

The abbot of St. Mary's, in York, and the sheriff at Nottingham were his *bêtes noires*. Munday and Chettle wrote a popular play in 1601, entitled *The Death of Robert, Earl of Huntington*.

Epitaph of Robin Hood.

Hear undernead dis laitl stean
Laiz robert earl of Huntingtun.
Near arcir ver az hie sa geud,
An pipl kauld im robin heud.
Sick utlawz az hi an iz men
Vil england nivr si agen.
Obiit 24 (? 14) kal dekembris, 1247.
Dr. Gale (dean of York).

Robin Hood's Fat Friar was Friar Tuck.

Robin Hood's Men, outlaws, freebooters.

There came sodainly twelve men all appareled in short cotes of Kentish Kendal [*green*] ... every one of them ... like outlaws or Robyn Hodes men.—Hall (*fo.* lvi. *b*).

Robin Redbreast. One tradition is that the robin pecked a thorn out of the crown of thorns when Christ was on His way to Calvary, and the blood which issued from the wound, falling on the bird, dyed its breast red.

Another tradition is that it carries in its bill dew to those shut up in the burning lake, and its breast is red from being scorched by the fire of Gehenna.

He brings cool dew in his little bill,
And lets it fall on the souls of sin;
You can see the mark on his red breast still,
Of fires that scorch as he drops it in.
J. G. Whittier, *The Robin*.

Robin Redbreasts, Bow Street officers. So called from their red vests.

Robin Roughhead, a poor cottager and farm laborer, the son of Lord Lackwit. On the death of his lordship, Robin Roughhead comes into the title and estates. This brings out the best qualities of his heart—liberality, benevolence and honesty. He marries Dolly, to whom he was already engaged, and becomes the good genius of the peasantry on his estate.—Allingham, *Fortune's Frolic*.

Robin and Makyne (2 *syl.*), an old Scotch pastoral. Robin is a shepherd, for whom Makyne sighs, but he turns a deaf ear to her, and she goes home to weep. In time, Robin sighs for Makyne, but she replies, "He who wills not when he may, when he wills he shall have nay."—Percy, *Reliques, etc.*, II.

Robin of Bagshot, *alias* Gordon, *alias* Bluff Bob, *alias* Carbuncle, *alias* Bob Booty, one of Macheath's gang of thieves, and a favorite of Mrs. Peachum's.—Gay, *The Beggar's Opera* (1727).

Robins (*Zerubbabel*), in Cromwell's troop.—Sir W. Scott, *Woodstock* (time, Commonwealth).

Robinson Cru'soe (2 *syl.*), a tale by Daniel Defoe. Robinson Crusoe ran away from home, and went to sea. Being wrecked, he led for many years a solitary existence on an uninhabited island of the tropics, and relieved the weariness of life by numberless contrivances. At length he met a human being, a young Indian, whom he saved from death on a Friday. He called him his "man Friday," and made him his companion and servant.

Defoe founded this story on the adventures of Alexander Selkirk, sailing-master of the *Cinque Ports Galley*, who was left by Captain Stradling on the desolate island of Juan Fernandez for four years and four months (1704-1709), when he was rescued by Captain Woodes Rogers and brought to England.

Robsart (*Amy*), countess of Leicester. She was betrothed to Edmund Tressilian. When the earl falls into disgrace at court for marrying Amy, Richard Varney loosens a trap-door at Cumnor Place; and Amy, rushing forward to greet her husband, falls into the abyss and is killed.

Sir Hugh Robsart, of Lidcote Hall, father of Amy.—Sir W. Scott, *Kenilworth* (time, Elizabeth).

Roc, a white bird of enormous size. Its strength is such that it will lift up an elephant from the ground and carry it to its mountain nest, where it will devour it. In the *Arabian Nights' Entertainments*, it was a roc which carried Sindbad the sailor from the island on which he had been deserted by his companions ("Second Voyage"). And it was a roc which carried Agib from the castle grounds of the ten young men who had lost their right eyes ("The Third Calender's Story"). Sindbad says one claw of the roc is as "big as the trunk of a large tree," and its egg is "fifty paces [*150 feet*] in circumference."

⁎⁎ The "rukh" of Madagascar, lays an egg equal to 148 hen's eggs.—*Comptes Rendus*, etc., xxxii. 101 (1851).

Rocco, the jailer sent with Fidelio (*Leonora*) to dig the grave of Fernando Florestan (*q.v.*)—Beethoven, *Fidelio* (1791).

Roch'dale (*Sir Simon*), of the manor-house. He is a J.P., but refuses to give justice to Job Thornberry, the old brazier, who demands that his son, Frank Rochdale, should marry Mary [Thornberry], whom he has seduced. At this crisis, Peregrine appears, and tells Sir Simon he is the elder brother, and, as such, is heir to the title and estates.

Frank Rochdale, son of the baronet, who has promised to marry Mary Thornberry, but Sir Simon wants him to marry Lady Caroline Braymore, who has £4000 a year. Lady Caroline marries the Hon. Tom Shuffleton, and Frank makes the best reparation he can by marrying Mary.—G. Colman, Jr., *John Bull* (1805).

Roche's Bird (*Sir Boyle*), which was "in two places at the same time." The tale is that Sir Boyle Roche said in the House of Commons, "Mr. Speaker, it is impossible I could have been in two places at once, unless I were a bird." This is a quotation from Jevon's play, *The Devil of a Wife* (seventeenth century).

Wife. I cannot be in two places at once.

Husband (Rowland). Surely no, unless thou wert a bird.

Rochecliffe (*Dr. Anthony*), formerly Joseph Albany, a plotting royalist.—Sir W. Scott, *Woodstock* (time, commonwealth).

Rochester (*The earl of*), the favorite of Charles II., introduced in high feather by Sir W. Scott in *Woodstock*, and in *Peveril of the Peak* in disgrace.

Rochester (*Edward*). Brusque, cynical lover of *Jane Eyre*. Having married in his early youth a woman who disgraces him and then goes crazy, he shuts her up at Thornhill, and goes abroad. He returns to find a governess there in charge of his child-ward; falls in love with her, and would marry her, but for the discovery of his insane wife. *Jane Eyre* leaves him, and is lost to him until he is almost blind from injuries received in trying to rescue his wife from burning Thornhill. *Jane* marries and ministers unto him.—Charlotte Brontë, *Jane Eyre* (1847).

Rock (*Dr. Richard*), a famous quack, who professed to cure every disease. He was short of stature and fat, wore a white three-tailed wig, nicely combed and frizzed upon each cheek, carried a cane, and halted in his gait.

Dr. Rock, F.U.N., never wore a hat.... He and Dr. Franks were at variance.... Rock cautioned the world to beware of bog-trotting quacks, while Franks called his rival "Dumplin' Dick." Head of Confucius, what profanation!—Goldsmith, *Citizen of the World* (1759).

Oh! when his nerves had received a shock,
Sir Isaac Newton might have gone to Rock.
Crabbe, *Borough* (1810).

Rocket. *He rose like a rocket, and fell like the stick.* Thomas Paine said this of Mr. Burke.

Roderick, the thirty-fourth and last of the Gothic kings of Spain, son of Theod´ofred and Rusilla. Having violated Florinda, daughter of Count Julian, he was driven from his throne by the Moors, and assumed the garb of a monk with the name of "Father Maccabee." He was present at the great battle of Covadonga, in which the Moors were cut to pieces, but what became of him afterwards no one knows. His helm, sword, and cuirass were found, so was his steed. Several generations passed away, when, in a hermitage near Viseu, a tomb was discovered, "which bore in ancient characters King Roderick's name;" but imagination must fill up the gap. He is spoken of as most popular.

Time has been
When not a tongue within the Pyrenees
Dared whisper in dispraise of Roderick's name,
Lest, if the conscious air had caught the sound,
The vengeance of the honest multitude
Should fall upon the traitorous head, and brand
For life-long infamy the lying lips.
Southey, *Roderick, etc.*, xv. (1814).

Roderick's Dog was called Theron.

Roderick's Horse was Orel´io.

Roderick (The Vision of Don). Roderick, the last of the Gothic kings of Spain, descended into an ancient vault near Toledo. This vault was similar to that in Greece, called the cave of Triphōnios, where was an oracle. In the vault Roderick saw a vision of Spanish history from his own reign to the beginning of the nineteenth century. *Period I*. The invasion of the Moors, with his own defeat and death. *Period II*. The Augustine age of Spain, and their conquests in the two Indies. *Period III*. The oppression of Spain by Bonaparte, and its succor by British aid.—Sir W. Scott, *The Vision of Don Roderick* (1811).

Roderick Dhu, an outlaw and chief of a banditti, which resolved to win back the spoil of the "Saxon spoiler." Fitz-James, a Saxon, met him and knew him not. He asked the Saxon why he was roaming unguarded over the mountains, and Fitz-James replied that he had sworn to combat with Roderick, the rebel, till death laid one of them prostrate. "Have, then, thy wish!" exclaimed the stranger, "for I am Roderick Dhu." As he spoke, the whole place bristled with armed men. Fitz-James stood with his back against a rock, and cried, "Come one, come all, this rock shall fly from its firm base as soon as I." Roderick, charmed with his daring, waved his hand, and all the band disappeared as mysteriously as they had appeared. Roderick then bade the Saxon fight, "For," said he, "that party will prove victorious which first slays an enemy." "Then," replied Fitz-James, "thy cause is hopeless, for Red Murdock is slain already." They fought, however, and Roderick was slain (canto v.).—Sir W. Scott, *The Lady of the Lake* (1810).

Roderick Random, a child of impulse, and a selfish libertine. His treatment of Strap is infamous and most heartless.—Smollett, *Roderick Random* (1748).

Rod′erigo or **Roderi′go** (3 *syl.*), a Venetian gentleman, in love with Desdemona. When Desdemona eloped with Othello, Roderigo hated the "noble Moor," and Ia′go took advantage of this temper for his own base ends.—Shakespeare, *Othello* (1611).

Roderigo's suspicious credulity and impatient submission to the cheats which he sees practised on him, and which, by persuasion, he suffers to be repeated, exhibit a strong picture of a weak mind betrayed by unlawful desires to a false friend.—Dr. Johnson.

Rodilardus, a huge cat, which attacked Panurge, and which he mistook for "a young, soft-chinned devil." The word means "gnaw-lard" (Latin, *rodĕre lardum*).—Rabelais, *Pantagruel*, iv. 67 (1545).

⁎ The marquis de Carabas." (See PUSS IN BOOTS.)

Rodrigo, king of Spain, conquered by the Moors. He saved his life by flight, and wandered to Guadaletê, where he begged food of a shepherd, and gave him in recompense his royal chain and ring. A hermit bade him, in penance, retire to a certain tomb full of snakes and toads, where, after three days, the hermit found him unhurt; so, going to his cell, he passed the night in prayer. Next morning, Rodrigo cried aloud to the hermit, "They eat me now; I feel the adder's bite." So his sin was atoned for, and he died.

⁎ This Rodrigo is Roderick, the last of the Goths.

Rodrigo, rival of Pe′dro, "the pilgrim," and captain of a band of outlaws.—Beaumont and Fletcher, *The Pilgrim* (1621).

Rodri′go de Mondragon (*Don*), a bully and tyrant, the self-constituted arbiter of all disputes in a tennis-court of Valladolid.

Don Rodrigo de Mondragon was about 30 years of age, of an ordinary make, but lean and muscular; he had two little twinkling eyes that rolled in his head, and threatened everybody he looked at; a very flat nose, placed between red whiskers that curled up to his very temples; and a manner of speaking so rough and passionate that his words struck terror into everybody.—Lesage, *Gil Blas*, ii. 5 (1715).

Rodhaver, the sweetheart of Zal, a Persian. Zal being about to scale her bower, she let down her long tresses to assist him, but Zal managed to fix his crook into a projecting beam, and thus made his way to the lady of his devotion.—Champion, *Ferdosi*.

Rodman (*Keeper, The*), an ex-colonel of the Federal army, who has become the keeper of a national cemetery at the south. "At sunrise, the keeper ran up the stars and stripes, and … he had taken money from his own store to buy a second flag for stormy weather, so that, rain or not, the colors should float over the dead.... It was simply a sense of the fitness of things." He deviates so far from his rule as to fall in love with a Southern girl, whose nearest relative he has nursed through his last illness. She despises him as a Yankee too much to suspect this; she will not even write her name as a visitor to the National Cemetery. She goes to Tennessee to teach school, and Rodman offers to buy the uprooted vines discarded by the new owner of her cottage. "Wuth about twenty-five cents, I guess," said the Maine man, handing them over.—Constance Fenimore Woolson (1880).

Rodmond, chief mate of the *Brittania*, son of a Northumbrian, engaged in the coal trade; a hardy, weather-beaten seaman, uneducated, "boisterous of manners," and regardless of truth, but tender-hearted. He was drowned when the ship struck on Cape Colonna, the most southern point of Attica.

Unskilled to argue, in dispute yet loud,
Bold without caution, without honors proud,
In art unschooled, each veteran rule he prized,
And all improvement haughtily despised.
Falconer, *The Shipwreck*, i. (1756).

Ro′dogune, **Rhodogune**, or **Rho′dogyne** (3 *syl*.), daughter of Phraa′tês, king of Parthia. She married Deme′trius Nica′nor (the husband of Cleopat′ra, queen of Syria) while in captivity.

⁎ P. Corneille has a tragedy on the subject entitled *Rodogune* (1646).

Rodolfo (*Il conte*). It is in the bedchamber of this count that Ami′na is discovered the night before her espousal to Elvi′no. Ugly suspicion is excited, but the count assures the young farmer that Amina walks in her sleep. While they are talking Amina is seen to get out of a window and walk along a narrow edge of the mill-roof while the huge wheel is rapidly revolving. She crosses a crazy bridge, and walks into the very midst of the spectators. In a few minutes she awakens and flies to the arms of her lover.—Bellini, *La Sonnambula* (opera, 1831).

Rodomont, king of Sarza or Algiers. He was Ulien's son, and called the "Mars of Africa." His lady-love was Dor′alis, princess of Grana′da, but she eloped with Mandricardo, king of Tartary. At Rogero's wedding Rodomont accused him of being a renegade and traitor, whereupon they fought, and Rodomont was slain.—*Orlando Innamorato* (1495); and *Orlando Furioso* (1516).

Who so meek? I'm sure I quake at the very thought of him; why, he's as fierce as Rodomont!—Dryden, *Spanish Fryar*, v. 2 (1680).

⁎ Rodomontade (4 *syl*.), from Rodomont, a bragging although a brave knight.

Rogel of Greece (*The Exploits and Adventures of*), part of the series called *Le Roman des Romans*, pertaining to "Am´adis of Gaul." This part was added by Feliciano de Silva.

Roger, the cook who "cowde roste, sethe, broille, and frie, make mortreux, and wel bake a pye."—Chaucer, *Canterbury Tales* (1388).

Roger (Sir), curate to "The Scornful Lady" (no name given).—Beaumont and Fletcher, *The Scornful Lady* (1616).

Roger Armstrong, clerical lover of Faith Gartney, and her preferred suitor.—A. D. T. Whitney, *Faith Gartney's Girlhood*.

Roger Bontemps, the personation of contentment with his station in life, and of the buoyancy of good hope. "There's a good time coming, John."

Vous pauvres, pleins d'enviè;
Vous rich, désireux;
Vous dont le char dévie
Après un cours heureux;
Vous qui perdrez peut-être
Des titres éclatans;
Eh! gai! prenez pour maitre
Le gros Roger Bontemps.
Béranger (1780-1856).

Ye poor, with envy goaded;
Ye rich, for more who long;
Ye who by fortune loaded
Find all things going wrong;
Ye who by some disaster
See all your cables break;
From henceforth, for your master
Sleek Roger Bontemps take.

Roger Chillingworth, deformed husband of Hester Prynne. He returns to Boston from a long sojourn with the Indians, and sees his wife in the pillory with a baby—not his—in her arms. From that instant he sets himself to work to discover the name of her seducer, and, suspecting Arthur Dimmesdale, attaches himself to the oft-ailing clergyman as his medical attendant. He it is who first suspects the existence of the cancer that is devouring the young clergyman's life, and when the horrible thing is revealed, kneels by the dying man with the bitter whisper, "Thou hast escaped me!"—Nathaniel Hawthorne, *The Scarlet Letter* (1850).

Roger de Coverley (*Sir*), an hypothetical baronet of Coverley or Cowley, near Oxford.—Addison, *The Spectator* (1711, 1712, 1714).

*** The prototype of this famous character was Sir John Pakington, seventh baronet of the line.

Roge´ro, brother of Marphi´sa; brought up by Atlantês, a magician. He married Brad´amant, the niece of Charlemagne. Rogero was converted to Christianity, and was baptized. His marriage with Bradamant and his election to the crown of Bulgaria concludes the poem.—Ariosto, *Orlando Furioso* (1516).

Who more brave than Rodomont? who more courteous than Rogero?—Cervantês, *Don Quixote*, I. i. (1605).

Rogero, son of Roberto Guiscardo, the Norman. Slain by Tisaphernês.—Tasso, *Jerusalem Delivered*, xx. (1575).

Rogero (3 *syl.*), a gentleman of Sicilia.—Shakespeare, *The Winter's Tale* (1604).

*** This is one of those characters which appear in the *dramatis personæ*, but are never introduced in the play. Rogero not only does not utter a word—he does not even enter the stage all through the drama. In the Globe edition his name is omitted. (See VIOLENTA.)

Rogers (*Mr.*), illiterate, tender-hearted, great-souled old father of *Louisiana*. When she begs his pardon for having been ashamed of, and having disowned him, he tells her, "It's *you* as should be a-forgivin' *me* ... I hadn't done ye no sort o' justice in the world, an' never could."—Frances Hodgson Burnett, *Louisiana* (1880).

Roget, the pastoral name of George Wither in the four "eglogues" called *The Shepheards Hunting* (1615). The first and last "eglogues" are dialogues between Roget and Willy, his young friend; in the second pastoral Cuddy is introduced, and in the third Alexis makes a fourth character. The subject of the first three is the reason of Roget's imprisonment, which, he says, is a hunt that gave great offence. This hunt is in reality a satire called *Abuses Stript and Whipt*. The fourth pastoral has for its subject Roget's love of poetry.

*** "Willy" is his friend, William Browne, of the Inner Temple (two years his junior), author of *Britannia's Pastorals*.

Roi Panade ("*king of slops*"), Louis XVIII. (1755, 1814-1824).

Roister Doister (*Ralph*), a vain, thoughtless, blustering fellow, in pursuit of Custance, a rich widow, but baffled in his endeavor.—Nicholas Udall, *Ralph Roister Doister* (the first English comedy, 1534).

Rokesmith (*John*), *alias* JOHN HARMON, secretary of Mr. Boffin. He lodged with the Wilfers, and ultimately married Bella Wilfer. John Rokesmith is described as "a dark gentleman, 30 at the utmost, with an expressive, one might say, a handsome face."—Dickens, *Our Mutual Friend* (1864).

※ For solution of the mystery, see vol. I. ii. 13.

Ro′land, count of Mans and knight of Blaives. His mother, Bertha, was Charlemagne's sister. Roland is represented as brave, devotedly loyal, unsuspicious, and somewhat too easily imposed npon. He was eight feet high, and had an open countenance. In Italian romance he is called Orlan′do. He was slain in the valley of Roncesvalles as he was leading the rear of his uncle's army from Spain to France. Charlemagne himself had reached St. Jean Pied de Port at the time, heard the blast of his nephew's horn, and knew it announced treachery, but was unable to render him assistance (A.D. 778).

Roland is the hero of Théroulde's *Chanson de Roland*; of Turpin's *Chronique*; of Bojardo's *Orlando Innamorato*; of Ariosto's *Orlando Furioso*; of Piccini's opera called *Roland* (1778); etc.

Roland's Horn, Olivant or Olifant. It was won from the giant Jatmund, and might be heard at the distance of thirty miles. Birds fell dead at its blast, and the whole Saracen army drew back in terror when they heard it. So loud it sounded, that the blast reached from Roncesvallês to St. Jean Pied de Port, a distance of several miles.

Roland lifts Olifant to his month and blows it with all his might. The mountains around are lofty, but high above them the sound of the horn arises [*at the third blast, it split in twain*].—*Song of Roland* (as sung by Taillefer, at the battle of Hastings). See Warton, *History of English Poetry*, v. I, sect. iii. 132 (1781).

Roland's Horse, Veillantif, called in Italian *Velian′tino* ("the little vigilant one").

In Italian romance, Orlando has another horse, called Brigliado′ro ("golden bridle").

Roland's Spear. Visitors are shown a spear in the cathedral of Pa′via, which they are told belonged to Roland.

Roland's Sword, Duran′dal, made by the fairies. To prevent its falling into the hands of the enemy, when Roland was attacked in the valley of Roncesvallês, he smote a rock with it, and it made in the solid rock a fissure some 300 feet in depth, called to this day *La Brêche de Roland*.

Then would I seek the Pyrenean breach,
Which Roland clove with huge two-handed sway,
And to the enormous labor left his name.
Wordsworth.

※ A sword is shown at Rocamadour, in the department of Lot (France), which visitors are assured was Roland's *Durandal*. But the romances says that Roland, dying, threw his sword into a poisoned stream.

Death of Roland. There is a tradition that Roland escaped the general slaughter in the defile of Roncesvallês, and died of starvation while trying to make his way across the mountains.—John de la Bruiere Champier, *De Cibaria*, xvi. 5.

Died like Roland, died of thirst.

Nonnulli qui de Gallicis rebus historias conscripserunt, non dubitarunt posteris significare Rolandum Caroli illius magni sororis filium, verum certe bellica gloria omnique fortitudine nobillissimum, post ingentem Hispanorum cædem prope Pyrenæi saltus juga, ubi insidiæ ab hoste collocatæ fuerint, siti miserrime extinctum. Inde nostri intolerabili siti et immiti volentes significare se torqueri, facete aiunt "Rolandi morte se perire."—John de la Bruiere Champier, *De Cibaria*, xvi. 5.

Roland (The Roman). Sicinius Dentātus is so called by Niebuhr. He is not unfrequently called "The Roman Achillês" (put to death B.C. 450).

Roland Blake. Hero of a war-novel of the same name.—Silas Weir Mitchell, M.D. (1886).

Roland and Oliver, the two most famous of the twelve paladins of Charlemagne. To give a "Roland for an Oliver" is to give tit for tat, to give another as good a drubbing as you receive.

Froissart, a countryman of ours [*the French*] records,
England all Olivers and Rowlands bred
During the time Edward the Third did reign.
Shakespeare, 1 *Henry VI.* act i. sc. 2 (1589).

Roland de Vaux (*Sir*), baron of Triermain, who wakes Gyneth from her long sleep of 500 years, and marries her.—Sir W. Scott, *Bridal of Triermain* (1813).

Rolando (*Signor*), a common railer against women, but brave, of a "happy wit and independent spirit." Rolando swore to marry no woman, but fell in love with Zam´ora, and married her, declaring "that she was no woman, but an angel."—J. Tobin, *The Honeymoon* (1804).

The resemblance between Rolando and Benedick will instantly occur to the mind.

Rolandseck Tower, opposite the Drachenfels. Roland was engaged to Aude, daughter of Sir Gerard and Lady Guibourg; but the lady, being told that Roland had been slain by Angoulaffre, the Saracen, retired to a convent. The paladin returned home full of glory, having slain the Saracen, and when he heard that his lady-love had taken the veil, he built Rolandseck Castle, which overlooks the convent, that he might at least *see* the lady to whom he could never be united. After the death of Aude, Roland "sought the battle-field again, and fell at Roncevall."—Campbell, *The Brave Roland*.

Roldan, "El encantado," Roldan made invulnerable by enchantment. The cleft "Roldan," in the summit of a high mountain in the kingdom of Valencia, was so called because it was made by a single back-stroke of Roldan's sword. The character is in two Spanish romances, authors unknown.—*Bernardo del Carpio* and *Roncesvalles*.

This book [*Rinaldo de Montalban*], and all others written on French matters, shall be deposited in some dry place ... except one called *Bernardo del Carpio*, and another called *Roncesvalles*, which shall certainly accompany the rest on the bonfire.—Cervantes, *Don Quixote*, I. i. 6 (1605).

Rolla, kinsman of the Inca Atali'ba, and the idol of the army. "In war a tiger chafed by the hunters' spears; in peace more gentle than the unweaned lamb" (act i. 1). A firm friend and most generous foe. Rolla is wounded in his attempt to rescue the infant child of Alonzo from the Spaniards, and dies. His grand funeral procession terminates the drama.—Sheridan, *Pizarro* (altered from Kotzebue, 1799).

Rolleston (*General*), father of Helen, in *Foul Play*, by Charles Reade.

Rollo, duke of Normandy, called "The Bloody Brother." He caused the death of his brother, Otto, and slew several others, some out of mere wantonness.—Beaumont and Fletcher, *The Bloody Brother* (1639).

Rollo, boy who is the hero of Jacob Abbott's celebrated and delightful "*Rollo Books*," embracing *Rollo Learning to Read*, *Rollo Learning to Work*, *Rollo at School*, *Rollo's Vacation*, etc., etc. (1840-1857).

Roman (*The*), Jean Dumont, the French painter, *Le Romain* (1700-1781).

Stephen Picart, the French engraver, *Le Romain* (1631-1721).

Giulio Pippi, called *Giulio Romano* (1492-1546).

Adrian von Roomen, mathematician, *Adriānus Romānus* (1561-1615).

Roman Achillês, Sicinius Dentātus (slain R.C. 450).

Roman Brevity. Cæsar imitated laconic brevity when he announced to Amintius his victory at Zela, in Asia Minor, over Pharna'cês, son of Mithridatês; *Veni, vidi, vici*.

Poins. I will imitate the honorable Roman in brevity.—Shakespeare, 2 *Henry IV*. act ii. sc. 2 (1598).

Sir Charles Napier is credited with a far more laconic despatch, on making himself master of Scinde, in 1843. Taking possession of Hyderabad, and outflanking Shere Mohammed by a series of most brilliant manœuvres, he is said to have written home this punning despatch: *Peccāvi* ("I have sinned" [Scinde]).

Roman Father (*The*), Horatius, father of the Horatii and of Horatia. The story of the tragedy is the well-known Roman legend about the Horatii and Curiatii. Horatius rejoices that his three sons have been selected to represent Rome, and sinks the affection of the father in love for his country. Horatia is the betrothed of Caius Curiatius, but is also beloved by Valerius, and when the Curiatii are selected to oppose her three brothers, she sends Valerius to him with a scarf, to induce him to forego the fight. Caius declines, and is slain. Horatia is distracted; they take from her every instrument of death, and therefore she resolves to provoke her surviving brother, Publius, to kill her. Meeting him in his triumph, she rebukes him for murdering her lover, scoffs at his "patriotism," and Publius kills her. Horatius now resigns Publius to execution for murder, but the king and Roman people rescue him.—W. Whitehead (1741).

⁎⁎ Corneille has a drama on the same subject, called *Les Horaces* (1639).

Roman des Romans (*Le*), a series of prose romances connected with Am´adis, of Gaul. So called by Gilbert Saunier.

Romans (*Last of the*), Rienzi, the tribune (1310-1354).

Charles James Fox (1749-1806).

Horace Walpole, *Ultimus Romanorum* (1717-1797).

Caius Cassius was so called by Brutus.

The last of all the Romans, fare thee well!
It is impossible that ever Rome
Should breed thy fellow.
Shakespeare, *Julius Cæsar*, act v. sc. 3. (1607).

Romans (*Most Learned of the*), Marcus Terentius Varro (B.C. 116-28).

Romance of the Rose, a poetical allegory, begun by Guillaume di Lorris in the latter part of the thirteenth century, and continued by Jean de Meung in the former half of the fourteenth century. The poet dreams that Dame Idleness conducts him to the palace of Pleasure, where he meets Love, whose attendant maidens are Sweet-looks, Courtesy, Youth, Joy, and Competence, by whom he is conducted to a bed of roses. He singles out one, when an arrow from Love's bow stretches him fainting on the ground, and he is carried off. When he comes to himself, he resolves, if possible, to find his rose, and Welcome promises to aid him; Shyness, Fear, and Slander obstruct him; and Reason advises him to give up the quest. Pity and Kindness show him the object of his search; but Jealousy seizes Welcome, and locks her in Fear Castle. Here the original poem ends. The sequel, somewhat longer than the twenty-four books of Homer's *Iliad*, takes up the tale from this point.

Roma´no, the old monk who took pity on Roderick in his flight (viii.), and went with him for refuge to a small hermitage on the sea-coast, where they remained for twelve months, when the old monk died.—Southey, *Roderick, The Last of the Goths*, i., ii. (1841).

Rome Does (*Do as*). The saying originated with Saint Ambrose (fourth century). It arose from the following diversity in the observance of Saturday:—The Milanese make it a feast, the Romans a fast. St. Ambrose, being asked what should be done in such a case, replied, "In matters of indifference, it is better to be guided by the general usage. When I am at Milan, I do not fast on Saturdays, but when I am at Rome, I do as they do at Rome."

Rome Saved by Geese. When the Gauls invaded Rome, a detachment in single file scaled the hill on which the capitol stood, so silently that the foremost man reached the summit without being challenged; but while striding over the rampart, some sacred geese were disturbed, and by their cackle aroused the guard. Marcus Manlius rushed to the wall, and hustled the Gaul over, thus saving the capitol.

A somewhat parallel case occurred in Ireland in the battle of Glinsaly, in Donegal. A party of the Irish would have surprised the Protestants if some wrens had not disturbed the guards by the noise they made in hopping about the drums and pecking on the parchment heads.—Aubrey, *Miscellanies*, 45.

Ro´meo, a son of Mon´tague (3 *syl.*), in love with Juliet, the daughter of Cap´ulet; but between the houses of Montague and Capulet there existed a deadly feud. As the families were irreconcilable, Juliet took a sleeping draught, that she might get away from her parents and elope with Romeo. Romeo, thinking her to be dead, killed himself; and when Juliet awoke and found her lover dead, she also killed herself.—Shakespeare, *Romeo and Juliet* (1598).

Romeo and Juliet, a tragedy by Shakespeare (1598). The tale is taken from *Rhomeo and Julietta*, a novel by Boisteau, in French, borrowed from an Italian story by Bandello (1554).

In 1562 Arthur Brooke produced the same tale in verse, called *The Tragicall History of Romeus and Juliet*. In 1567 Painter published a prose translation of Boisteau's novel.

Romola, superb woman, high-spirited, pure and single of heart, the idol and co-laborer of her scholarly father. She wrecks her life by the marriage with the fascinating Greek, Tito Melema.—George Eliot, *Romola*.

Romp (*The*), a comic opera altered from Bickerstaff's *Love in the City*. Priscilla Tomboy is "the romp," and the plot is given under that name.

A splendid portrait of Mrs. Jordan, in her character of "The Romp," hung over the mantelpiece in the dining-room [*of Adolphus Fitzclarence*].—Lord W. P. Lennox, *Celebrities, etc.*, i. 11.

Rom´uald (*St*). The Catalans had a great reverence for a hermit so called, and hearing that he was about to quit their country, called together a parish meeting, to consult how they might best retain him amongst them, "For," said they, "he will certainly be consecrated, and his relics will bring a fortune to us." So they agreed to strangle him; but their intention being told to the hermit, he secretly made his escape.—St. Foix, *Essais Historiques sur Paris*, v. 163.

*** Southey has a ballad on the subject.

Romulus (*The Second and Third*), Camillus and Marĭus. Also called "The Second and Third Founders of Rome."

Romulus and Remus, the twin sons of Silvia, a vestal virgin, and the god Mars. The infants were exposed in a cradle, and the floods carried the cradle to the foot of the Palatine. Here a wolf suckled them, till one Faustulus, the king's shepherd, took them to his wife, who brought them up. When grown to manhood, they slew Amulius, who had caused them to be exposed.

The Greek legend of Tyro is in many respects similar. This Tyro had an amour with Poseidon (as Silvia had with Mars), and two sons were born in both cases. Tyro's mother-in-law confined her in a dungeon, and exposed the two infants (Pelias and Neleus) in a boat on the river Enīpeus (3 *syl*.). Here they were discovered and brought up by a herdsman (Romulus and Remus were brought up by a shepherd), and when grown to manhood, they put to death their mother-in-law, who had caused them to be exposed (as Romulus and Remus put to death their great-uncle, Amulius).

Ron, the ebony spear of Prince Arthur.

The temper of his sword, the tried Excalibor,
The bigness and the length of Rone his noble spear,
With Pridwin his great shield.
Drayton, *Polyolbion*, iv. (1612).

Ronald (*Lord*), in love with Lady Clare, to whom he gave a lily-white doe. The day before the wedding nurse Alice told Lady Clare she was not "Lady

Clare" at all, but her own child. On hearing this, she dressed herself as a peasant girl, and went to Lord Ronald to release him from his engagement. Lord Ronald replied, "If you are not the heiress born, we will be married tomorrow, and you shall still be Lady Clare."—Tennyson, *Lady Clare*.

Ronaldson (*Neil*), the old ranzelman of Jarlshof (ch. vii.).—Sir W. Scott, *The Pirate* (time William III.).

Rondib´ilis, the physician consulted by Panurge, on the knotty question, "whether he ought to marry, or let it alone."—Rabelais, *Pantagruel* (1545).

⁎ This question, which Panurge was perpetually asking every one, of course refers to the celibacy of the clergy.

Rondo (*The Father of the*), Jean Baptiste Davaux.

Rope of Ocnus (*A*), profitless labor. Ocnus was always twisting a rope with unwearied diligence, but an ass ate it as fast as it was twisted.

⁎ This allegory means that Ocnus worked hard to earn money, which his wife squandered by her extravagance.

The work of Penelopê's web was "never ending, still beginning," because Penelopê pulled out at night all that she had spun during the day. Her object was to defer doing what she abhorred but knew not how to avoid.

Roper (*Margaret*), was buried with the head of her father, Sir Thomas More, between her hands.

Her who clasped in her last trance
Her murdered father's head.
Tennyson.

Roque (1 *syl.*), a blunt, kind-hearted old servitor to Donna Floranthe.—Colman, *The Mountaineers* (1793).

Roque Guinart, a freebooter, whose real name was Pedro Rocha Guinarda. He is introduced by Cervantês in *Don Quixote*.

Rosa, a village beauty, patronized by Lady Dedlock. She marries Mrs. Rouncewell's grandson.—C. Dickens, *Bleak House* (1853).

Rosabelle (3 *syl.*), the lady's-maid of Lady Geraldine. Rosabelle promised to marry L'Eclair, the orderly of Chevalier Florian.—W. Dimond, *The Foundling of the Forest*.

Rosalind (*i.e.* Rose Daniel), the shepherd lass who rejected Colin Clout (the poet Spenser) for Menalcas (John Florio, the lexicographer, 1579). Spenser was at the time in his twenty-sixth year. Being rejected by Rosalind, he did not marry till he was nearly 41, and then we are told that Elizabeth "was the name of his mother, queen and wife" (*Sonnet*, 74). In the *Faëry Queen*, "the country lass" (Rosalind) is introduced dancing with the Graces, and the poet says she is worthy to be the fourth (bk. vi. 10, 16). In 1595 appeared the *Epithala'mion*, in which the recent marriage is celebrated.—Ed. Spenser, *Shepheardes Calendar*, i., vi. (1579).

"Rosalinde" is an anagram for Rose Daniel, evidently a well-educated young lady of the north, and probably the "Lady Mirabella" of the *Faëry Queen*, vi. 7, 8. Spenser calls her "the widow's daughter of the glen" (ecl. iv.), supposed to be either Burnley or Colne, near Hurstwood, in Yorkshire. Ecl. i. is the plaint of Colin for the loss of Rosalind. Ecl. vi. is a dialogue between Colin and Hobbinol, his friend, in which Colin laments, and Hobbinol tries to comfort him. Ecl. xii. is a similar lament to ecl. i. Rose Daniel married John Florio, the lexicographer, the "Holofernês" of Shakespeare.

Rosalind, daughter of the banished duke who went to live in the forest of Arden. Rosalind was retained in her uncle's court as the companion of his daughter, Celia; but when the usurper banished her, Celia resolved to be her companion, and, for greater security, Rosalind dressed as a boy, and assumed the name of Ganymede, while Celia dressed as a peasant girl, and assumed the name of Aliēna. The two girls went to the forest of Arden, and lodged for a time in a hut; but they had not been long there when Orlando encountered them. Orlando and Rosalind had met before at a wrestling match, and the acquaintance was now renewed; Ganymede resumed her proper apparel, and the two were married, with the sanction of the duke.—Shakespeare, *As You Like It* (1598).

Nor shall the griefs of Lear be alleviated, or the charms and wit of Rosalind be abated by time.—N. Drake, M.D., *Shakespeare and His Times*, ii. 554 (1817).

Rosaline, the niece of Capulet, with whom Romeo was in love before he saw Juliet. Mercutio calls her "a pale-hearted wench," and Romeo says she did not "grace for grace and love for love allow," like Juliet.—Shakespeare, *Romeo and Juliet* (1598).

⁎⁎ Rosaline is frequently mentioned in the first act of the play, but is not one of the *dramatis personæ*.

Rosaline, a lady in attendance on the princess of France. A sharp wit was wedded to her will, and "two pitch balls were stuck in her face for eyes." Rosaline is called "a merry, nimble, stirring spirit." Biron, a lord in attendance on Ferdinand, king of Navarre, proposes marriage to her, but she replies:

You must be purged first, your sins are racked ...
Therefore if you my favor mean to get,
A twelvemonth shall you spend, and never rest,

But seek the weary beds of people sick.
Shakespeare, *Love's Labor's Lost* (1594).

Rosalu´ra, the airy daughter of Nantolet, beloved by Belleur.—Beaumont and Fletcher, *The Wild-goose Chase* (1652).

Ros´amond (*The Fair*), Jane Clifford, daughter of Walter, Lord Clifford. The lady was loved, not wisely, but too well, by Henry II., who kept her for concealment in a labyrinth at Woodstock. Queen Eleanor compelled the frail fair one to swallow poison (1777).

She was the fayre daughter of Walter, Lord Clifford.... Henry made for her a house of wonderfull working, so that no man or woman might come to her. This house was named "Labyrinthus," and was wrought like unto a knot, in a garden called a maze. But the queen came to her by a clue of thredde, and so dealt with her that she lived not long after. She was buried at Godstow, in a house of nunnes, with these verses upon her tombe:

Hic jacet in tumba Rosa mundi, non Rosa munda;
Non redolet, sed olet, quæ redolere solet.

Here Rose the graced, not Rose the chaste, reposes;
The smell that rises is no smell of roses.

*** The subject has been a great favorite with poets. We have in English the following tragedies:—*The Complaint of Rosamond*, by S. Daniel (before 1619); *Henry II.... with the Death of Rosamond*, either Bancroft or Mountford (1693); *Rosamond*, by Addison (1706); *Henry and Rosamond*, by Hawkins (1749); *Fair Rosamond*, by Tennyson (1879). In Italian, *Rosmonda*, by Rucellai (1525). In Spanish, *Rosmunda*, by Gil y Zarate (1840). We have also *Rosamond*, an opera, by Dr. Arne (1733); and *Rosamonde*, a poem in French, by C. Briffaut (1813). Sir Walter Scott has introduced the beautiful soiled dove in two of his novels—*The Talisman* and *Woodstock*.

*** Dryden says her name was *Jane*:

Jane Clifford was her name, as books aver:
"Fair Rosamond" was but her *nom de guerre*.

We rede that in Englande was a king that had a concubyne whose name was Rose, and for hir greate bewtye he cleped hir Rose à mounde (Rosa mundi), that is to say, Rose of the world, for him thought that she passed al wymen in bewtye.—R. Pynson (1493), subsequently printed by Wynken de Worde in 1496.

The *Rosemonde* of Alfieri is quite another person. (See ROSEMOND.)

Rosa´na, daughter of the Armenian queen who helped St. George to quench the seven lamps of the knight of the Black Castle.—R. Johnson, *The Seven Champions of Christendom*, ii. 8, 9 (1617).

Roscius (*Quintus*), the greatest of Roman actors (died B.C. 62).

What scene of death hath Roscius now to act?
Shakespeare, 3 *Henry VI.* act v. sc. 6 (1592).

Roscius (*The British*), Thomas Betterton (1635-1710), and David Garrick (1716-1779).

⁂ The earl of Southampton says that Richard Burbage "is famous as our English Roscius" (1566-1619).

Roscius (*The Irish*), Spranger Barry, "The Silver Tongued" (1719-1777).

Roscius (*The Young*), William Henry West Betty, who, in 1803, made his *début* in London. He was about 12 years of age, and in fifty-six nights realized £34,000. He died, aged 84, in 1874.

Roscius of France (*The*), Michel Boyron or Baron (1653-1729).

Roscrana, daughter of Cormac, king of Ireland (grandfather of that Cormac murdered by Cairbar). Roscra´na is called "the blue-eyed and white-handed maid," and was "like a spirit of heaven, half folded in the skirt of a cloud." Subsequently she was the wife of Fingal, king of Morven, and mother of Ossian, "king of bards."—Ossian, *Temora*, vi.

⁂ Cormac, the father of Roscrana, was great-grandfather of that Cormac who was reigning when Swaran made his invasion. The line ran thus: (1) Cormac I., (2) Cairbre, his son, (3) Artho, his son, (4) Cormac II., father-in-law of Fingal.

Rose, "the gardener's daughter," a story of happy first love, told in later years by an old man who had, in his younger days, trifled with the passion of love; but, like St. Augustin, was always "loving to love" (*amans amāre*), and was at length heart-smitten with Rose, whom he married. (See ALICE.)—Tennyson, *The Gardener's Daughter*.

Rose. Sir John Mandeville says that a Jewish maid of Bethlehem (whom Southey names Zillah) was beloved by one Ham´uel, a brutish sot. Zillah rejected his suit, and Hamuel, in revenge, accused the maiden of offences for which she was condemned to be burned alive. When brought to the stake, the flames burnt Hamuel to a cinder, but did no harm to Zillah. There she stood, in a garden of roses, for the brands which had been kindled became red roses, and those which had not caught fire became white ones. These are the first roses that ever bloomed on earth since the loss of paradise.

As the fyre began to brenne about hire, she made her preyeres to oure Lord ... and anon was the fayer quenched and oute, and brondes that weren brennynge becomen white roseres ... and theise werein the first roseres that ever ony man saughe.—Sir John Maundeville, *Voiage and Traivaile*.

Rose. According to Mussulman tradition, the rose is thus accounted for: When Mahomet took his journey to heaven, the sweat which fell on the earth from the prophet's forehead produced *White* roses, and that which fell from Al Borak´ (the animal he rode) produced *yellow* ones.

Rose.

The gentle name that shows
Her love, her loveliness, and bloom
(Her only epitaph a rose)
Is growing on her tomb!
John James Piatt, *Poems of House and Home* (1879).

Rose of Aragon (*The*), a drama by S. Knowles (1842). Olivia, daughter of Ruphi´no (a peasant), was married to Prince Alonzo of Aragon. The king would not recognize the match, but sent his son to the army, and made the cortez pass an act of divorce. A revolt having been organized, the king was dethroned, and Almagro was made regent. Almagro tried to marry Olivia, and to murder her father and brother, but the prince returning with the army made himself master of the city, Almagro died of poison, the marriage of the prince and peasant was recognized, the revolt was broken up, and order was restored.

Rose of Har´pocrate (3 *syl.*). Cupid gave Harpocrate a rose, to bribe him not to divulge the amours of his mother, Venus.

Red as a rose of Harpocrate.
E. B. Browning, *Isobel's Child*, iii.

Rose of Paradise. The roses which grew in paradise had no thorns. "Thorns and thistles" were unknown on earth till after the Fall (*Gen.* iii. 18). Both St. Ambrose and St. Basil note that the roses in Eden had no thorns, and Milton says, in Eden bloomed "Flowers of all hue, and without thorn the rose."—*Paradise Lost*, iv. 256 (1665).

Rose of Raby, the mother of Richard III. This was Cicely, daughter of Ralph de Nevill of Raby, earl of Westmoreland.

Rose Vaughan. Lover of "Yone" Willoughby, in *The Amber Gods*. He has super-refined and poetical tastes; delights and revels in beauty, and until he met Yone had admired her gentle sister. The siren, Yone, sets herself to win him and succeeds. Marriage disenchants him and the knowledge of this maddens her into something akin to hatred. Yet she dies begging him to kiss her. "I am your Yone! I forgot a little while,—but I love you, Rose, Rose!"—Harriet Prescott Spofford, *The Amber Gods* (1863).

Rose of York, the heir and head of the York faction.

When Warwick perished, Edmund de la Pole became the Rose of York, and if this foolish prince should be removed by death ... his young and clever brother [*Richard*] would be raised to the rank of Rose of York.—W. H. Dixon, *Two Queens*.

Roses (*War of the*). The origin of this expression is thus given by Shakespeare:

Plant. Let him that is a true-born gentleman ...
If he supposes that I have pleaded truth,
From off this briar pluck a white rose with me.

Somerset. Let him that is no coward, nor no flatterer,
But dare maintain the party of the truth,
Pluck a red rose from off this thorn with me.

Whereupon Warwick plucked a white rose and joined the Yorkists, while Suffolk plucked a red one and joined the Lancastrians.—Shakespeare, 1 *Henry VI.* act ii. sc. 4 (1589).

Rosemond, daughter of Cunimond, king of the Gepidæ. She was compelled to marry Alboin, king of the Lombards, who put her father to death A.D. 567. Alboin compelled her to drink from the skull of her own father, and Rosemond induced Peride´us (the secretary of Helmichild, her lover), to murder the wretch (573). She then married Helmichild, fled Ravenna, and sought to poison her second husband, that she might marry Longin, the exarch; but Helmichild, apprised of her intention, forced her to drink the mixture she had prepared for him. This lady is the heroine of Alfieri's tragedy called *Rosemonde* (1749-1803). (See ROSAMOND.)

Ro´sencrantz, a courtier in the court of Denmark, willing to sell or betray his friend and schoolfellow, Prince Hamlet, to please a king.—Shakespeare, *Hamlet* (1596).

Rosetta, the wicked sister of Brunetta and Blon´dina, the mothers of Cherry and Fairstar. She abetted the queen-mother in her wicked designs against the offspring of her two sisters, but, being found out, was imprisoned for life.—Comtesse D'Aunoy, *Fairy Tales* ("Princess Fairstar," 1682).

Rosetta, a bright, laughing little coquette, who runs away from home because her father wants her to marry young Meadows, whom she has never seen. She enters the service of Justice Woodcock. Now, it so happens that Sir William Meadows wishes his son to marry Rosetta, whom he has never seen, and he also runs away from home, and under the name of Thomas becomes gardener to Justice Woodcock. Rosetta and young Meadows here fall in love with each other, and the wishes of the two fathers are accomplished.—Isaac Bickerstaff, *Love in a Village* (1763).

In 1786 Mrs. Billington made her *début* in "Rosetta," at once dazzling the town with the brilliancy of her vocalization and the flush of her beauty.—C. R. Leslie.

Rosetta [Belmont], daughter of Sir Robert Belmont. Rosetta is high-spirited, witty, confident, and of good spirits. "If you told her a merry story, she would sigh; if a mournful one, she would laugh. For *yes* she would say 'no,' and for *no*, 'yes.'" She is in love with Colonel Raymond, but shows her love by teasing him, and Colonel Raymond is afraid of the capricious beauty.—Edward Moore, *The Foundling* (1748).

Rosiclear and Donzel del Phebo, the heroine and hero of the *Mirror of Knighthood*, a mediæval romance.

Rosinan´te (4 *syl.*), the steed of Don Quixote. The name implies "that the horse had risen from a mean condition to the highest honor a steed could achieve, for it was once a cart-horse, and was elevated into the charger of a knight-errant."—Cervantes, *Don Quixote*, I. ii. 1 (1605).

Rosinante was admirably drawn, so lean, lank, meagre, drooping, sharp-backed, and raw-boned, as to excite much curiosity and mirth.—Pt. I. ii. 1.

Rosiphele (3 *syl.*), princess of Armenia; of surpassing beauty, but insensible to love. She is made to submit to the yoke of Cupid, by a vision which befalls her on a May-day ramble.—Gower, *Confessio Amantis* (1393).

Rosmonda, a tragedy in Italian, by John R. Ruccellai (1525). This is one of the first regular tragedies of modern times. *Sophonisba*, by Trissino, preceded it, being produced in 1514, and performed in 1515.

Rosny (*Sabina*), the young wife of Lord Sensitive. "Of noble parents, who perished under the axe in France." The young orphan, "as much to be admired for her virtues, as to be pitied for her misfortunes," fled to Padua, where she met Lord Sensitive.—Cumberland, *First Love* (1796).

Ross (*Lord*), an officer in the king's army, under the duke of Monmouth.—Sir W. Scott, *Old Mortality* (time, Charles II.).

Ross (The Man of), John Kyrle, of Whitehouse, in Gloucestershire. So called because he resided in the village of Ross, Herefordshire. Kyrle was a man of unbounded benevolence, and beloved by all who knew him.

⁎ Pope celebrates him in his *Moral Essays*, iii. (1709).

Rosse (2 *syl.*), the sword which the dwarf Elberich gave to Otwit, king of Lombardy. It was so keen that it left no gap where it cut.

Balmung, the sword forged by Wieland, and given to Siegfried, was so keen that it clove Amilias in two without his knowing it, but when he attempted to move he fell asunder.

This sword to thee I give; it is all bright of hue,
Whatever it may cleave, no gap will there ensue.
From Almari I brought it, and Rossê is its name.
The Heldenbuch.

Rostocostojambedanesse (*M. N.*), author of *After Beef, Mustard.*—Rabelais, Pantagruel, ii. 7 (1533).

Rothmar, chief of Tromlo. He attacked the vassal kingdom of Croma, while the under-king, Crothar, was blind with age, resolving to annex it to his own dominion. Crothar's son, Fovar-Gormo, attacked the invader, but was defeated and slain. Not many days after, Ossian (one of the sons of Fingal) arrived with succors, renewed the battle, defeated the victorious army, and slew the invader.—Ossian, *Croma.*

Rothsay (*The duke of*) prince Robert, eldest son of Robert III. of Scotland.

Margaret, duchess of Rothsay.—Sir W. Scott, *Fair Maid of Perth* (time, Henry IV.).

Rou (*Le Roman de*), a metrical and mythical history, in Norman-French, of the dukes of Normandy, from Rollo downwards, by Robert Wace (author of *Le Brut*).

⁎⁎* Rou', that is, *Roul*, the same as Rollo.

Roubigné (*Julie de*), the heroine and title of a novel by Henry Mackenzie (1783).

Rougedragon (*Lady Rachel*), the former guardian of Lilias Redgauntlet.—Sir W. Scott, *Redgauntlet* (time, George III.).

Rouncewell (*Mrs.*), housekeeper at Chesney Wold to Lord and Lady Dedlock, to whom she is most faithfully attached.—C. Dickens, *Bleak House* (1823).

Round Table (*The*), a table made at Carduel, by Merlin, for Uther, the pendragon. Uther gave it to King Leodegraunce, of Camelyard, and when Arthur married Guinever (the daughter of Leodegraunce), he received the table with a hundred knights as a wedding present (pt. i. 45). The table would seat 150 knights (pt. iii. 36), and each seat was appropriated. One of them was called the "Siege Perilous," because it was fatal for any one to sit therein, except the knight who was destined to achieve the Holy Graal (pt. iii. 32).

King Arthur instituted an order of knighthood called "the knights of the Round Table," the chief of whom were Sir Launcelot, Sir Tristram, and Sir Lamerock, or Lamorake. The "Siege Perilous" was reserved for Sir Galahad, the son of Sir Launcelot by Elaine.—Sir T. Malory, *History of Prince Arthur* (1470).

⁎ There is a table shown at Winchester, as "Arthur's Round Table," but it corresponds in no respect with the Round Table described in the *History of Prince Arthur*. Round Tables are not unusual, as Dr. Percy has shown, with other kings in the times of chivalry. Thus, the king of Ireland, father of Christabelle, had his "knights of the Round Table."—See "Sir Cauline," in Percy's *Reliques*.

In the eighth year of Edward I., Roger de Mortimer established at Kenilworth, a Round Table for "the encouragement of military pastimes." Some seventy years later, Edward III. had his Round Table at Windsor; it was 200 feet in diameter.

Rousseau (*Jean Jacques*) used to say that all fables which ascribe speech and reason to dumb animals ought to be withheld from children, as being only vehicles of deception.

I shall not ask Jean Jacques Rousseau
If birds confabulate or no;
'Tis clear that they were always able
To hold discourse—at least in fable.
Cowper, *Pairing-Time Anticipated* (1782).

Roustam or **Rostam**, the Persian Hercules. He was the son of Zal, and a descendant of Djamshid At one time Roustam killed 1000 Tartars at a blow; he slew dragons, overcame devils, captured cities, and performed other marvellous exploits. This mighty man of strength fell into disgrace for refusing to receive the doctrines of Zoroaster, and died by the hand of one of his brothers named Scheghad (sixth century B.C.).

Routledge (*Harold*). First love of *Lilian Westbrook*, in *The Banker's Daughter*. They have a lover's quarrel and separate. Lilian, to save her father from poverty, marries another man. Meeting Harold in after years, her love revives. When he challenges a Frenchman who has spoken lightly of her, she follows him to the field in time to receive his last breath and sob in his ear—"I have loved you—you only—from the first."—Bronson Howard, *The Banker's Daughter*, (1878).

Rover, a dissolute young spark, who set off vice "as naughty but yet nice."—Mrs. Behn, *The Rover* (1680).

William Mountford [1660-1692] had so much in him of the agreeable, that when he played "The Rover," it was remarked by many, and particularly by Queen Mary, that it was dangerous to see him act—he made vice so alluring.—C. Dibdin, *History of the Stage*.

Rovewell (*Captain*), in love with Arethusa, daughter of Argus. The lady's father wanted her to marry Squire Cuckoo, who had a large estate; but Arethusa contrived to have her own way and marry Captain Rovewell, who turned out to be the son of Ned Worthy, who gave the bridegroom £30,000.—Carey, *Contrivances* (1715).

Rowe (*Nicholas*), poet-laureate (1673, 1714-1718). The monument in Westminster Abbey to this poet was by Rysbrack.

Rowena (*The lady*), of Hargettstanstede, a ward of Cedric the Saxon, of Rotherwood. She marries Ivanhoe.—Sir W. Scott, *Ivanhoe* (time, Richard I.).

Rowland (*Childe*), youngest brother of Helen. Under the guidance of Merlin, he undertook to bring back his sister from elf land, whither the fairies had carried her, and he succeeded in his perilous exploit.—*An Ancient Scotch Ballad*.

Rowland for an Oliver (*A*), a tit for tat; getting as good as you gave. Rowland (or Roland) and Oliver were two of Charlemagne's paladins, so much alike in prowess and exploits that they might be described as "fortemque Gyan, fortemque Cloanthum" (*Æneid*, i. 222).

Och! Mrs. Mustard-pot, have you found a Rowland for your Oliver at last?—T. Knight, *The Honest Thieves*.

Rowley, one of the retainers of Julia Avenel (2 *syl.*).—Sir W. Scott, *The Monastery* (time, Elizabeth).

Rowley (*Master*), formerly steward of Mr. Surface, Sr., the friend of Charles Surface, and the *fidus Achātēs* of Sir Oliver Surface, the rich uncle.—Sheridan, *School for Scandal* (1777).

Rowley (*Thomas*), the hypothetical priest of Bristol, said by Chatterton to have lived in the reigns of Henry VI. and Edward IV., and to have written certain poems, of which Chatterton himself was the author.

Rowley Overdees, a highwayman.—Sir W. Scott, *Guy Mannering* (time, George II.).

Roxa′na, daughter of Oxyartês of Bactria, and wife or concubine of Alexander the Great. Proud, imperious, and relentless, she loved Alexander with a madness of love; and being jealous of Statīra, daughter of King Darius, and wife of Alexander, she stabbed her and slew her.—N. Lee, *Alexander the Great* (1678).

So now am I as great as the famed Alexander; but my dear Statīra and Roxana, don't exert yourselves so much about me.—Mrs. Centlivre, *The Wonder*, iii. 1 (1714).

Roxa′na and Stati′ra. Dr. Doran says that Peg Woffington (as "Roxana"), jealous of Mrs. Bellamy (as "Statira") because she was better dressed, pulled her to the floor when she left the stage, and pummeled her with the handle of her dagger, screaming as she did so:

Nor he, nor heaven, shall shield thee from my justice.
Die, sorceress, die! and all my wrongs die with thee?
Table Traits.

Campbell tells a very similar story of Mrs. Barry ("Roxana") and Miss Boutwell ("Statira"). The stage-manager had given to Miss Boutwell a lace veil, and Mrs. Barry, out of jealousy, actually stabbed her rival in acting, and the dagger went a quarter of an inch through the stays into the flesh.

Royal Mottoes or LEGENDS.

Dieu et mon droit, Richard I.

Honi soit qui mal y pense, Edward III.

Semper eadem, Elizabeth and Anne.

Je maintiendrai, William III.

Royal Style of Address.

"My Liege," the usual style till the Lancastrian usurpation.

"Your Grace," Henry IV.

"Your Excellent Grace," Henry VI.

"Most High and Mighty Prince," Edward IV.

"Your Highness," Henry VII.

"Your Majesty," Henry VIII. So addressed in 1520, by François I.

"The King's Sacred Majesty," James I.

"Your Most Excellent Majesty," Charles II.

"Your Most Gracious Majesty," the present style.

Royal Titles.

WILLIAM I. called himself "Rex Anglorum, comes Normannorum et Cinomanentium."

WILLIAM II. called himself "Rex Anglorum," or "Monarchicus Britanniæ."

HENRY I. called himself "Rex Anglorum et dux Normannorum." Subsequent to 1106 we find "Dei gratia" introduced in charters.

HENRY II. called himself "Rex Anglorum, et dux Normannorum et Aquitannorum, et comes Andegavorum;" or "Rex Angliæ, dux Normanniæ et Aquitaniæ, et comes Andegaviæ."

RICHARD I. began his charters with "Dei gratia, rex Angliæ, et dux Normaniæ et Aquitaniæ, et comes Andegaviæ."

JOHN headed his charters with "Johannes, D.G. rex Angliæ, dominus Hiberniæ, dux Normanniæ et Aquitaniæ, et comes Andegaviæ." Instead of "Hiberniæ" we sometimes find "Iberniæ," and sometimes "Yberniæ."

HENRY III. followed the style of his father till October, 1259, when he adopted the form "D.G. rex Angliæ, dominus Hiberniæ, et dux Aquitaniæ."

EDWARD I. adopted the latter style. So did Edward II. till 1326, when he used the form "Rex Angliæ et dominus Hiberniæ." Edward I. for thirteen years headed his charters with "Edwardus, Dei gratia rex Angliæ, dominus Hiberniæ, et dux Aquitaniæ." But after 1337 the form ran thus: "Edwardus, D.G. rex Angliæ et Franciæ, dominus Hiberniæ, et dux Aquitaniæ;" and sometimes "Franciæ" stands before "Angliæ."

RICHARD II. began thus: "Richardus, D.G. rex Angliæ et Franciæ, et dominus Hiberniæ."

HENRY IV. continued the same style. So did HENRY V. till 1420, after which date he adopted the form, "Henricus, D.G. rex Angliæ, hæres et regens Franciæ, et dominus Hiberniæ."

HENRY VI. began, "Henricus, D.G. rex Angliæ et Franciæ, et dominus Hiberniæ."

EDWARD IV., EDWARD V., RICHARD III., HENRY VII. continued the same style.

From HENRY VIII. (1521) to GEORGE III. (1800) the royal style and title was "* by the grace of God, of Great Britain, France and Ireland, king, Defender of the Faith."

From GEORGE III. (1800) to the present day it has been, "* by the grace of God, of the United Kingdom of Great Britain and Ireland, king, Defender of the Faith."

Ru′bezahl, Number Nip, a famous mountain-spirit of Germany corresponding to our Puck.

Rubi, one of the cherubs or spirits of wisdom who was with Eve in Paradise. He loved Liris, who was young, proud, and most eager for knowledge. She asked her angel lover to let her see him in his full glory; so Rubi came to her in his cherubic splendor. Liris, rushing into his arms, was burnt to ashes; and the kiss she gave him became a brand upon his forehead, which shot unceasing agony into his brain.—T. Moore, *Loves of the Angels*, ii. (1822).

Ru′bicon (*Napoleon's*), Moscow. The invasion of Moscow was the beginning of Napoleon's fall.

Thou, Rome, who saw'st thy Cæsar's deeds outdone!
Alas! why passed he [*Napoleon*] too the Rubicon ...
Moscow! thou limit of his long career,
For which rude Charles had wept his frozen tear.
Byron, *Age of Bronze*, v. (1821).

. Charles XII. of Sweden formed the resolution of humbling Peter the Great (1709).

Rubo′nax, a man who hanged himself from mortification and annoyance at some verses written upon him by a poet.—Sir P. Sidney, *Defence of Poesie* (1595).

Rubrick (*The Rev. Mr.*), chaplain to the baron of Bradwardine.—Sir W. Scott, *Waverley* (time, George II.).

Ruby (*Lady*), the young widow of Lord Ruby. Her "first love" was Frederick Mowbray, and when a widow she married him. She is described as "young, blooming and wealthy, fresh and fine as a daisy."—Cumberland, *First Love* (1796).

Rucellai (*John*), *i.e.* Oricellarius, poet (1475-1525), son of Bernard Rucellai, of Florence, historian and diplomatist.

As hath been said by Rucellai.
Longfellow, *The Wayside Inn* (prelude, 1863).

Ruddymane (3 *syl.*), the name given by Sir Guyon to the babe rescued from Amavia, who had stabbed herself in grief at the death of her husband. So called because:

... in her streaming blood he [*the infant*] did embay his little hands.
Spenser, *Faëry Queen*, ii. 1, 3 (1590).

Rudge (*Barnaby*), a half-witted young man of three and twenty years old; rather spare, of a fair height and strong make. His hair, of which he had a great profusion, was red and hung in disorder about his face and shoulders. His face was pale, his eyes glassy and protruding. His dress was green, clumsily trimmed here and there with gaudy lace. A pair of tawdry ruffles dangled at his wrists, while his throat was nearly bare. His hat was ornamented with a cluster of peacock's feathers, limp, broken, and trailing down his back. Girded to his side was the steel hilt of an old sword, without blade or scabbard; and a few knee-ribbons completed his attire. He had a large raven named Grip, which he carried at his back in a basket, a most knowing imp, which used to cry out in a hoarse voice, "Halloa!" "I'm a devil!" "Never say die!" "Polly, put the kettle on!"

Barnaby joined the Gordon rioters for the proud pleasure of carrying a flag and wearing a blue bow. He was arrested and lodged in Newgate, from whence he made his escape, with other prisoners, when the jail was burnt down by the rioters; but both he and his father and Hugh, being betrayed by Dennis, the hangman, were recaptured, brought to trial, and condemned to death, but by the influence of *Gabriel Varden*, the locksmith, the poor half-witted lad was reprieved, and lived the rest of his life with his mother in a cottage and garden near the Maypole.

Here he lived, tending the poultry and the cattle, working in a garden of his own, and helping every one. He was known to every bird and beast about the place, and had a name for every one. Never was there a lighter-hearted husbandman, a creature more popular with young and old, a blither and more happy soul than Barnaby.—Ch. lxxxii.

Mr. Rudge, the father of Barnaby, supposed to have been murdered the same night as Mr. Haredale, to whom he was steward. The fact is that Rudge himself was the murderer both of Mr. Haredale and also of his faithful servant, to whom the crime was falsely attributed. After the murder, he was seen by many haunting the locality, and was supposed to be a ghost. He joined the Gordon rioters when they attacked and burnt to the ground the house of Mr. Haredale, the son of the murdered man, and being arrested (ch. lvi.), was sent to Newgate, but made his escape with the other prisoners when it was burnt down by the rioters. Being betrayed by Dennis, he was brought to trial for murder, but we are not told if he was executed (ch. lxxiii.). His name is not mentioned again, and probably he suffered death.

Mrs. [Mary] Rudge, mother of Barnaby, and very like him, "but where in his face there was wildness and vacancy, in hers there was the patient composure of long effort and quiet resignation." She was a widow. Her husband (steward at the Warren), who murdered his master, Mr. Haredale, and his servant, told her of his deed of blood a little before the birth of Barnaby, and the woman's face ever after inspired terror. It was thought for many years that Rudge had been murdered in defending his master, and Mrs. Rudge was allowed a pension by Mr. Haredale, son and heir of the murdered man. This pension she subsequently refused to take. After the reprieve of Barnaby, Mrs. Rudge lived with him in a cottage near the Maypole, and her last days were her happiest. C. Dickens, *Barnaby Rudge* (1841).

Ru´diger, a wealthy Hun, liegeman of Etzel, sent to conduct Kriemhild to Hungary. When Günther and his suite went to visit Kriemhild, Rudiger entertained them all most hospitably, and gave his daughter in marriage to Giselher (Kriemhild's brother). In the broil which ensued, Rudiger was killed fighting against Gernot, but Gernot dropped down dead at the same moment, "each by the other slain."—*Nibelungen Lied* (by the minnesingers, 1210).

Rudiger, a knight who came to Waldhurst in a boat drawn by a swan. Margaret fell in love with him. At every tournament he bore off the prize, and in everything excelled the youths about him. Margaret became his wife. A child was born. On the christening day, Rudiger carried it along the banks of the Rhine, and nothing that Margaret said could prevail on him to go home. Presently, the swan and boat came in sight, and carried all three to a desolate place, where was a deep cavern. Rudiger got on shore, still holding the babe, and Margaret followed. They reached the cave, two giant arms clasped Rudiger, Margaret sprang forward and seized the infant, but Rudiger was never seen more.—R. Southey, *Rudiger* (a ballad from Thomas Heywood's notes).

Rufus (or *the Red*), William II. of England (1057, 1087-1100).

Rugby, servant to Dr. Caius, in *Merry Wives of Windsor*, by Shakespeare.

Rugg, (*Mr.*) a lawyer living at Pentonville. A red-haired man, who wore a hat with a high crown and narrow brim. Mr. Pancks employed him to settle the business pertaining to the estate which had long lain unclaimed, to which Mr. Dorrit was heir-at-law. Mr. Rugg delighted in legal difficulties as much as a housewife in her jams and preserves.—C. Dickens, *Little Dorrit* (1857).

Ruggie´ro, a young Saracen knight, born of Christian parents. He fell in love with Bradamant (sister of Rinaldo), whom he ultimately married. Ruggiero is especially noted for possessing a hippogriff, or winged horse, and a shield of such dazzling splendor that it blinded those who looked on it. He threw away this shield into a well, because it enabled him to win victory too cheaply.—*Orlando Innamarato* (1495), and *Orlando Furioso* (1516).

Rukenaw (*Dame*), the ape's wife, in the beast-epic called *Reynard the Fox* (1498).

Rule a Wife and Have a Wife, a comedy by Beaumont and Fletcher (1640). Donna Margaritta, a lady of great wealth, wishes to marry in order to mask her intrigues, and seeks for a husband a man without spirit, whom she can mould to her will. Leon, the brother of Altea, is selected as the "softest fool in Spain," and the marriage takes place. After marriage, Leon shows himself firm, courageous, high-minded, but most affectionate. He "rules his wife" and her household with a masterly hand, wins the respect of every one, and the wife, wholly reclaimed, "loves, honors, and obeys" him.

Rumolt, the chief cook of Prince Günther of Burgundy.—*Nibelungen Lied*, 800 (1210).

Rumpelstilzchen [*Rumple.stiltz.skin*], an irritable, deformed dwarf. He aided a miller's daughter, who had been enjoined by the king to spin straw into gold; and the condition he made with her for this service, was that she should give him for wife her first daughter. The miller's daughter married the king, and when her first daughter was born, the mother grieved so bitterly that the dwarf consented to absolve her of her promise, if, within three days she could find out his name. The first day passed, but the secret was not discovered; the second passed with no better success; but on the third day, some of the queen's servants heard a strange voice singing:

Little dreams my dainty dame
Rumpelstilzchen is my name.

The queen, being told thereof, saved her child, and the dwarf killed himself from rage.—*German Popular Stories*.

Runa, the dog of Argon and Ruro, sons of Annir, king of Inis-Thona, an island of Scandinavia.—Ossian, *The War of Inis-Thorna*.

Runners.

1. Iphiclês, son of Phylakos and Klymĕnê. Hesiod says he could run over ears of corn without bending the stems; and Demarātos says he could run on the surface of the sea.—*Argonauts*, i. 60.

2. Camilla, queen of the Volsci, was so swift of foot that she could run over standing corn, without bending the ears, and over the sea without wetting her feet.—Virgil, *Æneid*, vii. 303; xi. 433.

Not so when swift Camilla scours the plain,
Flies o'er th' unbending corn, and skims along the main.
Pope.

3. Lădas, the swift runner of King Alexander. He ran so fast that he never left a foot-print on the ground.

4. Phidippĭdês, a professional courier, ran from Athens to Sparta (150 miles) in two days.

5. Theagĕnês, a native of Thasos, was noted for his swiftness of foot.

⁎⁎⁎ The Greek hemerodromos would run from twenty to thirty-six leagues in a day.

Runnymede, the *nom de plume* of Benj. Disraeli, in the *Times* (1805-1881).

Rupert, *i.e.* Major Roselheim, the betrothed of Meeta, "the maid of Mariendorpt."—S. Knowles, *The Maid of Mariendorpt* (1838).

Rupert (Prince), in the service of Charles II. Introduced by Sir W. Scott, in three of his novels.—*Woodstock*, *Legend of Montrose*, and *Peveril of the Peak*.

Rupert (Sir), in love with Catharine.—S. Knowles, *Love* (1840).

Rupert of Debate. Edward Geoffrey, earl of Derby, when he was Mr. Stanley, was so called by Lord Lytton (1799-1869).

Rupert Clare. Desperate lover, who skates with "handsome Madge" straight toward the rotten ice. Seeing their danger and his revengeful resolve, she shrieks out the name of her betrothed who, unknown to her and the rejected suitor, has followed them. "He hurls himself upon the pair," and rescues his affianced.

"The lovers stand with heart to heart,
'No more,' they cry, 'no more to part!'"
But still along the lone lagoon
The steel skates ring a ghostly tune,
And in the moonlight, pale and cold,
The panting lovers still behold
The self-appointed sacrifice
Skating toward the rotten ice!"
Fitz-James O'Brien, *Poems and Stories*.

Rush (*Friar*), a house-spirit, sent from the infernal regions in the seventeenth century to keep the monks and friars in the same state of wickedness they then were.

⁎⁎⁎ The legends of this roistering friar are of German origin. (*Bruder Rausch* means "Brother Tipple.")

Milton confounds "Jack-o'-Lantern" with Friar Rush. The latter was not a *field bogie* at all, and was never called "Jack." Probably Milton meant a friar with a rush-[light]." Sir Walter Scott also falls into the same error:

Better we had thro' mire and bush
Been lantern-led by Friar Rush.
Marmion (1808).

Rusil′la, mother of Roderick, the last of the Goths, and wife of Theodofred, rightful heir to the Spanish throne.—Southey, *Roderick, etc.* (1814).

Rusport (*Lady*), second wife of Sir Stephen Rusport, a City knight, and stepmother of Charlotte Rusport. Very proud, very mean, very dogmatical, and very vain. Without one spark of generosity or loving charity in her composition. She bribes her lawyer to destroy a will, but is thwarted in her dishonesty. Lady Rusport has a *tendresse* for Major O'Flaherty; but the major discovers the villainy of the old woman, and escapes from this Scylla.

Charlotte Rusport, step-daughter of Lady Rusport. An amiable, ingenuous, animated, handsome girl, in love with her cousin, Charles Dudley, whom she marries.—R. Cumberland, *The West Indian* (1771).

Russet (*Mr.*), the choleric old father of Harriot, on whom he dotes. He is so self-willed that he will not listen to reason, and has set his mind on his daughter marrying Sir Harry Beagle. She marries, however, Mr. Oakly.—(See HARRIOT.)—George Colman, *The Jealous Wife* (1761).

Russian Byron (*The*), Alexander Sergeiwitch Pushkin (1799-1837).

Russian History (*The Father of*), Nestor, a monk of Kiev. His *Chronicle* includes the years between 862 and 1116 (twelfth century).

Russian Murat (*The*), Michael Miloradowith (1770-1820).

Rust (*Martin*), an absurd old antiquary. "He likes no coins but those which have no head on them." He took a fancy to Juliet, the niece of Sir Thomas Lofty, but preferred his "Æneas, his precious relic of Troy," to the living beauty; and Juliet preferred Richard Bever to Mr. Rust; so matters were soon amicably adjusted.—Foote, *The Patron* (1764).

Rustam, chief of the Persian mythical heroes, son of Zâl "the Fair," king of India, and regular descendant of Benjamin, the beloved son of Jacob, the patriarch. He delivered King Caïcāus (4 *syl.*) from prison, but afterwards fell into disgrace because he refused to embrace the religious system of Zoroaster. Caïcaus sent his son, Asfendiar (or Isfendiar) to convert him, and, as persuasion availed nothing, the logic of single combat was resorted to. The fight lasted two days, and then Rustam discovered that Asfendiar bore a "charmed life," proof against all wounds. The valor of these two heroes is proverbial, and the Persian romances are full of their deeds of fight.

Rustam's Horse, Reksh.—Chardin, *Travels* (1686-1711).

In Matthew Arnold's poem, *Sohrab and Rustum*, Rustum fights with and overcomes Sohrab, and finds too late that he has slain his own son.

Rustam, son of Tamur, king of Persia. He had a trial of strength with Rustam, son of Zâl, which was to pull away from his adversary an iron ring. The combat was never decided, for Rustam could no more conquer Rustam than Roland could overcome Oliver.—Chardin, *Travels* (1686-1711).

Rusticus's Pig, the pig on which Rusticus fed daily, but which never diminished.

Two Christians, travelling in Poland, ... came to the door of Rustĭcus, a heathen peasant, who had killed a fat hog to celebrate the birth of a son. The pilgrims, being invited to partake of the feast, pronounced a blessing on what was left, which *never diminished in size or weight* from that moment, though all the family fed on it freely every day.—J. Brady, *Clavis Calendaria*, 183.

This, of course, is a parallelism to Elijah's miracle (1 *Kings* xvii. 11-16).

Rut (*Doctor*), in *The Magnetic Lady*, by Ben Jonson (1632).

Ruth, the friend of Arabella, an heiress, and ward of Justice Day. Ruth also is an orphan, the daughter of Sir Basil Thoroughgood, who died when she was two years old, leaving Justice Day trustee. Justice Day takes the estates, and brings up Ruth as his own daughter. Colonel Careless is her accepted *amé de cœur*.—T. Knight, *The Honest Thieves*.

Ruthven (*Lord*), one of the embassy from Queen Elizabeth to Mary Queen of Scots.—Sir W. Scott, *The Abbot* (time, Elizabeth).

Rutil'io, a merry gentleman, brother of Arnoldo.—Beaumont and Fletcher, *The Custom of the Country* (1647).

Rutland (*The Countess of*), wife of the earl of Essex, whom he married when he started for Ireland. The queen knew not of the marriage, and was heart-broken when she heard of it.—Henry Jones, *The Earl of Essex* (1745).

Rutland (*The duchess of*), of the court of Queen Elizabeth.—Sir W. Scott, *Kenilworth* (time Elizabeth).

Rutledge (*Archie*), constable at Osbaldistone Hall. Sir W. Scott, *Rob Roy* (time, George I.).

Rutledge (*Job*), a smuggler.—Sir W. Scott, *Redgauntlet* (time, George III.).

Rut'terkin, name of a cat, the spirit of a witch, sent at one time to torment the countess of Rutland (sixteenth century).

Ruy'dera, a duenna who had seven daughters and two nieces. They were imprisoned for 500 years in the cavern of Montesi'nos, in La Mancha, of Spain. Their ceaseless weeping stirred the compassion of Merlin, who converted them into lakes in the same province.—Cervantes, *Don Quixote*, II. ii. 6 (1615).

Ryence (*Sir*), king of Wales, Ireland, and many of the isles. When Arthur first mounted the throne, King Ryence, in scorn, sent a messenger to say "he had purfled a mantel with the beards of kings; but the mantel lacked one more beard to complete the lining, and he requested Arthur to send his beard by the messenger, or else he would come and take head and beard too." Part of the insolence was in this: Arthur at the time was too young to have a beard at all; and he made answer, "Tell your master, my beard at present is all too young for purfling; but I have an arm quite strong enough to drag him hither, unless he comes without delay to do me homage." By the advice of Merlin, the two brothers, Balin and Balan, set upon the insolent king, on his way to Lady De Vauce, overthrew him, slew "more than forty of his men, and the remnant fled." King Ryence craved for mercy; so "they laid him on a horse-litter, and sent him captive to King Arthur."—Sir T. Malory, *History of Prince Arthur*, i. 24, 34 (1470).

Rymar (*Mr. Robert*), poet at the Spa.—Sir W. Scott, *St. Ronan's Well* (time, George III.).

Ryno, youngest of the sons of Fingal, king of Morven. He fell in the battle of Lena between the Norsemen led by Swaran and the Irish led by Fingal.

"Rest!" said Fingal; "youngest of my sons, rest! Rest, O Ryno, on Lena! We, too, shall be no more. Warriors must one day fall."—Ossian, *Fingal*, v.

Ryparog´rapher of Wits, Rabelais (1495-1553).

⁎ Greek, *rupăros* ("foul, nasty"). Pliny calls Pyrĭcus the painter a "ryparographer."

Rython, a giant of Brittany, slain by King Arthur. (See RITHO.)

Rython, the mighty giant, slain,
By his good brand relieved Bretagne.
Sir W. Scott, *Bridal of Triermain*, ii. 11 (1813).

AADI or **SADI**, the Persian poet, called "The Nightingale of a Thousand Songs." His poems are *The Gulistan* or "Garden of Roses," *The Boston* or "Garden of Fruits," and *The Pend Nâmeh*, a moral poem. Saadi (1184-1263) was one of the "Four Monarchs of Eloquence."

Saba or **Zaba** (*The Queen of*), called Balkis. She came to the court of Solomon, and had by him a son named Melech. This queen of Ethiopia or Abyssinia is sometimes called Maqueda.—Zaga Zabo, *Ap. Damian. a Goes*.

The *Korân* (ch. xxvii.) tells us that Solomon summoned before him all the birds to the valley of ants, but the lapwing did not put in an appearance. Solomon was angry, and was about to issue an order of death, when the bird presented itself, saying, "I come from Saba, where I found a queen reigning in great magnificence, but she and her subjects worship the sun." On hearing this, Solomon sent back the lapwing to Saba with a letter, which the bird was to drop at the foot of the queen, commanding her to come at once, submit herself unto him, and accept from him the "true religion." So she came in great state, with a train of 500 slaves of each sex, bearing 500 "bricks of solid gold," a crown, and sundry other presents.

Sabbath-Breakers. The fish of the Red Sea used to come ashore on the eve of the Sabbath, to tempt the Jews to violate the day of rest. The offenders at length became so numerous that David, to deter others, turned the fish into apes.—Jallâlo´ddin.—*Al Zamakh.*

Sabellan Song, incantation. The Sabelli or Samnites were noted for their magic art and incantations.

Sabine (*Thĕ*). Numa, the Sabine, was taught the way to govern by Egĕrĭe, one of the Camēnæ (prophetic nymphs of ancient Italy). He used to meet her in a grove, in which was a well, afterwards dedicated by him to the Camenæ.

Our statues—she
That taught the Sabine how to rule.
Tennyson, *The Princess*, ii. (1830).

Sablonnière (*La*), the Tuilleries. The word means the "sand-pit." The *tuilleries* means the "tile-works." Nicolas de Neuville, in the fifteenth century, built a mansion in the vicinity, which he called the "Hotel des Tuilleries," and François I. bought the property for his mother in 1518.

Sabra, daughter of Ptolemy, king of Egypt. She was rescued by St. George from the hands of a giant, and ultimately married her deliverer. Sabra had three sons at a birth: Guy, Alexander, and David.

Here come I, St. George, the valiant man,
With naked sword and spear in han',
Who fought the dragon and brought him to slaughter,
And won fair Sabra thus, the king of Egypt's daughter.
Notes and Queries, December 21, 1878.

Sabreur (*Le Beau*), Joachim Murat (1767-1815).

Sab´rin, Sabre, or **Sabri´na**, the Severn, daughter of Locrine (son of Brute) and his concubine, Estrildis. His queen, Guendolen, vowed vengeance, and, having assembled an army, made war upon Locrine, who was slain. Guendolen now assumed the government, and commanded Estrildis and Sabrin to be cast into a river, since then called the Severn.—Geoffrey of Monmouth, *British History*, ii. 5 (1142).

(An exqusite description of Sabine, sitting in state as a queen, is given in the opening of song v. of Drayton's *Polyolbion*, and the tale of her metamorphosis is recorded at length in song vi. Milton in *Comus*, and Fletcher in *The Faithful Shepherdess*, refer to the transformation of Sabrina into a river.

Sabrina (*Aunt*). "Grim old maid in rusty bombazine gown and cap," whose strongest passion is family pride in the old homestead and farm which "her grandfather, a revolted cobbler from Rhode Island, had cleared and paid for at ten cents an acre."—Harold Frederic, *Seth's Brother's Wife* (1886).

Sabrinian Sea or *Severn Sea*, *i.e.* the Bristol Channel. Both terms occur not unfrequently in Drayton's *Polyolbion*.

Sacchini (*Antonio Maria Gaspare*), called "The Racine of Music," contemporary with Glück and Piccini (1735-1786).

Sacharissa. So Waller calls the Lady Dorothea Sidney, eldest daughter of the earl of Leicester, to whose hand he aspired. Sacharissa married the earl of Sunderland. (Greek, *sakchar*, "sugar.")

Sackbut, the landlord of a tavern, in Mrs. Centlivre's comedy, *A Bold Stroke for a Wife* (1717).

Sackingen (*The Trumpeter of*). Werner, a trumpeter, discourses such divine music upon his instrument as gains him access to a baronial castle, the good-will of the baron and the love of Margaret, the baron's daughter.—Victor Hugo, *The Trumpeter of Sackingen*.

Sacred Nine (*The*), the Muses, nine in number.

Fair daughters of the Sun, the Sacred Nine,
Here wake to ecstasy their harps divine.
Falconer, *The Shipwreck*, iii. 3 (1756).

Sacred War (*The*), a war undertaken by the Amphictyonic League for the defence of Delphi, against the Cirrhæans (B.C. 595-587).

The Sacred War, a war undertaken by the Athenians for the purpose of restoring Delphi to the Phocians (B.C. 448-447).

The Sacred War, a war undertaken by Philip of Macedon, as chief of the Amphictyonic League, for the purpose of wresting Delphi from the Phocians (B.C. 357).

Sa´cripant (*King*), king of Circassia, and a lover of Angelica.—Bojardo, *Orlando Innamorato* (1495); Ariosto, *Orlando Furioso* (1516).

With the same stratagem, Sacripant had his steed stolen from under him, by that notorious thief Brunello, at the siege of Albracca.—Cervantes, *Don Quixote*, I. iii. 9 (1605).

⁎⁎* The allusion is to Sancho Panza's ass, which was stolen from under him by the galley-slave, Gines de Passamonte.

Sacripant, a false, noisy, hectoring braggart; a kind of Pistol or Bobadil.—Tasso, *Secchia Rapita* (*i.e.* "Rape of the Bucket").

Sa´dak and Kalasra´de (4 *syl.*), Sadak, general of the forces of Am´urath, sultan of Turkey, lived with Kalasradê in retirement, and their home life was so happy that it aroused the jealousy of the sultan, who employed emissaries to set fire to their house, carry off Kalasradê to the seraglio, and seize the children. Sadak, not knowing who were the agents of these evils, laid his complaint before Amurath, and then learnt that Kalasradê was in the seraglio. The sultan swore not to force his love upon her till she had drowned the recollections of her past life by a draught of the waters of oblivion. Sadak was sent on this expedition. On his return, Amurath seized the goblet, and, quaffing its contents, found "that the waters of oblivion were the waters of death." He died, and Sadak was made sultan in his stead.—J. Ridley, *Tales of the Genii* ("Sadak and Kalasradê," ix. 1751).

Sadaroubay. So Eve is called in Indian mythology.

Saddletree (*Mr. Bartoline*), the learned saddler.

Mrs. Saddletree, the wife of Bartoline.—Sir W. Scott, *Heart of Midlothian* (time, George II.).

Sadha-Sing, the mourner of the desert.—Sir W. Scott, *The Surgeon's Daughter* (time, George II.).

Sæmund Sigfusson, surnamed "the Wise," an Icelandic priest and scald. He compiled the *Elder* or *Rythmical Edda*, often called *Sæmund's Edda*. This compilation contains not only mythological tales and moral sentences, but numerous sagas in verse or heroic lays, as those of Völung and Helgê, of Sigurd and Brynhilda, of Folsungs and Niflungs (pt. ii.). Probably his compilation contained all the mythological, heroic, and legendary lays extant at the period in which he lived (1054-1133).

Saga, the goddess of history.—*Scandinavian Mythology*.

Saga and Edda. The *Edda* is the Bible of the ancient Scandinavians. A saga is a book of instruction, generally, but not always, in the form of a tale, like a Welsh "mabinogi." In the *Edda* there are numerous sagas. As our Bible contains the history of the Jews, religious songs, moral proverbs, and religious stories, so the *Edda* contained the history of Norway, religious songs, a book of proverbs, and numerous stories. The original *Edda* was compiled and edited by Sæmund Sigfusson, an Icelandic priest and scald, in the eleventh century. It contains twenty-eight parts or books, all of which are in verse.

Two hundred years later, Snorro Sturleson, of Iceland, abridged, re-arranged, and reduced to prose the *Edda*, giving the various parts a kind of dramatic form, like the dialogues of Plato. It then became needful to distinguish these two works; so the old poetical compilation is the *Elder* or *Rythmical Edda*, and sometimes the *Sæmund Edda*, while the more modern work is called the *Younger* or *Prose Edda*, and sometimes the *Snorro Edda*. The *Younger Edda* is, however, partly original. Pt. i. is the old *Edda* reduced to prose, but pt. ii. is Sturleson's own collection. This part contains "The Discourse of Bragi" (the scald of the gods) on the origin of poetry; and here, too, we find the famous story called by the Germans the *Nibelungen Lied*.

Sagas. Besides the sagas contained in the *Eddas*, there are numerous others. Indeed, the whole saga literature extends over 200 volumes.

I. THE EDDA SAGAS. The *Edda* is divided into two parts and twenty-eight lays or poetical sagas. The first part relates to the gods and heroes of Scandinavia, creation, and the early history of Norway. The Scandinavian "Books of Genesis" are the "Voluspa Saga," or "prophecy of Vola" (about 230 verses), "Vafthrudner's Saga," and "Grimner's Saga." These three resemble the Sibylline books of ancient Rome, and give a description of chaos, the formation of the world, the creation of all animals (including dwarfs, giants and fairies), the general conflagration, and the renewal of the world, when, like the new Jerusalem, it will appear all glorious, and there shall in no wise enter therein "anything that defileth, neither whatsoever worketh abomination, or maketh a lie."

The "Book of Proverbs" in the *Edda* is called the "Hâvamâl Saga," and sometimes "The High Song of Odin."

The "Völsunga Saga" is a collection of lays about the early Teutonic heroes.

The "Saga of St. Olaf" is the history of this Norwegian king. He was a savage tyrant, hated by his subjects, but because he aided the priests in forcing Christianity on his subjects, he was canonized.

The other sagas in the *Edda* are "The Song of Lodbrok" or "Lodbrog," "Hervara Saga," the "Vilkina Saga," the "Blomsturvalla Saga," the "Ynglinga Saga" (all relating to Norway), the "Jomsvikingia Saga," and the "Knytlinga Saga" (which pertain to Denmark), the "Sturlunga Saga," and the "Eryrbiggia Saga" (which pertain to Iceland). All the above were compiled and edited by Sæmund Sigfusson, and are in verse; but Snorro Sturleson reduced them to prose in his prose version of the old *Edda*.

II. SAGAS NOT IN THE EDDA. Snorro Sturleson, at the close of the twelfth century, made the second great collection of chronicles in verse, called the *Heimskringla Saga*, or the book of the kings of Norway, from the remotest period to the year 1177. This is a most valuable record of the laws, customs, and manners of the ancient Scandinavians. Samuel Laing published his English translation of it in 1844.

1. *The Icelandic Sagas*. Besides the two Icelandic sagas collected by Sæmund Sigfusson, numerous others were subsequently embodied in the *Landama Bok*, set on foot by Ari hinn Frondê, and continued by various hands.

2. *Frithjof's Saga* contains the life and and adventures of Frithjof, of Iceland, who fell in love with Ingeborg, the beautiful wife of Hring, king of Norway. On the death of Hring, the young widow marries her Icelandic lover. Frithjof lived in the eighth century, and this saga was compiled at the beginning of the fourteenth century, a year or two after the *Heimskringla*. It is very interesting, because Tegnér, the Swedish poet, has selected it for his *Idylls* (1825), just as Tennyson has taken his idyllic stories from the *Morte d'Arthur* or the Welsh *Mabinogion*. Tegnér's *Idylls* were translated into English by Latham (1838), by Stephens (1841), and by Blackley (1857).

3. *The Swedish Saga*, or lay of Swedish "history," is the *Ingvars Saga*.

4. *The Russian Saga*, or lay of Russian legendary history, is the *Egmunds Saga*.

5. *The Folks-Sagas* are stories of romance. From this ancient collection we have derived our nursery tales of *Jack and the Bean-Stalk*, *Jack the Giant-Killer*, the *Giant who smelt the Blood of an Englishman*, *Blue Beard*, *Cinderella*, the *Little Old Woman cut Shorter*, the *Pig that wouldn't go over the Bridge*, *Puss in Boots*, and even the first sketches of *Whittington and His Cat*, and *Baron Munchausen*. (See Dasent, *Tales from the Norse*, 1859.)

6. *Sagas of Foreign origin*. Besides the rich stores of original tales, several foreign ones have been imported and translated into Norse, such as *Barlaham and Josaphat*, by Rudolph of Ems, one of the German minnesingers. On the other hand, the minnesingers borrowed from the Norse sagas their famous story embodied in the *Nibelungen Lied*, called the "German *Iliad*," which is from the second part of Snorro Sturleson's *Edda*.

Sagaman, a narrator of sagas. These ancient chroniclers differed from scalds in several respects. Scalds were minstrels, who celebrated in verse the exploits of living kings or national heroes; sagamen were tellers of legendary stories, either in prose or verse, like Scheherazādê, the narrator of the *Arabian Nights*, the mandarin, Fum-Hoam, the teller of the *Chinese Tales*, Moradbak, the teller of the *Oriental Tales*, Ferămorz, who told the tales to Lalla Rookh, and so on. Again, scalds resided at court, were attached to the royal suite, and followed the king in all his expeditions; but sagamen were free and unattached, and told their tales to prince or peasant, in lordly hall or at village wake.

Sage of Concord (*The*), Ralph Waldo Emerson, author of *Literary Ethics* (1838), *Poems* (1846), *Representative Men* (1850), *English Traits* (1856), and numerous other works (1803-1882).

In Mr. Emerson we have a poet and a profoundly religious man, who is really and entirely undaunted by the discoveries of science, past, present or prospective. In his case, poetry, with the joy of a Bacchanal, takes her graver brother, science, by the hand, and cheers him with immortal laughter. By Emerson scientific conceptions are continually transmuted into the finer forms and warmer lines of an ideal world.—Professor Tyndall, *Fragments of Science.*

Sage of Monticello (*The*), Thomas Jefferson, the third President of the United States, whose country seat was at Monticello.

As from the grave where Henry sleeps,
From Vernon's weeping willow,
And from the grassy pall which hides
The Sage of Monticello ...
Virginia, o'er thy land of slaves
A warning voice is swelling.
Whittier, *Voices of Freedom* (1836).

Sage of Samos (*The*), Pythagŏras, a native of Samos (B.C. 584-506).

Sages (*The Seven*). (See SEVEN WISE MEN OF GREECE.)

Sag´ittary, a monster, half man and half beast, described as "a terrible archer, who neighs like a horse, and with eyes of fire which strike men dead like lightning." Any deadly shot is a sagittary.—Guido delle Colonna (thirteenth century), *Historia Troyana Prosayce Composita* (translated by Lydgate).

The dreadful Sagittary,
Appals our numbers.
Shakespeare, *Troilus and Cressida* (1602).

(See also *Othello*, act i. sc. 1, 3. The barrack is so called from the figure of an archer over the door.)

Sagramour le De´sirus, a knight of the Round Table.—See *Launcelot du Lac* and *Morte d'Arthur.*

Sailor King (*The*), William IV. of Great Britain (1765, 1830-1837).

Saint (*The*), Kang-he, of China, who assumed the name of Chin-tsou-jin (1653, 1661-1722).

St. Aldobrand, the noble husband of Lady Imogine, murdered by Count Bertram, her quondam lover.—C. Maturin, *Bertram* (1816).

St. Alme (*Captain*), son of Darlemont, a merchant, guardian of Julio, count of Harancour. He pays his addresses to Marianne Franval, to whom he is ultimately married. Captain St. Alme is generous, high-spirited, and noble-minded.—Thomas Holcroft, *The Deaf and Dumb* (1785).

St. Andre, a fashionable dancing-master in the reign of Charles II.

St. Andre's feet ne'er kept more equal time.
Dryden, *MacFlecknoe* (1682).

St. Asaph (*The dean of*), in the court of Queen Elizabeth.—Sir W. Scott, *Kenilworth* (1821).

St. Basil Outwits the Devil. (See SINNER SAVED.)

St. Botolph (*The Prior of*). Sir W. Scott, *Ivanhoe* (time, Richard I.).

St. Cecili, **Cecily**, or **Cecile** (2 *syl.*), the daughter of noble Roman parents, and a Christian. She married Valirian. One day, she told her husband she had "an aungel ... that with gret love, wher so I wake or slepe, is redy ay my body for to kepe." Valirian requested to see this angel, and Cecile told him he must first go to St. Urban, and, being purged by him "fro synne, than [*then*] schul ye see that aungel." Valirian was accordingly "cristened" by St. Urban, returned home, and found the angel with two crowns, brought direct from paradise. One he gave to Cecile and one to Valirian, saying that "bothe with the palme of martirdom schullen come unto God's blisful feste." Valirian suffered martydom first; then Almachius, the Roman prefect, commanded his officers to "brenne Cecile in a bath of flammês red." She remained in the bath all day and night, yet, "sat she cold, and felte of it no woe." Then smote they her three strokes upon the neck, but could not smite her head off. She lingered on for three whole days, preaching and teaching, and then died. St. Urban buried her body privately by night, and the house he converted into a church, which he called the church of Cecily.—Chaucer, *Canterbury Tales* ("The Second Nun's Tale," 1388).

St. Christopher, a native of Lycia, very tall, and fearful to look at. He was so proud of his strength that he resolved to serve only the mightiest, and went in search of a worthy master. He first entered the service of the emperor; but one day, seeing his master cross himself for fear of the devil, he quitted his service for that of Satan. This new master he found was thrown into alarm at the sight of a cross; so he quitted him also, and went in search of the Saviour. One day, near a ferry, a little child accosted him, and begged the giant to carry him across the water. Christopher put the child on his back, but found every step he took the child grew heavier and heavier, till the burden was more than he could bear. As he sank beneath his load, the child told the giant he was Christ, and Christopher resolved to serve Christ and Him alone. He died three days afterwards, and was canonized. The Greek and Latin churches look on him as the protecting saint against floods, fire, and earthquake.—James de Voragine, *Golden Legends*, 100 (thirteenth century).

⁂ His body is said to be at Valencia, in Spain; one of his arms at Compostella; a jaw-bone at Astorga; a shoulder at St. Peter's, in Rome; and a tooth and rib at Venice. His day is May 9 in the Greek Church, and July 25 in the Latin. Of course, "the Christ-bearer" is an allegory. The gigantic bones called his relics may serve for "matters of faith" to give reality to the fable.

(His name before conversion was Offĕrus, but after he carried Christ across the ford, it was called Christ-Offerus, shortened into Christopher, which means "the Christ-bearer.")

St. Clare (*Augustin*), the kind, indulgent master of Uncle Tom. He was beloved by all his slaves.

Evangeline St. Clare, daughter of Mr. St. Clare. Evangeline was the good angel of the family, and was adored by Uncle Tom.

Miss Ophelia St. Clare, sister of Augustin.—Mrs. Harriet Beecher Stowe, *Uncle Tom's Cabin* (1852).

St. Distaff, an imaginary saint to whom January 7, or Twelfth Day is consecrated.

Partly worke and partly play
You must on St. Distaff's Day;
Give St. Distaff all the right,
Then give Christmas sport good night.
Wit Asporting in a Pleasant Grove of New Fancies (1657).

St. Filume′na or FILOMENA, a new saint of the Latin Church. Sabateli has a picture of this nineteenth-century saint, representing her as hovering over a group of sick and maimed, who are healed by her intercession. In 1802 a grave was found in the cemetery of St. Priscilla, and near it three tiles, with these words in red letters.

A re-arrangement of the tiles made the inscription, PAX TE-CUM, FI-LUMENA. That this was the correct rendering is quite certain, for the virgin martyr herself told a priest and a nun in a dream, that she was Fi[lia] Lumina, the daughter Lumina, *i.e.* the daughter of the Light of the world. In confirmation of this dream, as her bones were carried to Mugnano, the saint repaired her own skeleton, made her hair grow, and performed so many miracles, that those must indeed be hard of belief who can doubt the truth of the story.

St. George is the national saint of England, in consequence of the miraculous assistance rendered by him, to the arms of the Christians under Godfrey de Bouillon during the first crusade.

St. George's Sword, Askelon.

George he shaved the dragon's beard,
And Askelon was his razor.
Percy's *Reliques*, III. iii. 15.

St. George (*Le chevalier de*), James Francis Edward Stuart, called "The Old (or *elder*) Pretender" (1688-1766).

St. Graal. (See SANGRAAL.)

St. Leon, the hero of a novel of the same name, by W. Goodwin (1799). St. Leon becomes possessed of the "elixir of life," and of the "philosopher's stone;" but this knowledge, instead of bringing him wealth and happiness, is the source of misery and endless misfortunes.

Saint Maur, one of the attendants of Sir Reginald Front de Bœuf (a follower of Prince John).—Sir W. Scott, *Ivanhoe* (time, Richard I.).

St. Nicholas, the patron saint of boys. He is said to have been bishop of Myra, in Lycia, and his death is placed in the year 326.

Under his triple names of *St. Nicholas, Santa Claus* and *Kriss Kringle*, he fills good children's stockings on Christmas Eve. Clement C. Moore has made the annual visit of this saint "in a miniature sleigh drawn by eight tiny reindeer," the subject of his famous nursery poem beginning:

"'Twas the night before Christmas, and all through the house,
Not a creature was stirring, not even a mouse."
(1844).

St. Prieux, the *amant* of Julie, in Rousseau's novel entitled *Julie* ou *La Nouvelle Héloïse* (1760).

St. Ronan's Well, a novel by Sir W. Scott (1823). An inferior work; but it contains the character of Meg Dods, of the Clachan or Mowbray Arms inn, one of the very best low comic characters in the whole range of fiction.

St. Stephen's Chapel, properly the House of Commons, but sometimes applied to the two Houses of Parliament. So called by a figure of speech from St. Stephen's Chapel, built by King Stephen, rebuilt by Edward II. and III., and finally destroyed by fire in 1834. St. Stephen's Chapel was fitted up for the use of the House of Commons in the reign of Edward IV. The great council of the nation met before in the chapel-house of the abbey.

St. Swithin, tutor of King Alfred, and bishop of Winchester. The monks wished to bury him in the chancel of the minster; but the bishop had directed that his body should be interred under the open vault of heaven. Finding the monks resolved to disobey his injunction, he sent a heavy rain on July 15, the day assigned to the funeral ceremony, in consequence of which it was deferred from day to day for forty days. The monks then bethought them of the saint's injunction, and prepared to inter the body in the churchyard. St. Swithin smiled his approbation by sending a beautiful sunshiny day, in which all the robes of the heirarchy might be displayed without the least fear of being injured by untimely and untoward showers.

Saints (*Island of*), Ireland.

Saints (*Royal*).

David of Scotland (*, 1124-1153).

Edward the Confessor (1004, 1042-1066).

Edward the Martyr (961, 975-979).

Eric IX. of Sweden (*, 1155-1161).

Ethelred I., king of Wessex (*, 866-871).

Eugenius I., pope (*, 654-657).

Felix I., pope (*, 269-274).

Ferdinand III. of Castile and Leon (1200, 1217-1252).

Julius I., pope (*, 337-352).

Kâng-he, second of the Manchoo dynasty of China (*, 1661-1722).

Lawrence Justiniani, patriarch of Venice (1380, 1451-1465).

Leo IX., pope (1002, 1049-1054).

Louis IX. of France (1215, 1226-1270).

Olaus II. of Norway (992, 1000-1030).

Stephen I. of Hungary (979, 997-1038).

Saints for Diseases. These saints either ward off ills or help to relieve them, and should be invoked by those who trust their power:—

AGUE. St. Pernel cures.

BAD DREAMS. St. Christopher protects from.

BLEAR EYES. St. Otilic cures.

BLINDNESS. St. Thomas à Becket cures.

BOILS and BLAINS. St. Rooke cures.

CHASTITY. St. Susan protects.

CHILDREN'S DISEASES (*All*). St Blaise heals; and all cattle diseases. The bread consecrated on his day (February 3) and called "the Benediction of St. Blaise," should have been tried in the recent cattle plague.

CHOLERA. Oola Beebee is invoked by the Hindûs in this malady.

COLIC. St. Erasmus relieves.

DANCING MANIA. St. Vitus cures.

DEFILEMENT. St. Susan preserves from.

DISCOVERY OF LOST GOODS. St. Ethelbert and St Elian.

DOUBTS. St. Catherine resolves.

DYING. St. Barbara relieves.

EPILEPSY. St. Valentine cures.

FIRE. St. Agatha protects from it, but St. Florian should be invoked if it has already broken out.

FLOOD, FIRE, and EARTHQUAKE. St. Christopher saves from.

GOUT. St. Wolfgang, they say, is of more service than Blair's pills.

GRIPES. St. Erasmus cures.

IDIOCY. St. Gildas is the guardian angel of idiots.

INFAMY. St. Susan protects from.

INFECTION. St. Roque protects from.

LEPROSY. St. Lazarus, the beggar.

MADNESS. St. Dymphna cures.

MICE and RATS. St. Gertrude and St. Huldrick ward them off.

NIGHT ALARMS. St. Christopher protects from.

PLAGUE. St. Roch, they say, in this case is better than the "good bishop of Marseilles."

QUENCHING FIRE. St. Florian and St. Christopher should not be forgotten by fire-insurance companies.

QUINSY. St. Blaise will cure it sooner than tartarized antimony.

RICHES. St. Anne and St. Vincent help those who seek it. Gold-diggers should ask them for nuggets.

SCABS. St. Rooke cures.

SMALL-POX. St. Martin of Tours may be tried by those objecting to vaccination. In Hindûstan, Seetla wards it off.

SUDDEN DEATH. St. Martin saves from.

TEMPERANCE. Father Mathew is called "The Apostle of Temperance" (1790-1856).

TOOTH-ACHE. St. Appolline cures better than creosote.

VERMIN-DESTROYERS. St. Gertude and St. Huldrick.

WEALTH-BESTOWER. St. Anne, recommended to the sultan.

Saints of Places. The following are the patron saints of the cities, nations, or places set down:—

ABERDEEN, St. Nicholas (died 342). His day is December 6.

ABYSSINIA, St. Frumentius (died 360). His day is October 27.

ALEXANDRIA, St. Mark, who founded the church there (died A.D. 52). His day is April 25th.

ALPS (*The*), Felix Neff (1798-1829).

ANTIOCH, St. Margaret (died 275). Her day is July 20.

ARDENNES (*The*), St. Hubert (656-730). He is called "The Apostles of the Ardennes." His days are May 30 and November 3d.

ARMENIA, St. Gregory of Armenia (256-331). His day is September 30.

BATH, St. David, from whose benediction the waters of Bath received their warmth and medicinal qualities (480-544). His day is March 1.

BEAUVAIS, St. Lucian (died 290), called "The Apostle of Beauvais." His day is January 8.

BELGIUM, St. Boniface (680-755). His day is on June 5.

BOHEMIA, St. Wenceslaus.

BRUSSELS, the Virgin Mary; St. Gudule, who died 712. St. Gudule's day is January 8.

CAGLIARI (in Sardinia), St. Efisio or St. Ephesus.

CAPPADOCIA, St. Matthias (died A.D. 62). His day is February 24.

CARTHAGE, St. Perpetua (died 203). Her day is March 7.

COLOGNE, St. Ursula (died 452). Her day is October 21.

CORFU, St. Spiridion (fourth century). His day is December 14.

CREMONA, St. Margaret (died 275). Her day is July 20.

DENMARK, St. Anscharius (801-864), whose day is February 3; and St. Canute (died 1086), whose day is January 19.

EDINBURGH, St. Giles (died 550). His day is September 1.

ENGLAND, St. George (died 290). St. Bede calls Gregory the Great "The Apostle of England," but St. Augustin was "The Apostle of the English People" (died 607). St. George's day is April 23.

ETHIOPIA, St. Frumentius (died 360). His day is October 27.

FLANDERS, St. Peter (died 66). His day is June 29.

FLORENCE, St. John the Baptist (died A.D. 32). His days are June 24 and August 29.

Forests, St. Sylvester, because *silva*, in Latin, means "a wood." His day is June 20.

Forts, St. Barbara (died 335). Her day is December 4.

FRANCE, St. Denys (died 272). His day is October 9. St. Remi is called "The Great Apostle of the French" (439-535). His day is October 1.

FRANCONIA, St. Kilian (died 689). His day is July 8.

FRISELAND, St. Wilbrod or Willibrod (657-738), called "The Apostle of the Frisians." His day is November 7.

GAUL, St. Irenæus (130-200), whose day is June 28; and St. Martin (316-397), whose day is November 12; St. Denys is called "The Apostle of the Gauls."

GENOA, St. George of Cappadocia. His day is April 23.

GENTILES. St. Paul was "The Apostle of the Gentiles" (died A.D. 66). His days are January 25 and June 29.

GEORGIA, St. Nino, whose day is September 16.

GERMANY, St. Boniface, "Apostles of the Germans" (680-755), whose day is June 5; and St. Martin (316-397), whose day is November 11. (St. Boniface was called Winfred till Gregory II. changed the name.)

GLASGOW, St. Mungo, also called Kentigern (514-601).

Groves, St. Sylvester, because *silva*, in Latin, means "a wood." His day is June 20.

HIGHLANDERS, St. Columb (521-597). His day is June 9.

Hills, St. Barbara (died 335). Her day is December 4.

HOLLAND, the Virgin Mary. Her days are: her *Nativity*, November 21; *Visitation*, July 2; *Conception*, December 8; *Purification*, February 2; *Assumption*, August 15.

HUNGARY, St. Louis; Mary of Aquisgrana (*Aix-la-Chapelle*); and St. Anastatius (died 628), whose day is January 22.

INDIA, St. Bartolomé de las Casas (1474-1566); the Rev. J. Eliot (1603-1690); and Francis Xavier (1506-1552), called "The Apostle of the Indians," whose day is December 4.

IRELAND, St. Patrick (372-493). His day is March 17. (Some give his birth 387, and some his death 495).

ITALY, St. Anthony (251-356). His day is January 17.

LAPLAND, St. Nicholas (died 342). His day is December 6.

LICHFIELD, St. Chad, who lived there (died 672). His day is March 2.

LIEGE, St. Albert (died 1195). His day is November 21.

LISBON, St. Vincent (died 304). His translation to Lisbon is kept September 15.

LONDON, St. Paul, whose day is January 25; and St. Michael, whose day is September 29.

MOSCOW, St. Nicholas (died 342). His day is December 6.

Mountains, St. Barbara (died 335). Her day is December 4.

NAPLES, St. Januarius (died 291), whose day is September 19; and St. Thomas Aquīnas (1227-1274), whose days are March 7 and July 18.

NETHERLANDS, St. Armand (589-679).

NORTH (*The*), St. Ansgar (801-864), and Bernard Gilpin (1517-1583). NORWAY, St. Anscharius, called "The Apostle of the North" (801-864), whose day is February 3; and St. Olaus (992, 1000-1030).

OXFORD, St. Frideswide.

PADUA, St. Justina, whose day is October 7; and St. Anthony (1195-1231), whose day is June 13.

PARIS, St. Geneviève (419-512). Her day is January 3.

PEAK (*The*), Derbyshire, W. Bagshaw (1628-1702).

PICTS (*The*), St. Ninian (fourth century), whose day is September 16; and St. Columb (521-597), whose day is June 9.

PISA, San Ranieri.

POITIERS, St. Hilary (300-367). His day is January 14.

POLAND, St. Hedviga (1174-1243), whose day is October 15; and St. Stanislaus (died 1078), whose day is May 7.

PORTUGAL, St. Sebastian (250-288). His day is January 20.

PRUSSIA, St. Andrew, whose day is November 30; and St. Albert (died 1195), whose day is November 21.

ROCHESTER, St. Paulīnus (353-431). His day is June 22.

ROME, St. Peter and St. Paul. Both died on the same day of the month, June 29. The old tutelar deity was Mars.

RUSSIA, St. Nicholas, St. Andrew, St. George, and the Virgin Mary.

SARAGOSSA, St. Vincent, where he was born (died 304). His day is January 22.

SARDINIA, Mary the Virgin. Her days are: *Nativity*, November 21; *Visitation*, July 2; *Conception*, December 8; *Purification*, February 2; *Assumption*, August 15.

SCOTLAND, St. Andrew, because his remains were brought by Regulus into Fifeshire in 368. His day is November 30.

SEBASTIA (in Armenia), St. Blaise (died 316). His day is February 3.

SICILY, St. Agatha, where she was born (died 251. Her day is February 5. The old tutelar deity was Cerês.

SILESIA, St. Hedviga, also called Avoye (1174-1243). His day is October 15.

SLAVES or SLAVI, St. Cyril, called "The Apostle of the Slavi" (died 868). His day is February 14.

SPAIN, St. James the Greater (died A.D. 44). His day is July 24.

SWEDEN, St. Anscharius, St John, and St. Eric IX. (reigned 1155-1161).

SWITZERLAND, St. Gall (died 646). His day is October 16.

Valleys, St. Agatha (died 251). Her day is February 5.

VENICE, St. Mark, who was buried there. His day is April 25. St. Pantaleon, whose day is July 27; and St. Lawrence Justiniani (1380-1465).

VIENNA, St. Stephen (died A.D. 34). His day is December 26.

Vineyards, St. Urban (died 230). His day is May 25.

WALES, St. David, uncle of King Arthur (died 544). His day is March 1.

Woods, St. Silvester, because *silva*, in Latin, means "a wood." His day is June 20.

YORKSHIRE, St. Paulīnus (353-431). His day is June 22.

Saints for Special Classes of Persons, such as tradesmen, children, wives, idiots, students, etc.:—

ARCHERS, St. Sebastian, because he was shot by them.

ARMORERS, St. George of Cappadocia.

ARTISTS and the ARTS, St. Agatha; but St. Luke is the patron of painters, being himself one.

BAKERS, St. Winifred, who followed the trade.

BARBERS, St. Louis.

BARREN WOMEN. St. Margaret befriends them.

BEGGARS, St. Giles. Hence the outskirts of cities are often called "St. Giles."

BISHOPS, etc., St. Timothy and St. Titus (1 *Tim.* iii. 1; *Titus* i. 7).

BLIND FOLK, St. Thomas à Becket, and St. Lucy, who was deprived of her eyes by Paschasius.

BOOKSELLERS, St. John Port Latin.

BRIDES, St. Nicholas, because he threw three stockings, filled with wedding portions, into the chamber window of three virgins, that they might marry their sweethearts, and not live a life of sin for the sake of earning a living.

BURGLARS, St. Dismas, the penitent thief.

CANDLE and LAMP MAKERS, St. Lucy and Lucian. A pun upon *lux lucis* ("light").

CANNONEERS, St. Barbara, because she is generally represented in a fort or tower.

CAPTIVES, St. Barbara and St. Leonard.

CARPENTERS, St. Joseph, who was a carpenter.

CHILDREN, St. Felicitas and St. Nicholas. This latter saint restored to life some children, murdered by an inkeeper, of Myra, and pickled in a pork-tub.

COBBLERS, St. Crispin, who worked at the trade.

CRIPPLES, St. Giles, because he refused to be cured of an accidental lameness, that he might mortify his flesh.

DIVINES, St. Thomas Aquinas, author of *Somme de Theology*.

DOCTORS, St. Cosme, who was a surgeon in Cilicia.

DRUNKARDS. St. Martin, because St. Martin's Day (November 11) happened to be the day of the Vinalia, or feast of Bacchus. St. Urban protects.

DYING, St. Barbara.

FERRYMEN, St. Christopher, who was a ferryman.

FISHERMEN, St. Peter, who was a fisherman.

FOOLS, St. Maturin because the Greek word *matia* or *matê* means "folly."

FREE TRADE. R. Cobden is called "The Apostle of Free Trade" (1804-1865).

FREEMEN, St. John.

FULLERS, St. Sever, because the place so called, on the Adour, is or was famous for its tanneries and fulleries.

GOLDSMITHS, St. Eloy, who was a goldsmith.

HATTERS, St. William, the son of a hatter.

HOG and SWINEHERDS, St. Anthony. Pigs unfit for food used anciently to have their ears slit, but one of the proctors of St. Anthony's Hospital once tied a bell about the neck of a pig whose ear was slit, and no one ever attempted to injure it.

HOUSEWIVES, St. Osyth, especially to prevent their losing the keys, and to help them in finding these "tiny tormentors;" St. Martha, the sister of Lazarus.

HUNTSMEN, St. Hubert, who lived in the Ardennes, a famous hunting forest; and St. Eustace.

IDIOTS. St. Gildas restores them to their right senses.

INFANTS, St. Felicitas and St. Nicholas.

INFIDELS. Voltaire is called "The Apostle of Infidels" (1694-1778).

INSANE FOLKS, St. Dymphna.

LAWYERS, St. Yves Helori (in Sicily), who was called "The Advocate of the Poor," because he was always ready to defend them in the law courts gratuitously (1233-1303).

LEARNED MEN, St. Catherine, noted for her learning, and for converting certain philosophers, sent to convince the Christians of Alexandria of the folly of the Christian faith.

MADMEN, St. Dymphna.

MAIDENS, the Virgin Mary.

MARINERS, St. Christopher, who was a ferryman; and St. Nicholas, who was once in danger of shipwreck, and who, on one occasion, lulled a tempest for some pilgrims on their way to the Holy Land.

MILLERS, St. ARNOLD, the son of a miller.

MERCERS, St. Florian, the son of a mercer.

MOTHERS, the Virgin Mary; St. Margaret, for those who wish to be so. The girdle of St. Margaret, in St. Germain's, is placed round the waist of those who wish to be mothers.

MUSICIANS, St. Cecilia, who was an excellent musician.

NAILERS, St. Cloud, because *clou*, in French means "a nail."

NETMAKERS, St. James and St. John (*Matt.* iv. 21).

NURSES, St. Agatha.

PAINTERS, St. Luke, who was a painter.

PARISH CLERKS, St. Nicholas.

PARSONS, St. Thomas Aquinas, doctor of theology, at Paris.

PHYSICIANS, St. Cosme, who was a surgeon; St. Luke (*Col.* iv. 14).

PILGRIMS, St. Julian, St. Raphael, St. James of Compostella.

PINMAKERS, St. Sebastian, whose body was as full of arrows in his martydom as a pincushion is of pins.

POOR FOLKS, St. Giles, who affected indigence, thinking "poverty and suffering" a service acceptable to God.

PORTRAIT-PAINTERS and PHOTOGRAPHERS, St. Veronica, who had a handkerchief with the face of Jesus stamped on it.

POTTERS, St. Gore, who was a potter.

PRISONERS, St. Sebastian and St. Leonard.

SAGES, St. Cosme, St. Damian, and St. Katherine.

SAILORS, St. Nicholas and St. Christopher.

SCHOLARS, St. Katherine. (See "Learned Men.")

SCHOOL CHILDREN, St. Nicholas and St. Gregory.

SCOTCH REFORMERS. Knox is "The Apostle of the Scotch Reformers" (1505-72).

SEAMAN, St. Nicholas, who once was in danger of shipwreck; and St. Christopher, who was a ferryman.

SHEPHERDS and their FLOCKS, St. Windeline, who kept sheep, like David.

SHOEMAKERS, St. Crispin, who made shoes.

SILVERSMITHS, St. Eloy, who worked in gold and silver.

SLAVES, St. Cyril. This is a pun; he was "The Apostle of the Slavi."

SOOTHSAYERS, etc., St. Agabus (*Acts* xxi. 10).

SPORTSMEN, St. Hubert. (See "Huntsmen.")

STATUARIES, St. Veronica. (See above, "Portrait-painters.")

STONEMASONS, St. Peter, (*John* i. 42).

STUDENTS, St. Katherine, noted for her great learning.

SURGEONS, St. Cosme, who practised medicine in Cilicia gratuitously (died 310).

SWEETHEARTS, St. Valentine, because in the Middle Ages ladies held their "courts of love" about this time. (See VALENTINE.)

SWINEHERDS and SWINE, St. Anthony.

TAILORS, St. Goodman, who was a tailor.

TANNERS, St. Clement, the son of a tanner.

TAX-COLLECTORS, St. Matthew, (*Matt.* ix. 9).

TENTMAKERS, St. Paul and St. Aquila, who were tentmakers (*Acts* xviii. 3).

THIEVES, St. Dismas, the penitent thief. St. Ethelbert and St. Elian ward off thieves.

TRAVELLERS, St. Raphael, because he assumed the guise of a traveller in order to guide Tobias from Nineveh to Ragês (*Tobit* v.).

VINTNERS and VINEYARDS, St. Urban.

VIRGINS, St. Winifred and St. Nicholas.

WHEELWRIGHTS, St. Boniface, the son of a wheelwright.

WIGMAKERS, St. Louis.

WISE MEN, St. Cosme, St. Damian, and St. Catherine.

WOOLCOMBERS and STAPLERS, St. Blaise, who was torn to pieces by "combes of yren."

Sakhar, the devil who stole Solomon's signet. The tale is that Solomon, when he washed, entrusted his signet-ring to his favorite concubine, Amina. Sakhar one day assumed the appearance of Solomon, got possession of the ring, and sat on the throne as the king. During this usurpation, Solomon became a beggar, but in forty days Sakhar flew away, and flung the signet-ring into the sea. It was swallowed by a fish, the fish was caught and sold to Solomon, the ring was recovered, and Sakhar was thrown into the sea of Galilee with a great stone round his neck.—Jallâlo´ddin, *Al Zamakh*. (See FISH AND THE RING.)

Sa´kia, the dispenser of rain, one of the four gods of the Adites (2 *syl.*).

Sakia, we invoked for rain;
We called on Razeka for food;
They did not hear our prayers—they could not hear.
No cloud appeared in heaven,
No nightly dews came down.
Southey, *Thalaba, the Destroyer*, i. 24 (1797).

Sakunta´la, daughter of Viswamita and a water-nymph, abandoned by her parents, and brought up by a hermit. One day, King Dushyanta came to the hermitage, and persuaded Sakuntala to marry him. In due time a son was born, but Dushyanta left his bride at the hermitage. When the boy was six years old, his mother took him to the king, and Dushyanta recognized his wife by a ring which he had given her. Sakuntala was now publicly proclaimed queen, and the boy (whose name was Bhârata) became the founder of the glorious race of the Bhâratas.

This story forms the plot of the famous drama, *Sakuntala*, by Kâlidasa, well known to us through the translation of Sir W. Jones.

Sakya-Muni, the founder of Buddhism. Sakya is the family name of Siddharta, and *muni* means "a recluse." Buddha ("perfection") is a title given to Siddharta.

Sal´ace (3 *syl.*) or SALACIA, wife of Neptune, and mother of Triton.

Triton, who boasts his high Neptunian race,
Sprung from the god by Salace's embrace.
Camoens, *Lusiad*, vi. (1672).

Sal'adin, the soldan of the East. Sir W. Scott introduces him in *The Talisman*, first as Sheerkohf, emir of Kurdistan, and subsequently as Adonbeck el Hakim, the physician.

Salamanca *(The Bachelor of)*, the title and hero of a novel by Lesage. The name of the bachelor is Don Cherubim, who is placed in all sorts of situations suitable to the author's vein of satire (1704)

Sala'nio, a friend to Antonio and Bassānio.—Shakespeare, *Merchant of Venice* (1598).

Salari'no, a friend to Antonio and Bassānio.—Shakespeare, *Merchant of Venice* (1598).

Sa'leh. The Thamûdites (3 *syl.*), proposed that Sâleh should, by miracle, prove that Jehovah was a God superior to their own. Prince Jonda said he would believe it if Sâleh made a camel, big with young, come out of a certain rock which he pointed out. Sâleh did so, and Jonda was converted.

(The Thamûdites were idolaters, and Sâleh, the prophet, was sent to bring them back to the worship of Jehovah.)

Sâleh's Camel. The camel thus miraculously produced, used to go about the town, crying aloud, "Ho! every one that wanteth milk, let him come, and I will give it him."—Sale, *Al Korân*, vii. notes. (See *Isaiah* lv. 1).

Saleh, a son of Faras'chê (3 *syl.*) queen of a powerful under-sea empire. His sister was Gulna'rê (3 *syl.*), empress of Persia. Saleh asked the king of Samandal, another under-sea emperor, to give his daughter, Giauha'rê, in marriage to Prince Beder, son of Gulnarê; but the proud, passionate despot ordered the prince's head to be cut off for such presumptuous insolence. However, Saleh made his escape, invaded Samandal, took the king prisoner, and the marriage between Beder and the Princess Giauharê was duly celebrated.—*Arabian Nights* ("Beder and Giauharê").

Sa'lem, a young seraph, one of the two tutelar angels of the Virgin Mary and of John the Divine, "for God had given to John two tutelar angels, the chief of whom was Raph'ael, one of the most exalted seraphs of the hierarchy of heaven."—Klopstock, *The Messiah*, iii. (1748).

Sal'emal, the preserver in sickness, one of the four gods of the Adites (2 *syl.*).—D'Herbelot, *Bibliothèques Orientale* (1697).

Salian Franks. So called from the Isăla or Yssel, in Holland. They were a branch of the Sicambri; hence, when Clovis was baptized at Rheims, the old prelate addressed him as "Sigambrian," and said that "he must henceforth set at naught what he had hitherto worshipped, and worship what he had hitherto set at naught."

Salisbury (*Earl of*), William Longsword, natural son of Henry II. and Jane Clifford, "The Fair Rosamond."—Shakespeare, *King John* (1596); Sir W. Scott, *The Talisman* (time, Richard I.).

Sallust of France (*The*). César Vichard (1639-1692) was so called by Voltaire.

Salmigondin, or "Salmygondin," a lordship of Dipsody, given by Pantagruel to Panurge (2 *syl.*). Alcofribas, who had resided six months in the giant's mouth without his knowing it, was made castellan of the castle.—Rabelais, *Pantagruel*, ii. 32; iii. 2 (1533-45).

The lordship of Salmygodin was worth 67 million pounds sterling, per annum, in "certain rent," and an annual revenue for locusts and periwinkles, varying from £24,357 to 12 millions in a good year, when the exports of locusts and periwinkles were flourishing. Panurge, however, could not make the two ends meet. At the close of "less than fourteen days" he had forestalled three years' rent and revenue, and had to apply to Pantagruel to pay his debts.—*Pantagruel*, iii. 2.

Salmo´neus (3 *syl.*), king of Elis, wishing to be thought a god, used to imitate thunder and lightning by driving his chariot over a brazen bridge, and darting burning torches on every side. He was killed by lightning for his impiety and folly

Salmoneus, who while he his carroach drave
Over the brazen bridge of Elis' stream,
And did with artificial thunder brave
Jove, till he pierced him with a lightning beam.
Lord Brooke, *Treatise on Monarchie*, vi.

It was to be the literary Salmoneus of the political Jupiter.—Lord Lytton.

Sally in our Alley, subject of popular ballad of same name, by Henry Carew (1663-1743).

Sally (*red haired*), remembered love of a poor pioneer, whom the Indians have scalped and blinded. As he lies by the camp-fire, he bemoans his hard lot and wishes he had been left to die.

"It's twice dead not to see."
Rose Terry Cooke, *Poems* (1888).

Sally (*Kittredge*), black-eyed, rosy-cheeked country girl, Mara Linnotti's friend, and finally, the wife of Moses Pennell.—Harriet Beecher Stowe, *The Pearl of Orr's Island* (1860).

Salome and the Baptist. When Salomê delivered the head of John the Baptist to her mother, Herodias pulled out the tongue and stabbed it with her bodkin.

When the head of Cicero was delivered to Marc Antony, his wife, Fulvia, pulled out the tongue and stabbed it repeatedly with her bodkin.

Salvage Knight (*The*), Sir Arthegal, called Artegal, from bk. iv. 6. The hero of bk. v. (*Justice*).—Spenser, *Faëry Queen* (1596).

Salva'tor Rosa (*The English*) John Hamilton Mortimer (1741-1779.

Salvato're (4 *syl.*), Salva'tor Rosa, an Italian painter, especially noted for his scenes of brigands, etc. (1615-1673).

But, ever and anon, to soothe your vision,
Fatigued with these hereditary glories,
There rose a Carlo Dolce or a Titian,
Or wilder group of savage Salvatore's.
Byron, *Don Juan*, xiii. 71 (1824).

Sam, a gentleman, the friend of Francis'co.—Beaumont and Fletcher, *Mons. Thomas* (1619).

Sam; one of the Know-Nothings, or Native American party. One of "Uncle Sam's" sons.

Sam (*Dicky*), a Liverpool man.

Sam (*Uncle*), the United States of North America, or rather the government of the states personified. So called from Samuel Wilson, uncle of Ebenezer Wilson. Ebenezer was inspector of Elbert Anderson's store on the Hudson, and Samuel superintended the workmen. The stores were marked E·A. U·S. ("Elbert Anderson, United States"), but the workmen insisted that U·S. stood for Uncle Sam."—Mr. Frost.

Sam Kimper. Reformed convict who sets himself earnestly to work to lead a new life, toiling steadily at the shoemaker's bench, and *acting* his new religion. His only creed is to believe simply in the Saviour of sinners. "He" (the chaplain) "says to me—'Just believe in Jesus like you do in Andrew Jackson and you'll be right in the course of time. Believe that what He said was true, an' get your mind full of what He said, an' *keep it full*.'"—John Habberton, *All He Knew* (1890).

Sam Silverquill, one of the prisoners at Portanferry.—Sir W. Scott, *Guy Mannering* (time, George II.).

Sam Weller, servant of Mr. Pickwick. The impersonation of the shrewdness, quaint humor, and best qualities of cockney low life.—C. Dickens, *The Pickwick Papers* (1836).

Sa´mael (3 *syl.*), the prince of demons, who, in the guise of a serpant, tempted Eve in paradise. (See SAMIEL.)

Samarcand Apple, a perfect panacea of all diseases. It was bought by Prince Ahmed, and was instrumental in restoring Nouroun´nihar to perfect health, although at the very point of death.

In fact sir, there is no disease, however painful or dangerous, whether fever, pleurisy, plague, or any other disorder, but it will instantly cure; and that in the easiest possible way; it is simply to make the sick person smell of the apple.—*Arabian Nights*, ("Ahmed and Pari-Banou").

Sam´benites [*Sam´.be.neetz*], persons dressed in the *sambenito*, a yellow coat without sleeves, having devils painted on it. The sambenito was worn by "heretics" on their way to execution.

And blow us up i' the open streets.
Disguised in rumps, like sambenites.
S. Butler, *Hudibras*, iii. 2 (1678).

Sambo, any male of the negro race.

No race has shown such capabilities of adaptation to varying soil and circumstances as the negro. Alike to them the snows of Canada, the rocky land of New England or the gorgeous profusion of the Southern States. Sambo and Cuffey expand under them all.—Harriet Beecher Stowe.

Sam´eri (*Al*), the proselyte who cast the golden calf at the bidding of Aaron. After he had made it, he took up some dust on which Gabriel's horse had set its feet, threw it into the calf's mouth, and immediately the calf became animated and began to low. Al Beidâwi says that Al Sâmeri was not really a proper name, but that the real name of the artificer was Mûsa ebn Dhafar. Selden says Al Sameri means "keeper," and that Aaron was so called, because he was the *keeper* or "guardian of the people."—Selden, *De Diis Syris*, i. 4 (see *Al Korân*, ii. notes).

Sa´mian (*The Long-Haired*), Pythagoras or Budda Ghooroos, a native of Samos (sixth century B.C.).

Samian He´ra. Hera or Herê, wife of Zeus, was born at Samos. She was worshipped in Egypt as well as in Greece.

Samian Sage (The) Pythagoras, born at Samos (sixth century B.C.).

'Tis enough
In this late age, adventurous to have touched
Light on the numbers of the Samian Sage.
Thomson.

Samias´a, a seraph, in love with Aholiba´mah, the granddaughter of Cain. When the Flood came, the seraph carried off his *innamorata* to another planet.—Byron, *Heaven and Earth* (1819).

Sa´miel, the Black Huntsman of the Wolf's Glen, who gave to Der Freischütz seven balls, six of which were to hit whatever the marksman aimed at, but the seventh was to be at the disposal of Samiel. (See SAMAEL.)—Weber, *Der Freischütz* (libretto by Kind, 1822).

Samient, the female ambassador of Queen Mercilla to Queen Adicia (wife of the soldan). Adicia treated her with great contumely, thrust her out of doors, and induced two knights to insult her; but Sir Artegal, coming up, drove at one of the unmannerly knights with such fury as to knock him from his horse and break his neck.—Spenser, *Faëry Queen*, v. (1596).

(This refers to the treatment of the deputies sent by the states of Holland to Spain for the redress of grievances. Philip ("the soldan") detained the deputies as prisoners, disregarding the sacred rights of their office as ambassadors).

Sam´ma, the demoniac that John "the Beloved," could not exorcise. Jesus, coming from the Mount of Olives, rebuked Satan, who quitted "the possessed," and left him in his right mind.—Klopstock, *The Messiah*, ii. (1748).

Sammy Craddock, oracle of the Riggan coal-pits. Crabbed, wrinkled, sarcastic old fellow, whose self-conceit is immeasurable. "The biggest trouble I ha' is settlin' i' my moind what the world'll do when I turn up my toes to th' daisies, an' how the government'll mak' up their moinds who shall ha' th' honer o' payin' fer th' moniment."—Frances Hodgson Burnett, *That Lass o' Lowrie's* (1877).

Sampson, one of Capulet's servants.—Shakespeare, *Romeo and Juliet* (1597).

Sampson, a foolish advocate, kinsman of Judge Vertaigne (2 *syl.*).—Beaumont and Fletcher, *The Little French Lawyer* (1647).

Sampson (Mrs. Amanda Welsh), well-born Bohemian, financial adventurer and lobbyist. "She was still accustomed to at least a fair semblance of respect from the men who came to see her; women, it is to be noted, being not often seen within her walls."—Arlo Bates, *The Philistines* (1888).

Sampson (Dominie), or Abel Sampson, tutor to Harry Bertram, son of the laird of Ellangowan. One of the best creations of romance. His favorite exclamation is "Prodigious!" Dominie Sampson is very learned, simple and green. Sir Walter describes him as "a poor, modest, humble scholar, who had won his way through the classics, but fallen to the leeward in the voyage of life."—Sir W. Scott, *Guy Mannering* (time, George II.).

His appearance puritanical. Ragged black clothes, blue worsted stockings, pewter-headed long cane.—*Guy Mannering* (dramatized), i. 2.

Sampson (Dr.), eccentric Irish physician; inventor of *Chronothermalism*.—Charles Reade, *Very Hard Cash*.

Sampson (George), a friend of the Wilfer family. He adored Bella Wilfer, but married her youngest sister, Lavinia.—C. Dickens, *Our Mutual Friend* (1864).

Sampson (Nurse), dry-visaged, soft-hearted sick-nurse, whose adage is, "Somebody must eat drumsticks," and whose practice is based upon the formula.—A. D. T. Whitney, *Faith Gartney's Girlhood* (1863).

Samson (*The British*), Thomas Topham (1710-1749).

Samson Agonistes (4 *syl.*), "Samson, the Combatant," a sacred drama by Milton, showing Samson blinded and bound, but triumphant over his enemies, who sent for him to make sport by feats of strength on the feast of Dagon. Having amused the multitude for a time, he was allowed to rest awhile against the "grand stand," and, twining his arms round two of the supporting pillars, he pulled the whole edifice down, and died himself in the general devastation (1632).

Samson's Crown, an achievement of great renown, which costs the life of the doer thereof. Samson's greatest exploit was pulling down the "grand stand" occupied by the chief magnates of Philistia at the feast of Dagon. By this deed "he slew at his death more than [*all*] they which he slew in his life."—*Judges* xvi. 30.

And by self-ruin seek a Samson's crown.
Lord Brooke, *Inquisition upon Fame, etc.* (1554-1628).

San Bris (*Conte di*), father of Valenti´na. During the Bartholomew slaughter his daughter and her husband (Raoul) were both shot by a party of musketeers, under the count's command.—Meyerbeer, *Les Huguenots* (opera, 1836).

Sancha, daughter of Garcias, king of Navarre, and wife of Fernan Gonsalez, of Castile. Sancha twice saved the life of her husband: when he was cast into a dungeon by some personal enemies who waylaid him, she liberated him by bribing the jailer; and when he was incarcerated at Leon she effected his escape by changing clothes with him.

The countess of Nithsdale effected the escape of her husband from the Tower, in 1715, by changing clothes with him.

The Countess de Lavalette, in 1815, liberated her husband, under sentence of death, in the same way; but the terror she suffered so affected her nervous system that she lost her senses, and never afterwards recovered them.

San′chez II. of Castile, was killed at the battle of Zamo′ra, 1065.

It was when brave King Sanchez
Was before Zamora slain.
Longfellow, *The Challenge*.

Sanchi′ca, eldest daughter of Sancho and Teresa Panza.—Cervantes, *Don Quixote* (1605-15).

Sancho (*Don*), a rich old beau, uncle to Victoria. "He affects the misdemeanors of a youth, hides his baldness with amber locks, and complains of toothache, to make people believe that his teeth are not false ones." Don Sancho "loves in the style of Roderigo I."—Mrs. Cowley, *A Bold Stroke for a Husband* (1782).

Sancho Panza, the squire of Don Quixote. A short, pot-bellied peasant, with plenty of shrewdness and good common sense. He rode upon an ass which he dearly loved, and was noted for his proverbs.

Sancho Panza's Ass, Dapple.

Sancho Panza's Island-City, Barataria, where he was for a time governor.

Sancho Panza's Wife, Teresa [Cascajo] (pt. II. i. 5); Maria or Mary [Gutierez] (pt. II. iv. 7); Dame Juana [Gutierez] (pt. I. i. 7); and Joan (pt. I. iv. 21).—Cervantes, *Don Quixote* (1605-15).

*** The model painting of Sancho Panza is by Leslie; it is called "Sancho and the Duchess."

Sanchoni′athon or SANCHONIATHO. Nine books ascribed to this author are published at Bremen in 1838. The original was said to have been discovered in the convent of St. Maria de Merinhâo, by Colonel Pereira, a Portuguese; but it was soon ascertained that no such convent existed, that there was no colonel of the name Pereira in the Portuguese service, and that the paper bore the water-mark of the Osnabrück paper-mills. (See IMPOSTORS, LITERARY.)

Sanct-Cyr (*Hugh de*), the seneschal of King René, at Aix.—Sir W. Scott, *Anne of Geierstein* (time, Edward IV.).

Sancy Diamond (*The*) weighs 53-1/2 carats, and belonged to Charles "the Bold" of Burgundy. It was bought, in 1495, by Emmanuel of Portugal, and was sold, in 1580, by Don Antonio to the Sieur de Sancy, in whose family it remained for a century. The sieur deposited it with Henri IV. as a security for a loan of money. The servant entrusted with it, being attacked by robbers, swallowed it, and being murdered, the diamond was recovered by Nicholas de Harlay. We next hear of it in the possession of James II. of England, who carried it with him in his flight, in 1688. Louis XIV. bought it of him for £25,000. It was sold in the Revolution; Napoleon I. rebought it; in 1825 it was sold to Paul Demidoff for £80,000. The prince sold it, in 1830, to M. Levrat, administrator of the Mining Society; but as Levrat failed in his engagement, the diamond became, in 1832, the subject of a lawsuit, which was given in favor of the prince. We next hear of it in Bombay; in 1867 it was transmitted to England by the firm of Forbes and Co.; in 1873 it formed part of "the crown necklace," worn by Mary of Sachsen Altenburg, on her marriage with Albert of Prussia; 1876, in the investiture of the Star of India by the Prince of Wales, in Calcutta, Dr. W. H. Russel tells us it was worn as a pendant by the maharajah of Puttiala.

*** Streeter, in his book of *Precious Stones and Gems*, 120 (1877), tells us it belongs to the Czar of Russia, but if Dr. Russel is correct, it must have been sold to the maharajah.

Sand (*George*). Her birth name was Amantine Lucile Aurore Dupin, afterwards Dudevant (1803-1877).

San´dabar, an Arabian writer, about a century before the Christian era, famous for his *parables*.

It was rumored he could say
The *parables* of Sandabar.
Longfellow, *The Wayside Inn* (prelude 1863).

Sanford (*Marion*). Truth-loving, sincere, and simple-hearted woman, loyal in deed and thought to her traduced lover until time establishes his innocence.

A marked woman in general society; a woman who reigned, queen-like, over every heart, but among the circle of her relatives ... she was held to be little less than the angels.—Charles King, *Marion's Faith* (1886).

Sandford (*Harry*), the companion of Tommy Merton.—Thomas Day, *History of Sandford and Merton* (1783-9).

Sandpiper (*The*).

"Comrade, where wilt thou be to-night?
When the loosed storm breaks furiously?
My driftwood fire will burn so bright!

To what warm shelter can'st thou fly?
I do not fear for thee, 'though wroth
The tempest rushes through the sky.
For are we not GOD'S children both,
Thou little sandpiper and I?"
Celia Thaxter, *Drift-weed* (1878).

San´glamore (3 *syl.*), the sword of Braggadochio.—Spenser, *Faëry Queen*, iii. (1590).

Sanglier (*Sir*), a knight who insisted on changing wives with a squire, and when the lady objected, he cut off her head, and rode off with the squire's wife. Being brought before Sir Artegal, Sir Sanglier insisted that the living lady was his wife, and that the dead woman was the squire's wife. Sir Artegal commanded that the living and dead women should both be cut in twain, and half of each be given to the two litigants. To this Sir Sanglier gladly assented; but the squire objected, declaring it would be far better to give the lady to the knight than that she should suffer death. On this, Sir Artegal pronounced the living woman to be the squire's wife, and the dead one to be the knight's.—Spenser, *Faëry Queen*, v. 1 (1596).

("Sir Sanglier" is meant for Shan O'Neil, leader of the Irish insurgents in 1567. Of course this judgment is borrowed from that of Solomon, 1 *Kings* iii. 16-27.)

Sanglier des Ardennes, Guillaume de la Marck (1446-1485).

Sangraal, Sancgreal, etc., generally said to be the holy plate from which Christ ate at the Last Supper, brought to England by Joseph of Arimathy. Whatever it was, it appeared to King Arthur and his 150 knights of the Round Table, but suddenly vanished, and all the knights vowed they would go in quest thereof. Only three, Sir Bors, Sir Percivale and Sir Galahad, found it, and only Sir Galahad had touched it, but he soon died, and was borne by angels up into heaven. The Sangraal of Arthurian romance is "the dish" containing Christ transubstantiated by the sacrament of the Mass, and made visible to the bodily eye of man. This will appear quite obvious to the reader by the following extracts:—

Then anon they heard cracking and crying of thunder.... In the midst of the blast entered a sunbeam more clear by seven times than the day, and all they were alighted of the grace of the Holy Ghost.... Then there entered into the hall the Holy Grale covered with white samite, but there was none that could see it, nor who bare it, but the whole hall was full filled with good odors, and every knight had such meat and drink as he best loved in the world, and when the Holy Grale had been borne through the hall, then the holy vessel departed suddenly, and they wist not where it became.—Ch. 35.

Then looked they and saw a man come out of the holy vessel, that had all the signs of the passion of Christ, and he said ... "This is the holy dish wherein I ate the lamb on Sher-Thursday, and now hast thou seen it ... yet hast thou not seen it so openly as thou shalt see it in the city of Sarras ... therefore thou must go hence and bear with thee this holy vessel, for this night it shall depart from the realm of Logris ... and take with thee ... Sir Percivale and Sir Bors."—Ch. 101.

So departed Sir Galahad, and Sir Percivale and Sir Bors with him. And so they rode three days, and came to a river, and found a ship ... and when on board, they found in the midst the table of silver and the Sancgreall covered with red samite.... Then Sir Galahad laid him down and slept ... and when he woke ... he saw the city of Sarras (ch. 103).... At the year's end ... he saw before him the holy vessel, and a man kneeling upon his knees in the likeness of the bishop, which had about him a great fellowship of angels, as it had been Christ Himself ... and when he came to the sakering of the Mass, and had done, anon he called Sir Galahad, and said unto him, "Come forth ... and thou shalt see that which thou hast much desired to see" ... and he beheld spiritual things ... (ch. 104).—Sir T. Malory, *History of Prince Arthur*, iii. 35, 101, 104 (1470).

The earliest story of the Holy Graal was in verse (A.D. 1100), author unknown.

Chrétien de Troyes has a romance in eight-syllable verse on the same subject (1170).

Guiot's tale of *Titurel*, founder of Graalburg, and *Parzival*, prince thereof, belongs to the twelfth century.

Wolfram von Eschenbach, a minnesinger, took Guiot's tale as the foundation of his poem (thirteenth century).

In *Titurel the Younger* the subject is very fully treated.

Sir T. Malory (in pt. iii. of the *History of Prince Arthur*, translated in 1470 from the French) treats the subject in prose very fully.

R. S. Hawker has a poem on the *Sangraal*, but it was never completed.

Tennyson has an idyll called *The Holy Grail* (1858).

Boisserée published, in 1834, at Munich, a work *On the Description of the Temple of the Holy Graal*.

Sangra′do (*Doctor*), of Valladolid. This is the "Sagredo" of Espinel's romance called *Marcos de Obregon*. "The doctor was a tall, meagre, pale man, who had kept the shears of Clotho employed for forty years at least. He had a very solemn appearance, weighed his discourse, and used 'great pomp of words.' His reasonings were geometrical, and his opinions his own." Dr. Sangrado considered that blood was not needful for life, and that hot water could not be administered too plentifully into the system. Gil Blas became his servant and pupil, and was allowed to drink any quantity of water, but to eat only sparingly of beans, peas and stewed apples.

Dr. Hancock prescribed cold water and stewed prunes.

Dr. Rezio, of Barataria, allowed Sancho Panza to eat "a few wafers and a thin slice or two of quince."—Cervantes, *Don Quixote*, II. iii. 10 (1615).

Sansculottes (3 *syl.*), a low, riff-raff party in the great French Revolution, so shabby in dress that they were termed "the trouser-less." The *culotte* is the breeches, called *bræck* by the ancient Gauls, and *hauts-de-chausses* in the reign of Charles IX.

Sansculottism, red republicanism, or the revolutionary platform of the Sansculottes.

The duke of Brunswick, at the head of a large army, invaded France to restore Louis XVI. to the throne, and save legitimacy from the sacrilegious hands of sansculottism.—G. H. Lewes, *Story of Goethe's Life*.

Literary Sansculottism, literature of a low character, like that of the "Minerva Press," the "Leipsic Fair," "Hollywell Street," "Grub Street," and so on.

Sansfoy, a "faithless Saracen," who attacked the Red Cross Knight, but was slain by him. "He cared for neither God nor man." Sansfoy personifies infidelity.

Sansfoy, full large of limb and every joint
He was, and carëd not for God or man a point.
Spenser, *Faëry Queen*, i. 2 (1590).

Sansjoy, brother of Sansfoy. When he came to the court of Luciferă, he noticed the shield of Sansfoy on the arm of the Red Cross Knight, and his rage was so great that he was with difficulty restrained from running on the champion there and then, but Lucifera bade him defer the combat to the following day. Next day, the fight began, but just as the Red Cross Knight was about to deal his adversary a death-blow, Sansjoy was enveloped in a thick cloud, and carried off in the chariot of Night to the infernal regions, where Æsculapius healed him of his wounds.—Spenser, *Faëry Queen*, i. 4, 5 (1590).

(The reader will doubtless call to mind the combat of Menalāos and Paris, and remember how the Trojan was invested in a cloud and carried off by Venus under similar circumstances.—Homer, *Iliad*, iii.)

Sansloy (*"superstition"*), the brother of Sansfoy and Sansjoy. He carried off Una to the wilderness, but when the fauns and satyrs came to her rescue, he saved himself by flight.

⁎ The meaning of this allegory is this; Una (*truth*), separated from St. George (*holiness*), is deceived by Hypocrisy; and immediately Truth joins Hypocrisy it is carried away by Superstition. Spenser says the "simplicity of truth" abides with the common people, especially of the rural districts, it is lost to towns and the luxurious great. The historical reference is to Queen Mary, in whose reign Una (*the Reformation*) was carried captive, and religion, being mixed up with hypocrisy, degenerated into superstition, but the rural population adhered to the simplicity of the Protestant faith.—Spenser, *Faëry Queen*, i. 2 (1590).

Sansonetto, a Christian regent of Mecca, vicegerent of Charlemagne.—Ariosto, *Orlando Furioso* (1516).

Santa Klaus (1 *syl.*), the Dutch name of St. Nicholas, the patron saint of youth.

Santiago [*Sent.yah´.go*], the war-cry of Spain; adopted because St. James (*Sant Iago*) rendered, according to tradition, signal service to a Christian king of Spain in a battle against the Moors.

Santiago for Spain. This saint was James, son of Zebedee, brother of John. He was beheaded, and caught his head in his hands as it fell. The Jews were astonished, but when they touched the body they found it so cold that their hands and arms were paralyzed.—Francisco Xavier, *Añales de Galicia* (1733).

Santiago's Head. When Santiago went to Spain in his marble ship, he had no head on his body. The passage took seven days, and the ship was steered by the "presiding hand of Providence."—*España Sagrada*, xx. 6.

Santiago had two heads. One of his heads is at Braga, and one at Compostella.

Santiago lead the armies of Spain. Thirty-eight instances of the interference of this saint are gravely set down as facts in the *Chronicles of Galicia*, and this is super-added: "These instances are well known, but I hold it for certain that the appearances of Santiago in our victorious armies have been much more numerous, and in fact that every victory obtained by the Spaniards has been really achieved by this great captain." Once when the rider on the white horse was asked in battle who he was, he distinctly made answer, "I am the soldier of the King of kings, and my name is James."—Don Miguel Erce Gimenez, *Armas i Triunfos del Reino de Galicia*, 648-9.

The true name of this saint was Jacobo.... We have first shortened Santo Jacobo into *Santo Jac'o*. We clipped it again into *Sant' Jaco*, and by changing the *J* into *I* and the *c* into *g*, we get *Sant-Iago*. In household names we convert

Iago into *D'iago* or *Diago*, which we soften into *Diego*.—Ambrosio de Morales, *Coronica General de España*, ix. 7 sect. 2 (1586).

Santons, a body of religionists, also called *Abdals*, who pretended to be inspired with the most enthusiastic raptures of divine love. They were regarded by the vulgar as saints. Olearius, *Reisebeschreibung*, i. 971 (1647).

Sapphi′ra, a female liar.—*Acts* v. 1.

She is called the village Sapphira.—Crabbe.

Sappho, Greek poetess of the sixth century B.C., called "The Tenth Muse." Fragments of her verse remain which are very beautiful. She was the victim of unrequited love, and leaped to her death from the Leucadian Rock into the sea.

Sappho (The English), Mrs. Mary D. Robinson (1758-1800).

Sappho (The French), Mdlle. Scudéri (1607-1704).

Sappho (The Scotch), Catherine Cockburn (1679-1749).

Sappho of Toulouse, Clémence Isaure (2 *syl.*), who instituted, in 1490, *Les Jeux Floraux*. She is the authoress of a beautiful *Ode to Spring* (1463-1513).

Sapskull, a raw Yorkshire tike, son of Squire Sapskull, of Sapskull Hall. Sir Penurious Muckworm wishes him to marry his niece and ward, Arbella, but as Arbella loves Gaylove, a young barrister, the tike is played upon thus: Gaylove assumes to be Muckworm, and his lad, Slango, dresses up as a woman to pass for Arbella; and while Sapskull "marries" Slango, Gaylove, who assumes the dress and manners of the Yorkshire tike, marries Arbella. Of course, the trick is then discovered, and Sapskull returns to the home of his father, befooled but not married.—Carey, *The Honest Yorkshireman* (1736).

Saracen (*A*), in Arthurian romance, means any unbaptized person, regardless of nationality. Thus, Priamus, of Tuscany, is called a Saracen (pt. i. 96, 97); so is Sir Palomides, simply because he refused to be baptized till he had done some noble deed (pt. ii.).—Sir T. Malory, *History of Prince Arthur* (1470).

Sara Carroll. Devoted daughter of Major Carroll and firm ally of her dainty stepmother, Madame Carroll, in the latter's renewal of intercourse with her eldest son and concealment of his existence from her husband. Sara contrives that the mother shall be with the young man when he dies, and by becoming the go-between for the two, incurs the suspicions of her lover.—Constance Fenimore Woolson, *For the Major*.

Saragossa (*The Maid of*), Augustina Saragossa or Zaragoza, who, in 1808, when the city was invested by the French, mounted the battery in the place of her lover who had been shot. Lord Byron says, when he was at Seville, "the maid" used to walk daily on the prado, decorated with medals and orders, by command of the junta. Southey, *History of the Peninsular War* (1832).

Her lover sinks—she sheds no ill timed tear;
Her chief is slain—she fills his fatal post;
Her fellows flee—she checks their base career;
The foe retires—she heads the sallying host.
... the flying Gaul,
Foiled by a woman's hand before a battered wall.
Byron, *Childe Harold*, i. 56 (1809).

Sardanapa′lus, king of Nineveh and Assyria, noted for his luxury and voluptuousness. Arbācês, the Mede, conspired against him, and defeated him; whereupon his favorite slave, Myrra, induced him to immolate himself on a funeral pile. The beautiful slave, having set fire to the pile, leaped into the blazing mass, and was burnt to death with the king, her master (B.C. 817).—Byron, *Sardanapalus* (1619).

Sardanapa′lus of China (*The*), Cheo-tsin, who shut himself up in his palace with his queen, and then set fire to the building, that he might not fall into the hands of Woo-wong (B.C. 1154-1122).

(Cheo-tsin invented the chopsticks, and Woo-wong founded the Tchow dynasty.)

Sardanapa′lus of Germany (*The*), Wenceslas VI. or (IV.), king of Bohemia and emperor of Germany (1359, 1378-1419).

Sarell Gately. Shrewd, "capable" girl who "lives out" on the Heybrook farm.

"She was a young woman to take up responsibilities as she went along. She liked them. She became naturally a part of whatever was happening in her Troy; and wherever her temporary Troy might be, there was pretty sure to be something happening."—A. D. T. Whitney, *Odd or Even?* (1880).

Sassenach, a Saxon, an Englishman. (Welsh, *saesonig* adj. and *saesoniad* noun.)

I would, if I thought I'd be able to catch some of the Sassenachs in London.—*Very Far West Indeed*.

Satan, according to the *Talmud*, was once an archangel, but was cast out of heaven with one-third of the celestial host for refusing to do reverence to Adam.

In mediæval mythology, Satan holds the fifth rank of the nine demoniacal orders.

Johan Wier, in his *Præstigiis Dæmonum* (1564), makes Beëlzebub the sovereign of hell, and Satan leader of the opposition.

In legendary lore, Satan is drawn with horns and tail, saucer eyes, and claws; but Milton makes him a proud, selfish, ambitious chief, of gigantic size, beautiful, daring, and commanding. He declares his opinion that it is "better to reign in hell than serve in heaven." Defoe has written a *Political History of the Devil* (1726).

Satan, according to Milton, monarch of hell. His chief lords are Beëlzebub, Moloch, Chemos, Thammuz, Dagon, Rimmon, and Belial. His standard-bearer is Azaz´el.

He, above the rest
In shape and gesture proudly eminent,
Stood like a tower. His form had not yet lost
All her original brightness; nor appeared
Less than archangel ruined, and the excess
Of glory obscured ... but his face
Deep scars of thunder had intrenched, and care
Sat on his faded cheek ... cruel his eye, but cast
Signs of remorse.
Milton, *Paradise Lost*, i. 589, etc. (1665).

⁂ The word Satan means "enemy;" hence Milton says:

To whom the arch-enemy,
... in heaven called Satan.
Paradise Lost, i. 81 (1665).

Satanic School (*The*), a class of writers in the earlier part of the nineteenth century, who showed a scorn for all moral rules and the generally received dogmas of the Christian religion. The most eminent English writers of this school were Bulwer (afterwards Lord Lytton), Byron, Moore, and P. B. Shelley. Of French writers: Paul de Kock, Rousseau, George Sand, and Victor Hugo.

Satire (*Father of*), Archilŏchos of Paros (B.C. seventh century).

Satire (*Father of French*), Mathurin Regnier (1573-1613).

Satire (*Father of Roman*), Lucilius (B.C. 148-103).

Satiro-mastix, or *The Untrussing of the Humorous Poet*, a comedy by Thomas Dekker (1602). Ben Jonson, in 1601, had attacked Dekker in *The Poetaster*, where he calls himself "Horace," and Dekker "Cris´pinus." Next year (1602), Dekker replied with spirit to this attack, in a comedy entitled *Satiro-mastix*, where Jonson is called "Horace, junior."

Saturday. To the following English sovereigns from the establishment of the Tudor dynasty, Saturday has proved a fatal day:—

HENRY VII. died Saturday, April 21, 1509.

GEORGE II. died Saturday, October 27, 1760.

GEORGE III. died Saturday, January 29, 1820, but of his fifteen children only three died on a Saturday.

GEORGE IV. died Saturday, June 26, 1830, but the Princess Charlotte died on a Tuesday.

PRINCE ALBERT died Saturday, December 14, 1861. The duchess of Kent and the Princess Alice also died on a Saturday.

⁎ William III., Anne, and George I., all died on a Sunday; William IV. on a Tuesday.

Saturn, son of Heaven and Earth. He always swallowed his children immediately they were born, till his wife, Rhea, not liking to see all her children perish, concealed from him the birth of Jupiter, Neptune, and Pluto, and gave her husband large stones instead, which he swallowed without knowing the difference.

Much as old Saturn ate his progeny;
For when his pious consort gave him stones
In lieu of sons, of those he made no bones.
Byron, *Don Juan*, xiv. 1 (1824).

Saturn, an evil and malignant planet.

He is a genius full of gall, an author born under the planet Saturn, a malicious mortal whose pleasure consists in hating all the world.—Lesage, *Gil Blas*, v. 12 (1724).

The children born under the sayd Saturne shall be great jangeleres and chyders ... and they will never forgyve tyll they be revenged of theyr quarrell.—Ptholomeus, *Compost*.

Satyr. T. Woolner calls Charles II. "Charles the Satyr."

Next flared Charles Satyr's saturnalia
Of lady nymphs.
My Beautiful Lady.

⁎ The most famous statue of the satyrs is that by Praxitĕlês, of Athens, in the fourth century.

Satyrane (*Sir*), a blunt, but noble knight, who helps Una to escape from the fauns and satyrs.—Spenser, *Faëry Queen*, i. (1590).

And passion erst unknown, could gain
The breast of blunt Sir Satyrane.
Sir W. Scott.

※ "Sir Satyrane" is meant for Sir John Perrot, a natural son of Henry VIII., and lord deputy of Ireland, from 1583 to 1588; but, in 1590, he was in prison in the Tower for treason, and was beheaded in 1592.

Satyr'icon, a comic romance in Latin, by Petro'nius Ar'biter, in the first century. Very gross, but showing great power, beauty, and skill.

Saul, in Dryden's satire of *Absalom and Achitophel*, is meant for Oliver Cromwell. As Saul persecuted David, and drove him from Jerusalem, so Cromwell persecuted Charles II., and drove him from England.

... ere Saul they chose,
God was their king, and God they durst depose.
Pt. i. (1681).

※ This was the "divine right" of kings.

Saunders, groom of Sir Geoffrey Peveril of the Peak.—Sir W. Scott, *Peveril of the Peak* (time, Charles II.).

Saunders (Richard), the pseudonym of Dr. Franklin, adopted in *Poor Richard's Almanac*, begun in 1732.

Saunders Sweepclean, a king's messenger, at Knockwinnock Castle.—Sir W. Scott, *The Antiquary* (time George III.).

Saunderson (*Saunders*), butler, etc., to Mr. Cosmo Comyne Bradwardine, baron of Bradwardine and Tully Veolan.—Sir W. Scott, *Waverley* (time, George II.).

Saurid, king of Egypt, say the Coptites (2 *syl.*) built the pyramids 300 years before the Flood, and according to the same authority, the following inscription was engraved upon one of them:—

I, King Saurid, built the pyramids ... and finished them in six years. He that comes after me ... let him destroy them in 600 if he can ... I also covered them ... with satin, and let him cover them with matting.—Greaves, *Pyramidographia*, (seventeenth century).

Savage (*Captain*), a naval commander.—Captain Marryat, *Peter Simple* (1833).

Sav'il, steward to the elder Loveless.—Beaumont and Fletcher, *The Scornful Lady* (1616).

Sav´ille (2 *syl.*), the friend of Doricourt. He saves Lady Frances Touchwood from Courtall, and frustrates his infamous designs on the lady's honor.—Mrs. Cowley, *The Belle's Stratagem* (1780).

Saville (*Lord*), a young nobleman with Chiffinch (emissary of Charles II.).—Sir W. Scott, *Peveril of the Peak* (time Charles II.).

Saviour of Rome. C. Marĭus was so called after the overthrow of the Cimbri, July 30, B.C. 101.

Saviour of the Nations. So the duke of Wellington was termed after the overthrow of Bonaparte (1769-1852).

Oh, Wellington ... called "Saviour of the Nations!"
Byron, *Don Juan*, ix. 5 (1824).

Sawney, a corruption of Sandie, a contracted form of Alexander. Sawney means a Scotchman, as David a Welshman, John Bull an Englishman, Cousin Michael a German, Brother Jonathan a native of the United States, Macaire a Frenchman, Colin Tampon a Swiss, and so on.

Sawyer (*Bob*), a dissipated, struggling young medical practitioner, who tries to establish a practice at Bristol, but without success. Sam Weller calls him "Mr. Sawbones."—C. Dickens, *The Pickwick Papers* (1836)

Saxon Duke (*The*), mentioned by Butler in his *Hudibras*, was John Frederick, duke of Saxony, of whom Charles V. said, "Never saw I such a swine before."

Sboga (*Jean*), the hero of a romance by C. Nodier (1818), a leader of bandits, in the spirit of Lord Byron's *Corsair* and *Lara*.

Scadder (*General*), agent in the office of the "Eden Settlement." His peculiarity consisted in the two distinct expressions of his profile, for "one side seemed to be listening to what the other side was doing."—C. Dickens, *Martin Chuzzlewit* (1844).

Scalds, court poets and chroniclers of the ancient Scandinavians. They resided at court, were attached to the royal suite, and attended the king in all his wars. They also acted as ambassadors between hostile tribes, and their persons were held sacred. These bards celebrated in song the gods, the kings of Norway, and national heroes. Their lays or *vyses* were compiled in the eleventh century by Sæmund Sigfusson, a priest and scald of Iceland, and the compilation is called the *Elder* or *Rythmical Edda*.

Scallop-Shell (*The*). Every one knows that St. James's pilgrims are distinguished by scallop-shells, but it is a blunder to suppose that other pilgrims are privileged to wear them. Three of the popes have, by their bulls, distinctly confirmed this right to the Compostella pilgrim alone: viz., Pope Alexander III., Pope Gregory IX. and Pope Clement V.

Now, the escallop or scallop, is a shell-fish, like an oyster or large cockle; but Gwillim tells us what ignorant zoölogists have omitted to mention, that the bivalve is "engendered solely of dew and air. It has no blood at all; yet no food that man eats turns so soon into life-blood as the scallop."—*Display of Heraldy*, 171.

Scallop-shells used by Pilgrims. The reason why the scallop-shell is used by pilgrims is not generally known. The legend is this: When the marble ship which bore the headless body of St. James approached Bouzas, in Portugal, it happened to be the wedding day of the chief magnate of the village; and while the bridal party was at sport, the horse of the bridegroom became unmanageable, and plunged into the sea. The ship passed over the horse and its rider, and pursued its onward course, when, to the amazement of all, the horse and its rider emerged from the water uninjured, and the cloak of the rider was thickly covered with scallop-shells. All were dumbfounded, and knew not what to make of these marvels, but a voice from heaven exclaimed, "It is the will of God that all who henceforth make their vows to St. James, and go on pilgrimage, shall take with them scallop-shells; and all who do so shall be remembered in the day of judgment." On hearing this, the lord of the village, with the bride and bridegroom, were duly baptized, and Bouzas became a Christian Church.—*Sanctoral Portugues* (copied into the *Breviaries* of *Alcobaça and St. Cucufate*).

Cunctis mare cernentibus,
Sed a profundo ducitur;
Natus Regis submergitur,
Totus plenus conchilibus.
Hymn for St. James's day.

In sight of all the prince went down,
Into the deep sea dells;
In sight of all the prince emerged,
Covered with scallop-shells.

Scalping (*Rules for*). The Cheyennes, in scalping, remove from the part just over the left ear a piece of skin not larger than a silver dollar. The Arrapahoes take a similar piece from the region of the right ear. Others take the entire skin from the crown of the head, the forehead, or the nape of the neck. The Utes take the entire scalp from ear to ear, and from the forehead to the nape of the neck.

Scambister (*Eric*), the old butler of Magnus Troil, the udaller of Zetland.—Sir W. Scott, *The Pirate* (time, William III.).

⁎ A udaller is one who holds his lands by allodial tenure.

Scandal, a male character in *Love for Love*, by Congreve (1695).

Scandal (School for), a comedy by Sheridan (1777).

Scanderbeg. So George Castriota, an Albanian hero, was called. Amurath II. gave him the command of 5000 men, and such was his daring and success, that he was called Skander (*Alexander*). In the battle of Morava (1443) he deserted Amurath, and, joining the Albanians, won several battles over the Turks. At the instigation of Pius II. he headed a crusade against them, but died of a fever, before Mahomet II. arrived to oppose him (1404-1467). (Beg or Bey is the Turkish for "prince.")

Scanderbeg's sword needs Scanderbeg's arm. Mahomet II. "the Great" requested to see the scimitar which George Castriota used so successfully against the Ottomans in 1461. Being shown it, and wholly unable to draw it, he pronounced the weapon to be a hoax, but received for answer, "Scanderbeg's sword needs Scanderbeg's arm to wield it."

The Greeks had a similar saying, "None but Ulysses can draw Ulysses's bow."

Scapegoat *(The)*, a farce by John Poole. Ignatius Polyglot, a learned pundit, master of seventeen languages, is the tutor of Charles Eustace, aged 24 years. Charles has been clandestinely married for four years, and has a little son named Frederick. Circumstances have occurred which render the concealment of this marriage no longer decorous or possible, so he breaks it to his tutor, and conceals his young wife for the nonce in Polyglot's private room. Here she is detected by the housemaid, Molly Maggs, who tells her master, and old Eustace says, the only reparation a man can make in such circumstances is to marry the girl at once. "Just so," says the tutor. "Your son is the husband, and he is willing at once to acknowledge his wife and infant son."

Scapin, valet of Léandre, son of Seignior Géronte. (See FOURBERIES.)— Molière, *Les Fourberies de Scapin* (1671).

(Otway has made an English version of this play, called *The Cheats of Scapin*, in which Léandre is Anglicized into "Leander," Géronte is called "Gripe," and his friend, Argante, father of Zerbinette, is called "Thrifty," father of "Lucia."

Scapi'no, the cunning, knavish servant of Gratiano, the loquacious and pedantic Bolognese doctor.—*Italian Mask.*

Scar *(Little)*, son of Major and Madam Carroll, believed by his father to be legitimate, known by his mother to have been born during the lifetime of her first husband, although she had married the major, supposing herself a widow.—Constance Fenimore Woolson, *For the Major.*

Scar′amouch, a braggart and fool, most valiant in words, but constantly being drubbed by Harlequin. Scaramouch is a common character in Italian farce, originally meant in ridicule of the Spanish don, and therefore dressed in Spanish costume. Our clown is an imbecile old idiot, and wholly unlike the dashing poltroon of Italian pantomime. The best "Scaramouches" that ever lived were Tiberio Fiurelli, a Neapolitan (born 1608), and Gandini (eighteenth century).

Scar′borough Warning (*A*), a warning given too late to be taken advantage of. Fuller says the allusion is to an event which occurred in 1557, when Thomas Stafford seized upon Scarborough Castle, before the townsmen had any notice of his approach. Heywood says a "Scarborough warning" resembles what is now called Lynch law: punished first, and warned afterwards. Another solution is this: If ships passed the castle without saluting it by striking sail, it was customary to fire into them a shotted gun, by way of warning.

Be suërly seldom, and never for much ...
Or Scarborow warning, as ill I believe,
When ("Sir, I arrest ye") gets hold of thy sleeve.
T. Tusser, *Five Hundred Points of Good Husbandry*, x. 28 (1557).

Scarlet (*Will*), **Scadlock** or **Scathelocke**, one of the companions of Robin Hood.

"Take thy good bowe in thy hande," said Robyn.
"Let Moche wend with the
And so shall Wyllyam Scathelocke,
And no man abyde with me."
Ritson, *Robin Hood Ballads*, i. 1 (1520).

The tinker looking him about,
Robin his horn did blow;
Then came unto him Little John
And William Scadlock, too.
Ditto, ii. 7 (1656).

And there of him they made a
Good yeoman Robin Hood,
Scarlet and Little John,
And Little John, hey ho!
Ditto, appendix 2 (1790).

In the two dramas called *The First and Second Parts of Robin Hood*, by Anthony Munday and Henry Chettle, Scathlock or Scadlock, is called the brother of Will Scarlet.

... possible that Warman's spite ... doth hunt the lives
Of bonnie Scarlet and his brother, Scathlock.
Pt. i. (1597).

Then "enter Warman, with Scarlet and Scathlock bounde," but Warman is banished, and the brothers are liberated and pardoned.

Scarlet Woman (*The*), popery (*Rev*. xvii. 4).

And fulminated
Against the scarlet woman and her creed.
Tennyson, *Sea Dreams*.

Scathelocke (2 *syl.*) or **Scadlock**, one of the companions of Robin Hood. Either the brother of Will Scarlet or another spelling of the name. (See SCARLET.)

Scatterbury (*Juliet*). Ambitious New York woman, who lives in a flat and pretends to distant friends that she lives in a Fifth Avenue brown stone front; "an egregious follower of Ananias and Sapphira."—William Henry Bishop, *The Brown Stone Boy and Other Stories* (1888).

Scavenger's Daughter (*The*), an instrument of torture, invented by Sir William Skevington, lieutenant of the Tower in the reign of Henry VIII. "Scavenger" is a corruption of Skevington.

To kiss the scavenger's daughter, to suffer punishment by this instrument of torture, to be beheaded by a guillotine or some similar instrument.

Sceaf [*Sheef*], one of the ancestors of Woden. So called because in infancy he was laid on a wheatsheaf, and cast adrift in a boat; the boat stranded on the shores of Sleswig, and the infant, being considered a gift from the gods, was brought up for a future king.—*Beowulf* (an Anglo-Saxon epic, sixth century).

Scepticism (*Father of Modern*), Pierre Bayle (1647-1706).

Schacabac, "the hare-lipped," a man reduced to the point of starvation, invited to a feast by the rich Barmecide. Instead of victuals and drink, the rich man set before his guest empty dishes and empty glasses, pretending to enjoy the imaginary foods and drinks. Schacabac entered into the spirit of the joke, and did the same. He washed in imaginary water, ate of the imaginary delicacies, and praised the imaginary wine. Barmecide was so delighted with his guest, that he ordered in a substantial meal, of which he made Schacabac a most welcome partaker.—*Arabian Nights* ("The Barber's Sixth Brother"). (See SHACCABAC.)

Schah´riah, sultan of Persia. His wife being unfaithful, and his brother's wife too, Schahriah imagined that no woman was virtuous. He resolved, therefore, to marry a fresh wife every night, and to have her strangled at daybreak. Scheherazâdê, the vizier's daughter, married him notwithstanding, and contrived, an hour before daybreak, to begin a story to her sister, in the sultan's hearing, always breaking off before the story was finished. The sultan got interested in these tales; and, after a thousand and one nights, revoked his decree, and found in Scheherazâdê a faithful, intelligent, and loving wife.—*Arabian Nights' Entertainments.*

Schah´zaman, sultan of the "Island of the children of Khal´edan," situated in the open sea, some twenty day's sail from the coast of Persia. The sultan had a son, an only child, named Camaral´zaman, the most beautiful of mortals. Camaralzaman married Badoura, the most beautiful of women, the only daughter of Gaiour (2 *syl.*), emperor of China.—*Arabian Nights* ("Camaralzaman and Badoura").

Schaibar (2 *syl.*), brother of the fairy Pari-Banou. He was only eighteen inches in height, and had a huge hump both before and behind. His beard, though thirty feet long, never touched the ground, but projected forwards. His moustaches went back to his ears, and his little pig's eyes were buried in his enormous head. He wore a conical hat, and carried for quarterstaff an iron bar of 500 lbs. weight at least.—*Arabian Nights* ("Ahmed and Pari-Banou").

Schamir (*The*) that instrument or agent with which Solomon wrought the stones of the Temple, being forbidden to use any metal instrument for the purpose. Some say the Schamir´ was a worm; some that it was a stone; some that it was "a creature no bigger than a barleycorn, which nothing could resist."

Scheherazade [*Sha.ha´.ra.zah´.dê*], the hypothetical relater of the stories in the *Arabian Nights*. She was the elder daughter of the vizier of Persia. The sultan, Schahriah, exasperated at the infidelity of his wife, came to the hasty conclusion that no woman could be faithful; so he determined to marry a new wife every night, and strangle her at daybreak. Scheherazâdê, wishing to free Persia of this disgrace, requested to be made the sultan's wife, and succeeded in her wish. She was young and beautiful, of great courage and ready wit, well read, and an excellent memory, knew history, philosophy, and medicine, was besides a good poet, musician, and dancer. Scheherazâdê obtained permission of the sultan for her younger sister, Dinarzâdê, to sleep in the same chamber, and instructed her to say, one hour before daybreak, "Sister, relate to me one of those delightful stories which you know, as this will be the last time." Scheherazâdê then told the sultan (under pretence of speaking to her sister) a story, but always contrived to break off before the story was finished. The sultan, in order to hear the end of the story, spared her life till the next night. This went on for a thousand and one nights, when the sultan's resentment was worn out, and his admiration of his sultana was so great that he revoked his decree.—*Arabian Nights' Entertainments*. (See MORADBAK.)

Roused like the Sultana Scheherazadê, and forced into a story.—C. Dickens, *David Copperfield* (1849).

Schemseddin Mohammed, elder son of the vizier of Egypt, and brother of Noureddin Ali. He quarrelled with his brother on the subject of their two children's hypothetical marriage; but the brothers were not yet married, and children "were only in supposition." Noureddin Ali quitted Cairo, and travelled to Basora, where he married the vizier's daughter, and on the very same day Schemseddin married the daughter of one of the chief grandees of Cairo. On one and the same day a daughter was born to Schemseddin, and a son to his brother, Noureddin Ali. When Schemseddin's daughter was 20 years old, the sultan asked her in marriage, but the vizier told him she was betrothed to his brother's son, Bed´reddin Ali. At this reply, the sultan, in anger, swore she should be given in marriage to the "ugliest of his slaves;" and accordingly betrothed her to Hunchback, a groom, both ugly and deformed. By a fairy trick, Bedreddin Ali was substituted for the groom, but at daybreak was conveyed to Damascus. Here he turned pastry-cook, and was discovered by his mother by his cheese-cakes. Being restored to his country and his wife, he ended his life happily.—*Arabian Nights* ("Noureddin Ali," etc.). (See CHEESE-CAKES.)

Schemsel´nihar, the favorite sultana of Haroun-al-Raschid, caliph of Bagdad. She fell in love with Aboulhassan Ali ebn Becar, prince of Persia. From the first moment of their meeting they began to pine for each other, and fell sick. Though miles apart, they died at the same hour, and were both buried in the same grave.—*Arabian Nights* ("Aboulhassen and Schemselnihar").

Schlemihl (*Peter*), the hero of a popular German legend. Peter sells his shadow to an "old man in grey," who meets him while fretting under a disappointment. The name is a household term for one who makes a desperate and silly bargain.—Chamisso, *Peter Schlemihl* (1813).

Schmidt (*Mr.*), a German of kindly spirit and refined tastes, "in his talk gently cynical." "To know him a little was to dislike him, but to know him well was to love him." At the feet of a pretty Quaker dame, he laid an homage, which he felt to be hopeless of result, while he was schooled by sorrowful fortunes to accept the position as one which he hardly ever wished to change.—Silas Weir Mitchell, *Hephzibah Guinness* (1880).

Scholastic (*The*), Epipha′nius, an Italian scholar (sixth century).

Scholastic Doctor (*The*), Anselm, of Laon (1050-1117).

Scholey (*Lawrence*), servant at Burgh-Westra. His master is Magnus Troil, the udaller of Zetland.—Sir W. Scott, *The Pirate* (time, William III.).

*** Udaller, one who holds land by allodial tenure.

Schonfelt, lieutenant of Sir Archibald von Hagenbach, a German noble.—Sir W. Scott, *Anne of Geierstein* (time, Edward IV.).

School of Husbands, (*L'école des Maris*, "wives trained by men"), a comedy by Molière (1661). Ariste and Sganarelle, two brothers, bring up Léonor and Isabelle, two orphan sisters, according to their systems for making them in time their model wives. Sganarelle's system was to make the women dress plainly, live retired, attend to domestic duties, and have few indulgences. Ariste's system was to give the woman great liberty, and trust to her honor. Isabelle, brought up by Sganarelle, deceived him and married another; but Léonor, brought up by Ariste, made him a fond and faithful wife.

Sganarelle's plan:

J'entend que la mienne vive à ma fantaisie—
Que d'une serge honnête elle ait son vêtement,
Et ne porte le noir, qu' aux bons jours seulement;
Qu' enfermée au logis, en personne bien sage,
Elle s'applique toute aux choses du ménage,
A recoudre mon linge aux heures de loisir,
Ou bien à tricoter quelques bas par plasir;
Qu' aux discours des muguets elle ferme l'oreille,
Et ne sorte jamais sans avoir qui la veille.

Ariste's plan:

Leur sexe aime à jouir d'un peu de liberté;
On le retient fort mal par tant d'austérité;
Et les soins défiants les verroux et les grilles,
Ne font pas la vertu des femmes ni des filles;
C'est l'honneur qui les doit tenir dans le devoir,
Non la sévérité que nous leur faisons voir ...
Je trouve que le cœur est ce qu'il faut gagner.
Act i. 2.

School for Wives (*L'école des Femmes*, "training for wives"), a comedy by Molière (1662). Arnolphe has a crotchet about the proper training of girls to make good wives, and tries his scheme upon Agnes, whom he adopts from a peasant's cottage, and designs in due time to make his wife. He sends her from early childhood to a convent, where difference of sex and the conventions of society are wholly ignored. When removed from the convent she treats men as if they were schoolgirls, kisses them, plays with them, and treats them with girlish familiarity. The consequence is, a young man named Horace falls in love with her and makes her his wife, but Arnolphe loses his pains.

Schoolmen. (For a list of the schoolmen of each of the three periods, see *Dictionary of Phrase and Fable*, 794.)

Schoolmistress (*The*), a poem in Spenserian metre, by Shenstone (1758). The "schoolmistress" was Sarah Lloyd, who taught the poet himself in infancy. She lived in a thatched cottage, before which grew a birch tree, to which allusion is made in the poem.

There dwells, in lowly shed and mean attire,
A matron old, whom we schoolmistress name ...
And all in sight doth rise a birchen tree.
Stanzas 2, 3.

Schreckenwald (*Ital.*), steward of Count Albert.—Sir W. Scott, *Anne of Geierstein* (time, Edward IV.).

Schwaker (*Jonas*), jester of Leopold, archduke of Austria.—Sir W. Scott, *The Talisman* (time, Richard I.).

Scian Muse (*The*), Simon'dês, born at Scia, or Cea, now *Zia*, one of the Cyclades.

The Scian and the Teian Muse [*Anacreon*] ...
Have found the fame your shores refuse.
Byron, *Don Juan*, iii. ("The Isles of Greece," 1820).

Science (*The prince of*), Tehuhe, "The Aristotle of China" (died A.D. 1200).

Scio (now called *Chios*), one of the seven cities which claimed to be the birthplace of Homer. Hence he is sometimes called "Scio's Blind Old Bard." The seven cities referred to make an hexameter verse:

Smyrna, Chios, Colophôn, Salamis, Rhodos, Argos, Athenæ; *or*
Smyrna, Chios, Colophôn, Ithacâ, Pylos, Argos, Athenæ.
Antipater Sidonius, *A Greek Epigram*.

Sciol'to (3 *syl.*), a proud Genoese nobleman, the father of Calista. Calista was the bride of Altamont, a young man proud and fond of her, but it was discovered on the wedding day that she had been seduced by Lothario. This led to a series of calamities: (1) Lothario was killed in a duel by Altamont; (2) a street riot was created, in which Sciolto received his death-wound; and (3) Calista stabbed herself.—N. Rowe, *The Fair Penitent* (1703).

(In Italian, *Sciolto* forms but two syllables, but Rowe has made it three in every case.)

Scipio "dismissed the Iberian maid" (Milton, *Paradise Regained*, ii.). The poet refers to the tale of Scipio's restoring a captive princess to her lover, Allucius, and giving to her, as a wedding present, the money of her ransom. (See CONTINENCE.)

During his command in Spain a circumstance occurred which contributed more to his fame and glory than all his military exploits. At the taking of New Carthage, a lady of extraordinary beauty was brought to Scipio, who found himself greatly affected by her charms. Understanding, however, that she was betrothed to a Celtibērian prince named Allucius, he resolved to conquer his rising passion, and sent her to her lover without recompense. A silver shield, on which this interesting event is depicted, was found in the river Rhone by some fishermen in the seventeenth century.—Goldsmith, *History of Rome*, xiv. 3. (Whittaker's improved edition contains a fac-simile of the shield on p. 215.)

Scipio, son of the gypsy woman, Coscolīna, and the soldier, Torribio Scipio. Scipio becomes the secretary of Gil Blas, and settles down with him at "the castle of Lirias." His character and adventures are very similar to those of Gil Blas himself, but he never rises to the same level. Scipio begins by being a rogue, who pilfered and plundered all who employed him, but in the service of Gil Blas he was a model of fidelity and integrity.—Lesage, *Gil Blas* (1715).

Sciro′nian Rocks, between Meg′ara and Corinth. So called because the bones of Sciron, the robber of Attica, were changed into these rocks when Theseus (2 *syl.*) hurled him from a cliff into the sea. It was from these rocks that Ino cast herself into the Corinthian bay.—*Greek Fable.*

Scirum. The men of Scirum used to shoot against the stars.

Like ... men of wit bereaven,
Which howle and shoote against the lights of heaven.
Wm. Browne, Britannia's Pastorals, iv. (1613).

Scogan (*Henry*), M.A., a poet, contemporary with Chaucer. He lived in the reigns of Richard II., Henry IV., and probably Henry V. Among the gentry who had letters of protection to attend Richard II. in his expedition into Ireland, in 1399, is "Henricus Scogan, Armiger."—Tyrwhitt's *Chaucer*, v. 15 (1773).

Scogan? What was he?
Oh, a fine gentleman and a master of arts
Of Henry the Fourth's time, that made disguises
For the king's sons, and writ in ballad royal

Daintily well.
Ben Jonson, *The Fortunate Isles* (1626).

Scogan (John), the favorite jester and buffoon of Edward IV. "Scogan's jests" were published by Andrew Borde, a physician in the reign of Henry VIII.

The same Sir John [*Falstaff*], the very same. I saw him break Skogan's head at the court-gate, when he was a crack not thus high.—Shakespeare, 2 *Henry IV.* act iii. sc. 2.

⁎ Shakespeare has confounded Henry Scogan, M.A., the poet, who lived in the reign of Henry IV., with John Scogan, the jester, who lived about a century later, in the reign of Edward IV.; and, of course, Sir John Falstaff, could not have known him when "he was a mere crack."

Scogan's Jest. Scogan and some companions, being in lack of money, agreed to the following trick: A peasant, driving sheep, was accosted by one of the accomplices, who laid a wager that his sheep were hogs, and agreed to abide by the decision of the first person they met. This, of course, was Scogan, who instantly gave judgment against the herdsman.

A similar joke is related in the *Hitopadesa*, an abridged version of Pilpay's *Fables*. In this case, the "peasant" is represented by a Brahmin carrying a goat, and the joke was to persuade the Brahmin that he was carrying a dog. "How is this, friend," says one, "that you, a Brahmin, carry on your back such an unclean animal as a dog?" "It is not a dog," says the Brahmin, "but a goat;" and trudged on. Presently another made the same remark, and the Brahmin, beginning to doubt, took down the goat to look at it. Convinced that the creature was really a goat, he went on, when presently a third made the same remark. The Brahmin, now fully persuaded that his eyes were befooling him, threw down the goat and went away without it; whereupon the three companions took possession of it and cooked it.

In *Tyll Eulenspiegel* we have a similar hoax. Eulenspiegel sees a man with a piece of green cloth, which he resolves to obtain. He employs two confederates, both priests. Says Eulenspiegel to the man, "What a famous piece of blue cloth! Where did you get it?" "Blue, you fool! why, it is green." After a short contention, a bet is made, and the question in dispute is referred to the first comer. This was a confederate, and he at once decided that the cloth was blue. "You are both in the same boat," says the man, "which I will prove by the priest yonder." The question being put to the priest, is decided against the man, and the three rogues divide the cloth amongst them.

Another version is in novel 8 of Fortini. The joke was that certain kids he had for sale were capons.—See Dunlop, *History of Fiction*, viii. art. "Ser Giovanni."

Scone [*Skoon*], a palladium stone. It was erected in Icolmkil for the coronation of Fergus Eric, and was called the *Lia-Fail* of Ireland. Fergus, the son of Fergus Eric, who led the Dalriads to Argyllshire, removed it to Scone; and Edward I. took it to London. It still remains in Westminster Abbey, where it forms the support of Edward the Confessor's chair, which forms the coronation chair of the British monarchs.

Ni fallat fatum, Scoti, quocunque locatum
Invenient lapidem, regnare tenentur ibidem.
Lardner, *History of Scotland*, i. 67 (1832).

Where'er this stone is placed, the fates decree,
The Scottish race shall there the sovereigns be.

*** Of course, the "Scottish race" is the dynasty of the Stuarts and their successors.

Scotch Guards, in the service of the French kings, were called his *garde du corps*. The origin of the guard was this: When St. Louis entered upon his first crusade, he was twice saved from death by the valor of a small band of Scotch auxiliaries under the commands of the earls of March and Dunbar, Walter Stuart, and Sir David Lindsay. In gratitude thereof, it was resolved that "a standing guard of Scotchmen, recommended by the king of Scotland, should ever more form the body-guard of the king of France." This decree remained in force for five centuries.—Grant, *The Scottish Cavalier*, xx.

Scotland. So called, according to legend, from Scota, daughter of Pharaoh. What gives this legend especial interest is, that when Edward I. laid claim to the country as a fief of England, he pleaded that Brute, the British king, in the days of Eli and Samuel, had conquered it. The Scotch, in their defence, pleaded their independence in virtue of descent from Scota, daughter of Pharaoh. This is not fable, but sober history.—Rymer, *Fœdera*, I. ii. (1703).

Scotland a Fief of England. When Edward I. laid claim to Scotland as a fief of the English crown, his great plea was that it was awarded to Adelstan, by direct miracle, and, therefore, could never be alienated. His advocates seriously read from *The Life and Miracles of St. John of Beverley*, this extract: Adelstan went to drive back the Scotch, who had crossed the border, and, on reaching the Tyne, St. John of Beverley appeared to him, and bade him cross the river at daybreak. Adelstan obeyed, and reduced the whole kingdom to submission. On reaching Dunbar, in the return march, Adelstan prayed that some sign might be given, to testify to all ages that God had delivered the kingdom into his hands. Whereupon he was commanded to strike the basaltic rock with his sword. This did he, and the blade sank into the rock "as if it had been butter," cleaving it asunder for "an ell or more." As the cleft remains to the present hour, in testimony of this miracle, why, of course, *cela va sans dire.*—Rymer, *Fœdera*, I. ii. 771 (1703).

Scotland's Scourge, Edward I. His son, Edward II., buried him in Westminster Abbey, where his tomb is still to be seen, with the following inscription:—

Edwardus Longus, Scotorum Malleus, hic est.
(Our Longshanks, "Scotland's Scourge," lies here).
Drayton, *Polyolbion*, xvii. (1613).

So Longshanks, Scotland's Scourge, the land laid waste.
Ditto, xxix. (1622).

Scots (*scuite*, "a wanderer, a rover"), the inhabitants of the western coast of Scotland. As this part is very hilly and barren, it is unfit for tillage; and the inhabitants used to live a roving life on the produce of the chase, their chief employment being the rearing of cattle.

Scots (The Royal). The hundred cuirassiers, called *hommes des armes*, which formed the body-guard of the French king, were sent to Scotland in 1633, by Louis XIII., to attend the coronation of Charles I., at Edinburgh. On the outbreak of the civil war, eight years afterwards, these cuirassiers loyally adhered to the crown, and received the title of "The Royal Scots." At the downfall of the king, the *hommes des armes* returned to France.

Scott (*The Southern*). Ariosto is so called by Lord Byron.

First rose
The Tuscan father's "comedy divine" [*Danté*];
Then, not unequal to the Florentine,
The southern Scott, the minstrel who called forth
A new creation with his magic line,
And, like the Ariosto of the north [*Sir W. Scott*],
Sang ladye-love and war, romance and knightly worth.
Byron, *Childe Harold*, iv. 40 (1817).

⁂ Dante was born at Florence.

Scott of Belgium (*The Walter*), Hendrick Conscience (1812-).

Scottish Anacreon (*The*), Alexander Scot is so called by Pinkerton.

Scottish Boanerges (*The*), Robert and James Haldane (nineteenth century). Robert died 1842, aged 79, and James 1851.

Scottish Hogarth (*The*), David Allan (1744-1796).

Scottish Homer (*The*), William Wilkie, author of an epic poem in rhyme, entitled *The Epigoniad* (1753).

Scottish Solomon (*The*), James VI. of Scotland, subsequently called James I. of England (1566, 1603-1625).

✱✱ The French king called him far more aptly, "The Wisest Fool in Christendom."

Scottish Terriers (*The*), Sir David Wilkie (1785-1841).

Scottish Theoc'ritos (*The*), Allan Ramsay (1685-1758).

Scotus. There were two schoolmen of this name: (1) John Scotus *Erigena*, a native of Ireland, who died 886, in the reign of King Alfred; (2) John Duns Scotus, a Scotchman, who died 1308. Longfellow confounds these two in his *Golden Legend* when he attributes the Latin version of *St. Dionysius, the Areopagite*, to the latter schoolman.

And done into Latin by that Scottish beast,
Erigena Johannes.
Longfellow, *The Golden Legend* (1851).

Scourers, a class of dissolute young men, often of the better class, who infested the streets of London, in the seventeenth century, and thought it capital fun to break windows, upset sedan-chairs, beat quiet citizens, and molest young women. These young blades called themselves at different times, Muns, Hectors, Scourers, Nickers, Hawcabites, and Mohawks or Mohocks.

Scourge of Christians (*The*), Noureddin-Mahmûd, of Damascus (1116-1174).

Scourge of God (*The*), Attila, king of the Huns, called *Flagellum Dei* (died A.D. 453). Gensĕric, king of the Vandals, called *Virga Dei* (✱, reigned 429-477).

Scourge of Princes (*The*), Pietro Aretino, of Arezzo, a merciless satirist of kings and princes, but very obscene and licentious. He called himself "Aretino the Divine" (1492-1557).

Thus Aretin of late got reputation
By scourging kings, as Lucian did of old
By scorning gods.
Lord Brooke, *Inquisition Upon Fame* (1554-1628).

Suidas called Lucian "The Blasphemer;" and he added that he was torn to pieces by dogs for his impiety. Some of his works attack the heathen philosophy and religion. His *Jupiter Convicted* shows Jupiter to be powerless, and *Jupiter, the Tragedian*, shows Jupiter and the other gods to be myths (120-200).

Scourge of Scotland, Edward I., *Scotōrum Malleus* (1239, 1272-1307).

Scrape-All, a soapy, psalm-singing hypocrite, who combines with Cheatly to supply young heirs with cash at most exorbitant usury. (See CHEATLY.)—Shadwell, *Squire of Alsatia* (1688).

Scrape on, Gentlemen. Hadrian went once to the public baths, and, seeing an old soldier scraping himself with a potsherd, for want of a flesh-brush, sent him a sum of money. Next day the bath was crowded with potsherd scrapers; but the emperor said when he saw them, "Scrape on, gentlemen, but you will not scrape an acquaintance with me."

Scribble, an attorney's clerk, who tries to get married to Polly Honeycombe, a silly, novel-struck girl, but well off. He is happily foiled in his scheme, and Polly is saved from the consequences of a most unsuitable match.—G. Colman, the elder, *Polly Honeycombe* (1760).

Scrible′rus (*Cornelius*), father of Martinus. He was noted for his pedantry, and his odd whims about the education of his son.

Martīnus Scriblērus, a man of capacity, who had read everything; but his judgment was worthless, and his taste perverted.—(?) Arbuthnot, *Memoirs of the Extraordinary Life, Works, and Discoveries of Martin Scriblerus.*

⁎ These "memoirs" were intended to be the first instalment of a general satire on the false taste in literature prevalent in the time of Pope. The only parts of any moment that were written of this intended series, were Pope's *Treatise of the Bathos, or Art of Sinking in Poetry*, and his *Memoirs of P. P., Clerk of this Parish* (1727), in ridicule of Dr. Burnett's *History of His Own Time*. The *Dunciad* is, however, preceded by a *Prolegomena*, ascribed to Martinus Scriblerus, and contains his notes and illustrations on the poem, thus connecting this merciless satire with the original design.

Scriever (*Jock*), the apprentice of Duncan Macwheeble (bailie at Tully Veolan to Mr. Cosmo Comyne Bradwardine, baron of Bradwardine and Tully Veolan).—Sir W. Scott, *Waverley* (time George II.).

Scriptores Decem, a collection of ten ancient chronicles on English history, in one vol., folio, London, 1652, edited by Roger Twysden and John Selden. The volume contains: (1) Simeon Dunelmensis [Simeon of Durham], *Historia*; (2) Johannes Hagustaldensis [John of Hexham], *Historia Continuata*; (3) Richardus Hagustaldensis [Richard of Hexham], *De Gestis Regis Stephani*; (4) Ailredus Rievallensis [Ailred of Rieval], *Historia* (genealogy of the kings); (5) Radulphus de Diceto [Ralph of Diceto], *Abbreviationes Chronicorum* and *Ymagines Historiarum*; (6) Johannes Brompton, *Chronicon*; (7) Gervasius Dorobornensis [Gervais of Dover], *Chronica, etc.* (burning and repair of Dover Church; contentions between the monks of Canterbury and

Archbishop Baldwin; and lives of the archbishops of Canterbury); (8) Thomas Stubbs (a Dominican), *Chronica Pontificum ecc. Eboraci* [*i.e.* York]; (9) Guilielmus Thorn Cantuariensis [of Canterbury], *Chronica*; and (10) Henricus Knighton Leicestrensis [of Leicester], *Chronica*. (The last three are chronicles of "pontiffs" or archbishops.)

Scriptores Quinque, better known as *Scriptores Post Bedam*, published at Frankfürt, 1601, in one vol., folio, and containing: (1) Willielm Malmesburiensis, *De Gestis Regum Anglorum, Historiæ Novellæ*, and *De Gestis Pontificum Anglorum*; (2) Henry Huntindoniensis, *Historia*; (3) Roger Hovedeni [Hoveden], *Annales*; (4) Ethelwerd, *Chronica*; and (5) Ingulphus Croylandensis [of Croyland], *Historia*.

Scriptores Tres, three "hypothetical" writers on ancient history, which Dr. Bertram professed to have discovered between the years 1747 and 1757. They are called Richardus Corinensis [of Cirencester], *De Situ Britanniæ*; Gildas Badonĭcus; and Nennius Banchorensis [of Bangor].—J. E. Mayor, in his preface to *Ricardi de Cirencestria Speculum Historiale*, has laid bare this literary forgery.

Scripture. Parson Adams's wife said to her husband that in her opinion "it was blasphemous to talk of Scriptures out of church."—Fielding, *Joseph Andrews*.

A great impression in my youth
Was made by Mrs. Adams, where she cries,
"That Scriptures out of church are blasphemous."
Byron, *Don Juan*, xiii. 96 (1824).

Scroggen, a poor hack author, celebrated by Goldsmith in his *Description of an Author's Bedchamber*.

Scroggens, (*Giles*), a peasant, who courted Molly Bawn, but died just before the wedding day. Molly cried and cried for him, till she cried herself fast asleep. Fancying that she saw Giles Scroggens's ghost standing at her bedside, she exclaimed in terror, "What do you want?" "You for to come for to go along with me," replied the ghost. "I ben't dead, you fool!" said Molly; but the ghost rejoined, "Why, that's no rule." Then, clasping her round the waist, he exclaimed, "Come, come with me, ere morning beam." "I won't!" shrieked Molly, and woke to find "'twas nothing but a dream."—*A Comic Ballad.*

Scroggs (*Sir William*), one of the judges.—Sir W. Scott, *Peveril of the Peak* (time, Charles II.).

Scrooge (*Ebenezer*), partner, executor, and heir of old Jacob Marley, stockbroker. When first introduced, he is "a squeezing, grasping, covetous old hunks, sharp and hard as a flint;" without one particle of sympathy, loving no one, and by none beloved. One Christmas Day Ebenezer Scrooge sees three ghosts; The Ghost of Christmas Past; Ghost of Christmas Present; and the Ghost of Christmas To-come. The first takes him back to his young life, shows him what Christmas was to him when a schoolboy, and when he was an apprentice; reminds him of his courting a young girl, whom he forsook as he grew rich; and shows him that sweetheart of his young days married to another, and the mother of a happy family. The second ghost shows him the joyous home of his clerk, Bob Cratchit, who has nine people to keep on 15*s.* a week, and yet could find wherewithal to make merry on this day; it also shows him the family of his nephew, and of others. The third ghost shows him what would be his lot if he died as he then was, the prey of harpies, the jest of his friends on 'Change, the world's uncared-for waif. These visions wholly changed his nature, and he becomes benevolent, charitable, and cheerful, loving all, and by all beloved.—C. Dickens, *A Christmas Carol* (in five staves, 1843).

Scrow, the clerk of Lawyer Glossin.—Sir W. Scott, *Guy Mannering* (time George II.).

Scrub, a man-of-all-work to Lady Bountiful. He describes his duties thus;

Of a Monday I drive the coach, of a Tuesday I drive the plough, on Wednesday I follow the hounds, on Thursday I dun the tenants, on Friday I go to market, on Saturday I draw warrants, and on Sunday I draw beer.— Geo. Farquhar, *The Beaux' Stratagem*, iii. 4 (1707).

Scrubin´da, the lady who "lived by the scouring of pots in Dyot Street, Bloomsbury Square."

Oh, was I a quart, pint, or gill,
To be scrubbed by her delicate hands!...
My parlor that's next to the sky
I'd quit, her blest mansion to share;
So happy to live and to die
In Dyot Street, Bloomsbury Square.
W. B. Rhodes, *Bombastes Furioso* (1790).

Scruple, the friend of Random. He is too honest for a rogue, and too conscientious for a rake. At Calais he met Harriet, the elder daughter of Sir David Dunder, of Dunder Hall, near Dover, and fell in love with her. Scruple subsequently got invited to Dunder Hall, and was told that his Harriet was to be married next day to Lord Snolt, a stumpy, "gummy" fogey of five and forty. Harriet hated the idea, and agreed to elope with Scruple; but her father discovered by accident the intention, and intercepted it. However, to prevent scandal, he gave his consent to the union, and discovered that Scruple, both in family and fortune, was quite suitable for a son-in-law.—G. Colman, *Ways and Means* (1788).

Scu'damour (*Sir*), the knight beloved by Am'oret (whom Britomart delivered from Busyrane, the enchanter), and whom she ultimately married. He is called Scudamour (3 *syl.*) from [*e*]*scu d'amour* ("the shield of love"), which he carried (bk. iv. 10). This shield was hung by golden bands in the temple of Venus, and under it was written: "WHOSOEVER BE THIS SHIELD, FAIRE AMORET BE HIS." Sir Scudamour, determined to win the prize, had to fight with twenty combatants, overthrew them all, and the shield was his. When he saw Amoret in the company of Britomart, dressed as a knight, he was racked with jealousy, and went on his wanderings, accompanied by nurse Glaucê for "his squire;" but somewhat later, seeing Britomart, without her hemlet, he felt that his jealousy was groundless (bk. iv. 6). His tale is told by himself (bk. iv. 10).—Spenser, *Faëry Queen*, iii., iv. (1590-6).

Sculpture (*Father of French*), Jean Goujon (1510-1572). G. Pilon is so called also (1515-1590).

Scyld, the king of Denmark preceding Beowulf. The Anglo-Saxon epic poem called *Beowulf* (sixth century) begins with the death of Scyld.

At his appointed time, Scyld deceased, very decrepit, and went into the peace of the Lord. They ... bore him to the sea-shore as he himself requested.... There on the beach stood the ring-prowed ship, the vehicle of the noble ... ready to set out. They laid down the dear prince, the distributer of rings, in the bosom of the ship, the mighty one beside the mast ... they set up a golden ensign high overhead ... they gave him to the deep. Sad was their spirit, mournful their mood.—Kemble, *Beowulf* (an Anglo-Saxon poem, 1833).

Scylla and Charybdis. The former was a rock, in which dwelt Scylla, a hideous monster, encompassed with dogs and wolves. The latter was a whirlpool, into which Charybdis was metamorphosed.—*Classic Fable*.

Scythian (*That Brave*), Darius, the Persian. According to Herod'otus, all the south-east of Europe used to be called Scythia, and Xenophon calls the dwellers south of the Caspian Sea "Scythians," also. In fact, by Scythia was meant the south of Russia and west of Asia; hence, the Hungarians, a Tartar horde, settled on the east coast of the Caspian Sea, who, in 889, crossed into Europe, are spoken of as "Scythians," and Lord Brooke calls the Persians "Scythians." The reference below is to the following event in Persian history:—The death of Smerdis was kept for a time a profound secret, and one of the officers about the court who resembled him usurped the crown, calling himself brother of the late monarch. Seven of the high nobles conspired together, and slew the usurper, but it then became a question to which of the seven the crown should be offered. They did not toss for it, but they did much the same thing. They agreed to give the crown to him whose horse neighed first. Darius's horse won, and thus Darius became king of the Persian empire.

That brave Scythian,
Who found more sweetness in his horse's neighing
Than all the Phrygian, Dorian, Lydian playing.
Lord Brooke, (1554-1628).

*** Marlowe calls Tamburlaine of Tartary "a Scythian."

You shall hear the Scythian Tamburlaine
Threatening the world with high astounding terms.
Marlowe, *Tamburlaine* (prologue, 1587).

Scythian's Name (*The*). Humber or Humbert, king of the Huns, invaded England during the reign of Locrin, some 1000 years B.C. In his flight, he was drowned in the river Abus, which has ever since been called the Humber, after "the Scythian's name."—Geoffrey, *British History*, ii. 2 (1142); and Milton's *History of England*.

Or Humber loud that keeps the Scythian's name.
Milton, *Vacation Exercise* (1627).

Sea-Captain (*The*), a drama by Lord Lytton (1839). Norman, "the sea-captain," was the son of Lady Arundel by her first husband, who was murdered. He was born three days after his father's murder, and was brought up by Onslow, a village priest. At 14 he went to sea, and became the captain of a man-of-war. Lady Arundel married again, and had another son named Percy. She wished to ignore Norman, and to settle the title and estates on Percy, but it was not to be. Norman and Percy both loved Violet, a ward of Lady Arundel. Violet, however, loved Norman only. A scheme was laid to murder Norman, but failed; and at the end Norman was acknowledged by his mother, reconciled to his brother, and married to the ward.

Seaforth (*The earl of*), a royalist, in the service of King Charles I.—Sir W. Scott, *Legend of Montrose* (time, Charles I.).

Seasons (*The*), a descriptive poem in blank verse, by James Thomson, "Winter" (1726), "Summer" (1727), "Spring" (1728), "Autumn" (1730). "Winter" is inscribed to the earl of Wilmington; "Summer" to Mr. Doddington; "Spring" to the countess of Hertford; and "Autumn" to Mr. Onslow.

1. In "Winter," after describing the season, the poet introduces his episode of a traveller lost in a snowstorm, "the creeping cold lays him along the snow, a stiffened corse," of wife, of children, and of friends unseen. The whole book containing 1069 lines.

2. "Summer" begins with a description of the season, and the rural pursuits of haymaking and sheep-shearing; passes on to the hot noon, when "nature pants, and every stream looks languid." After describing the tumultuous character of the season in the torrid zone, he returns to England, and describes a thunder-storm, in which Celădon and Amelia are overtaken. The thunder growls, the lightnings flash, louder and louder crashes the aggravated roar, "convulsing heaven and earth." The maiden, terrified, clings to her lover for protection. "Fear not, sweet innocence," he says. "He who involves yon skies in darkness ever smiles on thee. 'Tis safety to be near thee, sure, and thus to clasp protection." As he speaks the words, a flash of lightning strikes the maid, and lays her a blackened corpse at the young man's feet. The poem concludes with the more peaceful scenery of a summer's evening, when the story of Damon and Musidōra is introduced. Damon had long loved the beautiful Musidora, but met with scant encouragement. One summer's evening he accidently came upon her bathing, and the respectful modesty of his love so won upon the damsel that she wrote upon a tree, "Damon, the time may come when you need not fly." The whole book contains 1804 lines.

3. In "Spring" the poet describes its general features, and its influence on the vegetable and animal world. He describes a garden with its harem of flowers, a grove with its orchestry of song-birds making melody in their love, the rough world of brutes, furious and fierce with their strong desire, and lastly man tempered by its infusive influence. The book contains 1173 lines.

4. In "Autumn" we are taken to the harvest-field, where the poet introduces a story similar to that of Ruth and Boaz. His Ruth he calls "Lavinia," and his Boaz "Palēmon." He then describes partridge and pheasant shooting, hare and fox hunting, all of which he condemns. After luxuriating in the orchard and vineyard, he speaks of the emigration of birds, the falling of the sear and yellow leaf, and concludes with a eulogy of country life. The whole book contains 1371 lines.

⁎ It is much to be regretted that the poet's order has not been preserved. The arrangement of the seasons into Spring, Summer, Autumn, and Winter, is unnatural, and mars the harmony of the poet's plan.

Seatonian Prize. The Rev. Thomas Seaton, Fellow of Clare Hall, Cambridge University, bequeathed the rents of his Kislingbury estate for a yearly prize of £40 to the best English poem on a sacred subject announced in January, and sent in on or before September 29 following.

Shall hoary Granta call her sable sons....
Shall these approach the Muse? Ah, no! she flies,
And even spurns the great Seatonian prize.
Byron, *English Bards and Scotch Reviewers* (1809).

Sebastes of Mytile´ne (4 *syl.*), the assassin in the "Immortal Guards."—Sir W. Scott, *Count Robert of Paris* (time, Rufus).

Sebastian, a young gentleman of Messalinê, brother to Viola. They were twins, and so much alike that they could not be distinguished except by their dress. Sebastian and his sister, being shipwrecked, escaped to Illyria. Here Sebastian was mistaken for his sister (who had assumed man's apparel), and was invited by the Countess Olivia to take shelter in her house from a street broil. Olivia was in love with Viola, and thinking Sebastian to be the object of her love, married him.—Shakespeare, *Twelfth Night* (1614).

Sebastian, brother of Alonso, king of Naples, in *The Tempest* (1609).

Sebastian, father of Valentine and Alice.—Beaumont and Fletcher, *Mons. Thomas* (1619).

Sebastian (Don), king of Portugal, is defeated in battle and taken prisoner by the Moors (1574). He is saved from death by Dorax, a noble Portuguese, then a renegade in the court of the emperor of Barbary. The train being dismissed, Dorax takes off his turban, assumes his Portuguese dress, and is recognized as Alonzo of Alcazar.—Dryden, *Don Sebastian* (1690).

The quarrel and reconcilation of Sebastian and Dorax [*alias Alonzo of Alcazar*] is a masterly copy from a similar scene between Brutus and Cassius [*in Shakespeare's Julius Cæsar*].—R. Chambers, *English Literature*, i. 380.

Don Sebastian, a name of terror to Moorish children.

Nor shall Sebastian's formidable name
Be longer used to still the crying babe.
Dryden, *Don Sebastian* (1690).

Sebastian I. of Brazil, who fell in the battle of Alcazarquebir in 1578. The legend is that he is not dead, but is patiently biding the fulness of time, when he will return, and make Brazil the chief kingdom of the earth. (See BARBAROSSA.)

Sebastoc´rator (*The*), the chief officer of state in the empire of Greece. Same as Protosebastos.—Sir W. Scott, *Count Robert of Paris* (time, Rufus).

Sebile (2 *syl.*), la Dame du Lac, in the romance called *Perceforest*. Her castle was surrounded by a river, on which rested so thick a fog that no one could see across it. Alexander the Great abode with her a fortnight to be cured of his wounds, and King Arthur was the result of this amour (vol. i. 42).

Secret Hill (*The*). Ossian said to Oscar, when he resigned to him the command of the morrow's battle, "Be thine the secret hill to-night," referring to the Gaelic custom of the commander of an army retiring to a secret hill the night before a battle, to hold communion with the ghosts of departed heroes.—Ossian, *Cathlin of Clutha*.

Secret Tribunal (*The*), the count of the Holy Vehme.—Sir W. Scott, *Anne of Geierstein* (time, Edward IV.).

Sedgwick (*Doomsday*), William Sedgwick, a fanatical "prophet" in the Commonwealth, who pretended that it had been revealed to him in a vision that the day of doom was at hand.

Sedillo, the licentiate, with whom Gil Blas took service as a footman. Sedillo was a gouty old gourmand of 69. Being ill, he sent for Dr. Sangrado, who took from him six porringers of blood every day, and dosed him incessantly with warm water, giving him two or three pints at a time, saying, "a patient cannot be blooded too much; for it is a great error to suppose that blood is needful for the preservation of life. Warm water," he maintained, "drunk in abundance, is the true specific in all distempers." When the licentiate died under this treatment, the doctor insisted it was because his patient had neither lost blood enough nor drunk enough warm water.—Lesage, *Gil Blas*, ii. 1, 2 (1715).

Sedley (*Mr.*), a wealthy London stock-broker, brought to ruin by the fall of the Funds just prior to the battle of Waterloo. The old merchant then tried to earn a meagre pittance by selling wine, coals, or lottery-tickets by commission, but his bad wine and cheap coals found but few customers.

Mrs. Sedley, wife of Mr. Sedley. A homely, kind-hearted motherly woman in her prosperous days, but soured by adversity, and quick to take offence.

Amelia Sedley, daughter of the stock-broker, educated at Miss Pinkerton's academy, Chiswick Mall, and engaged to Captain George Osborne, son of a rich London merchant. After the ruin of old Sedley, George married Amelia, and was disinherited by his father. He was adored by his young wife, but fell on the field of Waterloo. Amelia then returned to her father, and lived in great indigence, but Captain Dobbin greatly loved her, and did much to relieve her worst wants. Captain Dobbin rose in his profession to the rank of colonel, and married the young widow.

Joseph Sedley, a collector, of Boggley Wollah; a fat, sensual, conceited dandy, vain, shy, and vulgar. "His Excellency" fled from Brussels on the day of the battle between Napoleon and Wellington, and returned to Calcutta, where he bragged of his brave deeds, and made appear that he was Wellington's right hand; so that he obtained the sobriquet of "Waterloo Sedley." He again returned to England, and became the "patron" of Becky Sharp (then Mrs. Rawdon Crawley, but separated from her husband). But this lady proved a terrible dragon, fleeced him of all his money, and in six months he died under very suspicious circumstances.—Thackeray, *Vanity Fair* (1848).

Sedley (*Sir Charles*), in the court of Charles II.—Sir W. Scott, *Woodstock* (time, Commonwealth).

Seelencooper (*Captain*), superintendent of the military hospital at Ryde.—Sir W. Scott, *The Surgeon's Daughter* (time, George II.).

Seer (*The Poughkeepsie*), Andrew Jackson Davis.

Seicen´to (3 *syl.*), the sixteenth century of Italian notables, the period of bad taste and degenerate art. The degraded art is termed *Seicentista*, and the notables of the period the *Seicentisti*. The style of writing was inflated and bombastic, and that of art was what is termed "rococo." The chief poet was Marini (1569-1615), the chief painter Caravaggio (1569-1609), the chief sculptor Bernini (1593-1680), and the chief architect Borromini (1599-1667).

Sede, in Voltaire's tragedy of *Mahomet*, was the character in which Talma, the great French tragedian, made his *début* in 1787.

Seidel-Beckir, the most famous of all talismanists. He made three of extraordinary power: viz., a little golden fish, which would fetch from the sea whatever was desired of it; a poniard, which rendered the person who bore it invisible, and all others whom he wished to be so; and a steel ring, which enabled the wearer to read the secrets of another's heart.—Comte de Caylus, *Oriental Tales* ("The Four Talismans," 1743).

Sejanus (*Ælius*), a minister of Tibērius, and commander of the Prætorian Guards. His affability made him a great favorite. In order that he might be the foremost man of Rome, all the children and grandchildren of the emperor were put to death under sundry pretences. Drusus, the son of Tiberius, then fell a victim. He next persuaded the emperor to retire, and Tiberius went to Campania, leaving to Sejānus the sole management of affairs. He now called himself emperor; but Tiberius, roused from his lethargy, accused his minister of treason. The senate condemned him to be strangled, and his remains, being treated with the grossest insolence, were kicked into the Tiber, A.D. 31. This was the subject of Ben Jonson's first historical play, entitled *Sejanus* (1603).

Sejjin or **Sejn**, the record of all evil deeds, whether by men or the genii, kept by the recording angel. It also means that dungeon beneath the seventh earth, where Eblis and his companions are confined.

Verily, the register of the deeds of the wicked is surely in Sejjin.—Sale, *Al Korân*, lxxxiii.

Selby (*Captain*), an officer in the guards.—Sir W. Scott, *Peveril of the Peak* (time, Charles II.).

Self-Admiration Society (*The*). *Poets*: Morris, Rosetti and Swinburne. *Painters*: Brown, Mudon, Whistler and some others.

Selim, son of Abdallah, who was murdered by his brother, Giaffir (pacha of Aby´dos). After the death of his brother, Giaffir (2 *syl.*) took Selim under his charge and brought him up, but treated him with considerable cruelty. Giaffir had a daughter named Zuleika (3 *syl.*), with whom Selim fell in love; but Zuleika thought he was her brother. As soon as Giaffir discovered the attachment of the two cousins for each other, he informed his daughter that he intended her to marry Osmyn Bey; but Zuleika eloped with Selim, the pacha pursued them, Selim was shot, Zuleika killed herself, and Giaffir was left childless and alone.—Byron, *Bride of Abydos* (1813).

Selim, son of Acbar. Jehanguire was called Selim before his accession to the throne. He married Nourmahal, the "Light of the Haram," but a coolness rose up between them. One night Nourmahal entered the sultan's banquet-room as a lute-player, and so charmed young Selim that he exclaimed, "If Nourmahal had so sung, I could have forgiven her!" It was enough. Nourmahal threw off her disguise, and became reconciled to her husband.— T. Moore, *Lalla Rookh* ("Light of the Haram," 1817).

Selim, son of the Moorish king of Algiers. [Horush] Barbarossa, the Greek renegade, having made himself master of Algiers, slew the reigning king, but Selim escaped. After the lapse of seven years, he returned under the assumed name of Achmet, and headed an uprising of the Moors. The insurgents succeeded, Barbarossa was slain, the widowed Queen Zaphîra was restored to her husband's throne, and Selim, her son, married Irênê, daughter of Barbarossa.—J. Brown, *Barbarossa* (1742 or 1755).

Selim, friend of Etan (the supposed son of Zamti, the mandarin).—Murphy, *The Orphan of China* (1759).

Sel´ima, daughter of Bajazet, sultan of Turkey, in love with Prince Axalla, but promised by her father in marriage to Omar. When Selima refused to marry Omar, Bajazet would have slain her; but Tamerlane commanded both Bajazet and Omar to be seized. So every obstacle was removed from the union of Selima and Axalla.—N. Rowe, *Tamerlane* (1702).

Selima, one of the six Wise Men from the East, led by the guiding star to Jesus.—Klopstock, *The Messiah*, v. (1771).

Se´lith, one of the two guardian angels of the Virgin Mary, and of John the Divine.—Klopstock, *The Messiah*, ix. (1771).

Sellock (*Cisly*), a servant girl in the service of Lady and Sir Geoffrey Peveril, of the Peak.—Sir W. Scott, *Peveril of the Peak* (time, Charles II.).

Selvaggio, the father of Sir Industry, and the hero of Thomson's *Castle of Indolence*.

In Fairy-land there lived a knight of old,
Of feature stern, Selvaggio well y-clept;
A rough, unpolished man, robust and bold,
But wondrous poor. He neither sowed nor reaped;
No stores in summer for cold winter heaped.
In hunting all his days away he wore—
Now scorched by June, now in November steeped,
Now pinched by biting January sore.
He still in woods pursued the libbard and the boar.
Thomson, *Castle of Indolence*, ii. 5 (1745).

Sem'ele (3 *syl.*), ambitious of enjoying Jupiter in all his glory, perished from the sublime effulgence of the god. This is substantially the tale of the second story of T. Moore's *Loves of the Angels*. Liris requested her angel lover to come to her in all his angelic brightness; but was burnt to ashes as she fell into his embrace.

For majesty gives nought to subjects, ...
A royal smile, a guinea's glorious rays,
Like Semelê, would kill us with its blaze.
Peter Pindar [Dr. Wolcot], *Progress of Admiration* (1809).

Semi'da, the young man, the only son of a widow, raised from the dead by Jesus, as he was being carried from the walls of Nain. He was deeply in love with Cidli, the daughter of Jairus.

He was in the bloom of life. His hair hung in curls on his shoulders, and he appeared as beautiful as David, when, sitting by the stream of Bethlehem, he was ravished at the voice of God.—Klopstock, *The Messiah*, iv. (1771).

Semir'amis, queen of Assyria, wife of Ninus. She survived her husband, and reigned. The glory of her reign stands out so prominently that she quite eclipses all the monarchs of ancient Assyria. After a reign of forty-two years she resigned the crown to her son, Ninyas, and took her flight to heaven in the form of a dove. Semiramis was the daughter of Dercĕto, the fish-goddess, and a Syrian youth, and, being exposed in infancy, was brought up by doves.

Semiramis of the North, Margaret, daughter of Waldemar III. of Denmark. At the death of her father she succeeded him; by the death of her husband, Haco VIII., king of Norway, she succeeded to that kingdom also; and, having conquered Albert of Sweden, she added Sweden to her empire. Thus was she queen of Denmark, Norway and Sweden (1353-1412).

Semirămis of the North, Catherine of Russia, a powerful and ambitious sovereign, but in morals a law unto herself (1729-1796).

Semkail, the angel of the winds and waves.

I keep the winds in awe with the hand which you see in the air, and prevent the wind Haidge from coming forth. If I gave it freedom it would reduce the universe to powder. With my other hand I hinder the sea from overflowing, without which precaution it would cover the face of the whole earth.— Comte de Caylus, *Oriental Tales* ("History of Abdal Motalleb," 1743).

Semo (*Son of*), Cuthullin, general of the Irish tribes.

Sempro´nius, one of the "friends" of Timon of Athens, and "the first man that e'er received a gift from him." When Timon sent to borrow a sum of money of "his friend," he excused himself thus: As Timon did not think proper to apply to me first, but asked others before he sent to me, I consider his present application an insult. "Go," said he to the servant, "and tell your master:

Who bates mine honor shall not know my coin."
Shakespeare, *Timon of Athens*, act iii. sc. 3 (1600).

Sempronius, a treacherous friend of Cato while in Utĭca. Sempronius tried to mask his treason by excessive zeal and unmeasured animosity against Cæsar, with whom he was acting in alliance. He loved Marcia, Cato's daughter, but his love was not honorable love; and when he attempted to carry off the lady by force, he was slain by Juba, the Numidian prince.—J. Addison, *Cato* (1713).

I'll conceal
My thoughts in passion, 'tis the surest way.
I'll bellow out for Rome, and for my country,
And mouth at Cæsar till I shake the senate.
Your cold hypocrisy's a stale device,
A worn-out trick.
Act i. 1.

Sena´nus (*St.*), the saint who fled to the island of Scattery, and resolved that no woman should ever step upon the isle. An angel led St. Can´ara to the isle, but Senanus refused to admit her.—T. Moore, *Irish Melodies* ("St. Senanus and the Lady," 1814).

Sen´eca (*The Christian*), Bishop Hall, of Norwich (1574-1656).

Sene´na (3 *syl.*), a Welsh maiden, in love with Car´adoc. She dressed in boy's clothes, and, under the assumed name of Mervyn, became the page of the Princess Goervyl, that she might follow her lover to America, when Madoc colonized Caer-Madoc. Senena was promised in marriage to another; but when the wedding day arrived and all was ready, the bride was nowhere to be found.

> ... she doffed
> Her bridal robes, and clipt her golden locks,
> And put on boy's attire, thro' wood and wild
> To seek her own true love; and over sea,
> Forsaking all for him, she followed him.
> Southey, *Madoc*, ii. 23 (1805).

Sennac'herib, called by the Orientals King Moussal.—D'Herbelot, *Notes to the Korân* (seventeenth century).

Sennamar, a very skilful architect, who built at Hirah, for Nôman-al-Aôuar, king of Hirah, a most magnificent palace. In order that he might not build another equal or superior to it, for some other monarch, Nôman cast him headlong from the highest tower of the building.—D'Herbelot, *Bibliothèque Orientale* (1697).

⁎ A parallel tale is told of Neim'heid (2 *syl.*), who employed four architects to build for him a palace in Ireland, and then, jealous lest they should build one like it, or superior to it, for another monarch, he had them all privately put to death.—O'Halloran, *History of Ireland*.

Sensitive (*Lord*), a young nobleman of amorous proclivities, who marries Sabīna Rosny, a French refugee, in Padua, but leaves her, more from recklessness than wickedness. He comes to England and pays court to Lady Ruby, a rich young widow; but Lady Ruby knows of his marriage to the young French girl, and so hints at it that his lordship, who is no libertine, and has a great regard for his honor, sees that his marriage is known, and tells Lady Ruby he will start without delay to Padua, and bring his young wife home. This, however, was not needful, as Sabina was at the time the guest of Lady Ruby. She is called forth, and Lord Sensitive openly avows her to be his wife.—Cumberland, *First Love* (1796).

Sentimental Journey (*The*), by Laurence Sterne (1768). It was intended to be sentimental sketches of his tour through Italy in 1764, but he died soon after completing the first part. The tourist lands at Calais, and the first incident is his interview with a poor monk of St. Francis, who begged alms for his convent. Sterne refused to give anything, but his heart smote him for his churlishness to the meek old man. From Calais he goes to Montriul (Montreuil-sur-Mer) and thence to Nampont, near Cressy. Here occurred the incident, which is one of the most touching of all the sentimental sketches, that of "The Dead Ass." His next stage was Amiens, and thence to Paris. While looking at the Bastille, he heard a voice crying, "I can't get out! I can't get out!" He thought it was a child, but it was only a caged starling. This led him to reflect on the delights of liberty and miseries of captivity. Giving reins to his fancy, he imaged to himself a prisoner who for thirty years had been confined in a dungeon, during all which time "he had seen no sun, no moon, nor had the voice of kinsman breathed through his lattice." Carried away by his feelings, he burst into tears, for he "could not sustain the picture of confinement which his fancy had drawn." While at Paris, our tourist visited Versailles, and introduces an incident which he had witnessed some years previously at Rennes, in Brittany. It was that of a marquis reclaiming his sword and "patent of nobility." Any nobleman in France who engaged in trade, forfeited his rank; but there was a law in Brittany that a nobleman of reduced circumstances might deposit his sword temporarily with the local magistracy, and if better times dawned upon him, he might reclaim it. Sterne was present at one of these interesting ceremonies. A marquis had laid down his sword to mend his fortune by trade, and after a successful career at Martinico for twenty years, returned home, and reclaimed it. On receiving his deposit from the president, he drew it slowly from the scabbard, and, observing a spot of rust near the point, dropped a tear on it. As he wiped the blade lovingly, he remarked, "I shall find some other way to get it off." Returning to Paris, our tourist starts for Italy; but the book ends with his arrival at Moulines (Moulins). Some half a league from this city he encountered Maria, whose pathetic story had been told him by Mr. Shandy. She had lost her goat when Sterne saw her, but had instead a little dog named Silvio, led by a string. She was sitting under a poplar, playing on a pipe her vespers to the Virgin. Poor Maria had been crossed in love, or, to speak more strictly, the curé of Moulines had forbidden her banns, and the maiden lost her reason. Her story is exquisitely told, and Sterne says, "Could the traces be ever worn out of her brain, and those of Eliza out of mine, she should not only eat of my bread and drink of my cup, but Maria should lie in my bosom, and be unto me as a daughter."

Sentinel and St. Paul's Clock (*The*). The sentinel condemned to death by court-martial for falling asleep on his watch, but pardoned because he affirmed that he heard St. Paul's clock strike thirteen instead of twelve, was John Hatfield, who died at the age of 102, June, 1770.

Sentry (*Captain*), one of the members of the club under whose auspices the *Spectator* was professedly issued.

September Massacre (*The*), the slaughter of loyalists confined in the Abbaye. This massacre took place in Paris between September 2 and 5, 1792, on receipt of the news of the capture of Verdun. The number of victims was not less than 1200, and some place it as high as 4000.

September the Third was Cromwell's day. On September 3, 1650, he won the battle of Dunbar. On September 3, 1651, he won the battle of Worcester. On September 3, 1658, he died.

Seraphic Doctor (*The*), St. Bonaventura, placed by Dantê among the saints of his *Paradiso* (1221-1274).

Seraphic Saint (*The*), St. Francis d'Assisi (1182-1226).

Of all the saints, St. Francis was the most blameless and gentle.—Dean Milman.

Seraphina Arthuret (*Miss*), a papist. Her sister is Miss Angelica Arthuret.—Sir W. Scott, *Redgauntlet* (time, George III.).

Sera′pis, an Egyptian deity symbolizing the Nile, and fertility in general.

Seraskier′ (3 *syl.*), a name given by the Turks to a general of division, generally a pacha with two or three tails. (Persian, *seri asker*, "head of the army.")

... three thousand Moslems perished here,
And sixteen bayonets pierced the seraskier.
Byron, *Don Juan*, viii. 81 (1824).

Serb, a Servian or native of Servia.

Sereme′nes (4 *syl.*), brother-in-law of King Sardanapālus, to whom he entrusts his signet-ring to put down the rebellion headed by Arbācês, the Mede, and Belĕsis, the Chaldēan soothsayer. Seremēnês was slain in a battle with the insurgents.—Byron, *Sardanapalus* (1819).

Sere′na, allured by the mildness of the weather, went into the fields to gather wild flowers for a garland, when she was attacked by the Blatant Beast, who carried her off in its mouth. Her cries attracted to the spot Sir Calidore, who compelled the beast to drop its prey.—Spenser, *Faëry Queen*, vi. 3 (1596).

Sergis (*Sir*), the attendant on Irēna. He informs Sir Artegal that Irena is the captive of Grantorto, who has sworn to take her life within ten days, unless some knight will volunteer to be her champion, and in single combat prove her innocent of the crime laid to her charge.—Spenser, *Faëry Queen*, v. 11 (1596).

Sergius, a Nestorian monk, said to be the same as Boheira, who resided at Bosra, in Syria. This monk, we are told, helped Mahomet in writing the *Korân*. Some say it was Saïd or Felix Boheira.

Boheira's name, in the books of Christians, is Sergius.—Masudi, *History*, 24 (A.D. 956).

Serimner, the wild boar whose lard fed the vast multitude in Einheriar, the hall of Odin. Though fed on daily, the boar never diminished in size. Odin himself gave his own portion of the lard to his two wolves, Geri and Freki.—*Scandinavian Mythology*. (See RUSTICUS'S PIG.)

Seri′na, daughter of Lord Acasto, plighted to Chamont (the brother of Monimia, "the orphan").—Otway, *The Orphan* (1680).

Seriswattee, the Janus of Hindû mythology.

The Serpent and Satan. There is an Arabian tradition that the devil begged all the animals, one after another, to carry him into the garden, that he might speak to Adam and Eve, but they all refused except the serpent, who took him between two of its teeth. It was then the most beautiful of all the animals, and walked upon legs and feet.—Masudi, *History*, 22 (A.D. 956).

The Serpent's Punishment. The punishment of the serpent for tempting Eve was this: (1) Michael was commanded to cut off its legs; and (2) the serpent was doomed to feed on human excrements ever after.

Serpent d'Isabit, an enormous monster, whose head rested on the top of the Pic du Midi de Bigorre, its body filled the whole valley of Luz, St. Sauveur, and Gèdres, and its tail was coiled in the hollow below the cirque of Gavarnie. It fed once in three months, and supplied itself by making a very strong inspiration of its breath, whereupon every living thing around was drawn into its maw. It was ultimately killed by making a huge bonfire, and waking it from its torpor, when it became enraged, and drawing a deep breath, drew the bonfire into its maw, and died in agony.—Rev. W. Webster, *A Pyrenean Legend* (1877).

Served My God. WOLSEY said, in his fall, "Had I but served my God with half the zeal I served my king, He would not in mine age have left me naked to mine enemies."—Shakespeare, *Henry VIII.* act iii. sc. 2 (1601).

SAMRAH, when he was deposed from the government of Basorah by the Caliph Moawiyah, said, "If I had served God so well as I have served the caliph, He would never have condemned me to all eternity."

ANTONIO PEREZ, the favorite of Philip II. of Spain, said, "Mon zele etoit si grand vers ces benignes puissances [i.e. *Turin*] qui si j'en eusse eu autant pour Dieu, je ne doubte point qu'il ne m'eut deja recompensé de son paradis."

The earl of GOWRIE, when, in 1854, he was led to execution, said, "If I had served God as faithfully as I have done the king [*James VI.*], I should not have come to this end."—Spotswood, *History of the Church of Scotland*, 332, 333 (1653).

Sesostris (*The Modern*), Napoleon Bonaparte (1769, 1804-1815, 1821).

But where is he, the modern, mightier far,
Who, born no king, made monarchs draw his car;
The new Sesostris, whose unharnessed kings,
Freed from the bit, believe themselves with wings,
And spurn the dust o'er which they crawled of late,
Chained to the chariot of the chieftain's state?
Byron, *Age of Bronze* (1821).

. "Sesostris," in Fénelon's *Télémaque*, is meant for Louis XIV.

Set´ebos, a deity of the Patagonians.

His art is of such power,
It would control my dam's god Setebos.
Shakespeare, *The Tempest* (1609).

The giants, when they found themselves fettered, roared like bulls, and cried upon Setebos to help them.—Eden, *History of Travayle*.

Seth, a servant of the Jew at Ashby. Reuben is his fellow-servant.—Sir W. Scott, *Ivanhoe* (time, Richard I.).

Seth Fairchild. Young countryman, who is almost persuaded to be in love with Isabel, the wife of his brother, Albert. Albert is killed—it is supposed, accidentally—and Isabel, assuming that Seth has murdered him, and for her sake, promises to keep the deed secret. The horror of the supposition and her readiness to believe him capable of the crime, dispels Seth's unholy illusion and sends him back to his first love, who has always been his good angel.—Harold Frederic, *Seth's Brother's Wife* (1887).

Settle (*Elkana*), the poet, introduced by Sir W. Scott in *Peveril of the Peak* (time, Charles II.).

Seven Champions of Christendom (*The*): St. George for England; St. Andrew for Scotland; St. Patrick for Ireland; St. David for Wales; St. Denis for France; St. James for Spain; and St. Anthony for Italy.

. Richard Johnson wrote *The Famous History of the Seven Champions of Christendom* (1617).

Seven, Rienzi's Number.

October 7, Rienzi's foes yielded to his power.
7 months Rienzi reigned as tribune.
7 years he was absent in exile.
7 weeks of return saw him without an enemy (Oct. 7).
7 was the number of the crowns the Roman convents and the Roman council awarded him.

Seven Sleepers (*The*). The tale of these sleepers is told in divers manners. The best accounts are those in the *Korân* xviii., entitled, "The Cave, Revealed at Mecca;" *The Golden Legends*, by Jacques de Voragine; the *De Gloria Martyrum*, i. 9, by Gregory of Tours; and the *Oriental Tales*, by Comte de Caylus (1743).

Names of the Seven Sleepers. Gregory of Tours says their names were: Constantine, Dionysius, John, Maximian, Malchus, Martinian or Marcian, and Serapĭon. In the *Oriental Tales* the names given are: Jemlikha, Mekchilinia, Mechlima, Merlima, Debermouch, Charnouch, and the shepherd Keschetiouch. Their names are not given in the *Korân*.

Number of the Sleepers. Al Seyid, a Jacobite Christian of Najrân, says the sleepers were only three, with their dog; others maintain that their number was five, besides the dog; but Al Beidâwi, who is followed by most authorities, says they were seven, besides the dog.

Duration of the Sleep. The *Korân* says it was "300 years and nine years over;" the *Oriental Tales* say the same; but if Gregory of Tours is followed, the duration of the sleep was barely 230 years.

The Legend of the Seven Sleepers. (1) According to Gregory of Tours. Gregory says they were seven noble youths of Ephesus, who fled in the Decian persecution to a cave in Mount Celion, the mouth of which was blocked up by stones. After 230 years they were discovered, and awoke, but died within a few days, and were taken in a large stone coffin to Marseilles. Visitors are still shown, in St. Victor's Church, the stone coffin.

If there is any truth at all in the legend, it amounts to this: In A.D. 250, some youths (three or seven) suffered martyrdom under the Emperor Decius, "fell asleep in the Lord," and were buried in a cave of Mount Celion. In 479 (the reign of Theodosius) their bodies were discovered, and, being consecrated as holy relics, were removed to Marseilles.

(2) According to the *Oriental Tales*. Six Grecian youths were slaves in the palace of Dakiānos (*Decianus*, *Decius*). This Dakianos had risen from low degrees to kingly honors, and gave himself out to be a god. Jemlikha was led to doubt the divinity of his master, because he was unable to keep off a fly which persistently tormented him, and being roused to reflection, came to the conclusion that there must be a god to whom both Dakianos and the fly were subject. He communicated his thoughts to his companions, and they all fled from the Ephesian court till they met the shepherd Keschetiouch, whom they converted, and who showed them a cave, which no one but himself knew of. Here they fell asleep, and Dakianos, having discovered them, commanded the mouth of the cave to be closed up. Here the sleepers remained 309 years, at the expiration of which time they all awoke, but died a few hours afterwards.

The Dog of the Seven Sleepers. In the notes of the *Korân*, by Sale, the dog's name is Kratim, Kratimer, or Katmir. In the *Oriental Tales* it is Catnier, which looks like a clerical blunder for Catmer, only it occurs frequently. It is one of the ten animals admitted into Mahomet's paradise. The *Korân* tells us that the dog followed the seven young men into the cave, but they tried to drive him away, and even broke three of its legs with stones, when the dog said to them, "I love those who love God. Sleep, masters, and I will keep guard." In the *Oriental Tales* the dog is made to say, "You go to seek God, but am not I also a child of God?" Hearing this, the young men were so astounded, they went immediately, and carried the dog into the cave.

The Place of Sepulture of the Seven Sleepers. Gregory of Tours tells us that the bodies were removed from Mount Celion in a stone coffin to Marseilles. The *Korân*, with Sale's notes, informs us they were buried in the cave, and a chapel was built there to mark the site. (See SLEEPER.)

The Seven Sleepers turning on their sides. William of Malmesbury says that Edward the Confessor, in his mind's eye, saw the seven sleepers turn from their right sides to their left, and (he adds) whenever they turn on their sides, it indicates great disasters to Christendom.

Woe, woe to England! I have seen a vision:
The seven sleepers in the cave of Ephesus
Have turned from right to left.
Tennyson, *Harold*, i. 1.

Seven Wise Masters. Lucien, the son of Dolopathos, was placed under the charge of Virgil, and was tempted in manhood by his step-mother. He repelled her advances, and she accused him to the king of taking liberties with her. By consulting the stars it was discovered that if he could tide over seven days his life would be spared; so seven wise masters undertook to tell the king a tale each, in illustration of rash judgments. When they had all told their tales, the prince related, under the disguise of a tale, the story of the queen's wantonness; whereupon Lucien was restored to favor, and the queen was put to death.—Sandabar, *Parables* (contemporary with King Courou).

⁎⁎* John Rolland, of Dalkeith, has rendered this legend into Scotch verse. There is an Arabic version by Nasr Allah (twelfth century), borrowed from the Indian by Sandabar. In the Hebrew version by Rabbi Joel (1270), the legend is called *Kalilah and Dimnah*.

Seven Wise Men (*The*).

One of Plutarch's *brochures* in the *Moralia* is entitled "The Banquet of the Seven Wise Men," in which Periander is made to give an account of a contest at Chalcis between Homer and Hesiod, in which the latter wins the prize, and receives a tripod, on which he caused to be engraved this inscription:

This Hesiod vows to the Heliconian nine,
In Chalcis won from Homer the divine.

Seven Wise Men of Greece (*The*), seven Greeks of the sixth century B.C., noted for their maxims.

BIAS. His maxim was, "Most men are bad" ("There is none that doeth good, no, not one," *Psalm* xiv. 3): Οἱ πλέιους κακοί (fl. B.C. 550).

CHILO. "Consider the end:" Τέλος ὁρᾶν μακροῦ βίου (fl. B.C. 590).

CLEOBŪLOS. "Avoid extremes" (the golden mean): Ἄριστον μέτρον (fl. B.C. 580).

PERIANDER. "Nothing is impossible to industry" (patience and perseverance overcome mountains): Μελέτη τὸ πᾶν (B.C. 665-585).

PITTĂCOS. "Know thy opportunity" (seize time by the forelock): Καιρὸν γνῶθι (B.C. 652-569).

SOLON. "Know thyself:" Γνῶθι σεαυτὸν (B.C. 638-558).

THĀLES (2 *syl.*). "Suretyship is the forerunner of ruin." ("He that hateth suretyship is sure," *Prov.* xi. 15): Εγγύα, πάρα δ' ἄτη (B.C. 636-546).

First Solon, who made the Athenian laws,
While Chilo, in Sparta, was famed for his saws;
In Milētos did Thalês astronomy teach;
Bias used in Priēnê his morals to preach;
Cleobūlos of Lindos, was handsome and wise;
Mitylēnê, gainst thraldom saw Pittăcos rise;
Periander is said to have gained, thro' his court,
The title that Myson, the Chenian, ought.

⁎ It is Plato who says that Myson should take the place of Periander as one of the Seven Wise Men.

Seven Years.

Barbarossa changes his position in his sleep every seven years.

Charlemagne starts in his chair from sleep every seven years.

Ogier, the Dane, stamps his iron mace on the floor every seven years.

Olaf Redbeard of Sweden uncloses his eyes every seven years.

Seven Year's War (*The*), the war maintained by Frederick II. of Prussia against Austria, Russia, and France (1756-1763).

Seven Against Thebes (*The*). At the death of Œdĭpus, his two sons, Eteŏclês and Polynīcês, agreed to reign alternate years, but at the expiration of the first year Eteoclês refused to resign the crown to his brother. Whereupon, Polynicês induced six others to join him in besieging Thebes, but the expedition was a failure. The names of the seven Grecian chiefs who marched against Thebes were: Adrastos, Amphiarāos, Kapaneus, Hippomedon (*Argives*), Parthenopæos (*an Arcadian*), Polynicês (*a Theban*), and Tydeus (*an Æolian*). (See EPIGONI.)

Æschylos has a tragedy on the subject.

Severn, a corruption of Averne, daughter of Astrild. The legend is this: King Locryn was engaged to Gwendolen, daughter of Corīneus, but seeing Astrild (daughter of the king of Germany), who came to this island with Homber, king of Hungary, fell in love with her. While Corineus lived he durst not offend him, so he married Gwendolen, but kept Astrild as his mistress, and had by her a daughter (Averne). When Corineus died, he divorced Gwendolen, and declared Astrild queen, but Gwendolen summoned her vassals, dethroned Locryn, and caused both Astrild and Averne to be cast into the river, ever since called Severn fron Averne "the kinges dohter."

Sevier (*Dr.*), New Orleans physician. "His inner heart was all of flesh, but his demands for the rectitude of mankind pointed out like the muzzles of cannon through the embrasures of his virtues." He befriends the struggling Richlings, setting John upon his feet time and again, and in his last illness, never leaving him until he goes out and closes the door upon the dying man, reunited to his wife and child. Dr. Sevier finds work for the widow, and educates little Alice, named for his own dead wife.

"And oh! when they two, who have never joined hands on this earth, go to meet John and Alice,—which GOD grant may be at one and the same time,— what weeping there will be among GOD'S poor!"—George W. Cable, *Dr. Sevier* (1883).

Sewall (*Judge*) Colonial judge in Massachusetts. He has left in his diary a circumstantial account of his courtship of Madam Winthrop, also a curious "confession" made by him in church of the "Guilt contracted upon the opening of the late Commission of Oyer and Terminer, at Salem."—*Sewall Papers* (1697).

Sewall (*Rev. Mr.*). Boston clergyman, liberal in opinion, and large of heart. He counsels the Lapham parents in their family perplexities, and becomes the not-too-willing sponsor of Lemuel Barker, a rustic aspirant after literary honors.—W. L. Howells, *The Rise of Silas Lapham* and *The Minister's Charge*.

Sex. Milton says that spirits can assume either sex at pleasure, and Michael Psellus asserts that demons can take what sex, shape, and color they please, and can also contract or dilate their forms at pleasure.

For spirits when they please,
Can either sex assume, or both; so soft
And uncompounded is their essence pure;
Not tied or manacled with joint and limb,
Nor founded on the brittle strength of bones,
Like cumbrous flesh.
Paradise Lost, i. 423, etc. (1665).

Sex. Cæneus and Tire´sias were at one part of their lives of the male sex, and at another part of their lives of the female sex. (See these names.)

Iphis was first a woman, and then a man.—Ovid, *Metamorphoses*, ix. 12; xiv 699.

Sextus [Tarquinius]. There are several points of resemblance in the story of Sextus and that of Paris, son of Priam. (1) Paris was the guest of Menelāos, when he eloped with his wife, Helen; and Sextus was the guest of Lucretia when he defiled her. (2) The elopement of Helen was the cause of a national war between the Greek cities and the allied cities of Troy; and the defilement of Lucretia was the cause of a national war between Rome and the allied cities under Por´sena. (3) The contest between Greece and Troy terminated in the victory of Greece, the injured party; and the contest between Rome and the supporters of Tarquin terminated in favor of Rome, the injured party. (4) In the Trojan war, Paris, the aggressor, showed himself before the Trojan ranks, and defied the bravest of the Greeks to single combat, but when Menelaos appeared, he took to flight; and so Sextus rode vauntingly against the Roman host, but when Herminius appeared, fled to the rear like a coward. (5) In the Trojan contest, Priam and his sons fell in battle; and in the battle of Lake Regillus, Tarquin and his sons were slain.

⁎ Lord Macaulay has taken the "Battle of Lake Regillus" as the subject of one of his *Lays of Ancient Rome*. Another of his lays, called "Horatius," is the attempt of Porsĕna to re-establish Tarquin on the throne.

Seyd, pacha of the Morea, assassinated by Gulnare (2 *syl.*), his favorite concubine. Gulnare was rescued from the burning harem by Conrad, "the Corsair." Conrad, in the disguise of a dervise, was detected and seized in the palace of Seyd, and Gulnare, to effect his liberation, murdered the pacha.—Byron, *The Corsair* (1814).

Seyton (*Lord*), a supporter of Queen Mary's cause.

Catherine Seyton, daughter of Lord Seyton, a maid of honor in the Court of Queen Mary. She appears at Kinross village in disguise.

Henry Seyton, son of Lord Seyton.—Sir W. Scott, *The Abbot* (time, Elizabeth).

Sforza, of Lombardy. He with his two brothers (Achilles and Palamēdês) were in the squadron of adventurers in the allied Christian army.—Tasso, *Jerusalem Delivered* (1575).

*** The word Sforza means "force," and, according to tradition, was derived thus: Giacomuzzo Attendolo, the son of a day laborer, being desirous of going to the wars, consulted his hatchet, resolving to enlist if it stuck fast in the tree at which he flung it. He threw it with such *force* that the whole blade was completely buried in the trunk (fifteenth century).

Sforza (Ludov'ico), duke of Milan, surnamed "the More," from *mora*, "a mulberry" (because he had on his arm a birth-stain of a mulberry color). Ludovico was dotingly fond of his bride, Marcelia, and his love was amply returned; but during his absence in the camp, he left Francesco lord protector, and Francesco assailed the fidelity of the young duchess. Failing in his villainy, he accused her to the duke of playing the wanton with him, and the duke, in a fit of jealousy, slew her. Sforza was afterwards poisoned by Eugenia (sister of Francesco), whom he had seduced.

Nina Sforza, the duke's daughter.—Massinger, *The Duke of Milan* (1622).

*** This tragedy is obviously an imitation of Shakespeare's *Othello* (1611).

Sganarelle, the "cocu imaginaire," of Molière's comedy (1660). The plot runs thus: Célie was betrothed to Lélie, but her father, Gorgĭbus, insisted on her marrying Valère, because he was the richer man. Célie fainted on hearing this, and dropped her lover's miniature, which was picked up by Sganarelle's wife. Sganarelle, thinking it to be the portrait of a gallant, took possession of it, and Lélie asked him how he came by it. Sganarelle said he took it from his wife, and Lélie supposed that Célie had become the wife of Sganarelle. A series of misapprehensions arose thence: Célie supposed that Lélie had deserted her for Madame Sganarelle; Sganarelle supposed that his wife was unfaithful to him; madame supposed that her husband was an adorer of Célie; and Lélie supposed that Célie was the wife of Sganarelle. In time they met together, when Lélie charged Célie with being married to Sganarelle; both stared, an explanation followed, when a messenger arrived to say that Valère was married.—Molière, *Le Cocu Imaginaire*.

Sganarelle, younger brother of Ariste (2 *syl.*); a surly, domineering, conceited fellow, the dupe of the play. His brother says to him, "Cette farouche humeur à tous vos procédés inspire un air bizarre, et, jusques à l'habit, rend tout chez vous barbare." The father of Isabelle and Léonor, on his death-bed, committed them to the charge of Sganarelle and Ariste, who were either to marry them or dispose of them in marriage. Sganarelle chose Isabelle, but insisted on her dressing in serge, going to bed early, keeping at home, looking after the house, mending the linen, knitting socks, and never flirting with any one. The consequence was, she duped her guardian, and cajoled him into giving his signature to her marriage with Valère.—Molière, *L'Ecole des Maris*.

Sganarelle (3 *syl.*). At about 63 years of age, Sganarelle wished to marry Dorimène (3 *syl.*), daughter of Alcantor, a girl fond of dances, parties of pleasure, and all the active enjoyments of young life. Feeling some doubts about the wisdom of this step, he first consults a friend, who dissuades him, but, seeing the advice is rejected, replies "Do as you like." He next consults two philosophers, but they are so absorbed in their philosophy, that they pay no attention to him. He then asks the gypsies, who take his money and decamp with a dance. At length, he overhears Dorimène telling a young lover that she only marries the old dotard for his money, and that he cannot live above a few months; so he makes up his mind to decline the marriage. The father of the lady places the matter in his son's hands, and the young fire-eater, armed with two swords, goes at once to the old *fiancé*, and begs him to choose one. When Sganarelle declines to fight, the young man beats him soundly, and again bids him choose a sword. After two or three good beatings, Sganarelle consents to the marriage "forcé."—Molière, *Le Mariage Forcé* (1664).

Molière wrote *Sganarelle ou Le Cocu Imaginaire* (*q.v.*) as a supplement to this comedy.

*** This joke about marrying is borrowed from Rabelais, *Pantagruel*, iii. 35, etc. Panurge asks Trouillogan whether he would advise him to marry. The sage says "No." "But I wish to do so," says the prince. "Then do so, by all means," says the sage. "Which, then, would you advise?" asks Panurge. "Neither," says Trouillogan. "But," says Panurge, "that is not possible." "Then both," says the sage. After this, Panurge consults many others on the subject, and lastly the oracle of the Holy Bottle.

The plot of Molière's comedy is founded on an adventure recorded of the count of Grammont (*q.v.*). The count had promised marriage to la belle Hamilton, but deserted her, and tried to get to France. Being overtaken by the two brothers of the lady, they clapped their hands on their swords, and demanded if the count had not forgotten something or left something behind. "True," said the count; "I have forgotten to marry your sister;" and returned with the two brothers to repair this oversight.

Sganarelle, father of Lucinde. Anxious about his daughter because she has lost her vivacity and appetite, he sends for four physicians, who retire to consult upon the case, but talk only on indifferent topics. When Sganarelle asks the result of their deliberation, they all differ, both in regard to the disease, and the remedy to be applied. Lisette (the lady's maid) sends for Clitandre, the lover, who comes disguised as a quack doctor, tells Sganarelle that the young lady's disease must be acted on through the imagination, and prescribes a mock marriage. Sganarelle consents to the experiment, but Clitandre's assistant being a notary, the mock marriage proves to be a real one.—Molière, *L'Amour Médecin* (1665).

Sganarelle, husband of Martine. He is a faggot-maker, and has a quarrel with his wife, who vows to be even with him for striking her. Valère and Lucas (two domestics of Géronte) ask her to direct them to the house of a noted doctor. She sends them to her husband, and tells them he is so eccentric that he will deny being a doctor, but they must beat him well. So they find the faggot-maker, whom they beat soundly, till he consents to follow them. He is introduced to Lucinde, who pretends to be dumb, but, being a shrewd man, he soon finds out that the dumbness is only a pretence, and takes with him Léandre as an apothecary. The two lovers understand each other, and Lucinde is rapidly cured with "pills matrimoniac."—Molière, *Le Médecin Malgré Lui* (1666).

⁂ Sganarelle being asked by the father what he thinks is the matter with Lucinde, replies, "Entendez-vous le Latin?" "En aucune façon," says Géronte. "Vous n'entendez point le Latin?" "Non, monsieur." "That is a sad pity," says Sganarelle, "for the case may be briefly stated thus:

Cabricias arci thuram, catalamus, singulariter, nominativo, hæc musa, *la muse*, bonus, bona, bonum. Deus sanctus, estne oratio Latinas? etiam, *oui*, quare? *pourquoi?* quia substantivo et adjectivum concordat in generi, numerum, et casus." "Wonderful man!" says the father.—Act iii.

Sganarelle (3 *syl.*), valet to Don Juan. He remonstrates with his master on his evil ways, but is forbidden sternly to repeat his impertinent admonitions. His praise of tobacco, or rather snuff, is somewhat amusing:

Tabac est la passion des honnêtes gens; et qui vit sans tabac n'est pas digne de vivre. Non seulement il réjouit et purge les cerveaux humains, mais encore il instruit les ames à la vertu, et l'on apprend avec lui à devenir honnête homme ... il inspire des sentiments d'honneur à tous ceux qui en prennent.—Molière, *Don Juan*, i. 1 (1665).

Shaccabac, in *Blue Beard*. (See SCHACABAC.)

I have seen strange sights. I have seen Wilkinson play "Macbeth;" Matthews, "Othello;" Wrench, "George Barnwell;" Buckstone, "Iago;" Rayner, "Penruddock;" Keeley, "Shylock;" Liston, "Romeo" and "Octavian;" G. F. Cooke, "Mercutio;" John Kemble, "Archer;" Edmund Kean, clown in a pantomine; and C. Young, "Shaccabac."—*Record of a Stage Veteran*.

"Macbeth," "Othello," "Iago" (in *Othello*), "Shylock" (*Merchant of Venice*), "Romeo" and "Mercutio" (in *Romeo and Juliet*), all by Shakespeare: "George Barnwell" (Lillo's tragedy so called); "Penruddock" (in *The Wheel of Fortune*), by Cumberland); "Octavian" (in Colman's drama so called); "Archer" (in *The Beaux' Stratagem*, by Farquhar).

Shackfords (*The*). *Lemuel Shackford*, "a hard, avaricious, passionate man, holding his own way remorselessly.... A prominent character because of his wealth, endless lawsuits and eccentricity."

Richard Shackford, nephew of *Lemuel*, a frank, whole-souled young fellow, intent upon his profession, but willing to make everybody else comfortable as he wins his way up. He is accused, upon circumstantial evidence, of the murder of his uncle, but is extricated by his own sagacity, which enables him to fix the crime upon the true assassin.—T. B. Aldrich, *The Stillwater Tragedy* (1880).

Shaddai (*King*), who made war upon Diabolus for the regaining of Mansoul.—John Bunyan, *The Holy War* (1682).

Shade (*To fight in the*). Dieneces [*Di.en´.e.seez*], the Spartan, being told that the army of the Persians was so numerous that their arrows would shut out the sun, replied, "Thank the gods! we shall then fight in the shade."

Shadow (*Simon*), one of the recruits of the army of Sir John Falstaff. "A half-faced fellow," so thin that Sir John said, "A foeman might as well level his gun at the edge of a penknife" as at such a starveling.—Shakespeare, 2 *Henry IV*. act iii. sc. 2 (1598).

Shadrach, Meshach and Abednego were cast, by the command of Nebuchadnezzar, into a fiery furnace, but received no injury, although the furnace was made so hot that the heat thereof "slew those men" that took them to the furnace.-*Dan*. iii. 22.

By Nimrod's order, Abraham was bound and cast into a huge fire at Cûtha; but he was preserved from injury by the angel Gabriel, and only the cords which bound him were burnt. Yet so intense was the heat that above 2000 men were consumed thereby.—See *Gospel of Barnabas*, xxviii.; and Morgan, *Mahometanism Explained*, V. i. 4.

Shadwell (*Thomas*), the poet-laureate, was a great drunkard, and was said to be "round as a butt, and liquored every chink" (1640-1692).

Besides, his [*Shadwell's*] goodly fabric fills the eye,
And seems designed for thoughtless majesty.
Dryden, *MacFlecknoe* (1682).

⁎ Shadwell took opium, and died from taking too large a dose. Hence Pope says:

Benlowes, propitious still to blockheads, bows;
And Shadwell nods the poppy on his brows.
The Dunciad, iii. 21, 22 (1728).

Benlowes was a great patron of bad poets, and many have dedicated to him their lucubrations. Sometimes the name is shifted into "Benevolus."

Shaf′alus and Procrus. So Bottom, the weaver, calls Cephălus and Procris. (See CEPHALUS.)

Pyramus. Not Shafalus to Procrus was so true.

Thisbe. As Shafalus to Procrus; I to you.

Shakespeare, *Midsummer Night's Dream* (1592).

Shaftesbury (*Anthony Ashley Cooper, earl of*), introduced by Sir W. Scott in *Peveril of the Peak* (time, Charles II.).

Shafton (*Ned*), one of the prisoners in Newgate with old Sir Hildebrand Osbaldistone.—Sir W. Scott, *Rob Roy* (time, George I.).

Shafton (*Sir Piercie*), called "The knight of Wolverton," a fashionable cavaliero, grandson of old Overstitch, the tailor, of Holderness. Sir Piercie talks in the pedantic style of the Elizabethan courtiers.—Sir W. Scott, *The Monastery* (time, Elizabeth).

Shah (*The*), a famous diamond, weighing 86 carats. It was given by Chosroës, of Persia, to the Czar of Russia. (See DIAMONDS.)

Shakebag (*Dick*), a highwayman with Captain Colepepper.—Sir W. Scott, *Fortunes of Nigel* (time, James I.).

Shakespeare, introduced by Sir W. Scott in the ante-rooms of Greenwich Palace.—Sir W. Scott, *Kenilworth* (time, Elizabeth).

⁎ In *Woodstock* there is a conversation about Shakespeare.

Shakespeare's Home. He left London before 1613, and established himself at Stratford-on-Avon, in Warwickshire, where he was born (1564), and where he died (1616). In the diary of Mr. Ward, the vicar of Stratford, is this entry: "Shakspeare, Drayton and Ben Jonson had a merry meeting, and, it seems, drank too hard, for Shakspeare died of a fever then contracted." (Drayton died 1631, and Ben Jonson, 1637.) Probably Shakespeare died on his birthday, April 23.

Shakespeare's Monument, in Westminster Abbey, designed by Kent, and executed by Scheemakers, in 1742. The statue to Shakespeare in Drury Lane Theatre was by the same.

The statue of Shakespeare in the British Museum is by Roubiliac, and was bequeathed to the nation by Garrick. His best portrait is by Droeshout.

Shakespeare's Plays, quarto editions:

ROMEO AND JULIET: 1597, John Danter; 1599, Thomas Creede for Cuthbert Burby; 1609, 1637. Supposed to have been written, 1595.

KING RICHARD II.: 1597, Valentine Simmes for Andrew Wise; 1598, 1608 (with an additional scene); 1615, 1634.

KING RICHARD III.: 1597, ditto; 1598, 1602, 1612, 1622.

LOVE'S LABOR'S LOST; 1598, W. W. for Cuthbert Burby. Supposed to have been written, 1594.

KING HENRY IV. (pt. I): 1598, P. S. for Andrew Wise; 1599, 1604, 1608, 1613. Supposed to have been written, 1597.

KING HENRY IV. (pt. 2): 1600, V. S. for Andrew Wise and William Aspley; 1600. Supposed to have been written, 1598.

KING HENRY V.: 1600, Thomas Creede for Thomas Millington and John Busby; 1602, 1608. Supposed to have been written, 1599.

MIDSUMMER NIGHT'S DREAM: 1600, Thomas Fisher; 1600, James Roberts. Mentioned by Meres, 1598. Supposed to have been written, 1592.

MERCHANT OF VENICE: 1600, I. R. for Thomas Heyes; 1600, James Roberts; 1637. Mentioned by Meres, 1598.

MUCH ADO ABOUT NOTHING: 1600, V. S. for Andrew Wise and William Aspley.

MERRY WIVES OF WINDSOR: 1602, T. C. for Arthur Johnson; 1619. Supposed to have been written, 1596.

HAMLET: 1603, I. R. for N. L.; 1605, 1611. Supposed to have been written, 1597.

KING LEAR: 1608, A. for Nathaniel Butter; 1608, B. for ditto. Acted at Whitehall, 1607. Supposed to have been written, 1605.

TROILUS AND CRESSIDA: 1609, G. Eld for R. Bonian and H. Whalley (with a preface). Acted at court, 1609. Supposed to have been written, 1602.

OTHELLO: 1622, N. O. for Thomas Walkely. Acted at Harefield, 1602.

The rest of the dramas are:

All's Well that Ends Well, 1598. First title supposed to be *Love's Labor's Won*.

Antony and Cleopatra, 1608. No early mention made of this play.

As You Like It. Entered at Stationer's Hall, 1600.

Comedy of Errors, 1593. Mentioned by Meres, 1598.

Coriolanus, 1610. No early mention made of this play.

Cymbeline, 1605. No early mention made of this play.

1 *Henry VI.* Alluded to by Nash in *Pierce Penniless*, 1592.

2 *Henry VI.* Original title, *First Part of the Contention*, 1594.

3 *Henry VI.* Original title, *True Tragedy of Richard Duke of York*, 1595.

Henry VIII., 1601. Acted at the Globe Theatre, 1613.

John (King), 1596. Mentioned by Meres, 1598.

Julius Cæsar, 1607. No early mention made of this play.

Lear, 1605. Acted at Whitehall 1607. Printed 1608.

Macbeth, 1606. No early mention made of this play.

Measure for Measure, 1603. Acted at Whitehall 1604.

Merry Wives of Windsor, 1596. Printed 1602.

Pericles Prince of Tyre. Printed 1609.

Taming of the Shrew. (?) Acted at Henslow's Theatre, 1593. Entered at Stationer's Hall, 1607.

Tempest, 1609. Acted at Whitehall, 1611.

Timon of Athens, 1609. No early mention made of this play.

Titus Andronicus, 1593. Printed 1600.

Twelfth Night. Acted in the Middle Temple Hall, 1602.

Two Gentlemen of Verona, 1595. Mentioned by Meres 1598.

Winter's Tale, 1604. Acted at Whitehall, 1611.

First complete collection in folio; 1623, Isaac Jaggard and Ed. Blount; 1632, 1664, 1685. The second folio is of very little value.

Shakespeare's Parents. His father was John Shakespeare, a glover, who married Mary Arden, daughter of Robert Arden, Esq., of Bomich, a good country gentleman.

Shakespeare's Wife, Anne Hathaway, of Shottery, some eight years older than himself; daughter of a substantial yeoman.

Shakespeare's Children. One son, Hamnet, who died in his twelfth year (1585-1596). Two daughters, who survived him, Susanna and Judith, twin-born with Hamnet. Both his daughters married and had children, but the lines died out.

Voltaire says of Shakespeare: "Rimer had very good reason to say that Shakespeare *n'etait q'un vilain singe.*" Voltaire, in 1765, said, "Shakespeare is a savage with some imagination, whose plays can please only in London and Canada." In 1735 he wrote to M. de Cideville, "Shakespeare is the Corneille of London, but everywhere else he is a great fool (*grand fou d'ailleur*)."

Shakespeare of Divines (*The*), Jeremy Taylor (1613-1667).

Taylor, the Shakespeare of divines.—Emerson.

Shakespeare of Eloquence (*The*). The comte de Mirabeau was so called by Barnave (1749-1791).

Shakespeare of Germany (*The*), Augustus Frederick Ferdinand von Kotzebue (1761-1819).

Shakespeare of Prose Fiction (*The*). Richardson, the novelist, is so called by D'Israeli (1689-1761).

Shallow, a weak-minded country justice, cousin to Slender. He is a great braggart, and especially fond of boasting of the mad pranks of his younger days. It is said that Justice Shallow is a satirical portrait of Sir Thomas Lucy of Charlecote, who prosecuted Shakespeare for deer-stealing.—Shakespeare, *The Merry Wives of Windsor* (1596); and 2 *Henry IV.* (1598).

As wise as a justice of the quorum and custalorum in Shallow's time.—Macaulay.

Shallum, lord of a manor consisting of a long chain of rocks and mountains called Tirzah. Shallum was "of gentle disposition, and beloved both by God and man." He was the lover of Hilpa, a Chinese antediluvian princess, one of the 150 daughters of Zilpah, of the race of Cohu or Cain.—Addison, *Spectator*, viii. 584-5 (1712).

Shalott (*The lady of*), a poem by Tennyson, in four parts. Pt. i. tells us that the lady passed her life in the island of Shalott in great seclusion, and was known only by the peasantry. Pt. ii. tells us that she was weaving a magic web, and that a curse would fall on her if she looked down the river. Pt. iii. describes how Sir Lancelot rode to Camelot in all his bravery; and the lady gazed at him as he rode along. Pt. iv. tells us that the lady floated down the river in a boat called *The Lady of Shalott*, and died heart-broken on the way. Sir Lancelot came to gaze on the dead body, and exclaimed, "She has a lovely face, God in his mercy grant her grace!" This ballad was afterwards expanded into the *Idyll* called "Elaine, the Lily Maid of Astolat" (*q.v.*), the beautiful incident of Elaine and the barge being taken from the *History of Prince Arthur*, by Sir T. Malory.

"While my body is whole, let this letter be put into my right hand, and my hand bound fast with the letter until I be cold, and let me be put in a fair bed with all the richest clothes that I have about me, and so let my bed and all my rich clothes be laid with me in a chariot to the next place whereas the Thames is, and there let me be put in a barge, and but one man with me such as ye trust to steer me thither, and that my barge be covered with black samite over and over." ... So when she was dead, the corpse and the bed and all was led the next way unto to the Thames, and there a man and the corpse and all were put in a barge on the Thames, and so the man steered the barge to Westminster, and there he rowed a great while to and fro, or any man espied.—Pt. iii. 123.

King Arthur saw the body and had it buried, and Sir Lancelot made an offering, etc. (ch. 124); much the same as Tennyson has reproduced it in verse.

Shalott (The lady of). "It is not generally known that the lady of Shalott lived, last summer, in an attic at the east end of South Street." Thus begins a story of an incurable invalid, whose only amusement is watching street scenes reflected in a small mirror hung opposite the one window of her garret-room. A stone flung by a boy shatters the mirror, and the fragile creature never recovers from the shock.—Elizabeth Stuart Phelps, *The Lady of Shalott*.

Shamho′zai (3 *syl.*), the angel who debauched himself with women, repented, and hung himself up between earth and heaven.—Bereshit rabbi (in *Gen.* vi. 2).

⁂ Harût and Marût were two angels sent to be judges on earth. They judged righteously until Zohara appeared before them, when they fell in love with her, and were imprisoned in a cave near Babylon, where they are to abide till the day of judgment.

Shandy (*Tristram*), the nominal hero of Sterne's novel called *The Life and Opinions of Tristram Shandy, Gentleman* (1759). He is the son of Walter and Elizabeth Shandy.

Captain Shandy, better known as "Uncle Toby," the real hero of Sterne's novel. Captain Shandy was wounded at Namur, and retired on half-pay. He was benevolent and generous, brave as a lion but simple as a child, most gallant and most modest. Hazlitt says that "the character of Uncle Toby is the finest compliment ever paid to human nature." His modest love-passages with Widow Wadman, his kindly sympathy for Lieutenant Lefevre, and his military discussions, are wholly unrivalled.

Aunt Dinah [Shandy], Walter Shandy's aunt. She bequeathed to him £1000, which Walter fancied would enable him to carry out all the wild schemes with which his head was crammed.

Mrs. Elizabeth Shandy, mother of Tristram Shandy. The ideal of nonentity, individual from its very absence of individuality.

Walter Shandy, Tristram's father, a metaphysical Don Quixote, who believes in long noses and propitious names; but his son's nose was crushed, and his name, which should have been Trismegistus ("the most propitious"), was changed in christening to Tristram ("the most unlucky"). If much learning can make man mad, Walter Shandy was certainly mad in all the affairs of ordinary life. His wife was a blank sheet, and he himself a sheet so written on and crossed and rewritten that no one could decipher the manuscript.—L. Sterne, *The Life and Opinions of Tristram Shandy* (1759).

Sharp, the ordinary of Major Touchwood, who aids him in his transformation, but is himself puzzled to know which is the real and which the false colonel.—T. Dibdin, *What Next?*

Sharp (Rebecca), the orphan daughter of an artist. "She was small and slight in person, pale, sandy-haired, and with green eyes, habitually cast down, but very large, odd, and attractive when they looked up." Becky had the "dismal precocity of poverty," and, being engaged as governess in the family of Sir Pitt Crawley, bart., contrived to marry, clandestinely, his son, Captain Rawdon Crawley, and taught him how to live in splendor "upon nothing a year." Becky was an excellent singer and dancer, a capital talker and wheedler, and a most attractive, but unprincipled, selfish, and unscrupulous woman. Lord Steyne introduced her to court; but her conduct with this peer gave rise to a terrible scandal, which caused a separation between her and Rawdon, and made England too hot to hold her. She retired to the Continent, was reduced to a Bohemian life, but ultimately attached herself to Joseph Sedley, whom she contrived to strip of all his money, and who lived in dire terror of her, dying in six months under very suspicious circumstances.—Thackeray, *Vanity Fair* (1848).

Sharp (Timothy), the "lying valet" of Charles Gayless. His object is to make his master, who has not a sixpence in the world, pass for a man of wealth in the eyes of Melissa, to whom he is engaged.—Garrick, *The Lying Valet* (1741).

Sharp-Beak, the crow's wife, in the beast-epic called *Reynard the Fox* (1498).

Sharpe (*The Right Rev. James*), archbishop of St. Andrew's, murdered by John Balfour (a leader in the covenanters' army) and his party.—Sir W. Scott, *Old Mortality* (time, Charles II.).

Sharper (*Master*), the cutler in the Strand.—Sir W. Scott, *Peveril of the Peak* (time, Charles II.).

Sharpitlaw (*Gideon*), a police officer.—Sir W. Scott, *Heart of Midlothian* (time, George II.).

Shawonda′see, son of Mudjekeewis, and king of the south wind. Fat and lazy, listless and easy. Shawondasee loved a prairie maiden (the Dandelion), but was too indolent to woo her.—Longfellow, *Hiawatha* (1855).

She Stoops to Conquer, a comedy by Oliver Goldsmith (1773). Miss Hardcastle, knowing how bashful young Marlow is before ladies, *stoops* to the manners and condition of a barmaid, with whom he feels quite at his ease, and by this artifice wins the man of her choice.

⁎ It is said that when Goldsmith was about 16 years old, he set out for Edgworthstown, and finding night coming on when at Ardagh, asked a man "which was the best house in town"—meaning the best inn. The man, who was Cornelius O'Kelly, the great fencing-master, pointed to that of Mr. Ralph Fetherstone, as being the best house in the vicinity. Oliver entered the parlor, found the master of the mansion sitting over a good fire, and said he intended to pass the night there, and should like to have supper. Mr. Fetherstone happened to know Goldsmith's father, and, to humor the joke, pretended to be the landlord of "the public," nor did he reveal himself till next morning at breakfast, when Oliver called for his bill. It was not Sir Ralph Fetherstone, as is generally said, but Mr. Ralph Fetherstone, whose grandson was Sir Thomas.

Sheba. The queen of Sheba, or Saba (*i.e.* the Sabeans) came to visit Solomon, and tested his wisdom by sundry questions, but affirmed that his wisdom and wealth exceeded even her expectations.—1 *Kings* x.; 2 *Chron.* ix.

No, not to answer, madam, all those hard things
That Sheba came to ask of Solomon.
Tennyson, *The Princess*, ii.

⁎ The Arabs call her name Balkis, or Belkis; the Abyssinians, Macqueda; and others, Aazis.

Sheba (*The queen of*), a name given to Mde. Montreville (the Begum Mootee Mahul).—Sir W. Scott, *The Surgeon's Daughter* (time, George II.).

Shebdiz, the Persian Bucephalos, the favorite charger of Chosroës II., or Khosrou Parvis, of Persia (590-628).

Shedad, king of Ad, who built a most magnificent palace, and laid out a garden called "The Garden of Irem," like "the bowers of Eden." All men admired this palace and garden, except the prophet Houd, who told the king that the foundation of his palace was not secure. And so it was, that God, to punish his pride, first sent a drought of three years' duration, and then the Sarsar, or icy wind, for seven days, in which the garden was destroyed, the palace ruined, and Shedad, with all his subjects, died.

It is said that the palace of Shedad, or Shuddaud, took 500 years in building, and when it was finished the angel of death would not allow him even to enter his garden, but struck him dead, and the rose garden of Irem was ever after invisible to the eye of man.—Southey, *Thalaba, the Destroyer*, 1. (1797).

Sheep-Dog (*A*), a lady-companion, who occupies the back seat of the barouche, carries wraps, etc., goes to church with the lady,and "guards her from the wolves," as much as the lady wishes to be guarded, but no more.

"Rawdon," said Becky, ... "I must have a sheep-dog ... I mean a *moral* shepherd's dog ... to keep the wolves off me." ... "A sheep-dog, a companion! Becky Sharp with a sheep-dog! Isn't that good fun!"—Thackeray, *Vanity Fair*, xxxvii. (1848).

Sheep of the Prisons, a cant term in the French Revolution for a spy under the jailers.—C. Dickens, *A Tale of Two Cities*, iii. 7 (1859).

Sheep Tilted at. Don Quixote saw the dust of two flocks of sheep coming in opposite directions, and told Sancho they were two armies—one commanded by the Emperor Alifanfaron, sovereign of the island of Trap´oban, and the other by the king of the Garaman´teans, called "Pentap´olin with the Naked Arm." He said that Alifanfaron was in love with Pentapolin's daughter, but Pentapolin refused to sanction the alliance, because Alifanfaron was a Mohammedan. The mad knight rushed on the flock "led by Alifanfaron," and killed seven of the sheep, but was stunned by stones thrown at him by the shepherds. When Sancho told his master that the two armies were only two flocks of sheep, the knight replied that the enchanter Freston had "metamorphosed the two grand armies" in order to show his malice.—Cervantes, *Don Quixote*, I. iii. 4 (1605).

⁎ After the death of Achillês, Ajax and Ulysses both claimed the armor of Hector. The dispute was settled by the sons of Atreus (2 *syl.*), who awarded the prize to Ulysses. This so enraged Ajax that it drove him mad, and he fell upon a flock of sheep driven at night into the camp, supposing it to be an army led by Ulysses and the sons of Atreus. When he found out his mistake, he stabbed himself. This is the subject of a tragedy by Soph´oclês called *Ajax Mad.*

※ Orlando in his madness also fell foul of a flock of sheep.—Ariosto, *Orlando Furioso* (1516).

Sheffield (*The Bard of*), James Montgomery, author of *The Wanderer of Switzerland*, etc. (1771-1854).

With broken lyre and cheek serenely pale,
Lo! Sad Alcæus wanders down the vale ...
O'er his lost works let classic Sheffield weep;
May no rude hand disturb their early sleep!
Byron, *English Bards and Scotch Reviewers* (1809).

Sheila, pretty, simple-hearted girl, whose father is a magnate among his neighbors in the Orkney Islands. Sheila is won by a Londoner—Lavender by name—who visits her island home. He transplants the Northern wild flower into a London home, where she pines for a while, homesick and heart-sick. In time, her sound sense enables her to adjust herself to altered conditions, and her stronger nature raises and ennobles her husband's.—William Black, *A Princess of Thulè*.

Shelby (*Mr.*), Uncle Tom's first master. Being in commercial difficulties, he was obliged to sell his faithful slave. His son afterwards endeavored to buy Uncle Tom back again, but found that he had been whipped to death by the villain Legree.—Harriet Beecher Stowe, *Uncle Tom's Cabin* (1852).

Shell (*A*). Amongst the ancient Gaels a shell was emblematic of peace. Hence when Bosmi′na, Fingal's daughter, was sent to propitiate King Erragon, who had invaded Morven, she carried with her a "sparkling shell as a symbol of peace, and a golden arrow as a symbol of war."—Ossian, *The Battle of Lora*.

Shells, *i.e.*, hospitality. "Semo, king of shells" ("hospitality"). When Cuthullin invites Swaran to a banquet, his messenger says, "Cuthullin gives the joy of shells; come and partake the feast of Erin's blue-eyed chief." The ancient Gaels drank from shells; and hence such phrases as "chief of shells," "hall of shells," "king of shells," etc. (king of hospitality). "To rejoice in the shell" is to feast sumptuously and drink freely.

Shemus-an-Snachad, or "James of the Needle," M'Ivor's tailor at Edinburgh.—Sir W. Scott, *Waverley* (time, George II.).

Shepheardes Calendar (*The*), twelve eclogues in various metres, by Spenser, one for each month. *January*: Colin Clout (*Spenser*) bewails that Rosalind does not return his love, and compares his forlorn condition to the season itself. *February*: Cuddy, a lad, complains of the cold, and Thenot laments the degeneracy of pastoral life. *March*: Willie and Thomalin discourse of love (described as a person just aroused from sleep). *April*: Hobbinol sings a song on Eliza, queen of shepherds. *May*: Palinode (3 *syl.*) exhorts Piers to join the festivities of May, but Piers replies that good shepherds who seek their own indulgence expose their flocks to the wolves. He then relates the fable of the kid and her dam. *June*: Hobbinol exhorts Colin to greater cheerfulness, but Colin replies there is no cheer for him while Rosalind remains unkind and loves Menalcas better than himself. *July*: Morrel, a goat-herd, invites Thomalin to come with him to the uplands, but Thomalin replies that humility better becomes a shepherd (*i.e.*, a pastor or clergyman). *August*: Perigot and Willie contend in song, and Cuddy is appointed arbiter. *September*: Diggon Davie complains to Hobbinol of clerical abuses. *October*: On poetry, which Cuddy says has no encouragement, and laments that Colin neglects it, being crossed in love. *November*: Colin, being asked by Thenot to sing, excuses himself because of his grief for Dido, but finally he sings her elegy. *December*: Colin again complains that his heart is desolate because Rosalind loves him not (1579).

Shepheards Hunting (*The*), four "eglogues" by George Wither, while confined in the Marshalsea (1615). The shepherd, Roget, is the poet himself, and his "hunting" is a satire called *Abuses Stript and Whipt*, for which he was imprisoned. The first three eglogues are upon the subject of Roget's imprisonment, and the fourth is on his love of poetry. "Willy" is the poet's friend, William Browne, of the Inner Temple, author of *Britannia's Pastorals*. He was two years the junior of Wither.

Shepherd (*The*), Moses, who for forty years fed the flocks of Jethro, his father-in-law.

Sing, heavenly Muse, that on the secret top
Of Oreb or of Sinai, didst inspire
That shepherd who first taught the chosen seed,
"In the beginning," how the heaven and earth
Rose out of chaos.
Milton, *Paradise Lost*, i. (1665).

Shepherd (The Gentle), George Grenville, the statesman. One day, in addressing the House, George Grenville said, "Tell me where! tell me where!..." Pitt hummed the line of a song then very popular, beginning, "Gentle shepherd, tell me where!" and the whole House was convulsed with laughter (1712-1770).

*** Allan Ramsay has a beautiful Scotch pastoral called *The Gentle Shepherd* (1725).

Shepherd (John Claridge), the signature adopted by the author of *The Shepherd of Banbury's Rules to Judge of the Changes of Weather, etc.* (1744). Supposed to be Dr. John Campbell, author of *A Political Survey of Britain*.

Shepherd-Kings (*The*), or *Hyksos*. These Hyksos were a tribe of Cuthites driven from Assyria by Aralius and the Shemites. Their names were: (1) SAÏTÊS or Salâtês, called by the Arabs El-Weleed, and said to be a descendant of Esau (B.C. 1870-1851); (2) BEON, called by the Arabs Er-Reiyan, son of El-Weleed (B.C. 1851-1811); (3) APACHNAS (B.C. 1811-1750); (4) APŌPHIS, called by the Arabs Er-Reiyan II., in whose reign Joseph was sold into Egypt and was made viceroy (B.C. 1750-1700); (5) JANIAS (B.C. 1700-1651); (6) ASSETH (1651-1610). The Hyksos were driven out of Egypt by Amŏsis or Thetmosis, the founder of the eighteenth dynasty, and retired to Palestine, where they formed the chiefs or lords of the Philistines. (Hyksos is compounded of *hyk*, "king," and *sos*, "shepherd.")

. Apophis or Aphophis was not a shepherd-king, but a pharaoh or native ruler, who made Apachnas tributary, and succeeded him, but on the death of Aphophis the hyksos were restored.

Shepherd Lord (*The*), Lord Henry de Clifford, brought up by his mother as a shepherd to save him from the vengeance of the Yorkists. Henry VII. restored him to his birthright and estates (1455-1543).

The gracious fairy,
Who loved the shepherd lord to meet
In his wanderings solitary.
Wordsworth, *The White Doe of Rylstone* (1815).

Shepherd of Banbury. (See SHEPHERD, JOHN CLARIDGE.)

Shepherd of Filida.

"Preserve him, Mr. Nicholas, as thou wouldst a diamond. He is not a shepherd, but an elegant courtier," said the curé.—Cervantes, *Don Quixote*, I. i. 6 (1605).

Shepherd of Salisbury Plain (*The*), the hero and title of a religious tract by Hannah More. The shepherd is noted for his homely wisdom and simple piety. The academy figure of this shepherd was David Saunders, who, with his father, had kept sheep on the plain for a century.

Shepherd of the Ocean. So Colin Clout (*Spenser*) calls Sir Walter Raleigh in his *Colin Clout's Come Home Again* (1591).

Shepherdess (*The Faithful*), a pastoral drama by John Fletcher (1610). The "faithful shepherdess" is Corin, who remains faithful to her lover although dead. Milton has borrowed rather largely from this pastoral in his *Comus*.

Sheppard (*Jack*), immortalized for his burglaries and escapes from Newgate. He was the son of a carpenter in Spitalfields, and was an ardent, reckless and generous youth. Certainly the most popular criminal ever led to Tyburn for execution (1701-1724).

⁎ Daniel Defoe made *Jack Sheppard* the hero of a romance in 1724, and W. H. Ainsworth, in 1839.

Sherborne, in Dorsetshire, always brings ill luck to the possessor. It belonged at one time to the see of Canterbury, and Osmond pronounced a curse on any laymen who wrested it from the Church.

The first laymen who held these lands was the Protector Somerset, who was beheaded by Edward VI.

The next laymen was Sir Walter Raleigh, who was also beheaded.

At the death of Raleigh, James I. seized on the lands, and conferred them on Car, earl of Somerset, who died prematurely. His younger son, Carew, was attainted, committed to the Tower, and lost his estates by forfeiture.

⁎ James I. was no exception. He lost his eldest son, the prince of Wales, Charles I. was beheaded, James II. was forced to abdicate, and the two Pretenders consummated the ill luck of the family.

Sherborne is now in the possession of Digby, earl of Bristol.

(For other possessions which carry with them ill luck, see GOLD OF TOLOSA, GOLD OF NIBELUNGEN, GRAYSTEEL, HARMONIA'S NECKLACE, etc.)

Sheridan's Ride, the story of the brilliant dash of Sheridan upon Winchester, that turned the fortunes of the day in favor of the Federal forces. Early, in command of the Confederates, had driven the United States troops out of the town. When Sheridan met them, they were in full retreat.

"Hurrah! hurrah for horse and man,
And when their statues are placed on high,
Under the dome of the Union sky,
The American soldier's Temple of Fame,
There, with the glorious General's name
Be it said, in letters both bold and bright:—
Here is the steed that saved the day
By carrying Sheridan into the fight,
From Winchester—twenty miles away!'"
Thomas Buchanan Read, *Sheridan's Ride*.

Sheva, the philanthropic Jew, most modest, but most benevolent. He "stints his appetite to pamper his affections, and lives in poverty that the poor may live in plenty." Sheva is "the widows' friend, the orphans' father, the poor man's protector, and the universal dispenser of charity, but he ever shrank to let his left hand know what his right hand did." Ratcliffe's father rescued him at Cadiz, from an *auto da fe*, and Ratcliffe himself rescued him from a howling London mob. This noble heart settled £10,000 on Miss Ratcliffe at her marriage, and left Charles the heir of all his property.—Cumberland, *The Jew* (1776).

*** The Jews of England made up a very handsome purse, which they presented to the dramatist for this championship of their race.

Sheva, in the satire of *Absalom and Achitophel*, by Dryden and Tate, is designed for Sir Roger Lestrange, censor of the press, in the reign of Charles II. Sheva was one of David's scribes (2 *Sam*. xx. 25), and Sir Roger was editor of the *Observator*, in which he vindicated the court measures, for which he was knighted.

Than Sheva, none more loyal zeal have shown,
Wakeful as Judah's lion for the crown.
Tate, *Absalom and Achitophel*, ii. (1682).

Shib'boleth, the test pass-word of a secret society. When the Ephraimites tried to pass the Jordan, after their defeat by Jephthah, the guard tested whether they were Ephraimites or not, by asking them to say the word "Shibboleth," which the Ephraimites pronounced "Sibboleth" (*Judges* xii. 1-6).

In the Sicilian Vespers, a word was given as a test of nationality. Some dried peas (*ciceri*) were shown to a suspect: if he called them *cheecharee*, he was a Sicilian, and allowed to pass; but if *siseri*, he was a Frenchman, and was put to death.

In the great Danish slaughter on St. Bryce's Day (November 13, 1002), according to tradition, a similar test was made with the words "Chichester Church," which, being pronounced hard or soft, decided whether the speaker were Dane or Saxon.

Shield of Rome (*The*), Fabius "Cunctātor." Marcellus was called "The Sword of Rome." (See FABIUS.)

Shift (*Samuel*), a wonderful mimic, who, like Charles Mathews, the elder, could turn his face to anything. He is employed by Sir William Wealthy, to assist in saving his son, George, from ruin, and accordingly helps the young man in his money difficulties by becoming his agent. Ultimately, it is found that Sir George's father is his creditor, the young man is saved from ruin, marries, and becomes a reformed and honorable member of society, who has "sown his wild oats."—Foote, *The Minor* (1760).

Shilling (*To cut one off with a*). A tale is told of Charles and John Banister. John, having irritated his father, the old man said, "Jack, I'll cut you off with a shilling." To which the son replied, "I wish, dad, you would give it to me now."

✱✱✱ The same identical anecdote is told of Sheridan and his son Tom.

Shingle (*Solon*), prominent personage in J. S. Jones's farce, *The People's Lawyer*.

Ship (*The Intelligent*). *Ellīda* (Frithjof's ship) understood what was said to it; hence in the *Frithjof Saga* the son of Thornsten constantly addresses it, and the ship always obeys what is said to it.—Tegner, *Frithjof Saga*, x. (1825).

Shipton (*Mother*), the heroine of an ancient tale entitled *The Strange and Wonderful History and Prophecies of Mother Shipton*, etc.—T. Evan Preece.

Shipwreck (*The*), a poem in three cantos, by William Falconer (1762). Supposed to occupy six days. The ship was the *Britannia*, under the command of Albert, and bound for Venice. Being overtaken in a squall, she is driven out of her course from Candia, and four seamen are lost off the lee main-yardarm. A fearful storm greatly distresses the vessel and the captain gives command "to bear away." As she passes the island of St. George, the helmsman is struck blind by lightning. Bowsprit, foremast, and main-topmast being carried away, the officers try to save themselves on the wreck of the foremast. The ship splits on the projecting verge of Cape Colonna. The captain and all his crew are lost except Arion (*Falconer*), who is washed ashore, and being befriended by the natives, returns to England to tell this mournful story.

Shirley. Bright, independent heiress of Yorkshire, beautiful and courted, who chooses her own way and her own husband.—Charlotte Brontè, *Shirley*.

Shoo-King (*The*), the history of the Chinese monarchs, by Confucius. It begins with Yoo, B.C. 2205.

Shoolbred (*Dame*), the foster-mother of Henry Smith.—Sir W. Scott, *Fair Maid of Perth* (time, Henry IV.).

Shore (*Jane*), the heroine and title of a tragedy by N. Rowe (1312). Jane Shore was the wife of a London merchant, but left her husband to become the mistress of Edward IV. At the death of that monarch, Lord Hastings wished to obtain her, but she rejected his advances. This drew on her the jealous wrath of Alicia (Lord Hastings's mistress), who induced her to accuse Lord Hastings of want of allegiance to the lord protector. The duke of Gloucester commanded the instant execution of Hastings; and, accusing Jane Shore of having bewitched him, condemned her to wander about in a sheet, holding a taper in her hand, and decreed that any one who offered her food or shelter should be put to death. Jane continued an outcast for three days, when her husband came to her succor, but he was seized by Gloucester's myrmidons, and Jane Shore died.

Shoreditch (*Duke of*). Barlow, the favorite archer of Henry VIII., was so entitled by the Merry Monarch, in royal sport. Barlow's two skillful companions were created at the same time, "marquis of Islington," and "earl of Pancras."

Good king, make not good lord of Lincoln "duke of Shoreditche."—*The Poore Man's Petition to the Kinge* (art. xvi. 1603).

Shorne (*Sir John*) noted for his feat of conjuring the devil into a boot.

To Master John Shorne,
That blessêd man borne,
Which jugeleth with a bote;
I beschrewe his herte rote
That will trust him, and it be I.
Fantassie of Idolatrie.

Short-Lived Administration (*The*). the administration formed February 12, 1746, by William Pulteney. It lasted only two days.

Shortcake (*Mrs.*), the baker's wife, one of Mrs. Mailsetter's friends.—Sir W. Scott, *The Antiquary* (time, George III.).

Shortell (*Master*), the mercer at Liverpool.—Sir W. Scott, *Peveril of the Peak* (time, Charles II.).

Short'hose (2 *syl.*), a clown, servant to Lady Hartwell, the widow.— Beaumont and Fletcher, *Wit Without Money* (1539).

Shorthouse (*Tom*), epitaph of.

Hic Jacet Tom Shorthouse, *sine* Tom, *sine* Sheets, *sine* Riches;
Qui Vixit sine Gown, *sine* Cloak, *sine* Shirt, *sine* Breeches.
Old London (taken from the *Magna Britannia*)

Shovel-Boards or *Edward Shovel-Boards*, broad shillings of Edward III. Taylor, the water-poet, tells us "they were used for the most part at shoave-board."

... the unthrift every day,
With my face downwards do at shoave-board play.
Taylor, the water-poet (1580-1754).

Shewsberry (*Lord*), the earl marshall in the court of Queen Elizabeth.—Sir W. Scott, *Kenilworth* (time, Elizabeth).

Shufflebottom (*Abel*), a name assumed by Robert Southey in some of his amatory productions (1774-1843).

Shuffles (*Robert*). One of the "bad boys," whose misdemeanors and reformation are sketched in *Outward Bound,* by William T. Adams (Oliver Optic).

Shuffleton (*The Hon. Tom*), a man of very slender estate, who borrows of all who will lend, but always forgets to repay or return the loans. When spoken to about it, he interrupts the speaker before he comes to the point, and diverts the conversation to some other subject. He is one of the new school, always emotionless, looks on money as the *summum bonum*, and all as fair that puts money in his purse. The Hon. Tom Shuffleton marries Lady Caroline Braymore, who has £4000 a year. (See DIMANCHE.)—G. Colman, Jr., *John Bull*.

Shylock, the Jew, who lends Antonio (a Venetian merchant) 3000 ducats for three months, on these conditions: If repaid within the time, only the principal would be required; if not, the Jew should be at liberty to cut from Antonio's body a pound of flesh. The ships of Antonio being delayed by contrary winds, the merchant was unable to meet his bill, and the Jew claimed the forfeiture. Portia, in the dress of a law doctor, conducted the trial, and when the Jew was about to take his bond, reminded him that he must shed no drop of blood, nor must he cut either more or less than an exact pound. If these conditions were infringed his life would be forfeit. The Jew, feeling it to be impossible to exact the bond under such conditions, gave up the claim, but was heavily fined for seeking the life of a Venetian citizen.—Shakespeare, *The Merchant of Venice* (1598).

Among modern actors, *Henry Irving*, as Shylock, stands unsurpassed.

According to the kindred authority of Shylock, no man hates the thing he would not kill.—Sir W. Scott.

⁎ Paul Secchi tells us a similar tale: A merchant of Venice, having been informed by private letter that Drake had taken and plundered St. Domingo, sent word to Sampson Ceneda, a Jewish usurer. Ceneda would not believe it, and bet a pound of flesh it was not true. When the report was confirmed the pope told Secchi he might lawfully claim his bet if he chose, only he must draw no blood, nor take either more or less than an exact pound, on the penalty of being hanged.—Gregorio Leti, *Life of Sextus V*. (1666).

Sibbald, an attendant on the earl of Menteith.—Sir W. Scott, *Legend of Montrose* (time, Charles I.).

Sibylla, the sibyl. (See SIBYLS.)

And thou, Alecto, feede me wyth thy foode ...
And thou, Sibilla, when thou seest me faynte,
Addres thyselfe the gyde of my complaynte.
Sackville, *Mirrour for Magistraytes* ("Complaynte," etc., (1557).

Sibyls. Plato speaks of only *one* sibyl; Martian Capella says there were *two* (the *Erythræan* or *Cumæan* sibyl, and the *Phrygian*); Pliny speaks of the *three* sibyls; Jackson maintains, on the authority of Ælian, that there were *four*; Shakespeare speaks of the *nine* sibyls of old Rome (1 *Henry VI.* act i. sc. 2); Varro says they were *ten* (the sibyls of Libya, Samos, Cumæ (in Italy), Cumæ (in Asia Minor), Erythræ, Persia, Tiburtis, Delphi, Ancy´ra (in Phrygia), and Marpessa), in reference to which Rabelais says, "she may be the *eleventh* sibyl" (*Pantagruel*, iii. 16); the mediæval monks made the number to be *twelve*, and gave to each a distinct prophecy respecting Christ. But whatever the number, there was but *one* "sibyl of old Rome" (the Cumæan), who offered to Tarquin the nine Sibylline books.

Sibyl's Books (*The*). We are told that the sibyl of Cumæ (in Æŏlis) offered Tarquin nine volumes of predictions for a certain sum of money, but the king, deeming the price exorbitant, refused to purchase them; whereupon she burnt three of the volumes, and next year offered Tarquin the remaining six at the same price. Again he refused, and the sibyl burnt three more. The following year she again returned, and asked the original price for the three which remained. At the advice of the augurs the king purchased the books, and they were preserved with great care under guardians specially appointed for the purpose.

Sicilian Bull (*The*), the brazen bull invented by Perillos for the tyrant Phalăris, as an engine of torture. Perillos himself was the first victim enclosed in the bull.

As the Sicilian bull that rightfully
His cries echoed who had shaped the mould,
Did so rebellow with the voice of him
Tormented, that the brazen monster seemed
Pierced through with pain.
Dantê, *Hell*, xxvii. (1300).

Sicilian Vespers (*The*), the massacre of the French in Sicily, which began at Palermo, March 30, 1282, at the hour of vespers, on Easter Monday. This wholesale slaughter was provoked by the brutal conduct of Charles d'Anjou (the governor) and his soldiers towards the islanders.

A similar massacre of the Danes was made in England, on St. Bryce's Day (November 13), 1002.

Another similar slaughter took place at Bruges, March 24, 1302.

✳ The Bartholomew Massacre (Aug. 24, 1572) was a religious not a political movement.

Sicilien (*Le*) or L'AMOUR PEINTRE, a comedy by Molière (1667). The Sicilian is Don Pèdre, who has a Greek slave named Is´idore. This slave is loved by Adraste (2 *syl.*), a French gentleman, and the plot of the comedy, turns on the way that the Frenchman allures the Greek slave away from her master. Hearing that his friend Damon is going to make a portrait of Isidore, he gets him to write to Don Pèdre a letter of introduction, requesting that the bearer may be allowed to take the likeness. By this ruse, Adraste reveals his love to Isidore, and persuades her to elope. The next step is this: Zaïde (2 *syl.*), a young slave, pretends to have been ill-treated by Adraste, and runs to Don Pèdre to crave protection. The don bids her go in, while he intercedes with Adraste on her behalf. The Frenchman seems to relent, and Pèdre calls for Zaïde to come forth, but Isidore comes instead, wearing Zaïde's veil. Don Pèdre says to Adraste, "There, take her home, and use her well!" "I will," says Adraste, and leads off the Greek slave.

Siddartha, born at Gaya, in India, and known in Indian history as Buddha (*i.e.* "The Wise").

Sidney, the tutor and friend of Charles Egerton McSycophant. He loves Constantia, but conceals his passion for fear of paining Egerton, her accepted lover.—C. Macklin, *The Man of the World* (1764).

Sidney (*Sir Philip*). Sir Philip Sidney, though suffering extreme thirst from the agony of wounds, received in the battle of Zutphen, gave his own draught of water to a wounded private, lying at his side, saying, "Poor fellow, thy necessity is greater than mine."

A similar instance is recorded of Alexander "the Great," in the desert of Gedrosia.

David, fighting against the Philistines, became so parched with thirst, that he cried out, "Oh, that one would give me drink of the water of the well of Bethlehem, which is by the gate!" And the three mighty men broke through the host of the Philistines, and brought him water; nevertheless, he would not drink it, but poured it out unto the Lord.—2 *Sam.* xxiii. 15-17.

Sidney's Sister, Pembroke's Mother. Mary Herbert (born Sidney), countess of Pembroke, who died 1621.

Underneath this sable hearse
Lies the subject of all verse—
Sidney's sister, Pembroke's mother.
Death, ere thou hast slain another
Fair, and good, and learned as she,

Time shall throw his dart at thee.
Ben Jonson (1574-1637).

Sid´rophel, William Lily, the astrologer.

Quoth Ralph, "Not far from hence doth dwell
A cunning man, hight Sidrophel,
That deals in destiny's dark counsels,
And sage opinions of the moon sells;
To whom all people, far and near,
On deep importances repair."
S. Butler, *Hudibras*, ii. 3 (1664).

Siebel, Margheri´ta's rejected lover, in the opera of *Faust e Margherita*, by Gounod (1859).

Siége. *Mon siége est fait*, my opinion is fixed, and I cannot change it. This proverb rose thus: The abbé de Vertot wrote the history of a certain siege, and applied to a friend for some geographical particulars. These particulars did not arrive till the matter had passed the press; so the abbé remarked with a shrug, "Bah! mon siége est fait."

Siege Perilous (*The*). The Round Table contained sieges for 150 knights, but three of them were "reserved." Of these, two were posts of honor, but the third was reserved for him who was destined to achieve the quest of the Holy Graal. This seat was called "perilous," because if any one sat therein, except he for whom it was reserved, it would be his death. Every seat of the table bore the name of its rightful occupant, in letters of gold, and the name on the "Siege Perilous" was Sir Galahad (son of Sir Launcelot and Elaine).

Said Merlin, "There shall no man sit in the two void places but they that shall be of most worship. But in the *Siege Perilous* there shall no man sit but one, and if any other be so hardy as to do it, he shall be destroyed."—Pt. i. 48.

Then the old man made Sir Galahad unarm; and he put on him a coat of red sandel, with a mantel upon his shoulder furred with fine ermines ... and he brought him unto the Siege Perilous, when he sat beside Sir Launcelot. And the good old man lifted up the cloth, and found there these words written: THE SIEGE OF SIR GALAHAD.—Sir T. Malory, *History of Prince Arthur*, iii. 32 (1470).

Siege of Calais, a novel by Mde. de Tencin (1681-1749). George Colman has a drama with the same title.

Siege of Damascus. Damascus was besieged by the Arabs while Eu´menês was governor. The general of the Syrians was Pho´cyas, and of the Arabs, Caled. Phocyas asked Eumenês's permission to marry his daughter, Eudo´cia, but was sternly refused. After gaining several victories he fell into the hands of the Arabs, and then joined them in their siege in order to revenge himself on Eumenês. Eudocia fell into his power, but she refused to marry a traitor. Caled requested Phocyas to point out to him the governor's tent; on being refused, they fought, and Caled fell. Abudah, being now in chief command, made an honorable peace with the Syrians, Phocyas died, and Eudocia retired to a convent.—J. Hughes, *Siege of Damascus* (1720).

Siege of Rhodes, by Sir W. Davenant (1656).

Sieg´fried [*Seeg.freed*], hero of pt. i. of the *Nibelungen Lied*, the old German epic. Siegfried was a young warrior of peerless strength and beauty, invulnerable except in one spot between his shoulders. He vanquished the Nibelungs, and carried away their immense hoards of gold and precious stones. He wooed and won Kriemhild, the sister of Günther, king of Burgundy, but was treacherously killed by Hagan while stooping for a draught of water after a hunting expedition.

Siegfried had a cape, or cloak, which rendered him invisible, the gift of the dwarf, Alberich; and his sword, called Balmung, was forged by Wieland, blacksmith of the Teutonic gods.

This epic consists of a number of different lays by the old minnesingers, pieced together into a connected story as early as 1210. It is of Scandinavian origin, and is in the *Younger Edda*, amongst the "Völsunga Sagas" (compiled by Snorro, in the thirteenth century).

Siegfried's Birthplace. He was born in Phinecastle, then called Xanton.

Siegfried's Father and Mother. Siegfried was the youngest son of Siegmund and Sieglind, king and queen of the Netherlands.

Siegfried called Horny. He was called horny because, when he slew the dragon, he bathed in its blood, and became covered with a horny hide which was invulnerable. A linden leaf happened to fall on his back between his shoulder-blades, and, as the blood did not touch this spot, it remained vulnerable.—The minnesingers, *The Nibelungen Lied* (1210).

Sieg´fried von Lindenberg, the hero of a comic German romance by Müller (1779). Still popular and very amusing.

Sieglind [*Seeg.lind*], the mother of Siegfried, and wife of Siegmund, king of the Netherlands.—The minnesingers, *The Nibelungen Lied* (1210).

Siegmund [*Seeg.mund*], king of the Netherlands. His wife was Sieglind, and his son, Siegfried [*Seeg.freed*].—The minnesingers, *The Nibelungen Lied* (1210).

Sige´ro, "the Good," slain by Argantês. Argantês hurled his spear at Godfrey, but it struck Sigēro, who "rejoiced to suffer in his sovereign's place."—Tasso, *Jerusalem Delivered*, xi. (1575).

Sightly (*Captain*), a dashing young officer, who runs away with Priscilla Tomboy, but subsequently obtains her guardian's consent to marry her.—*The Romp* (altered from Bickerstaff's *Love in the City*).

Sigismonda, daughter of Tancred, king of Salerno. She fell in love with Guiscardo, her father's squire, revealed to him her love, and married him in a cavern attached to the palace. Tancred discovered them in each other's embrace, and gave secret orders to waylay the bridegroom and strangle him. He then went to Sigismonda, and reproved her for her degrading choice, which she boldly justified. Next day, she received a human heart in a gold casket, knew instinctively that it was Guiscardo's, and poisoned herself. Her father being sent for, she survived just long enough to request that she might be buried in the same grave as her young husband, and Tancred:

Too late repenting of his cruel deed,
One common sepulchre for both decreed;
Intombed the wretched pair in royal state,
And on their monument inscribed their fate.
Dryden, *Sigismonda and Guiscardo* (from Boccaccio).

Sigismund, emperor of Austria.—Sir W. Scott, *Anne of Geierstein* (time, Edward IV.).

Sigismunda, daughter of Siffrēdi, lord high chancellor of Sicily, and betrothed to Count Tancred. When King Roger died, he left the crown of Sicily to Tancred, on condition that he married Constantia, by which means the rival lines would be united, and the country saved from civil war. Tancred gave a tacit consent, intending to obtain a dispensation; but Sigismunda, in a moment of wounded pride, consented to marry Earl Osmond. When King Tancred obtained an interview with Sigismunda, to explain his conduct, Osmond challenged him, and they fought. Osmond fell, and when his wife ran to him, he thrust his sword into her and killed her.—J. Thomson, *Tancred and Sigismunda* (1745).

⁎ This tragedy is based on "The Baneful Marriage," an episode in *Gil Blas*, founded on fact.

Sigismunda, the heroine of Cervantes's last work of fiction. This tale is a tissue of episodes, full of most incredible adventures, astounding prodigies, impossible characters, and extravagant sentiments. It is said that Cervantes himself preferred it to his *Don Quixote*, just as Corneille preferred *Nicomede* to his *Cid*, and Milton *Paradise Regained* to his *Paradise Lost*.—*Encyc. Brit.*, Art. "Romance."

Sigurd, the hero of an old Scandinavian legend. Sigurd discovered Brynhild, encased in a complete armor, lying in a death-like sleep, to which she had been condemned by Odin. Sigurd woke her by opening her corselet, fell in love with her, promised to marry her, but deserted her for Gudrun. This ill-starred union was the cause of an *Iliad* of woes.

An analysis of this romance was published by Weber in his *Illustrations of Northern Antiquities* (1810).

Sijil (*Al*), the recording angel.

On that day we will roll up the heavens as the angel Al Sijil rolleth up the scroll wherein every man's actions are recorded.—*Al Korân*, xxi.

Sikes (*Bill*), a burglar, and one of Fagin's associates. Bill Sikes was a hardened, irreclaimable villian, but had a conscience which almost drove him mad after the murder of Nancy, who really loved him (ch. xlviii.) Bill Sikes (1 *syl.*) had an ill-conditioned savage dog, the beast-image of his master, which he kicked and loved, ill-treated and fondled.—C. Dickens, *Oliver Twist* (1837).

The French "Bill Sikes" is "Jean Hiroux," a creation of Henry Monnier.

Sikundra (*The*), a mausoleum about six miles from Agra, raised by Akhbah "the Great."

Silence, a country justice of asinine dullness when sober, but when in his cups of most uproarious mirth. He was in the commission of the peace with his cousin Robert Shallow.

Falstaff. I did not think Master Silence had been a man of this mettle.

Silence. Who, I? I have been merry twice and once, ere now.—Shakespeare, *2 Henry IV.*, act vi. sc. 3 (1598).

Sile′no, husband of Mysis; a kind-hearted man, who takes pity on Apollo when cast to earth by Jupiter, and gives him a home.—Kane O'Hara, *Midas* (1764).

Silent (*The*), William I., prince of Orange (1533-1584). It was the principle of Napoleon III., emperor of the French, to "hear, see, and say nothing."

Silent Man (*The*), the barber of Bagdad, the greatest chatterbox that ever lived. Being sent for to shave the head and beard of a young man who was to visit the cadi's daughter at noon, he kept him from daybreak to midday, prating, to the unspeakable annoyance of the customer. Being subsequently taken before the caliph, he ran on telling story after story about his six brothers. He was called the "Silent Man," because on one occasion, being accidentally taken up with ten robbers, he never said he was not one of the gang. His six brothers were Bacbouc, the hunchback, Bakbarah, the toothless, Bakac, the one-eyed, Alcouz, the blind, Alnaschar, the earless, and

Schacabac, the hare-lipped.—*Arabian Nights* ("The Barber," and "The Barber's Six Brothers").

Silent Woman (*The*), a comedy by Ben Jonson (1609). Morose, a miserly old fellow, who hates to hear any voice but his own, has a young nephew, Sir Dauphine, who wants to wring from him a third of his property; and the way he gains his point is this: He induces a lad to pretend to be a "silent woman." Morose is so delighted with the phenomenon that he consents to marry the prodigy; but the moment the ceremony is over, the boy-wife assumes the character of a virago, whose tongue is a ceaseless clack. Morose is in despair, and signs away a third of his property to his nephew, on condition of being rid of this intolerable pest. The trick is now revealed, Morose retires into private life, and Sir Dauphine remains master of the situation.

Sile′nus, son of Pan, chief of the sile′ni or older satyrs. Silēnus was the foster-father of Bacchus, the wine-god, and is described as a jovial old toper, with bald head, pug nose, and pimply face.

Old Silenus, bloated, drunken,
Led by his inebriate satyrs.
Longfellow, *Drinking Song*.

Silky, a Jew money-lender, swindler, and miser. (See SULKY.)

Yon cheat all day, tremble at night, and act the hypocrite the first thing in the morning.—T. Holcroft, *The Road to Ruin*, ii. 3 (1792).

Silly Billy, William IV. (1765, 1830-1837).

Silva (*Don Ruy Gomez de*), an old Spanish grandee, to whom Elvíra was betrothed; but she detested him, and loved Ernani, a bandit-captain. Charles V. tried to seduce her, and Silva, in his wrath, joined Ernani to depose the king. The plot being discovered, the conspirators were arrested, but, at the intercession of Elvira, were pardoned. The marriage of Ernani and Elvira was just about to be consummated, when a horn sounded. Ernani had bound himself, when Silva joined the bandit, to put an end to his life whenever summoned so to do by Silva; and the summons was to be given by the blast of a horn. Silva being relentless, Ernani kept his vow, and stabbed himself.—Verdi, *Ernani* (1841).

Silver-Fork School (*The*), a name given to a class of English novelists who gave undue importance to etiquette and the externals of social intercourse. The most distinguished are: Lady Blessington (1789-1849), Theodore Hook (1716-1796), Lord Lytton (1804-1873), and Mrs. Trollope (1790-1863).

Silver Pen. Eliza Meteyard was so called by Douglas Jerold, and she adopted the pseudonym (1816-1879).

Silver Star of Love (*The*), the star which appeared to Vasco da Gama, when his ships were tempest-tossed, through the malice of Bacchus. Immediately the star appeared, the tempest ceased, and there was a great calm.

The sky and ocean blending, each on fire,
Seemed as all Nature struggled to expire;
When now the Silver Star of Love appeared,
Bright in the east her radiant front she reared.
Camoens, *Lusiad*, vi. (1572).

Silver Tongued (*The*), Joshua Sylvester, translator of Du Bartas's *Divine Weeks and Works* (1563-1618).

William Bates, a puritan divine (1625-1699).

Henry Smith, preacher (1550-1600).

Anthony Hammond, the poet, called "Silver Tongue" (1668-1738).

Spranger Barry, the "Irish Roscius" (1719-1777).

Silverquill (*Sam*), one of the prisoners at Portanferry.—Sir W. Scott, *Guy Mannering* (time, George II.).

Silves de la Selva (*The Exploits and Adventures of*), part of the series called *Le Roman des Romans*, pertaining to "Am´adis of Gaul." This part was added by Feliciano de Silva.

Silvester (*Anne*), woman betrayed under promise of marriage, by *Geoffrey Delamayne*, a famous athlete. By a series of *contretemps*, Anne is made out to be the wife (according to Scotch law) of her dearest friend's betrothed, who visits her as Delamayne's emissary. She is released from the embarrassing position, by the exhibition of a letter from Delamayne, promising to marry her, written before *Arnold's* visit. Infuriated by the *exposé*, Delamayne tries to murder his wife, and is prevented by a crazy woman. Her sudden attack brings on apoplexy. Anne, as his widow, marries her old friend and defender, Sir Patrick Lundie.—Wilkie Collins, *Man and Wife* (1874).

Silvestre (2 *syl.*), valet of Octave (son of Argante, and brother of Zerbinette).—Molière, *Les Fourberies de Scapin* (1671).

Sil´via, daughter of the duke of Milan, and the lady-love of Valentine, one of the heroes of the play.—Shakespeare, *The Two Gentlemen of Verona* (1594).

Simmons (*Widow*), the seamstress; a neighbor of the Ramsays.—Sir W. Scott, *Fortunes of Nigel* (time, James I.).

Simon (*Martin*), proprietor of the village Bout du Monde, and miller of Grenoble. He is called "The king of Pelvoux," and in reality is the Baron de Peyras, who has given up all his estates to his nephew, the young chevalier,

Marcellin de Peyras, and retired to Grenoble, where he lived as a villager. Martin Simon is in secret possession of a gold-mine, left him by his father, with the stipulation that he should place it beyond the reach of any private man, on the day it becomes a "source of woe and crime." Rabisson, a travelling tinker, the only person who knows about it, being murdered, Simon is suspected; but Eusebe Noel confesses the crime. Simon then makes the mine over to the king of France, as it had proved the source both "of woe and crime."—E. Stirling, *The Gold Mine*, or *Miller of Grenoble* (1854).

Simonides, benevolent Jew, father of Esther, and friend of Ben Hur.—Lew Wallace, *Ben Hur: a Tale of the Christ* (1880).

Simon Pure, a young quaker from Pennsylvania, on a visit to Obadiah Prim (a Bristol Quaker, and one of the guardians of Anne Lovely, the heiress). Colonel Feignwell personated Simon Pure, and obtained Obadiah's consent to marry his ward. When the real Simon Pure presented himself, the colonel denounced him as an impostor; but after he had obtained the guardian's signature, he confessed the trick, and showed how he had obtained the consent of the other three guardians.—Mrs. Centlivre, *A Bold Stroke for a Wife* (1717).

*** This name has become a household word for "the real man," the *ipsissimus ego*.

Si´monie or SI´MONY, the friar, in the beast-epic of *Reynard the Fox* (1498). So called from Simon Magus (*Acts*. viii. 9-24.)

Simony (*Dr.*), in Foote's farce, called *The Cozeners*, was meant for Dr. Dodd.

Sim´org, a bird "which hath seen the world thrice destroyed." It is found in Kâf, but as Hafiz says, "searching for the simorg is like searching for the philosopher's stone." This does not agree with Beckford's account. (See SIMURGH.)

In Kâf the simorg hath its dwelling-place,
The all-knowing bird of ages, who hath seen
The world with all its children thrice destroyed.
Southey, *Thalaba, the Destroyer*, viii. 19 (1797).

Simpcox (*Saunder*), a lame man, who asserted he was born blind, and to whom St. Alban said, "Come, offer at my shrine, and I will help thee." Being brought before Humphrey, duke of Gloucester, the lord protector, he was asked how he became lame; and Simpcox replied he fell from a tree which he had climbed to gather plums for his wife. The duke then asked if his sight had been restored? "Yes," said the man; and, being shown divers colors, could readily distinguish between red, blue, brown, and so on. The duke told the rascal that a *blind* man does not climb trees to gather their fruits; and one born blind might, if his sight were restored, know that one color differed from another, but could not possibly know which was which. He then placed a stool before him and ordered the constables to whip him till he jumped over it; whereupon the lame man jumped over it, and ran off as fast as his legs could carry him. Sir Thomas More tells this story, and Shakespeare introduces it in 2 *Henry VI.* act ii. sc. 1 (1591).

Simple, the servant of Slender (cousin of Justice Shallow).—Shakespeare, *The Merry Wives of Windsor* (1596).

Simple (The), Charles III. of France (879, 893-929).

Simple (Peter), the hero and title of a novel by Captain Marryat (1833).

Simple Simon, a man more sinned against than sinning, whose misfortunes arose from his wife Margery's cruelty, which began the very morning of their marriage.

We do not know whether it is necessary to seek for a Teutonic or Northern original for this once popular book.—*Quarterly Review.*

Simpson *(Tam)*, the drunken barber.—Sir W. Scott, *St. Ronan's Well* (time, George III.).

Simson *(Jean)*, an old woman at Middlemas village.—Sir W. Scott, *The Surgeon's Daughter* (time, George II.).

Simurgh, a fabulous Eastern bird, endowed with reason and knowing all languages. It had seen the great cycle of 7000 years twelve times, and, during that period, it declared it had seen the earth wholly without inhabitant seven times.—W. Beckford, *Vathek* (notes, 1784). This does not agree with Southey's account. (See SIMORG.)

Sin, twin-keeper, with Death, of Hellgate. She sprang, full-grown, from the head of Satan.

Woman to the waist, and fair,
But ending foul in many a scaly fold
Voluminous and vast, a serpent armed
With mortal sting.
Milton, *Paradise Lost*, ii. (1665).

Sin´adone *(The lady of)*, metamorphosed by enchantment into a serpent. Sir Lybius (one of Arthur's knights) slew the enchantress, and the serpent, coiling about his neck, kissed him; whereupon the spell was broken, the serpent became a lovely princess, and Sir Lybius made her his wife.—*Libeaux* (a romance).

Sindbad, a merchant of Bagdad, who acquired great wealth by merchandise. He went seven voyages, which he related to a poor, discontented porter named Hindbad, to show him that wealth must be obtained by enterprise and personal exertion.

First Voyage. Being becalmed in the Indian Ocean, he and some others of the crew visited what they supposed to be an island, but which was in reality a huge whale asleep. They lighted a fire on the whale, and the heat woke the creature, which instantly dived under water. Sindbad was picked up by some merchants, and in due time returned home.

Second Voyage. Sindbad was left, during sleep, on a desert island, and discovered a roc's egg, "fifty paces in circumference." He fastened himself to the claw of the bird, and was deposited in the valley of diamonds. Next day some merchants came to the top of the crags, and threw into the valley huge joints of raw meat, to which the diamonds stuck, and when the eagles picked up the meat, the merchants scared them from their nests, and carried off the diamonds. Sindbad fastened himself to a piece of meat, was carried by an eagle to its nest, and, being rescued by the merchants, returned home laden with diamonds.

Third Voyage is the encounter with the Cyclops. (See ULYSSES AND POLYPHEMOS, where the account is given in detail.)

Fourth Voyage. Sindbad married a lady of rank in a strange island on which he was cast; and when his wife died he was buried alive with the dead body, according to the custom of the land. He made his way out of the catacomb, and returned to Bagdad greatly enriched by valuables rifled from the dead bodies.

Fifth Voyage. The ship in which he sailed was dashed to pieces by huge stones let down from the talons of two angry rocs. Sindbad swam to a desert inland, where he threw stones at the monkeys, and the monkeys threw back cocoa-nuts. On this island Sindbad encountered and killed the Old Man of the Sea.

Sixth Voyage. Sindbad visited the island of Serendib (or Ceylon), and climbed to the top of the mountain "where Adam was placed on his expulsion from paradise."

Seventh Voyage. He was attacked by corsairs, sold to slavery, and employed in shooting elephants from a tree. He discovered a tract of hill country completely covered with elephants' tusks, communicated his discovery to his master, obtained his liberty, and returned home.—*Arabian Nights* ("Sindbad the Sailor").

Sindbad, Ulysses, and the Cyclops. (See ULYSSES AND POLYPHEMOS.)

Sin'el, thane of Glamis, and father of Macbeth. He married the younger daughter of Malcolm II. of Scotland.

Sinfire, brilliant, seductive, and wicked heroine of Julian Hawthorne's novel of the same name.

Sing (*Sadha*), the mourner of the desert.—Sir W. Scott, *The Surgeon's Daughter* (time, George II.).

Sing de Racine (*Le*), Campistron, the French dramatic poet (1656-1723).

Singing Apple (*The*), in the deserts of Libya. This apple resembled a ruby crowned with a huge diamond, and had the gift of imparting wit to those who only smelt of it. Prince Cherry obtained it for Fairstar. (See SINGING TREE.)

The singing apple is as great an embellisher of wit as the dancing water is of beauty. Would you appear in public as a poet or prose writer, a wit or a philosopher, you only need smell it, and you are possessed at once of these rare gifts of genius.—Comtesse D'Aunoy, *Fairy Tales* ("Princess Fairstar," 1682).

Singing Tree (*The*), a tree, every leaf of which was a mouth, and all the leaves sang together in harmonious concert.—*Arabian Nights* ("The Two Sisters," the last story).

*** In the tale of *Cherry and Fairstar*, "the singing tree" is called "the singing apple" (*q.v.*).

Single-Speech Hamilton, William Gerard Hamilton, statesman (1729-1796). His first speech was delivered November 13, 1775, and his eloquence threw into the shade every orator except Pitt himself.

It was supposed that he had exhausted himself in that one speech, and had become physically incapable of making a second; so that afterwards, when he really did make a second, everybody was naturally disgusted, and most people dropped his acquaintance.—De Quincey (1786-1859).

Singleton (*Captain*), the hero of a novel by D. Defoe, called *The Adventures of Captain Singleton*.

Singular Doctor (*The*), William Occam, *Doctor Singularis et Invincibilis* (1276-1347).

*** The "Occam razor" was *entia non sunt multiplicanda*, "entities are not to be unnecessarily multiplied." In other words, elements, genera, and first principles are very few in number.

Sinner Saved (*A*). Cyra, daughter of Proterĭus of Cappadōcia, was on the point of taking the veil among Emmelia's sisterhood, and just before the day of renunciation, Elĕēmon, her father's freed slave, who loved her, sold himself to the devil, on condition of obtaining her for his wife. He signed the bond with a drop of his heart's blood, and carried about with him a little red spot on his bresst, as a perpetual reminder of the compact. The devil now sent a dream to Cyra, and another to her father, which caused them to change their plans; and on the very day that Cyra was to have taken the veil, she was given by St. Basil in marriage to Eleemon, with whom she lived happily for many years, and had a large family. One night, while her husband was asleep, Cyra saw the blood-red spot; she knew what it meant, and next day Eleemon told her the whole story. Cyra now bestirred herself to annul the compact, and went with her husband to St. Basil, to whom a free and full confession was made. Eleemon was shut up for a night in a cell, and Satan would have carried him off, but he clung to the foot of a crucifix. Next day Satan met St. Basil in the cathedral, and demanded his bond. St. Basil assured him the bond was illegal and invalid. The devil was foiled, the red mark vanished from the skin of Eleemon, a sinner was saved, and St. Basil came off victorious.—Amphilochius, *Life of St. Basil*. (See Rosweyde, *Vitæ Patrum*, 156-8.)

*** Southey has converted this legend into a ballad of nine lays (1829).

Sinon, the crafty Greek, who persuaded the Trojans to drag the Wooden Horse into their city.—Virgil, *Æneid*, ii.

Dantê, in his *Inferno*, places Sinon, with Potiphar's wife, Nimrod, and the rebellious giants, in the tenth pit of Malêbolgê.

Sin Saxon. Sprightly, sparkling personage, who appears, first as a saucy girl, then, as a vivacious young matron, in several of A. D. T. Whitney's books. She marries Frank Sherman.—A. D. T. Whitney, *Leslie Goldthwaite* and *The Other Girls*.

Sintram, the Greek hero of the German romance, *Sintram and His Companions*, by Baron Lamotte Fouqué.

Sintram's Sword, Welsung.

Sio´na, a seraph, to whom was committed the charge of Bartholomew, the apostle.—Klopstock, *The Messiah*, iii. (1748).

Siph´a, the guardian angel of Andrew, the brother of Simon Peter.—Klopstock, *The Messiah*, iii. (1748).

Si´phax, a soldier, in love with Princess Calis, sister of Astorax, king of Paphos. The princess is in love with Polydore, the brother of General Memnon, ("the mad brother").—Beaumont and Fletcher, *The Mad Lover* (1617).

Sir Oracle, a dictatorial prig; a dogmatic pedant.

I am Sir Oracle,
And when I ope my lips, let no dog bark.
Shakespeare, *Merchant of Venice*, act i. sc. 1 (1598).

Sirens, three sea-nymphs, whose usual abode was a small island near Cape Pelōrus, in Sicily. They enticed sailors ashore by their melodious singing, and then killed them. Their names are Parthenŏpê, Ligeia, and Leucothĕa.— *Greek Fable.*

Sirloin of Beef. James I., on his return from a hunting excursion, so much enjoyed his dinner, consisting of a loin of roast beef, that he laid his sword across it, and dubbed it Sir Loin. At Chingford, in Essex, is a place called "Friday Hill House," in one of the rooms of which is an oak table with a brass plate let into it, inscribed with the following words:—"ALL LOVERS OF ROAST BEEF WILL LIKE TO KNOW THAT ON THIS TABLE A LOIN WAS KNIGHTED BY KING JAMES THE FIRST ON HIS RETURN FROM HUNTING IN EPPING FOREST."

Knighting the loin of beef is also ascribed to Charles II.

Our second Charles, of fame facete,
On loin of beef did dine;
He held his sword, pleased, o'er the meat.
"Arise, thou famed Sir Loin."
Ballad of the New Sir John Barleycorn.

Sister Anne, sister of Fatĭma (the seventh and last wife of Bluebeard). Fatima, being condemned to death by her tyrannical husband, requested sister Anne to ascend to the highest tower of the castle to watch for her brothers, who were momentarily expected. Bluebeard kept roaring below stairs for Fatima to be quick; Fatima was constantly calling out from her chamber, "Sister Anne, do you see them coming?" and sister Anne was on the watch-tower, mistaking every cloud of dust for the mounted brothers. They arrived at last, rescued Fatima, and put Bluebeard to death.—Charles Perrault, *Contes* ("La Barbe Bleue," 1697).

This is a Scandinavian tale taken from the *Folks Sagas.*

Sis′yphos, in Latin **Sisyphus**, a king of Corinth, noted for his avarice and fraud. He was punished in the infernal regions by having to roll uphill a huge stone, which always rolled down again as soon as it reached the top. Sisyphos is a type of avarice, never satisfied. The avaricious man reaches the summit of his ambition, and no sooner does he so than he finds the object of his desire as far off as ever.

With many a weary step, and many a groan,
Up the high hill he heaves a huge round stone;

The huge round stone, returning with a bound,
Thunders impetuous down, and smokes along the ground.
Homer, *Odyssey*, xi. [Pope's trans.].

Sisyphus, in the Milesian tales, was doomed to die, but when Death came to him, the wily fellow contrived to fasten the unwelcome messenger in a chair, and then feasted him till old Spare-ribs grew as fat as a prize pig. In time, Pluto released Death, and Sisyphus was caught, but prayed that he might speak to his wife before he went to Hadês. The prayer was granted, and Sisyphus told his wife not to bury him, for though she might think him dead, he would not be really so. When he got to the infernal regions, he made the ghosts so merry with his jokes, that Pluto reproved him, and Sisyphus pleaded that, as he had not been buried, Pluto had no jurisdiction over him, nor could he even be ferried across the Styx. He then obtained leave to return to earth, that he might persuade his wife to bury him. Now, the wily old king had previously bribed Hermês, when he took him to Hadês, to induce Zeus to grant him life, provided he returned to earth again in the body; when, therefore, he did return, he demanded of Hermês the fulfillment of his promise, and Hermês induced Zeus to bestow on him life. Sisyphus was now allowed to return to earth, with a promise that he should never die again, till he himself implored for death. So he lived, and lived till he was weary of living, and when he went to Hadês the second time, he was allotted, by way of punishment, the task of rolling a huge stone to the top of a mountain. Orpheus (2 *syl.*), asked him how he could endure so ceaseless and vain an employment, and Sisyphus replied that he hoped ultimately to accomplish the task. "Never," exclaimed Orpheus; "it can never be done!" "Well, then," said Sisyphus, "mine is at worst but everlasting hope."—Lord Lytton, *Tales of Miletus*, ii.

Sitoph'agus (*"the wheat-eater"*), one of the mouse princes, who being wounded in the battle, crept into a ditch to avoid further injury or danger.

The lame Sitophagus, oppressed with pain,
Creeps from the desperate dangers of the plain;
And where the ditches rising weeds supply ...
There lurks the silent mouse relieved of heat,
And, safe embowered, avoids the chance of fate.
Parnell, *Battle of the Frogs and Mice*. iii. (about 1712).

The last two lines might be amended thus:

There lurks the trembling mouse with bated breath,
And, hid from sight, avoids his instant death.

Siward [*Se. 'ward*], the earl of Northumberland, and general of the English forces, acting against Macbeth.—Shakespeare, *Macbeth* (1606).

Six Chronicles (*The*). Dr. Giles compiled and edited six Old English Chronicles for Bohn's series in 1848. They are: Ethelwerd's *Chronicle*, Asser's *Life of Alfred*, Geoffrey of Monmouth's *British History*, *Gildas the Wise*, Nennius's *History of the Britons*, and Richard of Cirencester *On the Ancient State of Britain*. The last three were edited in 1757, by Professor Bertram, in his *Scriptores Tres*, but great doubt exists as to the genuineness of the chronicles contained in Dr. Bertram's compilation. (See THREE WRITERS.)

Sixteen-String-Jack, John Rann, a highwayman. He was a great fop, and wore sixteen tags to his breeches, eight at each knee (hanged 1774).

Dr. Johnson said that Gray's poetry towered above the ordinary run of verse, as Sixteen-String-Jack above the ordinary foot-pad.—Boswell, *Life of Johnson* (1791).

Skeffington, author of *Sleeping Beauty*, *Maids and Bachelors*, etc.

And sure *great* Skeffington must claim our praise
For skirtless coats, and skeletons of plays.
Byron, *English Bards and Scotch Reviewers* (1809).